W9-BDC-013

# Prentice Hall Brief Review

# United States History and Government

**Bonnie-Anne Briggs / Catherine Fish Petersen**

**Order Information**

Send orders to:
PEARSON CUSTOMER SERVICE
P.O. BOX 2500
LEBANON, IN 46052-3009

or

CALL TOLL FREE 1-800-848-9500
(8:00 A.M.-6:00 P.M. EST)

• Orders can be placed via phone

PEARSON

Acknowledgments appear on pages I-17–I-18, which constitute an extension of this copyright page.

**Copyright © 2011 Pearson Education, Inc., or its affiliates.** All Rights Reserved. Printed in the United States of America. This publication is protected by copyright, and permission should be obtained from the publisher prior to any prohibited reproduction, storage in a retrieval system, or transmission in any form or by any means, electronic, mechanical, photocopying, recording, or likewise. For information regarding permissions, write to Pearson Curriculum Group Rights & Permissions, One Lake Street, Upper Saddle River, New Jersey 07458.

Pearson, Prentice Hall, and Pearson Prentice Hall are trademarks, in the U.S. and/or other countries, of Pearson Education, Inc., or its affiliates.

Regents Examinations and questions appear courtesy of the New York State Education Department/ New York Regents Exam.

13-digit ISBN  978-0-13-316903-4
10-digit ISBN      0-13-316903-0

1 2 3 4 5 6 7 8 9 10  V011  14 13 12 11 10

# Table of Contents

**New York Standards**

Standard    Key Idea

## 4.2

# Table of Contents

# About This Book

This book has been written to help you, the student, review your United States history and government course in order to take the New York State Regents Examination in United States History and Government. The purpose of this book is to:

- help you focus on the key facts, themes, and concepts tested on the Regents Examination.
- familiarize you with the format of the Regents Examination.
- provide you with the test-taking skills you need to succeed on the Regents Examination.

## Content Review

Just like the New York State Core Curriculum, this book is organized into seven units.

- The concepts and content that are consistently tested are emphasized in this text.
- Special emphasis has been given to the second unit on United States government and constitutional history to 1865.
- The charts, maps, cartoons, timelines, and graphic organizers in this text will help reinforce your understanding of the content.
- *The Big Idea* notes at the beginning of each section organize the section content at a glance.
- *Key Themes and Concepts* notes summarize important content and link it to the key themes and concepts of United States history and government.

## Test-Taking Skills

You can practice your test-taking skills on a variety of Regents Examination questions throughout the book.

- A Pre-Test assessment helps you to measure your basic social studies skills and understandings, while providing Regents multiple-choice questions in addition to those in each unit in the book.
- Every multiple-choice question has been on a New York State Regents Examination.
- Document-Based Questions, Thematic Essay Questions, and multiple-choice questions are provided in each history and government unit of the book.
- **Six** Regents Examinations are provided for additional practice.
- An extensive Test-Taking Strategies section teaches you the skills and strategies you need for the exam.
- *Preparing for the Exam* notes in the margins help reinforce test-taking skills and strategies.
- The Reference Section provides charts, based on the New York core curriculum coordinated with what has been tested, that summarize the actions of each United States President, list important people in United States history, explain decisions in each of the Landmark Supreme Court Cases, and includes a Glossary.

# About the Authors

## Bonnie-Anne Briggs

Bonnie-Anne Briggs is a graduate of Nazareth College of Rochester and the State University of New York at Brockport. She retired in June 2002 from her position as teacher and Teacher-in-Charge of Social Studies (department head) at Gates Chili High School in suburban Rochester. She was an adjunct professor in social studies education at the State University of New York at Brockport from 1988 until 2005. Miss Briggs is a past President of the Rochester Area Council for the Social Studies. She is also a past officer of both the New York State Social Studies Supervisory Association and the New York State Council for the Social Studies. Miss Briggs is a recipient of the Rochester Area Council Distinguished Educator Award, the New York State Social Studies Supervisory Association Supervisor of the Year Award, the New York State Council for the Social Studies Distinguished Educator Award, and the Outstanding Alumni Award from Nazareth College of Rochester. She has been inducted into the Gates Chili High School Alumni Hall of Fame, and in 1993, she was a semifinalist for the New York State Teacher of the Year Award. Miss Briggs is currently a very active docent at the Susan B. Anthony House in Rochester, New York.

## Catherine Fish Petersen

Catherine Fish Petersen is a graduate of Wellesley College, Harvard University, and the State University of New York at Stony Brook. Ms. Petersen was the consultant to the New York State Education Department on the *Social Studies Resource Guide* and was their social studies consultant for the New York State Academy for Teaching and Learning. She also was an editor of the State publication, *Social Studies Instructional Strategies & Resources Pre K-Grade Six*. Before retirement, she chaired the Department of Humanities (Social Studies and English) in the East Islip School District on Long Island. Ms. Petersen is a past president of the New York State Social Studies Supervisory Association. She is also a past president, treasurer, and executive secretary of the Long Island Council for the Social Studies. She served on the Board of Directors of the New York State Council for the Social Studies. Ms. Petersen is a recipient of the Long Island Council for the Social Studies Presidential Leadership Award and its Gus Swift Outstanding Service to Social Studies Education Award, the New York State Social Studies Supervisory Association Supervisor of the Year Award and that organization's Special Service Award, as well as the Distinguished Social Studies Service Award from the New York State Council for the Social Studies.

## How to Succeed on the Regents Exam in United States History and Government

This section of the book is intended to help you prepare to take the Regents Examination itself. Other parts of the book review the contents of the course you have studied. This section includes hints about preparing for and actually taking the examination based on test-taking skills you have probably been developing for years in social studies classes. Read and think carefully about all parts of this section as you prepare for the examination.

## Preparing to take the Regents Examination

1. **Attend review sessions.** If review sessions are offered by your teacher or school, attend them. You will probably be reminded of something you studied earlier in the year and have not thought of since then. Review sessions also help you bring together the main ideas of the whole course.
2. **Find a study partner.** Two heads can be better than one. Try to review with a friend or a family member who can give you the chance to explain various parts of this course. You will have a better chance of remembering details if you have already explained them correctly to someone else. It has been said that the best way to learn something is to teach it to someone else.
3. **Do not "over-study."** As important as it is to review carefully and over a period of time for your exams, do not make the mistake of "over-studying" or cramming at the last minute. This could leave you exhausted and unable to think clearly during the exam itself. This exam is important enough for you to ask your employer for time off right before the test.
4. **Eat a good meal.** Eat something before the exam so your energy level stays high.
5. **Know the exam site.** Be sure you know the correct time and place of the examination. Arriving half an hour late can make the difference between passing and failing. Be sure someone else at your house has a schedule of your exams.
6. **Be prepared.** Bring several dark ink pens and pencils.
7. **Wear a watch, if possible.** You will need to pay close attention to the time during the exam, and you might be seated where you cannot see a clock.
8. **Stay for the full allotted time.** Come to the exam prepared to stay for the full three-hour examination period. Do not tell someone to pick you up in two hours—you will need all the time allowed. Don't sacrifice a year's worth of work to get outside faster on a nice day.

## Taking the Regents Examination

1. **Arrive on time.** Use a reliable method of getting to school so you can arrive early in the exam room. This will allow you to get your mind on the task at hand.
2. **Select a seat.** If you are allowed to select your own seat, be sure to choose one with the least distraction. Choose one away from doors or windows.
3. **Dress comfortably.** You will be sitting in one place for a long period of time, so be sure you are comfortably dressed.
4. **Listen to instructions.** Pay full attention to all instructions given by the proctor(s).

5. **Read directions carefully.** Read all directions written on the test booklet as you take the exam. If you have reviewed well, you will be familiar with the terms *discuss, explain, show,* and *describe.* Nonetheless, take the time to read carefully the instructions given to you on the test.

6. **Be an active test-taker.** Become a participant in the exam, not a spectator. You may write on the exam. Underline key ideas. You may write in the margins as you think about the questions. The idea is for you to interact with the exam. Other hints are given as you review the multiple-choice questions from the practice examination.

7. **DON'T leave blanks.** No credit can be given for a blank on either multiple-choice or essay questions. Write something. Write anything, but never leave an answer blank.

## The Multiple-Choice Section

Part I of the Regents Examination is made up of 50 multiple-choice questions. These questions tend to fall into certain categories that you can identify as you take an examination. The following is about identifying these categories and improving your ability to answer certain types of questions. These questions come from the June 2000 exam.

## Data-Based Questions

Data-based questions provide specific information to be used in answering a question or questions. You will probably not be able to answer the question(s) without this information, and you will also need to know some social studies background to help interpret the information. There are several types of data-based questions.

**Reading Passages** Some questions on the practice exam are based on a selected reading passage. These questions often require an ability to recognize opinions expressed in a passage.

If there are words you are unsure of in the selection, try to find a root word you know. Be sure to look for dates or other historical references to help you. You may write notes in the margin near the selection.

*Example:*

> "To take a single step beyond these specific [Constitutional] limits to the powers of Congress is to grasp unlimited power.
>
> "The power to create a [national] bank has not, in my opinion, been delegated to Congress by the Constitution. Supporters of the Bank Bill argue that a [national] bank would be a great convenience in collecting taxes. Even if this argument were true, the Constitution allows only for laws which are 'necessary,' not those which are merely 'convenient' for carrying out delegated powers."
>
> The speaker is basing his argument mainly on a strict interpretation of which provision of the federal Constitution?
> (1) Preamble
> (2) elastic clause
> (3) judicial review
> (4) apportionment of representatives

# Test-Taking Strategies

*Answer:* The correct answer is 2. The phrase "laws which are 'necessary'" near the end of the reading passage should help you make an association with the elastic clause or "necessary and proper" clause. As you read this book, you will find key vocabulary and social studies phrases highlighted throughout.

**Speaker Questions** Speaker questions present different reading passages by different people on the same topic. When answering speaker questions, follow these steps:

- Determine the theme or topic that all of the speakers are addressing.
- Read the questions before you study the speakers' statements too closely; often you do not have to read each speaker's viewpoint to answer a question.
- Be sure you are reading the correct speaker when answering each question.
- Take your time when answering speaker questions. You will probably need to go back and forth among the readings as you analyze the difference between speakers.

### Example:

*Speaker A:* "We cannot make the same mistakes that led to the sinking of the *Lusitania*. Freedom of the seas is important, but we must keep our ships away from possible danger."

*Speaker B:* "We should encourage Great Britain and France to follow a policy of appeasement."

*Speaker C:* "Continued isolation is the only alternative. Whichever way we turn in this conflict, we find an alien ideology."

*Speaker D:* "The future of the free world depends now on the United States and Great Britain. We must not only help win this war, but also ensure that no others occur in the future."

The speakers are most likely discussing the situation facing the United States just before
(1) the American Revolution
(2) the Spanish-American War
(3) World War II
(4) the Korean War

*Answer:* The correct answer is 3, World War II. Underline all hints such as the phrases *mistake of the* Lusitania, *freedom of the seas, Great Britain and France, appeasement, continued isolation,* and *future of the free world.* The correct answer cannot be the American Revolution or the Spanish-American War, because the sinking of the *Lusitania* occurred after both of those wars. The correct answer cannot be the Korean War, because the United States had abandoned its isolationist policy before the Korean War. All of the hints together indicate that these speakers are discussing the situation facing the United States just before World War II.

**Graphs** Graphs may appear in several forms—bar graphs, line graphs, or pie graphs. Some graphs may provide all of the information that you need to answer the question. Others may require you to draw upon your knowledge of social studies to interpret the graph.

*Example:*

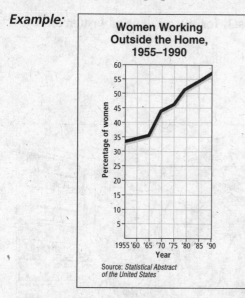

The trend shown in the graph was mainly the result of
(1) increases in immigration
(2) demands for more schoolteachers
(3) a buildup in the defense industry
(4) new social attitudes

*Answer:* The correct answer is 4. The graph indicates a steady increase in the number of women working outside the home between 1955 and 1990. You must draw upon your knowledge of U.S. history to provide the reason for this trend.

**Tables** Some questions require you to draw conclusions from information provided in tables. Be *very* careful to base your conclusions only on the information in the table unless the question specifically asks you to do otherwise. Be sure to note the source and date of the information given in the table.

Which statement is best supported by the chart?
(1) In the early 1900s, there was an increase in the number of immigrants who became farmers.
(2) In the early 1900s, people who lived in cities were more likely to vote than those who lived in rural areas.
(3) In 1920, more people lived in cities than on farms.
(4) In 1920, there were fewer women working in factories than on farms.

*Example:*

| Rural and Urban Populations in the United States | | |
|---|---|---|
| Year | Rural (thousands) | Urban (thousands) |
| 1860 | 25,227 | 6,217 |
| 1870 | 28,656 | 9,902 |
| 1880 | 36,026 | 14,130 |
| 1890 | 40,841 | 22,106 |
| 1900 | 45,835 | 30,160 |
| 1910 | 49,973 | 41,999 |
| 1920 | 51,553 | 54,158 |

*Source: Bureau of the Census*

*Answer:* The correct answer is 3. This question tests your ability to read the table, as well as your understanding of the words *urban* and *rural*. To answer a question such as this, eliminate all possible answers that do not have information given in the chart. For example, answer 1 mentions immigrants, but the table provides no information about immigrants.

# Test-Taking Strategies

**Political Cartoons** Some questions ask you to analyze and interpret a political cartoon. When analyzing a political cartoon, follow these steps:

- Study the caption.
- Look for a date.
- Read all words in the cartoon. Look closely for any small print written on figures or objects in the cartoon.
- Identify the symbolism used by the cartoonist.

*Example:*

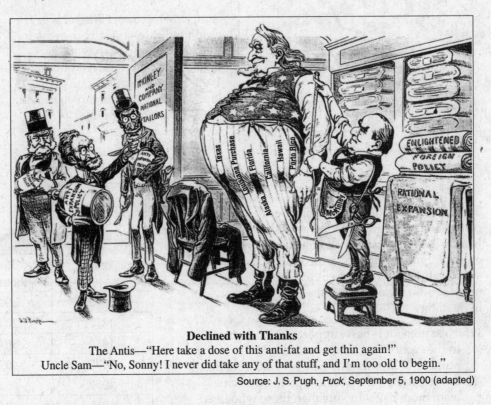

**Declined with Thanks**
The Antis—"Here take a dose of this anti-fat and get thin again!"
Uncle Sam—"No, Sonny! I never did take any of that stuff, and I'm too old to begin."

Source: J. S. Pugh, *Puck*, September 5, 1900 (adapted)

Which foreign policy is the main issue of this cartoon?
(1) containment
(2) imperialism
(3) internationalism
(4) neutrality

The correct answer is 2, imperialism. When analyzing this cartoon, be sure to look very carefully at all parts of the cartoon: the caption under the figures in the cartoon, the writing on the large figure representing Uncle Sam, the writing on the tailor (McKinley) and the material behind him, and the writing on the containers that the men at the door are carrying. The date of the cartoon (1900) is also an important hint about the answer.

**Outlines** Some questions ask you to complete a hypothetical outline.

***Example:***

> In an outline, one of these entries is a main topic and three are subtopics.
> Which is the main topic?
> (1) Alexander Hamilton's Economic Program
> (2) The Rise of National Political Parties
> (3) The Constitution's First Tests
> (4) John Adams's Stormy Presidency

*Answer:* In this question, you are simply asked to determine the main topic. Look for the most general answer. Recognize that the other choices would be subheads on the outline under the main topic. The right choice is 3 because 1, 2, and 4 are examples of the Constitution's first tests.

**Quotation Interpretation** This type of question asks you to explain the idea of a given quotation. Sometimes the date and speaker of the quotation are identified and sometimes not.

***Example:***

> "(Sec. 4.) Every person presenting himself for registration shall be able to read and write any section of the Constitution in the English language, and before he shall be entitled to vote, he shall have paid on or before the first day of March of the year in which he proposes to vote his poll tax as prescribed by law for the previous year."
>
> —*Public Laws of North Carolina, 1899, chapter 218*

> The principle purpose of this law was to
> (1) assure equality of voting rights for all peoples
> (2) encourage literacy for former enslaved people
> (3) prevent African Americans from using their suffrage rights
> (4) promote the racial integration of Southern society

*Answer:* The correct answer is 3. The date and place of origin of this quotation are important clues, which should remind you that Jim Crow laws were legal in much of the South at the end of the 1800s.

**Maps** When maps are given, be sure to look for the following:

- A key explaining any symbols used
- Dates
- Specific place locations
- Compass point for directions

**Timelines** A timeline is a graphic way of showing relationships among events over time. Questions dealing with timelines often ask you to draw a conclusion about a series of events. When answering timeline questions, be careful to focus on the time period shown; do not jump to a different era to answer the question.

## Other Multiple-Choice Questions

Many other types of multiple-choice questions appear on the Regents Examination.

**Headline Questions** In this type of question, you are given a few sample headlines that usually have to do with a common event. Your goal is to determine the connection between the headlines.

*Example:*

> **"Raise Tariffs!"**
> **"Buy American!"**
> **"Impose Import Quotas!"**
>
> Which policy do these slogans reflect?
> (1) militarism    (3) isolationism
> (2) protectionism    (4) détente

*Answer:* The correct answer is 2. The subject of all three headlines is economics and trade. The words and phrases *tariffs, buy American,* and *import quotas* suggest foreign trade. The only possible answer that deals with foreign trade is protectionism.

**Recall Questions** These questions require you to know specific information about people, events, topics, concepts, and vocabulary studied in the course. Throughout this review book, you will find many suggestions about test-taking strategies, as well as references to the many important people and events covered in this course. There is also a glossary at the end of this book to help you with vocabulary.

*Example:*

> At the Constitutional Convention of 1787, a bicameral legislature was proposed as the solution to the disagreement over
> (1) taxation within each state
> (2) control of interstate commerce
> (3) limits on the treaty-making power of a President
> (4) state representation in the national government

*Answer:* The correct answer is 4. The key to answering this question correctly is understanding the meaning of the term *bicameral legislature* and the reason for its proposal.

**Cause-and-Effect Questions** These questions test your understanding of the concepts of cause and effect. A cause is an event or action that brings about another event or action—an effect. Your study of history will have revealed that almost everything is either the cause or result of some event.

*Example:*

> Which factor contributed most directly to the settlement and development of the Great Plains after the Civil War?
> (1) freeing of the enslaved people in Southern states
> (2) construction of railroads west of the Mississippi River
> (3) influx of immigrants from eastern and southern Europe
> (4) hospitality of the American Indian tribes inhabiting the region

*Answer:* The correct answer is 2. The use of the newly developed railroad as transportation was key to the western development (choice 2). Choice 1 is wrong because the freed enslaved people did not move west, and 3 is wrong because those immigrants generally stayed in urban areas to work in factories. Note the word *hospitality* in choice 4. Few of the American Indian tribes welcomed the arrival of the settlers on the plains.

**Time Reference or Chronology Questions** These are questions that make reference to a particular time period. You rarely need to identify specific dates on Regents exams. However, you often do need to know the time sequence or order of events.

### Example:

In the period between World War I and World War II, which group made the greatest gains in political rights?
(1) African Americans
(2) women
(3) new immigrants
(4) Native Americans

*Answer:* The correct answer is 2. With a question like this, it is a good idea to write the dates of the period above the question so that you can focus on that specific time. Remember, a condition that was true in one time period may cease to exist in another time period. When answering this question, you should remember that the Nineteenth Amendment granting women the right to vote was passed in 1920 (between the wars). Not until well after World War II did the other groups make great gains in their political rights.

**Generalizations** These questions require you to make a general statement about a particular event, time period, or body of information. You are really being asked to draw a conclusion.

### Example:

A primary aim of the writers of the United States Constitution was to
(1) strengthen the power of the central government
(2) change from a government based on division of powers to one based on a single power
(3) develop a governmental system based on the principle of supremacy of the states
(4) weaken the power of the executive

*Answer:* The correct answer is 1. This question asks you to explain why the Constitution was written. To do so, you need to recall the problems of the Articles of Confederation. Choice 1 is correct because the Constitution does establish a strong central government.

**Fact and Opinion** These questions require you to find a statement that is clearly either fact or opinion. If you keep in mind that certain words such as *most important, most significant,* and *greatest contribution* signal opinions, you should have no trouble with this type of question. It is difficult to make true statements that include the words *always, never, all,* or *none.*

**Sources and References** Some questions test your ability to identify a valid source of information. A primary source is one written or told by someone who was present at an event. These sources can be biased, but they can also give a special insight into an event. Secondary sources, such as textbooks, are those that are written after an event.

**Questions About Social Scientists** Some questions ask about the jobs of certain types of social scientists. These might include the following:

*Historian:* a person who studies the past and makes judgments about why events happened and how they affected other events

*Economist:* a person who studies the monetary systems of countries or cultures. The work of economists is important to our understanding of events such as the Great Depression.

*Political scientist:* a person who studies the workings of government and politics. For example, political scientists analyze the results of elections to determine trends in voting patterns.

## The Thematic Essay

There will be one thematic essay on your examination. The score on the thematic essay ranges from 0 to 5 points, using a generic scoring rubric. You should become familiar with this rubric as you prepare for the exam, because it will help you learn how to write the most effective essay possible.

You will not have a choice of theme or topic, but you will have many choices within the provided list of suggested examples you may draw upon in writing your essay. You may choose examples that are not on the list of suggestions, but that approach may not be a good idea. The most frequently studied examples are the ones that are usually given in the suggestions. As an example, we will use the Thematic Essay Question from the June 2004 exam:

**Answers to the essay questions are to be written in the separate essay booklet.**

*Directions:*   Write a well-organized essay that includes an introduction, several paragraphs addressing the task below, and a conclusion.

Theme:   **Geography and United States Government Actions**

> Geographic factors often influence United States government actions, both foreign and domestic. Some of these factors include location, physical environment, movement of people, climate, and resources.

Task:

> Identify *two* actions taken by the United States government that were influenced by geographic factors, and for *each* action
> - Discuss the historical circumstances that resulted in the government action
> - Discuss the influence of a geographic factor on the action
> - Describe the impact of the government action on the United States

From your study of United States history, you may use any federal government action that was influenced by geography. Some suggestions you might wish to consider include the Louisiana Purchase (1803), issuance of the Monroe Doctrine (1823), passage of the Homestead Act (1862), decision to build the transcontinental railroad (1860s), acquisition of the Philippines (1898), decision to build the Panama Canal (early 1900s), and passage of the Interstate Highway Act (1956).

**You are *not* limited to these suggestions.**

Guidelines:

**In your essay, be sure to**
- Develop all aspects of the task
- Support the theme with relevant facts, examples, and details
- Use a logical and clear plan of organization, including an introduction and a conclusion that are beyond a restatement of the theme

**In developing your answer, be sure to keep these general definitions in mind:**

(a) <u>discuss</u> **means "to make observations about something using facts, reasoning, and argument; to present in some detail"**
(b) <u>describe</u> **means "to illustrate something in words or tell about it"**

## Blocking Essay Answers

Blocking an essay will help you organize your ideas before you write your answer. Organizing your thoughts before writing will help you earn more points on the essay and avoid leaving out parts of the essay. Experts in helping students prepare for tests know that the more involved you become with a test, the better you will do on it.

## Steps in Blocking an Essay

**1.** Underline the words that tell you what you need to do: *discuss, describe, explain,* and so on.
**2.** Study the directions next to each bulleted point (•).
**3.** Use those directions to form headings for your block.
**4.** Under each section of your block, write facts to help you answer that part of the question.
**5.** Review to see if you have completed all parts of the *Task*.
**6.** Check to see that your introduction and conclusion show thought and are not just a repetition of the ones you are given in the question.
**7.** When you have arranged all your facts in the section of the block, check to be sure you have not left any blocks empty.

# Test-Taking Strategies

## Sample Block

This chart blocks only one of the two required actions for the Thematic Essay Question that was on the June 2004 Regents examination.

| As an example, we will use the June 2004 exam: | Action | Discuss historical circumstances that resulted in government actions. | Discuss influence of a geographic factor (location, physical environment, actions, movement of people, climate resources) | Impact of action on United States. |
|---|---|---|---|---|
| | Louisiana Purchase | France wanted and needed to sell area much cheaper than the United States expected to buy; President Jefferson decided the government could purchase the land. | United States could expand to the west and end French presence on U. S. western border. | Gave United States chance to double size of territory to allow for future growth and exploration for new resources. United States set precedent that it could add additional territory. |

## Generic Thematic Essay Scoring Rubric

| Score of 5: | Score of 4: | Score of 3: |
|---|---|---|
| • Thoroughly develops all aspects of the task evenly and in depth<br>• Is more analytical than descriptive (analyzes, evaluates, and/or creates* information)<br>• Richly supports the theme with many relevant facts, examples, and details<br>• Demonstrates a logical and clear plan of organization; includes an introduction and a conclusion that are beyond a restatement of the theme | • Develops all aspects of the task but may do so somewhat unevenly<br>• Is both descriptive and analytical (applies, analyzes, evaluates, and/or creates information)<br>• Supports the theme with relevant facts, examples, and details<br>• Demonstrates a logical and clear plan of organization; includes an introduction and a conclusion that are beyond a restatement of the theme | • Develops all aspects of the task with little depth or develops most aspects of the task in some depth<br>• Is more descriptive than analytical (applies, may analyze, and/or evaluate information)<br>• Includes some relevant facts, examples, and details; may include some minor inaccuracies<br>• Demonstrates a satisfactory plan of organization; includes an introduction and a conclusion that may be a restatement of the theme |

| Score of 2: | Score of 1: | Score of 0: |
|---|---|---|
| • Minimally develops all aspects of the task or develops some aspects of the task in some depth<br>• Is primarily descriptive; may include faulty, weak, or isolated application or analysis<br>• Includes few relevant facts, examples, and details; may include some inaccuracies<br>• Demonstrates a general plan of organization; may lack focus; may contain digressions; may not clearly identify which aspect of the task is being addressed; may lack an introduction and/or a conclusion | • Minimally develops some aspects of the task<br>• Is descriptive; may lack understanding, application, or analysis<br>• Includes few relevant facts, examples, or details; may include inaccuracies<br>• May demonstrate a weakness in organization; may lack focus; may contain digressions; may not clearly identify which aspect of the task is being addressed; may lack an introduction and/or a conclusion | Fails to develop the task or may only refer to the theme in a general way; OR includes no relevant facts, examples, or details; OR includes only the theme, task, or suggestions as copied from the test booklet; OR is illegible; OR is blank |

# Document-Based Question

There will be one document-based question (DBQ) on the examination. The score on the document-based essay question ranges from 0 to 5 points, using a generic scoring rubric. You should become familiar with this rubric as you prepare for the exam, because it will help you learn how to write the most effective essay possible. The DBQ from the June 2004 exam is included here for you.

The DBQ has two important parts. Part A includes the scaffolding questions in which you examine documents individually and complete short-answer questions. Part B is the essay question in which you draw upon your analysis of the documents and your knowledge of United States history and government to write the essay. You must complete all sections of both parts. There are several steps you should take to ensure success in answering the DBQ:

- **Read the *Historical Context* section carefully.** This sets the time frame in which all parts of the question are set. It also limits the time period that you can write about in your answer. Remember to highlight or underline important data.
- **Read and understand the *Task*.** Read this part carefully to be sure that you complete all parts. Underline any parts of the test that you do not want to forget or overlook.
- **Do not leave any blanks on the scaffolding question section.** Any blanks you leave will cause you to lose points automatically.
- **Keep track of main ideas/block your essay.** As you work through the scaffolding questions, write down the main idea or ideas of each document on your scrap paper. Briefly listing the main ideas of each document will help you organize your thoughts so that you can successfully support your viewpoint in the essay. You may choose to organize the main ideas by creating a simple chart.

# Document-Based Question

In developing your answer, be sure to keep this general definition in mind:

> discuss means "to make observations about something using facts, reasoning, and argument; to present in some detail"

This question is based on the accompanying documents (1–8). The question is designed to test your ability to work with historical documents. Some of the documents have been edited for the purposes of the question. As you analyze the documents, take into account both the source of each document and any point of view that may be presented in the document.

**Historical Context:**

> The Civil War and the period of Reconstruction brought great social, political, and economic changes to American society. The effects of these changes continued into the twentieth century.

**Task:** Using information from the documents and your knowledge of United States history, answer the questions that follow each document in Part A. Your answers to the questions will help you write the Part B essay in which you will be asked to

> • Identify and discuss *one* social, *one* political, **AND** *one* economic change in American society that occurred as a result of the Civil War or the period of Reconstruction

## Part A: Short-Answer Questions

*Directions:* Analyze the documents and answer the short-answer questions that follow each document in the space provided.

### Document #1

> " . . . *All persons born or naturalized in the United States, and subject to the jurisdiction thereof, are citizens of the United States and of the State wherein they reside. No State shall make or enforce any law which shall abridge the privileges or immunities of citizens of the United States; nor shall any State deprive any person of life, liberty, or property, without due process of law; nor deny to any person within its jurisdiction the equal protection of the laws. . . .*"
>
> —**Fourteenth Amendment, Section 1, 1868**

1a. How does the Fourteenth Amendment define citizenship? [1]

_____

_____

Score ☐

b. During Reconstruction, how was the Fourteenth Amendment intended to help formerly enslaved persons? [1]

_____

_____

Score ☐

## Document #2

" . . . History does not furnish an example of emancipation under conditions less friendly to the emancipated class than this American example. Liberty came to the freedmen of the United States not in mercy, but in wrath [anger], not by moral choice but by military necessity, not by the generous action of the people among whom they were to live, and whose good-will was essential to the success of the measure, but by strangers, foreigners, invaders, trespassers, aliens, and enemies. The very manner of their emancipation invited to the heads of the freedmen the bitterest hostility of race and class. They were hated because they had been slaves, hated because they were now free, and hated because of those who had freed them. Nothing was to have been expected other than what has happened, and he is a poor student of the human heart who does not see that the old master class would naturally employ every power and means in their reach to make the great measure of emancipation unsuccessful and utterly odious [hateful]. It was born in the tempest and whirlwind [turmoil] of war, and has lived in a storm of violence and blood. When the Hebrews were emancipated, they were told to take spoil [goods or property] from the Egyptians. When the serfs of Russia were emancipated [in 1861], they were given three acres of ground upon which they could live and make a living. But not so when our slaves were emancipated. They were sent away empty-handed, without money, without friends, and without a foot of land to stand upon. Old and young, sick and well, were turned loose to the open sky, naked to their enemies. The old slave quarter that had before sheltered them and the fields that had yielded them corn were now denied them. The old master class, in its wrath, said, "Clear out! The Yankees have freed you, now let them feed and shelter you! . . .""

**Source: Frederick Douglass, *Life and Times of Frederick Douglass*, Park Publishing Co., 1881**

2. According to this document, what did Frederick Douglass identify as a problem with the way the United States government emancipated the enslaved persons? [1]

_____

_____

Score ☐

## Document #3

" . . . We believe you are not familiar with the description of the Ku Klux Klans riding nightly over the country, going from county to county, and in the county towns, spreading terror wherever they go by robbing, whipping, ravishing, and killing our people without provocation [reason], compelling [forcing] colored people to break the ice and bathe in the chilly waters of the Kentucky river."

"The [state] legislature has adjourned. They refused to enact any laws to suppress [stop] Ku-Klux disorder. We regard them [the Ku-Kluxers] as now being licensed to continue their dark and bloody deeds under cover of the dark night. They refuse to allow us to testify in the state courts where a white man is concerned. We find their deeds are perpetrated [carried out] only upon colored men and white Republicans. We also find that for our services to the government and our race we have become the special object of hatred and persecution at the hands of the Democratic Party. Our people are driven from their homes in great numbers, having no redress [relief from distress] only [except] the United States court, which is in many cases unable to reach them."

"We would state that we have been law-abiding citizens, pay our taxes, and in many parts of the state our people have been driven from the polls, refused the right to vote. Many have been slaughtered while attempting to vote. We ask, how long is this state of things to last? . . ."

—Petition to the United States Congress, March 25, 1871,
**Miscellaneous Documents of the United States Senate, 42nd Congress, 1st Session, 1871**

3a. Based on this document, identify *one* way the Ku Klux Klan terrorized African Americans. [1]

_____

Score [ ]

b. According to this document, how did the actions of the Ku Klux Klan affect African Americans' participation in the political process? [1]

_____

_____

Score [ ]

## Document #4

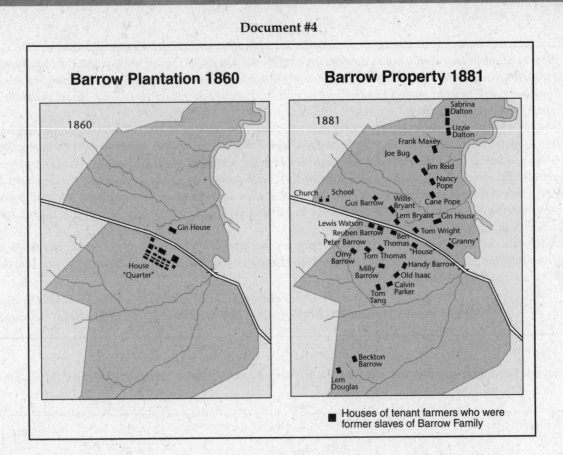

**Barrow Plantation 1860**

1860

Gin House

House "Quarter"

**Barrow Property 1881**

1881

Sabrina Dalton
Lizzie Dalton
Frank Maxey
Joe Bug
Jim Reid
Nancy Pope
Church   School
Gus Barrow
Willis Bryant
Cane Pope
Lem Bryant   Gin House
Lewis Watson
Reuben Barrow
Ben Thomas
Tom Wright
Peter Barrow
"Granny"
Omy Barrow
Tom Thomas
"House"
Milly Barrow
Handy Barrow
Old Isaac
Calvin Parker
Tom Tang
Beckton Barrow
Lem Douglas

■ Houses of tenant farmers who were
former slaves of Barrow Family

4. According to these illustrations, how did the economic role of African Americans change between 1860 and 1881? [1]

_____

_____

Score ☐

## Document #5

" . . . When we come to the New Industrial South the change is marvellous, and so vast and various that I scarcely know where to begin in a short paper that cannot go much into details. Instead of a South devoted to agriculture and politics, we find a South wide-awake to business, excited and even astonished at the development of its own immense resources in metals, marbles, coal, timber, fertilizers, eagerly laying lines of communication, rapidly opening mines, building furnaces, foundries [workplace where melted metal is poured into molds], and all sorts of shops for utilizing the native riches. It is like the discovery of a new world. When the Northerner finds great foundries in Virginia using only (with slight exceptions) the products of Virginia iron and coal mines; when he finds Alabama and Tennessee making iron so good and so cheap that it finds ready market in Pennsylvania; and foundries multiplying near the great furnaces for supplying Northern markets; when he finds cotton-mills running to full capacity on grades of cheap cottons universally in demand throughout the South and Southwest; when he finds small industries, such as paper-box factories and wooden bucket and tub factories, sending all they can make into the North and widely over the West; when he sees the loads of most beautiful marbles shipped North; when he learns that some of the largest and most important engines and mill machinery were made in Southern shops; when he finds in Richmond a "pole locomotive," made to run on logs laid end to end, and drag out from Michigan forests and Southern swamps lumber hitherto inaccessible; when he sees worn out highlands in Georgia and Carolina bear more cotton than ever before by help of a fertilizer the base of which is the cotton seed itself (worth more as a fertilizer than it was before the oil was extracted from it); when he sees a multitude of small shops giving employment to men, women, and children who never had any work of that sort to do before; and when he sees Roanoke iron cast in Richmond into car irons, and returned to a car factory in Roanoke which last year sold three hundred cars to the New York and New England Railroad—he begins to open his eyes. The South is manufacturing a great variety of things needed in the house, on the farm, and in the shops, for home consumption, and already sends to the North and West several manufactured products. With iron, coal, timber contiguous [adjoining] and easily obtained, the amount sent out is certain to increase as the labor becomes more skillful. The most striking industrial development today is in iron, coal, lumber, and marbles; the more encouraging for the self-sustaining life of the Southern people is the multiplication of small industries in nearly every city I visited. . . ."

**Source: Charles Dudley Warner, "The South Revisited,"**
*Harper's New Monthly Magazine* **(March 1887)**

5.  According to this passage, what was *one* economic change that had occurred in the South by 1887? [1]

_____

_____

Score ☐

## Document #6

### A Public Fountain in North Carolina, 1950

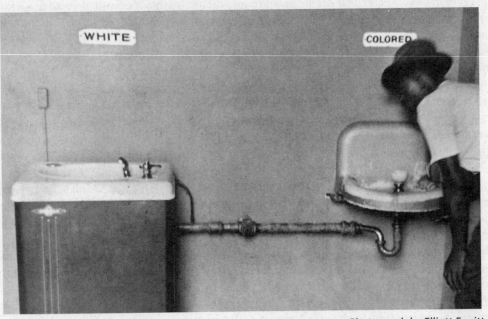

WHITE                    COLORED

—*Photograph by Elliott Erwitt*
*Source: Steve Kashwer,* The Civil Rights Movement:
A Photographic History, 1954–68, *Abbeville Press*

6.  What does this photograph show about the treatment of African Americans in the South after
    Reconstruction? [1]

_____

_____

Score ☐

**Document #7**

" . . . Since 1868 there has been a steady and persistent determination to eliminate us from the politics of the Southern States. We are not to be eliminated. Suffrage is a federal guaranty and not a privilege to be conferred [given] or withheld by the States. We contend for the principle of manhood suffrage as the most effective safeguard of citizenship. A disfranchised citizen [one who is deprived of the right to vote] is a pariah [outcast] in the body politic. We are not opposed to legitimate restriction of the suffrage, but we insist that restrictions shall apply alike to all citizens of all States. We are willing to accept an educational or property qualification, or both; and we contend that retroactive legislation depriving citizens of the suffrage rights is a hardship which should be speedily passed upon by the courts. We insist that neither of these was intended or is conserved [protected] by the new constitutions of Mississippi, South Carolina or Louisiana. Their framers intended and did disfranchise a majority of their citizenship [deprived them of the right to vote] because of "race and color" and "previous condition," and we therefore call upon the Congress to reduce the representation of those States in the Congress as provided and made mandatory by Section 2 of Article XIV of the Constitution. We call upon Afro-Americans everywhere to resist by all lawful means the determination to deprive them of their suffrage rights. If it is necessary to accomplish this vital purpose to divide their vote in a given State we advise that they divide it. The shibboleth [custom] of party must give way to the shibboleth of self-preservation. . . ."

— **Afro-American Council public statement, 1898**
**Source: Francis L. Broderick and August Meier,** *Negro Protest Thought in the Twentieth Century,*
**Bobbs-Merrill Company**

7.  What political problem is being described in this passage? [1]

_____

_____

Score ☐

## Document #8

We hold these truths to be self-evident: that all men are created equal.

Source: Robert Divine et al., America Past and Present, Addison Wesley (adapted)

**Parade in New York City sponsored by the NAACP in 1917**

8. What was the general goal of the marchers shown in this photograph? [1]

_____

_____

Score ☐

## Part B
## Essay

*Directions:* Write a well-organized essay that includes an introduction, several paragraphs, and a conclusion. Use evidence from *at least five* documents in your essay. Support your response with relevant facts, examples, and details. Include additional outside information.

**Historical Context:**

The Civil War and the period of Reconstruction brought great social, political, and economic changes to American society. The effects of these changes continued into the twentieth century.

**Task:** Using information from the documents and your knowledge of United States history, write an essay in which you

- Identify and discuss *one* social, *one* political, **AND** *one* economic change in American society that occurred as a result of the Civil War or the period of Reconstruction

**Guidelines:**

**In your essay, be sure to**
- Develop all aspects of the task
- Incorporate information from *at least five* documents
- Incorporate relevant outside information
- Support the theme with relevant facts, examples, and details
- Use a logical and clear plan of organization, including an introduction and a conclusion that are beyond a restatement of the theme

## Sample Block or Prewriting Outline

The chart below blocks the Document-Based Question from the June 2004 Regents examination used here.

## Writing the Document-Based Question

Use the list you created while answering the scaffolding questions to help guide the writing of your essay. Using the question from the June 2004 Regents, you should have a list of social, political, and economic changes from the given documents. Be sure to note that not all of the changes have to be positive and that some changes definitely had a negative impact on the Untied States.

In your essay, you should take care to draw as much information out of the documents as you can. However, you should also include other information from your knowledge of United States history if that information helps support your viewpoint. In the document-based question from the sample Regents examination, for example, you could also include information about other changes that occured such as the work of Martin Luther King, Jr., Rosa Parks, Civil Rights legislation of the 1960s, and so on.

Be sure to study carefully the *Guidelines* that are provided in the instructions on writing the document-based question. These *Guidelines* will remind you of what you must include in order to score the full five points for the essay.

| Document (number and source) | Type of Change (social, political, economic) | Specific Application |
|---|---|---|
| 1 14th Amendment | political | gave persons natural born or naturalized citizenship |
| 2 F. Douglass | economic | formerly enslaved persons that were not given land, money or other assistance to help them get started as free citizens |
| 3 Senate document | social and political | KKK depriving former enslaved persons of basic human rights, i.e. life, liberty as well as new political right to vote |
| 4 Plantation map | economic | enslaved persons had a right to be tenant farmers, big plantations had been subdivided, therefore change for the old "elite" or Master too |
| 5 Harper's Magazine | economic and social | multiple examples of new types of businesses in the south in 1887, iron foundries, cotton mills, train car production |
| 6 separate drinking fountain | social | illustrates separate AND unequal public facilities as recent as the 1950s and 60s |
| 7 Afro-American Council | political | changes did not always happen when they should have, some Southern states made their own laws to deprive African Americans of voting rights |
| 8 NAACP Parade | social, political, and economic | shows that in 1917 African Americans were using parades and demonstrations to protest their lack of right to be truly equal (note formal, business dress on marchers) |

# Generic Document Based Question Essay Scoring Rubric

| Score of 5: | Score of 4: | Score of 3: |
|---|---|---|
| • Thoroughly develops all aspects of the task evenly and in depth<br>• Is more analytical than descriptive (analyzes, evaluates, and/or creates information)<br>• Incorporates relevant information from *at least* xxx* documents<br>• Incorporates substantial relevant outside information<br>• Richly supports the theme with many relevant facts, examples, and details<br>• Demonstrates a logical and clear plan of organization; includes an introduction and a conclusion that are beyond a restatement of the theme | • Develops all aspects of the task but may do so somewhat unevenly<br>• Is both descriptive and analytical (applies, analyzes, evaluates, and/or creates information)<br>• Incorporates relevant information from at least xxx* documents<br>• Incorporates relevant outside information<br>• Supports the theme with relevant facts, examples, and details<br>• Demonstrates a logical and clear plan of organization; includes an introduction and a conclusion that are beyond a restatement of the theme | • Develops all aspects of the task with little depth *or* develops most aspects of the task in some depth<br>• Is more descriptive than analytical (applies, may analyze, and/or evaluate information)<br>• Incorporates some relevant information from some of the documents<br>• Incorporates limited relevant outside information<br>• Includes some relevant facts, examples, and details; may include some minor inaccuracies<br>• Demonstrates a satisfactory plan of organization; includes an introduction and a conclusion that may be a restatement of the theme |
| Score of 2: | Score of 1: | Score of 0: |
| • Minimally develops all aspects of the task *or* develops some aspects of the task in some depth<br>• Is primarily descriptive; may include faulty, weak, or isolated application or analysis<br>• Incorporates limited relevant information from the documents or consists primarily of relevant information copied from the documents<br>• Presents little or no relevant outside information<br>• Includes few relevant facts, examples, and details; may include some inaccuracies<br>• Demonstrates a general plan of organization; may lack focus; may contain digressions; may not clearly identify which aspect of the task is being addressed; may lack an introduction and/or a conclusion | • Minimally develops some aspects of the task<br>• Is descriptive; may lack understanding, application, or analysis<br>• Makes vague, unclear references to the documents or consists primarily of relevant and irrelevant information copied from the documents<br>• Presents no relevant outside information<br>• Includes few relevant facts, examples, or details; may include inaccuracies<br>• May demonstrate a weakness in organization; may lack focus; may contain digressions; may not clearly identify which aspect of the task is being addressed; may lack an introduction and/or a conclusion | Fails to develop the task or may only refer to the theme in a general way; *OR* includes no relevant facts, examples, or details; includes only the historical context and/or task as copies from the test booklet; *OR* includes only entire documents copied from the test booklet; *OR* is illegible; *OR* is blank |

* *xxx* means that the required number of documents varies by question but almost always means one more than half of the total number of documents given.

# Unit Pre-Tests

This section consists of seven Pre-Tests, one for each of the units in the New York State Core Curriculum in United States History and Government. In constructing these Pre-Tests, the authors' objective was to give you the opportunity to determine what you know about each unit before you begin to review the unit. The questions cover a range of topics within each unit. They focus on major understandings and often tested information. In addition, the Pre-Tests offer practice in social studies reading skills with the inclusion of many outline, headline, and speaker questions. The Pre-Tests can be supplemented with the maps, charts, graphs, cartoons, and accompanying questions throughout each unit that provide further opportunities to strengthen social studies skills.

These Pre-Tests are composed only of multiple choice questions that have appeared on previous Regents examinations. They do not duplicate any *Questions for Regents Practice* at the end of each unit, nor any multiple choice question on the six Regents Examinations in the book. Therefore, the Pre-Tests may also be used as additional practice questions following your review of the unit.

# Unit 1 Pre-Test

**Name** _____   **Date** _____

**Directions** Review the Test-Taking Strategies section of this book. Then answer the following questions, drawn from actual Regents examinations. For each statement or question, choose the number of the word or expression that, of those given, best completes the statement or answers the question.

1. Which type of map shows the most detailed information about Earth's natural features, such as rivers, lakes, and mountain ranges?
   (1) political
   (3) weather
   (2) demographic
   (4) physical

2. • Jamestown, founded in 1607
   • Plymouth colony, founded in 1620
   • New Amsterdam, founded in 1625

   These early colonial settlements were similar in that each was located
   (1) at the base of a mountain range
   (2) near the coastline
   (3) in an arid climate
   (4) on offshore islands

3. Because of the fertile land and long growing season, plantations in the Thirteen Colonies developed in
   (1) New England
   (2) the Middle Atlantic region
   (3) the South
   (4) the upper Mississippi River valley

4. Which geographic feature contributed the most to the development of commerce throughout colonial America?          *trade*
   (1) mountains
   (2) natural harbors
   (3) grasslands
   (4) interior lakes

5. Which heading best completes the partial outline below?

   > I. _____
   > A. Villages with town meetings
   > B. Small farms and commercial fishing
   > C. First American college

   (1) New England colonies
   (2) Middle colonies
   (3) Southern colonies
   (4) Spanish colonies

6. Which group benefited most from the United States acquisition of the port of New Orleans?
   (1) farmers in the Ohio River Valley
   (2) American Indians in the Southwest
   (3) fur trappers in the Columbia River valley
   (4) gold miners in Northern California

7. Acquiring New Orleans as part of the Louisiana Purchase was considered important to the development of the Mississippi and Ohio River Valleys because the city
   (1) provided protection from attacks by the Spanish
   (2) provided migrant workers for river valley farms
   (3) served as a port for American agricultural goods
   (4) served as the cultural center for the nation

8. In the early 1800s, the need for a water route to help farmers ship their products to market was one reason for the
   (1) Gadsden Purchase
   (2) Louisiana Purchase
   (3) Mexican Cession
   (4) Missouri Compromise

9. The relatively flat grassy region of the United States between the Mississippi River and the Rocky Mountains is known as the
   (1) Great Plains
   (3) Coastal Plain
   (2) Great Basin
   (4) Piedmont

10. In the 1800s, the Great Plains region of the United States was characterized primarily by
    (1) exceptionally high amounts of annual rainfall
    (2) heavily wooded forests covering most of the area
    (3) an extensive system of navigable rivers
    (4) vast expanses of native grasses

Copyright © Pearson Education, Inc., or its affiliates. All Rights Reserved

**Name** _____    **Date** _____

**Directions**  Review the Test-Taking Strategies section of this book. Then answer the following questions, drawn from actual Regents examinations. For each statement or question, choose the number of the word or expression that, of those given, best completes the statement or answers the question.

1.  Which heading best completes the partial outline below?

> I. _____
> A. Committees of Correspondence
> B. Nonimportation Agreements
> C. Boston Tea Party
> D. First Continental Congress

(1) Protests Against Slavery in the American Colonies

(2) British Parliamentary Actions to Punish Colonial Americans

(3) Colonial Responses to British Mercantile Policies

(4) Colonial Attempts to End the British Policy of Salutary Neglect

2.  In writing the *Declaration of Independence,* Thomas Jefferson was influenced most by John Locke's idea of

(1) due process of law

(2) natural rights

(3) the rights of the accused

(4) the right to privacy

3.  The Northwest Ordinance of 1787 set a precedent for other western territories by

(1) allowing slavery

(2) including voting rights for women

(3) providing a method for the creation of new states

(4) setting aside land for churches

**Base your answers to questions 4 and 5 on the statements below and on your knowledge of social studies.**

Speaker A:  A leader is not ultimately responsible to the people but to God, from whom the leader derives the right to govern.

Speaker B:  Each citizen is entitled to a voice in government. Therefore, government should be run by those representatives elected directly by the citizens so that the will of the citizens is expressed.

Speaker C:  History has taught us that the concentration of political power leads to the abuse of that power. Therefore, power should be divided among national, state, and local governments.

Speaker D:  Life is a struggle. Those who seize and maintain political power represent the strongest and most competent of that society and earn the right to govern.

4.  The principle of federalism contained in the Constitution of the United States is most consistent with the ideas of Speaker

(1) A              (3) C
(2) B              (4) D

5.  Over the course of its history, the United States has advanced the goal of Speaker B by

(1) upholding the separation of church and state

(2) adding constitutional amendments to expand voting rights

(3) expanding the role of the Supreme Court in government

(4) providing for the direct election of the President

6.  **"New Congress to Have Two Houses"**
    **"Slaves to Count as Three-Fifths of a Person"**
    **"President to be Chosen by Electoral Vote"**

Which conclusion about the Constitutional Convention is best supported by these headlines?

(1) The Framers of the Constitution were able to compromise on important issues.

(2) States that were small in area would lose power in the new Constitution.

(3) States with large populations controlled the outcome of the convention.

(4) The President and Congress would have equal power under the new constitution.

Copyright © Pearson Education, Inc., or its affiliates. All Rights Reserved

# Unit 2 Pre-Test *continued*

Name _____     Date _____

7. Which newspaper headline shows the operation of the system of checks and balances?

   (1) "Senate Rejects President's Choice of Supreme Court Justice"
   (2) "Florida To Gain Two Seats in the United States House of Representatives"
   (3) "Albany County Receives $4 Million from Congress for Transportation Development"
   (4) "New York State Rejects Federal Regulations on Drug Testing"

8. Which statement from the United States. Constitution is referred to as the elastic clause?

   (1) "All legislative powers herein granted shall be vested in a Congress of the United States. . . . "
   (2) "Congress shall make no law respecting an establishment of religion. . . . "
   (3) "All bills for raising revenue shall originate in the House of Representatives. . . . "
   (4) "Congress shall have power . . . to make all laws which shall be necessary and proper for carrying into execution the foregoing powers. . . . "

9. The decision in *Marbury* v. *Madison* (1803) expanded the power of the Supreme Court by

   (1) restricting the use of the elastic clause
   (2) establishing the power of judicial review
   (3) upholding the constitutionality of the National Bank
   (4) interpreting the interstate commerce clause

10. The major reason Antifederalists opposed ratification of the Constitution was because they believed

   (1) amending the Constitution was too easy
   (2) too much power was given to the states
   (3) a federal court system would be too weak
   (4) individual rights were not adequately protected

11. Which heading best completes the partial outline below?

   I. _____
   A. Political parties
   B. Committee system in Congress
   C. Judicial review
   D. President's cabinet

   (1) Unwritten Constitution
   (2) Constitutional Amendments
   (3) Electoral Process
   (4) Checks and Balances

12. Washington's Proclamation of Neutrality (1793), Jefferson's Embargo Act (1807), and the Monroe Doctrine (1823) were all efforts to

   (1) avoid political conflicts with European nations
   (2) directly support European revolutions
   (3) aid Great Britain in its war against France
   (4) promote military alliances

13. The slogan "Fifty-four forty or fight!," the annexation of Texas, and the Mexican War all relate to the

   (1) theory of nullification
   (2) practice of secession
   (3) belief in Manifest Destiny
   (4) idea of due process

14. As the United States acquired more land between 1803 and 1850, controversy over these territories focused on the

   (1) need for schools and colleges
   (2) failure to conserve natural resources
   (3) expansion of slavery
   (4) construction of transcontinental railroads

15. As the Civil War began, President Abraham Lincoln stated that his primary goal was to

   (1) end slavery
   (2) set new national boundaries
   (3) increase congressional powers
   (4) preserve the Union

Copyright © Pearson Education, Inc., or its affiliates. All Rights Reserved

Copyright © Pearson Education, Inc., or its affiliates. All Rights Reserved

**Name** _____  **Date** _____

**Directions** Review the Test-Taking Strategies section of this book. Then answer the following questions, drawn from actual Regents examinations. For each statement or question, choose the number of the word or expression that, of those given, best completes the statement or answers the question.

1. Constitutional amendments adopted during Reconstruction were intended to
   (1) provide legal and political rights for African Americans
   (2) end property and religious qualifications for voting
   (3) correct problems with the electoral college system
   (4) limit the number of terms of the President

2. In the South, the passage of Jim Crow laws in the 1870s and 1880s led directly to the
   (1) racial integration of public schools
   (2) decline of the Democratic party
   (3) organization of the Ku Klux Klan
   (4) segregation of public facilities

3. In an outline, which main topic would include the other three?
   (1) Erie Canal
   (2) Nineteenth-Century Internal Improvements
   (3) Transcontinental Railroad
   (4) National Road

4. The growth of big business in the late 1800s resulted in
   (1) a reduction in child labor
   (2) the elimination of the middle class
   (3) the widening of the economic gap between rich and poor
   (4) a shift in transportation investment from railroads to canals

5. Mark Twain labeled the late 1800s in the United States the "Gilded Age" to describe the
   (1) end of the practice of slavery
   (2) absence of international conflicts
   (3) extremes of wealth and poverty
   (4) achievements of the labor movement

6. During the late nineteenth century, which practices were used by employers against workers?
   (1) boycotts and lockouts
   (2) picketing and walkouts
   (3) blacklists and yellow-dog contracts
   (4) mass rallies and sit-down strikes

**Base your answers to questions 7 and 8 on the speakers' statements below and on your knowledge of social studies.**

Speaker A: "When demand ran high, and markets were scarce, he showed little mercy, broke his contracts for delivery and raised prices."

Speaker B: "The man of wealth must hold his fortune 'in trust' for the community and use it for philanthropic and charitable purposes."

Speaker C: "It is cruel to slander the rich because they have been successful. They have gone into great enterprises that have enriched the nation and the nation has enriched them."

Speaker D: "The fruits of the toil of millions are boldly stolen to build up colossal fortunes for the few, unprecedented in the history of mankind."

7. Which two speakers would most likely label late nineteenth-century industrialists as *robber barons*?
   (1) A and B          (3) B and C  own big busines
   (2) A and D          (4) C and D

8. The most valid conclusion that can be drawn from the different viewpoints of these speakers is that industrialists of the late nineteenth century
   (1) benefited and harmed society
   (2) treated their workers fairly
   (3) used illegal means to gain wealth
   (4) generally opposed the free-enterprise economic system

**Name** _____  **Date** _____

9. In the last half of the 1800s, which development led to the other three?
   (1) expansion of the middle class
   (2) growth of industrialization
   (3) formation of trusts
   (4) creation of labor unions

10. Which action by the federal government during the late 1800s is an example of nativism?
    (1) passage of the Chinese Exclusion Act
    (2) creation of tribal reservations in the East
    (3) grants of financial aid to western farmers
    (4) support for the construction of transcontinental railroads

**Base your answers to questions 11 and 12 on the speakers' statements below and on your knowledge of social studies.**

Speaker A: "Our nation has grown and prospered from the ideas and labor of immigrants. The nation has been enriched by immigrants from different nations who brought new ideas and lifestyles, which have become part of American culture."

Speaker B: "United States industries are competing with established European manufacturers. To prosper, American industries need the vast supply of unskilled labor that is provided by immigrants."

Speaker C: "Immigrants are taking jobs at low wages without regard for long hours and workers' safety. American workers must unite to end this unfair competition."

Speaker D: "Immigrants arrive in American cities poor and frightened. They are helped to find jobs or housing. These newcomers should show their gratitude at voting time."

11. Which speaker is most clearly expressing the melting pot theory?
    (1) A          (3) C
    (2) B          (4) D

12. Speaker D is expressing an opinion most like that of a
    (1) labor union member
    (2) religious leader
    (3) factory owner
    (4) political party boss

13. The Gentlemen's Agreement, literacy tests, and the quota system were all attempts by Congress to restrict
    (1) immigration
    (2) property ownership
    (3) voting rights
    (4) access to public education

14. In the ten years following the Civil War, a large numbers of former slaves earned a living by becoming
    (1) conductors on the Underground Railroad
    (2) workers in Northern factories
    (3) sharecroppers on Southern farms
    (4) gold miners in California

15. The tragedy of the Triangle Shirtwaist Company fire of 1911 drew national attention to the need to
    (1) restrict immigration from southern Europe
    (2) establish full-time fire departments
    (3) protect the safety of workers
    (4) improve conditions for tenement dwellers

16. During the late 1800s, many farmers supported the idea that free and unlimited coinage of silver would
    (1) end farm subsidies
    (2) help farmers to repay their loans
    (3) lead to lower prices for consumer goods
    (4) decrease prices for farmland

Copyright © Pearson Education, Inc., or its affiliates. All Rights Reserved

# Unit 4 Pre-Test

**Name** _____  **Date** _____

**Directions** Review the Test-Taking Strategies section of this book. Then answer the following questions, drawn from actual Regents examinations. For each statement or question, choose the number of the word or expression that, of those given, best completes the statement or answers the question.

1. Which development led to the other three?
   (1) growth of tenements and slums
   (2) shift from a rural to an urban lifestyle
   (3) rapid industrial growth
   (4) widespread use of child labor

2. During the Progressive Era, muckrakers published articles and novels primarily to
   (1) advance their own political careers
   (2) make Americans aware of problems in society
   (3) help the federal government become more efficient
   (4) provide entertainment for readers

3. Which heading best completes the partial outline below?

   > I. _____
   > A. Secret ballot
   > B. Direct election of senators
   > C. Recall
   > D. Referendum

   (1) Checks and Balances
   (2) Unwritten Constitution
   (3) Progressive Reforms
   (4) Universal Suffrage

4. Which long-awaited goal of the women's rights movement was achieved during the Progressive Era?
   (1) right to vote
   (2) right to own property
   (3) equal pay for equal work
   (4) equal access to employment and education

   **Base your answer to question 5 on the speakers' statements below and on your knowledge of social studies.**

   Speaker A: It is more important now to focus on vocational training and economic opportunities than on removing obstacles to social equality for African Americans.

   Speaker B: The Constitution is color-blind and recognizes no superior class in this country. All citizens are equal before the law.

   Speaker C: The American Negro [African American] must focus on the achievement of three goals: higher education, full political participation, and continued support for civil rights.

   Speaker D: African Americans should return home to Africa to establish their own independent nation free from white control.

5. During the early 1900s, reform leaders tried to advance the goals of Speaker C by
   (1) supporting passage of Jim Crow laws
   (2) forming the Tuskegee Institute in Alabama
   (3) avoiding attempts to overturn racial segregation in the courts
   (4) creating the National Association for the Advancement of Colored People (NAACP)

6. A similarity between the Bank of the United States, created in 1791, and the present-day Federal Reserve System is that both were established to
   (1) set tariff rates
   (2) regulate the money supply
   (3) achieve balanced budgets
   (4) restrict the gold supply

7. The Spanish-American War (1898) marked a turning point in United States foreign policy because the United States
   (1) developed a plan for peaceful coexistence
   (2) emerged as a major world power
   (3) pledged neutrality in future European conflicts
   (4) refused to become a colonial power

Copyright © Pearson Education, Inc., or its affiliates. All Rights Reserved

**Name** _____     **Date** _____

8. Which heading best completes the partial outline below?

> I. _____
> A. Sea power is the key to national greatness.
> B. United States missionaries spread Christian principles.
> C. The Anglo-Saxon civilization is the best in the world.
> D. Sugar plantations in Hawaii were developed by Americans.

(1) Reasons to Declare War on Spain
(2) Justification for American Imperialism
(3) Theodore Roosevelt's Political Platform
(4) Yellow Journalism in Newspapers

9. What was a major reason for United States entry into World War I?

(1) to overthrow the czarist government of Russia
(2) to keep Latin America from being attacked by Germany
(3) to maintain freedom of the seas
(4) to break up the colonial empires of the Allies

**Base your answers to questions 10 and 11 on the statements below that discuss immigration laws in the early twentieth century, and on your knowledge of social studies.**

Speaker A: A literacy test as a requirement for immigration to the United States is reasonable. Great numbers of uneducated workers take jobs and good wages from our workers.

Speaker B: Requiring literacy of immigrants is unfair. It will keep people out because they lacked the opportunity to gain an education.

Speaker C: A literacy test will allow more people from northern and western Europe to enter. They are similar to the majority of the United States population.

Speaker D: Literacy is not an issue. The real purpose of this law is to discriminate against immigrants from certain parts of the world.

10. Supporters of literacy tests to restrict immigration would most likely favor the views of Speakers

(1) A and C          (3) B and D
(2) B and C          (4) A and B

11. The immigrants referred to by Speaker D were mainly from

(1) Canada and Mexico
(2) South America
(3) western Europe
(4) southern and eastern Europe

12. In the case *Schenck* v. *United States* (1919), the United States Supreme Court settled the issue of limits on individual freedoms during wartime by establishing the

(1) clear and present danger test
(2) states' rights principle
(3) separate but equal doctrine
(4) popular sovereignty principle

13. One goal for a lasting peace that president Woodrow Wilson included in his Fourteen Points was

(1) establishing a League of Nations
(2) maintaining a permanent military force in Europe
(3) returning the United States to a policy of isolationism
(4) blaming Germany for causing World War I

14. Many senators who opposed United States membership in the League of Nations argued that joining the League would

(1) involve the nation in future military conflicts
(2) reduce freedom of the seas
(3) end the country's free-trade policy
(4) endanger the nation's military preparedness

Copyright © Pearson Education, Inc., or its affiliates. All Rights Reserved

# Unit 5 Pre-Test

**Name** _____  **Date** _____

Copyright © Pearson Education, Inc., or its affiliates. All Rights Reserved

**Directions** Review the Test-Taking Strategies section of this book. Then answer the following questions, drawn from actual Regents examinations. For each statement or question, choose the number of the word or expression that, of those given, best completes the statement or answers the question.

1. Improved mass-production techniques affected the American economy of the 1920s by

   (1) reducing prices of consumer goods
   (2) lowering the quality of most products
   (3) causing higher unemployment
   (4) decreasing the quantity of manufactured products

2. During most of the 1920s, which group experienced the most severe economic problems?

   (1) owners of small family farms
   (2) workers in the automobile industry
   (3) bankers in urban centers
   (4) entertainers in the field of radio

3. The Harlem Renaissance of the 1920s can best be described as

   (1) an organization created to help promote African American businesses
   (2) a movement that sought to draw people back to the inner cities
   (3) a relief program to provide jobs for minority workers
   (4) a period of great achievement by African-American writers, artists, and performers

4. The influence of nativism during the 1920s is best illustrated by the

   (1) increase in the popularity of the automobile
   (2) emergence of the flappers
   (3) expansion of trusts and monopolies
   (4) growth of the Ku Klux Klan

5. "Public Ignores Prohibition Restrictions"
   "Evolution and Creation Debated in Scopes Trial"
   "Women Bring Change to the Industrial Workforce"

   What do headlines such as these from the 1920s illustrate?

   (1) conflict between traditional and modern values
   (2) trend toward mass consumption of consumer goods
   (3) hostility of certain groups toward ethnic minorities
   (4) debate over the role of government in the economy

6. The Red Scare, the National Origins Acts of the 1920s, and the verdict in the Sacco and Vanzetti trial are examples of negative American attitudes toward

   (1) immigrants
   (2) business leaders
   (3) African Americans
   (4) labor union leaders

7. Statistics such as the gross domestic product, consumer price index, and unemployment rate are used to measure the

   (1) condition of the economy
   (2) amount of the federal budget deficit
   (3) balance of international trade
   (4) productivity of industry

8. Which heading would be most appropriate for the partial outline below?

   > I. _____
   >   A. Wages lagging behind the cost of living
   >   B. Overproduction of consumer goods
   >   C. Excessive buying on credit

   (1) Mercantilist Economic Theory
   (2) Features of a Bull Stock Market
   (3) Monopolistic Business Practices
   (4) Causes of the Great Depression

**Name** _____     **Date** _____

9. New Deal programs such as the Civilian Conservation Corps (CCC) and the Works Progress Administration (WPA) were primarily intended to help

(1) farmers

(2) homeowners

(3) businesses

(4) unemployed workers

10. Critics of the New Deal claimed that the Tennessee Valley Authority (TVA) and the Social Security System threatened the United States economy by

(1) applying socialist principles

(2) imposing unfair working hours

(3) decreasing government spending

(4) eroding antitrust laws

11. The Federal Deposit Insurance Corporation (FDIC) and the Securities and Exchange Commission (SEC), established during the New Deal, were important because they

(1) increased the supply of money in the economy

(2) guaranteed loans to failing businesses and banks

(3) attempted to restore public confidence in financial institutions

(4) provided grants to unemployed workers

12. President Franklin D. Roosevelt tried to pack the United States Supreme Court, but Congress did not support him. This situation is an example of

(1) Congress undermining the separation of powers

(2) the President using the unwritten constitution

(3) the use of the system of checks and balances

(4) how federalism was preserved by one branch of government

13. The National Labor Relations Act (Wagner Act) of 1935 strengthened labor unions because it legalized

(1) collective bargaining

(2) blacklisting

(3) the open shop

(4) the sit-down strike

14. The New Deal tried to solve many problems of the Great Depression by

(1) providing federal aid to many sectors of the economy

(2) reducing taxes on big business to stimulate job creation

(3) lowering federal spending to maintain a balanced budget

(4) decreasing foreign competition by raising tariffs

15. One similarity in the presidential administrations of Abraham Lincoln, Franklin D. Roosevelt, and Lyndon Johnson is that each

(1) maintained a foreign policy of neutrality

(2) expanded the power of the presidency

(3) removed Supreme Court Justices from office

(4) decreased the size of the military

16. A lasting effect of the New Deal has been a belief that government should

(1) own the principal means of producing goods and services

(2) allow natural market forces to determine economic conditions

(3) maintain a balanced federal budget during hard economic times

(4) assume responsibility for the well-being of its citizens

Copyright © Pearson Education, Inc., or its affiliates. All Rights Reserved

# Unit 6 Pre-Test

Name _____     Date _____

**Directions**  Review the Test-Taking Strategies section of this book. Then answer the following questions, drawn from actual Regents examinations. For each statement or question, choose the number of the word or expression that, of those given, best completes the statement or answers the question.

1. "Arms Sales to Warring Nations Banned"
   "Americans Forbidden to Travel on Ships of Warring Nations"
   "Loans to Nations at War Forbidden"
   "War Materials Sold Only on Cash-and-Carry Basis"

   These headlines from the 1930s reflect the efforts of the United States to

   (1) maintain freedom of the seas
   (2) send military supplies to the League of Nations
   (3) limit the spread of international communism
   (4) avoid participation in European wars

2. The Neutrality Acts passed by Congress in the mid-1930s were efforts to

   (1) avoid mistakes that led the country into World War I
   (2) create jobs for the unemployed in the military defense industry
   (3) support the League of Nations efforts to stop wars in Africa and Asia
   (4) help the democratic nations of Europe against Hitler and Mussolini

3. Why was the United States called the "arsenal of democracy" in 1940?

   (1) The leaders in the democratic nations of Europe were educated in the United States.
   (2) Most of the battles to defend worldwide democracy took place on American soil.
   (3) The United States supervised elections in European nations before the war.
   (4) The United States provided much of the weaponry needed to fight the Axis powers.

4. Shortly after entering World War II, the United States began the Manhattan Project to

   (1) work on the development of an atomic bomb
   (2) increase economic production to meet wartime demands
   (3) defend New York City against a nuclear attack
   (4) recruit men for the military services

5. A controversial issue that resulted from World War II was the

   (1) future role of the League of Nations
   (2) morality of nuclear warfare
   (3) commitment of troops without congressional approval
   (4) civilian control of the military

6. A main purpose of government-ordered rationing during World War II was to

   (1) increase foreign trade
   (2) limit the growth of industry
   (3) conserve raw materials for the war effort
   (4) encourage women to enter the workforce

7. The experiences of African Americans serving in the military forces during World War II influenced their postwar decision to

   (1) renew support for the principle of separate but equal
   (2) join the armed forces in record numbers
   (3) increase efforts to end racial discrimination
   (4) move back to the rural south

8. Which factor contributed to the internment of Japanese Americans during World War II?

   (1) labor shortage during the war
   (2) influence of racial prejudice
   (3) increase of terrorist activities on the West Coast
   (4) fear of loss of jobs to Japanese workers

9. The decision of the Supreme Court in *Korematsu* v. *United States* (1944) upheld the power of the president during wartime to

   (1) ban terrorists from entering the country
   (2) limit a group's civil liberties
   (3) stop mistreatment of resident legal aliens
   (4) deport persons who work for enemy nations

Copyright © Pearson Education, Inc., or its affiliates. All Rights Reserved

**Name** _____     **Date** _____

10. The GI Bill affected American society after World War II by

    (1) eliminating child labor

    (2) expanding voting rights

    (3) increasing spending on space exploration

    (4) extending educational and housing opportunities

11. Following World War II, Eleanor Roosevelt was most noted for her

    (1) support of racial segregation in the United States military

    (2) role in creating the United Nations Universal Declaration of Human Rights

    (3) opposition to the Truman Administration

    (4) efforts to end the use of land mines

12. The main foreign policy objective of the Marshall Plan (1948–1952) was to

    (1) stop communist aggression in Korea

    (2) fight poverty in Latin America

    (3) rebuild the economies of European nations

    (4) provide jobs for unemployed Americans

13. Which foreign policy decision by President Harry Truman is an example of the policy of containment?

    (1) relieving General MacArthur of his Korean command

    (2) recognizing the new nation of Israel

    (3) supporting the trials of war criminals in Germany and Japan

    (4) providing military aid to Greece and Turkey

14. During the Korean War, President Harry Truman removed General Douglas MacArthur from command because MacArthur

    (1) called for an immediate end to the war

    (2) refused to serve under the United Nations

    (3) lacked the experience to provide wartime leadership

    (4) threatened the constitutional principle of civilian control of the military

15. Which foreign policy term would be the most appropriate title for the partial outline below?

    > I. _____
    > A. Truman Doctrine
    > B. Marshall Plan
    > C. Berlin Blockade
    > D. Korean War

    (1) Imperialism          (3) Noninvolvement

    (2) Appeasement          (4) Containment

16. What was a major outcome of the Korean War (1950–1953)?

    (1) Korea continued to be a divided nation.

    (2) North Korea became an ally of the United States.

    (3) South Korea became a communist nation.

    (4) Control of Korea was turned over to the United Nations.

17. McCarthyism in the early 1950s resulted from

    (1) new commitments to civil rights for African Americans

    (2) opposition to the Marshall Plan

    (3) charges that Communists had infiltrated the United States government

    (4) increased public support for labor unions

18. During the early 1950s, the tactics of Senator Joseph McCarthy were criticized because he

    (1) violated important constitutional liberties

    (2) displayed racial prejudice in his questions

    (3) opposed the use of loyalty oaths

    (4) ignored evidence of Soviet spying

Copyright © Pearson Education, Inc., or its affiliates. All Rights Reserved

# Unit 7 Pre-Test

**Name** _____  **Date** _____

**Directions** Review the Test-Taking Strategies section of this book. Then answer the following questions, drawn from actual Regents examinations. For each statement or question, choose the number of the word or expression that, of those given, best completes the statement or answers the question.

1. In 1957, President Dwight D. Eisenhower sent federal troops to Little Rock, Arkansas, to
   (1) protect civil rights marchers
   (2) help African Americans register to vote
   (3) enforce a Supreme Court decision to desegregate public schools
   (4) end race riots resulting from a bus boycott

2. Which strategy did African American students use when they refused to leave a "whites only" lunch counter in Greensboro, North Carolina, in 1960?
   (1) economic boycott
   (2) hunger strike
   (3) petition drive
   (4) civil disobedience

3. The Equal Pay Act, the Title IX education amendment, and the proposed Equal Rights amendment (ERA) were primarily efforts to improve the status of
   (1) African Americans
   (2) American Indians
   (3) migrant workers
   (4) women

4. One reason for the creation of the Peace Corps by President John F. Kennedy was to
   (1) stop the spread of AIDS in Africa and Asia
   (2) gain control of territory in Latin America
   (3) provide workers for industrial nations
   (4) give support to developing nations

5. A major goal of President Lyndon Johnson's Great Society program was to
   (1) control economic inflation
   (2) end poverty in the United States
   (3) repeal several New Deal social programs
   (4) return responsibility for welfare programs to the states

6. **"Batista Driven from Power"**
   **"Bay of Pigs Invasion Fails"**
   **"U-2 Planes Reveal Soviet Missiles"**

   These headlines refer to the relationship between the United States and
   (1) Canada         (3) Mexico
   (2) Cuba           (4) Panama

7. United States involvement in the Vietnam War was based in part on a desire to
   (1) prevent renewed Japanese expansionism in the Pacific
   (2) assure access to an adequate supply of oil from the Middle East
   (3) contain communism in Southeast Asia
   (4) protect American business interests in China

8. The main goal of President Richard Nixon's foreign policy of détente was to
   (1) assure American victory in Vietnam
   (2) resolve conflicts in the Middle East
   (3) abolish the North Atlantic Treaty Organization (NATO)
   (4) improve relations with the Soviet Union

9. Which statement best describes an impact of the Watergate scandal on American society?
   (1) The modern environmental movement began.
   (2) Public trust in government declined.
   (3) Voter turnout in elections increased.
   (4) An economic recession ended.

10. A major policy of President Ronald Reagan's administration was to
    (1) reduce defense spending
    (2) lower federal income tax rates
    (3) end desegregation of public facilities
    (4) promote regulation of small businesses

Copyright © Pearson Education, Inc., or its affiliates. All Rights Reserved

# Unit 7 Pre-Test *continued*

**Name** _____     **Date** _____

11. **"Gorbachev Proposes Nuclear Arms Reductions"**
    **"Berliners Travel Freely Between East and West"**
    **"Russia Seeks To Join NATO"**

    These headlines are most closely associated with the

    (1) military arms race
    (2) decline of Cold War hostilities
    (3) failures of the containment policy
    (4) successes of communism in the Soviet Union

12. The North American Free Trade Agreement (NAFTA) and the General Agreement on Trade and Tariffs (GATT) have encouraged countries to

    (1) participate in the global economy
    (2) create a uniform international currency
    (3) accept similar wage and price controls
    (4) regulate multinational corporations

13. *The Jungle* by Upton Sinclair and *Unsafe at Any Speed* by Ralph Nader were both intended to

    (1) publicize the growing violence in American society
    (2) suggest that a poor person could get rich with hard work
    (3) encourage immigration reform
    (4) make the public aware of the poor quality of certain products

14. The dispute over counting Florida voter ballots in the presidential election of 2000 was settled by

    (1) an order of the governor of Florida
    (2) an agreement between the candidates
    (3) a vote of the United States Senate
    (4) a United States Supreme Court decision

15. The United States intervened in Haiti and Bosnia during the 1990s to

    (1) gain access to new markets
    (2) acquire colonies for an economic empire
    (3) stop conflicts within those nations
    (4) disrupt international drug trafficking

16. As the average age of the nation's population increases, there will be a need to

    (1) create more child care facilities
    (2) address the financing of Medicare
    (3) increase the number of public schools
    (4) reform immigration laws

Copyright © Pearson Education, Inc., or its affiliates. All Rights Reserved

# Geography and the Development of the United States

**Section 1:  Geography and the Development of the United States**

## Unit Overview

This unit provides a general review of the physical and cultural geography of the United States. It also reviews some of the ways in which geography has influenced the history of the country. Geographers use five themes to study an area. The five themes are location, place, movement, regions, and human-environment interaction.

These are some of the key questions relating to the nation's geography. Each question relates to one of the five geographic themes:

- Where is the United States located, both absolutely and relatively? How has the country's relative location changed over time?
- What are the physical and human characteristics of the United States?
- How have people, goods, and ideas moved between places?
- How are places within the United States similar to and different from other places?
- How have people in the United States interacted with the natural environment?

# Geography and the Development of the United States

The
# Big
# Idea

The physical geography of the United States has played a major role in the nation's development:

- Geography influences the development of both domestic and foreign policies of the United States.

- Today, geographic issues are linked to environmental issues such as air and water pollution, energy sources and uses, and waste disposal.

- The study of demographics and population trends is of ongoing importance throughout United States history.

## Key Themes and Concepts

As you review this unit, take special note of the following key themes and concepts:

**Physical Systems:** How have the nation's systems of mountains and waterways influenced the development of the United States?

**Immigration and Migration:** What have been the major patterns of immigration and movement of people over the course of the country's history?

**Places and Regions:** What different types of regions exist within the United States?

## Key Terms

| | | |
|---|---|---|
| geographers | Mississippi River | Manifest Destiny |
| geography | Appalachian | Sun Belt |
| demographic | Mountains | Pacific Northwest |
| Great Plains | Rocky Mountains | Great Lakes |
| Central Plains | population density | Middle Atlantic |
| Midwest | New England | Region |

## Location

**Geographers** describe the location of an area in both absolute and relative terms. An atlas is the best source for identifying both physical and political place locations as well as other demographic information.

### Absolute Location

In terms of its absolute location, the United States is located in the Northern and Western hemispheres. With the exception of Hawaii, the country is located on the continent of North America. The country is bordered by the Atlantic Ocean on the east and the Pacific Ocean on the west.

### Relative Location

Geographers also consider an area's relative location, or where it is located in relation to other places. For example, the United States is located south of Canada and north of Mexico. California is west of New York.

The relative location of a place can also change over time. For much of the country's history, Americans felt relatively isolated from Europe and Asia. Likewise, people in the West felt relatively isolated from the East.

Changes in transportation and communication technologies changed these perceptions. For example, the number of post offices in the nation leaped from 75 in 1790 to 8,450 in 1830. Regular mail delivery made it easier for people in distant places to communicate with one another. Improved communication and transportation helped tie together different parts of the country as it grew in both size and population.

**The United States: Political**

## Place

Geographers study both the physical and human characteristics of places. Both physical and human characteristics of the **geography** of the United States have had a huge impact on the development of the country. Geographers use a number of types of maps. Physical maps show land features such as rivers and mountains. Political maps illustrate state or country boundaries and various political divisions such as counties and cities. **Demographic** maps show the placement of groups of people by different categories such as age or income level or education. The ability to develop maps forecasting weather conditions has improved dramatically with the use of modern technology.

### Physical Characteristics

Physical characteristics include landforms, water bodies, vegetation, and climate. Because of its size, the United States has a wide variety of landforms. As the map on this page shows, the **Great Plains** and the **Central Plains** occupy the central regions of the country, also known as the **Midwest.** The rich soils and climate of the Midwest encouraged Americans to move to these regions, where they could acquire inexpensive farmland. The **Mississippi River** cuts through the Central Plains as it flows south to the Gulf of Mexico. Boats traveling along the Mississippi allowed farmers and traders to transport their goods to markets throughout the country.

Two mountain ranges run from north to south on either side of the Central Plains region. In the east are the lower, older **Appalachian Mountains.** In the west are the **Rocky Mountains.** The Rockies are a cordillera, or a related set of mountain ranges, that stretches from northern Alaska to Mexico, forming the longest mountain chain in North America.

**Analyzing Documents**

This map shows the fifty states of the United States.

- Where is New York located in relation to Florida?

- What types of regions are shown on this map?

- What two foreign countries share their borders with the United States?

# The United States and Canada: Physical

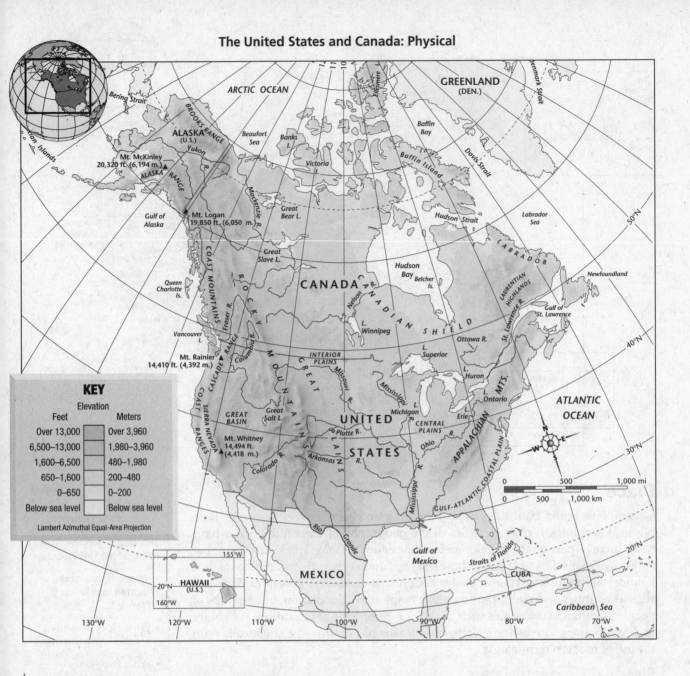

## KEY

### Elevation

| Feet | Meters |
|---|---|
| Over 13,000 | Over 3,960 |
| 6,500–13,000 | 1,980–3,960 |
| 1,600–6,500 | 480–1,980 |
| 650–1,600 | 200–480 |
| 0–650 | 0–200 |
| Below sea level | Below sea level |

Lambert Azimuthal Equal-Area Projection

## Analyzing Documents

Study the map on this page; then answer the following questions.

- What major landform occupies the central region of the United States?

- Which mountain range is higher, the Appalachian Mountains or the Rocky Mountains?

## Human Characteristics

Several waves of immigration have created a unique cultural mix of people in the United States. People from every region of the world have settled in the United States. As a result, the nation's human characteristics, such as language, religion, and customs, are varied. About half of all African Americans live in the South. About nine percent of southern residents are of Latino origin.

In general, **population density** is greater in the eastern half of the country. The most densely settled region of the country is the Northeast Corridor, which stretches along the east coast from Washington, D.C., to Boston, Massachusetts.

Compared with those in many nations of the world, people in the United States have long life expectancies, high per capita incomes, and high literacy rates.

# Movement

Geographers study the movement of people, goods, and ideas within an area. The movement of people into and within the United States over the course of history can be broken into the following large patterns.

## Bering Strait Land Bridge

Geographers believe that during the Ice Ages—between about 20,000 and 12,000 years ago—much of the earth's water was frozen into glaciers and ice sheets. As a result, ocean levels dropped, exposing a flat bridge of land between Alaska and eastern Asia where the Bering Strait is today. Over thousands of years, hunters from East Asia crossed the land bridge and gradually spread out over North and South America. These Paleo-Indians were the first humans in the Americas, ancestors of all the Native American peoples.

## European Exploration and Slavery

By the 1500s, better ships and navigation methods allowed European explorers to find their way to North America. The first European newcomers, mainly from Spain, settled in what are now Florida, the Southwest, and Mexico. About a century later, people from France and Great Britain set up colonies on the eastern coast of North America. In addition, millions of Africans were enslaved and brought unwillingly to North America. In the 1600s the earliest English settlements in the New World, from Plymouth in Massachusetts to New Amsterdam in New York to Jamestown, Virginia, were all located near the coastline or on rivers. **New England** earned its name as it is the location of some of the earliest colonies, Massachusetts, Rhode Island, and Connecticut and later New Hampshire, Vermont, and Maine. The geography of this area encouraged small farms and commercial fishing, whereas much further south, fertile land and a long growing season encouraged the development of plantations producing tobacco, cotton, rice, and indigo. Geographically, the Appalachian Mountains limited the movement of colonists westward until the middle of the eighteenth century. Later in the century by the end of the Revolutionary War, the western border of the United States was the Mississippi River.

## Movement and Migration

| Time Period | Location | Reason/s | Results: |
|---|---|---|---|
| 20,000 B.C. to 12,000 B.C. | Bering Strait, between Alaska and eastern Asia | Hunters in search of food and warmer climate | Settlement by Native Americans from Alaska south and west along the coastline |
| 1500s (A.D.) | Florida, Mexico | Spanish in search of gold, glory for their nation, and to spread Christianity | Spanish language and heritage in the settled areas, eventually including California and the American Southwest |
| 1600s–early 1700s | Coastal New England, New York, the Middle Atlantic and Southern colonies to Georgia | Religious freedom, farmland, coastal fishing resources, furs, minerals, | The Thirteen original British colonies developed |
| 1700s | Expansion westward over the Appalachian Mountains to the Mississippi River Valley | Population growth encouraged expansion westward | The concept of the frontier as the western boundary of the new country was extended further west |
| 1800s | Across the Great Plains and the Rocky Mountains to California | Continued growth of population, immigration | Manifest Destiny accepted as American right, acquisition of additional territory |

## United States Territorial Expansion, 1783–1853

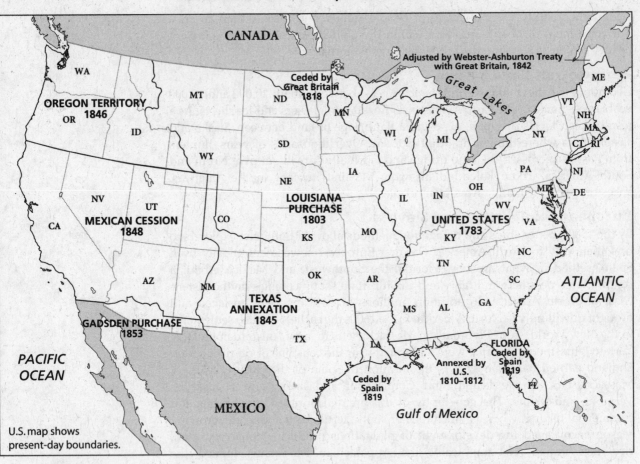

U.S. map shows present-day boundaries.

## Analyzing Documents

The movement of people from east to west put pressure on the government to expand the territory of the United States. Study the map above; then answer the following questions.

- What was the date of the Louisiana Purchase?

- When were the lands of the present-day states of Washington and Oregon added to the country's territory?

- Using the information on this map, describe the acquisition of present-day California.

## Migration from East to West

During the 1800s, the promise of land and gold led many Americans of European descent to move westward. Farmers along the Ohio and Mississippi River Valleys benefitted from the Louisiana Purchase and the acquisition of New Orleans as a port for American agricultural goods. Native Americans were forced from their lands to locations even further west. Rivers, turnpikes, canals, and railroads all played a part in the movement of people to the frontiers of the west. The flat grassy region between the Mississippi River and the Rocky Mountains is known as the Great Plains. This fertile farmland was a great attraction, and the Homestead Act of 1862 provided for the development of additional farms in the area. **Manifest Destiny** was the concept that expressed the American belief that the United States was destined to expand across North America. Throughout the seventeenth, eighteenth, and nineteenth centuries, the American frontier shifted further and further westward. The Atlantic Ocean to the east and the Pacific Ocean to the west enhanced the ability of the United States to maintain a policy of political neutrality for many years.

## African American Migration

African Americans moved from the South to the Northeast and Midwest in search of economic opportunities from about 1890 to 1920 and again during the 1940s.

## The Rise of the Sun Belt

Beginning around 1950, many Americans moved from the industrial cities of the North and Midwest to the so-called **Sun Belt**—the southern states stretching from Florida to California. Newcomers were attracted by job opportunities and warmer climates.

This population shift, along with its corresponding reapportionment of congressional seats, has given the South greater influence in American politics. Once a stronghold for Democrats, the South has become more strongly Republican and conservative.

# Regions

The continental United States from east to west covers a distance of over three thousand miles. The states of Hawaii in the Pacific Ocean and Alaska in the North Pacific expand the country's geographic dimensions. Given this huge size, it is not surprising that geographers can identify hundreds of regions within the country.

## Different Types of Regions

Geographers describe regions as places having at least one common characteristic. Regions can be defined by physical characteristics, such as landforms or climate. They can also be defined by cultural characteristics, such as the economy of the area or the political organization of the area. The map below shows regions that share similar economies or land use patterns. Political regions include towns, counties, cities, states, and the United States as a whole.

In the United States, geographers use terms to describe groups of states. They use "Midwest" to describe states such as Ohio, Indiana, and Illinois. They use **"Pacific Northwest"** to describe Oregon and Washington. They also refer to the states where the Rocky Mountains are as the "Rocky Mountain area." Climatic conditions can cause a region to be identified for its frequency of tornadoes, hurricanes, or snowstorms. The cultural characteristics of people might also designate a region, such as the region around Lancaster, Pennsylvania, where many Amish people live. As you study the history and development of the United States, think about how various immigrant groups gave certain regions distinctive names, for example, New York City's Chinatown.

### Analyzing Documents

Study the land-use map on this page; then answer the following questions.

- What is the major land use activity in the Midwest?

- How do the economic activities of the Pacific Northwest compare with those of the Northeast?

- Where are the most concentrated areas of manufacturing and trade located?

**Land Use in the United States**

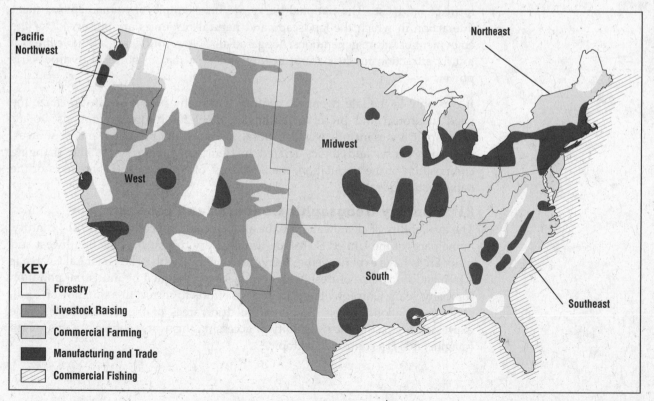

KEY
- Forestry
- Livestock Raising
- Commercial Farming
- Manufacturing and Trade
- Commercial Fishing

### Regions Within New York State

In New York State, some examples of regions include the **Great Lakes** region, the Adirondack Mountains, Long Island, the Finger Lakes, Manhattan, and the Capital District around Albany.

## Human-Environment Interaction

When studying an area, geographers also examine how people use the environment and how they have changed it. What are the consequences of those changes?

### Early Land Use Patterns

From the earliest days of settlement, Americans have been interacting with their environment to survive. When the Europeans began to settle along the Atlantic coast, they faced a range of climatic and geographic conditions. At various points in this nation's history, these conditions both encouraged and discouraged settlement. In some places, Native Americans assisted the Europeans in adapting to their unfamiliar surroundings.

The great Atlantic coastal plain fostered agricultural development in the **Middle Atlantic Region,** while further to the south, the long, hot summers gave rise to the tobacco and cotton industries. Settlers of coastal South Carolina drained swamps to create thriving rice plantations. The rocky soil of New England discouraged extensive farming, but the rich coastal waters encouraged the development of fishing and shipbuilding. The waterfalls in the area and elsewhere in the Middle Atlantic states encouraged the development of factories that could benefit from water power. These factories produced goods that were then traded all over the world. Port cities, such as Boston, New York, Charleston, Savannah, and New Orleans, developed as centers of this trade. Even today population density is impacted by geographic features. Coastal areas and river valleys tend to attract development much faster than deserts or mountainous areas.

### Tourism and Conservation

In addition to the land-use patterns shown on the map above, tourism is another form of land use. The national parks are an example of human-environment interaction in which the landscape and natural resources are preserved for the enjoyment of future generations. Niagara Falls, New York, leads a double life as a tourist attraction for its natural beauty and as a major source of hydroelectric power.

It was only in the late twentieth century that many people began to realize the need to protect and preserve the environment for future generations. Today, geographic issues include waste disposal, air and water pollution, energy sources, and energy use, and topics related to demographics, such as the changing composition of the population, the "graying" of America, and the effects of the baby boom generation.

### 21st Century Geographic Concerns and Interests

The availability of clean water will be an increasing concern into the 21st century. Some parts of the United States are usually very dry such as the Southwest and other areas have experienced extreme seasonal droughts. The Great Lakes area is a tremendous source of fresh water but has been plagued by industrial pollution for many years. Currently there are serious efforts to correct this situation on local, state, and national levels. Some of the drier areas of the United States have expressed interest in the possibility of accessing this water source. As you might imagine, this is a controversial topic.

# Looking Ahead

As you continue through this review book, you will have many opportunities to utilize the concepts of location, place, movement, regions, and human-environment interaction. Use the maps located in this unit and elsewhere in this text to help you draw conclusions about the impact geography has had and continues to have on the development of the United States.

In recent years the Regents examination has included multiple-choice questions, one Thematic Essay Question, and one Document-Based Question. This unit includes one Thematic Essay Question. To succeed on the Regents examination, you may need to review these pages after you have completed your United States History and Government course. If you are using this text as a review aid, try to answer as many of these questions as you can before you refer to the other sections of the text.

## Analyzing Documents

Study the climate map on this page; then answer the following questions.`

• Much of the southwestern United States has a hot, dry, arid climate and receives less than 10 inches of rainfall each year. Many people have been moving to this region in recent decades. How do you think climate affects the human-environment interaction in this region?

• Describe the climate of the southeastern half of the United States.

## The United States and Canada: Climate Regions

ARCTIC OCEAN
Bering Sea
ALASKA (U.S.)
Baffin Bay
Labrador Sea
Hudson Bay
CANADA
Vancouver
Calgary
Seattle
Montreal
Ottawa
PACIFIC OCEAN
HAWAII (U.S.)
San Francisco
UNITED STATES
Chicago
New York
Washington, D.C.
St. Louis
ATLANTIC OCEAN
Los Angeles
Dallas
MEXICO
Gulf of Mexico
Miami
Tropic of Cancer

KEY
☐ Tropical wet
☐ Tropical wet and dry
☐ Semiarid
☐ Arid
☐ Mediterranean
☐ Humid subtropical
☐ Marine west coast
☐ Humid continental
☐ Subarctic
☐ Tundra
☐ Highlands

Lambert Azimuthal Equal-Area Projection

# Thematic Essay Question

*Directions:* Write a well-organized essay that includes an introduction, several paragraphs addressing the task below, and a conclusion.

**Theme: Influence of Geographic Factors on Governmental Actions**

> Actions taken by the United States government have often been influenced by geographic factors. Some of these factors include location, climate, natural resources, and physical features.

**Task:**

> Identify *two* actions taken by the United States government that have been influenced by geographic factors and for *each*
>
> - State *one* reason the United States took the action
> - Describe how a geographic factor influenced the action
> - Discuss the impact of the action on the United States

You may use any action taken by the United States government that was influenced by a geographic factor. Some suggestions you might wish to consider include the Lewis and Clark expedition (1804–1806), issuance of the Monroe Doctrine (1823), Mexican War (1846–1848), Commodore Perry's opening of Japan (1853), passage of the Homestead Act (1862), purchase of Alaska (1867), construction of the Panama Canal (1904–1914), entry into World War II (1941), passage of the Interstate Highway Act (1956), and involvement in the Persian Gulf War (1991).

**You are *not* limited to these suggestions.**

**Guidelines:**

**In your essay, be sure to:**

- Develop all aspects of the task
- Support the theme with relevant facts, examples, and details
- Use a logical and clear plan of organization, including an introduction and a conclusion that are beyond a restatement of the theme

**In developing your answer, be sure to keep these general definitions in mind:**

(a) **describe means "to illustrate something in words or tell about it"**
(b) **discuss means "to make observations about something using facts, reasoning, and argument; to present in some detail"**

# Constitutional Foundations for the United States Democratic Republic

**Section 1:** **The Constitution: The Foundation of American Society**

**Section 2:** **The Constitution Tested: Nationalism and Sectionalism**

## Unit Overview

Unit 2 covers the period from the first English settlement in 1607 through the end of the Civil War in 1865. The focus of the unit is the Constitution of the United States—its historical and constitutional foundations, including the ways in which the nation's government, based on the Constitution, developed and was then tested.

Some of the key questions about the United States government and constitutional history through 1865 include:

- What was the influence of the colonial settlement pattern, colonists' experience living in the American colonies, colonial slavery, and Enlightenment thought on the development of the United States Constitution?

- What opinions about government were discussed and debated by the Framers? What compromises did they reach in order to create the Constitution and ensure approval by the states?

- What is the structure of the United States Constitution, and how does the government it describes function?

- What are the basic constitutional principles of American democracy? Why were they important when the Constitution was written? Why have they remained critical principles throughout United States history?

- How did the new nation go about putting its constitution into effect? What helped to build nationalism? What conflicting opinions about government were discussed and debated in those early years?

- How did sectionalism and slavery bring on a constitutional crisis that led the nation to civil war?

# The Constitution: The Foundation of American Society

The
# Big
# Idea

The Constitution is the foundation of American society. The United States:

• developed from thirteen English colonies.

• was influenced by the coming together of people from three different continents and cultures.

• developed its political system from British traditions and Enlightenment thinking, modified by the American colonial experience.

• won its independence in the American Revolution.

• bases its government on the 1789 Constitution.

• benefited from the actions of our first presidents as they put the new Constitution into effect.

• was influenced by the unwritten constitution that developed through interpretations, actions, court decisions, and customs.

## Section Overview

For centuries, North America was inhabited solely by Native Americans. Beginning in the sixteenth century, Europeans, mainly from Spain, France and England, came to the continent. The United States of America developed from thirteen colonies along the North American Atlantic coast, settled in the 1600s and 1700s by English and other Europeans, as well as by Africans brought as slaves.

In 1763, following the end of the French and Indian War, tensions between the colonies and England increased sharply. In 1776, after a year of fighting the British, the colonies issued the Declaration of Independence. The American Revolution resulted in victory for the former colonies.

They established a weak government under the Articles of Confederation, but in 1787 the leaders of the new nation wrote the United States Constitution. After ratification, the first government under the Constitution was formed. In its early years the new nation struggled to define itself, as political parties entered the debate over the meaning of the Constitution and how best to implement it.

## Key Themes and Concepts

Take special note of the following key themes and concepts:

**Diversity:** In what ways did the Native Americans, the Europeans, and the Africans who met in North America differ?

**Change** Why did the Thirteen British Colonies become an independent nation?

**Government** What is the basic structure and function of the government created by the United States Constitution?

**Constitutional Principles:** What are the basic principles that are the foundation of our democratic form of government?

**Citizenship** Under the Constitution, what are the basic rights and responsibilities of a citizen of the United States?

**Foreign Policy** What were the major influences on United States foreign policy in the first years of the new nation?

## Key People

Be sure you understand the significance of these key people:

| | | |
|---|---|---|
| John Locke | Patrick Henry | George Washington |
| Baron de Montesquieu | Samuel Adams | James Madison |
| Jean-Jacques Rousseau | Thomas Jefferson | Alexander Hamilton |
| Voltaire | Benjamin Franklin | John Marshall |
| John Peter Zenger | John Adams | James Monroe |

# Key Terms

Iroquois Confederacy
indentured servants
triangular trade
Middle Passage
democracy
republic
Magna Carta
writ of *habeas corpus*

Parliament
representative
  government
rule of law
natural rights
Enlightenment
social contract

charter
Mayflower Compact
salutary neglect
mercantilism
Articles of
  Confederation

# Key Supreme Court Cases

*Marbury* v. *Madison*, 1803
*McCulloch* v. *Maryland*, 1819
*Gibbons* v. *Ogden*, 1824

## Part 1 | The Historical Foundations of American Society and Government

Before examining the Constitution of the United States and the features that make it unique, it is important to understand the roots of the ideas in the document. To do that, we must start with the historical origins of the United States of America.

## The People and Peopling of the Thirteen American Colonies

The historical origins of the United States of America date from the settlement, in the seventeenth and eighteenth centuries, of thirteen English colonies along the North American Atlantic coast. There, the cultures of three different peoples came together—Native Americans (the original inhabitants), Europeans, and Africans (brought as enslaved people).

## Native Americans

Native Americans were the first people to occupy the Western Hemisphere. In the late 1400s, they numbered as many as 15 million in North America alone. The way of life of Native Americans was heavily influenced by the **environment.** The Native American lifestyle in present-day northeastern and southeastern United States was based on agriculture, hunting, and fishing. Trade was an important part of this economic system. Strong social organizations rested on ties between extended families, with women in positions of some power in those tribes that were agricultural.

### The Iroquois Confederacy

The most powerful government of the Eastern Woodlands Native Americans was the **Iroquois Confederacy,** formed in 1570, and made up of first five and then six Iroquois nations located in central and western New York. The Confederacy made it possible for the Iroquois to hold onto its lands against European pressure for almost two centuries, playing the English and French against each other.

### Trade and Alliances

Relations between colonists and Native Americans centered around trade and exchange, alliances, or warfare. The survival of **Jamestown,** founded in 1607 as

### Geography in History

• How did the environment influence the culture of Native Americans?

### Preparing for the Exam

On the examination, you will need to have a thorough understanding of important United States historical and governmental terms.

• What is a confederacy?

• What are two examples of confederacies in United States history?

the first permanent English settlement in North America is credited in part to the food supplied, in return for weapons, by the Algonquin tribes that made up the Powhatan Confederacy. Native Americans also offered food to the **Plymouth Colony,** settled in 1620, in order to gain the colony as an ally against other tribes. In the 1600s, the Iroquois fought the Hurons, the Eries, and then the French for control of the fur trade between the Great Lakes region and New York. The wars with France ended in 1701 when the Iroquois adopted a policy of neutrality toward both France and England.

Interactions between Native Americans and the settlers led to outbreaks of diseases, such as measles and smallpox, which decimated the Native American population. As the Native Americans became increasingly dependent on European products, their traditional culture weakened.

## Different Views and Values

Possession of the land was at the center of conflict between Native Americans and colonists. Native Americans held land in common and believed it should be used for the good of all. It could not be bought or sold, although the rights to the use of land could be transferred. The English valued individual ownership and had a tradition of buying and selling land.

There were other cultural differences. The European colonists believed in the superiority of their way of life and acted accordingly. They attempted to convert the Native Americans to Christianity and assumed that they would adopt an English lifestyle.

### Analyzing Documents

Examine the cartoon, then answer the following questions.

- Which groups do the speakers in this cartoon represent?

- What point is the cartoonist making about immigration to the United States?

## Warfare

In the 1600s, European settlers and Native Americans engaged in wars caused by the expansion of English settlements and fears of Native Americans for the survival of their culture. In tidewater Virginia, profitable tobacco farming led settlers to move westward into Native American lands. By 1646, after two wars, the Powhatan Confederacy was destroyed, unable to hold back the settlers' movement. In 1675 in New England, an alliance of Native American tribes launched King Philip's War. The colonists eliminated most Native Americans in southern New England. However, for the next 50 years, colonial expansion in New England was slowed.

In the 1700s, France and England competed for world power, fighting four wars for control in Europe, Asia, and North America. Because the French entered regions to trade furs, building forts rather than settlements, Native Americans tended to support them rather than the British who settled and farmed the land. **The French and Indian War** (1756–63) erupted when the English challenged the French for control of the land that is now Ohio and western Pennsylvania. The war pitted the British army and colonists against the French and their Native American allies. Toward the end of the war, the Iroquois, influenced by their earlier conflict with the French over trade, ended their neutrality and supported the British.

### Analyzing Documents

"I am now grown old , and must soon die; . . . Why should you take by force that from us which you can have by love? Why should you destroy us, who have provided you with food? . . . What is the cause of your jealousy? You see us unarmed, and willing to supply your wants, if you come in a friendly manner, not with swords and guns, as to invade an enemy."
—King Powhatan, 1609

• What is the answer to Powhatan's question, "What is the cause of your jealousy?"

## The Colonists

The oldest settlement in what is now the United States is Saint Augustine, in Florida (1565). Founded by the Spanish, it did not become part of the United States until 1819. What was to become the United States began with the settlement of Virginia in 1607. By 1732, with the charter of Georgia, there were a total of 13 British colonies.

### The Colonial Experience, 1607–1732

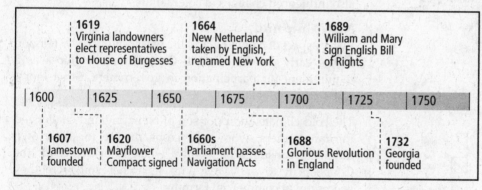

### Analyzing Documents

• How many years were there between the settling of the first and the last of the 13 English colonies?

• What major changes occurred in the colonies during that time?

### Who Came to the Colonies

The settlers were a diverse group. They included Africans brought against their will, Scots-Irish from northern Ireland, Germans, Portuguese, Swedes, Dutch, French, Welsh, Irish, Scots, Belgians, and Swiss. In the colonial period, a large number of European immigrants came as **indentured servants** who contracted to work as many as seven years to repay the cost of their passage.

Most of each colony's population, however, was English. This fact would greatly affect the nature of the government that developed in the United States.

### Why They Came

Just as the colonists represented many ethnic backgrounds, their motivations for coming to the colonies also varied.

Examine the map below
then answer the following
questions.

• By 1776, two thirds of the
population of the English
colonies lived no more
than 50 miles from the
ocean. Why?

• Which ethnic groups had
the largest settlements in
1770? Which had the
smallest settlements?

• Which natural harbors
in the Thirteen Colonies
contributed to the
development of
**commerce,** or trade
between cities, states,
and nations?

**Religious Reasons** Some colonies were founded for religious reasons, but the colonists represented different religions and had different motivations. Massachusetts, for example, was founded by Pilgrims, or Separatists, who had left the Church of England, and Puritans who wanted to reform it. Colonies controlled by the Puritans allowed no religious freedom. Rhode Island, on the other hand, permitted all religions including Judaism. Pennsylvania was founded as a refuge for Quakers and Maryland as a refuge for Roman Catholics.

**Economic Reasons** Economic motives were a major factor in the founding of Virginia, Delaware, and New Netherlands (later New York), as well as North and South Carolina. Georgia, the last of the colonies to be founded, was settled by debtors. Settlers in all colonies were drawn by the availability of land and the opportunity to own it.

**Political Reasons** Political events in seventeenth-century England influenced patterns of migration. Separatists and Puritans came to North America after having fallen into political disfavor because of their objections to the established Church of England and the king who headed it. After the monarchy was restored in 1660, colonies that included New Jersey and the Carolinas were founded on land granted by the king to his loyal supporters. Quakers, Catholics, French Huguenots, and Jews came to escape religious intolerance as well as governmental persecution.

## Colonial Settlement by Ethnic Group in 1770

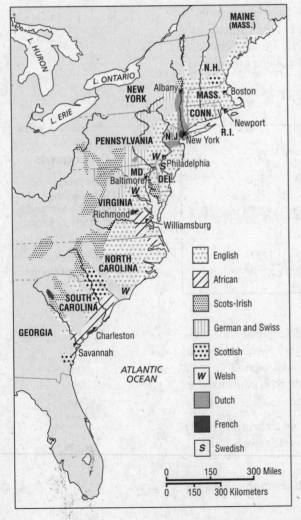

## What Influenced Their Experiences

Geography was a primary influence on the colonial way of life. So were the practices colonists brought from their homelands. Ethnic groups tended to settle together. Large distances and difficult transportation encouraged continuing family patterns, gender roles, and farming methods brought from Europe, although these were sometimes modified by the new environment. Native American and African cultures also influenced changes in colonial lifestyles.

## New England

Every aspect of New England life was influenced by religion in the early colonial period. Church membership was a requirement for participation in government. Strict moral codes were enforced.

The cold climate and poor soil of New England challenged Puritan farmers, who grew crops mostly for their own families' consumption. Only when they reached the Connecticut River Valley with its richer soil were they successful at commercial farming.

New England developed a diversified economy. Although farming was the most common occupation, New England also became the center of colonial shipping, with major ports at Boston and Salem. Fishing and ship building were among the related industries. Merchants and professionals made up the wealthiest social class.

## The Middle Colonies

The middle colonies had a diverse population, including Dutch, Germans, and Scots-Irish. These colonies, especially New York and Pennsylvania, benefited from more fertile soil. They exported wheat and corn, and this trade helped build New York and Philadelphia. Large numbers of tenant farmers—who rented rather than owned the land—lived in the Hudson River Valley of New York and in New Jersey.

## The Southern Colonies

Agriculture flourished in the southern colonies, which had a warmer climate and rich soil. The southern economy was based on crops grown for export, such as tobacco, rice, and indigo. They were cultivated first by indentured servants and then by enslaved Africans.

The wealthiest social class included Chesapeake tobacco planters and the owners of the Carolina rice plantations. The central role of plantation agriculture led to a growing dependence on slavery to support the economic, social, and political systems of the southern colonies.

### Comparing the Thirteen Colonies 1607–1760

| | New England Colonies MA, RI, CT, NH | Middle Colonies NY, NJ, PA, DE | Southern Colonies VA, MD, NC, SC, GA |
|---|---|---|---|
| Geography | cold winters, rocky soil, mountains, forests, rivers, natural harbors | less severe winters, fertile soil, rivers, natural harbors | mild, long growing season, fertile soil, tidal rivers, wide coastal plain |
| Early Colonists | English Pilgrims, mostly English Puritans | Dutch, English, Welsh, Germans, Scots-Irish, Irish, Swedes, French | English, enslaved Africans |
| Economy 17th to Mid-18th Centuries | diverse economy included small-scale farming, fishing, fur trade, shipbuilding, lumbering, trade and commerce, crafts, and industry. Major City: Boston | economy included medium-scale farming for cash crops of wheat, corn, and flax, as well as fur trade, trade, crafts, and industry. Major Cities: Philadelphia, New York | highly agricultural: economy included large plantations, which used indentured servants or slave labor, to produce cash crops of tobacco, rice, and indigo. Major City: Charleston, SC |
| Lifestyle | high literacy level, Protestant work ethic, town meetings; Colonial colleges: Harvard (the oldest), Yale, College of RI (Brown), Dartmouth | most regional diversity in religion and nationalities; Colonial colleges: Princeton, Pennsylvania, Columbia (King's), Rutgers (Queen's) | self-sufficient plantation life, few cities, least populated and developed region, small farmers largest social group; Colonial college: William and Mary |
| Influences on Gov't | 1620: Mayflower Compact (MA) 1639: Fundamental Orders of CT | 1683: NY Chapter of Liberties | 1619: House of Burgesses (VA) 1649: Act of Toleration (MD) |

# The Africans

By 1700, the institution of slavery—primarily involving Africans—already served to highlight the regional differences in the colonies.

## Origins of the Atlantic Slave Trade

The first enslaved people in the Americas were Native Americans. In the 1500s, the Spanish and Portuguese forced them to work in mines and on sugar plantations. After the Native American population declined as a result of European diseases, the Spanish, Portuguese, and French began enslaving West Africans. With the growth of tobacco, indigo, and rice plantations, the British colonies also began to participate in the slave trade. By the early 1700s, England controlled the Atlantic slave trade.

There was a two-way trade between England and the colonies for goods such as grains, fish, fur, wood products, tobacco, indigo, and rice, which the colonies exchanged for English manufactured goods. The slave trade, however, was a

**triangular trade.** New England merchants traded rum for enslaved people in West Africa. The enslaved people were sold in the West Indies for molasses or sugar, which was shipped to New England to make more rum.

## Geography in History

- Find a trade pattern that is an example of mercantilism.
- Find an example of the triangular trade.

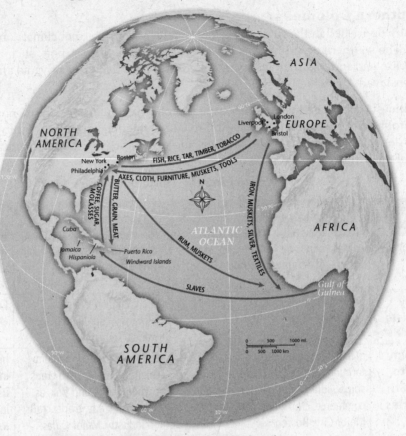

## Key Themes and Concepts

**Places and Regions**
- Slavery was more common in the southern colonies than in New England. Why?

## Development of Slavery in the Colonies

The first African enslaved people were brought to Virginia in 1619. At this time, most were considered indentured servants and were considered free when their contracts ended.

By 1700, a race-based definition of a slave that included restrictions and punishments, was written into law. Soon a **system of permanent slavery** was in place. It was a legal system that both discriminated against and exploited the Africans and African Americans. The slave system became central to the economic system of the South. It influenced not only the economy but also the social and political systems, affecting southerners of both races.

### Slavery

- This legalization of slavery coincided with an increased market for tobacco in **Virginia and the Chesapeake region,** and difficulty in obtaining European indentured servants. Working conditions on the Southern plantations alienated free workers.
- Slavery in **South Carolina and Georgia** was based on that of the Caribbean plantation system. Many of the settlers, along with their slaves, came from the West Indies. The Africans were enslaved from the time of their arrival. They were brought there to work on huge rice plantations. The slave code was the strictest in the colonies.
- Beginning in the 1800s, the **lower Mississippi Valley** contained the largest number of plantations, with 100 or more enslaved people. Cotton profits related directly to the amount of land cultivated, encouraging the slave system to grow.

- In contrast, the diverse economy, climate, and smaller farms in the **middle and northern colonies** meant slavery there was less common. At the end of the colonial period on the eve of the American Revolution, there were 50,000 enslaved people in the North compared with 400,000 in the South. While most enslaved people in the North, like those in the South, worked in agriculture, enslaved people in northern cities were often skilled tradesmen, domestic workers, and laborers. The slave codes were also milder than those of the southern colonies.

## Slave Resistance

Throughout the period in which slavery was legal, Africans and African Americans resisted their enslavement. On the slave ships during the voyage from Africa to America (called the **Middle Passage**), some staged revolts. Others chose starvation or drowning as an alternative to enslavement.

Even in the face of severe punishment, some enslaved Africans attempted escape. Small communities of escaped enslaved people formed in Spanish Florida, South Carolina, Georgia, and Virginia. Other enslaved people offered more subtle resistance, such as slowing down at work, pretending illness, or damaging tools and crops.

In colonial America, open rebellion was not very common. Two notable colonial revolts took place in New York City in 1712 and at the Stono River near Charleston, South Carolina, in 1739. Both rebellions were put down by local militia. Most of the enslaved people who survived were later executed.

## The Influence of Africa and African American Culture on Colonial Cultures

With succeeding generations, slaves lost some of their ethnic identity but many elements of their West African traditions became the basis of African American culture. Particularly important was maintenance of an extended family network that provided some stability in their lives. Some African words found their way into the English language, as did certain farming methods, foods, folk literature, and folk art. African building traditions of multiple small dwellings, front porches, and decorative iron work influenced southern colonial architecture. Some African musical styles and instruments, such as the banjo, continued to be incorporated into religious music and work songs. African musical traditions later influenced many forms of American music.

# Major Historical Influences on American Government

The government of each of the 13 colonies reflected ideas that came from the heritage of Western civilization. Those ideas were then modified by centuries of English thought and practice and by the American colonial experience.

## Ideas From Ancient Greece

The concept of **democracy,** or government by the people, began in the city-state of Athens (in what is now Greece) between 750 B.C. and 550 B.C. Athens had a direct democracy, one in which all eligible citizens participated in government.

## Ideas From Ancient Rome

The concept of republican government was established by the ancient Romans. In a **republic,** voters elect representatives who speak and act for other citizens in the business of government. These representatives are supposed to work for the common good. This form of government is sometimes called representative democracy.

## Reading Strategy

**Organizing Information**
- Many enslaved Africans found both peaceful and violent ways to resist their enslavement.

- What are two peaceful ways that slaves resisted?

1.

2.

- What are two violent ways that they resisted?

1.

2.

## Key Themes and Concepts

**Civic Values**
American political rights and governmental institutions had three major sources:

1. British constitutional, political, and historical traditions

2. Seventeenth- and eighteenth-century Enlightenment ideas

3. American colonial experience

- What is an example of how each source influenced the political rights and governmental institutions in the United States?

## Reading Strategy

**Reinforcing Main Ideas**
- Why is the writ of *habeas corpus* called the "Great Writ of Liberty"?

- Which two rights guaranteed in the U.S. Constitution can be traced directly to the English Bill of Rights?

## Influence of English Events and Documents

Other basic concepts of government and **common law** were established in England before or during the colonial period in America. The common-law system developed in England from customs and traditions enforced by court decisions. It became the basis of the legal system in nations that England colonized.

**Magna Carta** In 1215, English noblemen forced King John of England to agree to the Magna Carta, or Great Charter, a document that placed limits on his power to rule. For example, this document established the right to a trial by jury—but only for nobles.

**Petition of Right** In 1628, King Charles I signed the Petition of Right. It put in writing certain basic rights and legal traditions, such as a **writ of** *habeas corpus*—a court order requiring that a person be brought before a court and the court shown evidence why the person should be held for trial. It prevents arrest and imprisonment without a trial.

**The English Bill of Rights** In 1689, the Glorious Revolution ended a decades-long power struggle between the English **Parliament** and the monarchy. Parliament overthrew James II and replaced him with William and Mary, who were required to agree to the English Bill of Rights. This established that **representative government** and the **rule of law** outweighed the power of any monarch.

### Foundations of American Rights

| Rights | Sources of Rights | | | |
|---|---|---|---|---|
| | **Magna Carta (1215)** | **English Bill of Rights (1689)** | **Virginia Declaration of Rights (1776)** | **Bill of Rights (1791)** |
| Trial by jury | ✔ | ✔ | | ✔ |
| Due process | ✔ | ✔ | | ✔ |
| Private property | ✔ | | | ✔ |
| No unreasonable searches or seizures | | | ✔ | ✔ |
| No cruel punishment | | ✔ | ✔ | ✔ |
| No excessive bail or fines | | ✔ | | ✔ |
| Right to bear arms | | ✔ | | ✔ |
| Right to petition | | ✔ | | ✔ |
| Freedom of speech | | | ✔ | ✔ |
| Freedom of the press | | | ✔ | ✔ |
| Freedom of religion | | | ✔ | ✔ |

## 17th- and 18th-Century Enlightenment Thought

The Framers of the Constitution were also strongly influenced by the ideas of the philosophers of the **Enlightenment.** This intellectual movement held that reliance on reason and experience would lead to social progress.

**John Locke** John Locke's ideas influenced the Declaration of Independence, state constitutions, and the United States Constitution.

- **Locke** believed that people were born free with certain **natural rights,** including the rights to life, liberty, and property.
- Such rights predate any government and exist in the "state of nature."

- Locke stated that a **social contract** was formed between the people and their government in which people agree to form a state and grant to its government the powers necessary to protect their natural rights.
- Therefore, governments exist only with the **consent of the governed.**
- When a government fails to protect these rights, the contract has been broken and the people are free to change or even to replace or overthrow that government.

**The Baron de Montesquieu** The French philosopher Baron de Montesquieu believed that the British political system was successful because the power to govern was divided among the monarch and the two houses of Parliament. This division helped balance political power among the branches, so that no one branch had too much power.

**Jean-Jacques Rousseau** Another French philosopher, Jean-Jacques Rousseau, developed further the idea of a social contract. His arguments in support of government by the consent of the governed influenced the U.S. Declaration of Independence.

**Voltaire** A third important French philosopher, Voltaire, wrote *Philosophical Letters*, praising British institutions and rights. He wrote against religious intolerance and persecution.

## The Colonial Experience: Political Rights and Mercantile Relationships

During the colonial period, two important forces helped shape a uniquely American way of life:

- political ideas based on the English experience and on Enlightenment thinking,
- the colonists' experience thousands of miles from their home country.

### Colonial Charters and Self-Government

Twelve of the thirteen original colonies were founded based on charters issued by the British government. A **charter** provided legal authority to companies or individuals to start a colony. Most of the colonies were originally self-governing private enterprises, but by 1730, most became royal colonies. Even after England later centralized control, the colonies remained largely self-governing and independent.

### Colonial Principles and Practices of Government

The beliefs that colonists held about the proper role of government had a strong influence over the way they structured their governments.

**Limits on Government** The colonists believed that the power of government should be limited, in accordance with English laws and traditions. The colonists wrote laws based on the principle that government existed to protect people's natural rights. The rights to life, liberty, and protection of property were most often mentioned. As early as 1641 in Massachusetts, the right to own property and protect it from being illegally seized by the government was written into law. The right to vote helped to protect property rights.

**Enforceable Contracts** Colonists believed in the right to enter into contracts. Enforceable contracts between parties can be traced to the idea of a political compact, or contract. After the United States won independence, decisions of the Marshall Court protected individuals' right to enter into contracts.

### Analyzing Documents

*Men being, . . . by Nature, all free, equal and independent, no one can be ...subjected to the Political Power of another, without his own Consent. ...For when any number of Men have, by the consent of every individual, made a Community, they have made that community one Body, with a Power to Act as one Body, which is only by the will and determination of the majority . . .*
**Two Treatises on Government**
**John Locke, 1690**

- Compare this statement to the Mayflower Compact (1620) and to the Declaration of Independence (1776).

- What principle, basic to a democracy, do you find in all three documents?

### Key Themes and Concepts

**Constitutional Principles**
The following two cases deal with property rights and economic policy:

*Fletcher* v. *Peck* (1810) established that a state cannot interfere with constitutionally protected contract rights.

*Dartmouth College* v. *Woodward* (1819) extended constitutional protection of contracts to corporate charters.

- Why are *Fletcher* v. *Peck* and *Dartmouth College* v. *Woodward* important to economic freedom?

## Reading
### Strategy

**Formulating Questions**
From the context of the paragraph about the Zenger case, define what is meant by *seditious libel.*

## Analyzing
### Documents

*"We whose names are underwritten . . . covenant and combine ourselves together into a civil body politic, for our better ordering and preservation and furtherance of the ends aforesaid; and by virtue hereof to enact, constitute, and frame such just and equal laws, ordinances, acts, constitutions, offices from time to time as shall be thought most meet and convenient for the general good of the colony; unto which we promise all due submission and obedience."*
—*Mayflower Compact*

• What words indicate that this is a contract or compact?

• Is this to be a limited government?

**Freedom of the Press** Colonists believed there should be legal limits on government attempts to control what is written. In 1735, **John Peter Zenger,** a German immigrant to New York, was tried for **seditious libel** for accusing the governor of the colony of wrongdoing. Zenger's lawyer argued that no crime was committed when what Zenger had printed was true, and the jury found Zenger not guilty. Later, this case helped establish the principle of freedom of the press in the United States.

**Contract Theory of Government: Mayflower Compact** In 1620, before landing at Plymouth in present-day Massachusetts, an area outside of existing English authority, the Pilgrims signed the **Mayflower Compact.** This compact was a contract in which the colonists consented to be governed by a government that they created. It was the first plan for self-government and majority rule in the colonies. **The Fundamental Orders of Connecticut,** adopted in 1639, is another example of a colonial compact.

### Self-Government: Colonial Assemblies and Local Governments

The importance of self-government—of participation in government by representatives of the people—is seen in the colonial assemblies established in each colony. As early as 1619, Virginia colonists took the first step toward republican government when they instituted the colonies' first representative lawmaking body, the **House of Burgesses.** Most colonies established a bicameral, or two-house, legislature modeled after the two-house English Parliament.

Colonists also recognized the need for local governments. The county was the center of local government in most of the colonies. In New England, local government was at the town level, where the **town meeting** allowed citizens to govern themselves through **direct democracy.**

**Separation of Powers** A system of **separation of powers** developed in the colonies. Colonial charters divided government into three branches—the legislative, the executive, and the judicial. However, since colonial governors were usually appointed by the king and the judges by the governors, it was primarily through the colonial legislatures, elected by the people, that the colonists received their training in self government.

### Events Leading to the American Revolution

**1754**
French and Indian War begins; Albany Plan of Union

**1763**
France and Great Britain sign Treaty of Paris

**1765**
Parliament passes Stamp Act

**1773**
Tea Act; Boston Tea Party

1750     1755     1760     1765     1770     1775

**1759**
British capture Quebec

**1764**
Sugar Act

**1766**
Parliament repeals Stamp Act

**1774**
Intolerable Acts; First Continental Congress

## The Causes of the American Revolution

For almost a century before the outbreak of the American Revolution in 1775, England and France were involved in a rivalry for power, not only in Europe, but wherever the two nations had colonies. Preoccupied with France, England governed the colonies under a policy known as **salutary neglect,** or a healthy ignoring of the colonies. This policy resulted in the colonists gaining more independence in their trade practices and Great Britain benefiting from the colonies' economic prosperity. The colonies also exercised a large degree of self-government.

Before the Revolution, colonists saw themselves as British subjects and as New Yorkers, or Rhode Islanders, or Virginians. In 1754, Benjamin Franklin tried to get the colonies to join together as protection against the French. His **Albany Plan of Union,** modeled on the Iroquois Confederacy, was rejected by the colonies because each feared loss of power and independence.

**The Treaty of Paris of 1763,** marked Great Britain's victory over France in the Seven Years (or French and Indian) War. It also shifted the way power was distributed in North America. With French land in North America now in British hands, Native Americans could no longer benefit from balancing French and English interests against one another. The colonists felt their war efforts earned them the right to move into the newly acquired lands and saw less need for the protection of the British government. However, with the French wars ended, England changed its imperial policy toward the colonies. The Proclamation of 1763 prohibited expansion west of the ridge of the Appalachian Mountains. The British aim was to avoid conflicts between the colonists and Native Americans. The colonists deeply resented the Proclamation and often ignored it. In 1775, colonial resistance to post-1763 British policies resulted in the American Revolution.

**Land Claims After the French and Indian War, 1763**

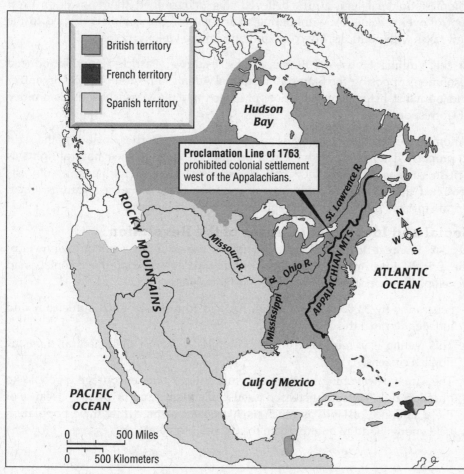

**Turning Point**

• Why is the Treaty of Paris of 1763 considered a turning point in history?

**Key Themes and Concepts**

**Change:**
• What caused the changes in British imperial policy after 1763?

• Why did the colonists resist those changes?

• What was the result of that resistance?

## Reading
### Strategy

**Organizing Information**
The American Revolution had economic, political, and social and ideological causes. List them, then identify those you consider the most significant.

1. Economic

2. Political

3. Social and Ideological

## Analyzing
### Documents

In May 1765, Patrick Henry voiced his opposition to the Stamp Act with a speech to the Virginia House of Burgesses. In that speech, he said:

*"Caesar had his Brutus; Charles the First, his Cromwell; and George the Third . . . may profit by their example. If this be treason, make the most of it."*

Brutus assassinated Caesar, and Cromwell defeated Charles I and had him beheaded.

- What is Patrick Henry's message?

- What might Patrick Henry have been implying but would not say?

## Economic Causes of the Revolution

As a result of the long struggle for power with France, Great Britain had secured control of a large portion of the continent. However, a large debt from the war remained. Great Britain also needed money to maintain a military force in the colonies in case of another French threat. Believing that the colonies should pay for their own defense, the British Parliament began to enforce the policy of mercantilism.

**Mercantilism** was an economic system during the sixteenth, seventeenth, and eighteenth centuries based on the belief that a strong nation was built by accumulating precious metals through increasing exports, protecting industries, and establishing colonies for the economic benefit of the home country. Colonies were to supply raw materials and markets, while restrictions were placed on colonial manufacturing and trade.

In 1764, Parliament passed the **Sugar Act** on foreign imports, and then in 1765 the **Stamp Act,** requiring a tax stamp on printed material, from newspapers to wills. Since the **Navigation Acts** of the late 1600s, the colonists, while often evading these regulations, had accepted the right of England to regulate trade. But the primary objective of these two acts was to raise money, and the colonists forced their repeal. Parliament then passed the **Townshend Acts.** These were seen as an economic threat because they differed from mercantilist practice by taxing imports from England, rather than from other nations.

## Political Causes of the Revolution

Some colonists also saw the Townshend Acts as a political threat. The money raised by the acts would be used to pay some of the English officials in the colonies. Colonial legislatures believed this undermined their power to exert control over officials by withholding their salaries. The colonists reacted to the new taxes with petitions, boycotts, and other more violent protests.

In the Virginia House of Burgesses, for example, **Patrick Henry** introduced resolutions opposing the Stamp Act. **Samuel Adams,** a Boston political organizer and journalist, helped create the Sons of Liberty and the Massachusetts Committee of Correspondence.

Colonists viewed these new taxes as a threat to their liberties, including the right to property. They charged that Great Britain had violated their **natural rights** as British citizens. Because they had no representation in Parliament, colonists reasoned that taxation could come only from the colonial legislatures. Great Britain insisted that Parliament represented all of its subjects.

## Social and Ideological Causes of the Revolution

Leaders in Great Britain failed to understand the colonists' fears of the power of the British government. They also did not recognize that the colonists had developed independent political lives and thoughts.

- Separation by 3,000 miles of ocean had led to a sense of self sufficiency and independence in the colonists.

- This feeling was reinforced by the colonists' belief in their natural rights as English citizens.

- The Great Awakening, a religious movement, had encouraged people to question authority and increased a sense of equality among people. Because of the abundance of land, as much as 90 percent of the white male population held enough land to qualify them for the right to vote.

# The American Revolution and the Declaration of Independence

## Resistance Leads to Crisis and War

In 1773, the issue of **taxation without representation** rose again when Parliament passed the Tea Act, which made British tea less expensive than tea imported by colonial tea merchants. Colonists protested by destroying three shiploads of British tea in the **Boston Tea Party.** The British government reacted with what the colonists called the **"Intolerable Acts"** of 1774. These acts punished Massachusetts by closing the port of Boston, forbidding town meetings, and reducing the powers of the legislature. More British troops were sent to occupy the colony and enforce the acts.

## The American Revolution and the Declaration of Independence, 1775–1783

| 1775 | 1777 | | 1783 |
|------|------|---|------|
| Second Continental Congress; Battles of Lexington and Concord | Battle of Saratoga | | Treaty of Paris |

| 1775 | 1777 | 1779 | 1781 | 1783 |

| | 1776 | | 1781 | |
|---|------|---|------|---|
| | *Common Sense* published; Declaration of Independence signed | | Cornwallis surrenders at Yorktown | |

### Analyzing Documents

Use the timeline to answer the following questions.

- How long did the American Revolution last?

- Was the Declaration of Independence issued before or after fighting began in the American Revolution?

## Colonial Efforts at Union

In the late summer of 1774, 12 of the colonies sent representatives to Philadelphia to plan a response to these British actions. This meeting became known as the **First Continental Congress.** After the start of the American Revolution in 1775 at Lexington and Concord, a **Second Continental Congress** met and took charge of the war effort.

While the colonies moved toward war and demands for independence, colonists were divided. Those known as **Tories** or **Loyalists** supported the king and obedience to English laws. Opposing independence, thousands left the United States at the end of the Revolution, including large numbers from New York.

## Decision for Independence

The decision to declare independence was made over a year after the American Revolution began. **Thomas Paine,** in his pamphlet, **Common Sense,** was influential in persuading the colonists to end their relationship with Great Britain.

In June 1776, Richard Henry Lee of Virginia presented a resolution to the Second Continental Congress calling for independence from Great Britain. The Congress appointed a committee (including Thomas Jefferson, Benjamin Franklin, and John Adams) to draft a formal declaration. The resulting **Declaration of Independence** was almost entirely the work of Thomas Jefferson. In writing the Declaration, Jefferson relied heavily on the Enlightenment ideas of John Locke's social contract theory and belief in natural rights. The delegates adopted the Declaration of Independence on July 4, which marks the birth of the United States of America.

### Reading Strategy

**Reading for Evidence**
*Common Sense,* 1776
*"We have boasted the protection of Great Britain, without considering, that her motive was interest not attachment; and that she did not protect us from our enemies on our account; but from her enemies on her own account. . . . A government of our own is our natural right: and . . . it is infinitely wiser and safer, to form a constitution of our own in a cool deliberate manner, while we have it in our power, than to trust such an interesting event to time and chance."*
—Thomas Paine,
Common *Sense,* 1776

- What is common sense to Paine?

| The PURPOSE of the Declaration: | The Declaration's KEY IDEAS OF GOVERNMENT: |
|---|---|
| • To announce to the world that the colonies were now a new, independent nation<br><br>• To explain and justify the reasons that the united colonies had decided to become the United States of America | • People have natural rights, including the rights to "Life, Liberty, and the pursuit of Happiness."<br><br>• When governments receive their power to govern "from the consent of the governed" by social contract or compact, that power is for the fundamental purpose of protecting the people's natural rights. |
| **The THREE PARTS of the Declaration:** | |
| • A theory of government<br><br>• A list of grievances against the King<br><br>• A formal resolution declaring independence | • When a government fails to protect and respect those rights, it is the "Right of the People to alter or to abolish" that government. |

## The Ideals of the Declaration of Independence

The ideals of the Declaration of Independence are still a goal for our nation. In 1791 the Bill of Rights again emphasized the importance of individual liberties and limits on government power first stated in the Declaration of Independence. Those ideals have also served to inspire people in other nations at other times during the French Revolution of the late 1700s, the South American independence movement in the early 1800s, and even twentieth century independence movements in Africa and Asia.

There was a fundamental contradiction between slavery and the Declaration's ideals of freedom and liberty. Locke's compact theory stated that no person may rule another without the consent of the other person. The colonists protested their treatment by England and chose freedom. Few made comparisons with the institution of slavery.

## Fighting the War for Independence

During the American Revolution, the Second Continental Congress served as the national government. The Congress had no constitutional basis but was created in a crisis and supported by popular opinion. It remained in place until 1781 when the Articles of Confederation went into effect.

The American Revolution pitted Great Britain, then the world's most powerful nation, against thirteen former colonies without financial resources and a regular army. The British army was larger in number, better trained, and aided by the Creek, Cherokee, and Shawnee in the South and most Iroquois in the North. It was disadvantaged by its use of European military techniques in America and by the behavior of its troops, which alienated many colonists in the territories it occupied.

Assembling and training the continental army (the colonists' army) was the achievement of **George Washington,** the colonial commander in chief. The continental army was reinforced as it moved from region to region by an untrained militia or home guard defending their homes.

The colonists were aided by an alliance with France, negotiated by Benjamin Franklin. Motivated by its ongoing rivalry with Great Britain, France supplied the colonists with military arms, troops, and naval support and engaged Great Britain in war elsewhere in the world.

The American victory at Saratoga helped bring the French into the war. They saw that the colonists might possibly win the war. The victory also prevented the

---

**Turning Point**

• Why is the Battle of Saratoga considered a turning point in the war?

British from isolating New England from the rest of the colonies by taking control of the Hudson River Valley and the area north of it to Canada.

The American Revolution lasted from 1775 to the surrender of the British at Yorktown in Virginia in 1781. A peace treaty, the **Treaty of Paris,** was negotiated by John Adams, John Jay, and Benjamin Franklin and was signed in 1783. In it Great Britain recognized the independence of the United States. The new nation's boundaries were set at Canada to the north, Spanish Florida to the south, and the Mississippi River to the west.

### Slavery, African Americans, and the Outcome of the American Revolution

Although African Americans fought on both sides during the American Revolution, more fought on the British side because of British promises of freedom from slavery. After first hesitating, Washington and the Continental Congress eventually recruited African Americans, as did state militias.

**Analyzing Documents**

**Reading for Evidence**
*"We have in common with all other men a natural and unalienable right to that freedom which the Great Parent of the Universe hath bestowed equally on all mankind, and which they have never forfeited by any compact or agreement whatsoever."*
*—From a petition of a group of slaves to the Massachusetts legislature, 1777*

• What evidence is there that the writers knew about Enlightenment ideas and the Declaration of Independence?

**Some Effects of the American Revolution**

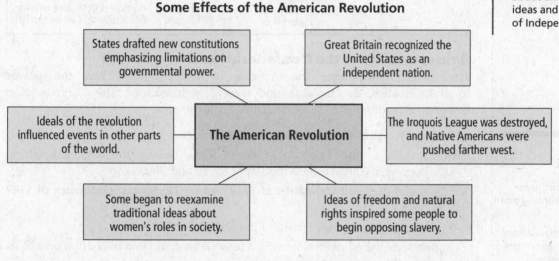

*The Revolution had important consequences for many groups of people.*

During the Revolution, some enslaved Africans in the South successfully escaped. Others were freed in return for military service. Some left the country with the British army, while others settled in northern cities and became part of a growing free African American population.

An antislavery movement led by Quakers started in the North before the Revolution. After the war, northern states passed laws that immediately or gradually abolished slavery. Although free, African Americans in the North still faced discrimination. Many were not allowed to vote, except in New England. There was segregation in public places, housing, and transportation.

**Reading Strategy**

**Reinforcing Main Ideas**
• Why did the Articles of Confederation create a weak national government?

## The Articles of Confederation, 1781–1789

The first constitution of the United States was the Articles of Confederation. This constitution, proposed by the Second Continental Congress in 1777, went into effect in 1781 after all 13 states had ratified, or approved, it. The Articles of Confederation reflected the colonists' fear of a strong central government and the desire of the individual states to protect their powers. As a result, the Articles created a weak national government.

## An Alliance of Independent States

The Articles set up a confederation among the 13 states. A confederation is an alliance of independent states in which the states give as much power as they choose to the central government, while keeping the greater part of the power and remaining sovereign. The Articles were more like a treaty among the states than a plan of centralized government.

### The Articles of Confederation, 1781–1789

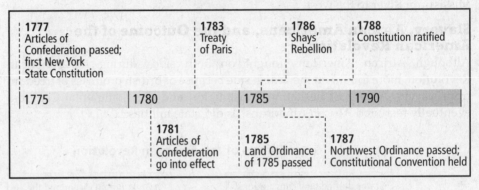

## Achievements of the Confederation Government

The government under the Articles of Confederation had the power to make treaties, declare war, and receive ambassadors. The Confederation Congress is credited with several notable achievements:

1. Successful conclusion of the American Revolution.
2. Negotiation of the Treaty of Paris of 1783, ending the war and setting U.S. borders at Canada, the Mississippi River, and Florida.
3. Passage of the **Land Ordinance of 1785** and the **Northwest Ordinance of 1787** pass, that
   - set a pattern of development of the Northwest Territory.
   - provided the guidelines by which new states could join the nation on a basis of equality with the thirteen original states.
   - prohibited slavery in the Northwest Territory.

### Turning Point

- Why is the Northwest Ordinance a turning point in history?
- How did that law affect the development of the rest of our nation?

### Preparing for the Exam

- Why was the period under the Articles of Confederation called the "critical period"?

## Weaknesses of the Confederation Government

The Confederation government proved too weak to deal with the problems during the **Critical Period** of the 1780s. There was no single national currency, because the states could also coin money. The Congress could not tax the people directly but had to ask the states for funds. The government lacked a president to direct operations. There was no national judiciary. Congress could raise an army only by requesting troops from the states.

The new nation soon suffered severe economic problems, while its government was unable to command respect at home or abroad. However, all 13 states had to agree before the Articles could be changed, so it was nearly impossible to change them.

# State Governments Based on Republican Principles

Between 1776 and 1787, 11 of the 13 states adopted new constitutions. State constitutions were based on republican principles creating a government grounded in representation of the people, and formed with the consent of the governed. Special state conventions were called so that the constitutions could be written by the people. When complete, they were ratified or approved by the voters.

Fears of a strong executive power led the Framers of the first state constitutions to emphasize limitations on power. The New York Constitution of 1777, which even included the text of the Declaration of Independence, gave most of the power to the legislature, rather than to a single person such as a governor. In New York as in most states, the legislature remained bicameral, rather than unicameral.

Some states granted more people the right to vote by lowering property qualifications. Some states gave the right to vote to property-owning African Americans and Native Americans. State constitutions, including the New York State Constitution, protected some individual rights, such as the right to religious freedom. In addition, the State government could not give money to any religion. This was part of a national movement to disestablish churches, which meant the end of government endorsement and financial support of any single religious group.

## Part 2 Writing and Ratifying the Constitution, 1787–1789

**Key Terms**

Constitutional Convention
representation
Great Compromise or Connecticut Plan

bicameral legislature
Three-Fifths Compromise
Commerce Compromise
Presidency Compromise

Federalists
ratification
Anti-Federalists
*The Federalist Papers*
Bill of Rights

**Analyzing Documents**

Reading for Evidence
• How were the state constitutions that were adopted after the American Revolution affected by the conflict and war with Great Britain?

• What ideas and features from state constitutions were included in the U.S. Constitution?

• What provision in the U.S. Constitution expressly supports disestablishment?

### Calling for a Constitutional Convention

By the middle of the 1780s, it was clear that the national government created by the Articles of Confederation was too weak. For example, in 1786 a group of debt-stricken farmers in Massachusetts turned to violence. Though short lived, **Shays' Rebellion** fueled fears of spreading national collapse and mob rule. Meanwhile, the new government faced increasing difficulty in regulating trade and dealing with the nation's debt. Some leaders also feared that the state legislatures had too much power; and that freedom outweighed order and stability. These problems led to a call for a **Constitutional Convention** in Philadelphia in May 1787 for "the sole and express purpose of amending the Articles of Confederation."

## The Constitutional Convention

### The Framers of the Constitution

Fifty-five delegates, representing all the states except Rhode Island, met in the Pennsylvania State House (now known as Independence Hall) in Philadelphia in May 1787 at the Constitutional Convention. The delegates were prominent lawyers, planters, and merchants at a time when most of the population were small farmers.

The most famous delegate was **George Washington,** who was elected president of the Constitutional Convention. Another well-known figure was **James Madison,** whom some consider to have had the most influence on the Constitution. Also attending were Benjamin Franklin and Alexander Hamilton, a strong nationalist from New York.

Some famous Americans from the Revolution were noticeably absent. Thomas Jefferson and John Adams were serving the country as diplomats in Europe. A few patriots, such as Patrick Henry, refused to attend because they suspected that

**Key Themes and Concepts**

Diversity
Certain groups of people were not represented at the Constitutional Convention.

• How does their absence explain some sections of the Constitution?

• Why were these groups absent?

**Reinforcing Main Ideas**
• What evidence is
there in the Articles of
Confederation that the
concern was preventing
threats to the liberties of
its citizens, rather than
creating an effective
national government?

• Why might the writers
of the Articles have
feared a strong central
government?

• What are the major
differences between the
governments created by
these two Constitutions?

the convention would try to create a strong national government, which they opposed. Still others were not selected by their states.

In addition, no women, Native Americans, African Americans, or poorer white men attended the Constitutional Convention. At that time, these groups had limited political and legal rights.

### Governments of the United States: 1781 and 1789

| How the Weaknesses of the Articles of Confederation Were Corrected by the Constitution | |
| --- | --- |
| **Articles of Confederation** | **Constitution of the United States** |
| • Confederacy: States, not national government, have most of the power.<br>• Congress lacked power to enforce laws.<br>• No executive officer to carry out the laws of Congress.<br>• No national courts. Only state courts exist.<br>• Congress is responsible to the states.<br>• Laws must be approved by 9 of 13 states.<br>• Congress has no power to tax.<br>• Congress can not regulate trade among the states.<br>• Each state coins its own money. There is no national currency.<br>• All 13 states must agree to an amendment. | • Federal system: Power to govern is divided between national and state government.<br>• The Constitution and acts of Congress take supremacy.<br>• A President heads the executive branch of the government.<br>• Both federal and state courts exist.<br>• Congress is responsible to the people.<br>• Laws require a majority vote in both houses of Congress.<br>• Congress has the power to levy and collect taxes.<br>• Congress is given sole control over interstate and foreign trade.<br>• Only the national government has the power to coin money.<br>• Amendment process involves both federal and state governments. |

## Key Compromises at the Convention

The delegates agreed that discussions would be kept secret in order to debate freely without outside pressure. They also decided not to revise the Articles of Confederation, but to write a new constitution instead.

Most of what we know about the Convention comes to us from Madison's notes. The delegates' task was to create a government with enough authority to govern effectively while protecting individual liberties. The debates involved much conflict and much compromise. In fact, the United States Constitution has been called a "bundle of compromises." Four key compromises made the Constitution possible.

### The Great Compromise, or Connecticut Plan

**Key Themes
and Concepts**

**Individuals, Groups,
Institutions**
At the Constitutional
Convention, four major
compromises were achieved.

• For each issue, how did
the compromise satisfy
each side?

• Why were the
compromises necessary?

• Why was slavery an issue
in two compromises?

The first issue to be resolved was that of **representation**. The delegates from Virginia proposed the Virginia Plan, which called for a bicameral legislature. A state's representation in each house would be based on its population. Larger states supported this plan. The smaller states favored the New Jersey Plan. This plan called for a unicameral legislature in which each state had equal representation.

The Virginia Plan served as the basis for much of the new Constitution. However, the matter of representation had to be settled by what is known as the **Great Compromise** or the **Connecticut Plan,** which gave something to both large and small states. The compromise created the Congress, a **bicameral legislature.** The states had equal representation in the upper house, or the Senate. In the lower house, or the House of Representatives, representation was based on population. In addition, all bills dealing with money would have to start in the House, but would need the approval of the Senate.

## The Three-Fifths Compromise

Meanwhile, a bitter debate continued over slavery and power. Southerners wanted enslaved people to be counted for purposes of deciding representation in the House, but not for purposes of determining taxes. The **Three-Fifths Compromise** stated that three fifths of the enslaved African Americans in a state would be counted for both representation and taxation purposes.

## The Commerce Compromise

Northerners wanted a government that could regulate trade. Southerners, however, feared that the importing of African slaves would be prohibited and that their agricultural exports would be taxed. Under the **Commerce Compromise** the delegates agreed that no export duties could be passed by Congress and that Congress could not prohibit the slave trade for 20 years.

## The Presidency Compromise

The delegates favoring a strong national government wanted a President elected directly by the people with a long term of office. Those favoring states' rights wanted a short term of office with state legislatures selecting the President. In the **Presidency Compromise,** the two sides agreed on a four-year term and the indirect election of the President through the **Electoral College** system.

**Reading Strategy**

**Organizing Information**
- Which groups stood in opposition to each other on the major issues at the Constitutional Convention?
- Why did they take their particular positions?

### Major Compromises of the Constitutional Convention

| Compromise | Issue | Solution |
|---|---|---|
| Connecticut Plan or Great Compromise | Equal or proportionate representation in Congress | Through a bicameral legislature, States would have equal representation in Senate, and representation in the House would depend on State's population. |
| Three-Fifths Compromise | Counting enslaved people within population to determine representation | Enslaved people were counted as three-fifths of one person, both for representation and taxation. |
| Commerce Compromise | Granting Congress the power to regulate foreign and interstate trade | Congress was forbidden to tax a State's exports, or take action against the slave trade for 20 years. |
| Presidency Compromise | Length of President's term of office and method of election | President would serve a four-year term and be elected by Electoral College rather than popular election, or selection by Congress or State governors. |

# Ratification of the Constitution

After months of debate in Philadelphia, delegates approved the Constitution of the United States. On September 17, 1787, thirty-nine of the delegates remaining in Philadelphia signed the Constitution. The fact that three, including George Mason, author of the Virginia Declaration of Rights, refused to sign gave an indication of the coming debate. The Framers had written that 9 of the 13 states must approve the Constitution for it to go into effect. Approval would be done through special conventions called in each state rather than through the state legislatures.

**Key Themes and Concepts**

**Government**
- Why was it essential that Virginia and New York be among those states that ratified the Constitution?
- In which states was there strong division of opinion about ratification?

| The Federalist Arguments | The Anti-Federalist Arguments |
|---|---|
| • Wanted a strong national government to provide order and protect the rights of people. | • Wanted a weak national government so that it would not threaten the rights of the people or the powers of the states. |
| • Claimed that a bill of rights was unnecessary because the new government's powers were limited by the Constitution. | • Wanted to add a bill of rights to protect the people against abuses of power by the federal government. |

## Analyzing Documents

*"Ambition must be made to counteract ambition . . . If men were angels, no government would be necessary. If angels were to govern men, neither external nor internal controls on government would be necessary. In framing a government which is to be administered by men over men, the great difficulty lies in this: you must first enable the government to control the governed; and in the next place oblige it to control itself."*
—James Madison,
*The Federalist Papers No. 51*

- Based on this quote, what was James Madison's view of the relationship between human nature and good government?

- Anti-Federalists opposed ratification because the Constitution shifted the balance of power between the national and state governments. How would Madison respond to this concern?

## The Great Debate and Ratification

Two groups formed in each state: the **Federalists**, who favored **ratification**, and the **Anti-Federalists**, who opposed it.

The first five states ratified the Constitution within a few months. By June 1788, nine states had given their approval—enough for ratification. But these did not include the states of Virginia and New York. The success of the new government depended upon acceptance of the Constitution by these two key states.

In Virginia, James Madison led the fight for ratification against the opposition of George Mason and Patrick Henry. Virginia approved the Constitution by ten votes but only with suggested amendments. New York was the next battleground. Here, **The Federalist Papers**—a series of pro-ratification essays by Alexander Hamilton, John Jay, and James Madison—helped turn the tide against the Anti-Federalists, led by Governor George Clinton. Ratification was by a margin of three votes. *The Federalist Papers* remains one of the finest statements on government and the Constitution ever written.

When the new government took office in 1789, Congress acted in response to concerns of the Anti-Federalists about the need for a **Bill of Rights** in the Constitution. James Madison prepared the first draft of these first ten amendments. By 1791 the states had ratified them.

## Part 3 What You Need to Know About the U.S. Constitution and Government

**Key Terms**

| | | |
|---|---|---|
| Preamble | unwritten constitution | census |
| popular sovereignty | delegated powers | Electoral College system |
| limited government | implied powers | bureaucracy |
| separation of powers | concurrent powers | jurisdiction |
| federal sysytem | reserved powers | judicial review |
| checks and balances | legislative | amendment |
| elastic clause | executive | due process of law |
| "necessary and proper" | judicial | equal protection clause |

## Preamble to the Constitution

The United States Constitution is a fundamental plan, or framework, clearly defining and limiting the powers of government. In the **Preamble,** or introduction, to the Constitution, the Framers defined their reasons for writing the document:

- To create a better, stronger national government
- To ensure a system of justice

- To provide for peace at home
- To provide for the defense of the nation
- To promote the well being of the people
- To secure liberty to the people and to future generations

## Basic Principles of the Constitution

The Constitution of the United States includes a number of important basic principles, which are listed below.

### Popular Sovereignty

Our Constitution is based on the principle of **popular sovereignty,** which means that the source of all power or authority to govern is the people. *Popular* means "of or by the people." *Sovereignty* means "supreme power." This type of government is a **democracy,** or government by the consent of the governed.

### Limited Government

Governmental powers are defined by the Constitution. In this way our government is limited by law. The U.S. Constitution, as well as state constitutions, places limits on state and national governments and governmental officials as well. No person is considered above the law.

### Federalism

The Constitution divides the power to govern between the states and the national government. This division of power between levels of government creates a **federal system** of government.

**Analyzing Documents**

*"We the People of the United States . . . do ordain and establish this Constitution for the United States."*
—Preamble to the U.S. Constitution

- According to the Preamble, who is creating this Constitution?

- In what other documents have we seen a concept that is restated here?

### System of Federalism

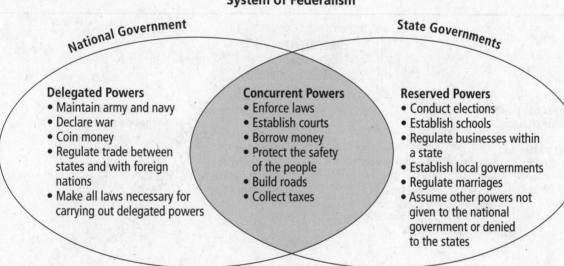

**National Government**

**State Governments**

**Delegated Powers**
- Maintain army and navy
- Declare war
- Coin money
- Regulate trade between states and with foreign nations
- Make all laws necessary for carrying out delegated powers

**Concurrent Powers**
- Enforce laws
- Establish courts
- Borrow money
- Protect the safety of the people
- Build roads
- Collect taxes

**Reserved Powers**
- Conduct elections
- Establish schools
- Regulate businesses within a state
- Establish local governments
- Regulate marriages
- Assume other powers not given to the national government or denied to the states

### Separation of Powers

The Constitution establishes the **separation of powers,** meaning that power to govern is divided among the legislative, executive, and judiciary branches to ensure that no single branch can dominate the government. Each branch takes its power directly from the Constitution, not from another branch.

## Three Branches of U.S. Government

| Legislative | Executive | Judicial |
|---|---|---|
| **Senate**<br>**House of Representatives** | **President**<br>**Vice President** | **Supreme Court**<br>**Federal Courts** |
| **Makes laws** | **Enforces laws and treaties** | **Explains and interprets laws** |
| • Overrides presidential vetoes<br>• Approves presidential appointments<br>• Approves treaties<br>• Taxes to provide services<br>• Provides for defense, declares war<br>• Regulates money and trade<br>• Impeaches officials | • Can veto laws<br>• Appoints high officials<br>• Conducts foreign policy<br>• Enforces laws and treaties<br>• Commander in chief of the military<br>• Recommends bills to Congress<br>• Reports the state of the Union to Congress | • Settles legal disputes between states<br>• Settles State and federal disputes<br>• Settles disputes between States and foreign countries<br>• Hears cases with ambassadors of foreign governments<br>• Settles disputes between individuals and Federal Government |

Source: U.S. Department of Justice

## Checks and Balances

In addition to separation of powers among the three branches of government, the constitution includes a system of **checks and balances.** Each branch of the national government has ways to check, or control, the other branches. This prevents one branch from gaining too much power.

### The Checks and Balances System

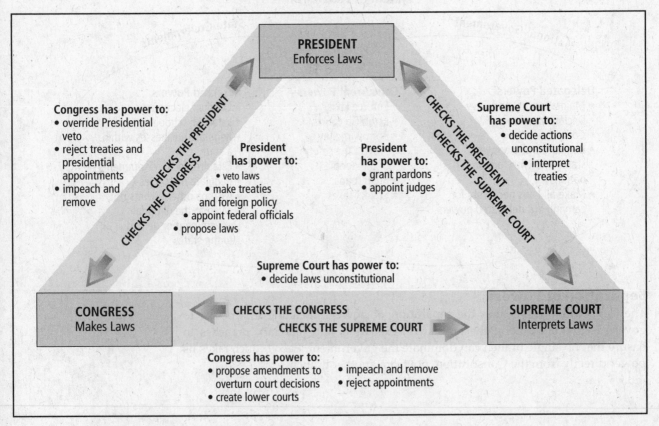

**PRESIDENT**
Enforces Laws

CHECKS THE PRESIDENT
CHECKS THE CONGRESS

CHECKS THE PRESIDENT
CHECKS THE SUPREME COURT

**Congress has power to:**
• override Presidential veto
• reject treaties and presidential appointments
• impeach and remove

**President has power to:**
• veto laws
• make treaties and foreign policy
• appoint federal officials
• propose laws

**President has power to:**
• grant pardons
• appoint judges

**Supreme Court has power to:**
• decide actions unconstitutional
• interpret treaties

**Supreme Court has power to:**
• decide laws unconstitutional

**CONGRESS**
Makes Laws

CHECKS THE CONGRESS
CHECKS THE SUPREME COURT

**SUPREME COURT**
Interprets Laws

**Congress has power to:**
• propose amendments to overturn court decisions
• create lower courts
• impeach and remove
• reject appointments

## Flexibility

The Constitution's flexibility allows it to meet changing conditions.

**The Elastic Clause** Article I, Section 8, Clause 18, known as the **elastic clause,** states that Congress can make all laws **"necessary and proper"** for carrying out the tasks listed in the Constitution.

**The Amendment Process** The Constitution may be formally changed with approval of both Congress and the states.

**Judicial Interpretation** The Supreme Court and lower federal courts review cases that involve possible conflicts with the Constitution and federal laws. This involves interpreting local, state, and federal laws, as well as executive actions.

**Unwritten Constitution** Congressional and executive interpretations and actions, court decisions, customs, and traditions form a so-called **unwritten constitution** to allow for Constitutional change and flexibility.

# Federalism in the Constitution

The Constitution divides the power to govern between the national and the state governments. Disputes between the national and state governments are settled by the courts, but the **Supremacy Clause** of Article VI of the Constitution makes the Constitution, federal laws, and treaties superior to state laws.

**The Supremacy Clause**

**Delegated Powers** Certain powers of the national government are spelled out in the Constitution. Most of these delegated powers are listed in Article I, Section 8. One example is the power of the national government to declare war.

**Implied Powers** Certain powers of the national government are not stated in writing. Their existence is implied by the **Elastic Clause.** One example of an implied power is the regulation of child labor; this power is implied by the delegated power to regulate interstate commerce.

**Denied Powers** Certain powers are denied to the national government, for example, the power to pass an export tax. Other powers are denied to the states, for example, the power to print money. Still other powers are denied to both national and state governments, for example, the power to deny the right to vote because of sex or race.

**Concurrent Powers** Certain powers belong to both national and state governments. One example of such a concurrent power is the power to tax.

**Reserved Powers** The reserved powers are neither delegated to the national government nor denied to the states. One example is the power to make divorce laws.

Federalism in Article IV is seen in the guarantee to each state of a republican form of government and protection against invasion and domestic violence. The amendment process in Article V, requires approval of both Congress and three quarters of the states. Article VII states that the new Constitution must first be approved or ratified by conventions of nine of the states.

### Key Themes and Concepts

**Government**
- Name an example of each type of power under federalism: a concurrent power, a delegated power, and a reserved power.
- What is the Supreme Law of the Land?

# The Basic Organization and Functions of Government Under the Constitution

The first three articles of the Constitution describe and define the powers of the **legislative, executive,** and **judicial** branches of the national government. These articles detail the separation of powers, while showing how each branch can check and balance the others.

## Preparing for the Exam

Some examination questions require you to read and interpret charts. Study the chart and answer this question.

- How does the term of a Supreme Court justice differ from those of other federal officeholders?

## Federal Officeholders

| Office | Number | Term | Selection | Requirements |
|---|---|---|---|---|
| Representative | at least 1 per state; based on state population | 2 years | elected by voters of congressional district | • age 25 or over<br>• citizen for 7 years<br>• resident of state in which elected |
| Senator | 2 per state | 6 years | original Constitution-elected by state legislature Amendment 17-elected by voters | • age 30 or over<br>• citizen for 9 years<br>• resident of state in which elected |
| President and Vice President | 1 | 4 years | elected by Electoral College | • age 35 or over<br>• natural-born citizen<br>• resident of U.S. for 14 years |
| Supreme Court Justice | 9 | Life | appointed by President with approval of the Senate | • no requirements in Constitution |

## Article I: The Legislative Branch

Article I establishes the United States Congress with its two houses—the Senate and the House of Representatives. Congress is the legislative, or lawmaking, branch of government. Article I gives the qualifications for election to Congress, the rights and privileges of members of Congress, and some basic operating procedures of both houses. The article also lists the powers delegated to Congress. These include the **"necessary and proper" or elastic clause,** which enables the government to adapt to changing times. Each house of Congress also has special duties that it alone can perform.

## Special Powers of the House and Senate

| House | Senate |
|---|---|
| • To select the President if no candidate receives a majority of the electoral vote | • To select the Vice President if no candidate has a majority of the electoral vote |
| • To bring impeachment charges | • To act as jury in cases of impeachment |
| • To originate all revenue (money) bills | • To ratify treaties (by a two-thirds vote) |
| | • To approve presidential appointments, including federal judges (by a majority vote) |

Article I briefly outlines how a bill becomes a federal law. This process requires the approval of each house and of the President. A presidential **veto,** or rejection, of a bill can be overridden by a two-thirds vote of each house. As the diagram on the next page shows, the process today is quite complex, and a bill must pass through numerous committees before becoming a law.

Congress does much of its work through committees—an important part of the **unwritten constitution.** Committees control what bills include and which come to the floor for a vote.

Due to its size, debate in the House is limited. The Senate is more flexible, usually permitting unlimited debate on a bill. At times, senators **filibuster,** or keep talking, until a majority of the Senate is forced to change or even drop the bill. In recent years, on major bills in the Senate, **cloture,** the votes of sixty senators, has been required to end a filibuster or a filibuster threat.

### The Powers of Congress as Stated (by Clause) in Article I, Section 8 of the United States Constitution

| Expressed Powers |
|---|
| **Peace Powers** |
| 1. To lay taxes<br>  a. Direct (not used since the War Between the States, except income tax)<br>  b. Indirect (customs [tariffs], excise for internal revenue)<br>2. To borrow money<br>3. To regulate foreign and interstate commerce<br>4. To establish naturalization and bankruptcy laws<br>5. To coin money and regulate its value; to regulate weights and measures<br>6. To punish counterfeiters of federal money and securities<br>7. To establish post offices and post roads<br>8. To grant patents and copyrights<br>9. To create courts inferior to the Supreme Court<br>10. To define and punish piracies and felonies on the high seas; to define and punish offenses against the law of nations<br>11. To exercise exclusive jurisdiction over the District of Columbia; to exercise exclusive jurisdiction over forts, dockyards, national parks, federal buildings, and the like |
| **War Powers** |
| 12. To declare war; to grant letters of marque and reprisal; to make rules concerning captures on land and water<br>13. To raise and support armies<br>14. To provide and maintain a navy<br>15. To make laws governing land and naval forces<br>16. To provide for calling forth the militia to execute federal laws, suppress insurrections, and repel invasions<br>17. To provide for organizing, arming, and disciplining the militia, and for its governing when in the service of the Union |
| **Implied Powers** |
| 18. To make all laws necessary and proper for carrying into execution the foregoing powers, such as:<br>  a. To define and provide punishment for federal crimes<br>  b. To establish the Federal Reserve System<br>  c. To improve rivers, canals, harbors, and other waterways<br>  d. To fix minimum wages, maximum hours of work |

# How Bills Become Laws

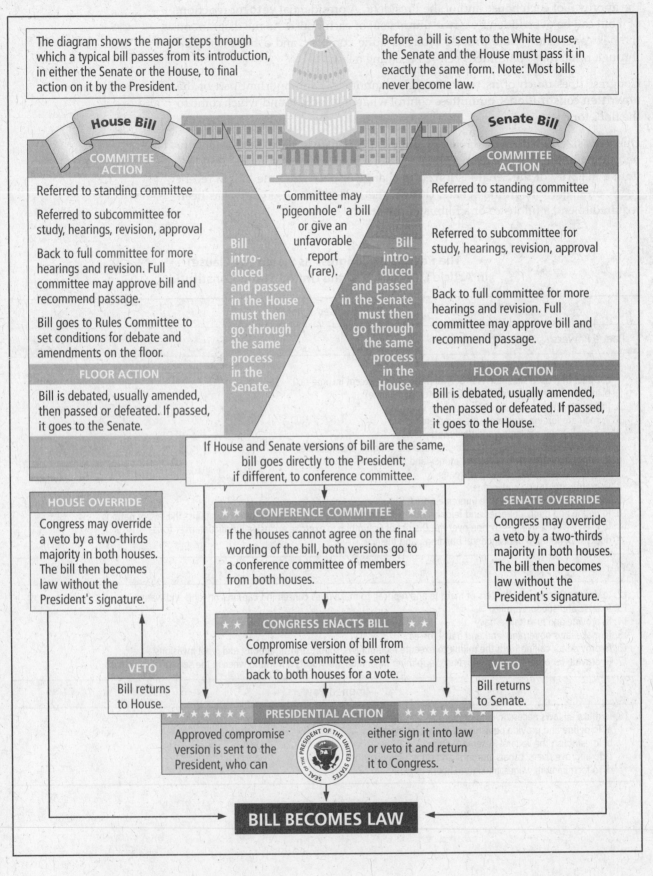

The diagram shows the major steps through which a typical bill passes from its introduction, in either the Senate or the House, to final action on it by the President.

Before a bill is sent to the White House, the Senate and the House must pass it in exactly the same form. Note: Most bills never become law.

## House Bill

### COMMITTEE ACTION

Referred to standing committee

Referred to subcommittee for study, hearings, revision, approval

Back to full committee for more hearings and revision. Full committee may approve bill and recommend passage.

Bill goes to Rules Committee to set conditions for debate and amendments on the floor.

### FLOOR ACTION

Bill is debated, usually amended, then passed or defeated. If passed, it goes to the Senate.

Bill introduced and passed in the House must then go through the same process in the Senate.

Committee may "pigeonhole" a bill or give an unfavorable report (rare).

Bill introduced and passed in the Senate must then go through the same process in the House.

## Senate Bill

### COMMITTEE ACTION

Referred to standing committee

Referred to subcommittee for study, hearings, revision, approval

Back to full committee for more hearings and revision. Full committee may approve bill and recommend passage.

### FLOOR ACTION

Bill is debated, usually amended, then passed or defeated. If passed, it goes to the House.

If House and Senate versions of bill are the same, bill goes directly to the President; if different, to conference committee.

### HOUSE OVERRIDE

Congress may override a veto by a two-thirds majority in both houses. The bill then becomes law without the President's signature.

### ★ ★ CONFERENCE COMMITTEE ★ ★

If the houses cannot agree on the final wording of the bill, both versions go to a conference committee of members from both houses.

### SENATE OVERRIDE

Congress may override a veto by a two-thirds majority in both houses. The bill then becomes law without the President's signature.

### ★ ★ CONGRESS ENACTS BILL ★ ★

Compromise version of bill from conference committee is sent back to both houses for a vote.

### VETO

Bill returns to House.

### VETO

Bill returns to Senate.

### ★ ★ ★ ★ ★ ★ PRESIDENTIAL ACTION ★ ★ ★ ★ ★ ★

Approved compromise version is sent to the President, who can

either sign it into law or veto it and return it to Congress.

## BILL BECOMES LAW

# Article II: The Executive Branch

Article II outlines the workings of the executive branch, including the method of electing the President as well as the powers and duties of the office.

## Electing the President

Article II describes the process by which the president is elected. The Twelfth, Twentieth, Twenty-second, Twenty-third, and Twenty-fifth Amendments have changed this process.

- A key compromise of the Constitutional Convention involved the method of electing the president. Under the resulting **Electoral College system,** voters cast their ballots for electors. Those electors cast the actual votes for President and Vice President. Each state was granted as many presidential electors as it had senators plus representatives. A candidate needs a majority of the electoral votes to become President. Today, that means 270 votes, a number that is one more than half of 538:
- the total number of senators (100)
- plus representatives (435)
- plus the three electoral votes given to Washington, D.C. by the 23rd amendment.

The Constitution requires that a **census,** or counting of the population, be taken every ten years. Changes to reflect shifts in population are then made in the number of representatives per state, which in turn affects the electoral vote. Today, data from the census is also used to make decisions about other national needs.

Customs and precedents influenced how the President is elected. After Washington's two terms, the formation of **political parties** forced changes in the election process. No longer did electors exercise their own judgments. Rather, they pledged in advance to vote for the presidential candidate of their party. Today, while the names of the presidential candidates appear on the ballot, voters are actually casting their ballots for electors chosen by each candidate's party.

By 1832, national conventions had become the method of selecting party candidates. Today **presidential primaries** and **caucuses** are held in each state to select most of the delegates to the national convention. Both parties also name their officials and office holders as delegates, which make up as many as 20 percent of Democratic Party delegates.

## Debating the Electoral College System

From the days of the Constitutional Convention, people have argued over the method of selecting the president.

**Reasons to Change the System** There are three major arguments against the Electoral College system.

1. It is a "winner-take-all" system. A winning candidate gets all the electoral votes in a state, no matter how close the popular vote is. Four times—in 1824, 1876, 1888, and 2000—the winner of the popular vote lost the presidency because he failed to win a majority of the electoral vote.
2. The less populated states are over-represented in the electoral college because every state has two electors for its two senators. It is estimated that the smallest states have a population of 175,000 to 330,000 per electoral vote while the ten largest states have a population of 573,000 to 703,000 per electoral vote.
3. In most states, electors are not required by law to vote for the candidate who wins in their state.

## Reading Strategy

**Analyzing Cause and Effect: Census**
The U.S. Constitution requires that a census of the population be taken every 10 years. The census is used to determine how many representatives each state will send to the House.

- What impact does the census have on the Electoral College?

- How is the 2010 census expected to impact each of the following states in the House and in the Electoral College? Florida, New York, Ohio, Texas

## Analyzing Documents

Use the text and the chart, "The Path to the Presidency," to determine what steps to the presidency are part of the Constitution and which have developed from custom.

# The Path to the Presidency

## First Step in a Presidential Campaign: Announcing Intention to Run

- Announcement made in person and/or on candidate's Web site a year or more before election.
- National and state campaign staffs organized; financial support and endorsements sought.

## The Campaign for Delegates Begins

- Candidate aims to win state party delegates to national nominating convention. Most states now hold primary elections to select some or all delegates. Some states hold caucuses (meetings) to name party members to district/state conventions which in turn elect some or all of the state's delegates to the national convention.
- Trend toward more and earlier primaries has accelerated pressure for money, media attention, and campaign travel. In 1968, fourteen primaries were held between March and June of election year; in 2008 more than 40 states held primary elections or caucuses between January and the end of March.

## Raising Money for the Primaries and General Election

- Earlier primaries increase costs of presidential election. More money needed to campaign in so many closely scheduled primaries and in a longer general election campaign period.
- Presidential candidates raise money in private meetings, fundraising events to meet the candidate, and appeals through letters, phone calls, and Web sites.
- Federal law provides public funding for both the primaries and general election and sets rules for raising and spending campaign money through the Federal Election Commission (FEC).
- Party committees, Political Action Committees (PACs), and 527s may, within limits, raise and spend money for voter registration, to get out the vote and promote issues, but not candidates.
- Candidates decide whether to accept partial public funding for primaries and/or full public funding for the general election with its restrictions on spending limits and on raising other funds.
- In 2008, the Republican nominee accepted public funding for the primaries and the general election. The Democratic candidate did not.
- The 2008 presidential primaries, plus the general election, cost more than 1.6 billion dollars.

## The National Convention: Selecting the Party Nominees

- Party nominees are chosen at conventions held in summer before November election.
- Having won a majority of delegate votes, nominee is usually known before convention.

## The Presidential Campaign

- Candidate plans strategy to win 270 of the 538 electoral votes needed to become President.
- Candidate concentrates time, and media attention on "contested" rather than "safe" states.
- Each state has as many votes as its senators plus representatives to equal 535 plus 3 electoral votes for Washington D.C. In 2000 election, Florida's electoral votes determined the presidency (271-266) even though Al Gore received more popular votes than G.W. Bush.
- After 2000 census, 12 House seats changed from Eastern and Midwestern states to Western and Southern states in a continuing population trend that shifted electoral votes as well.

## Election Day: Voters Choose the Electors Who Elect the President

- Voters cast ballots on Election Day—the Tuesday following first Monday in November.
- Voters decide which party's electors in each state will vote for President and Vice President on the Monday following the second Wednesday in December.
- The new President is sworn in (inaugurated) on January 20.

**Reasons to Keep the System** Despite such criticisms, the Electoral College system remains in use for three key reasons:

1. It is very difficult to amend the Constitution.
2. Small states would lose the advantage they now have of being over-represented in the electoral college; they would, therefore, oppose any change. It is also argued that at this time, the 11 most populous states control a majority of the Electoral College votes.
3. Changes in the Electoral College system might threaten the two-party political system. The fact that a presidential candidate needs a majority of the Electoral College vote, critics believe, prevents many small political parties from springing up.

## Presidential Roles and Powers

Article II describes the powers and duties of the President of the United States. Since power in the executive branch centers in one individual, a president can act swiftly in times of war and national crisis. In carrying out the duties of office, the president fills several different roles.

**Chief Executive** In this role, the President has the power to

- enforce or put the laws into effect.
- act as administrator of the huge federal bureaucracy.
- issue executive orders that have the effect of laws.
- appoint judges, diplomats, and other high government officials—some with Senate approval and others without.
- remove appointed government officials within the executive branch.

**Chief Diplomat** In this role, the President has the power to

- make treaties with the advice and consent of the Senate.
- make executive agreements with nations without Senate approval.
- extend or withdraw diplomatic recognition to a nation.

**Commander in Chief** In this role, the President has broad military powers that are shared with Congress. In times of war, these powers are even stronger.

**Chief Legislator** In this role of lawmaker, the President has the power to

- recommend legislation to Congress.
- veto potential laws.

**Chief of State** In addition to being head of the government, the President is also chief of state, the ceremonial head of government, and the symbol of all the people of the nation. He fills this role in such ceremonies as the laying of a wreath on the Tomb of the Unknowns.

**Judicial Powers** The President can grant reprieves, pardons, and amnesties, or pardons extended to groups rather than individuals.

**Head of the Party** The President is also the leader of the political party in power. The duties of this role are not mentioned in the Constitution because the party system developed through custom, making it part of the unwritten constitution.

## The Federal Bureaucracy

The federal **bureaucracy** consists of the administrative agencies and staff that put the decisions or policies of the government into effect. Such a bureaucracy has developed through legislation, executive action, and custom.

**Key Themes and Concepts**

**Government**
In the presidential election of 2000, George W. Bush became the fourth president to win the presidency without winning the popular vote. The other presidents were John Quincy Adams, elected in 1824; Rutherford B. Hayes, elected in 1876; and Benjamin Harrison, elected in 1888.

**Key Themes and Concepts**

**Government**
The executive branch is the largest branch of the government, as shown in the chart **The Government of the United States Under the Constitution** on the next page.

- Why is the executive branch so large?

- How were the departments and agencies shown created?

Most of the bureaucracy is part of the executive branch and includes the White House staff, 15 executive departments, and more than 200 independent agencies. This bureaucracy is explained in more detail in the following chart.

## The Government of the United States Under the Constitution

**Legislative**

### THE CONGRESS

Senate    House

- Architect of the Capitol
- General Accountability Office
- Government Printing Office
- Library of Congress
- United States Botanic Garden
- Office of Technology Assessment
- Congressional Budget Office

**Executive**

### THE PRESIDENT
### THE VICE PRESIDENT

**Executive Office of the President**

- White House Office
- Office of the Vice President
- Office of Management and Budget
- Council of Economic Advisers
- National Security Council
- Office of National Drug Control Policy
- Office of the United States Trade Representative
- Council on Environmental Quality
- Office of Science and Technology Policy
- Office of Administration
- Office of Policy Development

**Judicial**

### THE SUPREME COURT OF THE UNITED STATES

- Courts of Appeals
- District Courts
- Federal Claims Court
- Court of Appeals for the Federal Circuit
- Court of International Trade
- Territorial Courts
- Court of Appeals—Armed Forces
- Court of Veterans Appeals
- Administrative Office of the United States Courts
- Federal Judicial Center
- United States Tax Court
- U.S. Sentencing Commission

### Executive Departments

- State
- Treasury
- Defense
- Justice
- Interior

- Agriculture
- Commerce
- Labor
- Health and Human Services
- Housing and Urban Development

- Transportation
- Energy
- Education
- Veterans Affairs
- Homeland Security

### Selected Independent Establishments and Government Corporations

- Central Intelligence Agency
- Commission on Civil Rights
- Consumer Product Safety Commission
- Corporation for National and Community Service
- Defense Nuclear Facilities Safety Board
- Environmental Protection Agency
- Equal Employment Opportunity Commission
- Export-Import Bank of the U.S.
- Farm Credit Administration
- Federal Communications Commission

- Federal Deposit Insurance Corporation
- Federal Election Commission
- Federal Housing Finance Board
- Federal Maritime Commission
- Federal Mediation and Conciliation Service
- Federal Reserve System
- Federal Trade Commission
- General Services Administration
- National Science Foundation
- U.S. International Trade Commission
- Merit Systems Protection Board
- National Aeronautics and Space Administration

- National Labor Relations Board
- National Transportation Safety Board
- Nuclear Regulatory Commission
- Office of Government Ethics
- Securities and Exchange Commission
- Selective Service System
- Small Business Administration
- Social Security Administration
- Tennessee Valley Authority
- U.S. Postal Service

# Article III: The Judicial Branch

Article III of the Constitution creates the Supreme Court and gives Congress the power to create lower federal courts. The role of this judicial branch is to interpret the law. In addition to this national court system, each of the 50 states has its own court system.

## Jurisdiction

With two court systems—federal and state—the Constitution had to define the **jurisdiction,** or authority, of the federal courts in order to make clear which cases go to federal courts and which to state courts. The court that has the authority to hear a case is determined by two factors:

**Subject Matter** Federal courts hear cases involving federal laws, treaties, maritime law, and interpretation of the Constitution.

**Parties** Federal courts are directed to have jurisdiction if cases involve certain parties, or participants in a case. For example, cases involving representatives of foreign governments or states suing other states are tried in federal courts.

The Constitution states that in some types of cases, the Supreme Court will have original jurisdiction. This means the Supreme Court will hear the case first and make a decision. In most cases, the Supreme Court has appellate jurisdiction. This means that, in a lower court, if the losing side believes a judge made a mistake in applying the law in a case, that case may be appealed to a higher court. The Supreme Court hears only about 150 cases of the nearly 5,000 appealed to it each year.

## Judicial Review

The most important power of the federal courts is the right to **judicial review.** This power enables the courts to hear cases involving the application and interpretation of law. Laws that are judged not in keeping with the Constitution's intent are declared unconstitutional and void.

The Supreme Court is the final voice in interpreting the Constitution. The right of judicial review strengthened the power of the judiciary against the other two branches of government. Chief Justice John Marshall first stated the right of judicial review in the 1803 case of *Marbury* v. *Madison*.

## Amending the Constitution

Article V describes methods of amending, or formally changing, the Constitution. The purpose of an **amendment** process is to ensure that the government meets the

**Reading Strategy**

**Problem Solving**
• The process of amending the Constitution is an excellent example of federalism in practice. Why?

### The Formal Amendment Process (Four Methods)

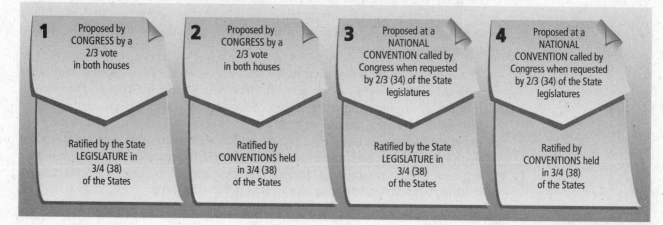

**1** Proposed by CONGRESS by a 2/3 vote in both houses → Ratified by the State LEGISLATURE in 3/4 (38) of the States

**2** Proposed by CONGRESS by a 2/3 vote in both houses → Ratified by CONVENTIONS held in 3/4 (38) of the States

**3** Proposed at a NATIONAL CONVENTION called by Congress when requested by 2/3 (34) of the State legislatures → Ratified by the State LEGISLATURE in 3/4 (38) of the States

**4** Proposed at a NATIONAL CONVENTION called by Congress when requested by 2/3 (34) of the State legislatures → Ratified by CONVENTIONS held in 3/4 (38) of the States

nation's changing needs. In accordance with the principle of federalism, both national and state governments are involved in the amendment process. In the most common method of amendment, Congress approves a proposed amendment by a two-thirds vote in each house. The amendment then goes to the state legislatures. If three quarters of them ratify it, the amendment becomes part of the Constitution. Twenty-six of the constitutional amendments have been adopted by this method. To date, only the Twenty-first Amendment has been ratified by special conventions called in the states.

## The Bill of Rights

The Bill of Rights is the name given to the first ten amendments to the Constitution adopted in 1791. They were added at the insistence of the Anti-Federalists. These amendments guarantee certain basic or fundamental rights of the people against the power of the federal government.

### The Bill of Rights

| Amendment | Subject |
|---|---|
| 1st | Guarantees freedom of religion, of speech, and of the press; the right to assemble peacefully; and the right to petition the government. |
| 2nd | Protects the right to possess firearms. |
| 3rd | Declares that the government may not require people to house soldiers during peacetime. |
| 4th | Protects people from unreasonable searches and seizures. |
| 5th | Includes protection against self incrimination and double jeopardy; guarantees due process of law. |
| 6th | Guarantees the right to a speedy, public trial, to confront witnesses, and to legal counsel. |
| 7th | Guarantees the right to trial by jury in most civil cases. |
| 8th | Prohibits excessive bail, fines, and "cruel and unusual" punishments. |
| 9th | Declares that rights not mentioned in the Constitution belong to the people. |
| 10th | Declares that powers not given to the national government belong to the states or to the people. |

## Extending Constitutional Protections

In the 200 years since the Bill of Rights was added to the Constitution, the rights of the people have been expanded by court decisions, by other amendments, and even by presidential actions. The Fourteenth Amendment contains the equal protection clause. Court interpretations have held that the Fourteenth Amendment extends the protections of most of the Bill of Rights against the states as well as the national government.

The courts have held that civil rights (as defined in the Bill of Rights and other amendments) are relative, not absolute. The courts have thus tried to balance an individual's rights against the rights of society and other individuals. In recent years, Bill of Rights issues such as privacy versus national security have been debated. Sometimes basic civil rights conflict with each other. For example, the Sixth Amendment right of the accused to confront witnesses might clash with a reporter's First Amendment, the right of freedom of the press to protect news sources. In such conflicts, the courts must decide the issue.

## Additional Constitutional Amendments

Between 1795 and 1992, an additional 17 amendments have been added to the Constitution. Note that the Thirteenth, Fourteenth, and Fifteenth Amendments were passed after the Civil War so that formerly enslaved people could become citizens, and to give them the right to vote. Four amendments—the Fifteenth, Nineteenth, Twenty-third, and Twenty-sixth—have expanded the right to vote.

### Amendments 11–27

| Amendment | Year Ratified | Subject |
|---|---|---|
| 11th | 1795 | Grants States immunity from certain lawsuits |
| 12th | 1804 | Separates voting for President and Vice President |
| 13th | 1865 | Abolishes slavery |
| 14th | 1868 | Defines citizenship; prohibits states from denying people due process and equal protection of the law including due process and equal protection |
| 15th | 1870 | Grants voting rights for African American men |
| 16th | 1913 | Gives Congress power to tax incomes |
| 17th | 1913 | Requires election of U.S. Senators by people of a state, not the state legislature |
| 18th | 1919 | Prohibits manufacture, sale, and transportation of alcoholic beverages |
| 19th | 1920 | Grants voting rights for women |
| 20th | 1933 | Shortens amount of time between election of a president and of Congress and start of their term of office |
| 21st | 1933 | Repeals Eighteenth Amendment |
| 22nd | 1951 | Limits president to two terms |
| 23rd | 1961 | Grants electoral votes and right to vote in presidential elections for the District of Columbia |
| 24th | 1964 | Abolishes poll taxes as qualification for voting in federal elections |
| 25th | 1967 | Sets procedure for determining presidential disability and succession, and for filling a vice-presidential vacancy |
| 26th | 1971 | Lowers voting age to 18 |
| 27th | 1992 | Bans mid-term congressional pay raises |

### Extending the Right to Vote

| Year | People Allowed to Vote |
|---|---|
| 1789 | White men over age 21 who meet property requirements (state laws) |
| Early 1800s–1850s | All white men over age 21 (state laws) |
| 1870 | African American men (15th Amendment) |
| 1920 | Women (19th Amendment) |
| 1961 | Citizens in the District of Columbia in presidential elections (23rd Amendment) |
| 1971 | Citizens age 18 or over (26th Amendment) |

**Analyzing Documents**

- Based on the chart what has been the most common way of extending the right to vote to more people?

# New York State Government Compared to the Federal Government

The government of New York has many similarities to the federal government. New York has a constitution and a Bill of Rights. The New York government has three branches. The executive branch is headed by the governor. The bicameral legislature has a Senate and an Assembly. The highest court in the judicial branch is the Court of Appeals.

Thirteen basic constitutional principles have endured since the ratification of the Constitution. These principles continue to be important to the development of American government and society.

## Constitutional Principle 1
### National Power—Limits and Potential

The powers of the federal government are limited. The Constitution states the powers held by each branch of government. The powers that are not delegated to the national government are reserved to the states or to the people (Tenth Amendment). The Bill of Rights also limits the government's interference with basic rights.

However, the powers of all three branches of the federal government have grown.
- Has the national government become too powerful?
- Do the limits placed on the national government make it incapable of dealing with the problems of the modern age?

### Examples of This Principle as a Recurring Theme in U.S. History

Need for a strong central government: debate over ratification
Loose vs. strict interpretation of the Constitution: Hamilton's financial plan, Louisiana Purchase
Conflict over slavery: 1820–1860
Civil War: establishing federal supremacy over the states
Imperialism: Spanish-American War, acquiring an overseas empire

Progressive movement: Theodore Roosevelt and Woodrow Wilson
Elastic clause: Pure Food and Drug Act, Social Security
Commerce clause: expanding powers of government
New Deal: expanding role of government
Great Society: demand for reform
New Federalism: less government involvement

## Constitutional Principle 2
### Federalism—Balance Between Nation and State

The Constitution created a new federal government that divided power between the states and the national government. The Constitution reserved certain powers to the states and to the people, but the Constitution and the laws and treaties of the United States are supreme to state laws.

- Is the power still balanced, or has it tilted to the federal government?
- Has the shift of power to the federal government become greater since the New Deal, or did Reagan's New Federalism reverse this trend?

### Examples of This Principle as a Recurring Theme in U.S. History

Marshall Supreme Court cases: *McCulloch* v. *Maryland*, *Gibbons* v. *Ogden*
John C. Calhoun: nullification, states' rights
Conflict over slavery: 1820–1860
Civil War: establishing federal supremacy over the states
Reconstruction: greater federal supremacy; 13th, 14th, and 15th Amendments

Populists and Progressive reform
New Deal legislation
Rights of minorities: *Brown* v. *Board of Education*
Fourteenth Amendment: extends Bill of Rights protections to states
Great Society, mid-1960s
New Federalism, 1980s

## Constitutional Principle 3
### The Judiciary—Interpreter of the Constitution or Shaper of Public Policy

The Judiciary interprets the law (Article III) and has the power to declare laws unconstitutional. This power of judicial review dates from Marshall's decision in *Marbury* v. *Madison,* which was based on Article III, and the supremacy clause in Article VI, which states that the Constitution is the "supreme law of the land."

- By acting when Congress has not acted, or by reversing congressional actions to favor the states, have the courts become lawmakers instead of law interpreters?
- If the courts did not have the power to shape public policy, would the Bill of Rights and democracy itself be endangered?

### Examples of This Principle as a Recurring Theme in U.S. History

*Marbury* v. *Madison:* judicial review strengthened judiciary, government, and national unity

Federal vs. state powers: *McCulloch* v. *Maryland, Gibbons* v. *Ogden*

Limiting protections and rights: *Dred Scott* v. *Sanford, Civil Rights Cases*

Reversals of decisions: *Plessy* v. *Ferguson, Brown* v. *Board of Education*

State vs. federal powers: *United States* v. *E.C. Knight Co., Lochner* v. *New York, Schechter Poultry* v. *United States*

Rights of accused: *Miranda* v. *Arizona, Gideon* v. *Wainwright*

First Amendment cases (freedom of speech, press, religion, assembly): *Engel* v. *Vitale, Schenck* v. *United States, New York Times Co.* v. *United States, Tinker* v. *Des Moines Independent Community School District*

Ninth Amendment privacy cases: *Roe* v. *Wade; Cruzan* v. *Director, Missouri Department of Health*

Checks and balances: *Watkins* v. *United States, United States* v. *Nixon*

## Constitutional Principle 4
### Civil Liberties—Protecting Individual Liberties From Government Abuses; the Balance Between Government and the Individual

A problem unique to a democratic government is how to balance the rights of the individual and the needs of society. The Constitution's Bill of Rights and Fourteenth Amendment guarantee certain basic rights, rights which predate any government. But these rights are not unlimited.

- What are the rights of the individual?
- Should government protect and/or extend the rights of the individual?
- Should government decide where the balance should be between individual and societal rights?

### Examples of This Principle as a Recurring Theme in U.S. History

Right to dissent: Alien & Sediton Acts; Virginia & Kentucky Resolutions

Equal protection clause: Fourteenth Amendment—*Civil Rights Cases, Heart of Atlanta Motel* v. *United States*

Freedom of speech v. "clear and present danger": *Schenck* v. *United States*

Relocation of Japanese Americans: *Korematsu* v. *United States*

Red Scare, McCarthyism: fear of subversion, the erosion of liberties *Watkins* v. *United States*

Testing for drug use: *Vernonia School District* v. *Acton*

Rights of individuals: effects of technology

Individual's rights v. security against terrorism: *Patriot Act, Foreign Intelligence Surveillance Act*

## Constitutional Principle 5
### Criminal Procedures—The Balance Between the Rights of the Accused and the Protection of the Community and Victims

This is a question of balancing the rights of individuals accused of crimes and those of citizens to be safe and secure.
- Why does an individual accused of a crime have rights?

- Are those rights easily defined?
- What are the rights of a victim of a crime?
- When do the rights of the accused interfere with society's ability to maintain law and order?

### Examples of This Principle as a Recurring Theme in U.S. History

Free press vs. the rights of the accused

Death penalty: individual rights v. rights of society

Writ of *habeas corpus:* purpose

Due process of law, search and seizure: *Mapp* v. *Ohio*

Students' rights and search and seizure: *New Jersey* v. *T.L.O.; Vernonia School District* v. *Acton*

Rights of the accused: *Miranda* v. *Arizona, Gideon* v. *Wainwright*

## Constitutional Principle 6
### Equality—Its Historic and Present Meaning as a Constitutional Value

This issue involves questions of who is equal and in what ways. When Jefferson wrote that "all men are created equal," he referred to the equality before the law of white, property-owning males. The equal protection clause of the Fourteenth Amendment and the due process clause of the Fifth Amendment were later interpreted to make equal justice more of a reality for all Americans.

- According to the Constitution, who is equal: men and women? All races? Rich and poor? Young and old?
- How has the Constitution expanded equality?
- Has equality been achieved?
- How are people equal: equal in opportunity? Before the law? In entitlements?

### Examples of This Principle as a Recurring Theme in U.S. History

Conflict over slavery: Constitutional Convention; 1820–1860
Passage of 13th, 14th, and 15th Amendments
Equal protection clause: 14th Amendment
Jim Crow laws: legal basis for segregation
*Plessy* v. *Ferguson*
*Brown* v. *Board of Education*
Martin Luther King, Jr.: Civil Rights Movement

19th-century women's rights movement
19th Amendment
1960s women's rights movement
Treatment of Native Americans: *Worcester* v. *Georgia*
Native American movement
New Deal: relief of human suffering
Great Society: help for less fortunate
Affirmative action: court decisions

## Constitutional Principle 7
### The Rights of Women Under the Constitution

Women are not mentioned in the Constitution except in the Nineteenth Amendment, which protects their right to vote.
- What is the historic and present meaning of equality for women as a constitutional value?

- How were these changes achieved?
- Are federal laws and court rulings sufficiently protective of the rights of women?
- Was there a need for the defeated Equal Rights Amendment?

### Examples of This Principle as a Recurring Theme in U.S. History

Elizabeth Cady Stanton and Susan B. Anthony: Women's suffrage movement
Seneca Falls: Women's rights movement
Effects of industrialization on the role of women

1960s women's rights movement
*Roe* v. *Wade*: Ninth amendment, right to privacy, abortion
Affirmative action and women

## Constitutional Principle 8
### The Rights of Ethnic and Racial Minority Groups Under the Constitution

The Constitution has not always protected ethnic, racial, and other minority groups. When first ratified, in fact, the Constitution contained clauses that protected slavery and the rights of slaveholders.
- Has the Constitution protected the rights of ethnic and racial minority groups?

- Has the Constitution protected the rights of economically powerful groups better than those of minority groups?
- Are the gains that minorities have made secure, or do such groups need more protection of their rights?
- How do we balance minority rights and rule by a majority?

### Examples of This Principle as a Recurring Theme in U.S. History

Conflict over slavery: Constitutional Convention; 1820–1860
Frederick Douglass: abolition movement
*Dred Scott* v. *Sanford*
Civil War: Emancipation Proclamation
Reconstruction: 13th, 14th, and 15th Amendments
Jim Crow laws, *Plessy* v. *Ferguson*: legal basis for segregation
Equal protection clause: 14th Amendment

*Brown* v. *Board of Education*
Martin Luther King, Jr.: Civil Rights Movement of 1960s
Restrictions on immigration: quota system, exclusion of Chinese and Japanese
Relocation of Japanese Americans: *Korematsu* v. *United States*
Native Americans: treaty rights, *Worcester* v. *Georgia*, Dawes Act, citizenship in 1924
Native American movement

## Constitutional Principle 9
### Presidential Power in Wartime and in Foreign Affairs

The Constitution gives the President the power to make treaties, as well as other major foreign-policy responsibilities. The President is also the commander in chief of the armed forces. The powers of the President have grown since the early days of the United States government, and they are even greater in wartime.

- Does the President have too much power, particularly since the Civil War?
- Are broad presidential powers necessary to conduct war and foreign affairs?

### Examples of This Principle as a Recurring Theme in U.S. History

George Washington: expanded governmental powers, Proclamation of Neutrality

Increase of presidential power during wartime by Lincoln, Wilson, and FDR.: *Schenck* v. *United States*, *Korematsu* v. *United States*

T. Roosevelt: increase of presidential power because of U.S. involvement in world affairs

T. Roosevelt: Roosevelt Corollary to Monroe Doctrine

Truman: decision to drop atomic bomb

Korean and Vietnam Wars: expanded presidential wartime powers

Kennedy: Cuban missile crisis

War Powers Act: a check on presidential power

Carter: Camp David Accords

G.H.W. Bush: Persian Gulf Crisis

Clinton: Somalia, Bosnia, Haiti, Yugoslavia

G.W. Bush: Bush Doctrine; presidential powers in wartime: writ of *Habeas Corpus*, wiretapping

## Constitutional Principle 10
### The Separation of Powers and the Effectiveness of Government

The Constitution established three branches of government with separate powers, as well as a system of checks and balances among them.
- Has the system of separation of powers and of checks and balances been effective in preventing dominance by one branch?

- Is this system necessary, or has it resulted in a badly-run government that is slow to respond to the needs of the people and the nation?

### Examples of This Principle as a Recurring Theme in U.S. History

Checks and balances: presidential veto

Judicial review: *Marbury* v. *Madison*

Reconstruction: period of legislative power

Checks and balances: Treaty of Versailles

Checks and balances: FDR and Supreme Court reorganization

Checks and balances: Vietnam War

Checks and balances: *Watkins* v. *United States*, *United States* v. *Nixon*

War Powers Act: check on presidential power

Watergate: government based on laws and not on an individual

Clinton: impeachment and acquittal

## Constitutional Principle 11
### Avenues of Representation

Since the Constitution was ratified, there has been a continuing expansion of the right to vote. However, while the system has become more democratic and more reflective of majority rule, the power of political parties and special interest groups has grown, as has the influence of technology.

- Has the federal government become more or less representative of "we the people"?

### Examples of This Principle as a Recurring Theme in U.S. History

Great Compromise: representation in Congress

Electoral college system

Direct election of senators

Passage of 15th, 19th, 24th, and 26th Amendments

19th-century and Progressive reform movements

Populist and Grange movements

Women's suffrage movement

Third parties' effect on the political process

"One man, one vote": effect on representative government

Campaign financing: public v. private, individual rights, rights of lobbyists and other special interests

Effects of technology: electronic voting; the Internet

## Constitutional Principle 12
### Property Rights and Economic Policy

The Constitution gives the government responsibility for promoting the general welfare and Congress the power to regulate commerce and taxes.

- Has government balanced its two roles as the promoter of capitalism and free enterprise and as the protector of the public from the abuses of business?

### *Examples of This Principle as a Recurring Theme in U.S. History*

Hamilton: government encouragement of business, national bank

Andrew Jackson: second national bank

Expanded interstate commerce clause: *Gibbons* v. *Ogden*; *Wabash, St. Louis & Pacific R.R.* v. *Illinois*

Weakened interstate commerce clause: *United States* v. *E.C. Knight Co., Lochner* v. *New York, Schechter Poultry* v. *United States*

Interstate commerce clause used against labor: *In Re Debs*

Antitrust activities: Sherman Antitrust Act, T. Roosevelt and W. Wilson, *Northern Securities Co.* v. *United States,* Clayton Antitrust Act

Federal Reserve: regulating monetary system

Government action for environmental and consumer protection

New Deal: government farm price supports

New Deal: collective bargaining, Wagner Act

Reagan: supply side economics, budget deficits

## Constitutional Principle 13
### Constitutional Change and Flexibility

The Constitution has adapted to changing circumstances over the years because of certain provisions built into it, such as the necessary and proper clause and the interstate commerce clause.

- Has the Constitution proven adaptable to changing times?

- Should the Constitution be easier to change?
- Has the amendment process, combined with judicial interpretation and the implied powers of the executive and legislative branches, kept the Constitution able to meet the challenges of the modern world?

### *Examples of This Principle as a Recurring Theme in United States History*

Washington: the unwritten constitution

Hamilton's bank plan: implied powers

Commerce clause: expansion of government authority, regulation of business, Federal Reserve System

Amendments and court decisions used to expand rights

Cabinet and congressional committees: custom and precedent

Role of political parties

## Part 5 Putting the Constitution Into Effect

**Key Terms**

| | | |
|---|---|---|
| unwritten constitution | protective tariff | loose constructionists |
| cabinet | neutrality | judicial review |
| "advise and consent" | Alien and Sedition Acts | Federalists |
| assumption | committee system | Democratic-Republicans |
| national bank | lobbying | foreign policy |
| excise tax | strict constructionists | Monroe Doctrine |

The Constitution was implemented, or put into effect, beginning in 1789 with George Washington's administration. Our leaders first needed to:

- create a sound financial foundation for the new nation.
- establish a solid political system.
- insure national security through foreign policy decisions.

Not all the actions that shaped our government in its early years grew directly out of the plan set down in the Constitution. From the time of our first presidents an **unwritten constitution** developed in response to changing times and circumstances. This unwritten constitution resulted from a combination of:

- executive interpretations and actions.
- congressional interpretations and actions.
- court decisions, especially judicial review.
- customs and traditions.
- the actions of political parties.

**Key Themes and Concepts**

**Government: Unwritten Constitution**
In the early years of the new nation, the United States government grew from the basic framework of the Constitution to a functioning governmental system. Provide an example of how interpretation, action, and custom each contributed to this process.

Interpretation:

Action:

Custom:

## First Years of the New Government, 1789–1820

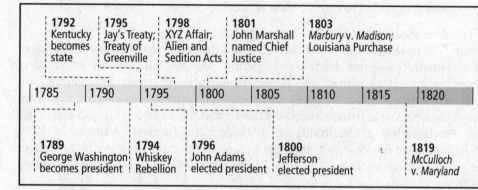

**1792** Kentucky becomes state

**1795** Jay's Treaty; Treaty of Greenville

**1798** XYZ Affair; Alien and Sedition Acts

**1801** John Marshall named Chief Justice

**1803** *Marbury* v. *Madison*; Louisiana Purchase

| 1785 | 1790 | 1795 | 1800 | 1805 | 1810 | 1815 | 1820 |

**1789** George Washington becomes president

**1794** Whiskey Rebellion

**1796** John Adams elected president

**1800** Jefferson elected president

**1819** *McCulloch* v. *Maryland*

# Executive Interpretation, Action, and Custom

## Executive Decision-Making

Starting with George Washington, when developing policy, presidents sought advice from the heads of the executive departments, who were called the President's **cabinet**. Today, the White House staff also plays a major role in this advisory process. The President appoints cabinet members with Senate approval but can dismiss a cabinet member without Senate approval.

The early presidents also consulted with congressional leaders when developing policies. Such **"advise and consent"** consultation is an informal procedure. Today, the Senate's official role often seems more "to consent" than "to advise" on presidential decisions. This method of advising the President has become custom.

## Developing a Financial Plan

With Washington's support, Alexander Hamilton, the first secretary of the treasury, set out to put the government on a sound economic footing. He proposed a plan that included four key elements:

**Assumption** Hamilton wanted the national government to pay off American Revolution war debts run up by the Continental Congress as well as the wartime debts of the states. Hamilton believed that this **assumption** of debt would establish the credit of the nation. Congress approved this plan.

**A National Bank** Hamilton wanted Congress to create a national bank, which he believed would win the government the support of the business community. Such a bank would also help the government in all of its financial dealings. Congress chartered a national bank in 1791.

**An Excise Tax** Hamilton proposed that the government raise operating revenues through an excise tax on whiskey.

**Analyzing Documents**

Hamilton used the **"necessary and proper"** clause to justify creating a national bank. Read the clause below, then answer the question.

*"[The Congress shall have the power] to make all laws which shall be necessary and proper for carrying into execution the foregoing powers, and all other powers vested by this Constitution in the government of the United States, or in any department or officer thereof."*
—U.S. Constitution, Article I, Section 8, Clause 18

- Was Hamilton justified in using the "necessary and proper" clause to create a national bank?

- Did the Supreme Court support his argument?

**A Protective Tariff** Hamilton called for a protective tariff to shield products of the nation's infant industries from foreign competition. Congress rejected the protective tariff but passed other tariffs to generate income for the government.

The Hamilton plan raised some controversy, but it put the new nation on a sound financial footing. It also encouraged the wealthy to support the government and built a solid foundation for the nation's future as an industrial power.

### The Whiskey Rebellion

In 1794, western Pennsylvania farmers protested and refused to pay excise tax on the whiskey they made from grain. Washington called out state militias and put down this "Whiskey Rebellion." There is debate today over how serious a threat this rebellion really was, but Washington's actions demonstrated that the new government intended to enforce federal law.

### Foreign Policy in the Federalist Era

## Geography in History

*"It is our true policy to steer clear of permanent alliances with any portion of the foreign world. . . ."*
—*Washington's Farewell Address, September 17, 1796*

- Why did Washington make this foreign policy?

- Why did geography make it possible for the United States to follow Washington's policy?

From 1789 to 1815, the French Revolution and the European wars that grew out of it put many pressures on the new nation. Washington and the other early presidents tried to protect the nation from such pressures. Washington, for example, supported the unpopular **Jay's Treaty,** an agreement designed to resolve conflicts with Great Britain and keep the United States from going to war. With his **Proclamation of Neutrality** in 1793 and his **Farewell Address** in 1796, Washington set the tone for United States foreign policy by warning of the danger of political alliances. Instead he urged the nation to follow a policy of **neutrality** in foreign affairs.

John Adams, the first vice president and second president, also understood the importance of keeping the new nation out of war. He settled rather than expand an undeclared naval war with France (1798–1800). His actions divided his own Federalist Party, which contributed to his failure to win a second term. But Adams, in resisting internal and external pressures for war and ending the 1778 alliance with France, made possible a peaceful and independent entry into the new century.

### Reacting to Dissent: The Alien and Sedition Acts

Taking advantage of the emotions stirred up by the French Revolution, the Federalists passed the **Alien and Sedition Acts** (1798), which were designed to strengthen the Federalist Party and weaken the Republican opposition. The Alien Acts made it more difficult to become a citizen and easier to arrest and deport any noncitizens thought to endanger national security. The Sedition Act made it easier to arrest a person for criticizing the government. Protests were made against these acts for challenging the freedom of speech and of the press. Madison and Jefferson in the Virginia and Kentucky Resolutions declared the acts dangerous to civil liberties and representative government.

### The Two-Term Presidency

## Key Themes and Concepts

**Presidential Decisions and Actions**
- What impact did Franklin D. Roosevelt's decision to run for a third and fourth term eventually have on the U.S. Constitution?

After serving two terms, Washington rejected a third term as president. In doing so, he established a tradition that was not broken until 1940 and 1944, when Franklin D. Roosevelt won a third and then a fourth term. Unhappiness over Roosevelt's break with tradition led to the passage of the Twenty-second Amendment that limits a President to two terms in office.

# Congressional Interpretation, Action, and Custom

### Creating Structures of Government

The Constitution supplied few details of how the machinery of government would operate, so early congressional actions helped set up that machinery. For example, the Constitution established only a Supreme Court. Congress, therefore, passed the **Judiciary Act of 1789,** creating the rest of the federal court system. Congress also created the first five executive departments—State, Treasury, War (Defense), Attorney General (Justice), and Postmaster General. Today, there are 15 departments and more than 200 independent agencies.

In 1789, Congress began the custom of assigning bills to committees. This developed into today's **committee system,** in which standing committees review all bills before sending them on to the full House or Senate. Congressional committees can also operate as investigative committees, gathering information in order to determine the need for new laws or to examine how current laws are working.

## Lobbying

Custom has led to **lobbying** by people representing special-interest groups who act to influence legislation and elect people who support the lobby group's views. Lobbying is protected by the First Amendment's right to petition but also regulated by federal law. The National Rifle Association and the National Association of Realtors are two examples of over 4,600 Political Action Committees (PACs) funded by lobby groups to seek access and influence.

## Strict vs. Loose Construction

**Hamilton's Financial Plan** Hamilton's proposal for a national bank started the first national debate between "strict" and "loose" constructionists. **Strict constructionists** favor a narrow interpretation of the Constitution, holding that government can do only those things the document specifically spells out. **Loose constructionists** favor a freer reading of the Constitution that gives government more room to act. Despite objections of such strict constructionists as Jefferson and Madison, Congress established the bank using the implied powers of the elastic clause.

**The Louisiana Purchase** In 1803, Jefferson had the chance to double the size of the nation through the **Louisiana Purchase.** However, supporting the purchase meant adopting a loose interpretation of the Constitution. Jefferson overcame his reluctance and backed the purchase. In addition to adding new lands, the

### Key Themes and Concepts

**Constitutional Principles**

- What major PACs are involved in election campaigns and what methods do they use to elect their candidates?

- How does federal law attempt to limit PACs?

- How might the Supreme Court ruling in *Citizens United* v. *FEC* impact future elections?

### The Louisiana Purchase, 1803

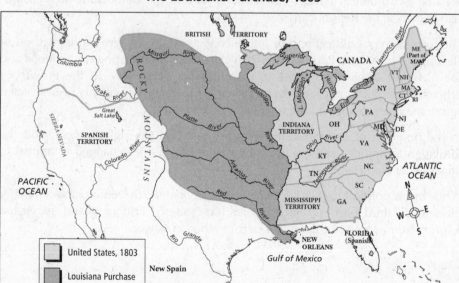

Map legend: United States, 1803; Louisiana Purchase

### Geography in History

"... is on the globe one spot, the possessor of which is our natural and habitual enemy. It is New Orleans, through which the produce of three-eighths of our territory must pass to market. . ."
— *Thomas Jefferson to Robert Livingston*

- Examine the map.

- Why did Jefferson agree to the Louisiana Purchase?

Louisiana Purchase gave the United States control of the vital port of New Orleans and the Mississippi River. This opened up a water route for Ohio River Valley farmers and others to ship their products to market.

## Judicial Interpretation of the Constitution

Under Chief Justice **John Marshall**, (1801–1835) a series of Supreme Court decisions strengthened the power of the national government and the authority of the judicial branch of government.

### The Marshall Court

- First, and most critically, Marshall led the Court in the 1803 decision in *Marbury v. Madison.* This decision established the court's most significant right—that of judicial review, the power to rule on the constitutionality of a law.
- The decision in *McCulloch v. Maryland,* 1819, upheld the creation of a national bank. The decision strengthened federal supremacy over state law, the use of the elastic clause, and national economic interests.
- Similarly, in 1824, the Marshall Court verdict in *Gibbons v. Ogden* expanded the powers of the national government in the area of commerce through a broad interpretation of the Congressional power to regulate interstate commerce. (Article I, Section 8)

### Activism v. Restraint

Those favoring **judicial activism** believe the Court should use this power to help make public policy. Those favoring **judicial restraint** believe that this power should be used only when there is an obvious violation of a particular part of the Constitution, opposing a policy-making role for the Court. In our history, the Court has been activist and restrained, irrespective of whether the Court was considered conservative or liberal. The Court has also been influenced by changes in the nation's social and political climate.

## Actions of Political Parties

Political parties developed through custom and tradition. The debate between **Federalists** and **Anti-Federalists** over ratification revealed the existence of differences of opinion on government. These differences led to the formation of the first two political parties—the **Federalists** and the **Democratic-Republicans,** also known as the Republicans.

The formation of political parties led to constitutional changes in the method of electing the president. Party politics also gave rise to nominating conventions and the pledging of electoral votes to a candidate. Today, due to the growth of primaries and party caucuses, the presidential candidate has usually been selected before the delegates attend the nominating convention.

In the first half of the 1800s, many more men had the right to vote, and the campaign techniques and organization of political parties changed to appeal to this broader electorate.

While major political parties have changed infrequently, the nation has seen many influential "third parties." Such parties have offered criticisms and suggested reforms later adopted by the major parties when in power.

**Key Themes and Concepts**

**Government**
Supreme Court decisions have affected the separation of powers in the federal system.

- How did *Marbury* v. *Madison* (1803) affect the separation of powers?

- Based on the Marshall Court's rulings, do you think Marshall was a Federalist or a Democratic-Republican?

**Analyzing Documents**

In *McCulloch v. Maryland*, (1819) the Court rejected the right of Maryland to tax the national bank. Chief Justice Marshall wrote, "The power to tax is the power to destroy." What did he mean?

## The First Political Parties

| Federalists | Democratic-Republicans |
|---|---|
| 1. Led by Alexander Hamilton, John Adams | 1. Led by Thomas Jefferson, James Madison |
| 2. Wealthy and well-educated should lead nation | 2. Believed people should hold the political power |
| 3. Believed in strong federal government | 3. Believed in smaller government and strong state's rights |
| 4. Favored order and unity | 4. Favored individual rights |
| 5. Favored economy based on manufacturing, shipping, and trade | 5. Favored economy based on agriculture |
| 6. Favored loose interpretation of Constitution | 6. Favored strict interpretation of Constitution |
| 7. Were pro-British, but pro-neutrality | 7. Pro-French, but pro-neutrality |
| 8. Favored national bank | 8. Opposed national bank |
| 9. Favored protective tariff | 9. Opposed protective tariff |

## Foreign Policy: 1800–1823

Events in Europe from 1789 to 1815 influenced domestic and foreign policies of the United States. Presidents maintained a **foreign policy** of American neutrality, staying out of European wars while insisting on the rights of the United States as a nation. The distance from Europe made it easier to keep out of European affairs. However, the right to trade with European nations remained a major concern because America's economic well-being depended on such trade.

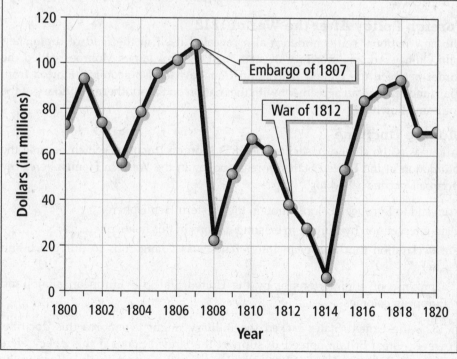

### United States Exports, 1800–1820

Embargo of 1807

War of 1812

Source: *Historical Statistics of the United States, Colonial Times to 1970*

## Analyzing Documents

Jefferson left instructions that his gravestone be inscribed:

"Author of the Declaration of Independence, the Statute of Virginia for Religious Freedom, and father of the University of Virginia."

- What does this tell you about a man who was both president and vice president of the United States, governor of Virginia, the first secretary of state, and the second minister to France?

## Preparing for the Exam

National self-interest is the prime motivation behind a nation's foreign policy.

- Did the motives behind American foreign policy change after the War of 1812? Why or why not?

## Analyzing Documents

- Examine the table. What effect did the War of 1812 have on U.S exports? Why?

## Reading Strategy

**Reading for Evidence**
Is the War of 1812 best described as

- a second war for independence?
- a war of expansion?
- a war for rights on the seas?

Explain your answer.

- How did geography affect whether a region of the United States supported or opposed the War of 1812?

## War of 1812

Meanwhile, Great Britain and France remained at war, and Great Britain outraged Americans by seizing American merchant ships trying to reach France. Congress passed the Embargo Act of 1807—which prohibited trade with other nations—in an attempt to force Great Britain and France to lift their blockades. New England, with its trade-based economy, was hit the hardest. Protests led to the repeal of the act in 1809.

Great Britain continued to violate American freedom of the seas, seizing American ships and impressing or forcing American sailors to serve in the British navy. Meanwhile, western and southern "War Hawks"—interested in expanding into British Canada and Spanish Florida—urged war. In 1812, Congress declared war on Great Britain. The war, however, was not supported by all Americans and provoked disputes among different sections of the nation.

Although the war ended in a draw in 1814, it produced some significant long-term results.

- The war reinforced the American belief that a policy of neutrality regarding European affairs was justified.
- Native American tribes in the West lost their ally, Great Britain, and were much less able to stand up to American expansion.
- American manufacturing began to grow, particularly in New England, when the United States was cut off from European imports.
- Opposing the war, in the face of a growing sense of nationalism, weakened the Federalist Party, which soon ceased to be a major factor in national politics.
- In Andrew Jackson and William Henry Harrison, the nation gained new war heroes. "The Star Spangled Banner" was inspired by the bombarding of Fort McHenry.

## Foreign Policy After the War of 1812

The new national self-confidence also revealed itself in the field of diplomacy. John Quincy Adams, secretary of state for President James Monroe, settled the border between the United States and Canada. He also acquired Florida from Spain and reached an agreement with that nation on the southern boundary of the Louisiana Purchase.

## Monroe Doctrine

Adams was the chief adviser for the 1823 **Monroe Doctrine,** which became the foundation of the United States' foreign policy in the Western Hemisphere. The Monroe Doctrine called for

- an end to European colonization in the Western Hemisphere.
- no intervention by Europe in existing nations in this hemisphere.
- a declaration that European interference was "dangerous to our peace and safety."
- a promise of noninterference by the United States in European affairs and European colonies.

In 1823, the United States lacked the military might to enforce this doctrine. However, Great Britain agreed to support the United States if this policy were challenged. By the end of the 1800s, the United States was actively enforcing the policy on its own.

## Preparing for the Exam

On the examination, you will need to understand the changing influences on United States foreign policy.

- How was the Monroe Doctrine influenced by each of the following?
- geography
- isolationism and neutrality
- United States national interests
- concerns of the new Latin American republics

**Multiple Choice**

*Directions:* Review the Test-Taking Strategies section of this book. Then answer the following questions, drawn from actual Regents examinations. For each statement or question, choose the *number* of the word or expression that, of those given, best completes the statement or answers the question.

1 "We hold these truths to be self-evident, that all men are created equal, that they are endowed by their Creator with certain unalienable rights, that among these are life, liberty, and the pursuit of happiness."

This quotation reflects beliefs mainly derived from

(1) the Magna Carta

(2) the divine right monarchs of Europe

(3) John Locke's theory of natural rights

(4) Marxist philosophy

**Base your answers to questions 2 and 3 on the quotation below and on your knowledge of social studies.**

"That to secure these rights, governments are instituted among men, deriving their just powers from the consent of the governed; that whenever any form of government becomes destructive of those ends, it is the right of the people to alter or abolish it, and to institute new government. . . ."

2 This quotation presents a justification for

(1) anarchy

(2) revolution

(3) despotism

(4) laissez faire

3 According to the quotation, governments get their authority from

(1) the people

(2) powerful leaders

(3) the justice system

(4) political parties

4 "The individual can be free *only* when the power of one governmental branch is balanced by the other two."

—*Baron de Montesquieu, 1735 (adapted)*

The idea expressed in this quotation is best illustrated by which aspect of the United States government?

(1) existence of a Cabinet

(2) separation of powers

(3) elastic clause

(4) executive privilege

5 In the colonial era, developments such as the New England town meetings and the establishment of the Virginia House of Burgesses represented

(1) colonial attempts to build a strong national government

(2) efforts by the British to strengthen their control over the colonies

(3) steps in the growth of representative democracy

(4) early social reform movements

6 "The only representatives of the people of these colonies are persons chosen therein by themselves; and that no taxes ever have been, or can be constitutionally imposed on them but by their respective legislatures."

—*Statement by the Stamp Act Congress, 1765*

What is a valid conclusion that can be drawn from this quotation?

(1) The colonial legislatures should be appointed by the English King with the consent of Parliament.

(2) Only the colonists' elected representatives should have the power to levy taxes.

(3) The English King should have the right to tax the colonists.

(4) The colonists should be opposed to all taxation.

7 One way in which the United States Constitution differed from the Articles of Confederation was that the Constitution

(1) created a national government having three branches

(2) provided for the direct election of the President by the voters

(3) made the amendment process more difficult

(4) increased the powers of the states

**Base your answers to questions 8 and 9 on the discussion below and on your knowledge of social studies.**

*Speaker A:* States must be represented in the national government solely on the basis of population. It is indeed the only fair situation.

*Speaker B:* The national legislature must be based on equal representation of the states to protect the interests of the small states.

*Speaker C:* States must accept the supremacy of the national government on all issues; otherwise, the system will fail.

*Speaker D:* The national Congress should consist of two houses: one in which representation is based on population, and one in which states are equally represented.

8 Which document was being written when this discussion most likely occurred?

(1) Declaration of Independence

(2) United States Constitution

(3) Covenant of the League of Nations

(4) Charter of the United Nations

9 Which speaker's idea about representation was actually included in the document that was written?

(1) A

(2) B

(3) C

(4) D

10 "We should consider we are providing a constitution for future generations of Americans, and not merely for the particular circumstances of the moment."

—*Delegate at the Constitutional Convention of 1787*

The writers of the Constitution best reflected this idea when they provided that

(1) Senators should be elected directly by the people

(2) three fifths of the slaves should be counted as part of the total population

(3) Congress shall make all laws necessary and proper to carry out its constitutional powers

(4) political parties should be established to represent various viewpoints

11 During the debates over the ratification of the United States Constitution, Federalists and Anti-Federalists disagreed most strongly over the

(1) division of powers between the national and state governments

(2) provision for admitting new states to the Union

(3) distribution of powers between the Senate and the House of Representatives

(4) method of amending the Constitution

**12** The main purpose of the Bill of Rights is to

(1) prevent governmental abuse of power

(2) increase the power of the Federal judiciary

(3) provide for separation of powers

(4) create a bicameral legislature

**13** The fact that the United States Constitution provided for federalism and a system of checks and balances suggests that

(1) the original thirteen states sought to dominate the national government

(2) its writers desired the national government to rule over the states

(3) its writers feared a concentration of political power

(4) the American people of that time supported a military government

**14** The United States Supreme Court is sometimes said to fulfill a legislative function because

(1) its members are appointed by the President

(2) its judgments may determine the effect of the law

(3) its members serve only so long as Congress approves

(4) it meets regularly with Congress to advise on the appropriateness of proposed laws

**15** Which quotation taken from the United States Constitution provides for limiting the power of government?

(1) "All persons born or naturalized in the United States . . . are citizens of the United States . . ."

(2) "This Constitution . . . shall be the supreme law of the land . . ."

(3) "The President shall be commander in chief of the army and navy . . ."

(4) "Congress shall make no law respecting an establishment of religion . . . or abridging the freedom of speech, or of the press . . ."

**16** Which action is an example of lobbying by a special interest group?

(1) labor union members threatening to strike if their company opens a factory in a foreign nation

(2) members of Congress introducing a bill that will provide for low-interest college loans

(3) a congressional committee investigating the activities of organized crime

(4) several lumber companies asking Senators to allow logging on Federal lands

**17** If the President has vetoed a bill, the United States Constitution provides that the bill will become a law when the bill is

(1) declared constitutional by the Supreme Court

(2) passed again by two-thirds of both houses of Congress

(3) approved by three-fourths of the State legislatures

(4) approved by a joint committee of Congress

**18** In the United States, the electoral college system affects the campaigns of major-party presidential candidates by influencing candidates to

(1) concentrate upon the states with large populations

(2) place more emphasis on controversial issues than on personality

(3) focus upon the states where winning by a large plurality is likely

(4) appeal to the electoral college members rather than to the general public

**19** The decision of President George Washington to use the state militia to put down the Whiskey Rebellion in 1794 demonstrated that the

(1) states were still the dominant power in the new nation

(2) President was becoming a military dictator

(3) Federal Government had no authority to impose an excise tax

(4) new National Government intended to enforce Federal laws

20 In United States history, which statement best represents the political ideology of Alexander Hamilton and the Federalists?

(1) Only the wealthy will survive in the economic system.

(2) A strong central government is essential for the economic growth of the nation.

(3) No one should have to pay taxes to the National Government.

(4) Elected officials should give public jobs to those who helped them into office.

21 The major role of political parties in the United States is to

(1) protect the American public from corrupt public officials

(2) insure that free and honest elections are held

(3) nominate candidates for public office and conduct campaigns

(4) meet constitutional requirements for choosing the President

22 The term "judicial review" refers to the power of

(1) the Supreme Court to determine the constitutionality of laws

(2) Congress to pass laws over the veto of the President

(3) the states to approve amendments to the Constitution

(4) the President to veto bills passed by Congress

23 In deciding to purchase the Louisiana Territory, President Thomas Jefferson had to overcome the problem of

(1) obtaining the support of Western settlers

(2) passing the constitutional amendment necessary to authorize the purchase

(3) avoiding a possible war with England over the purchase

(4) contradicting his belief in a strict interpretation of the Constitution

24 "The great rule of conduct for us in regard to foreign nations is, in extending our commercial relations to have with them as little political connection as possible."

—George Washington, Farewell Address, 1796

This statement helped establish the United States foreign policy called

(1) containment

(2) internationalism

(3) imperialism

(4) neutrality

25 The Monroe Doctrine declared that the United States would

(1) prevent the establishment of new European colonies anywhere in the world

(2) help colonies in North and South America adopt a democratic form of government

(3) view European interference in the Americas as a threat to the national interest of the United States

(4) prevent other nations from trading with South American nations

26 "Many, if not most, of our Indian wars have had their origin in broken promises and acts of injustice on our part."

The author of this statement would most likely agree that the history of United States treatment of Native Americans was primarily the result of

(1) prejudice toward Native American religions

(2) the desire for territorial expansion

(3) a refusal of Native Americans to negotiate treaties

(4) opposing economic and political systems

27 Which was the most important reason for the social mobility that existed in the English colonies of North America during the 18th century?

(1) absence of racial prejudice among the colonists

(2) existence of a strong cultural heritage

(3) early emphasis on rapid industrialization

(4) availability of land

28 Under mercantilism, the thirteen American colonies were expected to provide Great Britain with

(1) finished American-manufactured goods

(2) raw materials and markets for British products

(3) officials to represent colonial interests in Parliament

(4) laborers to work in British factories

29 Which feature of the United States government is based upon principles found in the Magna Carta and the Petition of Right?

(1) the levying of a personal income tax

(2) the power of Congress to declare war

(3) the power of the House of Representatives to originate all revenue bills

(4) Presidential veto power

30 In the eighteenth century, the British colonies in North America were most similar to Great Britain in their

(1) common law legal system

(2) countrywide established church

(3) opportunities for social mobility

(4) dependence upon manufacturing as the economic base

31 Which was most influential in making the idea of separation of church and state a part of the United States political tradition?

(1) the democratic heritage of ancient Athens

(2) the Roman Republic's principles of religious freedom

(3) practices of European colonial governments

(4) the diversity of the new nation's population

32 Which idea had a major influence on the authors of the Articles of Confederation?

(1) A strong central government threatens the rights of the people and the states.

(2) All people must be granted the right to vote.

(3) Three branches of government are needed to protect liberty.

(4) The central government must have the power to levy taxes and to control trade.

33 At the Constitutional Convention of 1787, the Three-fifths Compromise and the Great Compromise dealt with the issue of

(1) amendments to the Constitution

(2) women's rights

(3) representation in Congress

(4) the rights of the accused

34 In the 1780s, the publication of *The Federalist Papers* was intended to

(1) justify the American Revolution to the colonists

(2) provide a plan of operation for the delegates to the Constitutional Convention

(3) encourage ratification of the United States Constitution

(4) express support for the election of George Washington to the presidency

35 Under the United States Constitution, those powers not delegated to the federal government are

(1) exercised only by state governors

(2) concerned only with issues of taxation

(3) reserved to the states or to the people

(4) divided equally between the states and the national government

36 "The accumulation of all powers, legislative, executive, and judicial, in the same hands ... may justly be pronounced the very definition of tyranny."

The writers of the United States Constitution intended to prevent the situation described in this quotation by

(1) developing a system of checks and balances

(2) relying on an electoral college

(3) establishing political parties

(4) including the implies powers clause

37 Only a small number of amendments have been added to the United States Constitution mainly because the

(1) executive branch has feared a loss of power

(2) Constitution has been broadly interpreted and applied

(3) public has not objected to the government's use of its power

(4) Constitution is clear in its original intent and seldom needs amending

38 "The privilege of the writ of *habeas corpus* shall not be suspended, unless when in cases of rebellion or invasion the public safety may require it."

This provision is evidence that the writers of the United States Constitution

(1) wanted the President to have unlimited power during wartime

(2) wanted to balance individual liberty with the needs of the nation

(3) did not trust the common people to obey the laws

(4) expected the American people to oppose most government policies

**Four statements dealing with the formation of a new government are given below. Base your answers to questions 39 and 40 on these statements and on your knowledge of social studies.**

*Statement A:* Each person must be able to voice his or her concerns on all issues that involve this new nation and bear the responsibility for the decisions made.

*Statement B:* The power of this new nation must rest in a strong, stable group that makes important decisions with the approval, but not the participation, of all.

*Statement C:* There must be several governments within one nation to ensure adequate voice and responsibility to all.

*Statement D:* Individuals must not allow their freedoms to be swallowed by an all-powerful government.

39 Which statement best shows the desire for safeguards such as those in the Bill of Rights?

(1) A          (3) C

(2) B          (4) D

40 Which statement best represents the ideas of federalism?

(1) A          (3) C

(2) B          (4) D

*Directions:*  Write a well-organized essay that includes an introduction, several paragraphs addressing the task below, and a conclusion.

**Theme:**  **The Constitution and Change**

> The United States Constitution not only provides a basic framework government, but also allows for the flexibility to adapt to changes over time.

**Task:**

> - Identify *two* basic constitutional principles and discuss how each principle allows the government to adapt to changes in the United States
> - For *each* constitutional principle you discuss, describe a specific historical circumstance when the principle was used to meet the needs of American political, social, *or* economic life

You may use any constitutional principle from your study of United States history. Some suggestions you might wish to consider include: the amendment process; judicial review; equality; civil liberties; presidential power in foreign affairs; presidential power during wartime.

You are not limited to these suggestions.

**Guidelines:**

**In your essay, be sure to**
- Develop all aspects of the task
- Support the theme with relevant facts, examples, and details
- Use a logical and clear plan of organization, including an introduction and a conclusion that are beyond a restatement of the theme

**In developing your answer, be sure to keep these general definitions in mind:**

(a) <u>describe</u> means "to illustrate something in words or tell about it"
(b) <u>discuss</u> means "to make observations about something using facts, reasoning, and argument; to present in some detail"

# Thematic Essay Question 2

*Directions:* Write a well-organized essay that includes an introduction, several paragraphs addressing the task below, and a conclusion.

**Theme:** **Constitutional Principles and the Supreme Court**

> Throughout United States history, Supreme Court decisions concerning conflicts over constitutional issues have had a long-term effect on the nation.

**Task:**

> From your study of United States history, identify two Supreme Court decisions concerning conflicts over constitutional issues which have had a long-term effect on the nation. For each Supreme Court decision identified:
> * Describe the historical circumstances surrounding the Supreme Court decision
> * Discuss the extent to which the Supreme Court decision resolved the conflict over the constitutional issue
> * Discuss the long term impact of the Supreme Court decision

You may use any Supreme Court decision concerning conflicts over constitutional issues that has had a long-term effect on the nation. Some suggestions you might wish to consider include: *McCulloch* v. *Maryland* (1819) (federalism); *Marbury* v. *Madison* (1803) (role of the judiciary); *Gibbons* v. *Ogden* Dred (commerce); *Dred Scott* v. *Sanford* (separation of powers); *Schenck* v. *United States* (freedom of expression); *Gideon* v. *Wainwright* (right to legal counsel); *Heart of Atlanta Motel* v. *United States* (equal protection under the law).

You are not limited to these suggestions.

**Guidelines:**

**In your essay, be sure to**
* Develop all aspects of the task
* Support the theme with relevant facts, examples, and details
* Use a logical and clear plan of organization, including an introduction and a conclusion that are beyond a restatement of the theme

In developing your answer, be sure to keep these general definitions in mind:

    (a) <u>describe</u> means "to illustrate something in words or tell about it"
    (b) <u>discuss</u> means "to make observations about something using facts, reasoning, and argument; to present in some detail"

# The Constitution Tested: Nationalism and Sectionalism

## Section Overview

In the first half of the 1800s, the United States grew in size and population. The North, blessed with natural resources and a growing population, began industrializing. In the agricultural South, cotton became the dominant crop, and slavery became more firmly rooted in place.

As a new age of mass politics and reform dominated the 1830s and 1840s, tensions grew among the regions, pulling the North and the South apart. The southern states began to see their power and influence decreasing, and soon after the election of 1860, 11 states seceded from the Union. The Civil War that followed settled the constitutional question of federal supremacy versus states rights on the battlefields of Antietam and Gettsyburg.

## Key Themes and Concepts

**Factors of Production:** How did the transportation and industrial revolutions affect life in the United States?

**Civic Values:** What factors strengthened nationalism and democracy?

**Reform Movement:** What reform movements developed and what was their impact?

**Immigration and Migration:** How did immigration and migration west affect the development of our nation?

**Constitutional Principles:** What three constitutional principles were debated in the first half of the nineteenth century?

**Diversity:** What caused the sectionalism that led to the Civil War?

**Government:** How was the conflict over federalism resolved?

**Change:** What changes took place during the Civil War?

## Key People

| | | |
|---|---|---|
| John C. Calhoun | Elizabeth Cady | James Polk |
| Andrew Jackson | Stanton | John Brown |
| Martin Van Buren | Lucretia Mott | Abraham Lincoln |
| William Lloyd Garrison | Susan B. Anthony | Robert E. Lee |
| Frederick Douglass | Dorothea Dix | Ulysses S. Grant |
| Harriet Tubman | Meriwether Lewis | |
| Sojourner Truth | and William Clark | |

The
# Big Idea

In the early to mid-nineteenth century:

- the North and South developed different patterns of life and philosophies of government.

- immigration and territorial expansion produced growth and change.

- reform movements attempted to correct many of the injustices of American society.

- sectional differences led to a Civil War testing the Constitution.

## Key Terms

Whig Party
Democratic Party
American System
Industrial Revolution
Transportation
  Revolution
immigration
nativism
potato famine

slavery
spoils system
tariffs
National Bank
Removal Policy
Trail of Tears
abolitionist
Underground
  Railroad

Women's Rights
  Convention
Manifest Destiny
popular sovereignty
secede
Confederate States
  of America
Emancipation
  Proclamation

## Key Supreme Court Cases

*Worcester* v. *Georgia* (1832)
*Dred Scott* v. *Sanford* (1857)

## Part 1 | Testing the Constitution: Stress and Crisis

In the decades before the Civil War, some forces contributed to national unity, while others began splitting the nation apart.

### Nationalism and Sectionalism, 1820–1865

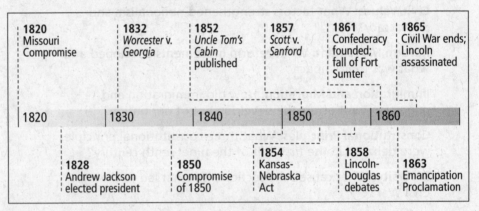

| 1820 | 1832 | 1852 | 1857 | 1861 | 1865 |
| Missouri Compromise | *Worcester* v. *Georgia* | *Uncle Tom's Cabin* published | *Scott* v. *Sanford* | Confederacy founded; fall of Fort Sumter | Civil War ends; Lincoln assassinated |

1820   1830   1840   1850   1860

| 1828 | 1850 | 1854 | 1858 | 1863 |
| Andrew Jackson elected president | Compromise of 1850 | Kansas-Nebraska Act | Lincoln-Douglas debates | Emancipation Proclamation |

### Reading Strategy

**Organizing Information**
List three factors that unified the United States between 1789 and 1861.

1.

2.

3.

## Factors Unifying the United States

The factors that unified the United States include the first and second two-party systems, the market economy and interstate commerce, and decisions of the Marshall Court.

Both the **first and second two-party systems** helped to unify the United States in part because they were national, not sectional, parties. The first two-party system consisted of the Federalists and the Democratic-Republicans, parties that offered different political philosophies and proposals for action. The second two-party system developed in 1834, when the new **Whig Party** opposed Andrew Jackson's party, now called the **Democratic Party.** Both parties ran campaigns that attracted interest and increased the numbers of those voting and involved in national issues.

The development of a market economy and increased interstate commerce helped to stimulate economic growth nationwide. In the 1800s, revolutions in transportation and technology led to industrialization and urbanization. Specialization was possible because people could now purchase what they did not make or grow. Banks expanded to provide the capital for investment and the funds needed for exchange of goods and services. Southern and western crops were exchanged for northern manufactured goods.

Decisions of the Marshall Court also promoted national unity. These decisions helped to encourage a national economy by expanding interstate commerce and protecting the validity of contracts.

### Comparing Household and Market Economies

| | Household Economy | Market Economy |
|---|---|---|
| Producers | Household | Industries |
| Labor | Members of the household produce a variety of goods at home. | Workers specialize in producing a certain product outside the home. They exchange their labor for cash. |
| Goods | Goods are made primarily to be used by the household. | Goods are sold on the open market for a profit. |

**Analyzing Documents**

Based on the table at left and your knowledge of American history, answer the following questions.

- How were workers affected by the change to a market economy?

- How did the shift to a market economy promote nationalism?

## The American System Supports a National Economy

Senator Henry Clay, supported by John Quincy Adams, designed a legislative program called the **"American System."** The program benefited the North, the South, and the West, and unified the nation by:

- establishing a better national transportation system to aid trade and national defense.
- setting the first protective tariff to encourage manufacturing and provide funds for improved transportation networks.
- creating a second national bank to promote the necessary financial support.

# Urban and Industrial Patterns in the North

The use of new technologies in manufacturing—particularly steam engines and machines to spin thread and weave cloth—gave rise to the **Industrial Revolution** in Great Britain during the 1700s. By the early 1800s, these new technologies reached the United States. Factory builders flocked to the North, particularly New England, because of its abundant supplies of iron, coal, and swiftly flowing rivers used for water power to operate machinery.

By 1860, northern factories had entered a worldwide competition for markets. While agriculture, especially in its westernmost states, continued to be a major part of its economy, the North began to take on a new identity as an urban manufacturing and commercial area. About 70 percent of national manufacturing was located in the North.

## The Transportation Revolution

A **Transportation Revolution** brought new technologies, innovations, and inventions that stimulated the development of transportation systems. As a result, northern markets were connected to western farmlands and westward migration accelerated. Railroads and canals, such as the Erie Canal in New York State, encouraged the growth of industry. The Erie Canal connected the Atlantic Ocean (at New York City) through the Great Lakes to the vast interior of the United States. One result was lower shipping costs. New York became a major port. Railroads later connected New York to other major cities and to the West. In the nineteenth century New York became the financial and industrial center of the nation.

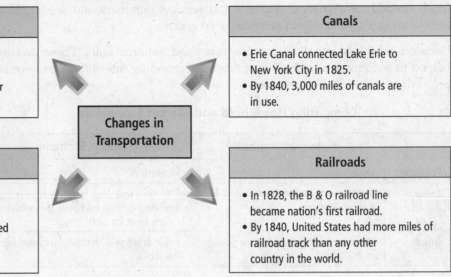

## The Transportation Revolution

**Steam Power**

- In 1807, Robert Fulton's *Clermont* steamed up the Hudson River.
- Steamships helped farmers ship their goods to markets around the world.

**Canals**

- Erie Canal connected Lake Erie to New York City in 1825.
- By 1840, 3,000 miles of canals are in use.

**Changes in Transportation**

**Roads**

- By 1833, the Cumberland Road ran from Maryland to Ohio.
- New roads of stone and gravel helped Americans move west.

**Railroads**

- In 1828, the B & O railroad line became nation's first railroad.
- By 1840, United States had more miles of railroad track than any other country in the world.

## The Factory System

By 1850, most American manufacturing was no longer done in homes and small shops, but instead in factories by workers using machines. This was called the factory system. The first mills were in New England, with the "model" Lowell mill the most well known. It employed white, teenage farm girls as its labor force, offering them an opportunity for financial independence. The girls lived at the mill in a highly regulated environment. Most planned to stay only a few years. Here the first work protests and strikes were organized against wage cuts.

By the 1840s and 1850s, the mills acquired a more permanent work force—Irish immigrant women who needed to work to help support their families. Working conditions were dictated by a strict routine. Twelve-hour days and six-day weeks were the routine. Gains made by the first union movements often were lost when demand for goods dropped in the fluctuating business cycle.

## Urban Problems

By 1860, nine of the ten largest cities in the nation were in the North. After 1840, immigrants made up the majority of the population in some cities. The gap between rich and poor widened, as a distinctive rich upper class and a poor working class developed in the cities. Private companies provided sanitation and water only to those who could afford to pay for these services. Cities were unsafe, and police forces did not begin to appear until the mid-1830s.

## Middle-Class and Working-Class Life in the North

**Industrialization** changed family life and gender roles. Previously, families worked together at home and on the farm, taking on different tasks according to gender. After industrialization, both working-class men and women worked, and their jobs also differed depending on their gender. More women worked as servants, more men in factories. The lives of middle-class men were often centered in the new business world, while middle-class women found their lives defined by the home. One of the few jobs considered proper for a single middle-class woman was teaching.

Working-class children usually had to make economic contributions to the family, but middle-class children did not. Childhood, as a specific stage in one's life, received new attention. Middle-class parents supported the growing movement for public schools.

### Key Themes and Concepts

**Change**
Cities grew tremendously during the first half of the 19th century. The population of New York City (Manhattan only), for example, soared from about 33,000 in 1790 to 124,000 in 1820, and about 516,000 by 1850.

## Urban and Rural Populations, 1800–1850

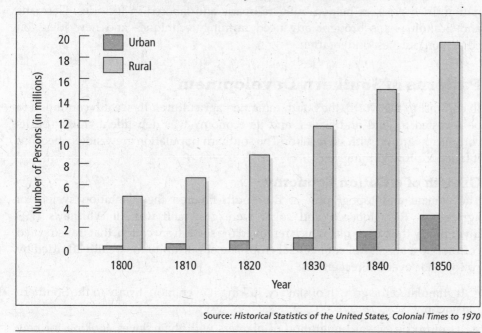

Source: *Historical Statistics of the United States, Colonial Times to 1970*

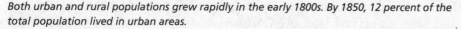

*Both urban and rural populations grew rapidly in the early 1800s. By 1850, 12 percent of the total population lived in urban areas.*

Free African Americans in the North continued to face racism and legal restrictions. Public places remained segregated. African Americans also faced discrimination in hiring. Women were more likely than men to find permanent work, most often as household helpers.

## Immigration

Until about 1850, most immigrants came from northern and western Europe, particularly Ireland and Germany. The Germans included many who were Jewish. Scandinavians, Dutch, Swiss, and English also immigrated. They generally settled in the North and the West because of greater economic opportunities there. The industrial economy was creating jobs so that there were few restrictions on **immigration.**

**Reasons for Immigration** Between 1845 and 1850, millions of Irish people came to the United States because of the **potato famine,** a period of mass starvation caused by failure of the potato crop. Many Germans came seeking peace and stability after the failed 1848 Revolution in Germany. Most immigrants arrived in search of better economic opportunities.

**Areas of Settlement** The Irish tended to settle in northeastern cities. Some Germans also stayed in cities, but many moved west to start farms, as did many Scandinavian immigrants.

**Difficulties They Faced** Irish and German Catholic immigrants often faced hostility from native-born Americans, some of whom feared economic competition from the newcomers. Others resented the Catholic or Jewish immigrants at a time when the nation was mostly Protestant. **Nativism,** or anti-immigrant feelings, was so strong that a political party called the **"Know Nothings,"** was formed to support the nativist political program. It campaigned to restrict immigration, electing as many as 100 congressmen. The party did very well in local elections in northern states.

### Preparing for the Exam

**Migrations:**
Throughout United States history there have been movements of people (migrations), voluntary and involuntary, into and within the nation. Some examples are:

- colonial settlement (1600s–1700s)
- forced migration of Native Americans (1800–1880)
- westward expansion (1840–1890)
- rural to urban migration (1870s–1920s)
- European immigration (1840–1860 and 1880–1910)
- migration of African Americans from the South to North (1900–1929)
- migration west from the Dust Bowl (1930s)
- suburbanization (1945–1960s)
- migration to the Sun Belt (1950-present)
- illegal immigration (1990-present)

### Key Themes and Concepts

**Immigration and Migration**
- Where did the immigrants of the first half of the nineteenth century come from?

- Why did they come to the United States?

- How did their reasons for coming differ from those of earlier immigrants? How were they the same?

- What reaction did these new immigrants face from native-born Americans?

**Contributions** Immigrants made significant contributions to the growth of this nation. Irish workers helped build railroads and labored in factories. Germans and Scandinavians brought advanced farming techniques and new ideas on education, such as kindergarten.

# Patterns of Southern Development

In contrast to the North, the South remained agricultural. Its wealth continued to be invested in land and slaves, and its economy was dependent chiefly on its cotton crop grown with slave labor. The southern population grew slowly because it failed to attract immigrants.

## Growth of a Cotton Economy

The climate and topography of the South favored the plantation system of agriculture. Rice, tobacco, and sugar were grown. It was **Eli Whitney's** 1793 invention of the **cotton gin,** which removed the seeds from cotton, that transformed cotton into a successful commercial crop. The opportunity for wealth afforded by cotton had several direct effects:

- It stimulated the growth of **slavery,** linking it even more firmly to the Southern economy.
- It spurred westward migration of planters with their slaves, looking for new land on which to grow cotton. Movement was into the Old Southwest, Alabama and Mississippi, and later even further west into Louisiana, Arkansas, and Texas.
- Cotton became important to the national economy, making up half of all exports.
- However, its agricultural base kept the South economically dependent on the North, both as a market for its crops and as a source of needed manufactured goods.

### The Growth of "King Cotton"

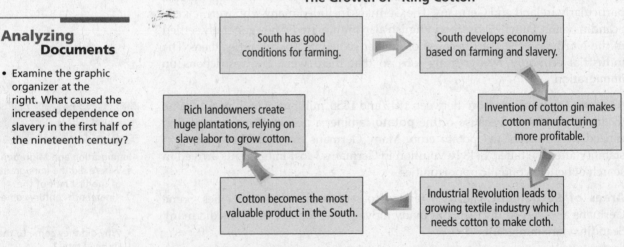

**Analyzing Documents**

- Examine the graphic organizer at the right. What caused the increased dependence on slavery in the first half of the nineteenth century?

*In the early 1800s, cotton became the South's most important crop.*

## Men and Women on Plantations

Slaveholding men dominated political, economic, and social life in the South. Planters' wives and daughters were responsible for the domestic sphere. They managed the care, feeding, and clothing of their families and the slave families as well.

## Life Under Slavery

Daily life for most slaves was very difficult. They had no control over their own lives or their children's lives, and they were at the mercy of the slaveholders or overseers. Slaves who worked as field hands often worked from dawn to sunset, while those who were house servants often worked long past sunset.

Slaves generally ate inexpensive food and wore rough clothing. Cabins housed one or two families. However, slaves were also a financial investment, and this affected their treatment. After the importing of slaves ended, the economic value of slaves increased, and their health care improved.

Slaves could not legally marry, but families remained central to the African American community. Parents instilled the importance of family in their children, while preparing them to cope with a life of slavery. Children were not educated and began work as young as eight years old. As planters moved westward in search of new lands for growing cotton, slave families were often tragically broken up.

The religious practices of slaves were a mixture of Protestant Christian and African elements. Music was an important part of worship services. Religion provided slaves with comfort and hope for salvation.

## Resistance

Resistance against slavery took many forms. Most protests took the forms of escape, self-mutilation, sabotage, or work slowdowns. Although open rebellions were rare, they instilled fear within the white slaveholding society. There were several notable slave revolts.

- In 1800, Gabriel Prosser's Conspiracy in Virginia, led by urban skilled workers, was discovered.
- In 1822, Denmark Vesey's plans to lead a South Carolina revolt were uncovered.
- In 1831, Nat Turner led a revolt in Virginia.

Rebellions led southern lawmakers to pass increasingly strict laws to maintain slavery. Freeing slaves became more difficult, and teaching a slave to read and write became illegal.

# The Age of Jackson

**Andrew Jackson** was twice elected President of the United States, serving from 1829 to 1837. He was the first president elected from a state other than one of the 13 original states. Jackson ran unsuccessfully for president in 1824. Out of four presidential candidates, none received a majority of the electoral votes. Although Jackson had the most popular votes and the most electoral votes, the House of Representatives selected **John Quincy Adams** as president. Jackson's party, the Democrats, got its support from middle-class and small farmers of the South and the West, and urban workers. Adam's party was strongest in the North.

## The Rise of Mass Politics

By the mid-1820s, most states had dropped their property qualifications for voting. In 1828, the number of voters was three times larger than it had been in 1824. Andrew Jackson, a popular hero of the War of 1812, appealed to these new voters and won both the electoral and the popular vote.

Selecting a presidential candidate became more democratic in 1832. Candidates were chosen for the first time by a national nominating convention, rather than a few party leaders.

**Reading Strategy**

**Reinforcing Main Ideas**
- What were some results of the expansion of slavery?

**Analyzing Documents**

*"This Fourth of July is yours, not mine. You may rejoice, I must mourn. . . . What, to the American slave, is your 4th of July? I answer; a day that reveals to him, more than any other days in the year, the gross injustice and cruelty to which he is the constant victim."*
—Frederick Douglass, Rochester, New York, 1852

- Why does Douglass find it impossible to celebrate the Fourth of July?
- How did slavery contradict the civic values expressed in the Declaration of Independence?

**Preparing for the Exam**

- What is the difference between popular and electoral vote?
- What happens when a candidate fails to win a majority of the electoral college?

Rallies, slogans, and often vicious written attacks marked the advent of mass politics. "Secret" ballots became popular, but parties printed them in colors so it was easy to tell for whom a person voted. Only after the Civil War did the truly secret ballot come into general use.

## The Spoils System and Civil Service Reform

The **spoils system,** which dates from the presidency of Andrew Jackson, gave government jobs to people who had worked to help their political party win the election. This method was called the spoils system because of the saying "To the victor belong the spoils (rewards)." In 1881, a party worker who had failed to get a government job killed President James Garfield. At that point, people began to demand reform, and the new president, Chester Arthur, supported it. The **Pendleton Act** of 1883 marked the beginning of **civil service reform.**

- It provided that competitive exams would be used to hire some government workers.
- It set up a commission to administer the tests.
- It banned the common practice of forcing government employees to give money to political parties.

# Growing Sectionalism

Sectionalism also developed in the United States during the first half of the nineteenth century as economic, social, and political differences pulled the nation in opposite directions.

## States' Rights v. Federal Supremacy

Debate raged over how the balance of power between the states and the federal government should be achieved. From 1820 to 1865 this debate focused on nullification, protective tariffs and the spread of slavery.

**The Tariff Issue** Southern states opposed protective **tariffs,** which resulted in higher prices paid for imported manufactured goods. The agricultural South saw northern industries as the chief beneficiaries of such tariffs.

John C. Calhoun of South Carolina, Jackson's first vice president, protested the **Tariff of 1828.** Calhoun argued that a state had the right to **nullify,** or declare void, any federal law that the state considered unconstitutional. A similar argument claiming states' right to interpret federal laws had been made by Madison and Jefferson in the Virginia and Kentucky Resolutions.

In 1832 a new, lower tariff was passed, but South Carolina still nullified the tariff. President Andrew Jackson declared South Carolina's actions treasonous.

The crisis was resolved after Congress agreed to a gradual lowering of the tariff and passed a Force Bill authorizing the use of federal troops in South Carolina to collect the tariff. South Carolina withdrew its nullification of the tariff. However, South Carolina then nullified the Force Bill, indicating that the issue was not permanently settled.

## The National Bank Issue—The Bank War

The Second Bank of the United States also provoked sectional differences. Most opposition to the **National Bank** came from southerners and westerners, who wanted a greater supply of money in circulation. They also resented the national bank's control over state banking.

### Key Themes and Concepts

**Economic Systems**
- Why did the South believe that the North benefited from a protective tariff?

- How did this debate increase sectional conflict?

### Preparing for the Exam

Give an example of a conflict in the pre-Civil War period involving each concept below.

Supremacy Clause, State's Rights, sectionalism, nationalism, nullification, secession

In 1832, President Jackson vetoed a bill to recharter the bank. He then withdrew federal money from the bank, effectively killing it. To Jackson and many of his followers, **the Second Bank of the United States** had symbolized privilege and the power of special northern interests.

## The Presidency of Andrew Jackson

### President Andrew Jackson

| |
|---|
| Fired more than 2,000 government workers and replaced them with his own supporters |
| Vetoed more acts of Congress than all six previous presidents combined |
| Closed Bank of the United States |
| Threatened to send huge army to South Carolina to force the state to obey tariff laws |
| Used Indian Removal Act to force 100,000 Native Americans from their homelands |

*Jackson's forceful actions earned him both strong support and angry opposition throughout the country.*

# Relations With Native Americans

As American settlers moved ever westward in the 1800s, conflict continued with the Native Americans who lived in these territories.

## Native American Cultural Survival Strategies

Native Americans tried a variety of strategies to cope and retain their land and culture.

- In the early 1800s, two Shawnee brothers, Prophet and Tecumseh, tried to build a **Pan-Indian Movement** in the Old Northwest, but this movement died with Tecumseh in the War of 1812.

- Meanwhile, a Seneca named Handsome Lake urged the Iroquois to adopt a lifestyle based on temperance, education, farming, and peace. This lifestyle became known as cultural revitalization.

- In 1813, Creeks attacked settlers in Georgia and Alabama in a series of raids, but in 1814, they were defeated at Horseshoe Bend, Alabama. The Southwest was then opened to settlement.

- The Cherokees attempted to survive and retain their culture through **cultural adaptation,** combining elements of Native American and European culture, including a written constitution. This strategy, however, did not save them.

## The Removal Policy

The federal government used a combination of treaties and force to move **Native Americans** to lands west of the Mississippi River. The treaties were worthless, because Native Americans were forced repeatedly to give up their land that had been guaranteed by treaty.

In the 1830s, President Andrew Jackson began his **Removal Policy** that forced all Native Americans to move west of the Mississippi. In 1832, the Cherokee went to court to prevent Georgia from taking their land. In **Worcester v. Georgia,** Chief Justice John Marshall ruled that Georgia had no authority over Cherokee territory, but Georgia simply ignored the ruling. In 1838, the U.S. Army rounded up the Cherokee and moved them west in a forced march known as the **Trail of Tears.**

**Analyzing Documents**

*"The consequences of a speedy removal will be important. . . . It will separate the Indians from immediate contact with settlements of whites; . . . and perhaps cause them . . . to cast off their savage habits and become an interesting, civilized, and Christian community."*
—President Andrew Jackson, 1830

- What does this quote reveal about Jackson's attitude toward Native Americans?

**Analyzing Documents**

*"We wish to remain on the land of our fathers. We have a perfect and original right to remain without interruption."*
—Cherokee public appeal, July 17, 1830

- What does this quote reveal about how the Cherokee viewed their possession of the land?

The Seminole of Florida were also faced with removal. A group fought the effort in the Second Seminole War. Many remained in Florida. By the 1840s, however, only scattered groups of Native Americans still lived in the East.

**Native American Land Transfer Before 1850**

### Analyzing Documents

Compare the map at right with the Territorial Expansion map on page 76.

- How does the map at right relate to the territorial expansion of the United States?

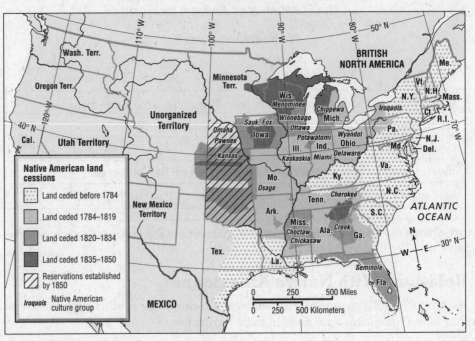

# The American Reform Tradition

In the early 1800s, great changes affected the way people lived and interacted with each other. The Industrial Revolution, urbanization, growth in immigration, westward expansion, and the cotton-based southern economy created opportunities as well as serious problems.

The Second Great Awakening, a religious revival movement, motivated reform with its emphasis on self-reliance, on one's ability to affect one's future and to improve the world. The movement called for self-improvement and for joining to fight forces of evil. The religious feelings that drove reform were reinforced by the Republican political belief in civic virtue—that a good citizen acts for the common good.

### Reform Movements

Many areas of American life inspired reform movements, including education and care of the mentally ill.

**Public Schools** Reformers recognized that if the people were to govern, they needed to be educated. Under the leadership of Horace Mann, Massachusetts led the nineteenth century drive for public education. Mann believed that every human being had the right to an education, and he developed an educational system with grade levels and teacher training. His ideas spread rapidly. By 1860, most people had at least an elementary education in all regions but the South. Educational opportunities for girls and young women also expanded.

**Care of the Mentally Ill** In the early 1800s, most mentally ill people were kept locked up in prisons. In the 1840s, a Massachusetts reformer named Dorothea Dix studied the poor treatment of the mentally ill and reported her findings to the state legislature, which authorized funds for state mental hospitals. Dix later worked with several other states that followed the example of Massachusetts.

**Other Reforms** Reformers also pushed for the creation of prisons, hospitals, orphanages, and institutions to care for physically disabled people. In addition, a strong temperance movement was organized to eliminate alcohol consumption.

## Abolition

In the 1820s, the **abolitionist** (or antislavery) movement grew as cotton production became more profitable and slavery spread. The abolitionist movement attracted a wide variety of activists, including African Americans such as Frederick Douglass, Harriet Tubman, and Sojourner Truth, and white activists such as Angelina and Sarah Grimké and William Lloyd Garrison.

Abolitionists organized the **Underground Railroad,** a series of safe houses where escaping slaves could rest safely as they made their way north and into Canada. Harriet Tubman, who made 19 trips to escort runaways, was a famous leader of the Underground Railroad.

Although the abolition movement was stronger in the North than in the South, not all northerners supported it. Some northern merchants feared that the abolition movement would further sour relations between the North and the South and harm trade. White workers feared the competition from escaped or freed slaves willing to work for lower wages.

## Women's Rights

By the 1830s, reform-minded women recognized that they faced discrimination, even within their own organizations. For example, the women delegates attending the 1840 World Anti-Slavery Convention were not allowed, after much debate, to participate in the convention.

The women's rights movement began officially in 1848, when Elizabeth Cady Stanton and Lucretia Mott organized the **Women's Rights Convention** in **Seneca Falls,** New York. There, the **Declaration of Sentiments** was issued. The first goal of this chiefly middle class movement was to end legal inequalities faced by married women. At this time, a husband had the legal right to control his wife's property, earnings, and children.

In 1853, Susan B. Anthony joined Stanton in the drive for women's rights. By the 1850s, the women's rights movement began focusing on winning the vote for women. Women's right to vote in national elections was not won until 1920.

# Territorial Expansion

From 1803 to 1853, the United States expanded to its present continental boundaries.

## Manifest Destiny

Many Americans believed in **Manifest Destiny,** the conviction that the United States had a divine mission:

- to expand to the Pacific Ocean and even to possess the entire North American continent.
- to spread the ideals of freedom and democracy.

What Americans saw as Manifest Destiny was viewed quite differently by the Native American and Mexican peoples, who were in possession of these western lands. Expansion increased national pride, but by raising serious questions about slavery, it also contributed to growing sectional tensions.

### Analyzing Documents

*On this subject, I do not wish to think, or speak, or write, with moderation. No!, no! Tell a man whose house is on fire, to give a moderate alarm; . . . tell the mother to gradually extricate [pull out] her babe from the fire into which it has fallen;—but urge me not to use moderation in a cause like the present. I am in earnest . . .—I will not retreat a single inch—AND I WILL BE HEARD.*
—William Lloyd Garrison,
The Liberator, 1831

- Based on this quote, how would you characterize Garrison's view of how slavery should be abolished?

### Analyzing Documents

*We hold these truths to be self-evident: that all men and women are created equal. . . . The history of mankind is a history of repeated injuries and usurpations [seizure of power] on the part of man toward woman, . . . [to establish] absolute tyranny over her. . . .*
—Declaration of Sentiments, 1848

- Which phrase did Stanton borrow from the Declaration of Independence? Why?

## People and Westward Expansion

The first Americans to move westward were **explorers,** such as Meriwether Lewis, William Clark, and Zebulon Pike, as well as naturalists, trappers, traders, and missionaries. These were followed by trailblazers and settlers who traveled westward along routes such as the Santa Fe and Oregon Trails. Mormons, led by Brigham Young, settled at the Great Salt Lake in 1846. In order to escape religious persecution, they selected a spot which placed them far from others. Discovery of gold and silver in California and other western territories accelerated settlement in those regions. Most settlers chose more prosperous lands in the far West, leaving the flat but dry and treeless Great Plains to be settled only after the 1860s.

### Territorial Expansion of the United States and Other Acquisitions

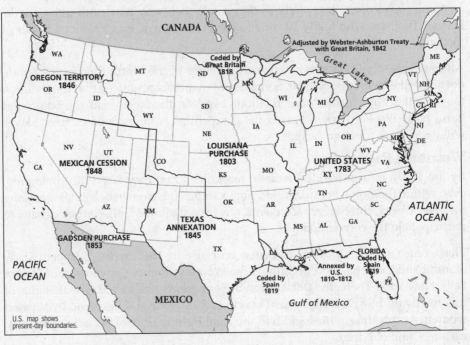

## Geography in History

Using the map at right and the map on page 74, answer the following questions.

- What was the effect of the Appalachian Mountains and Rocky Mountains on settlement?

- Why was the Great Plains the last region to be settled?

- How did the arid conditions affect the settlement of parts of the Mexican Cession?

## Analyzing Documents

In the 1840s, songs, writings, and slogans expressed responses to **Manifest Destiny.** Connect each example below to Manifest Destiny.

- James Polk: Fifty-four forty or fight!

- California: The Bear Flag Republic

- Henry D. Thoreau: *Civil Disobedience*

- U.S. Marines: "From the halls of Montezuma. . ."

## Lands Acquired Between 1783–1853

By 1853, the continental United States had expanded to its present boundaries. This expansion took place in several stages.

**Louisiana Purchase (1803)** This huge territory was acquired from France for $15 million. President Jefferson sent Meriwether Lewis and William Clark to explore this land in 1803. The information and maps they brought back contributed to expansion into this territory.

**Florida (1819)** This territory was acquired by treaty from Spain, satisfying southern expansionists. In the Adams-Onís Treaty, Spain also gave up its claims to the Pacific Northwest in return for the United States giving up its claims to Texas.

**Texas (1845)** The United States acquired Texas and what is now parts of New Mexico, Oklahoma, Colorado, Wyoming, and Kansas from Mexico by annexation. The Spanish had long established missions and settlements in Texas. After Mexico declared its independence from Spain in 1821, southern slaveholders and other American settlers moved into Texas. In 1836, the settlers declared independence from Mexico and created the Republic of Texas. Soon, Texas requested admission to the Union. However, President Jackson and then President **Martin Van Buren**

were concerned about the political effects of admitting another slave state as well as the diplomatic effects of admitting land claimed by Mexico. In 1845, after nine years of controversy, Texas joined the Union as a slave state during the administration of President James K. Polk.

**Oregon Country (1846)** What is now Oregon, Washington, Idaho, and parts of Montana and Wyoming, was gained from Great Britain in a compromise that continued the northern border set at the 49th parallel all the way to the coast.

**Mexican Cession (1848)** What is now California, Nevada, Utah, Arizona, and parts of New Mexico, Colorado, and Wyoming became part of the United States by the Treaty of Guadalupe Hidalgo, which ended the Mexican War (1846–1848). The Mexican War erupted in part because of Mexican objections to the Texas annexation and a dispute over the border between Texas and Mexico. President James Polk's outspoken desires to acquire California and the Southwest made it difficult to ease tensions with Mexico. After war broke out, national opinion was divided. Expansionists welcomed an opportunity to acquire more land. Northerners feared the future addition of more slave states. Some, such as Abraham Lincoln, saw it as a "war of conquest," others saw it as fulfilling *"Manifest Destiny."*

**Gadsden Purchase (1853)** This piece of land in southern Arizona and New Mexico was purchased from Mexico as a possible railroad route.

## Preparing for the Exam

While a treaty requires a two-thirds vote of the Senate, a joint resolution of Congress requires a majority of each house.

- Why did President James Polk push for Texas annexation?

## Part 2 The Constitution in Jeopardy: The American Civil War

Differences between the North and the South finally threatened the existence of the nation. The debate that followed on how slavery should be treated in new lands centered on constitutional issues.

## Great Constitutional Debates: The Slavery Issue

Until the Civil War, the Constitution had recognized and protected slavery in three ways: the Three-Fifths Compromise, the provision that Congress could not end the importing of slaves before 1808, and the fugitive slave clause. These compromises had been made in order to encourage southern states to ratify the Constitution. With the expansion of American territory in the West, controversy brewed over whether these new territories should allow slavery or not.

### Northern Views

Northerners who sought to stop the spread of slavery used several arguments:

1. The Constitution gave Congress jurisdiction, or power, over the territories.
2. Precedent, or previous acts, justified congressional action. Precedents included
   - the **Northwest Ordinance,** by which the Confederation Congress had banned slavery in the territory north of the Ohio River.
   - the **Missouri Compromise** of 1820, which had banned slavery in that part of the Louisiana Purchase north of 36° 30′ latitude.

### Southern Views

Because of the earlier constitutional compromises, Southerners insisted that slavery be permitted in the new territories. Constitutional equality, they said, applied only to whites. Slavery in the territories, they claimed, was legal for the following reasons:

### Reading Strategy

**Organizing Information** Below are eight events that led to the Civil War. Place them in order of occurrence.

- Compromise of 1850
- Confederacy formed
- *Dred Scott* v. *Sanford* decision
- John Brown's raid
- Kansas-Nebraska Act
- Lincoln elected president
- Missouri Compromise
- South Carolina secedes

1. Congress had no authority to prevent the extension of slavery into the territories.
2. Congress had a constitutional duty to protect slavery.

**Key Themes and Concepts**

**Constitutional Principles**
In 1836, southern members of Congress succeeded in passing the so-called gag rule, which prohibited the reading of any antislavery petitions in the House. The gag rule stayed in place for eight years.

• Why might abolitionists point to the gag rule as an example of how slavery threatened the rights of all Americans?

### Differences Between the North and the South

| | Northern States | Southern States |
|---|---|---|
| **Population** | 21.5 million | 9 million |
| **Number of Factories** | 110,100 | 20,600 |
| **Miles of Railroad** | 21,700 | 9,000 |
| **Bank Deposits** | $207 million | $47 million |
| **Cotton Production** | 4 thousand bales | 5 million bales |

*During the 1850s, differences between the North and the South continued to grow.*

**Key Themes and Concepts**

**Government**
Compromise is essential to democratic government.

• How did the Missouri Compromise postpone the clash between the North and the South?

• Why did the Compromise of 1850 satisfy neither side?

## The Compromise of 1850

Until 1850, with an equal number of slave and free states in the Union, the South maintained a balance of power in the Senate. That year, this balance was threatened when California, its rapid growth aided by the Gold Rush, applied to become a free state. The issue of slavery in the new territories was settled for a brief time by the **Compromise of 1850,** which included four key laws:

1. California entered the Union as a free state.
2. A stricter **Fugitive Slave Law** required that escaped slaves be returned.
3. Slave trade was prohibited in Washington D.C.
4. **Popular sovereignty,** or a vote of the people living in the territory, would determine whether a territory in the Mexican Cession was to be slave or free.

The Compromise of 1850 pleased no one. Some Northerners engaged in civil disobedience against the Fugitive Slave Law by protesting the return of runaway slaves and aiding slaves trying to reach the safety of Canada. The passage of this act is said to have motivated **Harriet Beecher Stowe** to write *Uncle Tom's Cabin.* The bestselling book of the nineteenth century, it influenced many to oppose slavery. The popular sovereignty provision was unclear. Would the vote to make a territory slave or free be held at the time the territory was settled or when it applied to become a state? This uncertainty led to further conflict.

## The Kansas-Nebraska Act

In 1820, the **Missouri Compromise** had prohibited slavery in the lands that made up Kansas and Nebraska. The Kansas-Nebraska Act of 1854 overturned the Missouri Compromise by allowing those territories to decide the question of slavery by popular sovereignty.

Violence erupted when pro- and antislavery people rushed into Kansas to vote on the issue. The territory was called **Bleeding Kansas** after a pro-slavery mob destroyed homes, stores, and offices in Lawrence, and John Brown's group killed pro-slavery settlers at Pottawatomie Creek. Violence extended to the U.S. Senate when, angered at a speech Sumner made, southern congressman Preston Brooks beat abolitionist Senator Charles Sumner in the Senate chamber.

## Rise of the Republican Party

Reactions to the Kansas-Nebraska Act led to changes in the political party system. One major party, the Whigs, split into northern and southern wings and soon died out. The Democrats were seriously weakened in the North. A new party, the Republicans, was founded to oppose the spread of slavery. It was a sectional rather than a national party and proclaimed a platform of "Free Soil, Free Labor, Free Men."

## The Dred Scott Case

In 1857 the Supreme Court gave its ruling on the question of slavery in the territories in *Dred Scott* v. *Sanford.* The ruling held that no African Americans, slave or free, were citizens, and therefore, they were not entitled to constitutional protection. The ruling also held that the Missouri Compromise was unconstitutional because Congress could not deprive people of their right to property—slaves—by banning slavery in any territory.

## The Lincoln-Douglas Debates

In Illinois in 1858, Abraham Lincoln, a Republican, challenged the well-known Senator Stephen A. Douglas, author of the **Kansas-Nebraska Act,** in the campaign for U.S. Senate. A series of debates were held, then the Illinois legislature reelected Douglas to the Senate. The **Lincoln-Douglas Debates** weakened Douglas in the South while making Lincoln a national political figure unacceptable to the South because of his position against the extension of slavery. Lincoln had accepted the Republican Senate nomination with a speech that included the famous lines:

"A house divided against itself cannot stand. I believe this government cannot endure, permanently half *slave* and half *free*. I do not expect the Union to be *dissolved*—I do not expect the house to *fall*—but I *do* expect it will cease to be divided. It will become *all* one thing or *all* the other."

## John Brown's Raid at Harper's Ferry

In 1859, John Brown led a small group in a raid against a federal arsenal in what is now West Virginia. His plan was to seize weapons and lead a slave uprising. Although he was unsuccessful and was later executed for treason, he became a Northern hero. The incident increased Southern distrust of the North.

## The Election of 1860

The election of 1860 showed clearly how divided the United States had become. The only remaining national party, the Democratic Party, split between the North and the South with each wing running a candidate. Abraham Lincoln, the first Republican to be elected President, received only 39 percent of the popular vote.

The election of a Northerner who opposed the extension of slavery drove some Southerners to threaten secession. To prevent secession, Senator John Crittenden of Kentucky proposed the **Crittenden Compromise,** which would have divided the nation, slave versus free territory, all the way to California, along the Missouri Compromise line. The compromise was defeated because congressional Republicans would not support it. Some did not believe that the South would go through with their threats to leave the Union.

## The Secession Crisis

In December 1860, South Carolina decided to **secede** from, or leave, the Union. By February 1861, six more Southern states seceded and, with South Carolina, formed the **Confederate States of America.**

President James Buchanan took no action to stop them. He stated that neither he nor Congress had the power to preserve the Union because it "rests upon public

## Analyzing Documents

*It is the opinion of the Court that the Act of Congress which prohibited a citizen from holding and owning property of this kind in the territory of the United States north of the line . . ., is not warranted by the Constitution, and is therefore void. . . .*
—Dred Scott v. Sanford, 1857

- What is meant by "property of this kind"?

- What act of Congress did this decision declare unconstitutional?

- Did the decision accelerate the march toward Civil War?

- Did it make the war inevitable? Why or why not?

## Preparing for the Exam

- Why did the "House Divided" speech hurt Lincoln in his Senate race but help him to be elected president?

opinion and can never be cemented by the blood of its citizens shed in war." Lincoln disagreed and denied that states could secede. In his First Inaugural Address in March 1861, Lincoln stated that "in view of the Constitution and the law, the Union is unbroken."

## Turning Point

The Election of 1860 can be considered a turning point in United States history. Examine the chart below and answer the question that follows.

### Election of 1860 Popular Vote

| Candidate | Popular Vote | % of Popular Vote |
|---|---|---|
| Lincoln | 1,865,593 | 39.5 |
| Douglas | 1,382,713 | 29.5 |
| Breckinridge | 848,356 | 18 |
| Bell | 592,906 | 13 |

### Election of Vote

| Candidate | Electoral Vote | % of Electoral Vote |
|---|---|---|
| Lincoln | 180 | 59 |
| Douglas | 12 | 4 |
| Breckinridge | 72 | 24 |
| Bell | 39 | 13 |

- Why did southern states respond to the election of 1860 by seceding from the Union?

## The Union and the Confederacy, 1861

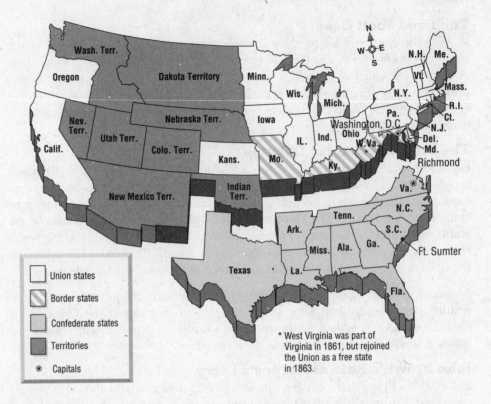

Union states
Border states
Confederate states
Territories
⊛ Capitals

* West Virginia was part of Virginia in 1861, but rejoined the Union as a free state in 1863.

## Analyzing Documents

Review the chart on page 78 and the map on this page.

- What advantages did the South have at the beginning of the Civil War? What advantages did the North have?

- How can the differences in the two areas best be explained?

- What advantages did each side have that are not seen on either the chart or the map?

- Why does the map show the border states differently? With which side did these states align?

## The Civil War

Lincoln's policy was to oppose secession but to take no military action until the South started fighting. In April 1861, the South seized Fort Sumter in Charleston Harbor, South Carolina. Lincoln called for troops to put down the rebellion. Four more southern states, including Virginia, seceded. The Civil War had begun.

### Great Constitutional Debates: Preservation of the Union

Once a state had entered the United States, did it have the right to leave? From the Southern view, the South had the right to secede because the United States had not protected Southern rights. (In this case, only the rights of the white population were being considered.) Lincoln took the position that states could not leave the Union. No minority could act to destroy the nation and its government.

### Lincoln's Aims and Actions

From the beginning of the secession crisis, Lincoln's goal was to preserve the Union. He took bold executive action to achieve this aim.

- He called out state militias, increased the size of the navy, ordered a naval blockade of the South, and approved funds for military expenses while Congress was not in session. Congress later gave its approval of these actions.

- He ordered the arrest of Southern sympathizers in Maryland and Delaware to prevent secession of those states. Failure to act might have meant the encircling of the capital by Confederate states.

- He suspended the writ of *habeas corpus* in areas not in rebellion. He later won congressional approval for this step.
- He declared martial law, which led to the arrests of thousands for suspected disloyalty.
- He censored newspapers and arrested publishers and editors.

## Constitutional Questions

Lincoln's actions broadened the power of the executive. They also raised troubling questions: Were such actions constitutional? Did they fall within the scope of the President's war powers, or were they dictatorial? Did the fact that some Northerners sympathized with the rebelling South justify the limiting of their civil rights? Did Lincoln set precedents for expanded executive action that later presidents might use in more questionable circumstances?

## Other Government Policies During the War

In order to help to finance the Civil War, a new federal banking system was created, establishing a national currency. The currency was backed by government bonds and issued by the new federal banks.

In 1862, the Congress passed three major acts to facilitate economic growth after the war ended, primarily by encouraging development of the Midwest and far west. Congress:

- passed the Pacific Railway Act authorizing the building of the **transcontinental railroad,** financed with public land grants and cash loans.
- passed the **Homestead Act,** providing for the settlement of western lands.
- approved the **Morrill Land Grant Act,** which gave public lands to states and territories to found agriculture, mechanical arts, and military science colleges.

## Military Strategy

The Confederate war strategy was to attack the Union army repeatedly, inflicting casualties and wearing it down until it lost the will to fight. The Confederacy hoped to gain aid and diplomatic recognition from Great Britain and France, two nations that relied on Southern cotton. Neither strategy was successful.

The Union relied on its superior resources and technology. Union ships blockaded Southern ports, preventing the Confederacy from importing food and military supplies. In 1863, General Ulysses S. Grant led the victorious Union forces at Vicksburg, Mississippi, giving the North control of the Mississippi and dividing the South. In 1864, Lincoln appointed Grant to head the Union forces. As the new commander, Grant's strategy was to destroy not only the Confederate army but also all Southern resources that supported the war effort.

## The Human Cost

The Civil War was the bloodiest war the United States has ever known. Some 600,000 Americans lost their lives as new military technologies and old diseases struck down soldiers and civilians. Families along the border between the Union and the Confederacy were particularly devastated, as family members fought on opposite sides.

The worst single day of the war occurred in 1862 at the **Battle of Antietam** in Maryland, where the Southern commander General Robert E. Lee attempted to invade Maryland. Some 5,000 soldiers died and more than 17,000 were wounded. In 1863, the three-day **Battle of Gettysburg** in Pennsylvania was the most costly battle of the war, leaving more than 50,000 dead and wounded on both sides.

**Key Themes and Concepts**

**Constitutional Principles**
Historically, presidential powers increase in times of war.

- How did Lincoln's presidential power increase during the Civil War?
- Name three other examples of increased presidential powers during wartime.
- Historically, how has the increase of presidential power during wartime been a threat to civil liberties?

## The Emancipation Proclamation

In 1863, Lincoln's **Emancipation Proclamation** freed all slaves in those areas still in rebellion against the Union. The Proclamation had largely a symbolic value. The Union could not enforce it, because it freed slaves only in areas under Confederate control.

Although African Americans had fought for the Union since the start of the war, after the Proclamation, their numbers in the Union military swelled. In all, more than 185,000 enlisted.

The Proclamation drew both criticism and praise. Some attacked it for freeing slaves only where the government could not enforce the decree, while permitting slavery where it could act. On the other hand, the Proclamation lessened the chances of European aid to the South. Most of all, it added a new humanitarian objective to the war.

## The Gettysburg Address

In November 1863, Lincoln dedicated the Union military cemetery at Gettysburg, just a few months after the battle there. His short speech summarized the meaning of the Civil War.

## The End of the War

The Battle of Gettysburg was the last time that the South attempted to invade the North. From then on, Lee fought a defensive war. The war ended in 1865 with Lee's surrender at Appomattox Court House.

## The Civil War on the Home Front

In the North, production in factories and on farms increased during the Civil War. Women and African Americans took more factory jobs to replace the white men who had gone to war. Women also ran the farms and raised money to help the wounded soldiers.

On both sides, women served as nurses, even in field hospitals. However, medicine was seen as a male profession, and even Clara Barton, founder of the American Red Cross, met with resistance.

The South lacked industrial support and a good transportation network. Furthermore, the Confederate government, led by Jefferson Davis, met opposition when calling for a military draft or attempting to collect food for the army.

In the South, the Northern blockade of Southern ports led to food shortages. Inflation soared. As in the North, women took over the work on the farms. On the plantations, they supervised the slaves. They also worked as government clerks and as teachers.

By the end of the Civil War, the South was devastated. The war left a legacy of bitterness and new problems. The dead on both sides included Lincoln himself, assassinated within days of the war's end.

## Analyzing Documents

*"Four score and seven years ago our fathers brought forth on this continent, a new nation, conceived in Liberty, and dedicated to the proposition that all men are created equal.*

*"Now we are engaged in a great civil war, testing whether that nation, or any nation so conceived and so dedicated, can long endure . . ."*

*"that we here highly resolve that these dead shall not have died in vain . . . and that government of the people, by the people, for the people, shall not perish from the earth."*
—Abraham Lincoln,
The Gettysburg Address

- For what event did Lincoln make the Gettysburg Address?

- Why did Lincoln refer back to the founding of the United States?

- In Lincoln's view, what was the purpose of the Civil War?

# Questions for Regents Practice

**Multiple Choice**

*Directions:* Review the Test-Taking Strategies section of this book. Then answer the following questions, drawn from actual Regents examinations. For each statement or question, choose the *number* of the word or expression that, of those given, best completes the statement or answers the question.

1  Base your answer to question 1 on the cartoon below and on your knowledge of social studies.

### "King Andrew the First"

The cartoonist is most clearly accusing President Jackson of which behavior?

(1) involving the United States in European wars

(2) exceeding the constitutional limits of his authority

(3) using government funds to support an extravagant lifestyle

(4) violating the Federal Constitution by granting titles of nobility

2  Which was most characteristic of the early factory systems in the United States?

(1) Factories provided workers with a voice in management and employment conditions.

(2) Women and children were not allowed to work in factories.

(3) Unsafe working conditions were common.

(4) Many workers had the opportunity to move up in social class.

**Base your answers to questions 3 and 4 on the quotation below and on your knowledge of social studies.**

"How can an industrialized Northeast, a plantation South, and a small farms West peacefully share the same nation?"

3  This quotation best describes the United States during which time period?

(1) Federal Era (1789–1800)

(2) Pre-Civil War (1820–1860)

(3) Era of Overseas Expansion (1898–1914)

(4) Great Depression of the 1930s

4  Which term can be most accurately applied to the situation in the quotation?

(1) sectionalism

(2) protectionism

(3) liberalism

(4) militarism

5 Which was most responsible for the rapid economic growth of New York City during the nineteeth century?

(1) presence of the New York Stock Exchange

(2) rise of domestic and foreign commerce

(3) rise of urban mass transportation

(4) migration of blacks from the rural South

6 In the United States, the belief in Manifest Destiny was most similar to later demands for

(1) restrictions on immigration

(2) a laissez-faire economic policy

(3) regulation of interstate commerce

(4) imperialistic expansion

7 In United States history, which characteristic was common to the War of 1812, the Mexican War, and the Spanish-American War?

(1) They were fought to promote democratic principles.

(2) Their aim was expansion of United States self-interest.

(3) They reflected conditions in Western Europe.

(4) They were necessary to protect national security.

**Base your answers to questions 8 and 9 on your knowledge of social studies and on the quotation below, from a speech made by a United States Senator in 1847.**

"What is the territory, Mr. President, which you propose to wrest from Mexico? It is consecrated to the heart of the Mexican by many a well-fought battle with his old Castilian master. His Bunker Hills, and Saratogas, and Yorktowns are there and shall he surrender that consecrated home of his affection to the Anglo-Saxon invaders? What do we want with it? The Senator from Michigan says he must have this. Why, my Christian brother, on what principle of justice?"

8 The parallel between the United States and Mexico which the Senator indicated in his speech was that both

(1) claimed Oregon

(2) disliked England

(3) had a revolutionary heritage

(4) were overcrowded

9 With which position would the speaker most likely have agreed?

(1) The United States should pressure Great Britain out of Oregon.

(2) The pursuit of a policy of manifest destiny is unfair.

(3) The annexation of Texas is justified because most of its population are settlers from the United States.

(4) The extension of United States democracy to parts of Mexico is divinely intended.

10 Laws requiring individuals to pass civil service examinations to obtain government jobs were enacted to

(1) eliminate patronage and corruption in government hiring

(2) allow the government to compete with private industry for employees

(3) support the development of public employee labor unions

(4) encourage the growth of local political parties

11 During the nineteenth century, the expansion of the population of the United States affected the lives of the Native Americans in that most

(1) moved to urban areas in large numbers

(2) sought to form alliances with other minority groups

(3) were forced to move westward

(4) chose to adopt the culture of the settlers

12 The reason for ending the importation of enslaved persons in the United States after 1807 was the

(1) success of the American colonial revolution against Great Britain

(2) rapid industrialization of the South

(3) replacement of slave labor by immigrant workers from eastern Europe

(4) passage of legislation that forbid the practice

13 The activities of Nat Turner and Denmark Vesey in the United States indicated that

(1) slave revolts occurred in the South

(2) cotton was a profitable crop

(3) political rivalries existed in the North

(4) slavery could be extended into the territories

14 A similarity between the pre-Civil War abolitionist movement and the Progressive movement is that both

(1) were mainly concerned with improving the status of African Americans

(2) worked to reduce income taxes

(3) contributed directly to the start of a major war

(4) sought to improve the conditions of poor or oppressed peoples

15 The main goal of the Seneca Falls Convention (1848) was to

(1) obtain equal rights for women

(2) make the public aware of environmental problems

(3 correct the abuses of big business

(4) organize the first labor union in the United States

16 "To the Honorable Senate and House of Representatives in Congress Assembled: We the undersigned, citizens of the United States, but deprived of some of the privileges and immunities of citizens, among which is the right to vote, beg leave to submit the following Resolution: . . ."

—*Susan B. Anthony, Elizabeth Cady Stanton (1873)*

This statement is an example of a citizen's constitutional right to

(1) petition for a redress of grievances

(2) seek election to public office

(3) receive a speedy, public trial

(4) assemble peacefully

**Base your answers to questions 17 and 18 on this excerpt from a resolution adopted at the Seneca Falls Convention in 1848 and on your knowledge of social studies.**

"We hold these truths to be self-evident: that all men and women are created equal; that they are endowed by their Creator with certain inalienable rights; that among these are life, liberty, and the pursuit of happiness. . . ."

17 Which document served as the most direct model for this resolution?

(1) Articles of Confederation

(2) Emancipation Proclamation

(3) United States Constitution

(4) Declaration of Independence

18 The philosophy stated in this resolution was based on the

(1) idea of rugged individualism

(2) natural rights theory

(3) theory of separation of powers

(4) "necessary and proper" clause of the United States Constitution

# Questions for Regents Practice

**19** "Compromise Enables Maine and Missouri to Enter Union" (1820)

"California Admitted to Union as Free State" (1850)

"Kansas-Nebraska Act Sets Up Popular Sovereignty" (1854)

Which issue is reflected in these headlines?

(1) enactment of protective tariffs

(2) extension of slavery

(3) voting rights for minorities

(4) universal public education

**20** "By the 1850s, the Constitution, originally framed as an instrument of national unity, had become a source of national discord."

This quotation suggests that

(1) vast differences of opinion existed over the issue of States rights

(2) the federal government had become more interested in foreign affairs than in domestic problems

(3) the Constitution had no provisions for governing new territories

(4) the Southern states continued to import slaves

**21** Which event was the immediate cause of the secession of several Southern states from the Union in 1860?

(1) the Dred Scott decision, which declared that all prior compromises on the extension of slavery into territories were unconstitutional

(2) the Missouri Compromise, which kept an even balance between the number of free and slave states

(3) the raid on the federal arsenal at Harper's Ferry, which was led by the militant abolitionist John Brown

(4) the election of President Abraham Lincoln, who opposed the spread of slavery into the territories

**22** "You have no oath registered in heaven to destroy the government, while I shall have the most solemn one to 'preserve, protect, and defend' it."

—*Abraham Lincoln, Inaugural Address, 1861*

When President Abraham Lincoln made this statement, he indicated his commitment to

(1) allow the Southern states to leave the Union

(2) defend the institution of slavery throughout the United States

(3) take strong action to maintain the Union

(4) make fundamental changes in the United States government

**23** "Restriction of free thought and free speech is the most dangerous of all subversions. It is the one un-American act that could easily defeat us."

In the United States, the danger identified in this statement was the greatest during the

(1) Age of Jackson

(2) Civil War

(3) Spanish-American War

(4) New Deal Era in the 1930s

**24** A major result of the Civil War was that the

(1) economic system of the South came to dominate the United States economy

(2) federal government's power over the states was strengthened

(3) members of Congress from Southern states gained control of the legislative branch

(4) nation's industrial development came to a standstill

**25** In the United States during the 1800s, the growth of industrialization resulted in

(1 the end of rural life and values

(2) a decline in the influence of big business

(3) a decrease in child labor

(4) the rising influence of the middle class

26  Which statement best explains why candidates for President of the United States are nominated during national nominating conventions?

(1) It is mandated by the U.S. Constitution.

(2) It is mandated by state constitutions.

(3) It is part of the United States political tradition.

(4) It was instituted by an act of Congress.

27  During the period from 1800 to 1865, the issues of states rights, tariffs, and slavery led most directly to the growth of

(1) imperialism

(2) sectionalism

(3) national unity

(4) industrialization

28  The United States Supreme Court decision in *Dred Scott* v. *Sanford* (1857) was important because it

(1) strengthened the determination of abolitionists to achieve their goals

(2) caused the immediate outbreak of the Civil War

(3) ended the importation of slaves into the United States

(4) increased the power of Congress to exclude slavery from the territories

29  Which argument did President Abraham Lincoln use against the secession of the Southern states?

(1) Slavery was not profitable.

(2) The government was a union of people and not of states.

(3) The Southern states did not permit their people to vote on secessions.

(4) As the Commander in Chief, he had the duty to defend the United States against foreign invasion.

30  Which situation was an immediate result of the United States Civil War?

(1) Women gained the right to vote as an acknowledgment of their role in the conflict.

(2) Secession was no longer regarded as an option to be exercised by states.

(3) Sectionalism disappeared as a force in American economic and political life.

(4) The South retained its pre-Civil War economic and social structure.

**Base your answer to questions 31 and 32 on the speakers' statements below and on your knowledge of social studies.**

*Speaker A:* "Secession from the Union caused this war, and all those who supported it must now be punished."

*Speaker B:* "The nation's wounds will heal most quickly if we forgive the Southerners and welcome them back into the Union."

*Speaker C:* "The freedmen must be given economic assistance and guaranteed the constitutional right to protect themselves."

*Speaker D:* "The war may have ended, but the fight must continue to preserve the system of white supremacy in the South."

31  Which speakers best represent the attitudes of the Radical Republicans who controlled Congress during Reconstruction?

(1) A and D

(2) A and C

(3) B and C

(4) B and D

32  The position taken by *Speaker B* is closest to the beliefs expressed by

(1) Abraham Lincoln

(2) Thaddeus Stevens

(3) the carpetbaggers

(4) the Ku Klux Klan

# Thematic Essay Question

**Directions:** Write a well-organized essay that includes an introduction, several paragraphs addressing the task below, and a conclusion.

**Theme:** Government: Federalism

> The United States Constitution created a new type of government—federalism—that divided power between the states and the national government. The proper balance of power under federalism has been debated throughout the history of the United States.

**Task:**

> From your study of United States history, identify *two* time periods in which there was an important debate about federalism. For *each* era or time period identified:
> - Identify a specific disagreement that occurred concerning the principle of federalism.
> - Discuss the historical circumstances surrounding the disagreement over federalism.
> - Describe the actions taken by each side during the disagreement over federalism.
> - Discuss the extent to which these actions were successful in resolving the disagreement.

You may use any time period in United States history in which there was an important debate about federalism. Some suggestions you might wish to consider include: the Supreme Court under John Marshall (1801–1835); the extension of slavery (1820–1860); Civil War (1861–1865); Reconstruction (1865–1876); Populist and Progressive reform movements (1890–1920); Franklin D. Roosevelt's New Deal (1933–1945); Civil Rights Movement (1950–1970); Ronald Reagan's New Federalism (1981–1989).

**You are *not* limited to these suggestions.**

**Guidelines:**

**In your essay, be sure to**
- Develop all aspects of the task
- Support the theme with relevant facts, examples, and details
- Use a logical and clear plan of organization, including an introduction and a conclusion that are beyond a restatement of the theme

**In developing your answer, be sure to keep these general definitions in mind:**

    (a) <u>describe</u> means "to illustrate something in words or tell about it"
    (b) <u>discuss</u> means "to make observations about something using facts, reasoning, and argument; to present in some detail"

# Document-Based Question

In developing your answers, be sure to keep this general definition in mind:

> (a) <u>discuss</u> means "to make observations about something using facts, reasoning, and argument; to present in some detail"

This question is based on the accompanying documents. The question is designed to test your ability to work with historical documents. Some of these documents have been edited for the purposes of this question. As you analyze the documents, take into account the source of each document and any point of view that may be presented in the document.

**Historical Context:**

> In May 1787, fifty-five delegates came together in Philadelphia to amend the Articles of Confederation. What they did was create a new Constitution, a plan of government designed to solve the governmental problems experienced under the Articles of Confederation. The Constitution they created has remained a flexible, living document that continues to guide this nation today.

**Task:** Using the information from the documents and your knowledge of United States history and government, answer the questions that follow each document in Part A. Your answers to the questions will help you write the Part B essay, in which you will be asked to

> Discuss how the Constitution was both:
> - a product of its time
> - a document that has had enough flexibility to meet the challenges of the future

# Document-Based Question

## Part A: Short Answer Questions

### Document #1

> "The United States in Congress assembled shall never engage in a war, . . . nor enter into any treaties or alliances, nor coin money, nor regulate the value thereof, . . . nor borrow money on the credit of the United States, nor appropriate money, . . . nor appoint a commander in chief of the army or navy, unless nine States assent [agree]."
>
> **—The Articles of Confederation**

1. Why might it be difficult for the government under the Articles of Confederation to be effective?

_____

_____

_____

### Document #2

| Year Ratified | Amendment Number | Excerpt from the Amendment |
|---|---|---|
| 1870 | 15 | "The right of the citizens of the United States to vote shall not be denied or abridged...on account of race, color, or previous condition of servitude." |
| 1920 | 19 | "The right of citizens of the United States to vote shall not be denied or abridged...on account of sex." |
| 1971 | 26 | "The right of citizens of the United States, who are eighteen years of age or older, to vote, shall not be denied or abridged..." |

2. How do these amendments demonstrate the ability of the Constitution to adapt to a change in attitude about who should have the right to vote?

_____

_____

_____

## Document #3

> "Representatives . . . shall be determined by adding to the . . . number of free persons . . . three fifths of all other persons [slaves]."
>
> —**U.S. Constitution, Article I, Section 2**

3. How was the debate over the counting of slaves for representation resolved in the Constitution?

_____

_____

_____

## Document #4

> "The accumulation of all powers, legislative, executive, and judiciary, in the same hands, whether one, a few, or many . . . may justly be pronounced the very definition of tyranny [cruel or unjust use of power]."
>
> —**James Madison,** *The Federalist Papers* **No. 47**

4. How might the system of checks and balances address the fears expressed in the quote by James Madison?

_____

_____

_____

# Document-Based Question

## Document #5

"So if a law be in opposition to the Constitution, if both the law and the Constitution apply to a particular case . . . the court must decide that case conformably [in agreement] to the law, disregarding the Constitution or conformably to the Constitution, disregarding the law, the court must determine which of these conflicting rules governs the case. This is the very essence of judicial duty. If, then, the courts are to regard the Constitution, and the Constitution is superior to any ordinary act, the Constitution and not such ordinary act, must govern the case to which both apply."

—*Marbury* v. *Madison* (1803)

5. How did the ruling in *Marbury* v. *Madison* expand the power of the Supreme Court?

_____

_____

_____

**Document #6**

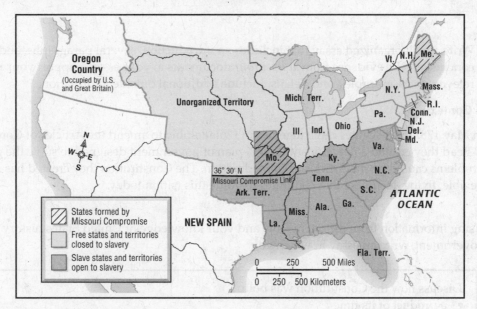

6. How does the map above demonstrate the ability of Congress to make laws to deal with the extension of slavery?

_____

_____

_____

## Part B

## Essay

*Directions:*   Write a well-organized essay that includes an introduction, several paragraphs, and a conclusion. Use evidence from *at least four* documents in your essay. Support your response with relevant facts, examples, and details. Include additional outside information.

### Historical Context:

In May 1787, 55 delegates came together in Philadelphia to amend the Articles of Confederation. Instead they created a new Constitution, a plan of government designed to solve the governmental problems caused by the Articles of Confederation. The Constitution they created has remained a flexible, living document that continues to guide this nation today.

**Task:**   Using information from the documents and your knowledge of United States history and government, write an essay in which you

> Discuss how the Constitution was both:
> - a product of its time
> - a document that has had enough flexibility to meet the challenges of the future

### Guidelines:

**In your essay, be sure to**
- Develop all aspects of the task
- Incorporate information from *at least four* documents
- Incorporate relevant outside information
- Support the theme with relevant facts, examples, and details
- Use a logical and clear plan of organization, including an introduction and a conclusion that are beyond a restatement of the theme

# Industrialization of the United States

## Unit Overview

The Civil War had torn the United States apart. With Union victory came the task of putting the nation back together. Yet the rebuilt nation would be a very different one. This unit reviews those changes that the Civil War brought to the United States. It also highlights how the shift from an agrarian to an industrial economy changed the United States and its people.

Some key questions to help you focus on the industrialization of the United States include:

- What social, political, and economic changes occurred as the nation sought to rebuild after the Civil War?
- What factors in the United States led to the shift from an agrarian to an industrial society, and what were the results of this shift?
- How did patterns of immigration to the United States change in the nineteenth and early twentieth centuries, and what did those changes mean for American society?

# The Reconstructed Nation

Reconstruction followed the Civil War in the South. During this period:

- President Abraham Lincoln was assassinated.
- President Andrew Johnson was impeached.
- African Americans won voting and political rights.
- Southern whites regained political control.

## Section Overview

After the Civil War, the nation faced the immense task of restoring the Union. Conflicting plans for Reconstruction produced bitter political battles that led to the impeachment of a president. Enormous resources were poured into rebuilding the shattered Southern economy. Meanwhile, new political gains for African Americans were gradually rolled back in the South as whites regained power.

## Key Themes and Concepts

As you review this section, take special note of the following key themes and concepts:

**Change** How did the nation rebuild and reunify after the Civil War?

**Citizenship** How did African Americans win political rights in the South?

**Places and Regions** How did white Southerners react to the terms of Reconstruction?

## Key People

As you review this section, be sure you understand the significance of these key people:

| | | |
|---|---|---|
| Andrew Johnson | Samuel Tilden | Thomas Nast |
| Ulysses S. Grant | Rutherford B. Hayes | W.E.B. Du Bois |
| William "Boss" Tweed | Booker T. Washington | |

## Key Terms

| | |
|---|---|
| Reconstruction | Compromise of 1877 |
| Radical Republicans | black codes |
| Radical Reconstruction | Ku Klux Klan |
| scalawags | poll taxes |
| carpetbaggers | literacy tests |
| Thirteenth Amendment | Freedmen's Bureau |
| Fourteenth Amendment | grandfather clauses |
| Fifteenth Amendment | segregation |
| solid South | Jim Crow laws |

## Key Supreme Court Cases

As you review this section, be sure you understand the significance of these key Supreme Court cases:

*The Civil Rights Cases* (1883)
*Plessy* v. *Ferguson* (1896)
*Brown* v. *Board of Education of Topeka, Kansas* (1954)

The effort to rebuild the Southern states and restore the Union was known as **Reconstruction,** a period that lasted from 1865 to 1877. Reconstruction required the rebuilding of the nation's economy as well as its government. With so much at stake, rival political factions—with competing plans for the future—waged bitter battles in Washington.

## Plans of Reconstruction

Several different plans for Reconstruction emerged during and after the war. Much debate about differing plans centered on who would control Reconstruction—the president or Congress.

### Lincoln's Plan

President Lincoln had begun planning for the restoration of the South long before the end of the war. His plan of Reconstruction was based on the idea that the Southern states had never left the Union. It featured the following elements:

- pardons to Southerners who swore oaths of loyalty to the United States
- recognition of new Southern state governments when 10 percent of those who had voted in the 1860 election took these oaths and when the states adopted new constitutions abolishing slavery

Lincoln was open to suggestions from Congress for changes in his plan, but his assassination in April 1865 meant he would never carry out his program.

### Johnson's Plan

Vice President Andrew Johnson became president after Lincoln's death. He intended to follow the broad outlines of Lincoln's plan. Johnson recognized four Southern state governments and prepared to readmit the others. These states would participate fully in Congress.

**Radical Republicans,** however, controlled Congress, and they wanted harsher terms for Reconstruction. Johnson's failure to consider congressional views on Reconstruction and his efforts to block radical plans finally led Republicans in Congress to attempt to impeach him. In 1868, the House charged the president with "high crimes and misdemeanors"—specifically, for violating the Tenure of Office Act. The Senate fell one vote short of the two-thirds vote required by the Constitution to remove a president from office. Although Johnson was acquitted, his political power was gone.

### Radical Reconstruction

Now the Republican-controlled Congress dictated the terms of Reconstruction. The chief features of this so-called Radical Reconstruction included:

- the division of the South into five military districts controlled by the U.S. Army, while new state constitutions and governments were being set up.
- the requirement of the new state governments to grant African American males the right to vote.
- the requirement of Southern states to ratify the Fourteenth Amendment. In addition to addressing several fundamental civil rights issues, the amendment prohibited many former Confederate government officials from holding office.

**Turning Point**
- Why is President Lincoln's assassination considered a turning point in history?

**Reading Strategy**

**Reinforcing Main Ideas**
- Why did Congress impeach President Johnson?

**Reading Strategy**

**Organizing Information**
During Radical Reconstruction, some groups of people exerted great power over the terms of Reconstruction, while others had very little power.

- Which groups had the largest roles in the Radical Reconstruction?
- Which had the smallest roles?

## Key Themes and Concepts

**Government**
- Which plan limited the voting rights of former Confederate officers?

## State Governments During Reconstruction

Immediately after the Civil War ended, white Southerners who had served in leadership positions before and during the Civil War tried to reassert their control of state and local governments. They were especially concerned with limiting the freedom and movement of former slaves.

When the radical plan of Reconstruction took effect, most of the former Confederate leaders—largely Democrats—were barred from holding office and voting. Republicans headed the new state governments that emerged and they were overwhelmingly supported by African Americans, who had recently won the right to vote. In many cases, African Americans themselves won election to office.

Many white Southerners deeply resented the federal government's imposition of Radical Reconstruction. They also resented the new Reconstruction governments and the role of African Americans in them. They branded the few white Southerners active in those governments as **scalawags** and the Republican Northerners who came to the South to take part in Reconstruction as **carpetbaggers.** White southerners sometimes used terror and violence in efforts to keep African Americans from taking part in government.

## New Constitutional Amendments

During the Reconstruction period, the states ratified three amendments to the Constitution:

- **Thirteenth Amendment** (1865)—abolished slavery in the United States
- **Fourteenth Amendment** (1868)—(1) declared that all native-born or naturalized people, including African Americans, were citizens; (2) forbade states to make laws that "abridge the privileges . . . of citizens" or that "deprive any person of life, liberty, or property, without due process of law" or that "deny to any person . . . the equal protection of the laws"; (3) limited the rights of former Confederate officers and government officials; and (4) promised to pay Civil War debts owed by the federal government, but declared Confederate debts to be void
- **Fifteenth Amendment** (1870)—declared that states could not keep citizens from voting because of "race, color, or previous condition of servitude" (slavery)

## Key Themes and Concepts

**Government**
During Reconstruction, three new amendments to the Constitution were ratified. In the space below, name these three amendments and provide the major provisions of each.

1.

2.

3.

## President Grant

The first presidential election after the end of the Civil War took place in 1868. Union war hero General Ulysses S. Grant ran as a Republican and won. Grant's strengths, however, were those of a military leader, not those of a politician or government leader. Scandals and corruption damaged Grant's administration, as business owners in the booming postwar economy offered bribes to politicians who would do favors for them. Among the most notorious scandals were:

- *Crédit Mobilier Scandal:* Railroad officials impoverished the railroad, then bribed members of Congress to block any investigation.
- *"Salary Grab":* Congress voted itself a 50 percent pay raise and added two years of "back pay." Public outcry forced repeal of this act.
- *"Whiskey Ring":* Whiskey distillers paid graft to federal tax collectors rather than pay tax on their liquor.

## Reading Strategy

**Analyzing Cause and Effect**
- Why were scandals common during President Grant's administration?

Political corruption was also common at state and local levels. Perhaps the most notorious figure was William "Boss" Tweed, who ran the Tammany Hall political machine in New York City in the 1860s and 1870s. The artist Thomas Nast attacked Tweed's behavior in a series of stinging cartoons that helped turn public opinion against Tweed.

# The End of Reconstruction

Corruption in the Grant administration weakened the political strength of the Republican party. In addition, by the early 1870s, all but a handful of former Confederates could vote again. Most of these white Southern males now voted Democratic in reaction to Radical Republican Reconstruction. For most of the next century, the Democratic party would dominate voting in the South, giving rise to the term **solid South.**

While nearly dying out in the South, the Republican party remained strong in the North and the Midwest. It focused on issues of interest to businessmen and farmers, such as keeping the money supply tight and tariffs on imports high.

## The Election of 1876

The emergence of the solid South gave the Democrats greater power in politics at the national level. In 1876, Democrats nominated Samuel Tilden, the governor of New York, to run for president against Republican Rutherford B. Hayes, the governor of Ohio.

Tilden clearly won the popular vote, but the electoral vote was contested. Four states sent in disputed election returns. Which votes were counted would determine the outcome of the election.

A special electoral commission was named to count the votes. The Republican majority on the commission gave all the electoral votes in question to Hayes, thus guaranteeing his victory.

In the **Compromise of 1877,** Democrats agreed to go along with the commission's decision in return for promises by Hayes to:

- withdraw remaining federal troops from the Southern states, thus ending the Reconstruction period.
- name a Southerner to his cabinet.
- support federal spending on internal improvements in the South.

The Compromise of 1877 effectively weakened the North's political victory in the Civil War, restoring to power many of the Southern families who, 16 years before, had formed the Confederacy and led it into war.

### Geography in History

- How did voting patterns in the South affect the presidential election of 1876?

### Preparing for the Exam

On the examination, you will need to understand the influences that brought Reconstruction to an end.

- Why do you think the Democrats agreed to support the Compromise of 1877?

### The Reconstructed Nation, 1865–1876

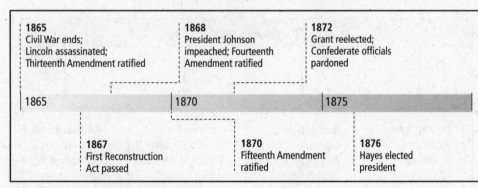

| 1865 | 1868 | 1872 |
| --- | --- | --- |
| Civil War ends; Lincoln assassinated; Thirteenth Amendment ratified | President Johnson impeached; Fourteenth Amendment ratified | Grant reelected; Confederate officials pardoned |

| 1865 | 1870 | 1875 |

| 1867 | 1870 | 1876 |
| --- | --- | --- |
| First Reconstruction Act passed | Fifteenth Amendment ratified | Hayes elected president |

### Analyzing Documents

Examine the timeline, then answer these questions.

- How many years passed between the end of the Civil War and the states' ratification of the Fifteenth Amendment?

- Which event occurred first: the impeachment of President Johnson or the election of President Hayes?

## White Control in the South

The withdrawal of federal troops enabled white Southerners to eliminate any political advances African Americans had made during Reconstruction. Various methods were used to curb the rights of African Americans, and by 1900, their civil rights had been sharply limited.

**Black Codes**  These measures, passed in most Southern states immediately after the Civil War, were based on old slave codes and aimed at keeping African Americans in conditions close to slavery. The black codes produced an angry reaction in the North that helped passage of the Radical Reconstruction program. Reconstruction governments in the South overturned these codes.

**Secret Societies**  White Southerners originally formed groups like the **Ku Klux Klan** to try to frighten African Americans and their supporters out of taking part in Reconstruction governments. The lawlessness and brutality demonstrated by these groups led the federal government to use the army against the societies. With the end of Reconstruction and the growth of white political power, the Klan and other similar groups played a less active role in the South. Such organizations, however, remain in existence to this day.

**Poll Taxes**  Southern states imposed a tax on every voter. Those who were too poor to pay poll taxes—including many African Americans—could not vote.

**Literacy Tests**  Some states required citizens to demonstrate that they could read and write before they voted. Often literacy tests involved interpreting a difficult part of the Constitution. Few African Americans could pass these tests because they had received little schooling. While the **Freedmen's Bureau,** created by Congress in 1865 to aid former slaves, established many schools for young African Americans, the bureau lasted only a few years. Thereafter, state laws forced African American children to attend separate schools that were poorly equipped and funded.

**Grandfather Clauses**  Poll taxes and literacy tests might have also kept poor and uneducated whites from voting. To prevent this, Southern states added grandfather clauses to their constitutions. These clauses allowed the son or grandson of a man eligible to vote in 1866 or 1867 to vote himself even if he could neither pay the tax nor pass the test. Since few African Americans could vote in 1867, the clause benefited whites almost exclusively.

**Jim Crow Laws**  Southern states also passed laws establishing social **segregation,** or the separation of people on the basis of race. Such Jim Crow laws forbade African Americans from sharing facilities with whites, such as railroad cars or water fountains. The passage of Jim Crow laws in the South after Reconstruction was aided in part by a narrow interpretation of the Fourteenth Amendment by the United States Supreme Court.

## Key Themes and Concepts

**Individuals, Groups, Institutions**
• Why did some white Southerners form secret societies such as the Ku Klux Klan?

## Reading Strategy

**Reading for Evidence**
• Reread the section entitled "White Control in the South." What were five major ways in which white Southerners reasserted their control in the South after Reconstruction?

*Jim Crow laws were a part of everyday life in the South after Reconstruction.*

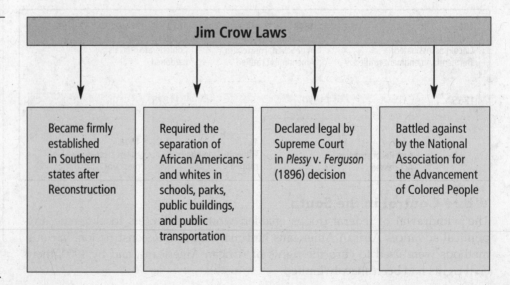

**Jim Crow Laws**

- Became firmly established in Southern states after Reconstruction
- Required the separation of African Americans and whites in schools, parks, public buildings, and public transportation
- Declared legal by Supreme Court in *Plessy* v. *Ferguson* (1896) decision
- Battled against by the National Association for the Advancement of Colored People

## The Supreme Court's Response

The Supreme Court did not interfere with efforts to restore white control in the South. In the 1883 *Civil Rights Cases*, the Court ruled that the Thirteenth Amendment abolished slavery but did not prohibit discrimination and that the Fourteenth Amendment prohibited discrimination by government but not by individuals. Later, in the landmark case of *Plessy v. Ferguson* (1896), the Court ruled that segregation was legal as long as African Americans had access to "equal but separate" facilities.

The Court's ruling in the *Plessy* case set a precedent that justified segregation in all public facilities—schools, hospitals, passenger terminals, and more—until the 1950s. It was not until the pivotal case of *Brown v. Board of Education of Topeka, Kansas* (1954) that the Supreme Court reversed the finding in *Plessy v. Ferguson* (1896). The *Brown* decision stated that educational facilities separated solely on the basis of race were by their nature unequal.

## African Americans Debate Their Future

Two prominent leaders offered contrasting strategies to improve the lives of African Americans. Booker T. Washington argued that African Americans should temporarily put aside their desire for political equality and instead focus on building economic security by gaining useful vocational skills. W.E.B. Du Bois called for the brightest African Americans to gain an advanced liberal arts education (rather than a vocational education) and then demand social and political equality. However, widespread discrimination against African Americans made either strategy difficult to follow.

### Key Themes and Concepts

**Constitutional Principles**
The following three cases deal with segregation and the Jim Crow laws:

*Civil Rights Cases* (1883) ruled that slavery was abolished but that discrimination by individuals was not prohibited by the Constitution.

*Plessy* v. *Ferguson* (1896) established segregation to be legal as long as "equal but separate" facilities were available to African Americans.

*Brown* v. *Board of Education of Topeka, Kansas* (1954) established that facilities separated by race were unequal.

• How did these three cases influence laws concerning segregation?

W.E.B. Du Bois                    Booker T. Washington

# The Rise of American Business, Industry, and Labor—1865–1920

## Big Idea

The United States developed a prosperous new economy based on the mass production of goods. During this period:

- economic development expanded in the North, but weakened in the South.

- entrepreneurs became wealthy and powerful.

- government began to regulate business.

- labor unions formed to improve working conditions.

## Section Overview

From Reconstruction through World War I, the United States developed a prosperous industrial economy that revolutionized American society. New machines made possible the mass production of goods. Industrial growth led to a new type of business, the corporation, headed by a rising class of enterprising industrialists such as Henry Ford. With little government interference, these corporate giants created new business structures, some legal and some not, that brought them fabulous wealth. They used their riches both to benefit society and to increase their power. Industries attracted a new type of laborer, the factory worker, who often worked long hours in hazardous conditions. These conditions spurred the growth of labor unions, which gradually gained the right to bargain with employers.

## Key Themes and Concepts

As you review this section, take special note of the following key themes and concepts:

**Science and Technology** How did technological developments lead to the growth of industrialization?

**Government** How did the government respond to the growth of powerful industries and to complaints about business practices?

**Factors of Production** What factors led to the growth of the labor movement, and what strategies did unions pursue?

## Key People

As you review this section, be sure you understand the significance of these key people:

| | | |
|---|---|---|
| Andrew Carnegie | Henry Ford | Charles Darwin |
| John D. Rockefeller | Horatio Alger | Terence Powderly |
| J. Pierpont Morgan | Adam Smith | Samuel Gompers |

## Key Terms

| | |
|---|---|
| transcontinental railroad | entrepreneurs |
| New South | assembly line |
| sharecroppers | laissez faire |
| tenant farmers | free enterprise system |
| capital | robber barons |
| corporations | Sherman Antitrust Act |
| monopoly | collective bargaining |
| merger | Haymarket Riot |
| trust | boycotts |

# Key Supreme Court Cases

As you review this section, be sure you understand the significance of these key Supreme Court cases:

*Munn* v. *Illinois* (1877)
*Wabash, St. Louis & Pacific Railway* v. *Illinois* (1886)
*United States* v. *E. C. Knight Company* (1895)
*In re Debs* (1895)

The Civil War changed the economies of the northern and southern regions of the United States. The Civil War stimulated economic growth in the North. Meanwhile, the South struggled to recover from the devastation of the war.

## Economic Developments in the North

The industrialization that had started before the war accelerated as northern factories rushed to keep up with the Union's demand for guns, ammunition, uniforms, and other necessary products. Improvements in railroad systems helped speed troop movements. Since so many northern farm workers entered the army, farms became more heavily mechanized, using fewer workers to produce more crops. Little of the fighting took place in the North, and the region was spared much physical destruction from the war.

After the war, the growing northern factories looked to overseas markets for their goods. Meanwhile, completion of the **transcontinental railroad**, authorized by the Pacific Railway Act of 1862, opened new markets in the West and brought products of western farms and mines east. The federal government encouraged the building of the transcontinental railroads by giving land to the railroad companies.

Economic growth attracted new waves of immigrants to the United States. Some sought farms in the West, but many found employment in the booming industries of the North.

## Economic Developments in the South

The Civil War ruined the South's economy. It ended slavery, thus killing the plantation system on which southern wealth was based. During the fighting, plantations had been burned, railroads ripped up, and the region's few factories destroyed.

After the war, many farmers and planters had to sell off parts of their land to pay off debts or to start over. These land-owners often found themselves in debt to banks or merchants. Yet despite such hardships, southern farmers again began to produce cotton and tobacco.

**Geography in History**
- What factors contributed to the development of factories in the North?

**Preparing for the Exam**

On the examination, you will need to understand important economic developments.

- What is the transcontinental railroad?

- How did it contribute to economic growth?

**Key Themes and Concepts**

**Places and Regions** New manufacturing technologies were less commonly used in the South than in the North. Why?

### Some Key Economic Issues in the Post-Civil War Era

| | NORTH | SOUTH |
|---|---|---|
| **industries** | continued rapid development financed by wartime growth; new interest in overseas markets | began slowly after the war, especially in textile and steel production; urban areas needed major reconstruction |
| **railroads** | crucial to economy; new transcontinental routes allowed the development of western markets | destroyed during the war; needed to be rebuilt, along with roads and bridges |
| **land use and agriculture** | farms began to mechanize and to increase production, providing food for the growing urban areas | plantation economy based on slavery ended; land destroyed by fighting; former slaves competed with destitute whites in search of land; tenant farming and sharecropping began |

Some southern leaders, however, believed that the South's economy should not rest simply on agriculture. They began to create a **New South,** with rebuilt railroads, new textile and steel mills, and, later, new industries, such as oil and coal production.

Despite these changes, the South lagged behind the North in economic growth. Agriculture still offered the most jobs, and many southerners, including large numbers of former slaves, had to farm land owned by others. These landless farmers included **sharecroppers,** who gave part of each year's crop to the landowner and received the rest as payment, and **tenant farmers,** who paid cash to rent land. A negative effect of the sharecropping system was that it kept formerly enslaved persons economically dependent.

Beginning in the 1880s, African Americans began a migration to the North in search of better jobs. This migration accelerated during and after World War I.

# Business Developments

Before the Civil War, sole proprietors, or single owners, and partnerships had controlled most American businesses. The mills and factories that came with industrialization, however, usually required greater **capital,** or money for investment, than one person or a few partners could raise.

## The Growth of Corporations

To raise capital for expansion, many businesses became corporations. A corporation is a business in which many investors own shares, usually called stocks. In exchange for their investment, each stockholder receives a dividend, or part of the corporation's profits.

Besides paying dividends, the corporations also limited investor losses. If a corporation failed, an investor lost only his or her investment and was not responsible for the corporation's debts.

The money raised by corporations speeded the growth of American industry. Among the fastest growing industries were transportation (railroads, urban transportation, and, later, automobiles), building materials (steel), energy (coal, oil, and electricity), and communications (telegraph and telephone).

## Other Forms of Business Organization

As the nation's economy boomed and industries grew larger in the late 1800s, other ways of organizing business appeared. Often the aim of such business organizations was to eliminate competition and dominate a particular area of the economy.

**Monopoly** A company or small group of companies that has complete control over a particular field of business is a monopoly. One example of a monopoly in the late 1800s was the E. C. Knight Sugar Company. Having a monopoly in a field often allowed a company to raise prices to almost any level it desired. Such abuses led to federal legislation aimed at curbing monopolies.

Some monopolies are permitted today. Public utility companies that provide gas, water, and electricity are examples of private companies that often have monopolies in their fields. Government agencies closely monitor the operations of such utilities.

**Conglomerate** A corporation that owns a group of unrelated companies is a conglomerate. Such conglomerates are usually formed by **merger,** the process by which one company acquires legal control over another. Mergers and

## Key Themes and Concepts

**Individuals, Groups, Institutions**
As the southern economy grew after the Civil War, some groups lagged behind others.

- Who were the sharecroppers?

- How did sharecroppers differ from tenant farmers?

## Key Themes and Concepts

**Economic Systems**
- What do you call a business in which many investors own shares?

Name two kinds of businesses that speeded the growth of American industry:

1.

2.

- What do you call a company that has complete control over a particular kind of business?

Name two examples:
1.

2.

- What do you call the merger of a group of unrelated companies?

Name an example:
1.

conglomerates are both legal and common today. General Electric, for example, is a conglomerate that has acquired many different divisions through mergers.

**Pool** Sometimes competing companies in one field entered into agreements to fix prices and divide business. Such an agreement was a pool. Railroad companies in the late 1800s formed such pools, which were later outlawed.

**Trust** A group of corporations in the same or related fields sometimes agreed to combine under a single board of trustees that controlled the actions of all the member corporations. This was a trust. Shareholders in the corporations received dividends from the trust but lost any say in its operation. The Standard Oil Trust was one example of such a combination. Trusts were later made illegal. Both trusts and pools were used by big business in an effort to limit competition.

**Holding Company** To get around the outlawing of trusts, corporations formed holding companies. The holding company bought controlling amounts of stock in different corporations rather than take operations over directly as a trust did.

### Innovations and Business Developments, 1868–1913

**Analyzing Documents**

Examine the timeline, then answer these questions.

- How many years passed between the formation of Standard Oil Trust and the formation of Carnegie Steel?

- Which event occurred first: the invention of the telephone or the introduction of the assembly line?

## Innovation

While these new forms of business organization helped young industries to get started and to maximize profits, other innovations enabled businesses to market their products more effectively. In urban areas, new department stores offered customers a wide variety of goods under one roof. For rural areas, retailers developed mail-order catalogs that saved customers a trip to faraway stores. The items offered in these stores and catalogs expanded as well, thanks to new inventions such as the vacuum cleaner, the telephone, the electric light bulb, the electric iron, and the safety razor.

## Entrepreneurs

These new forms of business organization and innovative ideas from inventors helped American industry grow in the late 1800s and early 1900s. Yet without the business knowledge and daring of certain individuals, that growth would have been much slower.

These individuals were **entrepreneurs,** people who take responsibility for the organization and operation of a new business venture. Entrepreneurs often risk large sums of venture capital in hopes of making enormous profits. The business decisions made by turn-of-the-century entrepreneurs had a great impact on the lives of most Americans. Some of the key entrepreneurs of the late 1800s and early 1900s are listed below.

**Andrew Carnegie** An immigrant from Scotland, Andrew Carnegie started work in a textile factory at age 12. He worked his way up through a variety of jobs and

**Reading Strategy**

**Organizing Information** In the space below, name four key entrepreneurs of the late 1800s and early 1900s and the industries each operated.

1.

2.

3.

4.

invested his money shrewdly. At age 38, Carnegie entered the steel industry, which was booming because of the growth of railroads. Carnegie sought to control all aspects of steelmaking and built his company into the world's largest steelmaker.

Carnegie sold his company in 1901 for a quarter billion dollars. He believed the wealthy had a duty to society and gave hundreds of millions to charities. He also underwrote the founding of free public libraries all across the country.

**John D. Rockefeller** Industrialist John D. Rockefeller entered the oil-refining business during the Civil War. He believed competition was wasteful and used ruthless methods to eliminate competitors. By 1882, his Standard Oil Company controlled over 90 percent of American oil refining. In 1882, he formed the Standard Oil Trust to control more aspects of oil production. Rockefeller also gave away hundreds of millions to charity.

**J. Pierpont Morgan** Trained as a banker, J. Pierpont Morgan profited by making loans to growing businesses. He took control of many bankrupt railroads in the late 1800s, reorganized them, and made a profit. He also controlled electrical, insurance, and shipping companies. Morgan bought Carnegie Steel in 1901, merged it with other companies, and created the United States Steel Corporation, the world's largest.

**Henry Ford** Entrepreneur Henry Ford revolutionized auto-making in 1913 by using a moving **assembly line** that permitted the mass production of cars, significantly lowering the cost of production. Ford also paid workers higher wages and set a standard that enabled laborers to afford such purchases.

## Attitudes Toward Business

Industrialization and the changes associated with it caused American attitudes toward business to alter in the late 1800s. Traditional attitudes, of course, still existed. They could be found in books by the popular writer Horatio Alger. Alger's novels describe poor boys who become rich through hard work and luck.

Alger's novels illustrate what is known as the Puritan work ethic. This is the belief, brought with the Puritans to colonial New England and embodied in the preaching of Puritan minister Cotton Mather, that hard work builds character and is its own reward.

The tremendous wealth some entrepreneurs gained during the late 1800s, as well as the cut-throat business methods they used, led some Americans to rethink their ideas on the meaning of business success. New philosophies tried to explain and justify both the accumulation of wealth and the practices used to achieve it.

**Laissez Faire** Many supporters of late 1800s business growth restated the older principle of laissez faire, or noninterference. Economist Adam Smith, in his 1776 book, *The Wealth of Nations*, and many other writers had supported this principle, which holds that government should not interfere in the economic workings of a nation. They believed that a **free enterprise system,** in which private individuals make the economic decisions, is most efficient.

During the late 1800s, economists restated the importance of laissez faire policies to economic growth. Government interference with business was minimal for much of this period, and entrepreneurs expanded their businesses and earned great wealth.

**Social Darwinism** Laissez faire capitalists found justification for their beliefs in new scientific theories being developed at that time. Naturalist Charles Darwin

*J. Pierpont Morgan*
Courtesy of the Library of Congress

**Preparing for the Exam**

- What system was based on the principle that private individuals should make economic decisions?

**Key Themes and Concepts**

**Human Systems**
Charles Darwin's theory of natural selection was simplified by philosophers and turned into a philosophy called Social Darwinism.

- How was Social Darwinism applied to business competition?

had developed a theory of evolution that described how animal species live or die by a process of natural selection. Other writers simplified Darwin's theories and created a philosophy called Social Darwinism.

Social Darwinists held that life was a struggle for the "survival of the fittest." Unregulated business competition would see weak businesses fail and healthy businesses thrive. Government action regulating business practices would interfere with the process of natural selection. Likewise, any government programs to aid the poor or workers would also violate natural "laws."

**Robber Barons or Philanthropists?** The philosophies described above and the growing gulf between rich and poor led some Americans to criticize laissez faire policies and those who profited from them. Critics condemned the wealthy entrepreneurs as robber barons, those who gained their wealth by ruthless methods in their dealings with competitors at the expense of the poor and the working class. The lavish lifestyles of the wealthy at this time fed such criticism. During this so-called Gilded Age, the rich spent freely to show off their wealth, a practice known as conspicuous consumption.

Public criticism and a sense of social responsibility led entrepreneurs to use a part of their wealth to aid society. People like Carnegie and Rockefeller became philanthropists, donating vast sums of money to charities and institutions such as schools, museums, libraries, and orchestras.

# Government Policies Toward Business

The federal government generally held a laissez faire attitude toward business for much of this period. Expanding industries and growing foreign trade seemed to justify such an attitude. In addition, many business leaders made financial contributions, legal and illegal, to the politicians who set federal policies.

A number of government policies were designed to aid the growth of business. These included loans and land grants to large railroad companies, high tariffs that discouraged competition from foreign manufacturers, tight limits on the amount of money in circulation, and few limits on immigration.

## Steps Toward Government Regulation

Several factors led the government to take the first steps in the late 1800s toward regulating business:

- periodic downturns in the national economy
- growing criticism of practices that saw big business profit at the expense of the poor and working class
- increasing grassroots political pressure for change

Although government intervention at this time had limited impact, it did set the course for more federal actions in years to come.

**Supreme Court Decisions** During the late 1800s, railroads developed a number of policies that discriminated against farmers and small shippers. These groups pressured some states to pass laws regulating railroad practices. The railroads sued to have such laws overturned.

In the 1877 case *Munn* v. *Illinois,* the Supreme Court upheld an Illinois law controlling grain elevator rates. The Court ruled that the Constitution recognized a state's right to a "police power" that permitted regulation of private property "affected with a public interest."

### Reading Strategy

**Reinforcing Main Ideas**
- What factors led the government toward regulating business in the late 1800s?

### Key Themes and Concepts

**Constitutional Principles**
Two landmark Supreme Court cases dealt with railroad regulation: *Munn* v. *Illinois* (1877) and *Wabash, St. Louis and Pacific Railway* v. *Illinois* (1886).

- How did these two cases influence railroad regulation?

In the 1886 case *Wabash, St. Louis & Pacific Railway Co.* v. *Illinois,* however, the Court ruled that states could not regulate railroad rates on portions of interstate routes that lay within their borders. Under the Constitution, only the federal government can regulate interstate trade. This decision meant that states could do little to regulate the railroads.

**Interstate Commerce Commission** In 1887, public pressure for reform of railroad policies led Congress to pass the Interstate Commerce Act. The act set up the Interstate Commerce Commission, an agency charged with ending such railroad abuses as pools and rebates, discounts only available to special customers. Although court decisions kept the commission ineffective for several years, its establishment set a precedent for federal regulation of interstate commerce.

**Sherman Antitrust Act** By the late 1800s, some large corporations and trusts had eliminated most competition and won almost total monopolies in their fields. Politicians heeded the public protests over the ensuing abuses. One result was the Sherman Antitrust Act of 1890. The act prohibited monopolies by declaring illegal any business combination or trust "in restraint of trade or commerce."

Yet when the federal government tried to enforce the act, the Supreme Court, in *United States* v. *E.C. Knight Company,* 1895, ruled that many businesses were exempt from the new law. In addition, some other corporations circumvented the act by forming holding companies rather than trusts. Once again, the precedent set by the act proved more important than the act itself.

## Labor Organizations

Business growth in the late 1800s brought generally higher wages to American workers. Yet periodic unemployment and poor working conditions remained a fact of life for workers. In addition, employers held enormous power over the lives of their workers and could lower wages and fire employees at will.

### The Growth of Unions

To improve conditions, increasing numbers of American workers formed labor unions beginning in the 1820s. As working conditions changed with industrialization, many more workers became interested in unions. "Eight hours for work, eight hours for sleep, eight hours for what we will" was a popular slogan that promoted a major goal of labor unions.

Americans had long understood the values of cooperation and association, and labor unions provided a means to put these values into action. In **collective bargaining,** union members representing workers negotiated labor issues with management. Instead of each worker trying to achieve individual aims, a united group would put pressure on management. Several early unions helped advance the cause of labor.

**Knights of Labor** Under the direction of Terence Powderly, the Knights of Labor, formed in 1869, welcomed skilled and unskilled workers as well as women and African Americans. The Knights fought for broad social reforms such as an eight-hour day for workers, an end to child labor, and equal opportunities and wages for women. As a rule, the union opposed strikes, but a successful strike against railroads in 1885 brought many new members. However, an antilabor feeling swept the nation after the **Haymarket Riot** in late 1886. The Knights declined in influence due to a series of unsuccessful strikes and competition from the American Federation of Labor.

**Key Themes and Concepts**

**Interdependence**
• What do you call the process through which union members represent workers in labor negotiations with management?

**American Federation of Labor** In 1886, Samuel Gompers formed the American Federation of Labor (AFL). The AFL was a collection of many different craft unions, unions of skilled workers in similar trades. In contrast to the Knights of Labor, the AFL fought for immediate goals such as better wages, hours, and working conditions. The policy that the AFL followed is known as *bread-and-butter unionism*. It so appealed to workers that AFL membership reached about a million by 1900, making the AFL the most powerful union in the nation. Nevertheless, groups such as women, immigrants, and African Americans generally were not welcome in the AFL.

**International Ladies' Garment Workers Union** Women made up the majority of workers in the garment industries. In 1900, the International Ladies' Garment Workers Union (ILGWU) was formed to represent the laborers who toiled in sweatshops. After a successful strike in 1910, the ILGWU soon became an important part of the AFL. In March 1911 a horrific fire at the Triangle Shirtwaist Company in New York City caused the deaths of almost 150 people, mostly young immigrant women. Dozens leapt to their deaths from upper stories to escape the burning building due to locked exits and inadequate fire escapes. This event gave further impetus to the work of the ILGWU.

## Labor Conflict

If collective bargaining failed, labor unions sometimes used **boycotts** against the employer or resorted to strikes, or work stoppages, to achieve their aims. Boycotts are still used today. They are an organized refusal to buy or use a product or service or to deal with a company or a group of companies. This type of protest is used as a means of forcing action by a company. Strikes sometimes ended in union victories; often, however, they led to violence as business owners sought state and even federal support to end walkouts. The strikes and labor-associated violence described below sometimes advanced the cause of labor and sometimes set it back. During the late 1800s when most efforts at **collective bargaining** failed, big business often used court injunctions against labor unions to force workers back to work. Other tactics used by big business were **blacklists** and **yellow dog contracts**. If a worker's name was put on a blacklist, it meant that the name was circulated to other companies or employers so that the person would not be hired because of his or her actions or beliefs. Big business also used yellow dog contracts, which forced workers to sign agreements stating that they would never join a labor union.

**Great Railway Strike** In 1877, a series of pay cuts for railroad workers led to a strike that spread across several states. At the request of state governors, President Rutherford B. Hayes sent federal troops to help end the strike. The workers gained little benefit from the strike, and owners took a harder position against unions.

**Haymarket Riot** A labor rally called by Chicago anarchists in 1886 ended with a bomb blast and riot that left many people dead, including seven police officers. Although the Knights of Labor had no responsibility for the violence, some public opinion blamed them.

**Homestead Strike** In 1892, union members at the Carnegie steel plant in Homestead, Pennsylvania, went on strike to protest a wage cut. Management brought in security guards to protect the plant. In the violence that followed, 16 people were killed. The National Guard finally ended the fighting and the strike. Fewer than 25 percent of the striking workers got their jobs back. The strike halted the union movement in the steel industry for 20 years.

## Reading Strategy

**Organizing Information** American workers began to form a number of labor unions in the 1800s. In the space below, name three different labor unions and describe the workers who joined each of them.

1.

2.

3.

## Preparing for the Exam

For the examination, you will need to understand the history of labor conflict in the United States.

Identify the outcome of each of the following strikes:

- Great Railway Strike (1877)
- Haymarket Riot (1886)
- Homestead Strike (1892)
- Pullman Strike (1894)
- Lawrence Textile Strike (1912)

*Pullman Strike*

**Pullman Strike** In 1894, a strike by railway-car makers in Illinois spread and tied up other rail lines. President Grover Cleveland sent in federal troops to end the strike. (The Supreme Court, in the 1895 case *In re Debs*, ruled that the president had the right to deploy the troops, even over the objection of the governor of Illinois.) Cleveland's action confirmed the belief of many that government favored the interests of business over those of labor. Both the Homestead Steel Strike and the Pullman Strike ended sooner than expected as a result of direct government intervention.

**Lawrence Textile Strike** The Industrial Workers of the World (IWW), a radical union of skilled and unskilled laborers, led a huge strike against the textile mills in Lawrence, Massachusetts, in 1912. The strike proved one of the greatest successes of that era, and workers won most of their demands.

### An Era of Strikes, Late 1800s

### Preparing for the Exam

A flowchart shows the steps in a process. Based on the text and the flowchart, answer the question.

- What were three reasons for tensions between workers and business owners?

1.

2.

3.

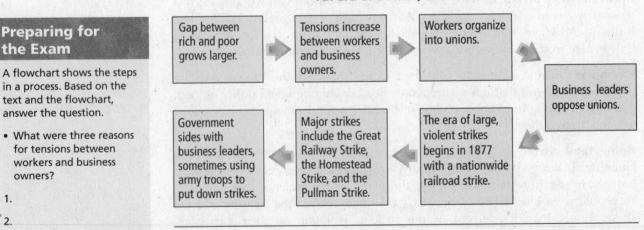

| Gap between rich and poor grows larger. | → | Tensions increase between workers and business owners. | → | Workers organize into unions. |

Business leaders oppose unions.

| Government sides with business leaders, sometimes using army troops to put down strikes. | ← | Major strikes include the Great Railway Strike, the Homestead Strike, and the Pullman Strike. | ← | The era of large, violent strikes begins in 1877 with a nationwide railroad strike. |

*Increasing tensions between workers and employers led to large, often violent strikes.*

# American Society Adjusts to Industrialization

## Section Overview

Industrialization and new building technologies triggered an explosion of urban growth that brought social changes, both good and bad. A prosperous middle class emerged, while urban crowding and disease took a heavy toll on the working poor, many of whom were immigrants. New arrivals came in waves, first from western Europe and Africa, then from eastern Europe and Asia. Despite widespread discrimination, many immigrants prospered. A growing United States population and a demand for new lands and resources lured Americans westward, reducing the Native American population and forcing them into ever-shrinking parcels of land. Western land was gobbled up by miners, ranchers, and a growing political force: farmers.

The
# Big
# Idea

Immigration and urbanization changed the United States dramatically. During the late 1800s:

• a prosperous middle class developed.

• cities became crowded and workers lived in unhealthful conditions.

• immigrants arrived from eastern Europe and Asia.

• women and other workers became a larger part of the workforce.

• settlers continued to move westward.

## Key Themes and Concepts

As you review this section, take special note of the following key themes and concepts:

**Change** What effects did industrialization and urbanization have on American culture, work life, and family life?

**Immigration and Migration** How did patterns of immigration change from colonial times through the early 1900s?

**Places and Regions** What types of land, resources, and economic opportunities caused Americans to move farther and farther westward?

## Key People

As you review this section, be sure you understand the significance of these key people:

John Dewey

Jane Addams

Frederick Jackson Turner

William Jennings Bryan

William McKinley

## Key Terms

tenements

political machines

settlement house movement

company towns

suffrage

ghettos

nativism

reservations

Dawes Act

Agricultural Revolution

Grange

Populist Party

free silver

Cities offered the best and the worst of life for newcomers from the countryside and from abroad. The dazzling skyscrapers and bustling streets were symbols of the new opportunities for prosperity in America. Yet behind the dazzle grew a darker side of city life.

# Industrialization and Urbanization

Industrialization and urbanization, the growth of cities, went hand in hand. Cities offered large numbers of workers for new factories. Cities provided transportation for raw materials and finished goods. As more plants were built, more workers moved to cities seeking jobs. In 1880, about a quarter of Americans lived in cities. By 1900, roughly 40 percent did. By 1920, more than half of all Americans lived in cities. This shift from rural to urban life had both positive and negative effects.

### Negative Effects of City Growth

Some of the negative effects of urbanization included crowded, unsanitary living conditions for workers, as well as corrupt city politics.

**Housing** Construction of decent housing often lagged behind the growth of city populations. Much city housing consisted of multifamily buildings called **tenements**. Immigrant and working-class families, who could pay little for rent, crowded into such buildings. These poorly maintained tenements deteriorated, and whole neighborhoods became slums. Crime flourished in such poor, congested neighborhoods.

**Health** Urban crowding helped spread disease. Water and sanitation facilities were often inadequate. Poor families could not afford proper diets and lacked knowledge of basic health procedures.

**Politics** **Political machines** took control of many city governments, partly by providing help to the growing number of poor immigrant voters and thereby gaining their support. Corruption increased, and money that could have been spent on public works often ended up in private pockets.

### Positive Effects of City Growth

Urbanization was aided and improved by new technologies in transportation, architecture, utilities, and sanitation. In addition, cities offered new cultural opportunities.

**New Technologies** Builders turned to new technologies to meet the challenge posed by huge numbers of people living together. Subways, elevated trains, and streetcars provided mass transportation. Steel girders and elevators made possible high-rise skyscrapers. Gas and electric lights brightened city streets and made them safer. Growing health problems forced officials to design and build new water and sewage systems.

**Cultural Advances** Public and private money funded new museums, concert halls, theaters, and parks. New printing presses turned out mass-circulation newspapers, magazines, and popular novels by authors such as Mark Twain and Horatio Alger. Public schools educated more students than ever before. Reformers, including the philosopher and educator John Dewey, improved the quality of teaching.

## Reading Strategy

**Analyzing Cause And Effect**

- How was industrialization related to urbanization?
- Did one process lead to the other, or were these processes interdependent?

## Reading Strategy

**Predicting Content**
The growth of cities had both positive and negative effects. Some of the negative effects included crowded and unsanitary living conditions for workers.

- How might these conditions change over time?
- How might they stay the same?

*An Urban Classroom*

**Community Improvement** Other reformers founded groups intended to correct the problems of society. In Chicago, Jane Addams started Hull House, a model project that led a **settlement house movement** to provide education and services to the poor. Political reformers sought to unseat corrupt political machines and see that public money was spent on improved services such as police and fire departments and new hospitals, rather than on graft.

**Preparing for the Exam**

Some examination questions require you to read and interpret charts. Study the chart and answer these questions.

- Approximately how much did the urban (city) population in the United States grow between 1860 and 1900?

- Did the rural population increase or decrease between 1870 and 1890?

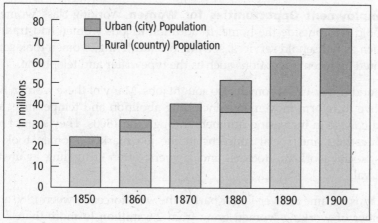

**Urban and Rural Population, 1850–1900**

Source: *Historical Statistics of the United States*

## The Urban Mixture

The people of these growing cities generally could be divided into three broad groups.

**Workers and the Poor** The largest group contained the workers and the poor. Most immigrants belonged to this group, whose members lived in slums and poorer neighborhoods. (Living conditions generally were better in the **company towns,** which were built and owned by a single employer, but workers in these towns were dependent on their employer for everything from housing to food to police protection.) Often workers lacked the time and money to go to theaters or museums or use other resources that cities provided.

**The Middle Class** As a result of industrialization, doctors, lawyers, office workers, and skilled laborers made up a growing middle class. Middle-class neighborhoods offered more spacious, better maintained housing. The middle-class people had both money and leisure time. Their homes contained the new consumer goods becoming available, such as sewing machines and phonographs. They could afford to go to concerts, attend increasingly popular football, basketball, or baseball games, and save money for their children's higher education.

**The Wealthy** Entrepreneurs and wealthy business people usually made the city their chief residence, although they often had summer estates outside it. The rich made up the smallest segment of urban society. They lived in large mansions or elegant apartment buildings. They often contributed to charities and cultural institutions such as opera companies and libraries. They could enjoy the broadest range of benefits of city life.

## Changes for Women, Families, and Workers

Industrialization and urbanization brought changes to the lives of women in all the classes. Many Americans had long held the view that the ideal woman devoted herself to home and family, instilling in her husband and children high moral

**Reading Strategy**

**Organizing Information**
- Into which three groups can the urban population of the late 1800s be divided?
- Which group was the largest?
- Which group was the smallest?

**Key Themes and Concepts**

**Change**
In the late 1800s, more women began to seek paid employment outside the home.

- What reasons led to this change?

- What kinds of new jobs did women seek outside the home?

values. In fact, usually only wealthy women could dedicate themselves full-time to such tasks.

In the late 1800s, more women began taking jobs outside the home, some out of economic necessity and others out of a desire for a larger role in society. These jobs provided added income and personal fulfillment but sometimes produced added stress for family members. For example, women who worked outside the home also were expected to continue performing most of the jobs in the home, and children often had to be cared for by relatives or neighbors during the day.

**New Employment Opportunities for Women** Working-class women often had to hold jobs outside the home. In addition to jobs women had traditionally filled, such as household services, sewing, or laundering, women took some new jobs created by recent inventions such as the typewriter and telephone.

Middle- and upper-class women also sought jobs. Many of these women had long been active in reform movements, including abolition and temperance, and had attended college in increasing numbers through the 1800s. They sought to apply their educations and social concerns in the job market. Women took jobs as teachers, social workers, doctors, and lawyers, often struggling against public disapproval.

Women thus became an ever-larger part of the workforce. Between 1880 and 1910, the number of working women grew from 2.6 million to more than 7 million. Conditions women met in the workplace—hostility, laws that barred them from certain jobs, unequal pay—led more women to seek legal remedies. To gain the political power to force change, however, women first needed to win the right to vote, called **suffrage.** The women's suffrage movement grew more active.

**Other Groups of Workers** Groups besides women faced problems in the workplace. Employers regularly discriminated against African American workers and workers who were older or disabled, refusing to hire them or keeping them in low-paying jobs.

Nor did laws protect children from dangerous and unhealthful work, such as in mines and factories. Nevertheless, many families were forced to send their children to work rather than school in order to help make ends meet.

# Immigration

The United States has always been a nation of immigrants. After the Civil War, however, industrialization drew an even greater flood of immigrants. From 1865 to 1900, some 13.5 million people arrived from abroad. During much of the nineteenth century, there were few restrictions on immigration as the growing numbers of factories provided job opportunities for cheap labor. Not until the 1920s would the numbers begin to dwindle. Immigration to the United States can be divided into three stages.

## Colonial Immigration

This period lasted from the arrival of the first people from England through the Declaration of Independence. The following features characterize this period of immigration.

**Colonial Immigrants** People from England made up the largest part of these immigrants. However, Scotch-Irish, German, Swedish, and Dutch also came in significant numbers. Large numbers of Africans were also part of the colonial immigration.

## Reading Strategy

**Problem Solving**
• How much did the number of working women grow between 1880 and 1910?
• What challenges did women face in the workplace?
• How did some women address those challenges?

## Key Themes and Concepts

**Individuals, Groups, Institutions**
• What other groups of workers also began working in the late 1800s? What kinds of conditions did they face?

## Key Themes and Concepts

**Immigration and Migration**
During the colonial period, a huge number of immigrants arrived in the United States. People from England, Germany, and Sweden, for example, made up a large number of these immigrants, but people from other countries came as well.

• What motivated immigrants in the colonial period to come to the United States?

**Reasons for Immigration** Some came seeking political and religious freedom. Others sought to improve their economic standing and their way of life. The Africans came unwillingly, as slaves.

**Areas of Settlement** English settlement spread along the Atlantic Coast from Maine to Georgia and inland to the Appalachians. Within this area, other ethnic groups became concentrated in certain regions. For example, many Dutch settled in New York and New Jersey, many Germans in Pennsylvania, and many Scotch-Irish in the backcountry areas of the Carolinas. Most Africans came at first to the Chesapeake region, then spread through the South.

**Difficulties They Faced** Immigrants came into conflict with the Native Americans. They also had to overcome the challenge of building homes, farms, and a new way of life in an unfamiliar region.

**Contributions** The immigrants succeeded in establishing a culture much like the one they had left in Europe, yet heavily influenced by the geographic factors they encountered in North America. In addition to their language, people coming from England brought forms of government, religions, family and cultural traditions, and economic patterns from their home country. Other groups contributed customs from their home country. All worked to build a successful economy in North America.

## Old Immigration

The old immigration covered the years from the establishment of the United States until around 1850. Most immigrants came from northern and western Europe, especially Ireland, Germany, and Scandinavia.

**Reasons for Immigration** Massive famine caused by failure of the potato crop drove millions of Irish immigrants to seek opportunity in the United States. Revolution in Germany caused many immigrants to seek peace and stability in America. Many people continued to arrive in search of better economic opportunity.

**Areas of Settlement** The Irish largely settled in cities in the Northeast. Some Germans also stayed in cities, but many moved west to start farms, as did a large number of Scandinavian immigrants.

**Difficulties They Faced** Irish and German Catholic immigrants often faced hostility on their arrival in the United States. Some Americans feared economic competition from the newcomers. Since at this time the nation was predominantly Protestant, resentment toward Catholics and Jews was also strong.

**Contributions** Irish workers helped build railroads and canals and labored in factories. Germans and Scandinavians brought, among other things, advanced farming techniques and new ideas on education such as kindergarten.

## New Immigration

The New Immigration covered the time from roughly 1870 to 1924. This period was marked by a shift in sources of immigration to southern and eastern Europe, especially the nations of Italy, Poland, and Russia. In addition, substantial numbers of Japanese and Chinese arrived.

**Reasons for Immigration** Hope of greater economic opportunity prompted many of these immigrants to come to America. Some also came seeking political freedom. Other groups, such as Russian Jews, sought religious freedom.

**Areas of Settlement** Most of the new immigrants settled in cities, especially industrial centers and ports, and often were concentrated in **ghettos,** or urban

**Geography in History**

**Organizing Information**
During the colonial period, in what areas did most English immigrants settle? List two other examples of immigrant groups and the areas in which they settled.

1.

2.

**Key Themes and Concepts**

**Immigration and Migration** "Old immigration" took place during the first half of the nineteenth century. People from northern and western Europe, Ireland, and Scandinavia, for example, made up a large number of these immigrants, but people came from other countries as well.

• What motivated immigrants in the colonial period to come to the United States?

**Geography in History**

**Organizing Information**
• Where did most Irish and German immigrants settle?

• What difficulties did these immigrant groups face?

## Immigrants

**Where they came from 1840–1860**

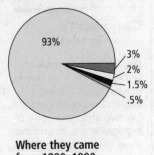

93%
3%
2%
1.5%
.5%

**Where they came from 1880–1900**

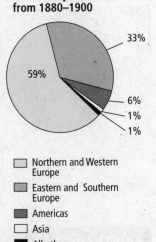

33%
59%
6%
1%
1%

- Northern and Western Europe
- Eastern and Southern Europe
- Americas
- Asia
- All others

Source: *Historical Statistics of the United States*

---

### Analyzing Documents

Examine the pie charts, then answer the following questions.

- What percentage of immigrants between 1840 and 1860 came from northern and western Europe?

- How much did the percentage of immigrants from eastern and southern Europe increase from the period 1840 to 1860 to the period 1880 to1900?

---

areas (usually poor) that are dominated by a single ethnic group. Asian immigrants tended to settle on the west coast, usually in California.

**Difficulties They Faced** Adjusting to life in the United States could cause strains in immigrant families. At school, immigrant children learned not only English but American tastes and customs. Immigrant parents often feared that their children were losing their religious and cultural heritage.

In addition, the growing numbers of new immigrants produced reactions of fear and hostility among many native-born Americans whose ancestors had come from very different backgrounds. Newcomers faced discrimination in jobs and housing. (As low-wage workers, they also competed against other minority groups, such as African Americans.) Popular pressure to limit immigration increased. Political party bosses often arranged assistance for newly arriving immigrants and in return expected those immigrants to show their gratitude by supporting that political party in elections.

**Contributions** The new immigrants found an abundance of jobs in the nation's expanding industries. Yet the steady stream of incoming workers to fill such jobs kept wages low. Young Italian and Jewish girls worked in the sweatshops of the garment industry. Poles and Slavs labored in the coal mines and steel mills of Pennsylvania and the Midwest. Chinese workers helped build the transcontinental railroad. These immigrants aided America's economic expansion and contributed to the nation's rich cultural diversity.

## Reaction Against Immigration

The flood of immigration in the late 1800s brought with it a new wave of **nativism.** This was the belief that native-born Americans and their ways of life were superior to immigrants and their ways of life. In the late 1800s, descendants of the old immigrants were often among the nativists protesting the arrival of new immigrants.

Nativists believed that immigrant languages, religions, and traditions would have a negative impact on American society. Nativist workers believed that the many new immigrants competing for jobs kept wages low. A series of downturns in the economy added to fears that immigrants would take jobs from native-born Americans.

Immigrants thus often met with prejudice and discrimination. Jokes and stereotypes about the newcomers were common. Nativists also tried to influence legislation against immigrants. Key developments in this area are included in the chart on the following page.

## Immigrants and American Society

Over the years, sociologists and others who studied immigration developed different theories on how immigrants were absorbed into the larger society.

**"Melting Pot" Theory** According to this theory, people from various cultures have met in the United States to form a new American culture. The contributions of individual groups are not easily distinguished. The resulting culture is more important than its parts.

**Assimilation** According to this theory, immigrants disappeared into an already established American culture. They gave up older languages and customs and became Americanized, adopting the appearances and attitudes of the larger society in order to be accepted. Immigrants from Africa and Asia, who looked least like nativist Americans, had the hardest time becoming assimilated.

## Reaction Against Immigration

- **Know-Nothing Party:** The party's members worked during the 1850s to limit the voting strength of immigrants, keep Catholics out of public office, and require a lengthy residence before citizenship. Also known as the American party, the Know-Nothing party achieved none of these goals and died out by the late 1850s.

- **Chinese Exclusion Act of 1882:** Some native-born Americans labelled immigration from Asia a "yellow peril." Under pressure from California, which had already barred the Chinese from owning property or working at certain jobs, Congress passed this law sharply limiting Chinese immigration.

- **"Gentlemen's Agreement":** In 1907 President Roosevelt reached an informal agreement with Japan under which that nation nearly halted the emigration of its people to the United States.

- **Literacy Tests:** In 1917 Congress enacted a law barring any immigrant who could not read or write.

- **Emergency Quota Act of 1921:** This law sharply limited the number of immigrants to the United States each year to about 350,000.

- **National Origins Act of 1924:** This law further reduced immigration and biased it in favor of those from northern and western Europe.

### Analyzing Documents

Examine the chart, then answer the following questions.

- How influential was the Know-Nothing party?
- What prompted Congress to pass the Chinese Exclusion Act of 1882?
- Which laws restricted the number of immigrants to the United States each year?

**Pluralism** This theory recognizes that groups do not always lose their distinctive characters. They can live side by side, with each group contributing in different ways to society. This approach is sometimes called the salad bowl theory, since groups, like different vegetables in a salad, remain identifiable but create a new, larger whole.

### Preparing for the Exam

Which sociological theory argues that different immigrant groups can live side-by-side without losing their distinctive characters?

## The American West in the Late 1800s

In 1893, Frederick Jackson Turner wrote in his paper "The Significance of the Frontier in American History" that the frontier, "and the advance of American settlement westward, explain American development." Turner claimed life in the West had given rise to inventiveness, independence, and unique American customs. (While other historians would argue instead that other factors, such as the nation's European heritage or economic abundance, were the key influences, Turner's thesis has had lasting influence.) In 1890, the government had announced that the West was closed. Industrialization had aided the settling of the West.

### The American West, 1862–1896

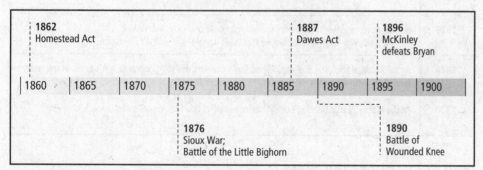

## Native Americans and Westward Expansion

The westward expansion of the late 1800s continued to create problems for the Native Americans who stood in its path. By the 1840s, only scattered groups of Native Americans still lived in the East. Most lived west of the Mississippi on lands that few whites wanted. The California gold rush, the building of the transcontinental railroad, and the discovery of rich farmland in the Great Plains changed this situation. Now white people began to move onto Native American lands in the West.

### Analyzing Documents

Examine the timeline, then answer the following questions.

- How many years passed between the Homestead Act and the Battle of Wounded Knee?
- Which event occurred first: the Battle of Little Bighorn or the passage of the Dawes Act?

## Key Themes and Concepts

**Government**
The Dawes Act was aimed at breaking up Native American tribes and reservations. It offered Native Americans who gave up tribal ways the deeds to their land and United States citizenship after 25 years.

- Was the Dawes Act fair to Native Americans?

- Did Native Americans support it?

## Turning Point

The decline of the Plains Indians can be traced to the following events:

- the Homestead Act

- the mass killing of buffalo

- the transcontinental railroad

## Analyzing Documents

American expansion onto Native American lands led to many wars and the near destruction of western Native American nations. The table outlines the struggle experienced by one tribe, the Sioux. Examine the chart, then answer the following questions.

- What caused the first Sioux War in 1865?

- How did the federal government respond to Sitting Bull's defeat of General Custer?

- How many Sioux were killed by American soldiers at the Massacre of Wounded Knee?

**Indian Wars** The Native Americans fought back. From the 1850s to 1890, a series of wars raged in the West. Gradually the Native Americans were forced to accept treaties that crowded them into smaller and smaller areas of land called **reservations.** Native American resistance was weakened by the greater numbers of whites with superior technology, and divisions among Native American peoples that did not permit a unified resistance. The defeat of the Sioux at Wounded Knee, South Dakota, in 1890 is usually considered the end of the Indian wars.

*Sitting Bull*

**Changing Government Policies** In victory, the federal government continued to display little understanding or respect for Native American cultures and values. Native Americans were given reservation land that rarely could produce adequate crops or support game for the people living on it. Reservations were located in sparsely populated areas of the west. Further, in 1887, Congress passed the **Dawes Act,** aimed at Americanizing the Native Americans. It proposed to break up tribes and reservations and to grant land directly to Native Americans as individuals and families. Native Americans who abandoned tribal ways would be granted deeds to their land and United States citizenship. Relatively few Native Americans accepted the terms of the Dawes Act. By 1900, the effect of these government policies had greatly reduced the size of the Native American population and had made them among the poorest Americans.

### The Sioux Wars

| | |
|---|---|
| **1865** | Federal government decides to build a road through Sioux territory. Sioux warriors resist violently, sparking Red Cloud's War. |
| **1867** | Red Cloud's War ends. Sioux agree to live on reservation in Dakota Territory. |
| **1875** | Federal government allows miners to search for gold on Sioux reservation.<br>Second Sioux War begins. Chief Sitting Bull leads many Sioux off the reservation. |
| **1876** | At the Battle of the Little Bighorn, Sitting Bull's warriors destroy General Custer's army. In response, federal government sends more troops to the region. Most Sioux agree to move to reservations. |
| **1890** | At the Massacre of Wounded Knee, American soldiers open fire on unarmed Sioux, killing 200. |

## The Economy of the West

An **Agricultural Revolution** with new technologies helped people who moved onto Native American lands exploit the wealth of the West. Railroads brought people and carried western crops and products to eastern markets. Barbed wire aided the growth of both farming and ranching. Steel plows cut tough prairie soil. Windmills pulled water to the surface of dry western lands. Mechanical reapers and farm tools allowed a smaller number of workers to plant and harvest larger crops.

The riches of the West, like the land itself, took many forms. In the Rocky Mountains, miners dug millions of dollars in gold, silver, copper, lead, and zinc ore. In the Great Plains, ranchers turned cattle raising into big business, as cowhands moved huge herds across the open ranges to rail lines. Farmers, too, were attracted to the Great Plains because of its rich topsoil and overcame heat, blizzards, droughts, insects, and occasional conflicts with ranchers to raise crops. Many settled lands claimed under the Homestead Act and later built huge farms. (Through the Homestead Act, as well as government land grants and other aid to large railroad companies, the federal government played a significant role in encouraging development of the resources of the West.) By the late 1800s, American farmers were raising enough to feed the nation and still export wheat and other crops. Mechanization of agriculture caused an increase in production.

Spurred by the expansion of mining, ranching, and farming, cities like Omaha, Denver, and San Francisco became some of the fastest-growing in the nation.

## Farmers, Populists, and Politics

Farmers gained more influence and power through two organizations: the Grange and the Populist party.

**The Grange** Many farmers facing the hardships and isolation of rural life joined the Grange. This organization, founded in 1867, was originally meant to develop social ties. However, poor economic conditions made farmers aware that railroad companies, which often stored farmers' crops and carried them to market, had great control over their livelihoods. To win back some of this control, the Grange began to press for political changes to limit the power of the railroads. Pressure from the Grange and other groups led to the state laws regulating railroads that were upheld in *Munn* v. *Illinois* and to the federal law creating the Interstate Commerce Commission.

**The Populist Party** Farmers and many factory workers realized that the best hope of winning more reforms was the formation of a new political party. In 1891, they founded the Populist Party, which had among its goals a graduated income tax, direct election of United States senators, government ownership of railroads, telegraphs, and telephones, and an eight hour day.

Courtesy of the Library of Congress

*William McKinley*

*William Jennings Bryan*

## Geography in History

- How was the economy of the West influenced by each of the following?

  Rocky Mountains
  Great Plains
  railroads
  Homestead Act

## Key Themes and Concepts

**Civic Values**
Many workers, both farm and factory, joined the Populist party, which had strong support from people rather than powerful politicians. List three goals of the Populist party.

1.

2.

3.

The new party had strong grassroots support—support directly from the people rather than established political figures. Populist candidates soon made strong showings in elections for state legislatures and for the United States Congress. Many of the ideas and goals of the Populists eventually became laws.

**The Election of 1896** The Populists made their strongest showing in the election of 1896, the first election to follow an economic depression that had begun in 1893. The chief Populist issue in the campaign was **free silver.** The free coinage of silver would produce cheap money, or currency inflated in value that would make it easier for farmers to pay off debts. William Jennings Bryan, who ran on both the Populist and Democratic tickets, argued tirelessly for this idea. Republican candidate William McKinley had the support of big business, which contributed heavily to his campaign. McKinley claimed the nation's economy was sound and opposed free silver.

## Reading Strategy

**Reinforcing Main Ideas**
• What changes did the outcome of the election of 1896 symbolize in the United States?

McKinley won the election by a fair margin. The nation's economy meanwhile improved, and the Populists disappeared as a political party. Yet, as has happened with other minor parties in American history, some of the Populists' ideas were later adopted by the other political parties.

The defeat of the Populists symbolized the great changes that had swept the nation since the Civil War. The economy had changed from agrarian to industrial. The United States was becoming a nation of cities rather than farms and villages. The West was closing and its influence coming to end. New immigrants were creating a new, complex, pluralistic culture in America. By 1900, the United States was entering both a new century and a modern age.

## Preparing for the Exam

During the election of 1896, the chief Populist party issue was free silver. Populist candidate William Jennings Bryan believed that the free coinage of silver would make it easier for farmers to pay off debts.

• Why do you think Republican candidate William McKinley opposed the idea of free silver?

### Some Late 19th Century Inventions That Changed American Life

| DATE | INVENTION | IMPACT ON CULTURE |
|------|-----------|-------------------|
| 1857 | passenger elevator | multi-story buildings could be built and by 1885 the first skyscraper was built in Chicago; escalators followed in 1891 |
| 1867 | barbed wire | allowed farmers to fence in the formerly open prairies |
| 1873 | Levi Strauss creates blue jeans, known as "Levi's" | heavy duty farm clothing was quickly successful and continued into the twenty-first century as a fashion garment |
| 1874 | first structural steel bridge | steel from the Carnegie Mills used in a triple arch design that spanned the Mississippi River at St. Louis, opened the way for other bridges |
| 1876 | telephone | increased speed and ease of communication for business, political, and social needs, aided in organization for farm groups and others |
| 1879 | earliest incandescent lights | before the end of the century, offices, homes, factories, and farms were affected by availability of longer hours of light |
| 1892 | first gas powered car and first gas powered tractor | earliest efforts at "horseless carriages" and farm equipment without animal helped spur further growth |

**Multiple Choice**

*Directions:* Review the Test-Taking Strategies section of this book. Then answer the following questions, drawn from actual Regents examinations. For each statement or question, choose the *number* of the word or expression that, of those given, best completes the statement or answers the question.

1 The literacy tests and poll taxes used in the southern states after 1870 were designed to

(1) ensure that only well-informed people voted

(2) prevent African Americans from voting

(3) provide an alternative to citizenship tests

(4) promote advances in public education

2 President Abraham Lincoln's post-Civil War plan for reconstruction of the South was based on the theory that the former Confederate states

(1) should be treated as conquered territories

(2) could be readmitted to the Union only by Congress

(3) had never actually left the Union

(4) must grant full equality to all people

3 During Reconstruction, what was a belief of the Radical Republicans?

(1) The former Confederate States should be brought back into the Union quickly.

(2) Reconstruction should force political and social reform in Southern states.

(3) The North and the South should take equal responsibility for causing the Civil War.

(4) The people who were freed from slavery should be denied equal civil rights.

4 One similarity between the Know-Nothings and the Ku Klux Klan is that both

(1) opposed the spread of communism

(2) exposed abuses in big business and government

(3) believed the problems of society were caused by the growth of labor unions

(4) fostered resentment against minority groups in American society

5 The most long-lasting victory for civil rights achieved during Reconstruction was the

(1) ratification of the thirteenth, fourteenth, and fifteenth amendments to the Constitution

(2) establishment of a strong two-party political system in the South

(3) increased prominence given to the Office of the President

(4) passage of Black Codes throughout the South

6 The solid South refers to the political situation in the post-Reconstruction South where

(1) most eligible voters supported the Prohibition party

(2) people who were freed from slavery held most government posts

(3) the Democratic party was dominant

(4) civil rights issues were strongly supported

7 Which statement best describes a major economic trend in the United States during the period from 1865 to 1900?

(1) Many business practices were developed to eliminate competition.

(2) Workers determined working conditions and factory output.

(3) The gross national product decreased steadily.

(4) Basic industries were taken over by the government.

8 An important result of industrialization in the United States was a growth in the

(1) influence of small family-owned businesses

(2) idea of socialism as the main political philosophy

(3) power of large corporations

(4) political power of small farmers

9 The Interstate Commerce Act, Sherman Antitrust Act, and Clayton Antitrust Act were attempts to limit

(1) business competition

(2) labor unions

(3) monopolies

(4) tariffs

10 Which factor that contributed to the economic growth of the United States in the period from 1865 to 1920 aroused the most opposition?

(1) growth of rapid transportation

(2) existence of democratic government

(3) mechanization of agriculture

(4) liberal immigration policies

11 Between 1865 and 1900, an issue that dominated national politics in the United States was

(1) slavery

(2) the rise of big business

(3) sectionalism

(4) environmental protection

12 During the second half of the nineteenth century, a major goal of new types of business organizations was to

(1) introduce safer and less expensive products to consumers

(2) consolidate the manufacture and distribution of products

(3) support the large number of government regulations

(4) compete successfully with Japanese imports

Base your answers to questions 13 and 14 on the chart below and on your knowledge of social studies.

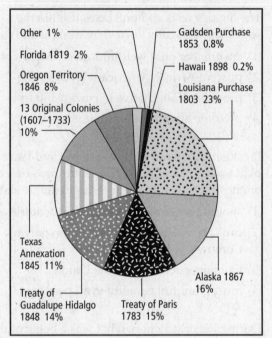

**American Territorial Growth**
(as a percentage of present United States territory)

13 Which territorial gain accounted for the largest increase in United States land growth?

(1) Treaty of Guadalupe Hidalgo

(2) Texas Annexation

(3) Louisiana Purchase

(4) purchase of Alaska

14 Which policy is best illustrated by the chart?

(1) isolationism

(2) manifest destiny

(3) containment

(4) globalization

**15** "[Buffalo hunters] have done more in the last two years, and will do more in the next year, to settle the . . . Indian question than the entire regular army has done in the last thirty years. . . . For the sake of peace let them kill, skin, and sell until the buffalo are destroyed."

—General Philip Sheridan

What was the result of the process described in this quotation?

(1) Native Americans were granted farmland under the Homestead Act.

(2) The disappearance of their economic base helped drive Native Americans onto reservations.

(3) Many Native Americans moved to eastern cities to work in factories.

(4) Most Native Americans migrated to Canada to find new ways to earn a living.

**16** "I am tired of fighting. . . . Hear me, my chiefs. I am tired. My heart is sick and sad. From where the sun now stands, I shall fight no more forever!"

—Chief Joseph, 1877

In this statement, Chief Joseph of the Nez Percé expressed his reluctant acceptance of a government policy of

(1) placing Native American tribes on reservations

(2) requiring Native Americans to settle west of the Mississippi River

(3) granting immediate citizenship to Native Americans

(4) forcing Native Americans to assimilate into American culture

Base your answer to question 17 on the graph below and on your knowledge of social studies.

**Farm and Non-farm Workers 1860–1900**

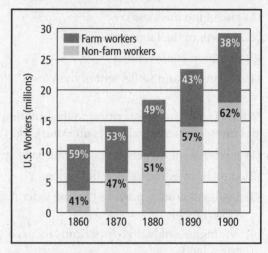

**17** Which development contributed most to the trends shown in this graph?

(1) industrialization

(2) westward migration

(3) commercial revolution

(4) trade restrictions

**18** A pioneer wanting to settle in the West in the 1870s would have benefited most from the

(1) Homestead Act

(2) Sherman Antitrust Act

(3) Interstate Commerce Act

(4) Agricultural Adjustment Act

**19** Unlike other minorities in the United States, Native Americans have some of their rights guaranteed by

(1) the Emancipation Proclamation

(2) treaties with the federal government

(3) the Declaration of Independence

(4) black codes

20 A belief in Manifest Destiny, the passage of the Dawes Act, and the completion of the transcontinental railroad are most closely associated with the

(1) rise of big business
(2) growth of the labor movement
(3) abolitionist movement
(4) expansion and settlement of the West

21 Which factor was most critical to the building of the transcontinental railroads after the Civil War?

(1) government ownership of the railroads
(2) capital investments by labor unions
(3) land and money provided by the federal government
(4) willingness of Native Americans to leave tribal lands

22 During the late 1800s, the growing of cash crops by an increasingly large number of farmers resulted in

(1) greater isolation of farmers from American economic life
(2) a shift from self-sufficiency to commercial farming
(3) less food available for export
(4) general economic prosperity for all farmers

23 As the United States became industrialized, an important effect of mechanization and the division of labor was that

(1) smaller industries had difficulty maintaining their competitiveness
(2) the price of most manufactured goods increased
(3) the demand to improve transportation systems decreased
(4) pools and trusts became less efficient forms of business organization

24 In the late 1800s, most strikes by unions were unsuccessful mainly because

(1) unions were generally considered to be unconstitutional
(2) government usually supported business instead of workers
(3) strikes had never been used before in labor disputes
(4) strikers failed to use militant tactics

25 The poll tax, the literacy test, and the actions of the Ku Klux Klan were all attempts to limit the effectiveness of

(1) the fourteenth and fifteenth amendments
(2) the Supreme Court's decision in *Brown* v. *Board of Education*
(3) civil rights legislation passed in all states after the Civil War
(4) immigration laws such as the Chinese Exclusion Act

26 The Rockefeller Foundation, Carnegie Hall, and the Morgan Library illustrate various ways that entrepreneurs and their descendants have

(1) suppressed the growth of labor unions
(2) supported philanthropic activities to benefit society
(3) applied scientific discoveries to industry
(4) attempted to undermine the United States economic system

27 The major reason the United States placed few restrictions on immigration during the early 1800s was that

(1) few Europeans wished to give up their economic security
(2) little opposition to immigration existed
(3) the growing economy needed a steady supply of cheap labor
(4) most immigrants spoke English and thus needed little or no education

# Thematic Essay Question

**Directions:** Write a well-organized essay that includes an introduction, several paragraphs addressing the task below, and a conclusion.

**Theme:** Industrialization

> The growth of industry in the nineteenth century had a major impact on many aspects of American society.

**Task:**

> Identify any *three* aspects of American society and for *each*.
>
> - Use specific examples to discuss how the growth of industry had an impact on that aspect of society.
> - Evaluate whether the role of industrialization had a positive or a negative effect and explain your reasoning using specific historic examples.

You may use any examples from your study of industrialization in the United States. Some suggestions you might wish to consider include: rise of organized labor, government involvement in the economy, status of the farmer, urbanization, or the role of women.

**You are *not* limited to these suggestions.**

**Guidelines:**

**In your essay, be sure to:**
- Develop all aspects of the task
- Support the theme with relevant facts, examples, and details
- Use a logical and clear plan of organization, including an introduction and a conclusion that are beyond a simple restatement of the theme

**In developing your answer, be sure to keep this general definition in mind:**

> **<u>discuss</u> means "to make observations about something using facts, reasoning, and argument; to present in some detail"**

# Document-Based Question

In developing your answers, be sure to keep this general definition in mind:

> discuss means "to make observations about something using facts, reasoning, and argument; to present in some detail"

This question is based on the accompanying documents. The question is designed to test your ability to work with historical documents. Some of the documents have been edited for the purposes of the question. As you analyze the documents, take into account the source of each document and any point of view that may be presented in the document.

**Historical Context:**

Extensive railroad construction in the 1800s transformed the United States by linking sections of the nation. This transformation had both positive and negative effects.

**Task:**   Using information from the documents and your knowledge of United States history, answer the questions that follow each document in Part A. Your answers to the questions will help you write the Part B essay, in which you will be asked to:

- Discuss the positive and negative effects of railroads in the United States during the 1800s

**Part A: Short Answer Questions**

*Directions:*    Analyze the documents and answer the short-answer questions that follow each document in the space provided.

### Document #1

*For half a century after Lewis and Clark's expedition, the Great Plains aroused little interest in the young nation. The plains were too dry for agriculture, people said. They were barren, forever a wasteland at the center of the continent. These ideas began to change in the years leading up to the Civil War. As the railroads were built westward, Americans realized how wrong they had been about the plains. Settlers in Kansas found no desert, but millions of acres of fertile soil. Cattlemen saw an open range for millions of cattle, a land of opportunity larger than even the Lone Star State. Of course, the plains were already inhabited by buffalo and Indians. But these meant little to the newcomers. Civilization, they believed, demanded that both be swept away and the land turned to "useful" purposes. How this came about is one of the saddest chapters in our history. . . .*

**Source: Albert Marrin, *Cowboys, Indians, and Gunfighters*, Atheneum**

1. According to this passage, how did the use of the railroads change people's opinions about the Great Plains?

_____

_____

### Document #2

*It was with a shock of abhorrence, therefore, that they discovered in 1871 the presence of railroad surveyors running a line through the valley of the Yellowstone. With Sitting Bull's approval, the young warriors immediately began a campaign of harassment, first letting the intruders know that they were not wanted there, and then driving them away. The reason the surveyors had come into this area was that the owners of the Northern Pacific Railroad had decided to change its route, abandoning the line through previously ceded lands and invading unceded lands without any consultation with the Indians. In 1872, the surveyors accompanied by a small military force came back to the Yellowstone country, and again Sitting Bull's followers drove them away. . .*

**Source: Dee Brown, *Hear That Lonesome Whistle Blow*, Henry Holt and Co.**

2. According to this document, why were Native American Indians hostile to the surveyors?

_____

_____

**Document #3**

3. What does this illustration show about the effect of the railroads on the buffalo herds?

_____

_____

_____

_____

## Document #4

*If nineteenth-century Monterey County owed much to the coming of the railroads, Santa Cruz County owed everything, for railroads constructed during the 1870s tied together the isolated communities along the north coast of Monterey Bay and launched an era of unparalleled development. . . .*

*Between 1875 and 1880 the Chinese built three separate railroads, laid forty-two miles of track, and drilled 2.6 miles of tunnels to stitch Santa Cruz County together and attach it permanently to the world beyond the Santa Cruz Mountains. The Chinese contributed not only their muscle and sweat, but their lives. At least fifty Chinese were killed in accidents while building those railroads. For every mile of railroad, one Chinese died. . . .*

*Chinese railroad workers on the Santa Cruz Railroad worked six ten-hour days a week and were paid one dollar a day. Two dollars per week was deducted from their pay for food, while expenses such as clothing and recreation chipped away at the remaining four dollars so that they averaged three dollars per week profit. . . .*

**Source: Sandy Lydon, *Chinese Gold: The Chinese in the Monterey Bay Region,*
Capitola Book Company**

4.  (a) According to this document, how did railroad development help Monterey and Santa Cruz counties?

_____

_____


   (b) Based on this document, state one working condition the Chinese experienced as they built the railroads.

_____

_____

## Document #5

Rich Farming Lands!

For Sale VERY CHEAP by the

## Union Pacific Railroad Company

The Best Investment! No Fluctuations!
Always Improving in Value.

The Wealth of the Country is made by the advance
in Real Estate.

NOW IS THE TIME!

### MILLIONS OF ACRES

Of the finest lands on the Continent, in Eastern
Nebraska, now for sale, Many of them never before
in Market, at prices that Defy Competition.

FIVE AND TEN YEARS' CREDIT GIVEN, WITH
INTEREST AT SIX PER CENT.

The Land Grant Bonds of the Company taken at par
for lands. ➞ Full particulars given, new Guide with
new Maps mailed free.

### THE PIONEER

A handsome illustrated paper, containing the
Homestead Law, sent free to all parts of the world.
Address

O.F. DAVIS,
Land Commissioner U.P.R.R.,
Omaha, Neb.

*—nineteenth-century broadside (adapted)*

5. According to the suggestions in this advertisement, how did railroads encourage settlement of the West?

_____

_____

_____

_____

**Document #6**

> ... That year (1877) there came a series of tumultuous strikes by railroad workers in a dozen cities; they shook the nation as no labor conflict in its history had done.
>
> It began with wage cuts on railroad after railroad, in tense situations of already low wages ($1.75 a day for brakemen working twelve hours), scheming and profiteering by the railroad companies, deaths and injuries among the workers— loss of hands, feet, fingers, the crushing of men between cars.
>
> At the Baltimore & Ohio station in Martinsburg, West Virginia, workers determined to fight the wage cut went on strike, uncoupled the engines, ran them into the roundhouse, and announced no more trains would leave Martinsburg until the 10 percent cut [in pay] was canceled. A crowd of support gathered, too many for the local police to disperse. B. & O. officials asked the governor for military protection, and he sent in militia. A train tried to get through, protected by the militia, and a striker, trying to derail it, exchanged gunfire with a militiaman attempting to stop him. The striker was shot in his thigh and his arm. His arm was amputated later that day, and nine days later he died.
>
> Six hundred freight trains now jammed the yards at Martinsburg. The West Virginia governor applied to newly elected President Rutherford Hayes for federal troops, saying the state militia was insufficient. In fact, the militia was not totally reliable, being composed of many railroad workers. Much of the U.S. Army was tied up in Indian battles in the West. Congress had not appropriated money for the army yet, but J. P. Morgan, August Belmont, and other bankers now offered to lend money to pay army officers (but no enlisted men). Federal troops arrived in Martinsburg, and the freight cars began to move. ...
>
> **Source: Howard Zinn, *A People's History of the United States*,**
> **Harper Collins Publishers**

6. According to this passage, why did the railroad workers go on strike in 1877?

_____

_____

_____

_____

### Document #7

*The policy which has been pursued has given us [the United States] the most efficient railway service and the lowest rates known in the world; but its recognized benefits have been attained at the cost of the most unwarranted discriminations, and its effect has been to build up the strong at the expense of the weak, to give the large dealer an advantage over the small trader, to make capital count for more than individual credit and enterprise, to concentrate business at great commercial centers, to necessitate combinations and aggregations of capital, to foster monopoly, to encourage the growth and extend the influence of corporate power, and to throw the control of the commerce of the country more and more into the hands of the few. . . .*

**Source: United States Senate, Select Committee on Interstate Commerce, 1886**

7. According to this document, how did the railroad owners engage in unfair business practices?

_____

_____

_____

_____

## Document #8

*We believe that the time has come when the railroad corporations will either own the people or the people must own the railroads; and, should the government enter upon the work of owning and managing all railroads, we should favor an amendment to the Constitution by which all persons engaged in the government service shall be placed under a civil service regulation of the most rigid character, so as to prevent the increase of the power of the national administration by the use of such additional government employees. . . . Transportation, being a means of exchange and a public necessity, the government should own and operate the railroads in the interest of the people. . . .*

**Source: Populist Party Platform, 1892**

8. According to the Populist Party platform, why should the government own the railroads?

_____

_____

_____

_____

# Document-Based Question

## Part B

### Essay

*Directions:* Write a well-organized essay that includes an introduction, several paragraphs, and a conclusion. Use evidence from at least **five** documents in the body of the essay. Support your response with relevant facts, examples, and details. Include additional outside information.

**Historical Context:**

> Extensive railroad construction in the 1800s transformed the United States by linking sections of the nation. This transformation had both positive and negative effects.

**Task:**

> Using information from the documents and your knowledge of United States history, write an essay in which you

---

- Discuss the positive and negative effects of railroads in the United States during the 1800s

---

**Guidelines:**

> **In your essay, be sure to:**
> - Address all aspects of the task by accurately analyzing and interpreting at least *five* documents
> - Incorporate information from the documents in the body of the essay
> - Incorporate relevant outside information
> - Support the theme with relevant facts, examples, and details
> - Use a logical and clear plan of organization
> - Introduce the theme by establishing a framework that is beyond a simple restatement of the *Task* or *Historical Context* and conclude with a summation of the theme

# The Progressive Movement:
## Responses to the Challenges Brought About by Industrialization and Urbanization

**Section 1:** Reform in America

**Section 2:** The Rise of American Power

## Unit Overview

Between the end of the Civil War and the turn of the twentieth century, the United States became a more industrialized and urbanized nation. These changes brought many benefits to society, but they created problems as well. In this unit, you will review how Americans responded to change, both at home and overseas, in the years from 1900 to 1920. This period is called the Progressive Era. The term comes from the word "progress" and indicates that Americans were reacting to problems by working for reform.

Some key questions to help you focus on the Progressive Era include:

* What were the pressures for reform that led to the Progressive movement?
* Who were the Progressives? What were their goals?
* How successful were the Progressives in meeting their goals?
* What were the causes of increased international involvement of the United States from 1890 to 1920?
* What were the effects of this involvement on the United States and other peoples around the world?

# Reform in America

The
**Big Idea**

The Progressive Era
was a period of reform
movements during which:

• Progressives promoted
political, economic, and
social reform.

• reforms were made
at the city, state, and
national levels.

• Progressive presidents
championed reform
nationwide.

• Progressive reforms laid
the groundwork for
future success.

## Section Overview

From the 1890s to 1920, a reform movement swept the nation as many people focused their energies on domestic reform, on improving conditions within the United States. The Progressive movement was made up of groups and individuals who worked to change the negative effects of industrialization and urbanization in the United States. Three Progressive presidents—Theodore Roosevelt, William Howard Taft, and Woodrow Wilson—implemented bold domestic reform programs at the national level.

## Key Themes and Concepts

As you review this section, take special note of the following key themes and concepts:

**Reform Movements** What conditions stirred Progressive reformers to action?

**Diversity** How did women and African Americans work for their own rights during the Progressive Era, and how successful were they?

**Environment** What environmental protections began in the Progressive Era?

**Government** What role did the government play in Progressive reform?

**Civic Values** In what ways were democratic values expanded by the Progressives?

**Culture and Intellectual Life** What social and moral changes did Progressives promote, and by what means?

**Science and Technology** What role did science and technology play in both creating and solving the problems the Progressives confronted?

## Key People

As you review this section, be sure you understand the significance of these key people:

| | | |
|---|---|---|
| Upton Sinclair | Margaret Sanger | Theodore Roosevelt |
| Jacob Riis | Booker T. Washington | Gifford Pinchot |
| Jane Addams | W.E.B. Du Bois | John Muir |
| Lincoln Steffens | Marcus Garvey | William Howard Taft |
| Carrie Chapman Catt | Ida B. Wells-Barnett | Woodrow Wilson |
| Alice Paul | Robert M. La Follette | |

# Key Terms

Progressive Era

muckrakers

prohibition

suffrage

initiative

referendum

recall

direct primary

direct election of senators

Square Deal

consumer protection

trust-busting

conservation

New Nationalism

New Freedom

graduated income tax

Federal Reserve System

## Preparing for the Exam

Movements can be traced throughout history. In Unit 2 you reviewed the birth of the American reform tradition. For the exam, you may need to identify and understand the different periods of reform in United States history.

- The Populists preceded the Progressives in the late nineteenth- and early twentieth-century reform movements.

- Reform continued under the New Deal of the 1930s and the period of reform in the 1960s.

# Key Supreme Court Cases

As you review this section, be sure you understand the significance of these key Supreme Court cases:

*Lochner* v. *New York* (1905)

*Muller* v. *Oregon* (1908)

*Northern Securities Co.* v. *United States* (1904)

# Pressures for Progressive Reform

By 1900, the United States was a rich and powerful nation. Industrialization, urbanization, and immigration had transformed the nation into a major world economy. The changes in American life, however, also brought problems. The Progressives' call for reform, which led to a period of time known as the **Progressive Era,** was a reaction to:

- powerful monopolies restricting competition and controlling prices.
- labor unrest and violence.
- unhealthy and unsafe living and working conditions.
- increasing gap between living standards of the rich and the poor.
- urban poverty, crime, congestion, and poor sanitation.
- political corruption and lack of government responsiveness.
- abuse of the nation's natural resources.

## Analyzing Documents

Using the information in this section and the timeline, answer the following questions.

- During whose presidency was the Supreme Court case *Lochner* v. *New York* (1905) decided?

- Which event on the timeline involved the creation of an organization that worked for the rights of African Americans?

- How did Sinclair's *The Jungle* lead to reform?

## Reform During the Progressive Era, 1901–1916

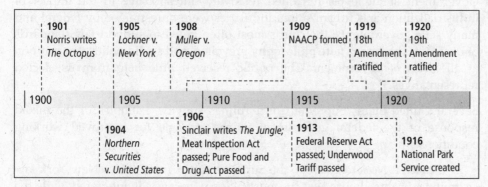

| 1901 | 1905 | 1908 | 1909 | 1919 | 1920 |
|---|---|---|---|---|---|
| Norris writes *The Octopus* | *Lochner* v. *New York* | *Muller* v. *Oregon* | NAACP formed | 18th Amendment ratified | 19th Amendment ratified |

1904 — *Northern Securities* v. *United States*

1906 — Sinclair writes *The Jungle*; Meat Inspection Act passed; Pure Food and Drug Act passed

1913 — Federal Reserve Act passed; Underwood Tariff passed

1916 — National Park Service created

## Effects of Business Practices

The corporate world grew increasingly wealthy and more powerful. Industrial leaders believed that economic success demonstrated fitness to lead, that Social Darwinism explained why some were rich and others were poor. Those who

## Geography
### in History

Some urban problems persist over time, while others arise as society develops. When answering the following questions, consider concerns in urban areas, such as waste disposal, water and air pollution, energy usage, and congestion.

- Which urban problems at the beginning of the 20th century continue to be problems today?

- What new problems have arisen?

### Key Themes and Concepts

**Government**
Two landmark Supreme Court cases that dealt with state laws limiting the number of working hours were *Lochner* v. *New York* (1905) and *Muller* v. *Oregon* (1908).

*"There is no reasonable ground for interfering with the liberty of a person or the right of free contract by determining the hours of labor . . . Clean and wholesome bread does not depend upon whether the baker works but ten hours per day or only sixty hours per week. . . ."*
—*Lochner* v. *New York* (1905)

- What seems to be the position of the Court on Progressive reform?

- How does the Court's action compare with the Supreme Court's decisions during the New Deal?

succeeded earned their position, and those who failed deserved their failure. Social Darwinists believed that the government should not intervene in this process, a belief consistent with the ideas of laissez faire economics.

## Conditions for Industrial Workers

Working conditions for factory workers continued to be harsh. Many laborers worked 60-hour weeks on machinery, often in unsafe, unhealthy conditions. Getting hurt on the job often resulted in the worker being fired. Workers earned low wages, and women and children were paid even less than male workers. Workers had little security because their employers could fire them at any time.

Soon, workers grew less tolerant of these terrible working conditions. Some tried to organize labor unions, but employers often fired those who did. Strikes were met with armed attacks from factory security guards and sometimes even federal troops.

## Life for the Urban Poor

The gap between living standards of the rich and the poor increased widely during this period. This gap was most apparent in the cities. As the rich grew richer, building lavish townhouses in relatively safe and clean neighborhoods, the poor grew even poorer. They lived in urban slums characterized by poverty, crime, congestion, and poor sanitation. Housing in the cities was segregated by social and economic status, by race, and often by ethnic background.

An elevated train in New York City

## Mixed Response of Government at All Levels

Government at all levels remained relatively unresponsive to the impact of industrialization and urbanization. Industries were unrestrained by federal and many state governments; the courts most often failed to support fair standards of business. The laissez faire philosophy prevailed, and so did political corruption at all levels of government. The public received little help from its elected representatives.

Several United States Supreme Court rulings provide examples of the mixed response of the federal government in the struggle for improved working conditions:

- In *Lochner* v. *New York* (1905), the Supreme Court ruled that a New York law limiting bakers' hours was unconstitutional because it interfered with the contract between employer and employee.

- In *Muller* v. *Oregon* (1908), the Court let stand an Oregon law limiting women to a ten-hour work day, ruling that the law was justified because it protected women's health. The effect of laws like this, however, was to keep women out of better paying jobs.

# Who Were the Progressives?

The Progressives set out to tackle the problems of their era. They did not form one single group. The Progressive movement was made up of many different movements, and the Progressives were many different kinds of Americans. Their commitment and their success varied from person to person and from cause to cause. They did have some things in common, however.

## Characteristics

The Progressives were influenced by the Populists but differed from them. While the Populists lived in the country or in small towns, the Progressives were largely city dwellers. Most of the Populists were farmers, who focused on farm problems. The Progressives tended to be educated professionals—doctors, lawyers, social workers, clergy, and teachers—with a wide range of concerns. The Progressive movement demonstrated the rising power and influence of America's middle class.

## Beliefs and Goals

Like all reformers, the Progressives were optimists. They believed that abuses of power by government and business could be ended. They believed that new developments in technology and science could be used to improve the basic institutions of American society—business, government, education, and family life. Progressives believed in capitalism and were concerned about the growth of socialism as a more radical reaction to the effects of industrialization. Progressives wanted to bypass party politics, which they saw as corrupt, but they had faith that a strong government could and should correct abuses and protect rights.

Not all Americans were Progressives or agreed with Progressive goals. Many business and political leaders opposed business regulation. They accepted the Social Darwinists' view that the vast differences in wealth and power in American society were the result of scientific forces that could not be changed. Many workers and farmers did not benefit from Progressive reform, nor did most African Americans, Asian immigrants, and Native Americans.

## Factors Aiding the Movement

Many Progressives worked with national voluntary organizations, which grew rapidly in the 1890s. The movement was centered in cities at a time when more of the population was living in cities. This helped communication among Progressives, as did the expanding telephone and telegraph systems. The availability of inexpensive mass-circulation magazines and newspapers also helped spread Progressive ideas. Finally, the Progressives were aided by an improved economy. The first decade of the twentieth century brought prosperity. Industrial profits, wages, and employment all rose; farmers thrived. The result was an optimistic climate and the financial resources to support reform.

# Progress Toward Social and Economic Reform and Consumer Protection

A wide variety of reform movements developed from the 1890s to the 1920s.

## The Muckrakers and Reform

**Muckrakers** helped bring reform issues to the attention of the public. Most were journalists and writers, but others were artists and photographers. Muckrakers investigated and exposed corruption and injustice through articles in mass-circulation magazines. They also wrote novels dramatizing situations that demanded reform.

## Geography in History

Throughout history, the middle class has developed with the growth of cities built around trade, commerce, and industry.

## Reading Strategy

**Organizing Information** As you review each of the reform movements of the Progressive Era, make lists comparing and contrasting the characteristics of each reform movement.

Causes:

Goals:

Leadership:

Influence:

Degree of success achieved:

## Key Themes and Concepts

- In what ways were the Progressive Era reform movements a continuation of the reform movement in the first half of the nineteenth century?

- How was Progressive Era reform different?

In 1906, the work of the muckrakers resulted in the passage of the Pure Food and Drug Act and the Meat Inspection Act—the first two acts of consumer protection legislation. The federal government passed these laws after it became clear that the unsanitary conditions exposed by Upton Sinclair's novel *The Jungle* were based on fact.

As time passed, the muckrakers' influence declined, partly because readers tired of their sensationalism. Nevertheless, their tradition has continued to the present day.

### Progressive Era Muckrakers

| Muckraker | Book/Article | Subject of Exposé |
|---|---|---|
| Frank Norris | *The Octopus* (1901) | monopolistic railroad practices in California |
| Ida Tarbell | *History of the Standard Oil Company* (1904) | ruthless practices of Standard Oil Company |
| Lincoln Steffens | *The Shame of the Cities* (1906) | political corruption in city government |
| Jacob Riis | *How the Other Half Lives* (1890) | conditions of the poor in New York's tenements |
| Upton Sinclair | *The Jungle* (1906) | dangerous and unsanitary conditions in meatpacking industry |

**Culture and Intellectual Life**
Media has played an investigative role at various times in United States history. Newspaper, radio, and television journalists provide a different view in order to balance that of governments, corporations, and other sources of power.

The muckraking tradition continued long after the Progressive Era. The publication by *The New York Times* of the Pentagon Papers and the reporting of the Watergate scandal by Bob Woodward and Carl Bernstein in *The Washington Post* are two late twentieth-century examples of the muckraking tradition.

• What are some current examples of investigative reporting on government or corporations using television or the Internet?

• What is the difference between investigative reporting and sensationalism in the media?

## Other Areas of Concern

Other people and groups also worked to bring Progressive reforms to American society.

**Problems of Poverty** Attempts to end the poverty, crowding, and disease in American cities began before 1900. Once the germ theory of disease was accepted, cities put more effort into improving water and sewage systems. A well-known urban reformer was Jacob Riis, who used writings and photographs to show the need for better housing for the poor. Some Protestant church leaders became part of the Social Gospel movement, which worked to help poor city dwellers. One goal of urban reformers was building codes that would require safer, better-lighted, better-ventilated, and more sanitary tenements.

**Social Settlement Movement** One early group of Progressive urban reformers was the settlement-house workers. Settlement houses, located in working-class slums, offered people—especially immigrants—education, child care, social activities, and help in finding jobs. Well-known settlement houses included Hull House in Chicago, founded by Jane Addams, and the Henry Street Settlement in New York City, founded by Lillian Wald.

**The Peace Movement** Addams and Wald were among the Americans who led peace groups, such as the Woman's Peace Party, in the period before and during World War I. Support of pacifism—the policy of opposition to war and fighting—weakened with America's entry into World War I in 1917 but was later revived. Pacifist Jeannette Rankin, the first woman elected to Congress (1916), voted against the entry of the United States entry into World War I (and World War II as well). For her pacifist efforts, Jane Addams won the Nobel Peace Prize in 1931.

**Temperance and Prohibition** The temperance movement, which opposed the use of alcoholic beverages, began in the 1820s. Over the years, its chief goal became **prohibition**—outlawing the manufacture and sale of alcoholic beverages. Under the leadership of Frances Willard, the Woman's Christian Temperance Union (WCTU), founded in 1874, was a strong advocate of prohibition. Its members included many Populists and Progressives. It joined with the Anti-Saloon League, and the two groups sought moral reform through prohibition. They believed that through prohibition, problems of poverty and disease could be eased, family life improved, and the national economy made more productive. The temperance

**Reading
Strategy**

**Analyzing Cause and Effect**
Use the text and the chart above to answer this question.

• What effect did the work of each muckraker have on Progressive reform?

crusade led to national prohibition with the adoption of the Eighteenth Amendment, which banned the manufacture, sale, and transportation of alcoholic beverages in the United States as of 1920.

**Child Labor** The National Child Labor Committee was formed in 1904 to rouse public opinion against child labor. The committee recognized the courts' opposition to child labor legislation as expressed in the Supreme Court's "freedom to contract" verdict in *Lochner* v. *New York* (1905) but successfully lobbied the federal government to create a Federal Children's Bureau (1912) to investigate child labor and pressured most states to set minimum wages and maximum hours for children. As a result of state laws and compulsory school attendance, by 1920 11.3 percent of children ages 10 to 15 were working, down from 18.2 percent in 1900.

## Women's Rights

Women were involved in all aspects of social reform, but **suffrage** for women continued to be the main goal of the women's rights movement in the Progressive Era. Women who had experienced success in other reform activities wanted to be able to vote. Furthermore, many suffragists thought that the women's vote would serve to correct various social problems.

**Women's Suffrage Movement** The women's suffrage movement began as part of a larger drive for women's rights in 1848 at Seneca Falls, New York. The intellectual leader was Elizabeth Cady Stanton, author of the Declaration of Sentiments. She was joined in the 1850s by Susan B. Anthony, who provided the driving leadership of the movement. In the 1860s, the women's suffrage movement split over the best way to achieve its goals. The more radical organization was led by Stanton and Anthony; the more moderate organization was headed by Lucy Stone and her husband Henry Blackwell. In 1890, the groups merged to form the National American Woman Suffrage Association (NAWSA).

Stanton died in 1902, and Anthony died in 1906, without achieving the objective of their life work. However, the Progressive spirit gave the movement a new surge. In the early 1900s, leadership of NAWSA and the campaign passed to Carrie Chapman Catt, who devised the strategy that was to secure women the vote. She concentrated on achieving the vote for women by a constitutional amendment while coordinating the national effort with a state-by-state movement to put more pressure on Congress and build grassroots support for ratification when the time came. NAWSA swelled to two million members.

**Reading Strategy**

**Reading for Evidence** Based on the information in the section "Women's Suffrage Movement," answer the following questions.

- How did suffragists change their tactics over time?

- What finally resulted in women winning the right to vote?

**Geography in History**

- Why is it significant that this map is dated 1920?

- In what region of the nation did women first receive the right to vote?

- In what regions did they have partial suffrage?

- What relationship is there between the pattern of suffrage and the pattern of migration and settlement of the states?

- What might explain that pattern?

### Women's Suffrage Before 1920

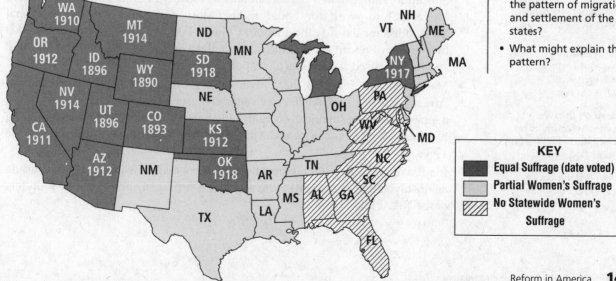

**KEY**
- Equal Suffrage (date voted)
- Partial Women's Suffrage
- No Statewide Women's Suffrage

## Key Themes and Concepts

### Civic Values

*"The right of citizens of the United States to vote shall not be denied or abridged by the United States or by any state on account of sex."*
—Section 1, Nineteenth Amendment

- Whose rights does this amendment protect?

- What are the other important steps in U.S. history in the extension of the right to vote?

## Key Themes and Concepts

### Diversity

A far-reaching debate among African Americans over goals and tactics took place between Booker T. Washington and W.E.B. Du Bois.

*". . . agitation of questions of social equality is of the extremest folly, and . . . progress in the enjoyment of all privileges that will come to us must be the result of severe and constant struggle rather than artificial forcing."*
—Booker T. Washington

*"I am resolved to be quiet and law abiding, but to refuse to cringe in body or soul, to resent deliberate insult, and to assert my just rights in the face of wanton aggression."*
—W.E.B. Du Bois

- Based on the two quotes, what belief do Washington and Du Bois share?

- What differences of opinion do they have?

Alice Paul led the more militant Congressional Union until she was expelled from NAWSA. She then formed the National Woman's Party. Paul alienated many women by her use of militant tactics and her campaigning against Woodrow Wilson for reelection in 1916. In the end, it was the highly visible activity of women during World War I that brought them the final public support needed. In 1920, the Nineteenth Amendment was ratified, giving women the right to vote.

**Education for Women** Another sign of women's progress was the growth of educational opportunities. Among women's colleges founded in the late 1800s were Vassar (1861), Wellesley (1870), and Smith (1871). State universities set up under the Morrill Act of 1862 were coeducational. By the early 1900s, one third of those attending college were women.

**The Fight for Birth Control** The women's movement also included a campaign for family planning through birth control. This campaign was led by Margaret Sanger, who began her work as a nurse caring for poor immigrant women in New York City. The American Birth Control League founded by Sanger later became the Planned Parenthood Federation. Sanger's movement was very controversial. She was arrested several times for sending information about contraception through the mail.

## The Rights of African Americans

The decades following the Civil War were a difficult time for African Americans. Laws prevented them from exercising their right to vote. In *Plessy* v. *Ferguson* (1896), the Supreme Court upheld the Jim Crow laws, which required segregated—"separate but equal"—public facilities for African Americans and whites. Lynchings by white mobs killed hundreds of African Americans.

Key African American leaders who worked to secure their people's rights are described below.

- Booker T. Washington, a former slave and founder of Tuskegee Institute, urged African Americans to get vocational training in order to establish themselves economically. This strategy, he believed, would increase their self-esteem and earn them respect from white society. Washington's policy, called accommodation, was expressed in an 1895 speech known as the Atlanta Compromise.

- W.E.B. Du Bois, a Harvard-educated professor, shared Washington's view of the importance of education but rejected accommodation. He felt that African Americans should protest unfair treatment and receive a broad, liberal education, rather than a vocational one. In 1905, Du Bois founded the Niagara Movement to work for equal rights. More successful was the National Association for the Advancement of Colored People (NAACP), started in 1909 by a group of reformers that included Du Bois and Jane Addams. The NAACP successfully used lawsuits as a weapon on behalf of civil rights.

- Marcus Garvey founded the Universal Negro Improvement Association, an African American nationalist and separatist group, in 1914. The group wanted a separate African American economy and urged African Americans to emigrate to Africa. Many of Garvey's ideas influenced the Black Power Movement of the 1960s.

- Ida B. Wells-Barnett was a journalist who launched a lifelong national crusade against lynching in the 1890s. She was also a suffragist and one of the founders of the NAACP.

### Rights of Others Facing Discrimination

In 1913, a group of American Jews established the Anti-Defamation League, an agency of the Jewish service organization B'nai B'rith ("Sons of the Covenant"), which had been founded in 1843. The Anti-Defamation League worked mainly to combat defamation, or libel and slander, directed against Jews. Later, its program was broadened to aim at securing the civil liberties of all Americans.

## Progressivism and Government Action

During the Progressive Era, political reform took place at all levels of government— city, state, and national.

### Reform of City Government

Given the Progressives' urban, middle-class roots, it is not surprising that they first concentrated their efforts on the governments of the cities in which they lived and in which they were influential citizens. They attacked political machines where they controlled government at the city and state levels, condemning practices such as accepting bribes in return for favors. In the 1890s, Americans interested in good government worked to elect reformist mayors. Success in doing so, however, did not always ensure permanent improvement. Progressives had to change not only the leader, but also the way city government worked.

Two new types of city government are associated with the Progressive movement. They were popular in small and medium-sized cities. In the city commissioner plan, the city is run by a group of commissioners, rather than by a mayor and city council. In the city manager plan, the city council hires a professional city manager to run the various municipal departments.

### Progressives Respond to Urban Problems

While some Progressives concentrated not only on making city governments more efficient and less corrupt, architects and city planners tried to improve the appearance of cities by constructing large, elaborate libraries, museums, and other public buildings. Progressive engineers recognized that the sudden and rapid growth of cities called for redesigning and improving needed city services such as sanitation, street lighting, and the water system. Still others worked to regulate these and other utilities or even turn them into publicly owned facilities.

### Reform of State Government

Progressives also acted to limit the power of boss-controlled political machines and powerful business interests at the state level. Progressives recognized that states exercised control over many of their cities. Extension of reform to the state, even the national level, was necessary to protect any gains made at the municipal level.

Progressive reforms often proved difficult to enforce, meeting opposition from business interests and the courts. Thus, changes in the way state governments worked were also part of the Progressive program. These changes, aimed at increasing citizen participation in government, included the following:

- The secret, or Australian, ballot lessens the chance of intimidation because it prevents party bosses (and anyone else) from knowing how people vote.
- The **initiative** is a system that allows voters to petition the legislature to consider a proposed law.
- In a **referendum,** voters, not the legislature, decide whether a given bill or constitutional amendment should be passed.

**Reading Strategy**

**Organizing Information**
To help you understand the various reforms at the city, state, and federal levels, create a chart that outlines the major reforms made at each level.

**Key Themes and Concepts**

**Government**
- Which do you consider the most important of the changes to increase citizen participation in government? Why?

- Has direct election stopped undue influence on U.S. senators?

- How have initiative and referendum been used by a special interest group?

- How has the direct primary changed the way in which we select a president?

- **Recall** is a form of petition used by voters to force elected officials out of office.
- A **direct primary** allows voters, rather than party leaders, to select the candidates who will run for office. In recent years the number of state convention delegates elected by a direct primary has increased to the point that the party's presidential nominee is known well before the national convention is held.
- Ratified in 1913, the Seventeenth Amendment provided for the direct election-election by the people-of United States senators. Up to this time senators had been elected by state legislatures, which were often controlled by corporations or political bosses.

Remember that the secret ballot, initiative, referendum, and **direct election of senators** were all parts of the Populist party program. Adoption of these reforms offers an example of how third parties can influence major parties.

## State Social, Economic, and Environmental Reforms

Wisconsin, under Governor Robert M. La Follette, was the model for Progressive reform. The State passed laws to regulate railroads, lobbying, and banking. It also started civil service reforms, shifted more of the tax burden to the wealthy and to corporations, required employers to compensate workers injured on the job, and provided for factory inspections.

Several other states passed laws like those of Wisconsin. In 1912 Massachusetts became the first state to pass a minimum wage law. Leading Progressive governors included Hiram Johnson of California, who reformed the railroad industry, and Theodore Roosevelt of New York. As governor of New York (1899–1900), Roosevelt, a friend of Jacob Riis and other Progressives, was concerned about social and economic reform. He supported the creation of the New York State Tenement Commission to investigate New York City tenements. He also worked to eliminate sweatshop factory conditions which forced women and children to work long hours for very low pay in dangerous conditions.

### The Presidents of the Progressive Era

| 1901 McKinley shot; Theodore Roosevelt succeeded as President | 1906 Square Deal | 1908 William Howard Taft elected President | 1913 16th, 17th Amendments ratified | 1914 Federal Trade Commission Act passed; Clayton Anti-trust Act passed | 1915 New Freedom |
|---|---|---|---|---|---|
| **1900** · **1903** · **1906** · **1909** · **1912** · **1915** · **1918** | | | | | |
| 1904 Theodore Roosevelt elected President | 1906 Meat Inspection Act passed | | 1912 T. Roosevelt forms Progressive Party; Woodrow Wilson elected President | 1916 Woodrow Wilson reelected President | |

## Theodore Roosevelt and the Square Deal

The first three Presidents of this century—Theodore Roosevelt, William Howard Taft, and Woodrow Wilson—are known as the Progressive Presidents. Roosevelt, elected Vice President in 1900, became President when President William McKinley was assassinated in 1901. He was elected in his own right in 1904.

Roosevelt saw his job as one of stewardship—leading the nation in the public interest, like a manager or supervisor. He believed that the President had any powers not specifically denied to the executive in the Constitution. Roosevelt's administration is often known as the Square Deal because of the many reforms made during his presidency.

## Key Themes and Concepts

### Government

*"…We must see that each man is given a square deal, because he is entitled to no more and shall receive no less."*
—T. Roosevelt, 1903

- What did Theodore Roosevelt mean by the Square Deal?

- What was meant by the stewardship theory of government?

- What did Wilson mean by the New Freedom?

- How did Theodore Roosevelt and Woodrow Wilson use the powers of the Presidency?

- What do you consider to be the most significant domestic reform made under, T. Roosevelt, Taft, Wilson?

## Consumer Protection

Although basically conservative, Roosevelt did not hesitate to use his presidential power of the presidency to deal directly with social and economic problems. He recognized the need for consumer protection, influencing passage in 1906 of the Pure Food and Drug Act and the Meat Inspection Act.

## Regulating Business

**Strengthening Railroad Legislation** Under pressure from Roosevelt, in 1903 Congress passed the Elkins Act, followed in 1906 by the Hepburn Act. The objective of both was to strengthen the Interstate Commerce Commission (ICC) and allow it to set railroad shipping rates. Also, the ICC's powers were expanded to include regulation of pipelines, ferries, bridges, and terminals. Some complained because the act allowed railroads to appeal to the courts. However, Roosevelt was often willing to compromise on details to make a larger point—in this case the right of government to regulate business.

**Trust-Busting** Roosevelt saw a difference between "good trusts," which were to be subject only to regulation, and "bad trusts," which were to be dissolved. The actions he took against big business earned him a reputation as someone who would do trust-busting. In 1903, Roosevelt convinced Congress to form the Bureau of Corporations within the Department of Commerce and Labor. He used the bureau to pressure corporations through investigations and publicity about their activities.

**The Northern Securities Case** By the end of the 1800s, the Northern Securities Company controlled the railroad system in the Pacific Northwest. In 1901, the Justice Department began prosecution of Northern Securities under the Sherman Antitrust Act. The case was eventually appealed to the Supreme Court. In its ruling in *Northern Securities Co.* v. *United States* (1904), the Supreme Court upheld the judgment against the company and ordered the company to be dissolved.

**The "Beef Trust"** Another government action using the Sherman Antitrust Act was directed against a group of meatpackers known as the "beef trust." This prosecution, too, was upheld by the Supreme Court, in *Swift & Co.* v. *United States* (1905). This decision gave the government broader powers under the Constitution's interstate commerce clause than the Court's ruling in the landmark case, *United States* v. *E.C. Knight Company* (1895).

## Analyzing Documents

Examine the cartoon, then answer the following questions.

- Who are the men at the desks?

- What place is pictured?

- Who do the large figures represent?

- Which constitutional amendment was the result of concern over the problem that is depicted in this cartoon?

## Labor Conditions

Roosevelt also achieved important reforms in working conditions.

**The Anthracite Coal Strike** In 1902, when Pennsylvania coal mine owners refused to negotiate with striking workers, Roosevelt threatened to send the army to take over the mines. The mine owners then agreed to arbitration, and the United Mine Workers, under John Mitchell, won shorter hours and higher wages but not recognition of their union. For the first time federal government in a labor dispute did not intervene solely on the side of management.

**Employers' Liability** One Progressive goal was to make employers assume more liability, or responsibility, for their workers. The Employers Liability Act of 1906 provided accident insurance for workers on interstate railroads and in Washington, D.C.

**Working Hours** Another Progressive goal was to limit workers' hours on the job. As you read above, in *Lochner* v. *New York* (1905) and *Muller* v. *Oregon* (1908), there were inconsistent results in conflicts between the rights of individuals and the rights of businesses.

## Conservation

As a naturalist, Theodore Roosevelt was interested in conservation, or protecting the nation's environment and its wilderness lands. His policies were influenced by the conservationists Gifford Pinchot and John Muir.

Before Roosevelt, the government's land policy put land in the private hands of homesteaders, railroads, and colleges. Roosevelt shifted this policy and kept some land under federal government protection. This was the philosophy of John Muir, a founder of the Sierra Club, who was also instrumental in the creation of Yosemite National Park.

**Key Themes and Concepts**

**Environment**
- How did Roosevelt's land policy differ from that of earlier presidents?

- What was the end result of Roosevelt's land policy by the time he left office?

- Roosevelt used the Forest Reserve Act of 1891 to place national forests under the control of the U.S. Forest Service, headed by conservationist Gifford Pinchot. A total of about 150 million acres of public lands was placed under the protection of the federal government. When Roosevelt left office, he had tripled the amount of land set aside for the public as national forests, national parks, wildlife refuges, and national monuments.

- The National (Newlands) Reclamation Act of 1902 set aside money from the sale of public lands to build dams and irrigation systems in the West.

- In 1908, Roosevelt called a national Conservation Congress, attended by hundreds of naturalists and conservationists as well as by 44 governors.

# Progressivism Under Taft

After Roosevelt declined to run for a third term, William Howard Taft succeeded him in 1909. Taft began his presidency with the support of Roosevelt and the Progressive wing of the Republican Party.

## Reforms Under Taft

Under Taft, the Justice Department brought twice as many suits against big business as it had under Roosevelt. One of the most important cases involved the Supreme Court's ruling in *Standard Oil Co. of New Jersey* v. *United States* (1911) held that the monopoly should be dissolved. But it also applied the so-called "rule of reason" to the Sherman Antitrust Act. There was a difference, said the Court, between "reasonable" and "unreasonable" business combinations. Size alone did not mean that a company was "unreasonable."

The Taft era witnessed other reforms, too. The Mann-Elkins Act of 1910 gave the ICC the power to regulate communication by telephone and telegraph. In 1913, the Sixteenth Amendment was ratified, authorizing Congress to impose an income tax.

## Problems for Taft

Taft, who was not as politically able as Roosevelt, soon ran into problems that split the Republican Party into a Taft faction and a Progressive faction. Like other Progressives, Taft wanted to lower tariffs, but he was unable to stand up to the Republican Congress that raised them with the Payne-Aldrich Act of 1909. Taft angered Progressives by calling the law "the best bill that the Republican party ever passed."

Taft ran into more trouble the following year when he dismissed Forest Service head Gifford Pinchot—a favorite of Progressive conservationists. Taft's secretary of the interior, Richard A. Ballinger, had allowed a group of business people to obtain several million acres of Alaskan public lands. Pinchot protested the action, and Taft fired him. Ballinger was identified with mining, lumbering, and ranching interests that wanted to develop the land for personal profit. They were supported by many senators from western states.

## Woodrow Wilson and the New Freedom

In 1912, Theodore Roosevelt challenged Taft for the Republican presidential nomination. When the nomination went to Taft, Roosevelt ran as the candidate of a third party, the Progressive or Bull Moose Party. Woodrow Wilson was the Democratic candidate, and Eugene Debs ran on the Socialist ticket.

Roosevelt offered what he called the **New Nationalism,** while Wilson called his program the **New Freedom.** Both were Progressive philosophies. Roosevelt, however, accepted social legislation and business regulation. The more traditional Wilson aimed for a return to competition in the marketplace with enforcement of antitrust laws. Wilson won the election of 1912 by a landslide of electoral votes, although he received only 41 percent of the popular vote. In 1916, he was reelected into office in an even closer race.

### Financial Reforms

Wilson accomplished two major financial reforms while in office. In 1913, he pressured Congress to pass the Underwood Tariff Act, which lowered tariffs for the first time since the Civil War. The law also provided for a **graduated income tax**—one that taxed larger incomes at a higher rate (6 percent) than it did lower ones (1 percent). This kind of tax, which takes a bigger share of higher incomes, is known as a progressive tax.

Also in 1913, the **Federal Reserve System** was created. This national banking system is divided into 12 districts, each with a Federal Reserve bank. The federal government could now (1) issue a new, sound currency—Federal Reserve notes; (2) control the amount of money in circulation and interest rates; and (3) shift money from one bank to another as needed. The Federal Reserve Board lowers interest rates to stimulate consumer spending in times of recession or raises interest rates to control inflation.

### Business Regulation

Wilson also achieved two important business regulations. The Federal Trade Commission Act of 1914 aimed to prevent unfair competition. It created a commission to investigate such practices as false advertising and mislabeling.

## Reading Strategy

**Formulating Questions**

Taft, a Progressive president, wanted to keep tariffs low, but when Congress raised tariffs with the Payne-Aldrich Act of 1909, he praised the bill.

• What might have prompted Taft to do this?

## Preparing for the Exam

Established in 1913, the Federal Reserve System created the first central banking system since the Second Bank of the United States. Twelve banks, rather than just one, exercised monetary controls.

• Who proposed the first national bank of the United States?

• Why was the Second Bank of the United States terminated?

• What is the primary role of the Federal Reserve System?

• What methods does it use to accomplish its goals?

## Federal Progressive Era Legislation

| Date | Legislation | Purpose |
|------|-------------|---------|
| 1890 | Sherman Antitrust Act | Outlawed monopolies and practices that result in restraint of trade, such as price fixing |
| 1902 | National (Newlands) Reclamation Act | Created to plan and develop irrigation projects |
| 1903 | Department of Commerce and Labor | Concerned with national issues of business, industry and labor; included Bureau of Corporations |
| 1903 | Elkins Act | Increased powers of Interstate Commerce Commission; declared rebates illegal |
| 1905 | United States Forest Service | Established to manage and protect the nation's water and timber resources |
| 1906 | Hepburn Act | Gave ICC greater power to investigate railroads and control rates |
| 1906 | Pure Food and Drug Act | Outlawed interstate transportation of impure or diluted foods and the deliberate mislabeling of foods and drugs |
| 1906 | Meat Inspection Act | Required federal inspection of meat processing to ensure sanitary conditions |
| 1910 | Mann-Elkins Act | Extended powers of ICC to include regulation of communication |
| 1913 | Department of Labor | Made cabinet department separate from Department of Commerce |
| 1913 | 16th Amendment | Passed by Congress in 1909; ratified in 1913; gave Congress power to levy an income tax |
| 1913 | 17th Amendment | Passed by Congress in 1912; ratified in 1913; provided for the direct election of senators |
| 1913 | Underwood Tariff Act | Lowered tariffs and created first graduated income tax |
| 1913 | Federal Reserve Act | Created a federal banking system to ensure national financial stability |
| 1914 | Federal Trade Commission Act | Created to prevent unfair competition, it had the power to investigate monopolies and stop false and misleading advertising |
| 1914 | Clayton Antitrust Act | Passed to restore business competition; strengthened Sherman Antitrust Act by making some specific practices of monopolies illegal |
| 1916 | National Park Service | Created to take over the administration of the nation's parks |
| 1919 | 18th Amendment | Passed by Congress in 1917, ratified in 1919; prohibited manufacture, transport, and sale of liquor (repealed in 1933) |
| 1920 | 19th Amendment | Passed by Congress in 1919; ratified in 1920; women gained the right to vote |
| 1920 | Women's Bureau | Created within the Department of Labor to promote the status of working women |

The Clayton Antitrust Act of 1914 strengthened the government's power to control business practices that threatened competition. Among other things, the act prohibited companies from price fixing and from buying stocks in competing firms. The Clayton Antitrust Act tried to end the practice of using antitrust laws against unions, but later Supreme Court decisions undercut this provision. Later in the twentieth century, federal prosecutions of alleged violations of antitrust laws continued against corporations such as AT&T and Microsoft.

### Other Reforms Under Wilson

- The Adamson Act (1916) set an eight-hour day for workers on railroads in interstate commerce.
- The Federal Farm Loan Act (1916) made low-interest loans available to farmers.
- The Keating-Owen Child Labor Act (1916) tried to outlaw child labor, but the Supreme Court ruled the law unconstitutional in the case of *Hammer* v. *Dagenhart* (1918).
- Ratification in 1919 of the Eighteenth Amendment prohibited the manufacture, sale, or transportation of liquor.
- Ratification of the Nineteenth Amendment in 1920 gave women the right to vote.

## End of the Progressive Era

The Progressive Era came to an end when the United States entered World War I. During the war, American priorities shifted to the war effort, and in the 1920s, the trend shifted away from reform and toward acceptance of society as it was.

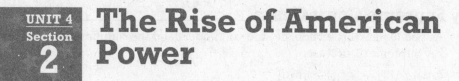

# The Rise of American Power

## Section Overview

The changes in the United States that led to Progressive reform at home also influenced American expansion overseas. From 1865–1920, a newly industrialized United States moved beyond the borders of North America to become an imperialist power on a global scale. Presidential power was a central issue, as was the shift in traditional foreign policy. Presidents Theodore Roosevelt and Woodrow Wilson dominated foreign policy as the nation involved itself in an interdependent world. Americans debated their motivations, their policies, and their effects on people at home and abroad.

## Key Themes and Concepts

As you review this section, take special note of the following key themes and concepts:

**Places and Regions** How did America's industrialization increase pressures for overseas expansion?

**Constitutional Principles** How did reactions to the Russian Revolution and World War I result in the restriction of some people's civil rights in the United States?

**Change** How did the United States change its traditional foreign policy in the early years of the twentieth century? In what ways did the nation continue policies of the past?

**Presidential Decisions and Actions** How did actions of Presidents Theodore Roosevelt and Woodrow Wilson increase both the power of the United States and the power of the presidency?

## Key People

As you review this section, be sure you understand the significance of these key people:

Frederick Jackson Turner

Henry Cabot Lodge

Matthew Perry

Theodore Roosevelt

William Howard Taft

Woodrow Wilson

## Key Terms

Open Door Policy

jingoism

imperialism

Roosevelt Corollary

dollar diplomacy

Fourteen Points

self-determination

Treaty of Versailles

League of Nations

reparations

The
# Big
# Idea

Between 1865 and 1920:

• the United States became a world power.

• U.S. territory was acquired by military conquest, treaty, purchase, and annexation.

• industrial and commercial expansion motivated expansion.

• the United States moved away from its traditional foreign policy.

• the transition to a world power increased feelings of nationalism in the nation, but it also caused debate and division.

## Key Supreme Court Cases

As you review this section, be sure you understand the significance of this key Supreme Court case:

*Schenck* v. *United States* (1919)

# Emerging Global Involvement

In the late 1800s and early 1900s, American expansion was in many ways a resumption of the expansionist drive that had been halted by the Civil War. A number of factors led the United States into greater global involvement in the late 1800s.

## New Technology

Improvements in transportation and communication technology shortened distances around the world. At the same time, other inventions accelerated industrial growth. Railroads connected factories and farms to Atlantic and Pacific ports, from which steamships carried goods to Europe, Latin America, and Asia. Communication was faster and easier thanks to the telegraph, telephone, and transatlantic cable. Communications technology quickly provided information on international markets and on events in other nations that might affect the United States. The world was becoming more interdependent.

## Drive for Markets and Raw Materials

Economics linked the domestic and foreign policy goals of the United States. Business leaders wanted raw materials from abroad. Both business leaders and farmers also wanted overseas markets. Overseas markets could provide economic stability, especially when, as in the 1890s, domestic consumption could not absorb the nation's output. At the same time, international competition increased as European nations, Japan, and the United States sought raw materials and markets. Foreign trade increased dramatically. High U.S. tariffs played a role in revolutions in Hawaii and in Cuba.

### United States Expansion, 1803–1867

| Date | Territory | How Acquired |
| --- | --- | --- |
| 1803 | Louisiana Purchase | purchased from France |
| 1819 | Florida | occupation, followed by treaty with Spain |
| 1845 | Texas | annexation by joint resolution of Congress |
| 1846 | Oregon Country | agreement with Great Britain |
| 1848 | Mexican Cession | Mexican War/treaty with Mexico |
| 1853 | Gadsden Purchase | purchase from Mexico |
| 1867 | Alaska | purchase from Russia |
| 1867 | Midway | annexation |

## Key Themes and Concepts

**Change**
Using the chart and the text, answer the following questions.

- Geographically, how do Alaska and Midway differ from the other territories on the chart?

- How did U.S. foreign policy between 1890 and 1919 change from previous policy directions?

- In what ways was it a continuation of existing foreign policy directions?

- How did the motives for expansion differ between the periods 1803–1867 and 1890–1914?

## Growth of Naval Power

The U.S. Navy began to expand in the 1880s, building steel-hulled warships with steam engines and the latest in weapons. Behind this growth was the urging of expansionists like Alfred T. Mahan, who argued that as foreign trade grew, a nation needed a strong navy to protect shipping routes. The navy, in turn, needed bases at which to refuel and restock supplies.

## Manifest Destiny and the Closing of the Frontier

As you will recall, the idea of Manifest Destiny took hold in the United States in the mid-1800s. Manifest Destiny is the idea that the United States had a divine mission to expand in order to spread the ideals of freedom and democracy.

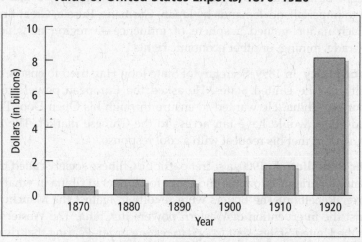

**Value of United States Exports, 1870–1920**

Dollars (in billions) — Year: 1870, 1880, 1890, 1900, 1910, 1920

Source: Historical Statistics of the United States, Colonial Times to 1970

**Analyzing Documents**

Bar graphs help you to compare quantities over a period of time. Based on the graph to the left, answer the following questions.

• What was the value of United States foreign trade

  in 1870?

  in 1900?

  in 1920?

This belief was fueled by historian Frederick Jackson Turner's frontier thesis. In a famous 1893 essay, Turner argued that the existence of a frontier throughout our history had been vital in shaping the American character. By 1893, Turner noted, that frontier no longer existed, an argument supported by the 1890 census. Some people interpreted this development to mean that Americans needed new frontiers beyond the current borders.

## Social Darwinism

Closely tied to Manifest Destiny was the idea that the American way of life was so superior that the United States was obliged to carry its benefits to other peoples. Few wondered whether these peoples wanted American "benefits," or recognized that this notion implied that other peoples and their ways of life were inferior. The belief in Anglo-Saxon superiority was a form of Social Darwinism. According to Social Darwinists, the law of nature resulted in the survival of superior people. Similarly, the same law led to the survival of superior nations, which are meant to dominate inferior nations. Few questioned the fact that no scientific evidence supported this theory.

## The Missionary Spirit

Another motive for expansion was the missionary spirit. It lay behind attempts to introduce Christianity and "civilization" to others, particularly in China, where the movement was strongest. The missionary impulse did result in certain improvements, such as the building of schools and hospitals. However, it also fostered a paternalistic view—one that saw the United States as a parent supervising weaker, less "developed" peoples. Underlying Manifest Destiny, Social Darwinism, and the missionary movement were nationalism, racism, and a strong sense of cultural superiority.

# The United States as a World Power: Asia and the Pacific

The role of the United States in Asia expanded because of the establishment of trade with China and Japan and the acquisition of Hawaii, Pacific bases, and the Philippines.

## China

American trade with China began in the 1780s through the port of Canton. By the late 1800s, however, Americans were afraid that their economic opportunities in

China might be limited. Throughout the nineteenth century, China had been subjected to imperialistic demands by Japan, Germany, Russia, Great Britain, and France. Each nation gained a sphere of influence—a region in which it had exclusive trade, mining, or other economic rights.

**Open Door Policy** In 1899, Secretary of State John Hay tried to ensure economic opportunity for the United States. He asked the European powers to keep an "open door" to China. He wanted to ensure through his Open Door Policy that the United States would have fair access to the Chinese market. The European powers, however, met his request with a cool response.

**The Boxer Rebellion** In 1900, a secret patriotic Chinese society called the Boxers attacked missionaries, diplomats, and other foreigners in China in what is known as the Boxer Rebellion. The Boxers were revolting against the Manchu Dynasty and against the intervention of Western powers in China. The Western powers, including the United States, sent troops to restore order. Fearing that rival nations would take even more Chinese land, Hay expanded the Open Door Policy to mean that the current boundaries of China should be preserved.

"The policy of the United States is to seek a solution which may bring about permanent safety and peace to China, preserve Chinese territorial and administrative entity, protect all rights guaranteed to friendly powers by treaty and international law, and safeguard for the world the principle of equal and impartial trade with all parts of the Chinese Empire."
—Open Door Policy, 1899

- Is this policy different from the principles of the Monroe Doctrine? If so, how?

- Why was it in American self-interest to call for the preservation of Chinese territorial and administrative integrity?

Examine the timeline to the right, then answer the following questions.

- Which event occurred first—Roosevelt's use of "Big Stick diplomacy" or the Spanish-American War?

- Which events are examples of use of force?

- What other methods of carrying out foreign policy are suggested?

## American Imperialism, 1867–1914

| 1867 Alaska purchased | 1889 Samoa agreement signed | 1900 "Big Stick diplomacy"; Boxer Rebellion | 1906 U.S. troops restore order in Cuba | 1914 Panama Canal opens |
|---|---|---|---|---|

| 1860 | 1870 | 1880 | 1890 | 1900 | 1910 | 1920 |
|---|---|---|---|---|---|---|

| 1880s U.S. trade abroad increases | 1899 Open Door Policy | 1898 Spanish-American War; Hawaii annexed | 1904 Roosevelt Corollary established | 1910 "Dollar diplomacy" |
|---|---|---|---|---|

## Japan

Japan had developed into a major economic power after 1854, the year Commodore Matthew Perry ended Japan's isolation by negotiating a treaty opening two Japanese ports to ships from the United States. Unlike China, Japan carried out a far-reaching modernization program making it a major economic power by 1900.

From 1900 to 1941, a key aim of American policy in Asia became protecting American economic, political, and territorial interests by providing the balance of power to restrict Japanese expansion.

- Japan displayed its growing strength by defeating Russia in the Russo-Japanese War of 1904–1905. President Theodore Roosevelt mediated the Treaty of Portsmouth in an effort to protect American possessions and interests in Asia. It was understood that Japan could remain in Manchuria and annex Korea. Japanese anger at the terms of the Treaty increased tensions between the two nations.

- United States agreement to the Japanese takeover of Korea was formalized in the 1905 Taft-Katsura Agreement. In return, Japan would not threaten the Philippines.

- United States–Japanese relations experienced a setback when, in 1906, the San Francisco schools placed Asian children in separate classes. The Japanese government condemned this segregation. In 1907, President Theodore Roosevelt achieved a compromise with Japanese officials called the Gentlemen's Agreement. This agreement ended school segregation in San Francisco but also restricted Japanese immigration to the United States.

- In 1908 the two nations also entered into the Root-Takahira Agreement in which the United States recognized Japan's interest in Manchuria, while the Japanese agreed to uphold the Open Door Policy and support China's *independence and integrity*. They each agreed to maintain the *status quo*, meaning no attempt would be made to seize the other's possessions.

## Hawaii

From the beginning of the nineteenth century, Americans – traders, whalers, missionaries – came to the Hawaii. Descendents of some of the missionaries developed important business interests there, namely sugar plantations. In 1887, the United States gained the right to establish a naval base at Pearl Harbor. By the 1890s Americans dominated the islands politically, economically, and militarily. But, until the 1890s, Hawaii remained an independent country ruled by a monarch.

Then, in 1890 a tariff law eliminated the favored status given in 1875 to Hawaiian sugar imports. The new law allowed all sugar to enter the United States duty free but gave sugar cane producers in the United States an incentive that encouraged the industry at home. This meant that Americans would be more likely to buy domestic sugar rather than Hawaiian sugar, and American planters in Hawaii would lose money.

At the same time, Americans in Hawaii feared Hawaiian nationalism led since 1891 by Queen Liliuokalani. Challenged both economically and politically, in 1893 American planters carried out a successful revolution against the Hawaiian ruler. They were aided by the chief United States diplomat to Hawaii and by American marines.

Against the wishes of the Hawaiian people, the American sugar growers asked that the United States annex Hawaii so that their sugar would be considered domestic and not foreign. But President Grover Cleveland opposed expansion by force. Hawaii remained in the hands of the American sugar interests as the independent Republic of Hawaii with Sanford B. Dole as president.

Not until 1898 during the Spanish-American War did it become a United States possession. It then became important as a military and commercial link to the Philippines and the rest of East Asia. Annexation was accomplished by a joint resolution of Congress rather than a treaty.

## Samoa

In 1878, the United States gained the rights to a naval station at Pago Pago in the Samoan Islands. The port was also used by Germany and Great Britain. Samoa was situated in the Pacific on the trade route to Australia. Conflicts arose among the three nations. In 1899, Germany and the United States divided Samoa.

# Imperialism: The Spanish-American War

In 1898, the United States began to acquire new territories, making it an imperial power. Most of these territorial gains resulted from the Spanish-American War.

## Underlying Causes of the Spanish-American War

There were several underlying causes of the war between Spain and the United States.

### Analyzing Documents

**Point of View**

*"…The Pacific is our ocean… And the Pacific is the ocean of the commerce of the future…The power that rules the Pacific, therefore, is the power that rules the world. And, with the Philippines, that power is and will forever be the American Republic."*
—Senator Albert J. Beveridge, 1900

- What does the speaker believe to be the source of world power for the United States? Why?

- How did the Open Door Policy and acquiring the Philippines affect United States foreign policy for the rest of the twentieth century?

### Analyzing Documents

In 1894, the United States Secretary of State said of the Samoan protectorate,

*"the first departure from our traditional and well established policy of avoiding entangling alliances with foreign powers in relation to objects remote from this hemisphere."*

- What traditional policy does the Secretary of State mean?

- What is the Secretary's position on U.S. expansionism? Why?

**Economic** United States business interests had invested $50 million in Cuba. Almost all of Cuba's sugar was exported to the United States. In 1894, the United States placed a high protective tariff on Cuban sugar, which had previously entered the nation duty free. Growers in Cuba lost millions because their sugar was no longer competitively priced. The result was economic chaos, which, combined with resentment of Spanish rule, set off a Cuban revolution against Spain in 1895. The revolution further endangered American investments.

**Humanitarian** Many Americans sympathized with the Cuban revolution and were appalled by the tactics of the Spanish military commander, Valeriano Weyler. He imprisoned hundreds of thousands of Cuban civilians in camps, where about 30 percent of them died from disease and starvation.

**Expansionist** American expansionists—including Theodore Roosevelt, Senator Henry Cabot Lodge, and Secretary of State John Hay—recognized that war offered an opportunity to seize territory from Spain, a weak nation.

## Immediate Causes of the Spanish-American War
In addition to the underlying causes of the Spanish-American War, several immediate events aroused Americans' emotions. These fed a growing **jingoism**— a super patriotism and demand for aggressive actions—that created a warlike mood.

**Yellow Journalism** In the late 1890s, two of the most famous American publishers, William Randolph Hearst of the *New York Morning Journal* and Joseph Pulitzer of the *New York World*, were battling for readers in a circulation war. Both newspapers printed the most sensational stories and pictures they could find about the horrors of the Cuban revolution. The stories often exaggerated and distorted events for emotional effect. This kind of sensationalism is called "yellow journalism."

**The de Lôme Letter** A personal letter written by the Spanish minister to the United States, Enrique Dupuy de Lôme, was printed in the *New York Journal* in February 1898. De Lôme's unfavorable comments—he called President McKinley "weak and catering to the rabble"—made it hard for the president and other political leaders to withstand demands for war.

**Sinking of the *Maine*** Less than a week after publication of the de Lôme letter, the United States battleship *Maine* exploded and sank in the harbor of Havana, Cuba, killing 266 Americans. The public blamed Spain, although a later investigation was never able to determine the cause of the explosion nor assign responsibility.

## Fighting the Spanish-American War
In April 1898, despite Spain's agreement to an armistice with Cuba, McKinley asked Congress to declare war. Congress complied. It also approved the Teller Amendment, which promised that the United States would not annex Cuba.

The war lasted four months, with fighting in both the Caribbean Sea and the Pacific Ocean. Of the 2,446 Americans who lost their lives, fewer than 400 were killed in combat; the rest died from infection and disease.

## The Results of the Spanish-American War
In December 1898 the terms of the Treaty of Paris negotiated with Spain:

- granted Cuba its independence.
- gave the Philippines to the United States in return for $20 million.
- ceded Puerto Rico and Guam to the United States.

---

### Analyzing Documents

The term *jingoism* comes from a British song of the 1870s:

*"We don't want to fight But by Jingo, if we do, We've got the men, we've got the ships, We've got the money too."*

- What does jingoism mean?

- What does nationalism mean?

- What is the difference between the two terms?

For the United States, the Treaty of Paris of 1898:

- led to the acquisition of many former Spanish territories that formed the basis of an American empire.
- set off a national debate among imperialists and anti-imperialists.
- increased American involvement in Latin America and Asia as the nation sought to protect its new lands.

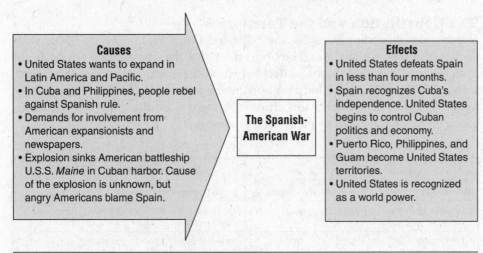

### The Spanish-American War

**Causes**
- United States wants to expand in Latin America and Pacific.
- In Cuba and Philippines, people rebel against Spanish rule.
- Demands for involvement from American expansionists and newspapers.
- Explosion sinks American battleship U.S.S. *Maine* in Cuban harbor. Cause of the explosion is unknown, but angry Americans blame Spain.

**The Spanish-American War**

**Effects**
- United States defeats Spain in less than four months.
- Spain recognizes Cuba's independence. United States begins to control Cuban politics and economy.
- Puerto Rico, Philippines, and Guam become United States territories.
- United States is recognized as a world power.

*With a quick victory in the Spanish-American War, the United States established itself as a new world power.*

**Analyzing Documents**

Examine the graphic organizer, then answer the following questions.

- Which are the *basic* causes of the war?
- Which are the *immediate* causes of the war?
- Which effects were long term?
- How was the War a turning point in United States history?

## Imperialism: The Great Debate

Ratification of the Treaty of Paris set off a great debate in the United States. As with all treaties, it had to be approved by a two-thirds vote of the Senate. The fundamental question was whether the United States should pursue imperialism—the policy of expanding a nation's power by foreign acquisitions.

### Debating Imperialism

Americans in both political parties, in all regions, and from all social classes could be found on either side of the debate. Progressives were also divided. Imperialists included Theodore Roosevelt, Senator Henry Cabot Lodge, and Alfred T. Mahan. Among the anti-imperialists were Andrew Carnegie, Mark Twain, Jane Addams, William Jennings Bryan, Booker T. Washington, and former Presidents Grover Cleveland and Benjamin Harrison.

**Analyzing Documents**

*"It has been a splendid little war; begun with the highest motives, carried out with magnificent intelligence and spirit."*
—Secretary of State John Hay, 1898

- How is this description of a war unusual?
- Why would anti-imperialists and pacifists object to this description?

### The American Empire During the Progressive Era, 1898–1917

| Date | Territory | How Acquired |
|------|-----------|--------------|
| 1898 | Hawaii | annexation after 1893 revolution |
| 1898 | Puerto Rico | gained from Spain after war |
| 1898 | Guam | gained from Spain after war |
| 1898 | Philippines | gained from Spain after war |
| 1899 | Samoa | treaty with Great Britain |
| 1899 | Wake Island | annexation |
| 1903 | Panama Canal Zone | treaty with Panama |
| 1917 | Virgin Islands | purchased from Denmark |

**Making Generalizations**
Self-interest is what determines a nation's foreign policy. Often that self-interest is mixed with idealism and nationalism.

Summarize the major reasons for the expansionism of the United States in the 1890s and early 1900s.

- Which reasons were based on self-interest, idealism, nationalism?

- How did the Hawaiians and Filipinos show their nationalism by their reactions to American actions and attitudes?

## Geography
### in History

1898: Guantanamo Bay in Cuba was site of first U.S. troop landing in Spanish-American War.

1901: Platt Amendment gave U.S. right to lease area "for use as coaling or naval station only."

1903: U.S.-Cuba Treaty continues lease of this first U.S. overseas naval base.

1934: Treaty is renegotiated. Can be broken only by "mutual consent" or U.S. abandonment.

2002: Under President G. W. Bush, part of base is used as a detention camp for "enemy combatants."

2009: President B. Obama orders the detention camp to be closed within one year.

2010: Closing is delayed by problem of relocating detainees.

## Acquiring the Philippines

In February 1899, the Senate approved the Treaty of Paris by a small margin. That January, Emilio Aguinaldo, who had been fighting the Spanish for Philippine independence, resisted annexation by the United States and declared the Philippines a republic. A bitter United States-Filipino war followed, lasting from 1899 until 1902. More than 4,000 Americans and some 16,000 Filipinos were killed in this war. An additional 200,000 Filipinos died from starvation and disease. Atrocities were committed by both sides. At the end of the war, the Philippines were under American control.

## The Constitution and the Territories

Imperialism was supported by the Supreme Court from 1901 to 1904, with decisions in the Insular Cases. The Court ruled that the Constitution applied only in those territories that Congress decided would be incorporated into the United States. The Court also held that people in annexed territories did not automatically have the rights of United States citizens. Congress would make that decision, based on the status given to a territorial possession.

| Imperialists' Point of View | Anti-Imperialists' Point of View |
|---|---|
| The United States needs colonies to compete economically. | Supporting an empire would be a financial burden. |
| To be a true world power, the United States needs colonies and naval bases. | The United States should concentrate its energies on solving problems at home. |
| It is the American destiny to expand, and its duty to care for poor, weak peoples. | Nonwhite people cannot be assimilated into American society. |
| To abandon territories makes the United States appear cowardly before the world. | An empire would involve the United States in more wars. |
| It is only honorable to keep land that Americans lost their lives to obtain. | It is a violation of democratic principles to annex land and not offer its people the same rights as those of U.S. citizens. |

## Governing the Territories

The United States set up different means of governing its new territories.

- **Hawaii** was made a territory in 1900, its first step to statehood in 1959.

- In 1916, the Jones Act promised the Philippines independence, but the law did not name a date. In 1934, the **Philippines** was promised independence in ten years. This promise was delayed because of World War II but was honored in 1946.

- The Foraker Act of 1900 provided for a Puerto Rican legislature elected by the people with a governor and council appointed by the American president. Puerto Ricans received United States citizenship in 1917. In 1952, the island became a commonwealth. This status gives **Puerto Rico** many rights of a state excluding sending representatives to Congress.

- U.S. troops remained in **Cuba** until 1902. American troops were sent to Cuba twice between 1902 and 1922. Cuban independence was limited by the Platt Amendment (1901), which remained part of the Cuban constitution until 1934. The amendment (1) required that the United States approve treaties between Cuba and other nations, (2) gave the United States the right to lease naval bases in Cuba, and (3) allowed the United States to intervene in Cuba to preserve order or peace.

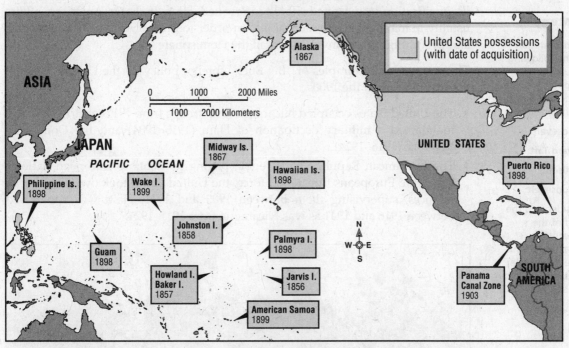

United States possessions (with date of acquisition)

ASIA

JAPAN

PACIFIC OCEAN

UNITED STATES

SOUTH AMERICA

Alaska 1867

Midway Is. 1867

Hawaiian Is. 1898

Puerto Rico 1898

Philippine Is. 1898

Wake I. 1899

Johnston I. 1858

Palmyra I. 1898

Guam 1898

Howland I. Baker I. 1857

Jarvis I. 1856

Panama Canal Zone 1903

American Samoa 1899

0   1000   2000 Miles
0   1000   2000 Kilometers

# America as a World Power: Latin America

Having acquired an empire, the United States found itself increasingly involved around the globe as it protected its new territories and interests. Of particular interest to the United States was Latin America.

## Expanding the Monroe Doctrine

The Monroe Doctrine of 1823 warned foreign powers to stay out of the Western Hemisphere. For several decades, the relatively weak United States seldom enforced the doctrine. It was used, however, to support the American annexation of Texas as well as the Mexican War. It was also used at the end of the Civil War against France, which had set up a puppet government in Mexico and refused to give in to American demands to withdraw. France withdrew only after the United States massed troops along the Mexican border.

**The Venezuelan Border Dispute** In 1895, the United States had an opportunity to reaffirm and expand the Monroe Doctrine. Great Britain and Venezuela were involved in a quarrel over the boundary between Venezuela and British Guiana (now Guyana). The United States offered to arbitrate, or help settle, the dispute. When Great Britain refused arbitration, the United States claimed that the British were violating the Monroe Doctrine and forced them to negotiate by threatening war. Secretary of State Richard Olney, in the Olney Interpretation of the Monroe Doctrine, claimed, "Today, the United States is practically sovereign of this continent."

**The Roosevelt Corollary** President Theodore Roosevelt, further reinforced, even reinterpreted, the Monroe Doctrine. Economic problems in Venezuela and the Dominican Republic led to threats of European intervention. In both cases, the United States stepped in to restore order. Roosevelt explained American policy in a 1904 message to Congress. If a nation in the Western Hemisphere is guilty of consistently behaving wrongly, he said, the Monroe Doctrine requires that the United States step in and act "as an international police power." This policy is known as the Roosevelt Corollary to the Monroe Doctrine.

## Geography in History

Based on the map above and the text, answer the following questions.

- Which United States acquisition was closest to Japan?

- Under what circumstances did the United States acquire the Philippines?

- What was particularly controversial about these circumstances?

**Organizing Information**
For each of the following presidents, summarize U.S. foreign policy in Latin America in the first half of the Twentieth Century.

**Theodore Roosevelt:**

**William Howard Taft:**

**Woodrow Wilson:**

**Franklin D. Roosevelt:**

- Which presidents in the second half of the twentieth century should be added to this list because they made important Latin American foreign policy decisions?

Theodore Roosevelt was famous for the statement, "Speak softly and carry a big stick." Examine the cartoon, then answer the questions that follow.

- What does the big stick in the cartoon represent?

- What evidence is there that in recent decades the Roosevelt Corollary was used in Latin America?

- The Roosevelt Corollary to the Monroe Doctrine stated that "Chronic wrongdoing . . . may force the United States, however, reluctantly . . . to the exercise of an international police power." How is his attitude expressed in the cartoon?

**The "Big Stick" Policy** With the Roosevelt Corollary to the Monroe Doctrine as its justification, the United States intervened often in Latin American affairs usually to maintain economic stability in order to protect American investments and prevent European involvement in the Hemisphere.

There are several examples of "Big Stick" foreign policy by the United States in the first decades of the 1900s.

- The United States occupied Nicaragua with troops from 1912 until 1933. It also maintained a military occupation of Haiti (1915–1934) and the Dominican Republic (1916–1924).

- The Dominican Republic had trouble paying its debts to European nations. When the Europeans threatened force, the United States took over Dominican finances, supervising them between 1905 and 1941. Haiti was supervised between 1916 and 1941 as was Nicaragua from 1911–1924.

**Dollar Diplomacy** President Taft's foreign policy approach was known as dollar diplomacy. This meant that the United States could help maintain orderly societies in other countries by increasing American investment in foreign economies. These investments tended to increase American intervention in foreign affairs.

**Intervention in Mexico** During the Mexican Revolution, President Wilson intervened in Mexico's affairs in order to protect huge U.S. investments there. He also believed in moral diplomacy—conducting foreign affairs in terms of judgments about right and wrong. In 1913, after Victoriano Huerta overthrew the Mexican president and had him murdered, Wilson refused to recognize Huerta's government. The next year, the U.S. Navy seized the port of Vera Cruz to prevent a German ship from landing its cargo of arms for Huerta. Wilson also sent a force into northern Mexico in 1916 in an attempt to capture Pancho Villa, a Mexican rebel whose border raid into New Mexico in 1916 led to American deaths.

**Latin American Reaction** The actions of the United States were met with protests from the Latin American nations. Cuba, Colombia, and other nations expressed their objections in strongly nationalistic language. The attitude of the United States left a heritage of distrust that persists today.

**The Good Neighbor Policy** Only under Presidents Herbert Hoover (1929–1933) and Franklin D. Roosevelt (1933–1945) did the United States try to improve its relations with Latin America. Roosevelt backed what came to be called the "good neighbor policy." This meant less emphasis on intervention and more on cooperation. However, American economic dominance of the region continued.

**The Panama Canal** Since the mid-1850s, the advantages of building a canal across the isthmus, or narrow piece of land connecting North and South America, were well recognized. The growth of United States commerce as well as the expansion of its navy increased pressure to be able to move navy and merchant ships quickly between the Atlantic and Pacific Oceans. The Spanish-American War and the management of the newly acquired empire heightened interest in the project.

Under Theodore Roosevelt, the United States settled on a route across Panama, which was part of Colombia. When Colombia seemed reluctant to agree to financial terms, Roosevelt encouraged Panamanians to revolt and declare their independence. The United States quickly negotiated a treaty with the new nation of Panama, which gave the United States a 99-year renewable lease on a ten-mile-wide strip of land, the Panama Canal Zone, across Panama.

Begun in 1904, building the canal was a mammoth task. Yellow fever and malaria caused delays as did the difficulty of moving more than 250 million cubic yards of soil. However, workers made the remarkable achievement of completing the canal ahead of schedule and under budget. The canal opened to traffic in 1914.

Responding to Panamanian demonstrations in 1979, the United States turned the Canal Zone over to the nation of Panama but continued to run the canal jointly with Panama. On December 31, 1999, the Canal itself was returned to Panama. By 2000, the Canal had less strategic and economic value because many commercial and naval ships were too large to pass through the locks.

# The United States and World War I

World War I began in Europe in 1914 and lasted until 1918. The United States did not enter the war until 1917. The financial and human costs of this devastating conflict were enormous.

## Causes of World War I

There were several factors that led to the outbreak of war in Europe.

**Nationalism** Strong nationalistic competition had developed among France, Great Britain, Russia, Austria-Hungary, and Germany, especially after the unification of Germany in 1871. There was also ethnic unrest within nations. For instance, the Czechs and Slovaks wanted to free themselves from Austro-Hungarian control.

**Imperialism** Several nations were involved in keen competition for markets and colonies throughout the world.

**The Alliance System** As national and imperial goals conflicted, two groups of nations organized against each other in an effort to maintain a balance of power. The Triple Alliance consisted of Germany, Austria-Hungary, and Italy. The Triple Entente was made up of France, Russia, and Great Britain. If fighting were to break out, members of either alliance were pledged to help each other. When the war began, Italy did not join with the Triple Alliance and in 1915 became a part of the Triple Entente.

**Militarism** The early 1900s witnessed a continual buildup of armies and navies. Germany, for instance, tripled naval construction in order to challenge Great Britain's control of the seas.

**Preparing for the Exam**

Before understanding how the United States became involved in World War I, it is important to review the basic causes of that war which began in 1914.

For each cause listed, give an example.

Nationalism:

Industrialism:

Imperialism:

Alliances:

Militarism:

## The United States and World War I

| 1910 | 1911 | 1912 | **1913**<br>Civil war<br>erupts in<br>Mexico<br>1913 | 1914 | **1915**<br>Germans<br>sink<br>*Lusitania*<br>1915 | 1916 | **1917**<br>U.S. enters war;<br>Espionage Act<br>passed<br>1917 | 1918 | **1919**<br>Senate rejects<br>Treaty of Versailles<br>1919 | 1920 |

**1914** War begins in Europe

**1916** Germany suspends submarine attacks

**1918** Fourteen Points announced; Germany surrenders

## United States Entry into World War I

War broke out in Europe in July 1914, after the heir to the Austro-Hungarian throne was assassinated. Because of the alliance system, most major European nations soon joined the conflict. The United States was officially neutral. In 1917, however, the United States was drawn into the war. There were several reasons for this.

**Cultural and Ethnic Links** Few Americans were truly neutral. Some sympathized with the Central Powers, dominated by Germany and Austria-Hungary. These included German-Americans because of ties to Germany and Irish-Americans because of anti-British feeling. The majority of Americans, however, favored the Allies, or the Triple Entente nations. Americans had long-standing cultural ties with Great Britain. Many also felt loyalty to our first ally, France.

### Analyzing Documents

Examine the map at right, then answer the following questions.

- Which nations were the Allied Powers?

- Which were the Central Powers?

- Which nations remained neutral?

### Europe During World War I: 1914–1918

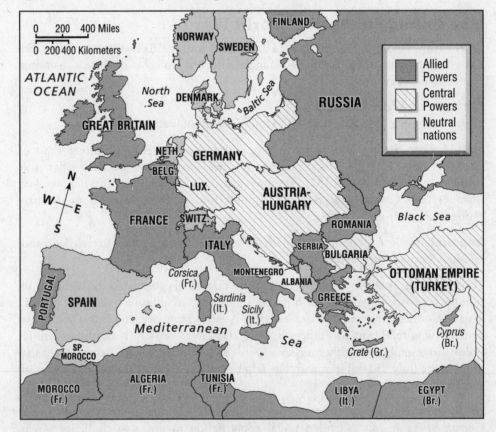

**Economic Ties** United States links to the Allies were economic as well as cultural. A British blockade of the North Sea effectively ended American exports to Germany, which dropped in value from about $345 million in 1914 to $29 million in 1916. Meanwhile, the value of trade with the Allies increased fourfold. American business and agriculture benefited from this trade, much of it financed by U.S. government loans to the Allies, totaling more than $2 billion by 1917.

Most Americans did not believe that trade with or loans to the Allies violated the nation's neutrality. In fact, President Wilson and his closest advisers were in favor of the Allies. However, even in the 1916 election for president, Wilson continued to proclaim American neutrality, campaigning on the slogan "He kept us out of war."

**Propaganda** Aided by their control of the transatlantic cable, the Allies conducted an effective propaganda campaign in the United States. They pictured the war as one of civilized, democratic nations against the barbaric monarchy of Germany.

**Freedom of the Seas and German Submarine Warfare** In 1915, determined to use its submarines to stop trade between the Allies and the United States and to break the British blockade, Germany announced a war zone around Great Britain. The German U-boats would sink enemy ships in the war zone. To avoid attack by error, neutral nations and their citizens should avoid the zone. Because a submarine is very vulnerable when surfaced, Germany ignored international law that required that a warship to stop and identify itself, then board a merchant or passenger ship and remove its crew and passengers before sinking it.

Germany's attempt to destroy the British blockade by attacking Allied ships was the single most important reason for American entrance into the war. Wilson insisted that America as a neutral nation had the right to trade with nations at war and to send its civilians on ships into war zones. He was defending the principle of freedom of the seas. This is the right of all nations to unrestricted travel in international waters in times of peace, except when limits are placed by international agreements, and the right of neutral nations to trade and its citizens to travel during war as well. The United States defense of this principle was a factor in the undeclared war with France in 1798, the Barbary Wars (1801–1805), the War of 1812, and World War I.

## Reading Strategy

**Analyzing Cause and Effect** Use the text and these three quotes to summarize the steps by which the United States entered World War I. Note the dates on each quote.

" . . . impartial in thought as well as in action."
—Woodrow Wilson, 1914

"He kept us out of war."
—Wilson campaign slogan, 1916

"The world must be made safe for democracy."
—Wilson request for declaration of war, April 2, 1917

- Did United States policy contradict Wilson's earlier statements and therefore involve the U.S. in the war, OR

- Did circumstances beyond the control of United States lead the nation to break its policy of neutrality?

## Analyzing Documents

American public opinion was extremely critical of Germany and its use of U-boats. Germany, however, did warn travelers—including passengers of the *Lusitania*—to stay out of the war zone.

- Who issued this notice? When? Where?

- Who is being warned, and what is the warning?

- What type of ship was the *Lusitania*?

- To what port was the *Lusitania* sailing?

- Was the ship British or American?

**Events of 1917 Lead to War** A series of events early in 1917 finally led to America's entry into World War I.

- On February 1, Germany announced a policy of unrestricted submarine warfare. It warned it would attack without warning all vessels headed for Allied ports. The main reason for Germany's decision was that the war was at a stalemate. Germany knew that its move would probably bring the United States into the war. However, Germany believed its U-boats, or submarines, could break the blockade and defeat the Allies before the United States could get troops to the battlefields.

- Two days later, the United States broke diplomatic relations with Germany. Tension and suspicion increased with the Zimmermann note of March 1. This was a message from the German foreign secretary, Arthur Zimmermann, to the German minister in Mexico. It urged a German military alliance with the Mexicans, promising them support in regaining their "lost territories" in the southwestern United States. When the message was made public, Americans reacted angrily.

- Five U.S. merchant ships were sunk by the Germans in March.

- Also in March, the Russian Revolution overthrew the czar. It appeared that more democratic forces would take control in Russia, so that if the United States went to war, it would be joining an alliance of democratic nations.

## Role of the United States in the War

**Preparedness** The United States entered World War I on the side of the Allies in April 1917. But earlier, in 1916, passage of the National Defense Act and the Navy Act began the expansion of the armed forces. The 1916 Revenue Act was also passed to pay for military expansion.

**The Draft Issue** Even before the entrance of the United States into World War I, the question of how to raise an army was being debated. Those favoring the draft saw it as being fair and democratic, with all Americans serving together. Those opposed to the draft—who preferred that military service be voluntary—viewed the draft as an example of the rich and educated exercising power over the poor, the working class, and immigrants. In May 1917, Congress passed the Selective Service Act, which established a draft. Eventually all males between the ages of 18 and 45 had to register. The constitutionality of the draft was challenged but upheld by the Supreme Court.

**American Expeditionary Force** By the end of the war, 4.8 million Americans had served in the armed forces, 2.8 million of them draftees. Eventually, over 2 million Americans served in France in a separate command, the American Expeditionary Force, led by General John J. Pershing.

The United States supplied fresh troops to a war in which both sides were exhausted by years of trench warfare. Neither side had moved more than a few miles, but casualties were in the millions. The entry of the United States tipped the scale in favor of the Allies. The United States lost about 51,000 men, far fewer than the millions lost by other nations.

**Analyzing Documents**

*"We shall endeavor to keep the United States neutral. In the event of this not succeeding, we make Mexico a proposal of alliance. . . : Make war together, make peace together, . . . and . . . Mexico is to reconquer the lost territory in Texas, New Mexico, and Arizona."*
—German foreign secretary Arthur Zimmermann, 1917

- What was Germany's first plan concerning the United States?

- If that plan failed, what did Germany propose to do in alliance with Mexico?

- What reaction would this note have had in the United States?

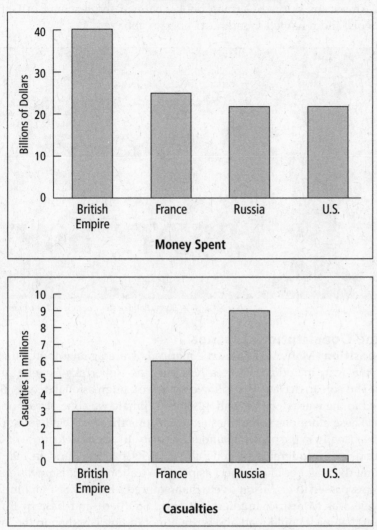

**Costs of the War for the Allies**

Money Spent

Casualties

Source: V.J. Esposito, A Concise History of World War I

## Analyzing Documents

Examine the graphs, then answer the questions that follow.

- Approximately how many casualties did Russia suffer in the war?

- Approximately how much money did the United States spend on the war?

**Mobilizing the Economy** To get the nation's economy geared up for war, certain economic operations were centralized and concentrated through a series of government agencies. Relying on the broad wartime powers of the president, Wilson used the Council of National Defense to oversee these agencies. Government control over the American economy increased during World War I. For the first time, the government entered fields such as housing and labor relations. It also supervised various public utilities, including the telephone and telegraph. About 16 percent of male workers went into the military, and their jobs were filled by women and African Americans.

**Patriotism** To President Wilson, World War I was a crusade. He believed that the Allies were fighting the war to end all wars, a war to make the world "safe for democracy." These idealistic goals helped make Wilson the Allies' moral leader. They also helped mobilize the American people to support the first conflict the United States had ever fought outside the Western Hemisphere. The nation geared up for the war with patriotic enthusiasm.

A propaganda campaign organized by the Committee on Public Information encouraged patriotism. Songs, posters, and pamphlets attacked Germany, urged the purchase of Liberty Bonds, and encouraged the conservation of resources.

## Reading Strategy

**Organizing Information** Suppose you were a member of Congress in 1917. You must decide whether the United States should go to war against Germany and the other Central Powers.

- Based on the information from this section, which events would influence your decision?

- How important to your decision is the policy of *Freedom of the Seas*?

Patriotism was accompanied by an outbreak of anti-German and anti-immigrant hysteria. Americans burned German books, banned the teaching of German in some schools, and renamed sauerkraut "liberty cabbage."

A Liberty Bond poster. *Courtesy of The Library of Congress*

## Wartime Constitutional Issues

**War Opposition** Many well-known Americans were against the United States entering the war, including Progressives such as Robert La Follette and Jane Addams. The vote to declare war followed intense Congressional debate. But once committed to the war effort, the nation's social climate was one of patriotism and nativism. These emotions sometimes led to actions that restricted some people's civil rights, usually in the name of national security. In addition to those of German background and immigrants in general, socialists pacifists, and in fact anyone questioning the war, became suspect as possible traitors. Nativism was expressed in a 1917 law passed over Wilson's veto that required a literacy test for immigrants. Its objective was to restrict immigration from Southern and Eastern Europe. It turned out that most could read and write, if not in English, then in the language of their homeland.

**The Espionage and Sedition Acts** Two broadly worded acts served to control and punish those who opposed the war effort. The Espionage Act of 1917 made it a crime to interfere with the draft and allowed the postmaster general to bar "treasonous" materials from the mail. The Sedition Act of 1918 made it a crime to speak or publish anything "disloyal, profane . . . or abusive" about the government, Constitution, flag, or military services of the United States.

Under these acts, the government prosecuted more than 2,000 Americans and sent 1,500 of them to jail. Pacifists, socialists, and others seen as extremists suffered the most. A special target was the Industrial Workers of the World (IWW), a radical union active in the West. Its leaders were arrested, its strikes broken up, and many of its members interned.

***Schenck* v. *United States*** In 1919, the Supreme Court ruled that free speech could be restricted during wartime in the landmark case *Schenck* v. *United States*. In a unanimous decision, Justice Oliver Wendell Holmes wrote, "Free speech would not protect a man falsely shouting "fire" in a theater and causing a panic." Holmes went on to say that Congress has the right to prevent words that would cause "a clear and present danger." That same year, the Court upheld the Sedition Act,

## Analyzing Documents

In wartime (particularly during the Civil War, World War I, and World War II), civil liberties were restricted. The Red Scare and McCarthyism that followed each of the world wars also led to violations of certain civil liberties.

*"Words can be weapons. . . . The question . . . is whether the words used are used in such circumstances and are of such nature as to create a clear and present danger that will bring about the substantial evils that Congress has a right to prevent."*
—*Schenck v. United States* (1919)

- According to this Supreme Court ruling, under what circumstances was it constitutional to restrict freedom of speech?

but in that decision the minority expressed concern that freedom of expression was endangered.

**The Red Scare 1918–1919** In November of 1917, a second revolution, this time by Bolsheviks, or communists, took place in Russia. The communist system was openly hostile to American values and beliefs, such as capitalism, private ownership of property, and certain freedoms. By 1918, an intense fear of communism swept the United States, and many Americans began to call for the imprisonment or exile of communists in the United States, even though the number of American communists was very small. This fear led some Americans to target others as well, including socialists, anarchists, labor leaders, and immigrants.

# The Search for Peace and Arms Control

World War I ended in November 1918 with an Allied victory. The United States, particularly President Wilson, played a major role in the peacemaking process.

## The Fourteen Points

Wilson had first suggested his own peace proposals in January 1918. His Fourteen Points included the following:

- Open, not secret, diplomacy
- Freedom of the seas
- Removal of trade barriers
- Arms reduction
- **Self-determination** of peoples—that is, letting various national groups make their own political decisions
- An "association of nations" to guarantee political independence and territorial integrity

## Wilson and the Treaty of Versailles

The Fourteen Points became the basis for the peace negotiations held at Versailles, France, beginning in January 1919. Wilson led the American delegation, thus becoming the first president of the United States to leave American soil while in office. Other Allied leaders included Georges Clemenceau of France, David Lloyd George of Great Britain, and Vittorio Orlando of Italy.

European nations, who had suffered far more than the United States, were cool to Wilson's plans. They wanted to be repaid for some of their losses, and some had made secret wartime deals involving territorial changes and money settlements that contradicted provisions of the Fourteen Points.

The most important agreement reached at Versailles was the treaty with Germany, the Treaty of Versailles. According to its provisions, Germany had to do the following:

- Accept complete responsibility for causing the war
- Pay huge **reparations** to the Allies
- Give up its military forces
- Cede lands to the new nations of Poland and Czechoslovakia
- Give up its overseas colonies

Wilson opposed many of the provisions of the Versailles Treaty and treaties with the other Central Powers. However, he was willing to compromise because the treaties provided for a new world organization, the **League of Nations.** The League, Wilson believed, would correct any problems caused by the peace treaties.

**Key Themes and Concepts**

**Government**
- Were Wilson's Fourteen Points a realistic basis for the peace treaty written at Versailles?

- Why did the Senate refuse to ratify the Treaty of Versailles?

- Was the failure to approve the Treaty of Versailles a turning back or a temporary halt in United States foreign policy?

## The League of Nations

The United States Senate had to approve the Versailles Treaty, and there Wilson ran into a great deal of opposition. Wilson had angered Republicans by excluding them from the American delegation to the Versailles Conference. Yet Republicans had a majority of seats in the Senate. The chairman of its foreign relations committee, Henry Cabot Lodge, distrusted and disliked Wilson. The feeling was mutual.

### Analyzing Documents

Examine the cartoon, then answer the following questions.

- Who is the man in the cartoon?
- What does the child represent?
- Who does the man want the child to play with?
- Why does the child want to play by himself?

**THE CHILD WHO WANTED TO PLAY BY HIMSELF.**
*President Wilson: "Now come along and enjoy yourself with the other nice children. I promised that you'd be the life and soul of the party."*

Some features of the League of Nations worried Americans. They feared, for instance, that the United States might be obligated to furnish troops to defend member nations.

Wilson stubbornly refused to allow any but the most minor changes in the Treaty of Versailles. He became increasingly moralistic and uncompromising.

When Wilson went on a speaking tour to gain popular support for the treaty, he collapsed and then suffered a stroke. His illness thereafter prevented him from playing an active role in the treaty debate.

The Senate voted several times on the Treaty of Versailles but always defeated it. The United States made a separate peace with Germany, and never did join the League. Fundamentally, the nation had voted to retain its traditional foreign policy of preferring nonintervention and of acting alone when it did choose to play a role.

## The Peace Movement: Women's International League for Peace and Freedom

Although the United States failed to join the League of Nations, there was still great concern in the United States about keeping the peace. During the Paris Peace Conference, for example, many American women met with others from around the world to form the Women's International League for Peace and Freedom. Jeannette Rankin, a prominent American pacifist, and reformer Jane Addams were among this group. Addams was voted the first president of the league.

The Women's International League for Peace and Freedom opposed peace terms that would create additional hostility among nations. The organization opposed the Treaty of Versailles for that reason, suggesting that its legacy would only be more war. Peace organizations wanted disarmament, arms control, and neutrality.

## Reparations and War Debts

In 1914, the United States had been a debtor nation, meaning that it owed more money to foreign nations than they owed to the United States. After World War I, the United States became the world's leading creditor nation, meaning that other countries owed more to the United States than it owed them. The nation was also the world's leading industrial producer, exporter, and financier. These changes were due in large part to money from the payment of war debts owed this nation by the former Allies.

During World War I, the European Allies borrowed a great deal of money from the United States in order to buy war supplies from American manufacturers. After the war, these debts became a source of conflict. European nations argued that their debts should be canceled because, while the United States had contributed money, Europe had paid a heavy price in lives. Nevertheless, the United States insisted on repayment.

A factor that made repayment difficult was U.S. protectionist policy. High American tariffs limited European trade with the United States and thus reduced earnings that might have been used to pay off war debts. These tariffs also led to retaliation by 26 nations, which raised their own tariff rates.

One step aimed at making repayment easier was the Dawes Plan, adopted in 1924. Under this plan, the United States lent funds to Germany so that it could make war reparations—money it owed to the European Allies as payment for economic losses during the war. The Allies would, in turn, use the funds to make payments on the war debts they owed the United States, as the diagram shows.

## Steps Toward Peace and Arms Control

In 1921, President Warren G. Harding hosted the Washington Naval Conference. The United States, Great Britain, France, Italy, and Japan agreed to set limits on the number of warships each nation could build. They also pledged to keep the peace in Asia and to protect the independence of China. The conference, however, failed to establish any means of enforcement.

In 1928, 15 nations met in Paris to sign the Kellogg-Briand Pact, which outlawed war except in self-defense. Enforcement provisions were missing from the pact, which 60 nations eventually signed.

Although the United States never joined the League of Nations or the World Court, it did send observers to League meetings. American judges also served on the World Court, which was based in Geneva, Switzerland.

### Postwar Loans and Debts

U.S. loans $ to Germany

Germany pays reparations to Allies

Allies pay war debts to U.S.

## Preparing for the Exam

The history of United States foreign policy can be viewed as a sequence of stages listed below.

**1776–1823**
Protecting national independence

**1824–1897**
Fulfilling Manifest Destiny

**1898–1918**
Emerging global involvement

**1919–1940**
Limiting international involvement

**1941 to the present**
Accepting world leadership

# Questions for Regents Practice

## Multiple Choice

*Directions:* Review the Test-Taking Strategies section of this book. Then answer the following questions, drawn from actual Regents examinations. For each statement or question, choose the *number* of the word or expression that, of those given, best completes the statement or answers the question.

1  In the late 1800s, which reason led the United States to give greater attention to the world beyond its borders?

   (1) fear of revolution in Latin America
   (2) fear of Russian expansion in Alaska
   (3) interest in finding places to settle surplus population
   (4) interest in obtaining markets for surplus goods

2  The United States government economic policy shifted away from laissez faire in the early 1900s. The main reason for this shift was the desire to

   (1) increase government ownership of major industries
   (2) make the United States more competitive with foreign economies
   (3) coordinate the economy for a war effort
   (4) reduce the abuses of big business

3  "Third parties in the United States are not . . . especially important in their own right, but only in terms of their influence on the major parties." Which is the most valid conclusion to be drawn from this quotation?

   (1) The contribution of third parties has been insignificant in American history.
   (2) The ideas of third parties have often been adopted by the two major parties.
   (3) Third-party leaders have often become the candidates of the major parties.
   (4) Third parties have failed to become important because they have been unable to develop new ideas.

4  Which is the most valid conclusion to be drawn from a study of the role of the Populist, Progressive, and Prohibition Parties in United States history?

   (1) Coalition government is a practical idea for United States society.
   (2) Improvements for racial minorities are often initiated by third parties.
   (3) Third-party platforms are often important in helping to bring about change.
   (4) Voters are most greatly influenced by the religious beliefs they hold.

5  In the United States, the term *muckraker* has been used to describe authors whose writings deal mainly with

   (1) criticizing the government's social welfare policies
   (2) publicizing constitutional issues relating to minorities' rights
   (3) advancing the cause of socialism
   (4) exposing social conditions in need of reform

6  Which event of the early 1900s is evidence that Upton Sinclair's novel *The Jungle* had an important impact on the United States?

   (1) adoption of reform in public education
   (2) passage of legislation limiting immigration
   (3) adoption of the Eighteenth Amendment establishing Prohibition
   (4) passage of legislation requiring federal inspection of meat

7 "All forms of life developed from earlier forms. In every case the fittest survived and the weak died out. It is the same for people and nations." This passage expresses a view most often found in

(1) fundamentalism

(2) Social Darwinism

(3) liberalism

(4) utopian socialism

8 Jacob Riis's photographs and the settlement house movement led by Jane Addams drew attention to the needs of the

(1) former slaves immediately after the Civil War

(2) farmers in the 1880s and 1890s

(3) urban poor in the late nineteenth and early twentieth centuries

(4) Japanese and Chinese laborers in the late 1800s

9 "In the period between the Civil War and World War I, often the first American to greet the sea-weary immigrants when they walked down the gangplank into the United States was a member of the local political machine. This considerate politician helped the immigrant through customs, got him a job, and lent him a few dollars until payday."

The process described in the quotation was a major benefit to the immigrant and to the nation because political machines

(1) encouraged new citizens to vote according to issues, not party labels

(2) helped provide a supply of cheap and willing labor for industry

(3) assisted the social, economic, and political assimilation of immigrants into the community

(4) helped to ensure honest government

10 Western territories were among the first to adopt laws granting political rights to women because the

(1) Native American heritage of matriarchy served as an example to territorial governors

(2) strongest women's rights movements began in the West

(3) settlers brought a tradition of women's suffrage to American homesteads

(4) hardships of pioneer life encouraged men and women to share responsibilities

11 A major purpose of the Federal Reserve System is to

(1) deal with the trade deficit through tariffs and quotas

(2) control the minimum wage

(3) establish the federal budget

(4) regulate interest rates and the money supply

12 The views of W.E.B. Du Bois clashed with those of Booker T. Washington because Du Bois insisted that African Americans should

(1) seek immediate equality of all types and resist any form of second-class citizenship

(2) pursue a policy of gradual integration

(3) accept racial segregation laws because they were constitutional

(4) learn a trade before pursuing political equality

13 Theodore Roosevelt's New Nationalism and Woodrow Wilson's New Freedom were designed primarily to

(1) increase the power and influence of the United States in foreign affairs

(2) reduce the role of government in the economy

(3) help the United States solve problems caused by industrialization

(4) protect the constitutional rights of religious and racial minorities

# Questions for Regents Practice

**14** Which statement reflects a foreign policy view held by both President James Monroe and President Theodore Roosevelt?

(1) Revolutionary movements in Western Europe must be stopped.

(2) Close economic ties with Asia must be maintained.

(3) Noninvolvement in world affairs is the wisest policy for the United States.

(4) United States influence in Latin America must be accepted by other countries.

Base your answers to questions 15 and 16 on the excerpt from the Progressive Party platform of 1912 below and on your knowledge of United States history.

"We of the Progressive Party here dedicate ourselves to the fulfillment of the duty laid upon us by our fathers to maintain the government of the people, by the people, and for the people whose foundations they laid. . . .

"To destroy this invisible government, to dissolve the unholy alliance between corrupt business and corrupt politics is the first task of statesmanship of the day."

**15** The phrase "invisible government" refers to the power exerted by

(1) the president's Cabinet

(2) the Supreme Court

(3) pressure groups

(4) minority parties in Congress

**16** The phrase "government of the people, by the people, and for the people" has been previously stated in the

(1) Declaration of Independence

(2) Bill of Rights

(3) preamble to the Constitution

(4) Gettysburg Address

**17** Which pair of terms represents two major causes of imperialism in the Nineteenth Century?

(1) industrialism and communism

(2) communism and fascism

(3) nationalism and industrialism

(4) collectivism and missionary zeal

**18** "The Constitution rides behind
And the Big Stick rides before
(Which is the rule of precedent
In the reign of Theodore)."

This rhyme from the early 1900s suggests that President Theodore Roosevelt

(1) relied heavily on the advice of his Cabinet and Congress

(2) failed to make adequate use of executive power

(3) developed strong foreign policies but neglected domestic needs

(4) ignored democratic principles in carrying out foreign policy

**19** During the late nineteenth century, some United States newspapers printed exaggerated accounts of Spanish cruelty in Cuba. These reports helped to bring about the Spanish-American War primarily by

(1) arousing public anger against Spain

(2) provoking the anger of the business community

(3) alienating the Spanish government

(4) encouraging the formation of Spanish revolutionary groups

20  In the late nineteenth and early twentieth Centuries, United States intervention in Latin America was motivated mainly by the United States desire to

(1) suppress Latin American movements for national independence

(2) reduce the influence of communism

(3) ensure the safety of its growing investments in the area

(4) counteract Spain's economic dominance of the area

21  The main reason the United States developed the Open Door Policy was to

(1) allow the United States to expand its trade with China

(2) demonstrate the positive features of democracy to Chinese leaders

(3) aid the Chinese nationalists in their struggle with the Chinese communists

(4) encourage Chinese workers to come to the United States

22  The "clear and present danger" ruling in the Supreme Court case *Schenck* v. *United States* (1919) confirmed the idea that

(1) prayer in public schools is unconstitutional

(2) racism in the United States is illegal

(3) interstate commerce can be regulated by state governments

(4) constitutional rights are not absolute

23  The main objective of President Woodrow Wilson's Fourteen Points was to

(1) establish a military alliance with European nations

(2) punish Germany for causing World War I

(3) provide for a just and lasting peace

(4) encourage open immigration in industrial nations

24  "Why, by interweaving our destiny with that of any part of Europe, entangle our peace and prosperity in the toils of European ambition, rivalship, interest, humor, or caprice?"

Which action by the United States best reflects the philosophy expressed in this quotation?

(1) passage of legislation restricting immigration

(2) rejection of the Treaty of Versailles

(3) enactment of the Lend-Lease Act

(4) approval of the United Nations Charter

25  "The chief opponents of the Versailles Treaty were dead men: Washington, Jefferson, and Madison."

This statement suggests that opposition in the United States to the Versailles Treaty was based on the

(1) rejection of Woodrow Wilson's Fourteen Points

(2) fear that the treaty would violate the tradition of noninvolvement

(3) belief that the treaty was too harsh on the Central Powers

(4) unhappiness of citizens with United States participation in World War I

26  The greatest contribution of the United States to world peace during the period between World War I and World War II was

(1) support of the League of Nations

(2) support of the disarmament movement

(3) membership in the World Court

(4) adoption of free trade

# Thematic Essay Question

*Directions:*   Write a well-organized essay that includes an introduction, several paragraphs addressing the task below, and a conclusion.

**Theme:**   **Foreign Policy**

> The primary aim of a nation's foreign policy is the self-interest of that nation. Throughout United States history, certain foreign policy actions have led to debate over whether they were in the national interest.

**Task:**

> From your study of United States history, identify *two* foreign policy actions that have led to debate over whether they were in the national interest.
> For *each* foreign policy action identified:
>
> - Discuss the historical circumstances that led the United States to take a specific foreign policy action
> - Describe the foreign policy action that was taken
> - Describe the opposing viewpoints about the role of national self-interest in that action
> - Evaluate whether the action taken succeeded in promoting the national self-interest

You may use any major controversial foreign policy action from your study of United States history. Some suggestions you might wish to consider include: War of 1812; Mexican War (1846–1848); acquisition of the Philippines (1898–1902); Roosevelt Corollary to the Monroe Doctrine (1904); Treaty of Versailles (1919); Lend-Lease Act (1941); Vietnam War; Persian Gulf Crisis (1990–1991).

**You are *not* limited to these suggestions.**

**Guidelines:**

**In your essay, be sure to**
- Develop all aspects of the task
- Support the theme with relevant facts, examples, and details
- Use a logical and clear plan of organization, including an introduction and a conclusion that are beyond a simple restatement of the theme.

**In developing your answer, be sure to keep these general definitions in mind:**

   (a)  **describe means "to illustrate something in words or tell about it"**
   (b)  **discuss means "to make observations about something using facts, reasoning, and arguments; to present in some detail"**
   (c)  **evaluate means "to examine and judge the significance, worth, or condition of; to determine the value of"**

# Document-Based Question

In developing your answers, be sure to keep this general definition in mind:

> <u>discuss</u> means "to make observations about something using facts, reasoning, and argument; to present in some detail.

This question is based on the accompanying documents. The question is designed to test your ability to work with historical documents. Some of the documents have been edited for the purposes of the question. As you analyze the documents, take into account the source of each document and any point of view that may be presented in the document.

**Historical Context:**

> As the United States transformed into an industrialized nation, the effects of this massive change were felt at all levels of society. Industrialization had long-term social, economic, and political effects on American society.

**Task:** Using information from the documents and your knowledge of United States history and government, answer the questions that follow each document in Part A. Your answers to the questions will help you write the Part B essay in which you will be asked to:

> • Discuss the social, economic, and political reactions to industrialization and urbanization in the United States from 1890 to 1920

## Part A: Short Answer

### Document #1

> *Today three-fourths of [New York's] people live in tenements. . . . The gang is the ripe fruit of tenement-house growth. It was born there, endowed with a heritage of instinctive hostility to restraint by a generation that sacrificed home to freedom, or left its country for its country's good. . . . New York's tough represents the essence of reaction against the old and the new oppression, nursed in the rank soil of its slums.*
>
> — **Jacob Riis,** *How the Other Half Lives*, **1890**

1. According to Jacob Riis, what problems developed as a result of urbanization?

_____

_____

## Document #2

> *I insist that the true object of all true education is not to make men carpenters, it is to make carpenters men. . . .*
> *The Talented Tenth of the Negro race must be made leaders of thought and missionaries of culture among their people.*
> *No others can do this work and Negro colleges must train men for it.*
>
> — **W.E.B. Du Bois**

2. According to Du Bois, what should be the role of well-educated African Americans in society?

_____

_____

_____

## Document #3

| Reform | Before the Reform | After the Reform |
|--------|-------------------|------------------|
| Primary | Party leaders pick candidates for state and local offices | Voters select party's candidates |
| Initiative | Only members of state legislatures can introduce bills | Votes can put bills before state legislatures |
| Referendum | Only legislators pass laws | Voters can vote on bills directly |
| Recall | Only courts or legislatures can remove corrupt officials | Voters can remove elected officials from office |

3. State one way in which Progressive legislation granted citizens greater participation in state governments.

_____

_____

_____

## Document #4

It shall be unlawful for any person engaged in commerce . . . to discriminate in price between different purchasers of commodities of like grade and quality . . . where the effect of such discrimination may be substantially to lessen competition or tend to create a monopoly. . . .

No person engaged in commerce . . . shall acquire . . . the whole or any part of the stock . . . where in any line of commerce or in any activity affecting commerce in any section of the country, the effect of such acquisition may be substantially to lessen competition, or to tend to create a monopoly.

— **Clayton Antitrust Act**

4. What effect did the Clayton Antitrust Act have on monopolies such as Standard Oil?

_____

_____

_____

## Document #5

### Value of United States Exports, 1870–1920

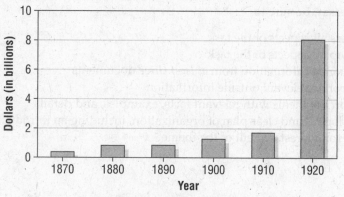

Source: *Historical Statistics of the United States, Colonial Times to 1970*

5. Based on this graph and your knowledge of United States history, how did industrialization affect the activity of American businesses in international markets?

_____

_____

_____

# Document-Based Question

## Part B

**Essay**

*Directions:*   Write a well-organized essay that includes an introduction, several paragraphs, and a conclusion. Use evidence from *at least **three*** documents in your essay. Support your response with relevant facts, examples, and details. Include additional outside information.

### Historical Context:

As the United States transformed into an industrialized nation, the effects of this massive change were felt at all levels of society. Industrialization had long-term social, economic, and political effects on American society.

### Task:

Using information from the documents and your knowledge of United States history and government, write an essay in which you:

---

- Discuss the social, economic, and political reactions to industrialization and urbanization in the United States from 1890 to 1920

---

### Guidelines:

#### In your essay, be sure to

- Address all aspects of the task.
- Develop all aspects of the task
- Incorporate information from *at least **three*** documents
- Incorporate relevant outside information
- Support the theme with relevant facts, examples, and details
- Use a logical and clear plan of organization, including an introduction and conclusion that are beyond a restatement of the theme.

# At Home and Abroad:
## Prosperity and Depression, 1917–1940

**Section 1:** War and Prosperity: 1917–1929

**Section 2:** The Great Depression

## Unit Overview

During the 1920s and 1930s, the United States completed the transition to a modern, urban, industrial nation. In the 1920s, the United States experienced sharp differences in income levels and shifts in cultural values, which created tensions in society and raised issues of civil liberties. At the end of that decade, the nation and the world plunged into a severe economic depression. President Franklin D. Roosevelt's New Deal programs in the 1930s attempted to overcome the effects of the Great Depression in the United States.

Some key questions to help you focus on America between the wars include:

• What tensions developed between the people who were a part of the traditional rural culture and those who were members of the new, urban-based society in the 1920s?

• What were the causes of the Great Depression, and how did that event affect the American people and their institutions?

# War and Prosperity: 1917–1929

The
# Big
# Idea

In the 1920s:

- the American people attempted to return to "normalcy" in foreign and domestic affairs.

- new technologies created a consumer goods economy based on mass consumption.

- the nation became increasingly urbanized, modernized, and commercialized.

- American society was unsettled by these rapid economic, social, and cultural changes.

- tensions developed between new and traditional lifestyles, while nativism resurfaced.

- a boom economy was not shared by all Americans and it came to an end with the 1929 stock market crash.

## Section Overview

The 1920s were a time of many changes in the economic and social aspects of life in the United States. Following World War I, the United States struggled to return to what President Harding called "normalcy." However, the impact of the war, the new age of consumerism, the automobile, and the growth of the suburbs contributed to the creation of a different and new national lifestyle.

While transportation and communications technology served to unite the nation, a clash of values between the new urban-centered life and the legacy of the traditional rural life caused uneasiness and conflict. In addition, all Americans did not share in the good times. Beneath the surface was an economy with structural flaws that brought the Roaring Twenties to an abrupt end with the stock market crash in October 1929.

## Key Themes and Concepts

As you review this section, take special note of the following key themes and concepts:

**Diversity** How did World War I affect women and minorities?

**Factors of Production** Were the 1920s a period of business boom or false prosperity?

**Culture and Intellectual Life** What social changes caused a clash of values during the twenties?

**Science and Technology** In the 1920s, how did new technology lead to social, economic, and political changes?

**Citizenship** In the 1920s, why were the civil liberties of socialists, anarchists, labor leaders, foreigners, Catholics, and African Americans threatened?

## Key Terms

| | |
|---|---|
| Great Migration | Harlem Renaissance |
| normalcy | Jazz Age |
| mass consumption | Red Scare |
| assembly line | quotas |
| consumer goods | Scopes Trial |
| flapper | |

## Key People

As you review this section, take special note of the following key people:

| | | |
|---|---|---|
| Warren G. Harding | Ernest Hemingway | Sinclair Lewis |
| Calvin Coolidge | Langston Hughes | A. Mitchell Palmer |
| Henry Ford | Zora Neale Hurston | Nicola Sacco |
| F. Scott Fitzgerald | Edward K. "Duke" Ellington | Bartolomeo Vanzetti |

# The Impact and Aftermath of War

World War I triggered a number of important changes in American society, most notably for some women and for many immigrants and African Americans. Some changes were subtle and gradual while others were immediate and dramatic.

## The Twenties

| | |
|---|---|
| **1921** Emergency Quota Act passed; Washington Conference began | **1924** Teapot Dome Scandal indictments; National Origins Act; Coolidge elected president |
| **1926** U.S. Marines oversee Nicaragua elections | **1928** U.S. signs Kellogg-Briand Pact |

1920 | 1921 | 1922 | 1923 | 1924 | 1925 | 1926 | 1927 | 1928 | 1929 | 1930

**1920** Warren G. Harding elected president

**1923** Calvin Coolidge succeeds Harding

**1925** Scopes Trial

**1927** Sacco and Vanzetti executed

**1929** Stock Market crash

## Analyzing Documents

Based on the timeline:

- How many years did Warren G. Harding serve as president?

- What event on the timeline is an example of a clash of values?

## Effects on Women and Minorities

As many men went off to fight in Europe, the roles and responsibilities of women were affected. Their family responsibilities increased. They contributed to the war effort as volunteers. Some women went to work in male-dominated fields, such as weapons factories. Many women served overseas with the Red Cross and the Salvation Army. Most, however, worked in traditionally female jobs, for which there was an increased demand. Only about five percent of the women entering the wartime workforce were new to work outside the home. At war's end, with the return of male workers, women were expected to quit their jobs or return to more traditional female work. Between 1910 and 1920, only 500,000 more women were added to the workforce.

The war had harsh consequences for immigrant families. Further immigration to the United States came to a halt. About 18 percent of the American troops were foreign-born. Yet, many immigrant families already in the country faced fierce social and job discrimination in an antiforeign climate whipped up by the war.

Most African American civil rights leaders supported World War I, and some 400,000 African American troops served in it. African American soldiers were assigned to segregated units and often worked as laborers. Discrimination was common.

## Preparing for the Exam

Examine the graphic below and use your knowledge of social studies to answer the following questions.

- What was the impact of post World War I conditions on different groups in American society?

- How did American business respond to the post World War I economic slowdown?

- Did any of these conditions exist after World War II? If so, what actions were taken in the late 1940s and 1950s?

### After World War I

**United States after the war**

- American economy slows as wartime production ends.
- Returning troops face difficult adjustment to civilian society.
- Many women and minority workers face loss of jobs as men return to workforce.
- Despite contributing to war effort, returning African American troops continue to face discrimination and segregation.
- Death and destruction of war leads to feelings of gloom among many Americans.

*After World War I, many Americans faced a difficult adjustment to peacetime life.*

### Geography
### in History

- Who participated in the Great Migration to the North from 1910 to 1930 and again in the 1940s?

- What were the reasons for it?

- What were the effects of it?

Where they saw combat, African American soldiers served with distinction. Several African American regiments fighting alongside of French troops were honored by that nation. Many returning African American soldiers questioned why the liberties and freedoms they had fought to preserve in Europe were denied them in their own country.

### Migration to the North

World War I accelerated the migration of African Americans to northern cities. This migration began after the Civil War. From about 1910 to 1920, southern agricultural jobs were lost to floods and to crop damage. About 500,000 African Americans moved from the South to jobs in the industrial North. Meanwhile in the North, workers were needed to meet war production goals. The flow of immigrant labor was ended by the fighting, creating an additional need for workers to replace those in uniform.

After the war, this **Great Migration** continued. Between 1910 and 1930 and again in the 1940s, almost two million African Americans left the South. Although they were usually able to improve their economic situation, they were still faced with discrimination and segregation. Competition for jobs and housing produced racial tensions that at times led to individual violence and to riots.

### The "Return to Normalcy," 1918–1921

After World War I, disillusioned Americans wanted to return to the traditional foreign policy of isolationism. The 1920 landslide election of Republican President Warren G. Harding and Vice President Calvin Coolidge represented the desire of many Americans to remove themselves from the pressures of world politics and the idealistic goals of the Progressives. While Progressivism continued, it was at a slower pace and reforms took place largely at the state and local levels.

#### Election of 1920

Republican Warren G. Harding 76% of electoral vote

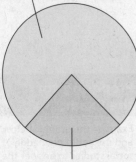

Democrat James M. Cox 24% of electoral vote

# The 1920s: Business Boom or False Prosperity?

For many Americans, postwar life did return to **normalcy.** Yet beneath the surface, troubling political and economic problems had begun to develop.

### Greed and Scandal Under Harding

Harding was an Ohio newspaper publisher with little experience in politics. Historians credit him for pardoning socialist Eugene V. Debs (who had been jailed for opposing the war) and for supporting antilynching legislation. Harding appointed some dedicated people to office, including Charles Evans Hughes as secretary of state.

However, the president also gave political jobs to members of the so-called Ohio Gang, corrupt associates who took advantage of him. After Harding's death in 1923, the public learned of several scandals during his administration.

- *Theft:* The head of the Veterans Bureau was convicted of selling hospital supplies for his own profit. He was imprisoned and fined.

- *Fraud:* The Alien Property Custodian was imprisoned for selling former German property for private profit.

- *The Teapot Dome Scandal:* Secretary of the Interior Albert Fall was convicted of accepting bribes from two oil executives in exchange for allowing them to lease government-owned petroleum reserves. One of the oil fields was at Teapot Dome, Wyoming.

### Analyzing
### Documents

*"America's present need is not heroics, but healing, not nostrums [remedies] but normalcy, not revolution but restoration, not surgery but serenity."*
—*Warren G. Harding*

Examine the pie graph and the quotation.

- How does the pie graph support the statement that the 1920 election was a landslide in favor of "normalcy"?

## Under Coolidge, Prosperity for Some

Calvin Coolidge became president when Harding died in office in 1923. In the 1924 election, Coolidge was returned to office. Coolidge is best known for his laissez-faire approach to the economy and his strong commitment to business interests. Coolidge retained financier Andrew Mellon as secretary of the treasury. Mellon acted on the philosophy that government's role was to serve business.

**Recession** The end of World War I was followed by a recession caused by the shift from a wartime to a peacetime economy. Production, farm income, and exports fell. Unemployment rose, reaching 11.7 percent in 1921. For farmers, in particular, hardship continued throughout the decade.

*Calvin Coolidge*

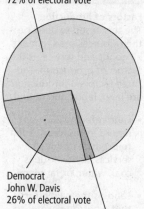

**Election of 1924**

Republican Calvin Coolidge
72% of electoral vote

Democrat
John W. Davis
26% of electoral vote

Progressive Party
Robert M. La Follette
2% of electoral vote

**Recovery** In other sectors of the economy, however, a period of economic recovery had begun by 1923, when Coolidge became President. The years between 1923 and 1929 were seen as a time of booming business. The Gross National Product (GNP) rose 40 percent. Per capita income went up 30 percent. With little inflation, actual purchasing power—and therefore the standard of living—increased. At the time, few people questioned this Coolidge prosperity.

**Pro-Business Policies** Some groups, especially big corporations and the wealthy, benefited greatly from Coolidge prosperity. For example:

- businesses and the wealthiest citizens were helped by tax laws that reduced personal income tax rates, particularly for upper income groups, removed most excise taxes, and lowered corporate income taxes.
- the government reduced the national debt and balanced the budget by raising tariffs and demanding repayment of war debts.
- tariff rates were raised in a return to protectionism. Republicans argued that higher tariffs would limit foreign imports, thus protecting United States industry and agriculture from foreign competition, but the actual effect was to weaken the world economy.
- regulatory agencies such as the Federal Reserve Board, the Federal Trade Commission, and the Interstate Commerce Commission were staffed with people who saw their role as assisting business rather than regulating it.
- a relaxed attitude toward corporate mergers was supported by the executive branch and by the Supreme Court. By 1929, about 1,300 corporations produced three fourths of all American manufactured goods, and 200 companies owned half the nation's wealth.

## Economic Boom Bypasses Others

Coolidge prosperity was not for everyone. Key segments of the population failed to share in the general rise in living standards.

**Labor** Strikes had dropped sharply during World War I, mainly because the Wilson government supported collective bargaining in return for a no-strike pledge. Membership in the American Federation of Labor grew, and wages for war industry employees rose sharply. However, inflation wiped out any real gains in buying power.

### Preparing for the Exam

You will need to understand certain important economic terms on the exam.

The **Gross National Product** (GNP) is the total value of all goods and services produced in one year.

**Per Capita Income** means income per individual; it is based on the national income divided by the population.

### Reading Strategy

**Reading for Evidence**
What evidence is presented in the text to support the following statement?

"Important segments of the population failed to share in the general rise in living standards."

## Key Themes and Concepts

**Factors of Production**
The term used to describe the resources used to make all goods and services is the *factors of production*. The three factors of production are land, labor, and capital.

- *Land* refers to all natural resources needed to produce goods and services. Land includes coal, water, or farmland.

- *Labor* is the paid effort that a person devotes to a task. Labor can include the medical aid provided by a doctor as well as the tasks performed by an assembly-line worker.

- *Capital* is any human-made resource used to produce other goods and services. Physical capital includes factory buildings and tools, while human capital includes workers' knowledge and experience.

The 1920s saw a reversal of any union gains. Strikes in the steel, mining, and railroad industries failed, in part because the government used not only troops to end the strikes but also injunctions, which are court orders that prohibit specified actions. The Supreme Court also ruled against child labor laws and against minimum wages for women and children. In addition, some companies began to offer health and life insurance in hopes of lessening workers' interest in unions. The strategy often worked. Membership in labor unions fell from a high of about 5 million in 1921 to under 3.5 million in 1929.

While the labor movement weakened in the 1920s, conditions improved for many workers. After 1923, unemployment averaged 5 percent or less. Worker productivity rose over 40 percent. In general, however, real wages for workers increased only slightly during this period, boosted primarily by wages of workers in the new industries such as communications and automobile manufacturing. This situation meant that they could not afford to buy many of the new consumer goods.

**Farmers** The only farmers to benefit from Coolidge prosperity were those involved in large commercial operations. Small farmers were hurt by a combination of factors.

- Farmers expanded production during World War I in response to rising prices and the demand for food. They added to their acreage and bought more farm machinery.
- New machinery and new farm techniques increased farmers' crop yield per acre.
- After the war, when European farms began producing again, American farmers were growing too much. With overproduction the prices of both farm products and farmland decreased dramatically.
- Net farm income fell 50 percent during the 1920s. As farm income fell, many farmers lost their land when they could not make their mortgage payments. As a result, the number of farmers declined, too. By 1930, only about 20 percent of the labor force made a living by farming.

**Native Americans** During the 1920s, Native Americans had the highest unemployment rate of any group and the shortest average life span. Most lived on reservations, without the basics, such as heat and running water.

**African Americans** African Americans who migrated to the North enjoyed a higher standard of living than in the South. However, they still earned less than white workers and experienced a higher rate of unemployment.

## Stock Market Speculation

The economic recovery helped produce a surge of investment in the stock market. Optimistic business and government leaders saw no end to the boom. They encouraged everyone to play the bull market—that is, the rising stock market. Some families invested their life savings. The profits rolled in—for a while.

Yet the new wealth flowed from a stock market with a deeply flawed structure. Many stocks were traded on margin. This meant that buyers could purchase stocks by making only small down payments in cash—sometimes as low as 5 percent of the value of the stocks. They borrowed the rest from brokers and counted on their profits to repay the loans. The system worked as long as the profits continued.

# Mass Consumption

The 1920s were a time of mass consumption—huge quantities of manufactured goods were available, and many people had more money to spend on them.

## The Effects of New Industries on American Life

### The Automobile Industry:

1. stimulated the steel, rubber, paint, glass, and oil industries
2. accelerated a middle-class move to the suburbs that fueled a real estate boom
3. led to an increase in highways and a decline in railroad construction and use
4. caused tractors to replace horses on farms
5. increased social equality as low prices made cars available to Americans at almost all income levels
6. stimulated installment buying
7. contributed to growing sophistication of advertising techniques
8. expanded cities into larger urban areas
9. stimulated development of services such as gas stations, motels, supermarkets, and shopping malls
10. gave greater independence to women and teenagers, changing family life

### The Electrical Industry:

1. changed homes, businesses, and cities through electric lights
2. helped double business productivity through electric power
3. transformed life and leisure with electric-powered durable goods such as washing machines, stoves, vacuum cleaners, refrigerators, and irons
4. stimulated installment buying
5. connected people and eased rural isolation through the telephone

### Radio and Motion Pictures:

1. helped erase regional differences and homogenize American culture
2. increased people's expectations, often unrealistically
3. helped end rural isolation
4. helped popularize ragtime and jazz
5. provided an outlet for advertising
6. increased interest in politics and spectator sports
7. created nationally known celebrities—stars of radio, sports, and movies

## Role of Technology

Technology, combined with new marketing strategies, best explains the transformation of American society in the 1920s. Led by Henry Ford and the automobile industry, mass production and the moving **assembly line** resulted in uniform products produced at lower costs.

These new technologies made possible a consumer-oriented economy, one in which more goods, costing less, were available to more Americans. Encouraged by a boom in advertising, families spent a smaller portion of their income on necessities and a larger proportion on new **consumer goods** such as appliances, radios, and ready-to-wear clothing. Often these goods were purchased over time through installment buying.

## Growing Cultural Homogenization

The new technology also made American culture more homogeneous, or uniform. Americans from one coast to the other tended to use the same products, wear the same styles, see the same movies, and listen to the same music. Regional and class differences were blurred, and individualism became less important than conformity.

## Key Themes and Concepts

**Science and Technology**
In the 1920s, radio, movies, and telephones helped produce a more homogenized national culture in which regional differences became less distinct.

- According to the chart, in what ways did the automobile, electrical industry, radio, and motion pictures influence the lifestyle of the 1920s?

- What technology since the 1920s has resulted in further national and even international homogenization?

## Reading Strategy

**Formulating Questions**
Consider that in the 1920s:

- 15 million cars were sold.

- 80 percent were bought on credit.

- a Model T Ford cost $290 in 1920.

- more than 63 percent of U.S. homes had electricity by the end of the decade.

- 10 million families owned radios by 1929.

In addition to these facts, what information do you need in order to have a more complete picture of the effect of new technologies in the 1920s?

*Cars on a city street*

Source: *Courtesy of the Library of Congress*

## Suburban Growth

With over half the population living in places with populations of more than 2,500 people, the United States in the 1920s was an urban rather than a rural nation for the first time in its history. Only the Great Depression ended the building boom that was part of this growth. The automobile made it possible to draw people to suburbs that grew even faster than cities. New regional, political, and economic units developed, resulting in the present-day conflict between urban and suburban needs, priorities, and values.

## Shifting Cultural Values

During the 1920s, American society experienced a struggle with social change as it became an urban, industrial nation. Changes in lifestyle, values, morals, and manners increased tension and conflict. Wealth, possessions, having fun, and sexual freedom—ideas influenced by the psychology of Sigmund Freud—were the new values.

**Leisure** With a shorter work week and with more paid vacation, Americans had more leisure time. Movies such as *The Ten Commandments* and the first movie with sound, *The Jazz Singer*, drew millions of people a week to theaters during the 1920s. Americans idolized Charlie Chaplin and other movie stars. They also admired sports figures, such as Babe Ruth. After his 1927 solo transatlantic flight, Charles Lindbergh became an overnight hero. Listening to the radio and to records were two other popular pastimes. Games such as bridge, crossword puzzles, and the board game of mah-jongg swept the country.

The popular image of young women in the 1920s was the **flapper,** a young, pretty woman with bobbed hair and raised hemlines. She drank alcohol, she smoked, and she thought for herself.

### Analyzing Documents

- What information from the graph helps you to gain a more complete picture of the effect of the automobile industry in the 1920s?

**Passenger Car Sales, 1920–1929**

Source: *Historical Statistics of the United States, Colonial Times to 1970*

The flapper was featured in movies, magazines, advertising, and novels, such as those of F. Scott Fitzgerald. The flapper was an expression of women's new sense of independence, a statement of change, even rebellion. As such, the flapper represented another example in the debate over traditional versus modern values that was dividing the nation.

**Literature** The conflict and concern created by changing American values also saw expression in literature. American writers of the 1920s protested the effects of technology and mass consumption. They criticized the business mentality, the conformity of the times, and the preoccupation with material things. Some writers, such as Ernest Hemingway, became expatriates, leaving the United States to settle in Europe. Often called the Lost Generation, these writers of the twenties produced some of the most enduring works of American literature.

**Harlem Renaissance** One of the most important cultural movements of the 1920s was the Harlem Renaissance, led by a group of African American writers in the New York City neighborhood of Harlem. These creative intellectual figures—mainly well-educated members of the middle class—felt alienated from the society of the 1920s. In their works they called for action against bigotry and expressed pride in African American culture and identity. Outstanding literary figures of the Harlem Renaissance include W.E.B. Du Bois, Langston Hughes, Zora Neale Hurston, and Alain Locke.

The Great Depression of the 1930s ended the Harlem Renaissance, cutting the sales of books and literary magazines. However, during the civil rights movement of the 1960s, the writers of the Harlem Renaissance and their works attracted renewed interest.

African American artists, musicians, and dancers also participated in the Harlem Renaissance. Black musicians in the South blended elements of African, European, and American music to create the distinctive sounds of jazz and the blues. This music was carried all over the country and abroad.

Edward K. "Duke" Ellington is one of the towering figures in jazz. Ellington recorded and composed music, performed on the piano, and conducted his own orchestra until his death in 1974. Bessie Smith, known as the "Empress of the Blues," was one of the most popular singers of the 1920s. This new music, to which people danced such daring new steps as the Charleston, became so popular that the period of the 1920s is often called the **Jazz Age.**

### Leading Writers of the 1920s

| | | |
|---|---|---|
| Willa Cather | novelist | *My Antonia* |
| F. Scott Fitzgerald | novelist | *The Great Gatsby* |
| Ernest Hemingway | novelist | *A Farewell to Arms* |
| Langston Hughes | poet, novelist | *The Weary Blues* |
| Zora Neale Hurston | novelist, folklorist | *Their Eyes Were Watching God* |
| Sinclair Lewis | novelist | *Main Street, Babbitt* |
| Eugene O'Neill | playwright | *Desire Under the Elms* |
| Edith Wharton | novelist | *The Age of Innocence* |

**Analyzing Documents**

*"We build our temples for tomorrow, strong as we know how, and we stand on the top of the mountain, free within ourselves."*
—Langston Hughes, on the Harlem Renaissance in The Big Sea

- What ideas of the Harlem Renaissance are expressed in this quote?

**Key Themes and Concepts**

**Culture and Intellectual Life**
The cultural and intellectual life of a time period reflects the era's social, economic, and political mood.

- How did the work of each writer in the chart reflect the 1920s?

- How did the Harlem Renaissance express the feelings of its participants?

- How did it have an influence beyond its time?

## Women's Changing Roles

The conflict between modern and traditional values in the 1920s also found expression in the contradictory roles of women.

**Women in the Workforce** Throughout the 1920s, the number of women in the workforce increased steadily. By 1930, 10.7 million women were working outside the home, making up 22 percent of the workforce. Most working women were single, widowed, or divorced. While, by 1930, about one in six married women worked—more than ever before—90 percent continued to remain at home.

By 1930, women earned 40 percent of the bachelor degrees awarded. Many of them became teachers, nurses, and social workers, traditional female occupations. Fewer than 20 percent worked in the better-paying skilled factory jobs. Changes in technology and scientific management created opportunities for women in white-collar and service industry jobs. These low-paying, low-status, and low-mobility-occupations included work as secretaries, salespeople, telephone operators, and beauticians. Because these jobs were labeled "female only," even in hard times, women were able to be hired for these and other new occupations.

One important gain for working women was the creation in 1920 of the Women's Bureau, part of the federal Department of Labor. It tried to improve working conditions for women from inside the government and provided data about working women.

**Involvement in Politics** In 1920, women voted in a national election for the first time. However, their vote did not have a distinctive effect on the outcome. Women did not vote in large numbers, nor did they vote as a bloc. To encourage women to play a greater part in politics, the National American Woman Suffrage Association reorganized itself as the nonpartisan League of Women Voters.

**Health, Rights, and Working Conditions** The divisions of the 1920s were reflected in the fate of two pieces of legislation. Encouraged by women reformers, Congress passed the Sheppard-Towner Act in 1921. With the aim of reducing infant mortality, the law provided for public health centers where women could learn about nutrition and health care. The program came to an end in 1929, largely because of opposition from the American Medical Association.

An equal rights amendment to the Constitution, proposed by Alice Paul in 1923, led to bitter disagreement among women. Many feminists supported it, but other feminists opposed it because they believed it would do away with special laws protecting female workers.

**Daily Life** Contrary to the image of the flapper, women were still restricted by economic, political, and social limits. In some ways, technology made life easier in the 1920s, especially for middle class women. With electric washing machines, vacuum cleaners, stoves, and refrigerators, household chores did not require so much time, and there was less need for servants. On the other hand, the typical homemaker now was expected to handle almost all the household tasks herself and to meet higher standards of cleanliness.

**Emphasis on Wife Rather Than Mother** The role of the woman as wife received increased importance. Women did have more choices in life. Families changed during this period, and divorce and family planning became more acceptable. However, divorce laws continued to favor men, and wives were expected to stay at home rather than work outside the home. Family size decreased; only 20 percent of women who married during the 1920s had five or more children. The family, which in earlier times had been a producing unit,

## Key Themes and Concepts

**Diversity**
In the 1920s women were workers, flappers, wives, mothers, voters, students, and housewives. In what ways were their lives different from the lives of women during the following periods in history?

- the first half of the nineteenth century
- the second half of the nineteenth century
- the Progressive Era
- World War I
- the Great Depression
- World War II
- the 1950s
- the 1960s and 1970s
- today

growing and processing much of its food, was now a consuming unit. Marketing and advertising appeals flooded the media, encouraging consumers to buy more goods.

## Constitutional and Legal Issues

Major constitutional and legal issues divided Americans in the 1920s. Many issues reflected the struggle between modern and traditional values and showed how international affairs affected domestic policies and attitudes. For some Americans, these tensions took the form of nativism, racism, and intolerance of differences in religion and politics.

### Threats to Civil Liberties

In the 1920s, the Red Scare and the Ku Klux Klan threatened the civil liberties of some Americans.

**The Red Scare 1918–1919** The imposition of stern measures to suppress dissent after World War I in a crusade against internal enemies was known as the Red Scare. It was fueled by the November 1917 Bolshevik Revolution, an uprising of Communists in Russia. In the United States, Communists made up only one half of one percent of the population, but many of them were targeted by the crackdown, as were various other groups viewed as un-American. Among them were socialists, anarchists, labor leaders, and foreigners.

The Red Scare was led by Attorney General A. Mitchell Palmer. It was sparked by several events that took place after the war ended. Race riots erupted in more than 25 cities. In Boston, a series of labor strikes climaxed with a walkout by the police. Several unexplained bombings added to the hysteria. All these events were seen as part of a Communist conspiracy.

The attorney general ordered the first so-called Palmer Raids late in 1919. In 33 cities, police without warrants raided the headquarters of Communists and other organizations. Eventually they arrested more than 4,000 people, holding them without charges and denying them legal counsel. Some 560 aliens were deported. Palmer's extreme actions and statements soon turned the public against him. However, the Red Scare had lingering effects, discouraging many Americans from speaking their minds freely in open debate, thus squelching their constitutional right to freedom of speech.

**Sacco and Vanzetti** Closely linked to the Red Scare was the case of Nicola Sacco and Bartolomeo Vanzetti. These two Italian immigrants—admitted anarchists— were convicted of murder in 1921 in connection with a Massachusetts robbery. Many people questioned the evidence against Sacco and Vanzetti, concluding that the two men were convicted more for their beliefs and their Italian origin than for a crime. In spite of mass demonstrations and appeals, the two men were executed in 1927. The governor of Massachusetts eventually cleared the two men in 1977, some 50 years later.

**The Ku Klux Klan** Antiforeign attitudes encouraged a revival of the Ku Klux Klan. The first organization, active during Reconstruction, had died out in the late 1800s. A reorganized Klan, formed in 1915, grew slowly until 1920. In that year, it added 100,000 members. The Klan of the 1920s targeted not only African Americans but also Catholics, Jews, and immigrants. To the Klan, the only true Americans were white, Protestant, and American-born. In 1925, membership peaked at two million.

### Preparing for the Exam

Remember that fear of foreigners and foreign ideas has been an issue that has arisen many times throughout United States history.

- 1790s: Alien and Sedition Acts

- 1840s: nativism and the Know-Nothings

- 1917–1918: suppression of dissent during World War I

- 1920s: Ku Klux Klan, Sacco and Vanzetti case, National Origins Quota Acts

- 1940s: internment of Japanese Americans during World War II

- 1950s: McCarthyism

*Immigrants at Ellis Island*

# Restrictions on Immigration

The nativism expressed in the Red Scare, the Sacco-Vanzetti case, and the new Klan was also evident in 1920s immigration legislation. Immigration had resumed after World War I, but there was less of a need for workers. In the post-war recession, immigrants were seen as taking jobs from returning soldiers and somehow threatening American values. The nativist climate led to the Immigration Act of 1924. This act established a system of national **quotas,** which limited the number of immigrants from each country. These quotas deliberately kept the totals for eastern and southern Europe low and excluded all immigration from Asia.

**Immigration to the United States, 1921 and 1926**

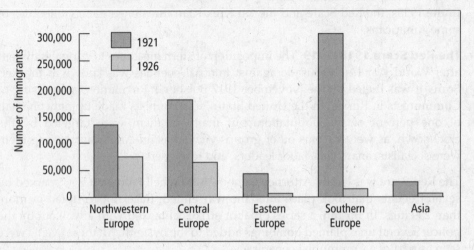

## Key Themes and Concepts

**Immigration and Migration**
During the 1920s, immigration from the western hemisphere was not limited. Large numbers of Mexicans moved into southwestern cities and Puerto Ricans moved into New York City, most in search of economic opportunities.

- What are the most dramatic changes pictured on the chart at right?

- What changes were made to immigration laws in the 1920s? Why?

## Prohibition

Both the rebirth of the Klan and the movement to restrict immigration reflected the struggle in the 1920s between what some saw as old, rural American values and the new values of a changing urban, industrialized culture. However, the clash between these two sets of values did not divide on the basis of where one lived.

For example, the movement for Prohibition, a ban on the sale and consumption of alcoholic beverages, was not confined to rural America, though it received much support there. The Eighteenth Amendment, allowing Prohibition, became part of the Constitution in 1919. Congress passed the Volstead Act to implement Prohibition, but the law turned out to be unenforceable. Most Americans were simply unwilling to accept a total ban on alcohol. Furthermore, it stimulated crime, encouraging smuggling and bootlegging, the illegal manufacture and sale of alcoholic beverages. In 1933, the Twenty-first Amendment ending Prohibition was ratified.

## Preparing for the Exam

Prohibition turned out to be unenforceable because too many Americans were unwilling to accept it. The massive evasion of this law is often compared to the reaction to the 1850 Fugitive Slave Law. In 1933, the Twenty-first Amendment repealed the Eighteenth Amendment.

## The Scopes Trial

The 1925 Scopes Trial, held in Dayton, Tennessee, received nationwide attention because it pitted the scientific ideas of Darwinian evolution against the Protestant fundamentalist view of biblical creationism. John Scopes, a biology teacher, had deliberately violated a state law forbidding anyone to teach the theory of evolution. Scopes was represented by a famous trial lawyer, Clarence Darrow. The prosecution relied on the assistance of William Jennings Bryan, a three-time presidential candidate and firm believer in fundamentalist Christianity. Although Scopes was convicted and fined $100, Bryan's confused testimony weakened fundamentalist arguments.

# UNIT 5
## Section 2

# The Great Depression

## Section Overview

The 1930s were dominated by the Great Depression. Worldwide in scope, the Great Depression affected virtually every aspect of American life. With roots in unregulated stock market speculation, a flawed banking system, and the overproduction of goods, the Great Depression was triggered by the stock market crash in 1929. Banks failed, and many people lost their life savings. The losses shut down businesses, producing widespread unemployment, homelessness, and hunger.

President Herbert Hoover's response to the Great Depression proved ineffective. In 1933, President Franklin D. Roosevelt's New Deal launched ambitious programs of relief, recovery, and reform. The New Deal dramatically increased the role and responsibility of government in American social and economic life and strengthened the power of the presidency. The entry of the United States into World War II in 1941 put a final end to the nation's worst economic collapse. Today, the Great Depression remains the benchmark against which an economic crisis is measured.

## Key Themes and Concepts

As you review this section, take special note of the following key themes and concepts:

**Factors of Production** What were the causes of the Great Depression?

**Economic Systems** Which New Deal actions were intended to reform the United States economic system?

**Government** How did the New Deal change the nineteenth-century role of government in the United States?

**Culture and Intellectual Life** How did the depression affect daily life and culture in America?

**Diversity** How did the New Deal affect organized labor, minorities, and women?

## Key Terms

| | |
|---|---|
| Great Stock Market Crash | Bonus Army |
| speculation | Hoovervilles |
| on margin | Dust Bowl |
| Great Depression | New Deal |
| overproduction | bank holiday |
| underconsumption | collective bargaining |
| distribution of wealth | court-packing proposal |
| "trickle down" economics | |

## The Big Idea

In the 1930s:

- fundamental weaknesses in the national and world economies caused the stock market crash and the Great Depression that followed.

- the Great Depression dominated every aspect of political, social, and economic life of the 1930s.

- President Herbert Hoover's efforts toward economic recovery did not succeed.

- President Franklin Roosevelt's New Deal worked for relief, recovery, and reform.

- the New Deal was based on the belief that government had a responsibility for the social and economic well-being of its citizens.

- President Franklin Roosevelt's New Deal provided relief but only limited recovery, and left a legacy of economic and social reform laws.

## Key People

As you review this section, take special note of the following key people:

Herbert Hoover

John Steinbeck

Franklin Delano Roosevelt

Frances Perkins

Harry Hopkins

Eleanor Roosevelt

John L. Lewis

Mary McLeod Bethune

John Maynard Keynes

Huey Long

## Key Supreme Court Cases

As you review this section, take special note of the following key Supreme Court case:

*Schechter Poultry Corporation* v. *United States* (1935)

### Analyzing Documents

According to the timeline:

- which event on the timeline resulted in a migration of farmers?

- which was a law passed to benefit workers?

- which act was passed to provide a "safety net"?

- which acts were passed to provide banking and investment reform?

**The Great Depression**

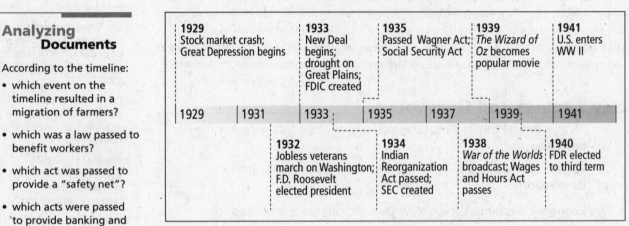

| 1929 | 1933 | 1935 | 1939 | 1941 |
|---|---|---|---|---|
| Stock market crash; Great Depression begins | New Deal begins; drought on Great Plains; FDIC created | Passed Wagner Act; Social Security Act | *The Wizard of Oz* becomes popular movie | U.S. enters WW II |

| 1929 | 1931 | 1933 | 1935 | 1937 | 1939 | 1941 |

| 1932 | 1934 | 1938 | 1940 |
|---|---|---|---|
| Jobless veterans march on Washington; F.D. Roosevelt elected president | Indian Reorganization Act passed; SEC created | *War of the Worlds* broadcast; Wages and Hours Act passes | FDR elected to third term |

## The Great Stock Market Crash

The end of the prosperity of the 1920s was marked by a series of plunges in the United States stock market in the fall of 1929 known as the Great Stock Market Crash. Throughout the 1920s, the stock market had grown on **speculation** by people who bought **on margin,** and, in fact, owned only a small portion of their stocks. Many could not meet margin calls, demands to put up the money to cover their loans. The result was panic selling. On October 29 (Black Tuesday) alone, stock values fell $14 billion. They dropped lower and lower in the weeks months, and years that followed, reaching bottom in July 1932. By then the market had fallen 89 percent from its September 1929 high point.

The stock market crash triggered the start of the **Great Depression.** It shattered the national sense of optimism and confidence of the 1920s. The crash dramatically exposed the fact that the national economy had serious weaknesses.

## Causes of the Great Depression

The Great Depression was caused by an unsound economy—**overproduction** and **underconsumption,** overexpansion of credit, and fragile corporate structures— combined with ineffective government action. The growing interdependence of international trade and banking made the effects even more damaging.

### Preparing for the Exam

Underconsumption or overproduction means that people buy fewer goods than are produced. In other words, supply is greater than demand.

## The Stock Market Crash

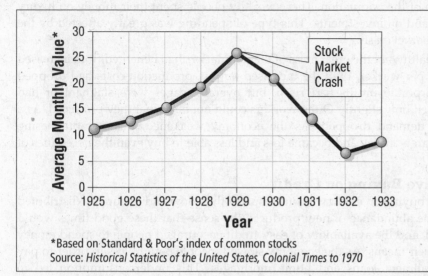

*Based on Standard & Poor's index of common stocks
Source: *Historical Statistics of the United States, Colonial Times to 1970*

### Analyzing Documents

Based on the graph and your knowledge of social studies, answer the following questions.

- When did the stock market crash occur?

- In what year did stock prices reach their lowest point?

- What role did speculation play in the crash?

- What is the relationship of the stock market crash to the Great Depression?

## Weaknesses in the Overall Economy

Weaknesses in the economy had existed before 1929 and were expanding.

- The agricultural sector had been depressed throughout the 1920s, with a worldwide drop in prices.

- Unemployment plagued the railroad, coal, and textile industries well before 1929.

- Speculation in real estate and the resulting building boom had declined.

- The number of bank failures was rising as farmers, people speculating in stocks, and consumers buying on credit could not repay their loans.

- As early as the summer of 1929, the economy showed signs of underconsumption. Inventories of unsold goods began to accumulate in warehouses as consumer demand slowed.

## Unequal Distribution of Income

Contributing to underconsumption and to the weakness of the economy was an unequal distribution of wealth.

- In the 1920s, at a time that a family needed an annual income of $2500 to have a modest standard of living, over 60 percent of American families lived on only $2000 per year—just enough to cover basic needs. Some 40 percent of all families had an income of less than $1,500, which put them below the poverty line. At the same time, the 24,000 richest families in the nation had a total income *three times as large* as the total income of the 6 million poorest families. In short, while 1 percent of the population owned 59 percent of the nation's wealth, 87 percent of the population owned only 10 percent of the wealth.

### Income Distribution in the United States, 1929

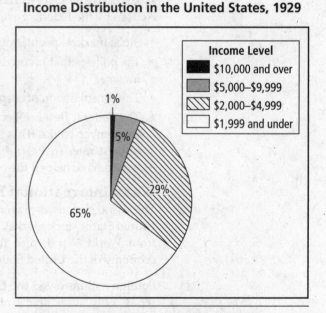

*How does the pie graph support the statement that underconsumption contributed to the weaknesses in the economy that led to the depression?*

- As a result, the economy was dependent on the spending of a very small portion of the population. These wealthy people spent their money on luxury goods and on investments. This type of spending was greatly affected by the stock market crash.
- The wealthy, not the great mass of the population, had benefited from increased output per worker. With the increased output, production costs had dropped and corporate profits had risen, but overall, wages were stagnant or had increased only slightly. Often workers could not buy what they produced. As a result, demand dropped. As the economy weakened, this non-purchasing group grew in size and became less and less able to buy even the necessities of life.

### Excessive Buying on Credit

Excessive buying on credit was one result of these low and unequally distributed wages. The abundance of new products, the sense that these good times would never end, and the availability of easy credit encouraged people to spend money beyond their means. As the economy slowed, people bought less in order to pay their installment loans and home mortgages. This underconsumption led to decreased production and a rise in unemployment.

### Weak Corporate Structure

The stock market crash set off the collapse of the nation's business structure. Business consolidations of the 1920s resulted in a few large companies in each industry. Holding companies controlled the stock of many different corporations and depended on the earnings of the various companies they held. This was a very fragile system, because when one company collapsed, it affected—in a domino fashion—the rest of the holding company.

### Weak Banking Structure

Some 6,000 banks failed in the 1920s. Many were rural banks that failed when farmers were unable to repay loans. Large banks were also vulnerable because they held inadequate reserves, investing too much in the stock market and making risky loans.

### Inadequate Government Policies

Actions by the federal government contributed to the depression.

- Stock market speculation was unregulated by the government.
- Tax policies that favored the wealthy resulted in further uneven distribution of income.
- The consolidation of corporations was not challenged under antitrust laws.
- The Federal Reserve Board allowed a low discount rate—the interest charged to member banks. This policy led to stock speculation. The board then raised interest rates in 1931, discouraging spending at just the time when spending would have helped the economy.

### Weak International Economy

The world's economies were affected by the collapse triggered by the crash of the United States stock market. Many European economies had never fully recovered from World War I, and the international economy depended heavily on the economy of the United States.

Foreign nations owed the United States money from World War I that they could repay only after the United States bought their goods and made foreign investments and loans. In June 1930, Congress passed the Hawley-Smoot Act, raising tariffs on agricultural and manufactured goods to the highest levels in

American history. However, high American tariffs kept out goods from overseas and led to high foreign tariffs. Meanwhile, Americans invested at home rather than abroad.

When the economy slowed, the United States made even fewer foreign investments and had less money to lend. This meant that foreign nations had less money to buy American goods and often defaulted on loans. The international nature of the banking system can be seen by the fact that banks in both Europe and the United States failed as a result of defaults on loans.

### Some Economic Changes Between 1928 and 1932
**(Figures in millions unless otherwise noted)**

| | 1928 | 1929 | 1930 | 1931 | 1932 |
|---|---|---|---|---|---|
| **A.** United States exports (merchandise) | $5,030 | $5,157 | $3,781 | $2,378 | $1,576 |
| **B.** Spending for new housing | $4,195 | $3,040 | $1,570 | $1,320 | $485 |
| **C.** Farm spending for lime and fertilizer | $318 | $300 | $297 | $202 | $118 |
| **D.** Federal spending | $2,933 | $3,127 | $3,320 | $3,578 | $4,659 |
| **E.** Cash receipts from farming | $10,991 | $11,312 | $9,055 | $6,331 | $4,748 |
| **F.** Lumber production (billions of board ft.) | 36.8 | 38.7 | 29.4 | 20 | 13.5 |
| **G.** Unemployment (in thousands) | 2,080 | 1,550 | 4,340 | 8,020 | 12,060 |
| **H.** Average weekly earnings of production workers in manufacturing (actual dollars) | $24.97 | $25.03 | $23.25 | $20.87 | $17.05 |

## Hoover's Response to the Great Depression, 1929–1933

Herbert Hoover was the president who first had to deal with the deepening depression. Hoover had taken office in 1929, after having served as Coolidge's secretary of commerce. An engineer by training, Hoover was a good businessman, a self-made millionaire, and a humanitarian. During and after World War I, he had an international reputation as a leader of a successful relief effort to aid starving Europeans and to help Europe recover economically.

### Hoover's Economic Plan
In order to improve economic conditions, Hoover:

- tried to restore confidence in the American economy with such statements as "Prosperity is just around the corner."
- altered his view that government should not become directly involved in the economy. He promoted programs that aided businesses, on the theory that as businesses recovered, economic benefits would **trickle down** to the workers and consumers.
- allowed the organization of the Reconstruction Finance Corporation (1932) to lend money to railroads, mortgage and insurance companies, and banks on the verge of bankruptcy.
- set a precedent for Franklin Roosevelt's New Deal with his use of federal works projects to create jobs and stimulate the economy.
- obtained voluntary agreements from businesses not to lower wages or prices. However, as companies increasingly faced collapse, they often could not honor these promises.
- halted the payment of war debts by European nations.

### Analyzing Documents

Examine the chart and then answer the following questions.

- How much did spending for new housing change between 1928 and 1932?

- What does the drop in U.S. exports indicate about the nature of the depression?

- How much did unemployment increase between 1928 and 1932?

- Based on this chart, which year was the economy in its most serious state?

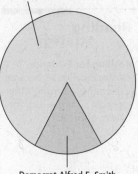

**Election of 1928**

Republican Herbert C. Hoover
84% of electoral vote

Democrat Alfred E. Smith
16% of electoral vote

*"Our Republican leaders tell us economic laws . . . cause panics which no one could prevent. But while they prate of [chatter about] economic laws, men and women are starving . . . I pledge you, I pledge myself, to a new deal for the American people."*
—F. D. Roosevelt, 1932

*"The urgent question today is the prompt balancing of the budget. When that is accomplished, I propose to support adequate measures for relief of distress and unemployment."*
—Herbert Hoover, 1932

Both of these statements were made during the 1932 presidential campaign.

- Which speech has a greater sense of urgency?

- Which man is more optimistic? Why?

- What is the clearest difference in their approach to the Great Depression?

## Reading
### Strategy

**Reading for Evidence**
- After individuals became unemployed, what other people or organizations were affected?

## Failure of Hoover's Program

Despite these efforts, Hoover's refusal to provide direct relief damaged his image as the nation's leader. Also damaging was his insistence, in the face of worsening conditions, that the economy was actually improving.

In the summer of 1932, thousands of unemployed World War I veterans and their families set up camps in Washington, D.C., to demand early payment of the bonus due to them for their war service. When the bill was defeated by Congress, most of **Bonus Army,** as they were called, refused to leave town. Hoover insisted that the veterans were influenced by Communists and other agitators. He called out the army to break up the Bonus Army's camps and disperse the veterans. The newspaper photographs showing tanks and tear gas being used against war veterans destroyed what little popularity Hoover had left.

Herbert Hoover took many steps to use the power of the federal government to stop the growing depression. In the end, his efforts were too little. It was not until 1932 that he changed some of his views, agreeing to increase federal spending to fight the depression. At the same time, he remained opposed to direct relief for the homeless and unemployed and supported raising taxes to balance the federal budget. Historians still debate whether he should be praised for the efforts he did make or condemned for not going far enough. Hoover's ability to act was limited by his inability to grasp the depth and breadth of the economic crisis and by his beliefs. For example:

- He had great faith in the American economic system, insisting that the forces of the market would eventually set the economy right again.
- He believed in voluntary rather than governmental action to solve problems of society.
- He believed in self-help and opposed direct relief on the grounds that it would destroy people's "rugged individualism."

## The Human Impact of the Great Depression

The Great Depression had a profound effect on all Americans.

### Unemployment

By 1932, some 12 million people—25 percent of the American labor force—were unemployed. The human toll was seen in long "bread lines" at soup kitchens. Relief efforts by organizations such as the Red Cross were limited, because voluntary contributions slowed down. As banks failed, people lost their savings; as companies failed, people lost their jobs as well.

African Americans and unskilled workers were the first to experience unemployment. In 1931, African American unemployment was estimated as 30 to 60 percent greater than white unemployment. Women were criticized for working while men could not find jobs. In truth, female occupations, usually in service sectors such as nursing and clerical work, were less affected than positions in manufacturing that were usually given to men. Family life was disrupted as parents looked for ways to stretch what money the family had. Families moved in with relatives. Marriages were postponed. The birth rate dropped, as did college enrollment.

### Urban Life

In many cities, families who had lost their homes lived in unheated shacks they had built of cardboard, tin, or crates. These communities became known as **Hoovervilles.** Some people slept under old newspapers called "Hoover blankets."

## Unemployment, 1929–1940 (in millions)

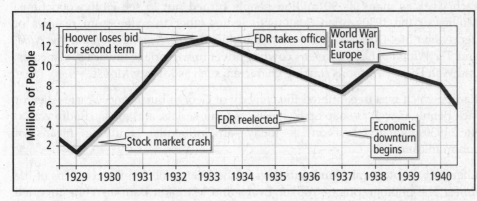

*Graph labels:*
- Hoover loses bid for second term
- FDR takes office
- World War II starts in Europe
- Stock market crash
- FDR reelected
- Economic downturn begins

*Y-axis: Millions of People (2, 4, 6, 8, 10, 12, 14)*
*X-axis: 1929 1930 1931 1932 1933 1934 1935 1936 1937 1938 1939 1940*

### Analyzing Documents

Based on the graph, what was the relationship between the unemployment rate and Hoover's defeat in the election of 1932?

Others slept in city parks. People selling apples and shoelaces on the street became a common sight. Cases of malnutrition, tuberculosis, and typhoid increased, as did deaths from starvation and suicide. Parents often went hungry to give what food they had to their children.

### Rural Life

With more people unable to buy food, farmers found that their already depressed income dropped by one half. Farm foreclosure sales grew in number. The farmers' desperate situation only worsened in the 1930s with seven years of drought in parts of Texas, Oklahoma, Kansas, Colorado, and New Mexico, a region that became known as the **Dust Bowl.** The drought, combined with poor farming methods, resulted in the loss of the topsoil, which was whipped into giant dust storms that swept across the Great Plains. Devastation in the Dust Bowl created a group of migrant farmers called "Okies" who moved to California in search of work. Their sufferings were made famous in John Steinbeck's novel *The Grapes of Wrath.*

### The Culture of the Great Depression

The sufferings of people during the Great Depression changed the popular culture of the 1930s, as people sought inexpensive and escapist leisure activities.

Spectator sports, especially baseball, remained popular, but fewer people could afford to attend. Instead, they played miniature golf, softball, pinball machines, the new board game Monopoly®, or they read comic books. Dick Tracy was one of the most popular comic strips of the decade.

### Geography in History

Starting in the late 1800s, farmers using steel plows cut through the thick grasses that covered the Great Plains. They grew wheat in areas too dry to grow corn. After World War I, when farm prices dropped, farmers responded by overfarming—clearing more land and growing more wheat. The 1930s were a decade of drought. For seven years, winds blew the top soil, no longer protected by the grass cover, east from New Mexico, Texas, Oklahoma, Colorado, and Kansas to the Atlantic and beyond. Sixty percent lost their farms.

- How do the problems of farmers in the 1920s and 1930s compare with farmers' problems of the the 1880s, the 1950s, the 1980s, and today?

*A bread line*

## Reading Strategy

**Formulating Questions**
Reread the section about the culture of the Great Depression, then answer the following questions.

- What forms of entertainment were most popular during the Great Depression?

- Why were these forms of entertainment so popular?

- How did the tone of popular entertainment (such as movies and radio) differ from that of art and literature?

About one third of the nation's movie theaters closed during the depression, but each week as many as 90 million people turned out to see Hollywood films. Movies of the 1930s often dealt with issues other than the grim realities of depression life. Depression-era movies included *King Kong, Gone With the Wind*, and *The Wizard of Oz*, as well as cowboy adventures, serials, musicals, comedies, and Walt Disney cartoons starring characters such as Mickey Mouse.

Radio, which was free, offered the comedy of George Burns and Gracie Allen or Jack Benny, as well as soap operas, news, sports, serials, and music. Radio was to the 1930s what television is today—an influential, unifying means of communication.

Literature, photography, and paintings of the 1930s reflected the concerns of the times. The photographs of Walker Evans and Margaret Bourke-White revealed the suffering of the people. Bourke-White's work appeared in *Life* magazine, which for decades depicted American life in pictures. Government programs provided work for artists, writers, and actors through theater and art projects. Artists painted murals on public buildings. Writers wrote histories and guidebooks about various regions. Actors appeared in plays funded by the Federal Theater Project. Dancers performed, and orchestras played.

Some novels, such as those of John Dos Passos or John Steinbeck, protested the life of the 1930s. Other works, such as those of William Faulkner, were less political. Langston Hughes continued to write about African Americans, especially the poor and working class. He also wrote a novel about life in Chicago, which succeeded Harlem in the 1930s and 1940s as the center of African American culture.

Music of the 1930s continued to be dominated by jazz created by Louis Armstrong, Duke Ellington, and other musicians. It was also the age of big swing bands, such as those of Glenn Miller and Benny Goodman. The musical became a popular form of theater, with music by greats such as George Gershwin, Irving Berlin, Cole Porter, and Jerome Kern.

## Franklin Delano Roosevelt

> "I pledge you, I pledge myself, to a new deal for the American people."
>
> —*Franklin Delano Roosevelt*

**Election of 1932**

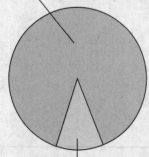

Democrat Franklin D. Roosevelt 89% of electoral vote

Republican Herbert C. Hoover 11% of electoral vote

In 1932, Franklin Delano Roosevelt was elected the thirty-second president. He was educated at Harvard University and the School of Law at Columbia University. He served as a Democrat in the New York State legislature, as assistant secretary of the navy under Woodrow Wilson, and as governor of New York before being elected president. He served as president throughout the rest of the depression and most of World War II, until his death in 1945.

### Restoring Public Confidence

Franklin Roosevelt is ranked by historians as one of the greatest presidents in American history. He inspired support and confidence in people. He was a master politician—intelligent, energetic, self-confident, charming, and optimistic. He had been tested by polio, which had left him in a wheelchair but made him tougher, more patient, and more compassionate.

Roosevelt, popularly called FDR, was also a master communicator. He held press conferences and effectively used the radio for "fireside chats" with the American public. He involved the public emotionally in his explanations of what he was doing to solve the nation's economic problems. He was able to convince people that he had confidence in himself and in the nation as well as genuine concern for the people.

FDR was controversial. While many respected and even loved him, others saw him as taking on almost dictatorial powers for himself and for the government. His attempt to make major changes in the Supreme Court is one example of controversy in his administration.

Another is his decision to break the so-called unwritten Constitution and run for a third term in 1940. Roosevelt ran for and was elected to a fourth term in 1944. He died in office in 1945. In 1951, the Twenty-second Amendment was added to the Constitution, limiting a president to two terms in office. Some saw it as a reaction against Roosevelt.

## Preparing to Lead the Nation

In the months between his election and his inauguration, Roosevelt surrounded himself with a group of formal and informal advisers. His cabinet members included Postmaster James Farley, Secretary of State Cordell Hull, and the first woman to hold a Cabinet post, Frances Perkins, as secretary of labor. FDR's informal advisers, known as the "brain trust," were a group of intellectuals and lawyers, several of whom were Columbia University professors. They favored reform and strongly influenced Roosevelt's administration. The most well-known brain trust member was social worker Harry Hopkins.

### Analyzing Documents

The two cartoons offer two points of view on FDR and the New Deal.

- Which cartoonist supports FDR's policies and which one opposes them?

- What is your evidence?

**Old Reliable**          **Alphabet Agencies Dance to FDR's Tune**

Source: Berryman, Graff Collection Apr. 12, 1938

## FDR's Eyes and Ears: Eleanor Roosevelt

Another major influence on Roosevelt was his wife, Eleanor Roosevelt. She was a humanitarian, active on behalf of women and minorities, especially African Americans. As First Lady, she became an important political figure in the nation. Through her travels, she served as the president's eyes and ears, but what he heard and saw was filtered through her progressive views and sensitivity to the plight of others. She helped to mold policy in several ways: through intervention with her husband on behalf of social reform; through her syndicated newspaper column; and through her travels and speeches around the nation. After Franklin Roosevelt's death in 1945, Eleanor Roosevelt became a leader in the issue of human rights, playing a key role in the creation of the 1948 Universal Declaration of Human Rights.

## The New Deal in Action: Relief, Recovery, Reform

Roosevelt's program to combat the problems caused by the depression was called the New Deal. The programs of the New Deal had the following goals:

- relief for those people who were suffering
- recovery for the economy, so it could grow again
- reform measures to avoid future depressions

### Relief Legislation of the New Deal

Congress passed a wide range of relief legislation as part of the New Deal.

**Emergency Banking Act, 1933** Roosevelt's first act as president was to close the nation's banks by declaring a **bank holiday** in order to stop the collapse of the national banking system. The time was used to assure the public that it could have confidence in the banks once they reopened. The law required the examination of banks to ensure that only financially sound banks were operating. In the same month, Roosevelt began to take the United States off of the gold standard.

**Federal Emergency Relief Act (FERA), 1933** Between 1933 and 1935, some $500,000 was provided for distribution by states and cities for direct relief and work projects for hungry, homeless, and unemployed people.

**Public Works Administration (PWA), 1933** Operating from 1933 until 1939, the PWA provided jobs through construction projects, such as bridges, housing, hospitals, schools, and aircraft carriers. The PWA also moved government money into the economy. It was hoped that this "pump priming" would create jobs, revive production, and lead to more consumer spending.

**Civilian Conservation Corps (CCC), 1933** Between 1933 and 1942, the CCC provided work for 2.5 million young men ages 18 to 25 conserving natural resources. Only 8,000 young women joined the CCC.

**Works Progress Administration (WPA), 1935** From 1935 until 1943, the WPA provided jobs for 25 percent of adult Americans. The agency was created to replace direct relief with public works projects. The WPA spent more government money than any other program. While WPA workers built roads, bridges, airports, public buildings, playgrounds, and golf courses, the program also offered work to writers, artists, musicians, scholars, and actors. Critics attacked the cultural work projects in particular. Others criticized the WPA for being inequitable. With WPA employment limited to one member of a family, only women who were heads of households were eligible for WPA jobs. However, the WPA provided jobs for over 8.5 million people who left a legacy in books, works of art, and public buildings, bridges, tunnels, and stadiums still in use.

*A WPA sign*

### Recovery Legislation of the New Deal

Congress also passed a wide range of recovery legislation as part of the New Deal.

## Some Major New Deal Programs

| Program | Initials | Begun | Purpose |
|---|---|---|---|
| Civilian Conservation Corps | CCC | 1933 | provided jobs to young men to plant trees, build bridges and parks, and set up flood control projects |
| Tennessee Valley Authority | TVA | 1933 | built dams to prevent flooding and to provide cheap electric power to seven southern states through regional planning; set up schools and health centers |
| Federal Emergency Relief Administration | FERA | 1933 | gave money to states and cities for aid to the unemployed and needy |
| Agricultural Adjustment Administration | AAA | 1933 | paid farmers not to grow certain crops; between 1933 and 1937 farm prices doubled; first AAA declared unconstitutional in 1936 |
| National Recovery Administration | NRA | 1933 | enforced codes that regulated wages, prices, and working conditions; in 1935, Supreme Court ruled law unconstitutional |
| Public Works Administration | PWA | 1933 | built ports, schools, aircraft carriers, and other large scale public work projects |
| Federal Deposit Insurance Corporation | FDIC | 1933 | insured savings accounts in banks approved by government; part of Glass-Steagall Banking Act that also separated commercial and investment banking |
| Securities Exchange Act | SEC | 1934 | set up Securities and Exchange Commission to oversee stock market and stock advisors |
| Rural Electrification Administration | REA | 1935 | loaned money to extend electricity to rural farmers |
| Works Progress Administration | WPA | 1935 | employed men and women to build hospitals, schools, parks, and airports; employed artists, writers, and musicians |
| Social Security Act | SSA | 1935 | set up a system of insurance for elderly, unemployed, and disabled; later added benefits for surviving spouses and children |
| National Labor Relations Act (Wagner Act) | NLRA | 1935 | gave labor right to form unions, and to collective bargaining; set up a Board (NLRB) to monitor elections, and enforce law |
| Fair Labor Standards Act (Wages and Hours Act) | FLSA | 1938 | set a minimum wage and a maximum work week and banned child labor in businesses in interstate commerce |

### Reading Strategy

**Organizing Information** Organize the information on the chart to categorize those programs that provided for:

1. Relief
2. Recovery
3. Reform

**National Industrial Recovery Act, 1933** The National Recovery Administration (NRA) had the authority to work with businesses to help them recover. The NRA set "codes of fair competition" within industries to maintain prices, minimum wages, and maximum hours. The public was encouraged to buy from companies that followed the NRA codes. The NRA was not popular, however. Some consumers complained that the NRA plan raised prices. Companies opposed the provisions giving unions the right to organize. Small companies felt at a disadvantage compared to larger companies. The NIRA was declared unconstitutional in 1935.

**Home Owners Loan Corporation (HOLC), 1933** This agency was created to help homeowners save their houses from foreclosure. It provided funds to pay off mortgages and financed over one million new long-term mortgages at lower, fixed-interest rates.

**First Agricultural Adjustment Act (AAA), 1933** The aim of the AAA was to raise farmers' income by cutting the amount of surplus crops and livestock. In that way, farmers would be able to sell their crops at the same prices of the years 1909–1914, a time when farm prices were high. The government paid farmers for reducing the number of acres they planted. The plan was financed through a processing tax on companies that made the wheat, corn, cotton, hogs, milk, and

### Preparing for the Exam

The purpose of agricultural price supports is to keep the prices of farm products at a reasonable and stable level. By paying farmers to reduce the number of acres they plant, the government helps reduce the supply of farm products. When demand stays the same for the reduced supply, prices will rise.

- Does this type of a program still exist today?

- If so, in what form?

tobacco into consumer products. Large farmers, rather than small farmers and tenant farmers, benefited from the AAA. The public was outraged at the destruction of crops and animals in order to keep production down. However, farm prices did increase. Although the AAA was declared unconstitutional in 1936, the principle of farm price supports had been established. The AAA was replaced with a law that encouraged using soil conservation methods.

**Federal Housing Administration (FHA), 1934** The FHA was created by the National Housing Act to insure bank mortgages. These mortgages were often for 20 to 30 years and at down payments of only 10 percent.

**Second Agricultural Adjustment Act (AAA), 1938** The second AAA was passed in response to a drop in farm prices in 1938. The government paid farmers to store portions of overproduced crops until the price reached the level of prices from 1909 to 1914. In spite of New Deal efforts, America's farmers did not regain prosperity until the 1940s, when World War II brought increased demand for food.

## Reform Legislation of the New Deal

Congress also passed a wide range of reform legislation as part of the New Deal.

**Glass-Steagall Banking Act, 1933** This law created the Federal Deposit Insurance Corporation (FDIC), which guaranteed individual bank deposits up to $5,000, an amount that had increased up to $100,000 by 2008. In 2009, Congress temporarily raised the insurance coverage for a depositor per bank up to $250,000. The Glass-Steagall Act separated investment banks from commercial ones, prohibiting commercial banks from involvement in securities markets. In 1999 Congress repealed this portion of the law. The Glass-Steagall Act also increased the powers of the Federal Reserve Board so that it had more control over speculation on credit.

**Securities Exchange Act, 1934** This act created the Securities and Exchange Commission (SEC), which had the authority to regulate stock exchanges and investment advisers. SEC powers included the right to bring action against those found practicing fraud. The SEC could require financial information about stocks and bonds before they were sold.

**Social Security Act, 1935** The 1935 Social Security Act was a combination of public assistance and insurance. The law had three main parts: (1) It provided old-age insurance, paid by a tax on both the employer and employee while the employee was working. The worker and employer, not the government, funded this part of social security. (2) It provided unemployment insurance for workers, paid by employers. (3) It gave assistance to dependent children and to the elderly, ill, and handicapped.

**National Labor Relations Act (Wagner Act), 1935** The Wagner Act, named for its author, New York Senator Robert Wagner, guaranteed labor the right to form unions and to practice **collective bargaining.** It created the National Labor Relations Board (NLRB) to ensure that elections to select unions were conducted fairly. The NLRB could also halt practices such as blacklisting, made illegal by this law.

**Fair Labor Standards Act, 1938** This law, also called the Wages and Hours Act, set a minimum wage (originally 25 cents per hour) and a maximum work week (originally 44 hours) for workers in industries involved in interstate commerce. The law also banned child labor in interstate commerce. It is one of many examples of New Deal legislation passed using the power given to Congress to regulate interstate commerce.

## Key Themes and Concepts

**Government**

*"Every qualified person shall be entitled to receive, with respect to the period beginning on the date he attains the age of sixty-five . . . an old-age benefit. . . ."*
—*Social Security Act, 1935*

• What was the reason for the Social Security Act?

• How was it funded?

• What are current concerns and proposals regarding social security?

## Analyzing Documents

*"Employees shall have the right of self-organization, to form, join, or assist labor organizations, to bargain collectively through representatives of their own choosing. . . ."*
—*National Labor Relations Act (Wagner Act) July 5, 1935*

• Why can this act be called the "Magna Carta of Labor"?

• What were some of the obstacles that organized labor faced prior to this act?

# The New Deal and Organized Labor

Roosevelt was interested in helping workers primarily through social legislation, such as social security. He also wanted to work cooperatively with business, as seen in the NRA legislation. When the NRA was ruled unconstitutional, and with it the part that ensured labor the right to form unions, Roosevelt turned to the Wagner Act as a means of aiding labor. By 1935, he had turned away from business and saw organized labor unions as a force in society that would balance the power of big business.

This pro-labor attitude of the New Deal resulted in an increase in union membership of more than 1.5 million members between 1933 and 1935. After the Wagner Act became law in 1935, membership grew another 3 million. By 1938, it had reached 7 million organized workers. These gains took place during a split within organized labor over how to unionize workers.

The American Federation of Labor (AFL), whose craft unions of skilled workers had dominated the labor movement since 1886, was challenged for control by a new union organized by industry. These new unions organized all workers, skilled and unskilled, in a given industry, such as textiles, coal, steel, and automobiles, much like the old Knights of Labor. But unlike the Knights, the industrial unions concentrated on "bread and butter" issues of wages, hours, and working conditions. Led by John L. Lewis, head of the United Mine Workers, the new industrial unions formed the Committee for Industrial Organization (CIO) within the AFL. In 1937 the CIO became a separate union, the Congress of Industrial Organizations (CIO).

In addition to the way it organized workers, the CIO differed from the AFL because its members included women, African Americans, and immigrants from southern and eastern Europe. These groups made up a large percentage of the unskilled work force that comprised the CIO unions. Despite their differences, the two organizations merged in 1955 to form the powerful AFL-CIO.

The 1930s were marked by a series of bitter strikes as the CIO attempted to unionize large industries, including the steel and automobile industries. Union workers demanded that companies enter into collective bargaining. Often police and company-paid guards used force against strikers. The workers made effective use of the sit down strike, a tactic in which they remained in the plant but refused to work until their demands were met.

# The New Deal's Effects on Minorities and Women

The New Deal legislation affected Native Americans, African Americans, Latinos, and women in a variety of ways.

## Native Americans and the New Deal

In 1924, Native Americans were finally granted citizenship by Congress. However, Native Americans continued to suffer under the government policy of forced assimilation enacted in 1887 by the Dawes Act. It aimed at breaking up the tribal structure of Native American life and forcing Native Americans to become landowning farmers. The Native Americans lost an additional 90 million acres of land between 1887 and 1934.

Under Roosevelt and the New Deal, government policy changed to one of tribal restoration. The 1934 Indian Reorganization Act, also called the Wheeler-Howard Act, was passed largely through the efforts of Roosevelt's commissioner of Indian affairs, John Collier. The bill's aim was to restore tribal self-government as well as

## Analyzing Documents

*"They picked me up about eight different times and threw me on my back on the concrete. While I was on the ground they kicked me in the face, head, and other parts of my body . . . I never raised a hand."*
—Walter Reuther, 1937 Ford Motor Company strike

- Did the Wagner Act resolve problems between management and labor?

- What is your evidence?

## Preparing for the Exam

**Native Americans and the New Deal**
- Compare the Indian Reorganization Act of 1934 to the Dawes Act of 1887 in terms of goals and Native Americans' reactions.

Native American languages, customs, and religious freedom. Another New Deal program provided for the education of Native American children under the Bureau of Indian Affairs.

## African Americans and the New Deal

African Americans were not a well-organized interest group in the 1930s. Therefore, they benefited less from the New Deal than did other groups. Roosevelt was not a strong advocate of civil rights, in part because he did not want to alienate southern Democrats in Congress, whose votes he needed to pass New Deal legislation. He did not support African American efforts to abolish the poll tax or to pass an antilynching law. Lynchings, in fact, increased during the 1930s.

However, within the New Deal programs, Eleanor Roosevelt and Harry Hopkins gave strong support to African Americans. As many as 50 African Americans were appointed to posts in various New Deal agencies. The most influential among them was Mary McLeod Bethune, who served in the National Youth Administration. While African Americans protested discrimination within New Deal programs, some 40 percent of the nation's African Americans received help through a New Deal program. Many moved from the Republican Party to the Democratic Party during the New Deal.

## Latinos and the New Deal

Many Latinos worked in agriculture and were hit particularly hard by the depression. "Okies" fleeing the Dust Bowl competed with Mexicans and Mexican Americans for migrant farmwork in California. While the New Deal provided relief for these workers, the government's policy was to stop immigration and return to Mexico any unemployed noncitizens.

## Women and the New Deal

Like African Americans, women were not an organized group during the 1930s. As you have read, women experienced less unemployment during this period, because they worked in low-paying female-only jobs less affected by the depression. Single women and female heads of families made up a large portion of the female workforce. Women earned about 50 cents for every dollar a man was paid, and they were often expected to give up jobs to male heads of families. The belief that the proper work for women was that of a wife and mother remained strong. Many New Deal programs simply would not hire women.

While women made little progress in the workplace, the New Deal did help women in government. Eleanor Roosevelt, Frances Perkins, and Mary McLeod Bethune were only a few of the women visibly active in the New Deal administration. More women also ran for and won political office although they were still far outnumbered by men.

## The 1936 Election Mandate

In his first term, Roosevelt won the support of large numbers of Americans. Popular belief in him and in his New Deal program that seemed to offer something to everyone translated into votes. Roosevelt carefully built what is known as the New Deal coalition, a voting bloc that embraced the solid Democratic South, new immigrant workers, the big cities, African Americans who had previously voted Republican, organized labor, the elderly, and farmers who usually voted Republican.

This coalition emerged in the 1936 election, when Roosevelt was reelected to a second term. Roosevelt received a mandate, or a clear endorsement, from the electorate, carrying all but two states. This shift in the two-party system was to dominate American politics over the next generation.

## Reading Strategy

**Organizing Information**
The New Deal affected various groups in different ways. To help you understand how different people were affected by the New Deal, create a chart showing the impact of the New Deal on:

• African Americans.

• Latinos.

• women.

**Stages of the New Deal**

1. **1933–early 1935:** New Deal legislation dealt with relief and recovery. Much of this legislation was passed in the "First Hundred Days" after FDR took office in March 1933. The 1934 Congressional elections increased the size of the Democratic majority in each house, which helped the New Deal legislative effort.

2. **1935 and early 1936:** Often called the "Second Hundred Days" or the "Second New Deal," this period's legislation focused more on social reform.

3. **1936 election:** This year is considered the high point of the New Deal.

4. **1937–1938:** A recession led to a new collapse in the weak economy that had just been starting to improve. The recession was due in part to New Deal cutbacks in spending after the 1936 election.

5. **1938:** By 1938 the New Deal had ended due to increased opposition in Congress and preoccupation with the danger of world war. Unemployment did not improve significantly until World War II created jobs in the production of war goods.

### Analyzing Documents

Examine the chart at left, then answer the following questions.

- What was the significance of the "First Hundred Days"?

- What is meant by the term *Second New Deal*, and what did it accomplish?

- Why did the economy weaken in 1937 and 1938?

- What ultimately caused the unemployment rate to improve?

## New Deal Generates Controversy

Roosevelt and his New Deal mobilized the government and the nation to fight the effects of the Great Depression. His program for relief, recovery, and reform provoked controversy. Criticisms came from those who felt that it was too radical or went too far as well as from those who felt its programs were too conservative or did not go far enough.

### FDR's Policy Strategies

Roosevelt was a pragmatist. That means he did not come to office committed to a single theory or set of beliefs but rather was a man of action, interested in whatever worked to solve a problem. In short, he was an experimenter. The New Deal showed his willingness to make choices based on trial and error in order to solve problems.

FDR was influenced by Populist and Progressive philosophies of using the government to solve social and economic problems. He also used ideas of the Hoover administration and lessons learned in mobilizing the nation to fight World War I. The strategies used by the New Deal included:

- passing relief measures that involved the federal government in the nation's economy to a greater degree than ever before. This direct governmental action was justified by using the commerce and elastic clauses of the Constitution.

- taking fiscal action to stimulate the economy and lower unemployment by lowering taxes and increasing government spending.

- assuming responsibility for the general welfare by protecting people against risks that they could not handle on their own.

- increasing the regulatory role of the federal government over banks, businesses, and the stock exchange.

- adopting deficit spending as an economic means of reviving the economy. This policy was based on the theories of economist John Maynard Keynes, who argued that the government must spend huge amounts of money to encourage production levels and purchasing power to increase. This policy, Keynes argued, would result in economic recovery.

### Preparing for the Exam

Compare the New Deal to other reform movements, such as Progressivism and the Great Society.

- Do they too appear to have stages?

## Analyzing Documents

Use the chart and your knowledge of social studies to answer the following questions.

- What is the definition of a *budget deficit*?

- In what year was the budget deficit the largest?

- What caused this increase in the budget deficit?

Review the New Deal programs to determine on what these funds were spent.

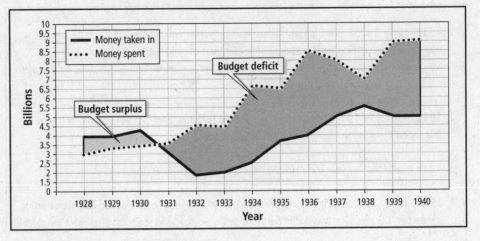

## Key Themes and Concepts

**Constitutional Principles**
The Supreme Court's ruling in *Schechter Poultry* v. *United States* (1935) declared the NRA unconstitutional. This decision was based in part on a narrow definition of the interstate commerce clause. It also considered this law a violation of separation of powers.

- Review *Gibbons* v. *Ogden* (1824) regarding interpretation of the interstate commerce clause.

- Review *Marbury* v. *Madison* regarding separation of powers.

- When else has the interstate commerce clause produced controversy?

- What is meant by separation of powers?

# Constitutional Issues

## Supreme Court Reaction

Throughout the New Deal, the Supreme Court majority practiced judicial restraint, narrowly interpreting the interstate commerce clause and striking down many of FDR's programs, which were based on a broad interpretation of that part of the Constitution. In a series of decisions, the Court ruled that several key New Deal laws were unconstitutional.

**Supreme Court and the NRA** The National Recovery Act (NRA) was declared unconstitutional in *Schechter Poultry Corporation* v. *United States (1935)*. The Court ruled that the law illegally gave Congress power to regulate intrastate commerce (or commerce within a single state) and violated the separation of powers by giving the legislative powers to the executive branch.

**Supreme Court and the AAA** In *United States* v. *Butler* (1936), the Supreme Court struck down the Agricultural Adjustment Act (AAA) on the grounds that agriculture was a local, not an interstate, matter under the provisions of the Tenth Amendment.

## Tennessee Valley Authority (TVA), 1933: Model Yardstick or Creeping Socialism?

The federally funded TVA provided jobs, cheap electricity, and flood control to poor rural areas of seven states through dam construction on the Tennessee River and its tributaries. The TVA was made possible through the efforts of Republican Senator George Norris of Nebraska. The TVA was praised as a bold experiment in government intervention to meet regional needs. It was attacked as "creeping socialism."

## FDR's "Court-Packing" Proposal: Failure and Success

Supreme Court opposition to FDR's programs continued with the Court consistently vetoing New Deal legislation. Franklin Roosevelt asked Congress to approve a law that would permit the president to increase the number of judges from nine to fifteen if the judges refused to retire at the age of 70.

The Judicial Reorganization Bill—or the **"court-packing" plan,** as its opponents called it—was intended to make the Supreme Court approve the New Deal laws. It never became law because it would have threatened the separation of powers and the system of checks and balances. The Supreme Court did not void another New Deal law and Roosevelt eventually appointed seven Supreme Court justices.

THE INGENIOUS QUARTERBACK!

## The Third Term Controversy

Several constitutional questions were raised during the New Deal years, among them the third term controversy when, in 1940, President Roosevelt challenged the unwritten constitution, winning both a third and a fourth term (1944). In 1951, the Twenty-second Amendment, setting a two-term limit for president, was ratified. Historians debate whether the amendment was solely a political reaction against Roosevelt and whether it makes a president a "lame duck" from the moment of the second inauguration.

# Political Opposition

In his first two terms, Roosevelt's strongest opposition was from big business. In 1934, a group of conservative Democratic and Republican business owners and politicians, including former presidential candidate Al Smith, formed the American Liberty League. It claimed that Roosevelt was exercising too much power as president. It attacked the New Deal because its programs were being financed through deficit spending. The group expressed fear that the American free enterprise system was being destroyed.

Radical groups such as the Communist Party also offered alternatives to the New Deal but failed to gain any major public support. At its peak in 1938, the Communist Party of the United States of America had only 55,000 members, and its 1936 presidential candidate won only 80,000 votes. Meanwhile, the pro-Nazi German-American Bund became active, as did the Black Shirts, fascists who supported the views of Italian dictator Benito Mussolini.

## Analyzing
### Documents

Using the table below and the text, answer the following questions.

- Who are some specific people who voiced the criticisms shown in the graphic summary?

- What evidence is there to support each of these positions?

Compare these positions with these comments about FDR and the New Deal:

*"...A hundred years from now, when historians look back at it, they will say that old things didn't work. What ran through the New Deal was finding a way to make them work."*
—Gardiner C. Means government financial advisor, New Deal

*"Roosevelt is the only President we ever had that thought the Constitution belonged to the pore [poor] man too..."*
—George Dobbin, Mill worker 1939

The Socialist Party in America drew some rising support, although some members began to vote for Roosevelt. The party was led by Eugene Debs and Norman Thomas, the party's presidential candidate. Unlike the Communist Party, the Socialists believed in the use of democratic means to make changes in the American economic structure.

As frustration grew in the face of the prolonged depression, various individuals entered the political scene, each criticizing the New Deal and often offering simplistic solutions to the economic crisis. These men were called "homegrown demagogues" because their philosophies did not come from a foreign nation and because they appealed to people's emotions and prejudice. These demagogues included:

- Francis E. Townsend, who created a financially impossible plan to provide government pensions for the elderly.
- Father Charles E. Coughlin, a Catholic priest who blamed business owners, especially Jewish ones, for the economic crisis.
- **Huey Long**, a powerful United States senator from Louisiana, who proposed that income and inheritance taxes on the wealthy be used to give each American a $2,500 income, a car, and a college education. Long was assassinated in 1935.

### Critics of the New Deal

| Women and African Americans | Progressives and Socialists | Republicans and other political opponents |
|---|---|---|
| New Deal programs offered more opportunities to white men than to women and minorities. Women and African Americans were paid less for the same work. | New Deal programs were not doing enough to solve the nation's problems. More should have been done to distribute the nation's wealth among all Americans. | Government was becoming too powerful. The Constitution was threatened. FDR was like a dictator. New Deal taxes on the wealthy were unfair. New Deal programs were too much like socialism. |

## Evaluating the New Deal

Most historians agree on the following assessment of the New Deal:

- World War II was largely responsible for ending the Great Depression. The New Deal improved but did not solve unemployment, the farm crisis, or underconsumption.
- Nevertheless, the New Deal did help people cope with the effects of the Great Depression while preventing economic and social disaster.
- The New Deal restored confidence in government while it brought more power to the presidency and the federal government.
- The government assumed a role and a responsibility in more aspects of the economic and social life of its citizens.
- The New Deal preserved the free-enterprise system, instituting reforms to provide stability and encourage growth.
- The deficit spending of the New Deal raised the national debt.

**Multiple Choice**

*Directions:* Review the Test-Taking Strategies section of this book. Then answer the following questions, drawn from actual Regents examinations. For each statement or question, choose the *number* of the word or expression that, of those given, best completes the statement or answers the question.

1 Which was a major problem faced by United States farmers in both the 1890s and 1920s?

(1) lagging technology

(2) lack of tariff protection

(3) overproduction of basic staples

(4) inflationary currency

2 In which respect were the decades of the 1920s and the 1960s in the United States most similar?

(1) organized militancy by ethnic minorities

(2) public concern with pollution of the environment

(3) widespread government activity dealing with social issues

(4) significant changes in manners and morals

3 What was the one similarity between the Red Scare following World War I and the Cold War following World War II?

(1) Fear of communism led to the suppression of the civil liberties of some Americans.

(2) Large numbers of Russian revolutionaries settled in the United States.

(3) Congressional investigations proved that the federal government was heavily infiltrated by Communist spies.

(4) Renewed fighting between wartime enemies was a constant threat.

4 Which is most commonly associated with the presidencies of Ulysses S. Grant and Warren G. Harding?

(1) depression in business

(2) corruption of public officials

(3) humanitarian reforms

(4) territorial expansion

5 In the United States, the widespread disregard of the fugitive slave laws and of Prohibition laws most clearly indicated that

(1) strongly held values are difficult to regulate

(2) the federal government is generally unable to enforce its own laws

(3) little respect is given to the legal system

(4) the judicial system is too lenient in its treatment of offenders

6 A major reason for the isolationist trend in the United States following World War I was

(1) a desire to continue the reforms of the Progressives

(2) the public's desire to end most trade with other nations

(3) the failure of the United States to gain new territory

(4) a disillusionment over the failure to achieve United States goals in the postwar world

7 The "boom" years of the 1920s were characterized by

(1) a decrease in both agricultural surpluses and farm foreclosures

(2) limited investment capital and declining numbers of workers in the labor force

(3) widespread use of the automobile and an increase in buying

(4) increased regulation of the marketplace by both federal and state governments

8  The racial segregation and poverty experienced by African Americans in the South during the 1920s led them to

(1) move to the North in great numbers to find factory jobs

(2) join with whites in strong national movements to protest unjust laws

(3) evolve their own strong labor movement

(4) support federal programs that gave them their own farmland

9  The Harlem Renaissance of the 1920s was a period when African Americans

(1) left the United States in large numbers to settle in Nigeria

(2) created noteworthy works of art and literature

(3) migrated to the West in search of land and jobs

(4) used civil disobedience to fight segregation in the armed forces

10  In the 1920s, the Sacco and Vanzetti case, the Red Scare, and the activities of the Ku Klux Klan all represented

(1) threats to civil liberties

(2) victories over discrimination and persecution

(3) support for the Prohibition movement

(4) greater social freedom for Americans

11  The conviction of John Scopes in 1925 for teaching about evolution supported the ideas of those Americans who

(1) believed in religious freedom and the separation of church and state

(2) hoped to lessen the differences between rural and urban lifestyles

(3) wanted to promote traditional fundamentalist values

(4) favored the changes resulting from the new technology of the 1920s

12  One important cause of the Great Depression in the United States was that by the end of the 1920s

(1) the government controlled almost every aspect of the economy

(2) tariffs were so low that foreign products had forced many United States companies out of business

(3) investors were too cautious and put their money only into government bonds

(4) factories and farms were able to produce far more than buyers could afford to purchase

13  President Herbert Hoover's refusal to provide funds for the unemployed during the Depression was based on his belief that

(1) the unemployment problem was not serious

(2) workers would not accept government assistance

(3) labor unions should provide for the unemployed

(4) federal relief programs would destroy individual initiative

14  Which is a valid conclusion based on a study of the presidencies of Thomas Jefferson and Franklin D. Roosevelt?

(1) Strong third parties develop when the two major parties ignore popular demands.

(2) Presidential success depends mainly on a sympathetic Supreme Court.

(3) Economic crisis can force a president to suspend basic civil liberties.

(4) A president's political program may change in the face of current needs.

15  The rapid, worldwide spread of the Great Depression of the 1930s was evidence of

(1) the failure of government job programs

(2) global financial interdependence

(3) a shortage of American factories making consumer goods

(4) the negative effects of unrestricted immigration

**16** Which New Deal reforms most directly targeted the basic problem of the victims of the Dust Bowl?

(1) guaranteeing workers the right to organize and bargain collectively

(2) regulating the sale of stocks and bonds

(3) providing farmers low-cost loans and parity payments

(4) raising individual and corporate income tax rates

**17** Deficit spending by the federal government as a means of reviving the economy is based on the idea that

(1) purchasing power will increase and economic growth will be stimulated

(2) only the national government can operate businesses efficiently

(3) the national government should turn its revenue over to the states

(4) lower interest rates will encourage investment

**18** The main purpose of the New Deal measures such as the Securities and Exchange Commission (SEC) and the Federal Deposit Insurance Corporation (FDIC) was to

(1) provide immediate employment opportunities

(2) develop rules to limit speculation and safeguard savings

(3) enable the federal government to take over failing industries

(4) assure a guaranteed income for American families

**19** During President Franklin D. Roosevelt's administration, which situation was viewed by critics as a threat to the principle of separation of powers?

(1) changing the date of the presidential inauguration

(2) congressional support of banking legislation

(3) proposing the expansion of Supreme Court membership

(4) passage of Social Security legislation

**20** "Section 202. (a) Every qualified individual shall be entitled to receive . . . on the date he attains the age of sixty-five . . . and ending on the date of his death, an old-age benefit. . . ."

A major purpose of this section of federal legislation was to

(1) guarantee an annual income to experienced employees

(2) assure adequate medical care for the elderly

(3) reward workers for their support of the union movement

(4) provide economic assistance to retired workers

**21** The popularity of escapist novels and movies during the Great Depression is evidence that

(1) the Great Depression was not really a time of economic distress

(2) popular culture is shaped by economic and social conditions

(3) American society did not try to solve the problems of the Great Depression

(4) the greatest employment opportunities for the average person in the 1930s were in the field of entertainment

**22** A major effect of the National Labor Relations Act (Wagner Act, 1935) was that labor unions

(1) were soon controlled by large corporations

(2) experienced increasing difficulty in gaining new members

(3) obtained the right to bargain collectively

(4) lost the right to strike

**23** The effectiveness of the New Deal in ending the Great Depression is difficult to measure because

(1) President Franklin D. Roosevelt died during his fourth term

(2) United States involvement in World War II rapidly accelerated economic growth

(3) the Supreme Court declared most New Deal laws unconstitutional

(4) later presidents failed to support most New Deal reforms

**24** Many opponents of New Deal programs claimed that these programs violated the American tradition of

(1) welfare capitalism

(2) governmental regulation of business

(3) collective bargaining

(4) individual responsibility

**25** A lasting result of the New Deal in the United States has been the

(1) reduction of the national debt

(2) control of stock prices by the federal government

(3) joint effort of business and labor to strengthen the presidency

(4) assumption by the federal government of greater responsibility for the nation's well-being

**26** The process of collective bargaining is best described as

(1) meetings of joint congressional committees to achieve compromise on different versions of a proposed law

(2) diplomatic strategies used to make treaties between two nations

(3) discussions between labor union leaders and management to agree on a contract for workers

(4) negotiations between a multinational company and a nation with which the company wishes to do business

**27** Which generalization most accurately describes the literary works of Langston Hughes, Sinclair Lewis, and John Steinbeck?

(1) Politics and art seldom mix well.

(2) The best literature concerns the lives of the wealthy.

(3) Literature often reflects the times in which it is created.

(4) Traditional American themes are the most popular.

**28** An immediate result of the Supreme Court decision in *Schechter Poultry* v. *United States* was that

(1) some aspects of the New Deal were declared unconstitutional

(2) state governments took over relief agencies

(3) Congress was forced to abandon efforts to improve the economy

(4) the constitutional authority of the president was greatly expanded

# Thematic Essay Question

**Directions:** Write a well-organized essay that includes an introduction, several paragraphs addressing the task below, and a conclusion.

**Theme:** **Reform Movements**

> Throughout United States history, there have been times when movements or programs have developed in response to demands for political, economic, or social reform.

**Task:**

> From your study of United States history, identify *two* movements or programs that developed in response to demands for reform. For *each* movement or program identified:
>
> - State one problem that led to the movement or program
> - Describe a specific reform advocated by the movement or program to deal with the problem
> - Discuss the tactics or means used by supporters of the movement or program to achieve the specific reform
> - Evaluate the extent to which the movement or program reform was successful

You may use any major reform movement or program from your study of United States history. Some suggestions you might wish to consider include: abolitionist movement (1830–1865); temperance movement (1830–1933); women's movement (1848–1920); Progressivism (1900–1920); New Deal (1933–1945); Great Society (1960s); Native American movement (1960–present).

**You are *not* limited to these suggestions.**

**Guidelines:**

> **In your essay, be sure to**
> - Develop all aspects of the task
> - Support the theme with relevant facts, examples, and details
> - Use a logical and clear plan of organization, including an introduction and a conclusion that are beyond a simple restatement of the theme

**In developing your answer, be sure to keep these general definitions in mind:**

(a) <u>describe</u> means "to illustrate something in words or tell about it"
(b) <u>discuss</u> means "to make observations about something using facts, reasoning, and argument; to present in some detail"
(c) <u>evaluate</u> means "to examine and judge the significance, worth, or condition of; to determine the value of"

# Document-Based Question

In developing your answers, be sure to keep this general definition in mind:

**discuss** means "to make observations about something using facts, reasoning, and argument; to present in some detail"

This question is based on the accompanying documents. The question is designed to test your ability to work with historical documents. Some of the documents have been edited for the purposes of the question. As you analyze the documents, take into account the source of each document and any point of view that may be presented in the document.

**Historical Context:**

The federal government responded quite differently to the prosperity of the 1920s and the Great Depression that followed. Roosevelt's New Deal was not only a decisive plan to combat the Depression, but it also marked a new direction in the role of government in managing the economy—a role that is still being debated today.

**Task:** Using information from the documents and your knowledge of United States history and government, answer the questions that follow each document in Part A. Your answers to the questions will help you write the Part B essay in which you will be asked to

- Discuss the response of the United States government to the Great Depression. In your essay, include a discussion of how this response can be considered a turning point in the role of the federal government in managing the economy

## Part A: Short Answer

### Document #1

" . . . we must have tax reform. The method of raising tax revenue ought not to impede the transaction of business; it ought to encourage it. I am opposed to extremely high taxes, . . . because they are bad for the country, and because they are wrong. We cannot finance the country through any system of injustice, even if we attempt to inflict it on the rich. . . . The wise and judicious course to follow in taxation and economic legislation is not to destroy those already who have secured success, but to create conditions under which everyone will have a better chance to be successful."

—Calvin Coolidge, *Inaugural Address*, March 4, 1925

1. According to this quote, how did Calvin Coolidge feel about the role of government in managing business?

_____

_____

## Document #2

### Economic Impact of the Great Depression

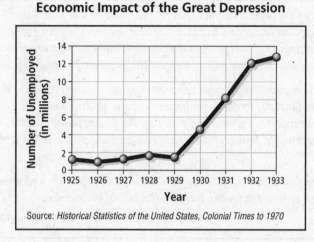

Source: *Historical Statistics of the United States, Colonial Times to 1970*

2. Based on the chart above, what effect did the stock market crash of 1929 have on the overall economy of the United States?

_____

_____

_____

## Document #3

*"I have recounted to you in other speeches, and it is a matter of general information, that for at least two years after the crash, the only efforts by the [Hoover] administration to cope with the distress of unemployment were to deny its existence."*

**—Franklin D. Roosevelt, 1932**

3. Based on this quote that Roosevelt made during the 1932 presidential campaign, how did Roosevelt evaluate the efforts made by the Hoover administration to resolve the nation's economic problems?

_____

_____

_____

# Document-Based Question

## Document #4

"So, first of all, let me assert my firm belief that the only thing we have to fear is fear itself—nameless, unreasoning, unjustified terror which paralyzes needed efforts to convert retreat into advance. In every dark hour of our national life a leadership of frankness and vigor has met with that understanding and support of the people themselves which is essential to victory. I am convinced that you will again give that support to leadership in these critical days.

In such a spirit on my part and on yours we face our common difficulties. They concern, thank God, only material things. Values have shrunken to fantastic levels; taxes have risen; our ability to pay has fallen; government of all kinds is faced by serious curtailment of income; the means of exchange are frozen in the currents of trade; the withered leaves of industrial enterprise lie on every side; farmers find no markets for their produce; the savings of many years in thousands of families are gone.

More important, a host of unemployed citizens face the grim problem of existence, and an equally great number toil with little return. Only a foolish optimist can deny the dark realities of the moment."

—Franklin D. Roosevelt, *First Inaugural Address*, March 4, 1933

4. In this excerpt from FDR's first inaugural speech, how did he attempt to win the support of the American people for his leadership during the economic crisis of the Great Depression?

_____

_____

_____

5. According to the above cartoon, how did some Americans view the New Deal?

_____

_____

_____

# Document-Based Question

## Part B

## Essay

*Directions:* Write a well-organized essay that includes an introduction, several paragraphs, and a conclusion. Use evidence from *at least three* documents in your essay. Support your response with relevant facts, examples, and details. Include additional outside information.

### Historical Context:

The federal government responded quite differently to the prosperity of the 1920s and the Great Depression that followed. Roosevelt's New Deal was not only a decisive plan to combat the Depression, but it also marked a new direction in the role of government in managing the economy—a role that is still being debated today.

### Task:

Using information from the documents and your knowledge of United States history and government, write an essay in which you

- Discuss the response of the United States government to the Great Depression.
- Include a discussion of how this response can be considered a turning point in the role of the federal government in managing the economy.

### Guidelines:

**In your essay, be sure to**
- Develop all aspects of the task
- Incorporate information from *at least three* documents
- Incorporate relevant outside information
- Support the theme with relevant facts, examples, and details
- Use a logical and clear plan of organization, including an introduction and a conclusion that are beyond a restatement of the theme

# The United States in an Age of Global Crisis
## Responsibility and Cooperation

**Section 1:** Peace in Peril, 1933–1950

**Section 2:** Peace with Problems, 1945–1960

## Unit Overview

This unit covers the time period from 1933 to 1960, a period that included the Great Depression, World War II, and the Cold War. This unit focuses on American foreign policy and how it affected life in the United States during those years.

Some of the key questions about the history of the United States during this period include:

- What caused the United States to change its foreign policy from isolationism and neutrality to a growing commitment to global involvement?

- Why did the world go to war from 1939 until 1945? How and when did the United States become involved in the conflict? How did the Allies strategize to end the war? How did World War II affect the lives of Americans on the home front?

- Why did the United States and the Soviet Union change from being allies in World War II to enemies during the Cold War?

- How did the United States try to stop the spread of communism in Europe and Asia? How did the desire to halt the spread of communism lead the United States into war in Korea? What effects did the fear of communism have within the United States?

# Peace in Peril, 1933–1950

The
# Big
# Idea

The United States fought on the side of the Allies in World War II. The United States:

- entered the war in 1941 when the Japanese bombed Pearl Harbor in Hawaii.

- fought in Europe and defeated the Germans.

- fought in Asia and defeated the Japanese.

- emerged from the war as a world leader.

## Section Overview

In the 1930s, great changes were happening in Europe and Asia. Totalitarian regimes rose to power in Germany, Italy, and Japan, threatening the freedom of nations on their borders. In 1939, the German invasion of Poland launched World War II, which quickly engulfed Europe and much of Asia. The United States, still embracing isolationism, tried to maintain neutrality, but the 1941 Japanese bombing of Pearl Harbor drew the nation into the conflict. Four more years of bloody fighting in Europe and Asia left millions of soldiers and civilians dead and hundreds of cities damaged or destroyed. The United States suffered relatively light losses in comparison to other nations, and it emerged as a world leader with a growing commitment to international involvement.

## Key Themes and Concepts

As you review this section, take special note of the following key themes and concepts:

**Presidential Decisions and Actions** How did Presidents Roosevelt and Truman influence the events and outcomes of World War II?

**Foreign Policy** How did world events change American foreign policy from one of isolationism to a growing commitment to global involvement?

**Diversity** How did World War II change the lives of women, African Americans, and Japanese Americans?

## Key People

| | |
|---|---|
| Franklin D. Roosevelt | Robert Oppenheimer |
| Adolf Hitler | Harry S. Truman |
| Benito Mussolini | Joseph Stalin |
| Francisco Franco | Winston Churchill |

## Key Terms

| | | |
|---|---|---|
| totalitarian | Allies | Rosie the Riveter |
| fascism | Axis Powers | Nisei |
| appeasement | Manhattan Project | WRA camps |
| Lend-Lease Act | Holocaust | |

In the 1920s and 1930s, the United States pursued a policy of neutrality and isolationism. In order to understand the reasons for this policy, we must examine the lingering impact of World War I.

# Isolationist Sentiment After World War I

The United States had been reluctant to enter World War I. Fighting had begun in Europe in 1914, and the United States stayed out of the war until 1917. Between April 1917, when the United States formally declared war, and Germany's surrender in November 1918, some 48,000 American soldiers were killed in battle, 2,900 were declared missing in action, and 56,000 soldiers died of disease. These losses were far less than those of the European nations, some of which had lost millions of soldiers and civilians. Nevertheless, the American losses were great enough to cause Americans to take a close look at the reasons for the entry of the United States into the war and at the nation's foreign policy.

## Isolation and Neutrality

Isolationism and neutrality are similar foreign policies, but an important difference exists between them. Isolationism is a national foreign policy of remaining apart from political or economic entanglements with other countries. Strict isolationists do not support any type of contact with other countries, including economic ties or trade activities.

When a country chooses a policy of neutrality, it deliberately takes no side in a dispute or controversy. Countries following this path are often referred to as being nonaligned or noninvolved. Neutral nations do not limit their trading activities with other nations, unless a trading partnership would limit that country's ability to stay politically noninvolved.

### Events Preceding American Involvement in World War II

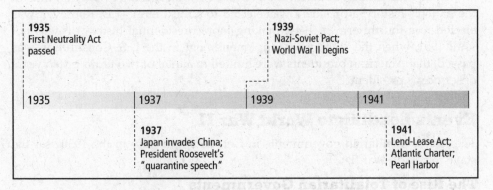

**1935**
First Neutrality Act passed

**1939**
Nazi-Soviet Pact;
World War II begins

1935     1937     1939     1941

**1937**
Japan invades China;
President Roosevelt's
"quarantine speech"

**1941**
Lend-Lease Act;
Atlantic Charter;
Pearl Harbor

## Historical Roots of Isolationism and Neutrality

The roots of isolationist and neutralistic sentiments in the United States can be traced to the late eighteenth and early nineteenth centuries.

**Precedents Set by George Washington** As president, George Washington set the precedent of American neutrality—but not isolationism. He knew that trade was necessary for the new nation, but that alliances might force it into war.

In 1793, Washington issued his Proclamation of Neutrality, making it clear that the United States would not offer aid during the French Revolution. In his farewell address of 1796, Washington warned the nation to avoid "entangling alliances," or political commitments to other nations, although he supported economic ties to other countries.

**Monroe Doctrine** The Monroe Doctrine reinforced the neutrality of the United States toward Europe. In 1823, President Monroe stated that the United States would not interfere in European affairs. He also warned European powers to remain out of the affairs of nations in the Western Hemisphere.

## Geography in History

- How did the United States' location relative to Europe and Asia contribute to isolationist sentiment before and after World War I?

## Preparing for the Exam

Many questions on the exam will require you to distinguish between similar concepts and terms.

What is the difference between isolationism and neutrality?

## Reading Strategy

**Reinforcing Main Ideas**
- How did the Monroe Doctrine contribute to isolationist and neutralistic sentiments in the United States prior to World War II?

## Isolationism in the 1930s

In 1934, when the United States was trying to recover from the worst economic depression in its history, Senator Gerald Nye led an investigation into the reasons the United States entered World War I. The committee concluded that the United States had gone to war at the encouragement of financiers and armament makers, eager for profits. As a result of this investigation, many Americans supported a return to isolationism.

In 1935, the Senate refused to allow the United States to join the World Court. That same year, Congress passed the first of a series of neutrality acts, which prevented Americans from making loans to nations at war. Any sales of goods to such nations were strictly on a **"cash and carry"** basis. In 1937, President Roosevelt made his famous quarantine speech, in which he stated that the United States would attempt to quarantine the warring nation "patients" in order to protect the rest of the world.

**Presidential Election of 1940** In 1940, President Franklin D. Roosevelt faced a challenge no other president had faced. He had helped the nation to survive the worst depression in its history while watching the rise of dictators in Europe and Asia. Roosevelt was at the end of his second term as president of the United States. Since the precedent set by President George Washington, no president had served more than two terms. This practice was not set by law at that time but was considered a respected tradition. Roosevelt surprised the nation by campaigning for and accepting the Democratic Party's nomination for a third term. He ran against Republican Wendell L. Wilkie, who appealed to many voters but not to anywhere near enough to defeat the popular F.D. Roosevelt. For the first time in the nation's history, a president was elected to a third term. (F.D. Roosevelt was elected to a fourth term in 1944, making more presidential history.) It was not until 1951, when the Twenty-second Amendment to the U.S. Constitution was passed, that American presidents were limited to a total of two terms or ten years of service as president.

# Events Leading to World War II

The rise of totalitarian governments in Germany and Italy in the 1930s set the stage for World War II.

## The Rise of Totalitarian Governments

In totalitarian governments, one political party has complete control over the government and bans all other parties. Totalitarian governments rely on terror to suppress individual rights and silence opposition.

In Germany and Italy, totalitarian governments were established based on the philosophy of **fascism.** Fascism places the importance of the nation above all else, and individual rights and freedoms are lost. Nazi Germany (led by Adolf Hitler) and fascist Italy (led by Benito Mussolini) were two fascist governments characterized by extreme nationalism, racism, and militarism (desire to go to war).

Hitler and Mussolini provided military assistance to Francisco Franco, a fascist leader in Spain who was attempting to overthrow the republican government. The devastating Spanish Civil War that erupted in 1936 became a "dress rehearsal" for World War II. The war in Spain was a testing ground for new weapons and military strategies that were used in World War II.

In the United States, opinions about support for the Spanish Civil War were divided. Some Americans traveled to Spain to fight for the republican cause. The United States government, however, continued to pursue a policy of neutrality.

## Key Themes and Concepts

**Foreign Policy**
The Neutrality Acts passed in 1935, 1936, and 1937 declared that the United States would withhold weapons and loans of money from all nations at war and that U.S. citizens who traveled on ships belonging to nations at war did so at their own risk. The acts also required that nonmilitary goods sold to nations at war be paid for in cash and transported by the purchaser.

• What events in the nation's history caused the government to be wary of Americans' involvement in ocean trade and travel?

## Preparing for the Exam

One way to remember the meaning of the term *totalitarianism* is from the word *total*: totalitarian governments have total control over every aspect of life. They suppress all individual rights and silence all opposition with threats. Fascism places the importance of the nation above individual rights.

• What is the relationship between totalitarianism and fascism?

Congress passed a resolution forbidding the export of arms to either side in 1937. Franco won the Spanish Civil War in 1939, established a fascist government, and remained leader of Spain until his death in 1975.

## Major World Events, 1918–1941

- **1918** Germany surrenders. World War I is concluded.

- **1919** Germany signs the Treaty of Versailles. The United States refuses to approve the Treaty of Versailles.

- **1921** Great Britain, France, and Japan attend the Washington Naval Conference on limiting arms. The conference produces the Four Power and Nine Power treaties.

- **1922** Benito Mussolini becomes Italy's fascist dictator. The USSR is officially formed, following the communist victory in the Russian Revolution.

- **1923** Adolf Hitler writes *Mein Kampf* in prison.

- **1924** In the USSR, Lenin dies. Stalin continues his rise to power.

- **1928** The Kellogg-Briand Pact outlawing war is signed by 62 nations. The pact contains no method of enforcement.

- **1929** The most serious economic depression in history begins, continuing through the 1930s.

- **1930** Japan occupies Manchuria.

- **1932** Japan seizes Shanghai. The United States issues the Stimson Doctrine, condemning Japanese aggression against Manchuria.

- **1933** Hitler assumes power in Germany. Japan announces its withdrawal from the League of Nations. President Roosevelt announces the Good Neighbor Policy in Latin America. The USSR is formally recognized by the United States. Nazi Germany begins operation of the first concentration camp at Dachau, near Munich.

- **1935** Italy invades Ethiopia. The United States passes the first Neutrality Act.

- **1936** Hitler reoccupies the Rhineland. The German/Italian Axis is formed. The Spanish Civil War begins (ending in 1939). The United States passes the second Neutrality Act. The United States votes for nonintervention at the Pan-American Conference.

- **1937** Japan invades China. Japan sinks an American gunboat in Chinese waters. The United States passes the third Neutrality Act, including a "cash and carry" plan.

- **1938** Germany annexes Austria (the *Anschluss*). Hitler demands the Sudetenland of Czechoslovakia. Great Britain, France, and Germany sign the Munich Pact, giving in to Hitler's demands.

- **1939** A German/Soviet nonaggression pact is signed. Japanese and American relations are deadlocked. The United States Senate refuses to grant aid to Great Britain or France. Hitler invades Poland, marking the beginning of World War II.

- **1940** Germany occupies Norway, Denmark, the Netherlands, Belgium, Luxembourg, and France. Germany attacks Great Britain. Japan joins the Axis Powers. President Roosevelt arranges to supply destroyers to Great Britain. Congress passes the Selective Training and Service Act, the first peacetime draft in United States history.

- **1941** Germany invades the USSR. The United States passes the Lend-Lease Act, granting aid to countries whose defense was seen as critical to the defense of the United States. President Roosevelt and Prime Minister Churchill agree to the Atlantic Charter. Japan attacks the United States at Pearl Harbor. The United States enters World War II.

## Analyzing Documents

Examine the chart then answer these questions.

- How might dissatisfaction with the outcome of World War I and economic depression have contributed to the rise of dictators in Italy and Germany?

- Which events described in the chart represent actions of appeasement on the part of France and Great Britain?

## Major World Events, 1918–1941

The chart "Major World Events, 1918–1941" summarizes the major events between the end of World War I and the entry of the United States into World War II. As you review the chart, look for relationships between events in order to understand how certain events caused others that occurred later.

Some events in the chart are so significant that they require further discussion.

**1938 Munich Agreement** With this agreement, Great Britain and France allowed Germany to annex the Sudetenland, a region of Czechoslovakia with a large German-speaking population. Hitler convinced the British prime minister Neville Chamberlain and the French premier Édouard Daladier that Germany would make no further territorial demands in Czechoslovakia after annexing the Sudetenland. When Chamberlain returned to Great Britain with this agreement, he told the world that he had achieved "peace for our time." Six months later, however, Hitler seized the rest of Czechoslovakia.

### Key Themes and Concepts

**Foreign Policy**
President Roosevelt explained the Lend-Lease Act to the American people through the use of a simple comparison:

If your neighbor's house is on fire, you don't sell him a hose. You lend it to him and take it back after the fire is out.

How did the Lend-Lease Act lead to greater U.S. involvement in the war?

### Key Themes and Concepts

**Science and Technology**
• How did advances in aviation technology contribute to changes in American isolationist sentiments?

### Reading Strategy

**Organizing Information**
• Who were the three major Allied Powers?

1.

2.

3.

• Who were the three major Axis Powers?

1.

2.

3.

Great Britain and France had resorted to the policy of **appeasement,** which means to agree to the demands of a potential enemy in order to keep the peace. Hitler demonstrated by his action that he could not be permanently appeased, and the world learned a costly lesson.

**Lend-Lease Act** Although the United States was officially committed to a policy of neutrality, President Roosevelt soon found a way around the Neutrality Acts to provide aid, including warships, to Great Britain. In 1941, Roosevelt convinced Congress to pass the **Lend-Lease Act,** which allowed the United States to sell or lend war materials to "any country whose defense the President deems vital to the defense of the United States." Roosevelt said that the nation would become the "arsenal of democracy," supplying arms to those who were fighting for freedom.

**Japan's Attack on Pearl Harbor** The United States did not enter World War II until 1941. President Roosevelt had promised that the United States would not fight in a war in which the country was not directly involved. However, on December 7, 1941, Japanese war planes attacked the U.S. Navy fleet at Pearl Harbor, Hawaii. Roosevelt called the attack a day that would "live in infamy," a day that Americans would never forget. This surprise attack shattered the American belief that the Atlantic and Pacific Oceans would safely isolate the United States from fighting in Europe and Asia. The attack on Pearl Harbor fueled American nationalism and patriotism. The day after the attack, Congress agreed to President Roosevelt's request to declare war on Japan. As a nation recently recovering from its worst economic depression in its history, the United States financed a great part of its involvement in World War II with the sale of government war bonds.

# World War II in Review

World War II began in 1939, when German forces invaded Poland. The United States entered the war two years later, after the Japanese attacked Pearl Harbor. War in Europe ended in May 1945, and fighting in the Pacific ended on August 14, 1945, when the Japanese surrender brought World War II to a conclusion.

## Major Powers

The war pitted 26 nations united together as the **Allies** against eight **Axis Powers.** The major powers among the Allies were Great Britain, the Soviet Union, and the United States. Germany, Italy, and Japan were the major Axis nations. Leaders of the major powers are listed below.

### Leaders During World War II

| Allies | |
|---|---|
| • Great Britain | Winston Churchill, Prime Minister |
| • USSR | Joseph Stalin, Communist dictator |
| • United States | Franklin D. Roosevelt, President until his death in April 1945 |
| | Harry S. Truman, President following Roosevelt's death |
| | Dwight D. Eisenhower, Supreme Commander of Allied troops in Europe |
| | Douglas MacArthur, Commander of the Allied troops in the Pacific |
| • France | Charles de Gaulle, leader of the Free French during the Nazi occupation |

| Axis Powers | |
|---|---|
| • Germany | Adolf Hitler, leader of the National Socialist German Workers' Party (Nazis), known as "Der Führer" ("The Leader") |
| • Italy | Benito Mussolini, Fascist dictator known as "Il Duce" ("The Leader") |
| • Japan | Emperor Hirohito |
| | Tojo Hideki, General and Prime Minister |

## Major Events

World War II was fought primarily in two major regions: Europe and North Africa, and in the Pacific. Major military engagements and turning points in World War II are presented on the next two pages.

### Europe During World War II

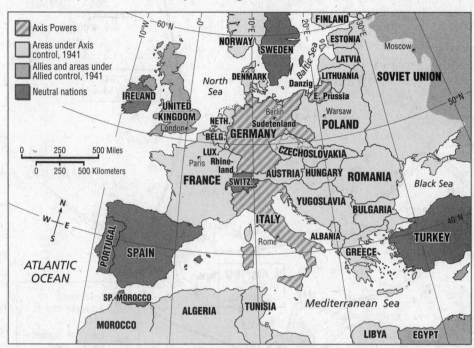

### Major Events of World War II

- **1939** Germany invades Poland with a rapid attack by armored vehicles supported by airplanes. This is known as a blitzkrieg, or "lightning war."

- **1940** Denmark, Norway, Belgium, the Netherlands, and much of northern France fall to Nazi invasion. Battle of Britain—months of terrifying air raids by Germany against Great Britain known as the blitz.

- **1941** Germany invades the Soviet Union. The siege of Leningrad begins and lasts 17 months. Japan attacks Pearl Harbor, Hawaii. The United States enters the war.

- **1941–1942** Japan seizes the Philippines, Burma, Singapore, the Dutch East Indies, and French Indochina. Japan continues to press southward toward Australia.

- **1942** Battle of Midway in the Pacific. The United States regains naval superiority in the Pacific.

- **1942–1943** Battle of Stalingrad. German troops are forced to surrender after thousands have been killed. This battle marks a turning point in the East and allows Russian soldiers to begin to move west.

- **1943** In North Africa, Allied troops defeat Axis armies for control of the Mediterranean Sea and the Suez Canal.

- **June 6, 1944** Allied invasions of Normandy, France, across the English Channel. This was the largest such invasion in history, involving over 150,000 soldiers. This invasion was known by the code name Operation Overlord and the D-Day Invasion.

- **1944–1945** Bitter fighting in the Pacific (for example at Leyte, Iwo Jima, and Okinawa) costs thousands of American lives.

- **December 1944** Battle of the Bulge. A surprisingly strong response by German troops slows the movement of Allied forces eastward to Germany.

- **April 12, 1945** Franklin Roosevelt dies unexpectedly from a cerebral hemorrhage.

- **April 1945** Allied troops from the East and West meet at the Elbe River in Germany. Hitler commits suicide.

- **May 8, 1945** The end of war in Europe, celebrated as V-E Day (Victory in Europe).

- **August 6, 1945** The United States drops an atomic bomb on the Japanese city of Hiroshima.

- **August 9, 1945** The United States drops an atomic bomb on the Japanese city of Nagasaki.

- **August 14, 1945** Hirohito announces Japan's defeat to the Japanese people.

- **September 2, 1945** Japan formally surrenders.

### Analyzing Documents

Examine the timeline. Then answer the following questions.

- What was the significance of the Battle of Midway?

- Which ended first, the war in Europe or the war in the Pacific?

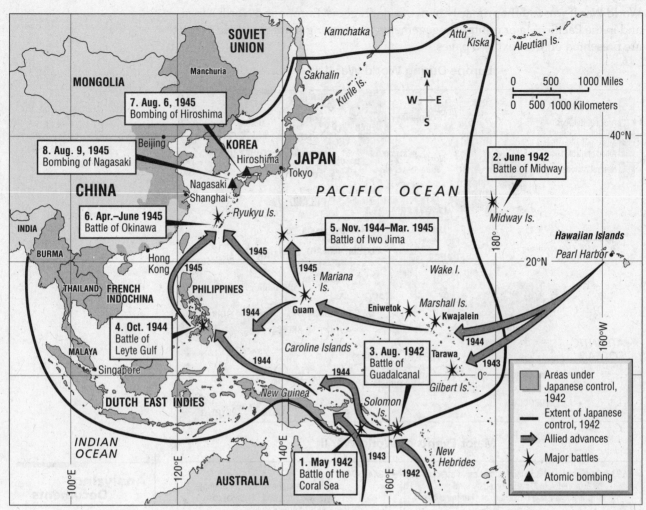

## World War II in the Pacific

**7. Aug. 6, 1945** Bombing of Hiroshima

**8. Aug. 9, 1945** Bombing of Nagasaki

**6. Apr.–June 1945** Battle of Okinawa

**5. Nov. 1944–Mar. 1945** Battle of Iwo Jima

**2. June 1942** Battle of Midway

**4. Oct. 1944** Battle of Leyte Gulf

**3. Aug. 1942** Battle of Guadalcanal

**1. May 1942** Battle of the Coral Sea

Areas under Japanese control, 1942

Extent of Japanese control, 1942

Allied advances

Major battles

Atomic bombing

### Wartime Diplomacy

During the war, leaders of the Allied nations met in a series of conferences to discuss wartime strategies and plans for the postwar world. Key meetings are described below.

**Atlantic Charter Meeting, 1941** Roosevelt and Churchill met on battleships in the North Atlantic to agree on certain principles for building a lasting peace and establishing free governments in the world. The document containing these agreements was called the Atlantic Charter.

**Casablanca, 1943** Roosevelt met with Churchill to plan "victory on all fronts." They used the term "unconditional surrender" to describe the anticipated victory.

**Cairo, 1943** Roosevelt, Churchill, and Chiang Kai-shek of China discussed the Normandy invasion.

**Tehran Conference, 1943** Roosevelt and Churchill met with Stalin to discuss war strategy and plans for the postwar world.

**Yalta, 1945** Roosevelt, Churchill, and Stalin outlined the division of postwar Germany into spheres of influence and planned for the trials of war criminals. The Soviet Union promised to enter the war against Japan.

**Potsdam, 1945** Allied leaders (with Truman now replacing Roosevelt) warned Japan to surrender to prevent utter destruction.

## Reading Strategy

**Analyzing Cause and Effect**
At Yalta, Roosevelt, Churchill, and Stalin agreed to split Germany into four zones, each under the control of one of the major Allies. Stalin promised to allow elections in the nations his army liberated from the Germans in Eastern Europe. Stalin did not fulfill this promise.

- How did the agreements at Yalta set the stage for the problems that later arose during the Cold War?

## The Atomic Bomb

In an effort to bring the war to a speedy conclusion and to prevent further destruction and loss of life, Allied leaders decided to embark on an atomic research project.

**The Manhattan Project** In the spring of 1943, a group of scientists from the United States, Canada, Great Britain, and other European countries began work on the top-secret atomic research program known as the **Manhattan Project.** The research was done primarily at Los Alamos, New Mexico, under the direction of Dr. Robert Oppenheimer. Many scientists involved in the project were refugees from Hitler's Germany. By July 1945, the first atomic bomb was tested in New Mexico. The success of this project enabled the United States to determine the ultimate use of the new weapon.

**The Bombings of Hiroshima and Nagasaki** Within days after the first atomic test, Allied leaders warned Japan to surrender or face "prompt and utter destruction." Since no surrender occurred, President Truman made the decision to drop atomic bombs on the Japanese cities of Hiroshima and Nagasaki. The bombs killed more than 100,000 Japanese instantly, and thousands more died later from radiation sickness. For a time after World War II, the United States held a monopoly on atomic weapons. The world had entered the atomic age. A controversial issue that resulted from World War II was the morality of nuclear warfare. The topic continues to be debated in the twenty-first century.

**Japan Surrenders** Within days of the devastating bombings of Hiroshima and Nagasaki, Japan formally surrendered, and World War II came to an end. Following Japan's surrender, the United States occupied Japan under the leadership of General Douglas MacArthur. A new constitutional monarchy introduced democratic reforms. Emperor Hirohito retained his throne, but only as a figurehead.

**Turning Point**

Several alternatives were considered before dropping the atomic bombs on Hiroshima and Nagasaki, Japan. The final decision rested with President Truman who made the decision to use the bombs to end the war as quickly as possible and thereby save American lives.

- Why might the dropping of the atomic bombs be considered a turning point in American history?

### Casualties in World War II

| Country | Military Dead | Military Wounded | Civilian Dead |
|---|---|---|---|
| Great Britain | 373,000 | 475,000 | 93,000 |
| France | 213,000 | 400,000 | 108,000 |
| Soviet Union | 11,000,000 | 14,102,000 | 7,000,000 |
| United States | 292,000 | 671,000 | * |
| Germany | 3,500,000 | 5,000,000 | 780,000 |
| Italy | 242,000 | 66,000 | 153,000 |
| Japan | 1,300,000 | 4,000,000 | 672,000 |

All figures are estimates    * Very small number of civilian dead

**Analyzing Documents**

Study the chart at left, then answer the following question.

- Which country had the greatest number of military casualties during World War II?

# The Holocaust

When Adolf Hitler rose to power in Germany, he did so by finding a scapegoat, someone to blame for Germany's problems after World War I. By appealing to anti-Semitism, feelings of hatred against Jewish people, Hitler encouraged the Germans to turn viciously on all Jewish citizens.

**Individuals, Groups, Institutions**
During the Holocaust, individuals were singled out for persecution because of their membership in a group. Institutions were developed, and individuals were put in place within those institutions to carry out the atrocities of the Holocaust. Genocide is the deliberate murder of an entire people.

List two other examples of genocide in the twentieth century.

1.

2.

## The "Final Solution"

Early in his rise to power, Hitler had seized Jewish property, homes, and businesses and barred Jews from many jobs. At the Wannsee Conference of 1942, the Nazis set as a primary goal the total extermination, or genocide, of all Jews under their domination. This effort was to be kept secret from the German people and from the rest of the world. Hitler's plan to eliminate the Jews was known to the Nazis as the Final Solution.

## The Horror of Concentration Camps

In the 1930s, the Nazis began to build concentration camps to isolate Jews and other groups from society and provide slave labor for industry. As Hitler's conquest of Europe continued, the camps became factories of death. More than six million Jews were killed in the camps as were another four million people— dissenters, Gypsies, homosexuals, the mentally and physically handicapped, Protestant ministers, and Catholic priests. Today, concentration camp names such as Auschwitz, Treblinka, and Dachau stand as memorials to the incredible human suffering and death of this time, a period now called the **Holocaust.**

The United States and other nations failed to take strong action to rescue Jews from Nazi Germany before World War II. In 1939, the *St. Louis*, a passenger ship carrying more than 900 Jewish refugees, left Europe for Cuba, but when they arrived, most of the refugees were denied permission to land there. The refugees were also denied permission to enter the United States, and the ship was forced to return to Europe. Most of the ship's passengers eventually were killed in the Holocaust.

After war broke out, the Allies still failed to speak out forcefully against the treatment of Jews or to make direct attempts to stop the genocide. Only toward the end of the war did the United States create the War Refugee Board to provide aid for Holocaust survivors.

**Reading Strategy**

• What important legal precedent was set at the Nuremberg trials?

## War Crimes Trials

A final chapter to the Holocaust occurred in Nuremberg, Germany, in 1945 and 1946. At that time an international military court tried 24 high-level Nazis for atrocities committed during World War II. By finding former Nazis guilty of "crimes against humanity," a precedent was established that soldiers, officers, and national leaders could be held responsible for such brutal actions. Escaped Nazis who were found after the end of the war—even decades later—were also brought to trial for war-related crimes.

Among the most infamous Nazis who were tried and convicted was Adolf Eichmann. He was captured in Argentina in 1960 and tried in Israel for the torture and deaths of millions of Jews. Eichmann was convicted of crimes against humanity and was hanged in 1962. Klaus Barbie, known as the "Butcher of Lyon" (France), was also apprehended and tried in 1987 for his wartime brutality against Jews.

War crime trials in Japan led to the execution of former premier Tojo and six other war leaders. About 4,000 other Japanese war criminals were also convicted and received prison sentences.

# American Patriotism

After the United States entered the war, the nation moved to full-scale wartime production and mobilization of the armed forces. Americans rallied behind the war effort.

With the exception of the attack on Pearl Harbor and battles on several Pacific islands, World War II was not fought on American soil. Nonetheless, America's coastal areas and large cities held blackout drills in case of attack. Americans supported the war effort by rationing food, gasoline, and other necessities and luxuries. During World War II, the federal government used rationing to provide more resources for the military. Rationing means that the availability of many consumer goods was very limited. Government campaigns encouraged Americans to have "meatless Tuesdays," and many Americans planted "victory gardens" to increase the food supply. Hollywood entertainers made special presentations to persuade citizens to buy war bonds to help the government finance the war.

## The Role of American Women

World War II brought dramatic changes to the lives of American women in the military and in the civilian workforce.

**In the Military** During the war, more than 200,000 women joined the military services. Women served in separate units from men, such as the Women's Army Corps (WAC), and performed vital military duties. They operated radios and repaired planes and vehicles. They were also assigned, along with men, to clerical duties.

**In the Civilian Workforce** When millions of men joined the military, employment opportunities opened up to women. Many women took jobs that had once been open to men only. More than five million women eventually worked in factories devoted to wartime production, although their pay never came close to equaling men's pay. One song about a woman named Rosie the Riveter became popular during the war years because it captured the sense of duty and patriotism felt by millions of women. The term **"Rosie the Riveter"** became a slang term for all women who worked in wartime factories.

### Key Themes and Concepts

**Economic Systems**
Between 1939 and 1945, federal spending increased from $9.4 billion to $95.2 billion. The government financed about 41 percent of the war costs by increasing taxes. The rest of the money needed was borrowed from banks, private investors, and the public. Such deficit spending—government spending of borrowed money—turned the depressed economy of the 1930s around almost overnight. It also created a huge national debt.

*Women factory workers*

**Preparing for the Exam**

- What trend emerged following World War II in regard to women's participation in the labor force?

**Resulting Change** Women's wartime work resulted in important changes in employment and lifestyle, even after the war. Before the war, most employed American women were young and unmarried. During the war, large numbers of married women and mothers who had never worked outside the home took jobs. This trend continued after the war. Although many women willingly returned to the roles of wife and mother at the end of the war, thousands more remained in the workforce, which improved their standard of living.

The entry of women into the paid workforce during World War II marked the beginning of a long-term trend. Women continued to enter the workforce throughout the rest of the century. New issues became important. For example, child care became important during the war years, and it remains an important issue today.

## African Americans

The experiences of African Americans during the war years provided the foundation of the civil rights movement of the 1950s and 1960s.

**Reading Strategy**

**Predicting Content**
- How might the experiences of African Americans during World War II have contributed to the rise of the civil rights movement during the 1950s?

**In the Military** Nearly one million African American men and women served in the military during World War II. Military units were segregated, and initially, African American soldiers were limited to support roles. Once the war went on, these soldiers soon saw combat, and many became distinguished themselves. One example of such heroism were the Tuskegee Airmen, the first black military pilots. These 994 fighter pilots were some of the most decorated fliers of the war effort, but they fought two wars, one overseas against a foreign enemy and the other against racism at home. In 1948, President Truman showed his support for civil rights by issuing Executive Order 9981, which led to the end of racial segregation in the military.

**At Home** In the 1940s, many southern African Americans began moving to northern cities in search of economic opportunity and freedom from discrimination. However, they met discrimination in the North. Race riots broke out in Detroit and New York City in the summer of 1943. Membership in civil rights organizations grew as African Americans struggled against discrimination.

African Americans experienced gains during the war years. Politically, their migration north had made them a significant voting bloc in urban areas. Economically, new jobs in war industries brought many African Americans the chance to earn more than they ever had before. Despite these gains, African Americans experienced discrimination and inequality in salaries in the workplace. The black press urged that the struggle for freedom be fought on two fronts—overseas and at home as well.

## Japanese Americans

Thousands of Japanese Americans faced hardship and economic losses after the attack on Pearl Harbor.

**Immigration to America** Immigrants from Japan began arriving in the United States in the early 1900s. These immigrants settled mainly on the west coast of the United States. By 1941, thousands of Americans of Japanese descent, called **Nisei**, had been born in the United States and were American citizens. Many had never been to Japan, and many had no desire to go there.

**Wartime Relocation Authority (WRA)** After the Japanese attack on Pearl Harbor, many Americans feared that Japanese Americans presented a threat to national security. Anti-Japanese sentiment grew, and in 1942 President Roosevelt issued Executive Order 9066, establishing military zones for the imprisonment of

Japanese Americans. More than 100,000 people of Japanese descent were forced to leave their homes and move to **WRA camps,** hastily constructed military-style barracks ringed with barbed wire and guarded by troops.

Ansel Adams

*High-school recess period, Manzanar Relocation Center, CA*

**Preparing for the Exam**

"It is a fact that the Japanese navy has been reconnoitering [investigating] the Pacific Coast. . . . It is [a] fact that communication takes place between the enemy at sea and enemy agents on land."

• Would the writer of this excerpt have supported the Supreme Court's decision in *Korematsu* v. *United States?*

***Korematsu* v. *United States*** In the 1944 landmark case *Korematsu* v. *United States*, the Supreme Court upheld the forced evacuation as a reasonable wartime emergency measure. However, no acts of Japanese-American sabotage or treason were ever identified, and thousands of Nisei fought honorably in the war. Almost 50 years after World War II, the United States government admitted that the wartime relocation program had been unjust. In 1988, Congress voted to pay $20,000 to each of the approximately 60,000 surviving Americans who had been interned. The first payments were made in 1990, and the government also issued a formal apology.

**Nisei Soldiers** Despite the injustices endured by Japanese Americans, thousands proved their loyalty by serving in the U.S. armed forces, primarily in Europe. The 442nd Regimental Combat Team, made up entirely of Japanese Americans, won more medals for bravery than any other unit of its size in the war.

**Key Themes and Concepts**

**Diversity**
The Korematsu Case shared a similarity with *Plessy* v. *Ferguson* (1896) in that specific groups were being targeted by the government based on race or ethnicity.

# Demobilization

During the war, American factories, geared up for wartime production, had helped the nation recover from the Great Depression. Now the challenge was to convert from a wartime to a peacetime society. The United States underwent a period of demobilization, or the movement from a military to a civilian status. The United States armed forces reduced from 12 million members to 1.5 million. Factories that had made planes and tanks now began producing consumer goods. It also meant ensuring that the nation would not slip back into depression.

**Truman's Legislative Program** During President Truman's administration, legislation was passed to deal with different issues raised by demobilization. Truman's legislative program aimed at promoting full employment, a higher minimum wage, greater unemployment compensation for workers without jobs, housing assistance, and other items was known as the **Fair Deal,** a play on words from Franklin Roosevelt's New Deal.

**Servicemen's Readjustment Act (The GI Bill of Rights)** This act authorized billions of dollars to pay for veterans' benefits, such as college education, medical treatment, unemployment insurance, and home and business loans. The GI Bill made it possible for more people to attend college and buy homes than ever before.

**Employment Act of 1946** This act made full employment a national goal and set up a Council of Economic Advisors to guide the president on economic matters.

**An End to Price Controls** Wartime legislation had put controls on the prices of most goods. In 1946, the government moved to end most such controls. However, the end of controls coupled with a tax cut caused a rapid increase in inflation. For example, food prices soared 25 percent in just two years.

**The Taft-Hartley Act** Workers' wages could not keep up with inflation after the war. Major strikes were held as unions pushed for higher wages. Antiunion feelings grew and led Congress to pass the Taft-Hartley Act over Truman's veto. The act:

- provided an 80-day "cooling-off" period through which the president could delay a strike that threatened national welfare.
- barred the closed shop, under which workers had to belong to a union before being hired.
- allowed states to pass "right-to-work laws," which said workers could take jobs and not have to join a union.
- banned union contributions to political campaigns.
- required union leaders to swear they were not communists.

## National Security Concerns

During Truman's administration, the National Security Act of 1947 was passed. This created the National Military Establishment, which later became the Department of Defense. The act also created the Central Intelligence Agency to oversee intelligence gathering activities. Truman also issued an executive order banning discrimination in the armed forces.

## The Baby Boom

In addition to problems caused by converting to a peacetime economy, the nation also experienced the largest population explosion in its history. The economic hardships of the Great Depression that had encouraged smaller families were gone. Families grew larger. This "baby boom" led to the expansion of many public services, especially schools. The rapid growth in personal income in the decade after World War II also contributed to an expansion of the middle class. You will learn more about the long-term effects of the baby boom in the next unit.

## The Election of 1948

Many voters had become dissatisfied with Truman's presidency because of inflation, strikes, Truman's actions on civil rights, and the developing cold war. Polls predicted that the Republican candidate, Governor Thomas Dewey of New York, would defeat Truman easily in the 1948 presidential election. Yet Truman pulled off one of the greatest upsets in American political history by winning reelection. He then attempted to build on this victory by proposing a program called the Fair Deal that aimed to extend reforms started under FDR's New Deal.

### Preparing for the Exam

The Taft-Hartley Act of 1947 was a setback for organized labor. It gave the president the power to delay (through court injunction) any strike that took place within an industry that the President deemed important to the nation's health or safety.

### Key Themes and Concepts

**Change**
- How did the prosperity of the 1940s and 1950s influence the nation's population growth rate?

# Peace with Problems, 1945–1960

## Section Overview

The end of World War II brought the desire to prevent such devastation from ever happening again. The United Nations was established to help nations find peaceful solutions to conflicts. Meanwhile, the uneasy wartime alliance between the United States and the Soviet Union dissolved as the Cold War took hold. As communism spread through the efforts of the Soviet Union and later China, the United States worked to strengthen its influence in Western Europe and Asia by providing economic aid and building strategic alliances. A growing anxiety about the spread of communism led the United States to become more deeply involved in global affairs, while also fearing a communist influence at home.

## Key Themes and Concepts

As you review this section, take special note of the following key themes and concepts:

**Change** Why did the United States and the Soviet Union change from being allies in World War II to enemies during the Cold War?

**Foreign Policy** How did the United States use economic aid to build its influence in Europe and Asia?

**Constitutional Principles** How did the fear of communism lead to the violations of some people's civil rights in the United States?

## Key People

| | |
|---|---|
| Eleanor Roosevelt | Douglas MacArthur |
| George C. Marshall | Alger Hiss |
| Mao Zedong | Joseph McCarthy |
| Chiang Kai-shek | Ethel and Julius Rosenberg |

## Key Terms

| | |
|---|---|
| containment | NATO |
| "iron curtain" | Warsaw Pact |
| Truman Doctrine | 38th parallel |
| Marshall Plan | HUAC |
| Cold War | |

The United States emerged from World War II as the world's greatest military power. Compared to other nations, it had suffered relatively little physical destruction. For a short time, the United States held a monopoly on the ability to use nuclear power. After World War II, the United States was aware of its strength as a nation and its responsibility to preserve world peace.

## The Big Idea

The post-World War II hostilities between the United States and the Soviet Union are together known as the Cold War.

The Cold War:

- lasted from about 1946 to 1991.

- was brought about by competition between the United States and the Soviet Union for power and influence in the world.

- consisted of political and economic conflict and military tensions throughout the globe.

## The United States and the World, 1945–1954

| 1945 | | 1949 | | 1953 | |
|---|---|---|---|---|---|
| World War II ends | | NATO formed | | Cease-fire in Korea | |

| 1945 | 1947 | 1949 | 1951 | 1953 | 1955 |
|---|---|---|---|---|---|

| | 1947 | | 1950 | | 1954 |
|---|---|---|---|---|---|
| | Marshall Plan; Truman Doctrine | | Korean War begins; Rosenbergs arrested | | McCarthy censured by Senate |

## Analyzing Documents

Review the timeline, then answer the following questions.

- How long did the Korean War last?

- In what year was NATO formed?

# The United Nations

American foreign policy changed dramatically as a result of World War II. Even before the conclusion of the war, the United States began planning for an international peacekeeping organization. Plans were made at the Yalta Conference for a United Nations Conference to be held in San Francisco in April 1945. The Soviet Union, under the leadership of Joseph Stalin, agreed to participate in planning the new organization which would be known as the United Nations. The United States Senate approved the United Nations Charter by a vote of 82 to 2.

## Organization of the United Nations

The structure of the United Nations (UN) includes a General Assembly of all its members and a Security Council of 15 members. The Security Council consists of ten rotating member nations and five permanent members. (The original permanent members were the United States, Great Britain, the Soviet Union, China, and France. After the breakup of the Soviet Union, the Russian Federation became a permanent member.)

The General Assembly serves as a forum for world leaders to speak on a variety of concerns. Although the UN has become militarily involved in a number of world crises, most of its members would agree that its greatest accomplishments have been in fighting hunger and disease and in promoting education. The headquarters of the United Nations is in New York City.

## Reading Strategy

**Organizing Information**
- Who are the five permanent members of the United Nations Security Council?

1.

2.

3.

4.

5.

## The United Nations

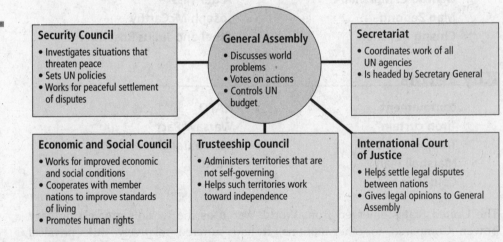

**Security Council**
- Investigates situations that threaten peace
- Sets UN policies
- Works for peaceful settlement of disputes

**General Assembly**
- Discusses world problems
- Votes on actions
- Controls UN budget

**Secretariat**
- Coordinates work of all UN agencies
- Is headed by Secretary General

**Economic and Social Council**
- Works for improved economic and social conditions
- Cooperates with member nations to improve standards of living
- Promotes human rights

**Trusteeship Council**
- Administers territories that are not self-governing
- Helps such territories work toward independence

**International Court of Justice**
- Helps settle legal disputes between nations
- Gives legal opinions to General Assembly

## Analyzing Documents

Study the chart, then answer the following questions.

- Which branch of the United Nations would help two countries resolve a legal dispute?

- Which branch sets UN policies?

**Universal Declaration of Human Rights** In 1946, President Truman appointed former first lady Eleanor Roosevelt as a United Nations delegate, the only woman in the American delegation. The committee that Eleanor Roosevelt led authored the Universal Declaration of Human Rights, a proclamation that is still part of the guiding philosophy of the UN today. In the postwar years, people all over the world were especially eager to have an international organization succeed at defining human rights for all people.

## Containment as a Foreign Policy

American foreign policy after World War II was influenced by two factors: the willingness of the United States to become involved in international peacekeeping efforts and its determination to prevent the spread of communism.

### Growing Distrust of the Soviet Union

In 1939, Germany and the Soviet Union had signed a nonaggression treaty, but after Germany violated the pact, the Soviet Union sought a new alliance to protect itself from Germany. The United States then allied with the Soviet Union throughout World War II. Although they were allies, American and Soviet leaders did not fully trust one another. After the war, it became apparent that the only common goal shared by the United States and the Soviet Union was the defeat of the Axis powers.

After World War II, the Soviet Union was viewed as a grave threat to the security of the noncommunist world. In defeating Nazi Germany, the Soviets had moved troops into the nations of Eastern Europe. After the war, the Soviet Union actively supported communist governments in those nations.

The United States, which had emerged as a superpower nation, took on the task of limiting communist expansion—a policy known as **containment.** The goal of containment was to confine communism to the area in which it already existed—the Soviet Union and the Eastern European nations. American presidential power increased during this time period as the United States sought to carry out this policy.

Following are key foreign policy developments related to the containment of communism immediately after World War II.

**Reading Strategy**

**Reinforcing Main Ideas** Containment of communism to the areas where it already existed was a central tenant of American foreign policy during the Cold War.

- How did communism spread to Eastern Europe?

- What had Stalin promised at Yalta in regards to Eastern Europe?

**Analyzing Documents**

Examine the cartoon at left, then answer the following questions.

- What major world event has recently ended?

- Describe the buildings below the climber.

- Why is the climber named "Europe"?

- What is the importance of the climber's rope?

- What does the caption mean?

In one or two sentences, write a summary of the idea this cartoon is conveying.

**The Way Back**

## Churchill's "Iron Curtain" Speech

In his 1946 speech at Westminster College in Fulton, Missouri, Prime Minister Winston Churchill of Great Britain cautioned the world about the threat of communist expansion. He warned that "from Stettin in the Baltic to Trieste in the Adriatic, an iron curtain has descended across the Continent." Churchill's phrase "iron curtain" drew a clear picture of the postwar world. There had come to be recognizable division between the free Western Europe and the communist Eastern Europe.

## The Truman Doctrine

Before World War II, Great Britain had been a powerful force in the Mediterranean. The tremendous losses and expense of World War II, however, weakened Great Britain's influence there. The Soviet Union, which had long been striving for access to the Mediterranean Sea by way of the Turkish straits, sought to extend its influence in the area.

The Soviets supported communist rebels in their attempt to topple the government of Greece. This led the United States to try to contain the spread of communism in the Mediterranean region. On March 12, 1947, President Truman asked Congress for $400 million in aid to Turkey and Greece. He called on the United States to support free people in resisting control by armed minorities or outside pressures. Truman believed that the failure of the United States to act at this time would endanger both the nation and the free world.

Congress approved Truman's request. By 1950, more than $660 million had been spent in aid to Turkey and Greece. This policy of economic and military aid became known as the **Truman Doctrine.** It represents a major step in the evolution of American foreign policy further away from isolationism and neutrality.

## The Marshall Plan

World War II left much of Europe in ruins. Major cities and industrial centers were destroyed. Survivors of the war struggled to find food, shelter, and clothing. Dissatisfaction with such conditions grew rapidly. In many war-torn countries, the Communist Party seemed to offer solutions to such problems.

To prevent the spread of communist influence in Europe, General George C. Marshall, secretary of state under President Truman, announced a new economic-aid program called the **Marshall Plan.** In a speech delivered on June 5, 1947, Marshall announced that the United States was against "hunger, poverty, desperation, and chaos." Between 1948 and 1952, about $13 billion in economic aid was allocated by the Republican-dominated Congress for the rebuilding of Europe under the Marshall Plan. The largest amount went to Great Britain, France, Italy, and West Germany.

This aid enabled Western Europe to begin consumer production once more and to build prosperous economies. Both Western Europe and the United States felt that with stabilized and improving economies, communist expansion would be halted.

## The Beginning of the Cold War: Germany 1948–1949

At the end of World War II, Germany was divided into four zones of occupation controlled by Great Britain, France, the Soviet Union, and the United States. Berlin, the capital of Germany, was located in the Russian sector. However, the city was divided into four sections, each controlled by one of the four Allies. Disagreements during this period of occupation marked the beginning of the Cold War, a period of tension between the United States and the Soviet Union from the end of World War II to 1991.

---

### Geography in History

Stalin wanted control of the Dardanelles, a narrow strait in Turkey, because it would give Soviet ports on the Black Sea access to the Mediterranean.

### Analyzing Documents

*"In these circumstances, it is clear that the main element of any United States policy toward the Soviet Union must be that of a long-term, patient but firm and vigilant containment of Russian expansive tendencies."*
—American diplomat George Kennan, July 1947

• In what ways were the Truman Doctrine and the Marshall Plan examples of "long-term, patient but firm and vigilant" containment of communism?

---

**The Berlin Blockade** The United States, France, and Great Britain cooperated in governing the western sectors of Germany. Unable to reach agreement with the Soviet Union over the eventual unification of Germany, the three western powers decided to unify their zones without the Soviet zone. In 1949, the Federal Republic of Germany, commonly known as West Germany, was established. The Soviets opposed the establishment of this separate government. Prior to that on June 24, 1948, the Soviets had cut off all access to West Berlin by blockading the roads leading to the city, all of which had to go through the Soviet-controlled sector of Germany. The Soviets hoped that the blockade would force the western powers out of Berlin.

**The Berlin Airlift** The United States, Great Britain, and France would not back down. Recognizing that West Berlin could not get supplies by road anymore, the western powers began an airlift of food, clothing, coal, medicine, and other necessities to the city. Almost a year later, on May 12, 1949, the Soviets recognized their defeat in the area and ended the blockade. Shortly afterward, the Soviets announced the formation of the German Democratic Republic, commonly known as East Germany. In 1955, West Germany was given full sovereignty. The West had learned once again that although World War II was over, its struggle against aggressor nations was not.

## Point Four Program

The United States recognized that the Soviet Union's expansionist aims were targeted not only at Europe but at developing nations of the world as well. In 1950, Congress approved President Truman's Point Four Program, which provided nearly $400 million for technical development programs in Latin America, Asia, and Africa. The Point Four Program was designed to modernize and strengthen the economies of developing nations and thereby discourage the growth of communism.

## The North Atlantic Treaty Organization

The United States and other Western European nations also fought the spread of communism by forming alliances. In April 1949, the United States and 11 other western nations signed a collective security agreement called the North Atlantic Treaty. This agreement bound the participating nations to act together for their common defense. Members pledged that an attack on any one of them would be considered an attack on all of them. Defense arrangements were coordinated through the North Atlantic Treaty Organization **(NATO)**. The Soviets later formed an opposing alliance with seven Eastern European nations under the **Warsaw Pact.**

In 1949, President Truman announced that the Soviet Union had successfully exploded an atomic bomb. Fearing the power that this gave the Soviets, the United States worked to strengthen its influence in the world by committing several billion dollars in assistance to countries in Western Europe and elsewhere.

## European Cooperation

In order to rebuild and strengthen their economies after the war, Western European nations made ever-increasing efforts at economic cooperation. In 1951, the European Coal and Steel Community formed to enable six European nations to set prices and regulate the coal and steel industries. By 1957, the scope of economic cooperation had broadened to include efforts to improve transportation and eliminate tariff barriers within Europe. Those same six nations signed a treaty in 1957 to form the European Economic Community (EEC), also known as the Common Market. As economic cooperation continued to broaden, this organization later transformed into the European Union (EU) that exists today.

### Reading Strategy

**Organizing Information**
Who controlled the four zones of occupation in Germany following World War II?

1.

2.

3.

4.

- In which zone was the capital Berlin located?

- Which zones were combined to form West Germany?

- How did the Soviets attempt to take control of Berlin?

### Key Themes and Concepts

**Foreign Policy**
NATO represented the principle of mutual military assistance or collective security. By joining NATO, the United States dropped its opposition to military treaties with Europe for the first time since the Monroe Doctrine. As a member of NATO the United States became actively involved in European affairs.

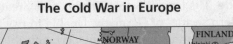

**The Cold War in Europe**

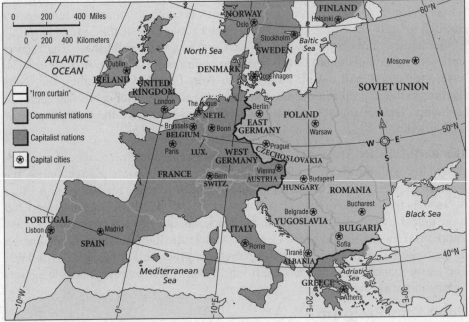

## Analyzing Documents

After losing more than 20 million people during the war and suffering wide-spread destruction, the Soviet Union was determined to rebuild in ways that would protect its own interests. One way was to establish satellite nations, countries subject to Soviet domination, on the western borders of the Soviet Union.

- How does this map illustrate the Soviet Union's desire to protect itself from non-communist rivals?

## Reading Strategy

**Analyzing Cause And Effect**

- How might the victory of the communists in the Chinese civil war in 1949 have contributed to United States involvement in the Korean War in 1950?

The European Union has experienced many changes in recent years. The European Parliament, the legislative branch of the EU, now has the power to approve or reject the EU's budget. In 1999, eleven member states began using a common currency called the euro. The EU continues to grapple with such key issues as increasing employment opportunities for citizens in all member nations. The EU today has 15 member states and is preparing for the admission of new members from eastern and southern Europe.

# Containment in Asia

During World War II, the United States had been an ally of China and an enemy of Japan. After World War II, the United States reversed its political alliances in Asia. With its new constitutional democracy, Japan became an American ally. Meanwhile, a communist takeover in China made the United States increasingly suspicious of and hostile to that nation.

## Communist Victory in China

In the 1930s, China had plunged into civil war. Mao Zedong, leader of the communist forces in China, sought to defeat the nationalist regime of Chiang Kai-shek. In 1949, the communist forces defeated the nationalists and renamed the now communist-led country the People's Republic of China. Chiang Kai-shek and the nationalists fled to the island of Taiwan.

The United States was alarmed by this development because it feared that communism would spread beyond China. Because the United States had overseen the initial rebuilding of postwar Japan and had helped put a new constitutional democracy in place, it did not want to see communism spread to Japan. Support for Japan was now seen as a way of offsetting communist China's influence in Asia.

## The Korean War

During World War II, Korea had been occupied by Japan. At the end of the war, Korea was divided along the **38th parallel,** or line of latitude. The northern zone was under the influence of the Soviet Union, and the southern zone was controlled by the United States. By 1948, the southern zone had elected an anticommunist government headed by Syngman Rhee and was now called the Republic of Korea. In the northern zone, now named the Democratic People's Republic of Korea, a communist government ruled.

**Fighting Begins** North Korea invaded South Korea in 1950 in an attempt to unify the country. President Truman responded to this invasion by committing American troops to major involvement in the Korean conflict.

**MacArthur in Command** General Douglas MacArthur, a World War II hero, was sent to command the United States military in Korea. Troops from the United States, along with small numbers of soldiers from other UN member nations, were soon involved in battles as fierce as those of World War II. A particularly devastating loss came at the Yalu River, when Chinese forces entered the conflict and pushed UN troops south. By the middle of 1951, the war had reached a stalemate. Fighting continued, but neither side was able to advance successfully.

Disagreement over the objectives and military strategies of the Korean War caused a major conflict between President Truman and General MacArthur. Although Truman was a civilian, the Constitution makes the president the commander in chief of the armed forces. When General MacArthur disagreed with Truman publicly about the conduct of the war, the President recalled him to the United States and dismissed him from command.

**Reading Strategy**

**Organizing Information**
- Who fought on the side of communist North Korea during the Korean War?
- Who fought on the side of anticommunist South Korea during the Korean War?

*President Harry Truman (left) and General Douglas MacArthur*

**Hostilities End** Although truce talks began in June 1951, no resolution was reached before the American presidential election of 1952. During that campaign the Republican candidate, World War II hero Dwight D. Eisenhower, promised that if he were elected president he would go to Korea to aid in the peace negotiations. Eisenhower won the election and did keep his campaign promise, but a truce or cease-fire was not officially signed until July 27, 1953.

The war in Korea lasted for more than three years and cost more than $15 billion. Approximately 34,000 Americans and one million Koreans and Chinese died in the conflict. At the end of the Korean War, Korea remained a divided nation and has continued in that political situation into the twenty-first century.

**New Directions** The policy of containment took a different course with American involvement in the Korean conflict. Early containment efforts focused primarily on economic aid programs. With the Korean War, the United States now showed

**Key Themes and Concepts**

**Civic Values**
The Korean War caused enormous frustration at home. When the truce was signed in 1953, Korea remained divided at almost exactly the same place as before the war, near the 38th parallel. Americans wondered why more than 54,000 of their soldiers had been killed and 113,000 wounded for such limited results. Some Americans wondered if their government was serious about stopping communism.

**Key Themes and Concepts**

**Foreign Policy**
- In what way did the Korean War mark a change in the U.S. policy of containment?

its willingness to undertake military action to contain communism if it was necessary. American experiences in Korea were a warning of future global confrontations between democratic and communist opponents.

# The Cold War at Home

Even as the United States defended democratic freedoms worldwide, sometimes those same freedoms were in danger at home. The spreading of communism to China and the apparent growing strength of the Soviet Union led some Americans to fear that communism could spread to the United States. This fear led some Americans to take actions that violated the civil rights of others.

Many Americans charged that communist agents were trying to subvert, or destroy, the American political system. Other Americans responded that the actions of anticommunists were more subversive of American values and more dangerous to the nation.

## Looking for Communists

The fear of communism in the United States had its roots in the period before World War II. Anticommunist activity began in the 1930s.

**HUAC** In 1938, the House Un-American Activities Committee (HUAC) was formed as a temporary investigative unit to look into communist activity in the United States. HUAC operated for more than 30 years. Its well-publicized probe of the movie industry in the 1940s and 1950s led to the blacklisting, or cutting off from employment, of many actors, writers, and directors.

**Reading Strategy**

**Reinforcing Main Ideas**
Americans' fears of communism resulted from the fact that communists were openly hostile to American beliefs and values such as capitalism, private ownership of land and business, and First Amendment freedoms.

- What other foreign and domestic events contributed to Americans' fears of the spread of communism?

J. Edgar Hoover, director of the Federal Bureau of Investigation, often aided HUAC investigations. Critics argued that Hoover conducted anticommunist activities that often violated the civil rights of Americans.

**The Smith Act** In 1940, Congress passed the Smith Act, which made it illegal for anyone to advocate "overthrowing . . . any government in the United States by force" or to "affiliate" with groups that called for such action.

In the 1951 landmark case of *Dennis* v. *United States*, the Supreme Court upheld the Smith Act. Eugene Dennis, general secretary of the Communist Party in the United States, and ten others were convicted of advocating the violent overthrow of the government.

Two court decisions in 1957 weakened the intent of the Smith Act. In *Watkins* v. *United States*, the court ruled the HUAC could not punish witnesses who refused to cooperate with its investigations. In *Yates* v. *United States*, the court ruled that the Smith Act applied only to those who teach or advocate direct "action" to overthrow government, not to those who merely advocate it in principle.

**The Loyalty Program** In 1947, President Truman fueled anticommunist feelings by ordering a Loyalty Review Board to conduct security checks on thousands of government employees. Those whose loyalty was considered doubtful were dismissed.

In the early 1950s, Robert Oppenheimer, who had led the research to develop the atomic bomb, voiced his opposition to building the new, more destructive hydrogen bomb. This action and his past association with others whose loyalty was being questioned led to a government hearing about his own loyalty. He was determined to be a "loyal citizen," but his security clearance was removed, and he was barred from future government research.

**The Hiss Case** The Alger Hiss case led many Americans to believe that there was a reason to fear that there were communists in the government. In 1948, Alger Hiss, a former adviser to President Roosevelt, was charged with having been a Communist spy during the 1930s. Whittaker Chambers, a former Communist party member, made these charges, which Hiss denied. A congressional committee investigated them.

A young Republican committee member from California, Richard Nixon, believed that Hiss was guilty. Nixon's pursuit of the case and Hiss's eventual conviction on perjury charges made Nixon a national figure. The conviction also added weight to Republican charges that Roosevelt and Truman had not been alert enough to the dangers of communism.

## McCarthyism

Against this political background, Senator Joseph McCarthy of Wisconsin began his own hunt for communists. In 1950, McCarthy charged he had a list of State Department employees known to be communists. Over the next four years, McCarthy went on to charge that many other people and government agencies had been corrupted by communism.

McCarthy made bold accusations without any evidence. This tactic became known as "McCarthyism." He ruined the reputations of many people he carelessly accused of being communists. Meanwhile, the Rosenberg case and congressional legislation helped win public support for McCarthy's actions.

**The Rosenberg Case** In 1950, Ethel and Julius Rosenberg and Morton Sobell were charged with giving atomic secrets to the Soviets during World War II. After a highly controversial trial, they were convicted of espionage. The Rosenbergs were sentenced to death and Sobell to prison. The Rosenbergs were executed in 1953.

**Congressional Legislation** In the same year the Rosenbergs were arrested, Congress passed the McCarran Internal Security Act. The law aimed at limiting the actions of anyone the government considered a threat to United States security. The McCarran-Walter Act of 1952 restricted the immigration of persons from communist-dominated nations in Asia and southern and central Europe. President Truman vetoed the bill, but Congress passed it over his veto.

**McCarthy's Fall** In 1954, McCarthy charged that even the army was full of communists. He held televised investigations into these charges. For the first time, millions of Americans saw McCarthy's bullying tactics for themselves. His public support quickly faded, and in December 1954, the Senate censured, or denounced, him for "conduct unbecoming a member." The fall of McCarthy ended the red scare of the 1950s, although anticommunist attitudes lingered as the Cold War continued to drag on. During this time the tactics of Senator McCarthy were criticized because he violated important constitutional liberties. The term McCarthyism has come to mean the use of methods of investigation and accusation that are regarded as unfair, in order to suppress opposition.

**Preparing for the Exam**

- What was the outcome of the Alger Hiss case and what was its significance?

**Key Themes and Concepts**

**Constitutional Principles** Although many people knew that Senator McCarthy's claims were exaggerated at best, he was still able to gain power and ruin the lives of many people.

- How did McCarthy contribute to the suppression of free speech and open, honest debate?

**Preparing for the Exam**

McCarthyism during the 1950s had many similarities to the Red Scare following World War I.

- How were the actions of Attorney General A. Mitchell Palmer and McCarthy similar?

# Questions for Regents Practice

## Multiple Choice

*Directions:* Review the Test-Taking Strategies section of this book. Then answer the following questions, drawn from actual Regents examinations. For each statement or question, choose the *number* of the word or expression that, of those given, best completes the statement or answers the question.

1 United States senators who opposed the Treaty of Versailles objected mainly to

(1) United States membership in the League of Nations

(2) payment of reparations by Germany to the Allied nations

(3) the transfer of Germany's colonial possessions to the League of Nations

(4) the creation of new and independent nations in Eastern Europe

2 A major reason for the United States neutrality in the 1930s was the nation's

(1) belief in the domino theory

(2) disillusionment resulting from World War I

(3) strong approval of political conditions in Europe

(4) military and naval superiority

3 At the outbreak of both World War I and World War II in Europe, public opinion in the United States generally favored

(1) remaining neutral

(2) entering the war on the side of the Allies

(3) invading Europe in order to acquire territory

(4) settling the conflict through an international peace organization

4 Isolationism as a foreign policy is more difficult to achieve in the twentieth century than in prior times mainly because

(1) the increase in the world's population has forced people to live more closely together

(2) there are more sovereign nations today than in the past

(3) modern technology had made nations more interdependent

(4) public opinion on issues is more easily disregarded

5 The appeasement policy followed by Western European leaders in the late 1930s was based primarily on the belief that war could be avoided by

(1) satisfying Hitler's desire for territorial expansion

(2) encouraging communist expansion into Nazi Germany

(3) limiting the development of Germany's armed forces

(4) appealing to the League of Nations for international cooperation

6 Which event led directly to United States entry into World War II?

(1) invasion of Poland by Germany and Russia

(2) attack on France by Italy

(3) sinking of the *Lusitania* by Germany

(4) attack on Pearl Harbor by Japan

Base your answer to question 7 on the announcement below and on your knowledge of social studies.

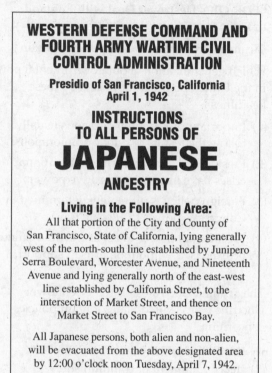

**WESTERN DEFENSE COMMAND AND FOURTH ARMY WARTIME CIVIL CONTROL ADMINISTRATION**

Presidio of San Francisco, California
April 1, 1942

**INSTRUCTIONS TO ALL PERSONS OF**

# JAPANESE

ANCESTRY

**Living in the Following Area:**

All that portion of the City and County of San Francisco, State of California, lying generally west of the north-south line established by Junipero Serra Boulevard, Worcester Avenue, and Nineteenth Avenue and lying generally north of the east-west line established by California Street, to the intersection of Market Street, and thence on Market Street to San Francisco Bay.

All Japanese persons, both alien and non-alien, will be evacuated from the above designated area by 12:00 o'clock noon Tuesday, April 7, 1942.

**7** During World War II, the action required by this announcement was based largely on

(1) racial prejudice

(2) a labor shortage

(3) the needs for skilled workers in defense industries

(4) a desire to protect Japanese Americans from military attack

**8** The rulings of the Supreme Court in *Dred Scott v. Sanford* (1857), *Plessy v. Ferguson* (1896), and *Korematsu v. United States* (1944) all demonstrate that the Supreme Court has

(1) continued to extend voting rights to minorities

(2) protected itself from internal dissent

(3) sometimes failed to protect the rights of minorities

(4) often imposed restrictions on free speech during wartime

**9** An important effect of World War II on United States foreign policy was a

(1) refusal to become involved in world affairs

(2) smaller role for the president in foreign policy and national security issues

(3) stronger commitment to collective security and world leadership

(4) willingness to intervene only when the national economy is involved

**10** After World War II, the United States was better able than its allies to adjust its economy from wartime to peacetime because the United States

(1) possessed nuclear weapons

(2) raised tariffs on imports

(3) had collected its war debts from the Allies

(4) had suffered no widespread wartime destruction

**11** What was a major effect of World War II on women and minorities in the United States?

(1) They were drafted into the military.

(2) They had new opportunities in the workforce.

(3) They received equal voting rights for the first time.

(4) They were granted equal pay for equal work.

# Questions for Regents Practice

Base your answers to questions 12 and 13 on the speakers' conversation below and on your knowledge of social studies.

*Speaker A:* "We must provide arms to the legitimate governments of Greece and Turkey if they are to defeat Soviet-sponsored subversion."

*Speaker B:* "The first priority is to help rebuild the postwar economies of European countries so that democratic governments can survive."

*Speaker C:* "Our main goal is to create a system of collective security agreements to deal with any military threats."

*Speaker D:* "We must continue to build both our nuclear and our conventional arsenals if we are to have any hope of world peace."

**12** The central concern of all the speakers is
   (1) the containment of communism
   (2) the defeat of the Axis Powers in World War II
   (3) a ban on the proliferation of nuclear weapons
   (4) the support of United Nations peacekeeping efforts

**13** These speakers' statements would most likely have been made during the presidential administration of
   (1) Franklin D. Roosevelt
   (2) Harry S. Truman
   (3) John F. Kennedy
   (4) Richard M. Nixon

**14** "Wilson Orders Controls on U.S. Industry to Fight War Against Germany"

   "FDR OK's Destroyer Deal with England to Fight Sub Threat"

   "Truman Orders Airlift of Supplies to Berlin"

   Which generalization about governmental power in the United States is supported by these headlines?
   (1) Important presidential decisions usually follow the results of public opinion polls.
   (2) Presidential actions during international crises have increased executive power.
   (3) Foreign policy is ultimately determined by Congress's power to allocate funds.
   (4) Presidential power to act in wartime cannot be exercised without bipartisan support.

**15** The Truman Doctrine and the Eisenhower Doctrine were United States foreign policies concerning
   (1) the international balance of payments
   (2) the containment of communism
   (3) worldwide environmental pollution
   (4) nuclear disarmament

**16** The North Atlantic Treaty Organization (NATO) and the Truman Doctrine were attempts to carry out a United States foreign policy of
   (1) brinkmanship
   (2) containment
   (3) appeasement
   (4) neutrality

17　After World War II, relations between the Soviet Union and the United States were marked by

(1) conflicts where the superpowers supported opposing sides, but did not confront each other directly

(2) refusal to negotiate on any issues

(3) slow but steady decreases in military forces and armaments

(4) reliance on international peace organizations to resolve disputes

18　The Red Scare and McCarthyism were similar in that both

(1) advocated the development of the arts and sciences

(2) supported United States foreign aid programs

(3) encouraged nativist ideas

(4) promoted economic development

19　The NATO alliance, Truman Doctrine, and Marshall Plan were all attempts to

(1) contain the spread of communism

(2) give military assistance to China

(3) defend United Nations peacekeeping forces

(4) bring peace to the Middle East

20　During the 1950s, Senator Joseph McCarthy held congressional hearings to expose suspected

(1) Nazis

(2) members of organized crime

(3) terrorists

(4) communists

21　The Cold War developed after World War II as a result of

(1) a decrease in arms production

(2) the collapse of the United Nations

(3) Japan's new economic growth

(4) tension between the superpowers

22　The need for an international peacekeeping organization after World War II resulted in the development of the

(1) Red Cross

(2) League of Nations

(3) United Nations

(4) Alliance for Progress

23　"We Americans live in a world we can no longer dominate, but from which we cannot isolate ourselves." The author of this quotation is saying that the United States should

(1) become less dependent on foreign nations

(2) realize that it is no longer a world power

(3) recognize important changes in international relations

(4) increase its economic and military strength

24　What was a major goal of United States foreign policy in Europe after 1945?

(1) development of nuclear weapons for World War II Allies of the United States

(2) liberation of nations under the control of the Soviet Union

(3) military support for nationalist movements within individual European nations

(4) promotion of international cooperation through political and economic agreements

25　In its dependence upon members to enforce human rights declarations, the United Nations most closely resembles the

(1) Soviet Union under Joseph Stalin

(2) United States under the federal Constitution

(3) United States under the Articles of Confederation

(4) Japanese government before World War II

# Thematic Essay Question

**Directions:** Write a well-organized essay that includes an introduction, several paragraphs addressing the task below, and a conclusion.

**Theme:** Foreign Policy

> The primary aim of a nation's foreign policy is the self-interest of that nation. Throughout United States history, certain foreign policy actions have led to debate over whether they were in the national interest.

**Task:**

> - Identify *three* different foreign policies that have been followed by the United States.
> - Discuss a specific application of that policy by the United States.
> - Include in your discussion one reason the United States applied that policy and one result of the application of that policy.

You may use any example from your study of United States foreign policy actions during the twentieth century. Some suggestions you might wish to consider include: isolationism, containment, formation of military alliances, reliance upon international alliances, and nonrecognition.

**You are *not* limited to these suggestions.**

**Guidelines:**

**In your essay, be sure to**

- Develop all aspects of the task
- Support the theme with relevant facts, examples, and details
- Use a logical and clear plan of organization, including an introduction and a conclusion that are beyond a restatement of the theme

**In developing your answer, be sure to keep this general definition in mind:**

<u>discuss</u> means "to make observations about something using facts, reasoning, and argument; to present in some detail"

In developing your answers, be sure to keep this general definition in mind:

> <u>discuss</u> means "to make observations about something using facts, reasoning, and argument; to present in some detail.

This question is based on the accompanying documents. The question is designed to test your ability to work with historical documents. Some of the documents have been edited for the purposes of the question. As you analyze the documents, take into account the source of each document and any point of view that may be presented in the document.

### Historical Context:

> World events after 1939 drew the United States into greater international involvement. These events forced the United States to abandon its isolationist foreign policy in favor of more active global involvement.

**Task:** Using information from the documents and your knowledge of United States history and government, answer the questions that follow each document in Part A. Your answers to the questions will help you write the Part B essay in which you will be asked to:

> • Discuss how the need for military security and the protection of democratic ideals have shaped American foreign policy since 1939

# Document-Based Question

### Document #1

"Yesterday, December 7, 1941, a date which will live in infamy, the United States of America was suddenly and deliberately attacked by naval and air forces of the Empire of Japan.

"The attack yesterday on the Hawaiian Islands has caused severe damage to American naval and military forces. Very many American lives have been lost. In addition, American ships have been reported torpedoed on the high seas between San Francisco and Honolulu.

"As Commander in Chief of the Army and Navy I have directed that all measures be taken for our defense. . . . I believe I interpret the will of the Congress and of the people when I assert that we will not only defend ourselves to the uttermost but will make very certain that this form of treachery shall never endanger us again.

"I ask that the Congress declare that, since the unprovoked and dastardly attack by Japan on Sunday, December 7, a state of war has existed between the United States and the Japanese Empire."

—**Franklin D. Roosevelt,** *Address to Congress,* **December 8, 1941**

1. Why did President Roosevelt believe that the attack on Pearl Harbor justified the United States officially declaring war on Japan?

_____

_____

_____

## Document #2

2. This cartoon represents Roosevelt, Stalin, and Churchill at the Yalta Conference. What does their activity in this cartoon say about their accomplishments at Yalta?

_____

_____

## Document #3

"[The Soviet Union] cannot be easily defeated or discouraged by a single victory on the part of its opponents . . . but only by intelligent long-range policies . . . no less steady in their purpose . . . than those of the Soviet Union itself. In these circumstances, it is clear that the main element of any United States policy toward the Soviet Union must be that of a long-term, patient but firm and vigilant containment of Russian expansive tendencies."

**—Foreign service officer George Kennan, July 1947**

3. What foreign policy position did Kennan believe the United States should take toward the Soviet Union?

_____

_____

_____

# Document-Based Question

## Document #4

> "The Parties agree that an armed attack against one or more of them in Europe or North America shall be considered an attack against them all and consequently they agree that, if such an armed attack occurs, each of them, in exercise of the right of individual or collective self-defense. . . will assist the Party or Parties so attacked by taking . . . such action as it deems necessary, including the use of armed force, to restore and maintain the security of the North Atlantic area."
>
> —**The North Atlantic Treaty, April 4, 1949**

4. How did joining NATO demonstrate the long-term commitment of the United States to international involvement?

_____

_____

_____

_____

## Document #5

> "I believe that it must be the policy of the United States to support free peoples who are resisting attempted subjugation [takeover] by armed minorities or by outside pressures. . . . I believe that our help should be primarily through economic and financial aid, which is essential to economic stability and orderly political processes. . . .
>
> "I therefore ask the Congress to provide authority for assistance to Greece and Turkey in the amount of $400,000,000. . . .
>
> "The free peoples of the world look to us for support in maintaining their freedoms. If we falter in our leadership, we may endanger the peace of the world—and we shall surely endanger the welfare of our own nation. Great responsibilities have been placed upon us by the swift movement of events. I am confident that the Congress will face these responsibilities squarely."
>
> —**President Harry S. Truman, *Address Before a Joint Session of Congress*, March 12, 1947**

5. Based on this quote, why did President Truman believe that the United States should help Greece and Turkey in their fight against a communist takeover?

_____

_____

Document #6

| | Flights | Cargo (short tons) | | | |
|---|---|---|---|---|---|
| | | Total | Food | Coal | Other |
| USA | 189,963 | 1,783,573 | 296,319 | 1,421,119 | 66,135 |
| UK | 87,841 | 541,937 | 240,386 | 164,911 | 136,640 |
| France | 424 | 896 | unknown | unknown | unknown |
| Total | 278,228 | 2,326,406 | | | |

Berlin Airlift Statistics, 1948–1949

6. How does the chart above demonstrate the commitment that the United States made to prevent the Soviet Union from crippling West Berlin in the blockade of 1948–1949?

_____

_____

Document #7

"Our purpose in the Persian Gulf remains constant: to drive Iraq out of Kuwait, to restore Kuwait's legitimate government, and to ensure the stability and security of this critical region. Let me make clear what I mean by the region's stability and security. . . . We seek a Persian Gulf where conflict is no longer the rule, where the strong are neither tempted nor able to intimidate the weak.

"Most Americans know instinctively why we are in the Gulf. They know we had to stop [Iraqi leader] Saddam [Hussein] now, not later. . . .They know we must make sure that control of the world's oil resources does not fall into his hands, only to finance further aggression. They know that we need to build a new, enduring peace, based not on arms races and confrontation but on shared principles and the rule of law."

—**President George Bush,** *State of the Union Address,* **January 29, 1991**

7. According to this quote, why did President Bush believe that American involvement in the Persian Gulf War was necessary?

_____

_____

# Document-Based Question

## Part B

### Essay

*Directions:*   Write a well-organized essay that includes an introduction, several paragraphs, and a conclusion. Use evidence from *at least four* documents in the body of the essay. Support your response with relevant facts, examples, and details. Include additional outside information.

**Historical Context:**

World events after 1939 drew the United States into greater international involvement. These events forced the United States to abandon its isolationist foreign policy in favor of more active global involvement.

**Task:**   Using information from the documents and your knowledge of United States history and government, write an essay in which you:

- Discuss how the need for military security and the protection of democratic ideals have shaped American foreign policy since 1939

**Guidelines:**

**In your essay, be sure to**

- Develop all aspects of the task
- Incorporate information from *at least four* documents
- Incorporate relevant outside information
- Support the theme with relevant facts, examples, and details
- Use a logical and clear plan of organization, including an introduction and conclusion that are beyond a restatement of the theme

# The World in Uncertain Times, 1950–the Present

## Unit Overview

The foreign policies that began after World War II continued to shape America's response to events abroad for decades. The policy of containment, begun under President Truman, eventually led the United States into its longest war, one that caused deep splits within American society.

During the period from the 1950s to the present, life changed at home for Americans. An expanding civil rights movement, a major constitutional crisis, new technologies, and a changing economic picture are some of the highlights of these years.

Some key questions to help you focus on this time period include:

- How did the foreign policy concerns of the United States become more global in scope?
- What were the goals and the achievements of the Civil Rights Movement?
- How did the war in Vietnam affect American society?
- How did relations of the United States with the Soviet Union change under Presidents Reagan and Bush?
- Why is September 11, 2001, considered a major turning point in United States history?
- What are some of the major challenges that the nation will face in years to come?

# Containment Abroad and Consensus at Home: 1945–1960

The
# Big Idea

Foreign policy, especially the Cold War, influenced events in the 1950s. During this period:

- President Eisenhower attempted to limit communism.

- policies toward Asia, the Middle East, and Latin America took shape.

- the economy of the United States improved.

- African Americans renewed their struggle for civil rights.

## Section Overview

During the 1950s, the Cold War intensified and spread to new locations around the world. Meanwhile, the new economic prosperity allowed many Americans to enjoy greater wealth and leisure than their parents had. At the same time, the Civil Rights Movement intensified as African Americans demanded justice and equality.

## Key Themes and Concepts

As you review this section, take special note of the following key themes and concepts:

**Foreign Policy**  How did tensions between the United States and the Soviet Union increase and decrease during Eisenhower's presidency?

**Citizenship**  How did African Americans begin to organize the Civil Rights Movement?

**Economic Systems**  Who benefited from the "Eisenhower prosperity," and who did not?

## Key People

Dwight D. Eisenhower

Nikita Khrushchev

Fidel Castro

Jackie Robinson

Rosa Parks

Martin Luther King, Jr.

## Key Terms

balance of power

brinkmanship

arms race

Sputnik

domino theory

Eisenhower Doctrine

suburbanization

Civil Rights Movement

## Key Supreme Court Cases

*Brown* v. *Board of Education of Topeka, Kansas* (1954)

## The Cold War Continues

The United States emerged from World War II as the strongest nation in the world. It controlled the atomic bomb, and its economy was undamaged by the destruction of war. The Soviet Union, however, quickly became America's chief rival. By 1949, it too had the atomic bomb. It had also taken control of most of the nations of Eastern Europe and was seeking to extend its influence elsewhere.

President Harry S. Truman began the policy of containment after the war in an attempt to limit the spread of communism. As the United States and the Soviet

Union—the two world superpowers—attempted to maintain a **balance of power,** a cold war developed.

### The Cold War, 1950–1960

| 1950 Korean War begins | 1953 Korean War ends | 1956 Suez crisis begins; Hungarian revolt | 1960 U-2 shot down over USSR |
|---|---|---|---|

| 1950 | 1952 | 1954 | 1956 | 1958 | 1960 |
|---|---|---|---|---|---|

| 1952 Dwight D. Eisenhower elected president | 1955 Summit conference in Geneva | 1959 Castro wins power in Cuba |
|---|---|---|

**Analyzing Documents**

Examine the timeline, then answer the following questions.

- Did the Korean War begin before or after Eisenhower became president?

- Which events on the timeline took place in Europe?

## Eisenhower's Foreign Policy

As President, Dwight D. Eisenhower continued Truman's basic policy of containment. However, he and his secretary of state John Foster Dulles introduced some new ideas.

**Massive Retaliation** Eisenhower worried that defense spending would bankrupt the nation. Yet he feared that the Soviets might see cutbacks in military spending as a sign of weakness.

Eisenhower and Dulles instead devised a "new look" for the nation's defense. The United States would rely more heavily on air power and nuclear weapons than on ground troops. Dulles announced a policy of massive retaliation. This meant that the United States would consider the use of nuclear weapons to halt aggression if it believed the nation's interests were threatened.

Dulles further stated that the nation must be ready to go "to the brink of war" in order to preserve world peace. This policy of **brinkmanship** greatly increased world tensions during the 1950s.

**The Arms Race** The United States and the Soviet Union began an arms race, stockpiling nuclear and nonnuclear weapons. The United States exploded a hydrogen bomb in 1952, and the Soviets tested one a year later. Both nations rushed to develop missiles capable of carrying nuclear weapons. The balance of power became a balance of terror.

In 1953, Eisenhower announced the Atoms for Peace Plan at the United Nations. The plan called for United Nations supervision of a world search to find peaceful uses for nuclear technology. The Soviet Union refused to participate.

In 1957, the Soviets launched a satellite, **Sputnik,** into orbit around the earth. The arms race then became a space race as the United States rushed to launch its own satellites, some for military purposes.

## Foreign Policy in Asia

Asia became a major area of concern for United States foreign policy. The Communist victory in China in 1949 raised fears of further Communist expansion. The war in Korea, even though it ended in what was basically a draw in 1953, added to these fears.

**The Domino Theory** As Communists took control of the governments of China and, later, some nations of Southeast Asia, American worries about Communist

## Key Themes and Concepts

**Interdependence**
• In 1954, the Central Intelligence Agency tried to overthrow the government of Iran and restore the country's former ruler, the shah. Why?

expansion increased. Eisenhower stated that the United States must resist further aggression in the region and explained what came to be known as the domino theory. The nations of Asia, he said, were like a row of dominoes standing on end. If one fell to communism, the rest were sure to follow.

**SEATO** One way to resist aggression, Dulles claimed, was through alliances. To mirror the formation of NATO in Europe, Dulles in 1954 pushed for the creation of the Southeast Asia Treaty Organization (SEATO). Its original members— Pakistan, Thailand, the Philippines, Australia, New Zealand, Great Britain, and the United States—pledged to meet any "common danger" from Communist aggression.

### Foreign Policy in the Middle East

The Middle East was the scene of several outbreaks of trouble during the Eisenhower administration.

**Iran** In 1954, the prime minister of Iran tried to nationalize that country's foreign-owned oil industry. The United States, through the Central Intelligence Agency, secretly arranged the overthrow of the prime minister's government and the restoration of the shah to the throne of Iran. This action helped secure America's supply of oil at the time but caused problems for the nation in years to come.

### Geography in History

• Nasser's seizure of the Suez Canal sparked a crisis that involved Great Britain, France, and Israel. Why was the Suez Canal so important to these nations?

**Egypt** Gamal Abdel Nasser, president of Egypt, had counted on economic support from the Soviet Union and the United States to build a huge dam at Aswan on the Nile River. Nasser's friendliness to the Soviet Union led the United States to withdraw its support. Nasser then nationalized the Suez Canal, which was run by a British and French company. He planned to use revenues from the canal to pay for the dam.

Great Britain and France, joined by Israel, sent troops to seize the canal. Fearing that fighting would spread through the region, both the United States and the Soviet Union supported a United Nations resolution condemning the attack. Great Britain, France, and Israel withdrew, and the canal remained under Egyptian control.

**The Eisenhower Doctrine** Troubles in the Middle East led Congress to adopt what became known as the Eisenhower Doctrine in 1957. The United States pledged to help any Middle Eastern nation resist Communist aggression.

**Lebanon** In 1958, the Eisenhower Doctrine was tested when the governments of Lebanon and Jordan asked for help. The United States sent marines to Lebanon, and Great Britain sent troops to Jordan to help restore political calm in those nations.

### Foreign Policy in Latin America

## Preparing for the Exam

On the examination, you will need to understand United States foreign policy during the 1950s in the Middle East.

What is the Eisenhower Doctrine? List two countries to which it is applied.

1.

2.

Troubles also flared up closer to home during Eisenhower's time in office. Three instances are especially notable.

**Guatemala** The CIA staged a successful covert operation in Guatemala in 1954. It arranged a revolt that toppled a government considered to be too friendly to Communists.

**Nixon's Tour** In 1958, Vice President Richard Nixon went on a goodwill tour of Latin America. In Peru and Venezuela, however, angry mobs surrounded his limousine, throwing rocks and eggs at it. This event revealed the strong anti-American feelings that had built up in Latin America in response to repeated interventions in the region by the United States.

**Cuba** In 1956, Fidel Castro began a revolt against the government of Cuban dictator Fulgencio Batista. When the revolt ended with Castro's victory in 1959, the United States quickly recognized the new government.

Castro, however, soon adopted policies that angered the Eisenhower administration. He limited civil liberties and imprisoned political opponents. He also nationalized key industries and turned to the Soviet Union for aid.

Large numbers of Cubans fled Castro's rule, with many settling in southern Florida. Some worked actively to end Castro's rule. Meanwhile, they became one more immigrant group that contributed to the richness of the American multicultural experience.

## Changing Relations With the Soviet Union

Tensions between the United States and the Soviet Union rose and fell during Eisenhower's time in office.

**New Soviet Leadership** Joseph Stalin, leader of the Soviet Union since the 1920s, died in 1953. In time, Nikita Khrushchev took over as the head of the Soviet government. This change marked a temporary easing of Cold War tensions as the Soviets began to focus more on improving conditions within their nation.

**Peaceful Coexistence** Relations between the superpowers gradually improved. In 1955, the leaders of the United States, the Soviet Union, Great Britain, and France held the first summit meeting since World War II in Geneva, Switzerland. The superpower leaders began talks on disarmament that, in time, led to a suspension of nuclear testing.

**Poland and Hungary** In 1956, riots by Polish workers won concessions from the Communist Polish government. Inspired by this, students and workers in Hungary began demonstrations that fall that ended with the Soviet Union sending tanks and troops to bring that nation firmly back under Communist control. The suppression of the Hungarian revolt cooled relations between the United States and the Soviet Union.

**Camp David** Relations improved again by 1959. Khrushchev visited the United States, and he and Eisenhower held lengthy talks at Camp David, the presidential retreat near Washington, D.C. The spirit of goodwill that grew at these talks encouraged the leaders to announce another summit meeting in Paris in 1960.

**The U-2 Incident** The Paris summit proved a disaster. Shortly before it opened, the Soviet military shot down an American U-2 aircraft deep in Soviet territory. The pilot admitted that he had been spying on Soviet military bases.

Eisenhower said that he had approved the U-2 flights and promised to suspend them. Khrushchev denounced the United States and demanded an apology. Eisenhower refused, and the summit collapsed before it really started.

In summary, Eisenhower's foreign policy was primarily a continuation of Truman's containment policy. Many of the events of the 1950s can be compared to kettles ready to boil over in the 1960s. In later years, the Eisenhower administration was criticized by some as not being aware enough of the struggles of developing nations and of their desires to end colonial rule.

## Reading Strategy

**Analyzing Cause and Effect**
- Why did the policies of Fidel Castro anger the Eisenhower administration?

## Key Themes and Concepts

**Foreign Policy**
Relations between the United States and the Soviet Union changed several times during the 1950s. Following the death of Soviet leader Joseph Stalin in 1953, the new Soviet leader Nikita Khrushchev focused more on improving conditions within his nation. This eased Cold War tensions.

- What event rekindled the Cold War in 1956?

## Turning Point

- Why is the U-2 incident considered a turning point in U.S.-Soviet relations?

# An Improving Economy at Home

When Dwight Eisenhower became president in 1953, he was the first Republican president since 1933—the year Herbert Hoover left office during one of the worst years of the Great Depression. Since that time, Democrats Franklin D. Roosevelt and Harry S. Truman had called for New Deal and New Society policies that had vastly increased both the federal government's spending and its role in society.

## Eisenhower's Economic Policies

Eisenhower had a deep dislike for strong centralized government. In addition, he generally believed policies that were good for big business were good for the nation as a whole.

**Eisenhower's Domestic Policies** Eisenhower attempted to cut back on the federal government's size and power. He reduced spending for defense and foreign aid.

Eisenhower did recognize that many social programs begun under the New Deal were very popular. He extended some of these and, in some cases, started new programs. The Social Security program was expanded to include seven million more people, and a new cabinet post, the Department of Health, Education, and Welfare, was created.

**The Farm Problem** Conditions on the nation's farms pulled Eisenhower between his desire to cut government spending and his wish to extend some social programs. Farm production had been increasing while prices for agricultural products had been declining. During the twentieth century the number of farms and the number of Americans employed in agriculture decreased significantly. At the same time, individual farm sizes were increasing.

Farmers had been receiving payments from the federal government to make up for changes in market conditions. Eisenhower's secretary of agriculture wanted to be able to cut such payments. Farmers protested, and in 1956, Congress approved a new program that paid farmers for not planting crops. Both types of payments are called subsidies, or direct payments by a government to private individuals.

## "Eisenhower Prosperity" and Consumer Spending

Despite the problems noted above, the American people commonly prospered during the 1950s. There were several reasons for this.

- During World War II, Americans had worked hard and generally earned good wages. Because of rationing and shortages, however, they could usually spend their money only on basic necessities.
- By war's end, Americans had accumulated huge amounts of capital—wealth in the form of money or property. They were ready to spend this capital on consumer goods.
- By the 1950s, wartime price controls were over, and factories had converted from the production of military supplies to the production of consumer goods.

**New Homes** The postwar years saw the start of a **"baby boom."** The growth in family size, the accumulation of capital, and the availability of government loans to veterans brought a rapid increase in home building.

**Suburbs** Much new home building was done in areas surrounding major cities (urban areas). These areas are called suburbs. The suburbs offered limited jobs and services for their residents, most of whom worked in the cities. The suburbs grew rapidly. Levittown, New York, for example, became a symbol of **suburbanization,** with some 17,000 tract houses built in four years. By the 1960s, almost a third of all Americans lived in suburbs.

## Key Themes and Concepts

**Presidential Decisions and Actions**
President Eisenhower believed that what was good for business benefited the United States as a whole. He attempted to limit the federal government's power but expanded several social programs, including Social Security.

- Why did farm conditions present a problem for Eisenhower?

- How did Congress resolve the problem?

## Reading Strategy

**Reinforcing Main Ideas**
- How did the growth of suburbs contribute to the decline of many cities?

*Refrigerator-Freezers!*

# THE FINAL FROST BARRIER!

IT'S HERE!
A FROST-PROOF
FOOD FREEZER!
NO FROST!
NO FROST-LOCKED
FOODS!
NO DEFROSTING!

**You'll feel like a queen . . .**
- Trim Upright Freezer with award-winning Sheer Look and embossed white-bright Lacework Styling.
- Takes so little floor space—only 32 inches wide—yet this 16 cu. ft. Frost-Proof Imperial Freezer shown, stores 560 lbs. of food.

- Serve family meals in minutes. Be always ready for guests.
- Shop once a week. Enjoy bulk buying that cuts food bills.
- Cook and bake in quantity. Enjoy "free" days.
- Freeze leftovers, like stew, turkey, cake, enjoy them weeks later.
- Have fun freezing your own fruits and vegetables; fish and game, too.

**DESIGNED WITH YOU IN MIND!**

## Analyzing Documents

Examine the advertisement, then answer the questions.

- What product is the advertisement promoting?

- Who is the advertisement targeting? What clues lead you to this conclusion?

- What does this advertisement suggest about the U.S. economy at the time?

- How is this advertisement similar to ads you see today? How is it different?

The growth of suburbs contributed to the decline of many cities. As people moved out of cities to suburbs, fewer taxpayers remained to help pay for essential services. At the same time, a greater concentration of poorer people in the cities increased the demand for many social services.

**Automobiles** Cars made the growth of suburbs possible, and suburbs increased the demand for cars. Since public transportation systems grew more slowly than suburbs, people in suburbs relied increasingly on their cars. Increased demand for automobiles benefited many areas of the nation's economy. Factories turned out the steel, glass, and rubber that went into new cars. Refineries also produced oil and gas that powered them.

The federal government stepped into the transportation picture with passage of the Federal Highway Act of 1956. This provided funding for what became a 44,000-mile network of interstate highways.

**A Nation on the Move** Americans moved from central cities to suburbs. They also moved to new areas of the country. Many people moved from the industrialized but decaying cities of the Northeast and the Midwest and from the farms of the Midwest to the Sun Belt. This was the name given to the states of the South and the West—including Florida, Texas, Arizona, and California—that experienced a faster than average population growth beginning in the postwar years.

The sun and warm climate of these states enticed both retirees and businesses that wished to relocate. As this region grew, it attracted more industry and prompted both population and job loss in what came to be called the Rust Belt. This region

## Reading Strategy

**Formulating Questions**
The increase in demand for cars benefited many industries, such as the steel and oil industries. Increased automobile ownership also made it possible for people to live in suburbs without public transportation, because the government provided funding for an extensive highway network.

- What were some of the negative consequences of this increased reliance on cars?

## Geography in History

In which areas of the United States did the population grow most quickly during in the 1950s? Give examples of three states that experienced rapid growth.

1.

2.

3.

included the states of the Northeast (including New York and Massachusetts) and the Midwest (including Ohio and Michigan).

**Analyzing Documents**

• Examine the bar graph at right. Between which two years did the number of homes with television sets increase most dramatically?

**Homes With Television Sets, 1948–1960**

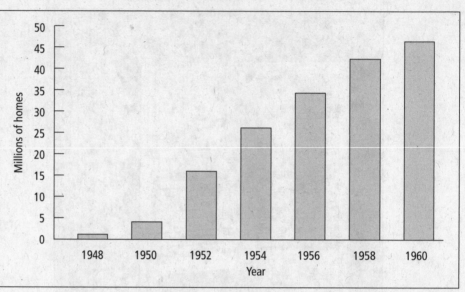

Source: *Statistical Abstract of the United States*

**Television** After limited broadcasting in 1939, national broadcasting began in 1946. Television became the leading form of popular entertainment, and its growth, both as a source of amusement and a tool for learning, has continued to the present day.

# A Renewed Struggle for Civil Rights

**Turning Point**

• Why is it considered a turning point in the struggle for civil rights when Jackie Robinson joined the Brooklyn Dodgers?

Since the period of Reconstruction after the Civil War, African Americans faced discrimination, especially in southern states. Jim Crow laws limited the freedoms of African Americans. For generations, white southerners continued to maintain economic, social, and political control over the South.

## Beginnings of Change

Until well into the twentieth century, much of the South was segregated, or separated by race. Although such segregation was less apparent in the North, African Americans were generally restricted to poorer neighborhoods and lower-paying jobs. Although African Americans fought for change, until the 1950s their gains were limited.

**Reading Strategy**

**Organizing Information**
The struggle to secure African American civil rights required the efforts of countless dedicated activists, organizers, and political leaders. What are two changes that President Truman made that had an impact on civil rights?

1.

2.

Not until 1947, for example, were African Americans permitted to play on major league baseball teams in this country. In that year, Jackie Robinson joined the Brooklyn Dodgers. This was one sign that public attitudes on segregation were beginning to change.

**Truman's Policies on Civil Rights** President Truman appointed a presidential commission on civil rights in 1946. Based on its report, Truman called for the establishment of a fair employment practices commission. Congress, however, failed to act on the idea.

Using his powers as commander in chief, Truman issued an executive order banning segregation in the armed forces. He also strengthened the Justice Department's civil rights division, which aided blacks who challenged segregation in the courts.

## Civil Rights Milestones

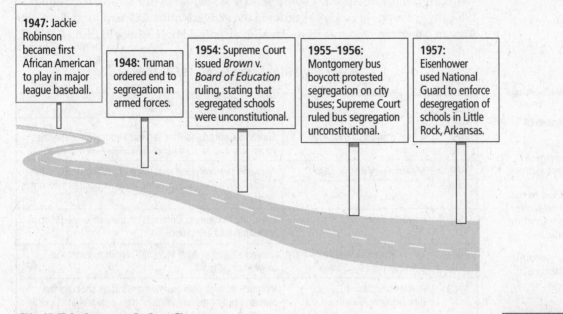

**1947:** Jackie Robinson became first African American to play in major league baseball.

**1948:** Truman ordered end to segregation in armed forces.

**1954:** Supreme Court issued *Brown* v. *Board of Education* ruling, stating that segregated schools were unconstitutional.

**1955–1956:** Montgomery bus boycott protested segregation on city buses; Supreme Court ruled bus segregation unconstitutional.

**1957:** Eisenhower used National Guard to enforce desegregation of schools in Little Rock, Arkansas.

## Civil Rights and the Courts

In the 1950s, the Supreme Court made several important decisions concerning the civil rights of African Americans.

**The Warren Court** In 1953, a vacancy occurred on the Supreme Court. President Eisenhower then appointed Earl Warren, former governor of California, as chief justice. Warren presided over the Supreme Court until 1969. During that period, the Court reached a number of decisions that deeply affected many areas of American life. Among the most far-reaching of the Warren Court's decisions were those dealing with civil rights for African Americans.

***Brown* v. *Board of Education*** Only a year after he became chief justice, Warren presided over the court as it reached a landmark decision in *Brown* v. *Board of Education of Topeka, Kansas* (1954). The Supreme Court actually combined five cases related to overturning state laws that allowed for school segregation in Kansas, Delaware, South Carolina, Virginia, and also in Washington, D.C. There were nearly 200 plaintiffs, including Oliver Brown for whom the case was named. Linda Brown, a young African American student, requested the right to attend a local all-white school in her Topeka neighborhood, rather than attend an all-black school that was further away.

The 1896 *Plessy* v. *Ferguson* decision had held that separate but equal public facilities were legal. Schools were such public facilities, and Brown was refused admittance to the all-white school.

The National Association for the Advancement of Colored People (NAACP) joined the case and appealed it all the way to the Supreme Court. In a unanimous decision, the Court reversed its ruling in *Plessy* v. *Ferguson* and held that in the field of public education, "the doctrine of separate but equal has no place."

**Little Rock** Although the Brown case opened the door for desegregation, integration did not follow immediately. Many Americans were shocked by the decision. In the South, whites began campaigns of "massive resistance" to public school desegregation.

### Key Themes and Concepts

**Constitutional Principles**
*Brown* v. *Board of Education of Topeka, Kansas (1954)* established that facilities separated by race were unequal. The decision reversed *Plessy* v. *Ferguson* (1896) and made integration of schools possible.

- How did the governor of Arkansas respond to *Brown* v. *Board of Education of Topeka, Kansas*?

### Key Themes and Concepts

**Government**
President Eisenhower was acting in his role as Commander in Chief when he sent troops to Little Rock.

Although the Supreme Court had ordered that school integration go forward "with all deliberate speed," many school systems openly defied the ruling. In 1957, the governor of Arkansas ordered the state's National Guard to prevent nine African American students from attending Central High School in Little Rock.

## Major Civil Rights Protests, 1954–1965

### Analyzing Documents

The table outlines some of the major civil rights protests from 1954 to 1965.

- Which protest led to the rise of Dr. Martin Luther King, Jr., as an important civil rights leader?

- Which three key protests occurred in Alabama?

| Year | Event | Outcome |
|------|-------|---------|
| 1954 | *Brown v. Board of Education* | Supreme Court ruled that separate educational facilities for whites and African Americans are inherently unequal. |
| 1955–1956 | Montgomery Bus Boycott | Alabama bus company was forced to desegregate its buses. Martin Luther King, Jr., emerged as an important civil rights leader. |
| 1961 | Freedom Rides | Interstate Commerce Commission banned segregation in interstate transportation. |
| 1963 | James Meredith sues University of Mississippi for admission | Supreme Court upheld Meredith's right to enter the all-white institution. |
| 1963 | Protest marches in Birmingham, Alabama | Violence against peaceful demonstrators shocked the nation. Under pressure, Birmingham desegregated public facilities. |
| 1963 | March on Washington | More than 200,000 people demonstrated in an impressive display of support for civil rights. |
| 1965 | Selma March (Alabama) | State troopers attacked marchers. President Johnson used federal force to protect route from Selma to Montgomery and thousands joined march. |

President Eisenhower was reluctant to step in, but the governor's defiance was a direct challenge to the Constitution. Eisenhower placed the Arkansas National Guard under federal control and then used it to enforce integration. When President Eisenhower sent federal troops, he acted in his presidential role as Commander in Chief. At the end of the school year, the governor continued his defiance by ordering all city high schools closed for the following year. The tactic failed, however, and in 1959 the first racially integrated class graduated from Central High School.

## African American Activism

Public facilities of all kinds were segregated in the South—schools, movie theaters, lunch counters, drinking fountains, restrooms, buses, and trains. Rather than wait for court rulings to end segregation, in the 1950s, African Americans began to organize the **Civil Rights Movement.**

**The Montgomery Bus Boycott** In Montgomery, Alabama, in 1955, an African American seamstress named **Rosa Parks** refused to give up her seat to a white man and move to the back of the bus, as was required by law. She was arrested for violating the law, and her action inspired a boycott of the city's buses.

**Martin Luther King, Jr.,** a young Baptist minister, emerged as a leader of the protest. King had studied the nonviolent methods of Mohandas Gandhi and Henry David Thoreau. His dynamic speaking style drew the attention and support of large numbers of people.

### Key Themes and Concepts

**Individuals, Groups, Institutions**
African Americans began to take direct action to end segregation following *Brown* v. *Board of Education* (1954). Boycotts of schools, lunch counters, and buses, for example, began.

- How did the actions of Rosa Parks and Martin Luther King, Jr., change attitudes toward segregation?

The boycott lasted 381 days. In the end, the Supreme Court ruled that segregation of public buses was illegal. Although Parks had not planned her action that day, her stand against injustice led the way for others.

## Civil Rights Legislation

Congress also made some moves to ensure civil rights for African Americans. In August 1957, it passed the first civil rights act since Reconstruction. The bill created a permanent commission for civil rights and increased federal efforts to ensure blacks the right to vote. Another bill in 1960 further strengthened voting rights.

Although these bills had only limited effectiveness, they did mark the beginning of change. Martin Luther King, Jr., once remarked that it was impossible to legislate what was in a person's heart, but that laws can restrain the heartless. During this time some southern Senators attempted to delay passage of civil rights legislation by using a filibuster. This is an effort by one or more senators to speak continuously on the floor of the Senate until support for their view can be gained or until the Senate leaders decide to delay the proposed bill. Filibusters may last several weeks and can be ended only by a special vote called cloture which can close debate.

# Decade of Change: 1960s

The
# Big
# Idea

The 1960s were a tumultuous era in American society. During this period:

- the struggle for civil rights continued.

- the women's rights movement organized.

- other groups, including Native Americans, struggled for equality.

- New Frontier and Great Society programs expanded upon the New Deal of the 1930s.

- the Cold War affected foreign policy in Latin America.

## Section Overview

In the early 1960s, the continuing pressure of African American civil rights groups, plus growing public sympathy, forced the passage of new legislation. Women, Latino Americans, Native Americans, and disabled Americans adapted civil rights tactics to achieve their own goals of equality. Meanwhile, the cold war tensions between the United States and the Soviet Union continued, as the two nations came into conflict in Germany and Cuba. So much fear was created by Cold War tensions that average citizens built bomb shelters in their backyards or basements. Local communities erected model shelters to serve as examples of how to prepare for an attack.

## Key Themes and Concepts

As you review this section, take special note of the following key themes and concepts:

**Citizenship** How did the African American Civil Rights Movement inspire others to struggle to achieve greater equality?

**Government** How did Presidents Kennedy and Johnson continue and expand upon traditions from the New Deal of the 1930s?

**Foreign Policy** How did the antagonism between the United States and the Soviet Union bring the two nations to the brink of war?

## Key People

| | | |
|---|---|---|
| James Meredith | John F. Kennedy | Cesar Chavez |
| Medgar Evers | Lyndon B. Johnson | |
| Betty Friedan | Malcolm X | |

## Key Terms

| | |
|---|---|
| civil disobedience | mainstreaming |
| Civil Rights Act of 1964 | Americans with Disabilities |
| Voting Rights Act of 1965 | Act of 1990 |
| Equal Rights Amendment | New Frontier |
| affirmative action | Great Society |
| United Farm Workers | Cuban Missile Crisis |
| American Indian Movement | Berlin Wall |

# Key Supreme Court Cases

*Heart of Atlanta Motel* v. *United States* (1964)
*Roe* v. *Wade* (1973)
*Regents of the University of California* v. *Bakke* (1979)

For additional cases, see the Landmark Supreme Court Cases chart in the Reference Section.

## The 1960s

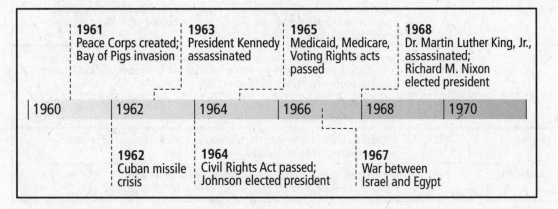

**1961**
Peace Corps created; Bay of Pigs invasion

**1963**
President Kennedy assassinated

**1965**
Medicaid, Medicare, Voting Rights acts passed

**1968**
Dr. Martin Luther King, Jr., assassinated; Richard M. Nixon elected president

1960  1962  1964  1966  1968  1970

**1962**
Cuban missile crisis

**1964**
Civil Rights Act passed; Johnson elected president

**1967**
War between Israel and Egypt

# The Struggle for Civil Rights Continues

During the 1960s, the struggle of African Americans to win equality before the law grew more intense. In their fight, African Americans were seeking to overcome a heritage of racism that had been a part of American thought and tradition for more than 300 years.

By the 1960s, however, many African Americans were working together for the common goal of justice and equality. The successes they gained would deeply affect many parts of American society.

### African Americans Organize

African Americans formed a number of different groups that used a variety of approaches in the attempt to achieve justice and equality. In the early 1960s, many groups followed the nonviolent methods introduced by Dr. Martin Luther King, Jr., and the Southern Christian Leadership Conference (SCLC), an organization of clergy who shifted the leadership of the Civil Rights Movement to the South.

**Election of 1960**

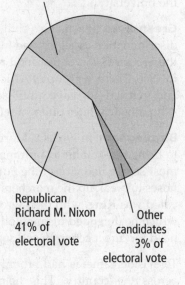

Democrat John F. Kennedy 56% of electoral vote

Republican Richard M. Nixon 41% of electoral vote

Other candidates 3% of electoral vote

Many civil rights activists used a form of protest called **civil disobedience.** This means the deliberate breaking of a law to show a belief that the law is unjust. For example, they attempted to use segregated facilities at interstate train stations and bus depots. Usually they were arrested for such acts; often they were beaten.

## Major African American Organizations

| Organization | Date of Founding | Background |
|---|---|---|
| National Association for the Advancement of Colored People (NAACP) | 1909 | Organized by black and white progressives; W. E. B. Du Bois an early leader; favored court challenges to segregation; appealed primarily to the professional and college-educated |
| National Urban League | 1910 | Began as the Urban League; devoted to empowering African Americans to enter the economic and social mainstream, and to secure economic self-reliance, equality, power, and civil rights |
| The Nation of Islam | 1930 | Known as Black Muslims, founded as a black separatist religious group; became the voice of black nationalism in the 1960s; Muhammad Ali converted in 1964; Malcolm X, a leading spokesperson, assassinated in 1965 |
| Congress of Racial Equality (CORE) | 1942 | Became best known for the "freedom rides" of the 1960s, efforts to desegregate interstate transportation |
| Southern Christian Leadership Conference (SCLC) | 1957 | Founded by Martin Luther King, Jr., to encourage nonviolent passive resistance; organized black Christian churches |
| Student Nonviolent Coordinating Committee (SNCC) | 1960 | In early days, used nonviolent civil disobedience in sit-ins and boycotts; later supported the idea of "black power" put forward by Stokely Carmichael |

**James Meredith** The push to integrate education continued. In 1962, James Meredith, an African American Air Force veteran, made headlines when he tried to enroll at the all-white University of Mississippi. The governor of the state personally tried to stop Meredith from enrolling. Riots broke out, and federal marshals and the National Guard were called up. Although he had to overcome continued harassment, Meredith did finally enter and eventually graduate from the university.

**Greensboro** Practicing civil disobedience, demonstrators protested such discrimination as segregated lunch counters and buses. Sit-ins at lunch counters— the 1960s version of fast-food restaurants—began at Greensboro, North Carolina, in 1960. There, a group of African Americans sat at a "whites only" lunch counter and refused to leave until served. As such protests became popular, some sympathetic whites often joined the sit-ins.

**Birmingham** In 1963, Dr. Martin Luther King, Jr., and the SCLC began a campaign to bring integration to Birmingham, Alabama, which many considered to be the most segregated city in the South. At a protest march, police used dogs and fire hoses to break up the marchers and arrested more than 2,000 people. One of those jailed was King, who then wrote his famous "Letter from a Birmingham Jail," in which he defended his methods of nonviolent civil disobedience and restated the need for direct action to end segregation.

Television cameras had brought the scenes of violence in Birmingham to people across the country. This helped build support for the growing civil rights movement. In Birmingham, the protests eventually resulted in the desegregation of city facilities.

**Medgar Evers** White reaction to African American protests sometimes turned deadly. Medgar Evers, field secretary of the NAACP, had been working to desegregate Jackson, Mississippi. In June 1963, Evers was murdered by a sniper outside his home.

*The March on Washington*

**University of Alabama** Also in June 1963, Governor George Wallace of Alabama vowed to stop two African American students from registering at the state university. Pressure from President Kennedy and the later arrival of the National Guard forced Wallace to back down. The two students enrolled peacefully.

**The March on Washington** The growing civil rights movement moved President Kennedy to deliver a televised speech to the nation in June 1963 on the need to guarantee the civil rights of African Americans. This marked the first speech by a president specifically on this issue. Eight days later, he sent the most comprehensive civil rights bill in the nation's history to Congress.

Civil rights groups organized a huge march on Washington, D.C., in August 1963, to show support for the bill. At the march, Dr. Martin Luther King, Jr., delivered his famous "I have a dream" speech to a crowd of more than 200,000 participants. In the speech, he eloquently expressed his hopes for a unified America.

Not all Americans shared King's dream, however. Just a few weeks after the March on Washington, white terrorists bombed an African American church in Birmingham, killing four young girls.

**Johnson and the Civil Rights Act** After the assassination of John F. Kennedy in November 1963, the new president, Lyndon Johnson, recognized the urgency of pushing forward with civil rights legislation. Johnson worked tirelessly for the passage of the bill, and in July 1964, he signed the **Civil Rights Act of 1964,** the most sweeping civil rights law in American history. The bill called for:

- protection of voting rights for all Americans.
- opening of public facilities (restaurants, hotels, stores, restrooms) to people of all races.
- a commission to protect equal job opportunities for all Americans.

Passage of the Civil Rights Act came just months after ratification of the Twenty-fourth Amendment to the Constitution, which abolished the poll tax in federal

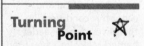

**Turning Point** ☆

- Why is the Civil Rights Act of 1964 considered a turning point in the struggle for civil rights?

elections. A poll tax was a fee that had to be paid before a person could vote. The poll tax had prevented poorer Americans—including many African Americans—from exercising their legal right to vote.

The Civil Rights Act of 1964 outlawed race discrimination in public accommodations, including motels that refused rooms to African Americans. In the landmark Supreme Court case *Heart of Atlanta Motel* v. *United States* (1964), racial segregation of private facilities engaged in interstate commerce was found unconstitutional. Title VIII of the Civil Rights Act of 1968, also known as the **Fair Housing Act,** prohibits discrimination in the sale, rental, or financing of dwellings based on race, color, national origin, sex, or familial status.

**The Voting Rights Act of 1965** Many southern states continued to resist civil rights legislation and Supreme Court rulings. Southern resistance to civil rights laws angered Johnson. He proposed new legislation, which was passed as the Voting Rights Act of 1965. This bill:

- put an end to literacy tests—tests of a person's ability to read and write that had often been misused to bar African American voters.
- authorized federal examiners to register voters in areas suspected of denying African Americans the right to vote.
- directed the attorney general of the United States to take legal action against states that continued to use poll taxes in state elections.

**Changes in the Civil Rights Movement** The summer of 1964 was known as "Freedom Summer" for its many demonstrations, protests, voter registration drives, and the March on Washington. Freedom Summer and the passage of the Voting Rights Act a year later marked highpoints of the Civil Rights Movement.

By the mid-1960s, some civil rights activists became frustrated that the new legislation had not improved conditions enough. Some demanded "Black Power," stressing that African Americans should take total control of the political and economic aspects of their lives. Some advocated the use of violence. Meanwhile, more moderate leaders continued to call for nonviolent methods of protest. These splits weakened the effectiveness of the Civil Rights Movement.

A new, more militant leader, **Malcolm X,** began to attract a following from African Americans who were frustrated by the pace of the Civil Rights Movement. Malcolm X spoke against integration, instead promoting black nationalism, a belief in the separate identity and racial unity of the African American community. A member of the separatist group Nation of Islam until 1964, Malcolm X broke with that group to form his own religious organization, called Muslim Mosque, Inc. After a pilgrimage to the Muslim holy city of Mecca in Saudi Arabia, during which he saw millions of Muslims of all races worshipping peacefully together, he changed his views about integration and began to work toward a more unified civil rights movement. He had made enemies, though, and in February 1965, he was assassinated at a New York City rally.

In 1964 and 1965, frustration at the discrimination in housing, education, and employment boiled over into riots in New York City, Rochester, and the Watts neighborhood of Los Angeles. In Watts alone, 34 people were killed, and more than a thousand were injured.

The federal government set up the Kerner Commission to investigate the cause of the rioting. It concluded that the riots were a result of the anger that had been building in many of America's inner cities.

**Reading Strategy**★

**Organizing Information**
In the space below, list three provisions of the Voting Rights Act of 1965. Which do you think is the most significant? Why?

1.

2.

3.

**Key Themes and Concepts**

**Individuals, Groups, Institutions**
In the 1960s, many African Americans felt that they should take more control over the political and economic conditions in their lives. A new leader named Malcolm X emerged and began to attract attention from more militant individuals.

- How were Malcolm X's beliefs different from those of Martin Luther King, Jr.?

**Assassinations** Dr. Martin Luther King, Jr., had been awarded the Nobel Peace Prize in 1964 "for the furtherance of brotherhood among men." He remained a leading speaker for African American rights, even as splits developed in the Civil Rights Movement.

As a supporter of the underprivileged and the needy, King went to Memphis, Tennessee, in April 1968 to back a sanitation workers' strike. There he was shot and killed by a white assassin. The death of the leading spokesperson for nonviolence set off new rounds of rioting in American cities.

Just two months after King's death, Senator Robert F. Kennedy, brother of the late president and now a presidential candidate committed to civil rights, was assassinated. The shock of these deaths and the increasing urban violence made the goals of King and the Kennedys seem far off to many Americans.

## The Women's Rights Movement

Like African Americans, women had long been denied equal rights in the United States. The successes of the African American Civil Rights Movement in the 1960s highlighted the need for organized action by women to achieve similar goals.

### Past Successes, New Goals

The women's rights movement was not just a product of the 1960s. The struggle for equality had been a long one. Some of the key events in the struggle are listed below.

1848 The Seneca Falls Convention marked the beginning of the organized women's rights movement in this nation.

1868 Passage of the Fifteenth Amendment granted the vote to African American men but not to any women. Susan B. Anthony arranged to have a women's suffrage amendment introduced in Congress. It was defeated there, but Anthony and others continued the fight.

1920 Ratification of the Nineteenth Amendment gave women the right to vote.

1940s Thousands of women took jobs in war-related industries.

By the 1960s, women had exercised the right to vote for 40 years, yet women still had not achieved equal status with men economically and socially. Women's groups renewed demands for a variety of goals including more job opportunities, equality of pay with men, and an end to discrimination based on sex.

Presidents Kennedy and Johnson appointed no women to major posts in their administrations. Yet in those years, fundamental changes occurred.

- More and more women entered fields that men had traditionally dominated, such as law, medicine, engineering, and the sciences.
- In 1963, **Betty Friedan** wrote ***The Feminine Mystique***, a book arguing that society had forced American women out of the job market and back into the home after World War II. The book was influential because it energized a new women's rights movement. Friedan said that not all women were content with the role of homemaker and that more job opportunities should be open to women.
- Title VII of the Civil Rights Act of 1964 barred job discrimination on the basis of sex as well as race.
- The National Organization for Women (NOW) formed in 1966 to push for legislation guaranteeing equality for women.

## Turning Point

- Why is the assassination of Martin Luther King, Jr., in 1968 considered a turning point in history?

## Reading Strategy

**Organizing Information**
- List five important events of the women's rights movement of the 1960s and early 1970s.

- Which event do you consider to be the most significant? Why?

## Analyzing Documents

- According to the line graph below, between which years did the number of women working outside the home first exceed 50 percent?

**Women Working Outside the Home, 1955–1990**

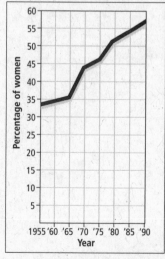

Source: *Statistical Abstract of the United States*

- Congress approved the **Equal Rights Amendment** (ERA) in 1972 and sent it to the states for ratification. This proposed amendment has never been ratified. The amendment stated "equality of rights under the law shall not be denied or abridged by the United States or any state on account of sex."
- The Equal Opportunity Act of 1972 (Equal Pay Act) required employers to pay equal wages for equal work.
- Title IX of the Educational Amendments Act of 1972 gave female college athletes the right to the same financial support as male athletes.

In the landmark case of *Roe v. Wade* (1973), the Supreme Court ruled that a woman's right to terminate a pregnancy is constitutionally protected. Laws making abortion a crime were overturned because they violated a woman's right to privacy; the Supreme Court held that the states could only limit abortion after the first six months of pregnancy. Challenges to the decision in *Roe* v. *Wade* have continued for decades afterward.

## Analyzing Documents

Examine the bar graph at right, then answer the questions.

- During the period 1950–1975, did the gap between men's and women's incomes appear to be widening or narrowing?

- What might explain this trend?

**Median Income of Men and Women, 1950–1975**

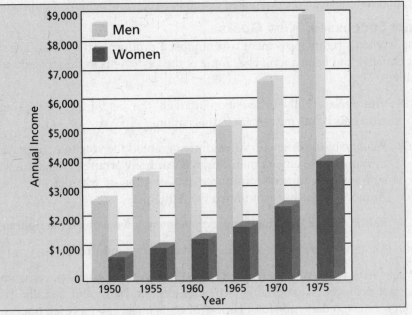

Source: *Statistical Abstract of the United States*

**Affirmative Action** Some of the laws guaranteeing equal opportunities for women, African Americans, and other minority groups called for affirmative action. This meant taking positive steps to eliminate the effects of past discrimination in hiring. In practice, it often meant giving preference to members of such groups when hiring workers or accepting applicants to schools. These affirmative action programs were begun during the Johnson administration of the 1960s.

**Women's Rights Vocabulary** The term *feminism* refers to the belief that women should have the same economic, social, and political rights as men. The women's rights movement is sometimes called the feminist movement.

The term *sexism* refers to beliefs or practices that discriminate against a person on the basis of sex. The women's movement directed its efforts at removing sexist terminology, practices, and literature from American business and education.

Adapted from The New Yorker

"Founding Fathers? How come no Founding Mothers?"

### Analyzing Documents

Examine the cartoon at left, which features a painting by John Trumbull that shows the signing of the Declaration of Independence.

- What criticism about this painting are the two characters giving?

The term *glass ceiling* was used to describe a mid-level position to which women might be promoted in many jobs but which allowed women to see upper-level, better-paying positions that were held by men and were not open to women. This type of unspoken discrimination occurred in all types of employment and can still be found today.

## Setbacks for the Women's Rights Movement

Not all Americans supported the women's rights movement. Some argued that women already had equal rights. Others claimed that those goals undermined "traditional" values. In 1971, President Nixon vetoed a bill that would have provided for a national system of day care for the children of working mothers. His reason for vetoing the bill was that he believed that the family rather than the government should be responsible for the care of children.

Critics also charged that affirmative action programs were a kind of reverse discrimination, in which white males lost chances at jobs to less-qualified women and members of minority groups. In 1979, the Supreme Court ruled in *Regents of the University of California* v. *Bakke* that the school used racial quotas when deciding on applicants to medical school. This meant that Allan Bakke was rejected admission to the medical school in favor of less-qualified applicants. The Court ruled that Bakke had been denied equal protection under the Fourteenth Amendment. It nevertheless found that other affirmative action programs may be constitutional.

The proposed ERA generated tremendous controversy. Opponents claimed that the women's rights movement had led to rising divorce rates, increasing numbers of abortions, and the growing acceptance and recognition of homosexuality—all threats to traditional values, said critics. Ratification of the ERA, they argued, would cause still more problems for American society. By the 1982 deadline, the ERA was three states short of ratification and thus was defeated.

In the late 1980s and 1990s, women's groups began to demand legal protection against physical and mental abuse directed toward both women and children. Lawsuits began to occur to protest sexual harassment, especially in the workplace.

### Reading Strategy

**Formulating Questions**
- Why might some women support the women's rights movement of the 1960s, while others might oppose it?

### Preparing for the Exam

- Why did the proposed Equal Rights Amendment cause controversy?

# Other Groups Struggle for Their Rights

In addition to the African American and women's civil rights movements, Latinos, Native Americans, and disabled Americans fought for equality and justice.

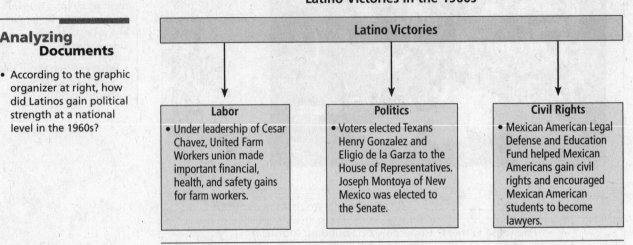

**Latino Victories in the 1960s**

Latinos began to organize against discrimination in the 1960s.

**Analyzing Documents**

- According to the graphic organizer at right, how did Latinos gain political strength at a national level in the 1960s?

**Turning Point**

The 1966 case of *Miranda* v. *Arizona* established the rights of the accused prior to questioning. The accused must be informed that he or she may remain silent and has the right to a lawyer.

**Key Themes and Concepts**

**Government**
- How did the federal government change its policies toward Native Americans in the early 1900s? What were the effects of these changes?

## Latinos

Latinos—people whose family origins are in the Spanish-speaking nations of Latin America—have often been denied equal opportunities in employment, education, and housing. The largest group of Latinos is Mexican Americans, often known as Chicanos.

By the early 1960s, large numbers of Chicanos were employed as farm workers, often migrants. They faced problems of discrimination, poor pay, and hazardous working conditions. In 1962, a Chicano named Cesar Chavez emerged as a labor leader, starting a union for migrant farm workers, a union that became the **United Farm Workers.** Chavez's work was especially helpful to grape and lettuce pickers in their struggle for higher wages and better working conditions.

Chavez, like Dr. Martin Luther King, Jr., believed in nonviolent methods. Chavez continued to serve as spokesperson for farm workers until his death in 1993. He helped raise the self-esteem of the nation's growing Latino population by making their contributions to the American economy and culture more visible.

## Native Americans

In the twentieth century, some conditions for Native Americans had improved. They were granted full citizenship in 1924. Franklin Roosevelt's Indian Reorganization Act of 1934 (Wheeler-Howard Act), known as the Indian New Deal, revised earlier government policies to rebuild tribes and promote tribal cultures. As the circumstances of the Native Americans improved, their population began to increase.

Nevertheless, conditions remained poor for many Native Americans. The per capita income of Native Americans was well below the poverty level. Rates of alcoholism and suicide were the highest of any ethnic group in the United States. Unemployment rates were far higher than the national average, and the high-school dropout rate was near 50 percent.

**Native Americans Organize** In the early 1950s, Congress had enacted legislation to lessen government control over reservations, but this led to the loss of property by many Native Americans and forced some onto welfare. During the Johnson administration, the government tried to improve conditions by starting new programs to raise the standard of housing and to provide medical facilities, educational institutions, and vocational training.

Native Americans began demanding greater responsibility in making decisions that affected their lives. Native Americans took inspiration from the African American Civil Rights Movement. They began to call for "Red Power" and formed the **American Indian Movement** (AIM) to further their goals.

In 1969, a group of militant Native Americans seized Alcatraz Island in San Francisco Bay with the demand that it be turned into an Indian cultural center. In 1972, members of AIM occupied the Bureau of Indian Affairs in Washington, D. C., demanding rights and property they said were guaranteed to them under earlier treaties. In 1973, AIM members occupied the reservation village of Wounded Knee, South Dakota, site of the last battle in the Indian wars of the 1800s. The takeover lasted two months, with the militants demanding changes in policies toward Native Americans.

Although these actions did not always achieve Native Americans' goals, the agitation did draw attention to their problems. Throughout the 1970s, court decisions tried to remedy earlier treaty violations. By 1989, Native Americans had been awarded more than $80 million as compensation for lost land.

In addition, government policies changed again. The Indian Self-Determination and Education Assistance Act of 1975 gave Native Americans more control over reservations. Also, the post of Assistant Secretary of the Interior for Indian Affairs was created in 1975 to protect Native American interests.

**New York State and Native Americans** Some major court cases involving Native American rights have taken place in New York State. For example, in *County of Oneida* v. *Oneida Indian Nation of New York State* (1985), the Supreme Court ruled that Native Americans had a right to sue to enforce their original land rights. The Court further stated that New York's purchase of 872 acres from the Oneida Indians in 1795 was illegal, because it was neither witnessed by federal agents nor approved by Congress. Both these steps were required under the federal Indian Trade and Non-Intercourse Act of 1793. Such court decisions have encouraged other Native American groups in New York State and across the nation to sue for return of lost lands.

More recent controversies have arisen in northern New York regarding the St. Regis Indian Reservation, or Akwesasne Mohawk Reservation as it is also known. Violence erupted on the 14,000-acre reservation, which stretches into southern Canada, in the spring of 1990. At issue was gambling on the reservation. The incident involved questions of which Native American group controlled reservation policy as well as the role New York State has in dealing with the reservation.

## Disabled Americans

Americans with disabilities have endured a long struggle to gain their full rights in American society. In the nation's early years, care of the handicapped was usually left to their families, often resulting in the neglect or abuse. Reformers began to work for change in the early 1800s. For example, in Massachusetts, Dorothea Dix led a campaign to improve conditions for mentally ill people, resulting in the founding of more than 30 state institutions to care for them.

### Preparing for the Exam

- What problems did Native Americans face in the 1960s and 1970s?

- How did they draw attention to their plight?

### Key Themes and Concepts

**Constitutional Principles**
The Supreme Court case *County of Oneida* v. *Oneida Indian Nation of New York State* (1985) established that Native American tribes had the right to sue state governments to reclaim their tribal lands.

- Why is *County of Oneida* v. *Oneida Indian Nation of New York State* important in the struggle for Native American equality?

### Reading Strategy

**Reinforcing Main Ideas**
- How has the view of people with handicaps changed from the nation's early years to today?

Educational opportunities for hearing-impaired students were gradually widened. Gallaudet College in Washington, D.C., was founded in 1857, and today that institution is internationally recognized for its educational programs for hearing-impaired students. In the late 1980s, its students successfully demonstrated to win the appointment of a hearing-impaired person as president of the college. In New York State, the National Technical Institute for the Deaf at the Rochester Institute of Technology is another school for the hearing impaired whose programs have won wide recognition. The school provides deaf students with college training in technical and scientific fields.

Educational opportunities were also widened for visually-impaired students. In 1829, the Perkins School for the Blind opened in Boston and quickly became a model for schools elsewhere. Although such schools still exist and serve important functions, many visually-impaired students today attend regular schools under a practice called **mainstreaming.** The idea behind mainstreaming is to bring handicapped students out of the isolation of special schools and into the "mainstream" of student life.

**New Programs for People With Disabilities** The federal government has been especially active in setting out new programs and policies for people with disabilities.

• President Kennedy established the Presidential Commission on Mental Retardation to study and highlight the problems of the mentally handicapped individuals in American society.

• President Kennedy also backed the establishment of the Special Olympics to provide both a showcase and encouragement for athletes with handicapping conditions.

• The Rehabilitation Act of 1973, Section 504, barred discrimination against people with disabilities in any programs, activities, and facilities that were supported by federal funds.

• The Education for All Handicapped Children Act of 1975 ensured a free, appropriate education for children with disabilities, including special education and related services.

Reading
**Strategy**

**Analyzing Cause and Effect**
• How did the Americans With Disabilities Act (1990) change the lives of people with handicaps?

• The **Americans With Disabilities Act of 1990** prohibited discrimination in employment, public accommodation, transportation, state and local government services, and telecommunications. Benefits of the act included greater accessibility to public buildings and transportation for people who use wheelchairs and the availability of electronic devices to allow hearing-impaired people to use telephones and enjoy movies.

Activism by disabled veterans, especially from the Vietnam War, drew increased attention to the needs of people with disabilities. Celebrities have also taken up the cause of working for increased congressional funding of medical research. Some examples include Elizabeth Taylor for AIDS research, the late Christopher Reeve for spinal cord injuries research, and Michael J. Fox for Parkinson's disease research.

Schools began to mainstream students with disabilities into regular classrooms. Students who previously might have attended special schools with other students with similar disabilities have begun to attend regular public schools in a major attempt at deinstitutionalization. These efforts are known as programs of inclusion.

# The New Frontier and the Great Society

Not all legislation on domestic issues during the 1960s concerned civil rights. President Kennedy's programs, known as the New Frontier, and President Johnson's, known as the Great Society, continued and expanded upon traditions begun during Franklin Roosevelt's New Deal of the 1930s.

## Kennedy's New Frontier

- *The Space Program* Following the successful launch of a Soviet cosmonaut, the first man in space, in 1961, President Kennedy committed the nation to a space program with the goal of landing a person on the moon by the end of the 1960s. In July 1969, six years after Kennedy's death, that goal was met when astronaut Neil Armstrong stepped onto the moon's surface. The effort had cost some $25.4 billion.

- *The Peace Corps* This program sent thousands of American volunteers to developing nations where they trained local people in technical, educational, and health programs. The Peace Corps program was intended to offset the growth of communism in such nations. The program is still in existence.

## Johnson's Great Society

- *The VISTA Program* The Volunteers in Service to America (VISTA) program was meant as a domestic Peace Corps, aiding poor citizens in rural and impoverished areas.

- *The Office of Economic Opportunity* Set up in 1964, this was the directing agency in President Johnson's War on Poverty. Its branches included Project Head Start (to provide education for preschoolers from low-income families), Project Upward Bound (to assist high-school students from low-income families to attend college), and the Job Corps (to provide vocational training for high-school dropouts.)

President Kennedy and Vice President Johnson

- *The Elementary and Secondary Education Act* This 1965 measure provided more than $1 billion in federal aid to education, with the greatest share going to school districts with large numbers of students from low-income families. Sections of the bill required that schools accepting the money be integrated.

- *Medicare* Amendments to the Social Security Act provided health insurance and some types of health care to those over the age of 65. A Medicaid program provided states with funds to help the needy who were not covered by Medicare.

- *Department of Housing and Urban Development* This cabinet post was meant to oversee federal efforts to improve housing and aid economic development of cities. Its first head, Robert C. Weaver, was the first African American to hold a cabinet post.

- *Food Stamp Program* With the Food Stamp Act of 1964, Johnson continued a program of assistance for low-income families to purchase food, which had originally begun in 1939 and existed until 1943. Kennedy issued the first executive order for Food Stamps in 1961. That was replaced and increased by the Act of 1964. In the decades following, various adjustments were made to the program (FSP). By August 2008, an all-time non-disaster high of 29 million Americans per month were part of the program. In October 2008, the name of the program was changed to Supplemental Nutrition Assistance Program (SNAP).

## Preparing for the Exam

On the examination, you will need to understand the major domestic programs of the 1960s.

In the space below, give two provisions of President Kennedy's "New Frontier" program and the reasons for these provisions.

1.

2.

## Key Themes and Concepts

**Government**
Johnson's domestic programs are an example of the concept of change. He often referred to his efforts as the **War on Poverty.** Today, 40 years later, Medicare is changing as it struggles to meet the needs of the growing senior citizen population.

## Key Themes and Concepts

**Foreign Policy**
In the 1960s, the United States had an uneasy relationship with many Latin American nations. While Presidents Kennedy and Johnson supported the Cold War policies begun under President Truman, Kennedy hoped to warm ties with Latin America through the Alliance for Progress. However, economic development funds from this program tended to support repressive, anticommunist governments.

- Why was the Bay of Pigs invasion of Cuba considered a failure?

# Foreign Policy in the 1960s

United States foreign policy under Kennedy and Johnson continued Truman's cold war policy of containment of communism. In Section 3, you will review how this policy led the nation into the **Vietnam War.** In this section, you will see how cold war concerns affected other aspects of the United States foreign policy in the 1960s.

## A History of Involvement

As you remember, the United States has been deeply involved in the affairs of Latin America since early in its history. Latin American nations often resented such intervention, and United States policies have left a legacy of anger and hostility.

Some of the key events in United States-Latin American relations are listed on the next page. For additional discussion of these events, see Unit 3, Section 2.

## Kennedy and Latin America

Some of President Kennedy's most significant foreign policy decisions involved Latin America.

**The Alliance for Progress** Kennedy hoped to improve relations with Latin America and stop the spread of communism there through the Alliance for Progress, which pledged $20 billion to help economic development in the region. However, funds often went to aid repressive governments simply because they were anticommunist.

**The Bay of Pigs** After President Kennedy took office, he approved a CIA plan to overthrow Fidel Castro, the Communist leader of Cuba. The plan called for Cuban exiles—supplied with U.S. arms, material, and training—to invade Cuba and set off a popular uprising against Castro. The invasion took place on April 17, 1961, at a location called the Bay of Pigs, about 90 miles from Havana. No uprising followed, and Castro's troops quickly crushed the invading forces, to the embarrassment of Kennedy and the United States government.

### Key Developments in United States-Latin American Relations

## Key Themes and Concepts

Examine the table at right, then answer these questions.

- Which event resulted in the United States becoming an imperial nation?

- Which development was intended to improve relations with Latin American nations?

| | |
|---|---|
| **The Monroe Doctrine** | In 1823, President Monroe warned the nations of Europe not to interfere with the nations of the Western Hemisphere, thus assuming the role of protector of the Western Hemisphere. However, this policy earned the United States a negative image in much of Latin America. |
| **Spanish-American War (1898)** | Victory in a war with Spain brought the United States an overseas empire. It also increased the nation's role in Latin America by giving it possession of Puerto Rico and much control over the government of Cuba. |
| **Panama Canal (1901–1914)** | The United States gained control over land where it wanted to build a canal by interfering in the internal affairs of Colombia. As a result, the United States made many enemies in Latin America. |
| **Roosevelt Corollary (1904)** | Under this addition to the Monroe Doctrine, President Theodore Roosevelt claimed the United States had the right to intervene in the affairs of Latin American nations guilty of "chronic wrongdoing." |
| **"Dollar Diplomacy" (early 1900s)** | President Taft planned to increase U.S. influence in Latin America through economic investment backed by military force. |
| **"Good Neighbor" Policy (1933)** | President Franklin Roosevelt made an effort to improve relations with Latin America by stressing increased cooperation. |

**The Cuban Missile Crisis** Fearing another U.S. invasion attempt, Castro agreed to a Soviet plan to base nuclear missiles aimed at the United States in Cuba. Kennedy learned of the plan while the bases were under construction. On October 22, 1962, he announced a naval blockade of Cuba and demanded that the Soviets withdraw the missiles. The Cuban Missile Crisis brought the United States and the Soviet Union to the brink of war, but the Soviets backed down and withdrew their missiles.

Kennedy had clearly demonstrated that the United States would not tolerate a Soviet presence in the Western Hemisphere just 90 miles from its shores. By doing so, Kennedy also helped the nation recover some of the prestige it had lost in the failed Bay of Pigs invasion.

### U.S. Soviet Tensions, 1961–1963

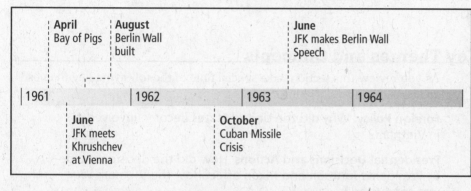

In 1963, the United States, Soviet Union, and Great Britain signed a **Nuclear Test Ban Treaty** in which they agreed not to test nuclear weapons in the air, in outer space, or under the sea. Underground testing was permitted.

## Kennedy and Berlin

Since World War II, the division of Germany into a Communist East Germany and a democratic West Germany had added to cold war tensions. President Kennedy and Soviet Premier Nikita Khrushchev met in Austria in June 1961 to discuss relations between the United States and the Soviet Union. Khrushchev thought that the Bay of Pigs disaster revealed American weakness, and he tried to threaten Kennedy into removing NATO troops from Europe. Instead, Kennedy increased U.S. military and financial commitment to West Germany.

Response to the American moves came in August 1961 when the East German government built a wall between East and West Berlin. The **Berlin Wall** was meant to stop the flood of East Germans escaping to freedom in the West and quickly became a symbol of tyranny. In June 1963, Kennedy visited West Berlin, renewing the American commitment to defend that city and Western Europe. In a famous speech, he said that he and all people who wanted freedom were citizens of Berlin.

The Berlin Wall stood as a strong cold war symbol until 1989. In that year, political change sweeping through Eastern Europe led East Germany to tear down the wall. By October 1990, the rapid political changes in the region had led to the reunification of the two Germanys as a single nation for the first time since the end of World War II.

**Impact of Kennedy's Death** Kennedy's energetic voice for world democracy, and his multilingual wife, Jacqueline, helped to make friends for the United States in many areas of the world. His tragic and unexpected assassination in November 1963 caused an outpouring of grief from around the world, as dozens of foreign heads of state came hurriedly to Washington, D.C., for Kennedy's funeral.

## Turning Point

• Why is the Cuban missile crisis of 1962 considered a turning point in U.S.-Soviet relations?

## Analyzing Documents

Examine the timeline then answer these questions.

• How many years passed between the fall of the Berlin Wall and the reunification of Germany?

• Which event occurred first: the meeting between President Kennedy and Soviet Premier Khrushchev, or the building of the Berlin Wall?

# Limits of Power: Turmoil at Home and Abroad: 1965–1972

The
# Big Idea

Fears of Communist expansion in Southeast Asia led to the United States' involvement in the Vietnam War. During this period:

- President Johnson escalated the war.

- student protests became part of the anti-war movement.

- the political and social upheaval of the 1960s divided Americans.

- President Nixon oversaw a cease fire agreement that allowed for U.S. withdrawal from Vietnam.

## Section Overview

The fear of Communist expansion led the United States to become increasingly involved in Southeast Asia. This involvement led to the Vietnam War—the longest war in United States history. As the war dragged on, American support began to erode. The combination of negative public opinion and the inability of the military to achieve clear-cut victory led to a gradual withdrawal from the war. Meanwhile, great social and cultural changes were taking place in many parts of American society.

## Key Themes and Concepts

As you review this section, take special note of the following key themes and concepts:

**Foreign Policy** Why did the United States become involved in Vietnam?

**Presidential Decisions and Actions** How did the decisions made by Presidents Johnson and Nixon affect how the Vietnam War was conducted?

**Change** What social and cultural changes developed in the 1960s?

**Constitutional Principles** How did Congress limit the power of the President in wartime?

## Key People

Lyndon B. Johnson          Richard Nixon          Henry Kissinger

## Key Terms

| | |
|---|---|
| Gulf of Tonkin Resolution | Vietnamization |
| hawks | War Powers Act |
| doves | |

Fear of Communist expansion led the United States to become deeply involved in Southeast Asia. Review the chart on the next page to learn about the growing involvement of the United States in this region.

| Date | Event |
|---|---|
| September 1945 | World War II ended in Asia; Ho Chi Minh, a member of the Communist party since 1920, proclaimed the Democratic Republic of Vietnam. |
| 1946–1949 | France, which had controlled Vietnam since the nineteeth century, appointed a "puppet leader" named Bao Dai, who was ineffective against the power of Ho Chi Minh. |
| 1949 | Mao Zedong declared the (Communist) People's Republic of China; recognized the Vietnamese government of Ho Chi Minh in 1950. |
| 1950–1953 | United States fought in the Korean War and provided the French with financial aid in their struggle to hang onto Vietnam. |
| 1953–1954 | President Eisenhower debated how far the United States should go in backing the French. |
| 1954 | The forces of Ho Chi Minh defeated the French at Dienbienphu; Geneva Accords divided Vietnam at the 17th parallel; North and South Vietnam agreed to hold elections in 1956 to reunite the country; the United States joined with seven Asian and European nations in the Southeast Asia Treaty Organization (SEATO), an anticommunist pact which extended protection to Vietnam. |
| 1955 | United States under President Eisenhower increased aid to South Vietnam. |
| 1956 | South Vietnamese President Ngo Dinh Diem, fearing the popularity of Ho Chi Minh, refused to hold elections scheduled under the Geneva Accords. |
| 1960 | Ho Chi Minh recognized the Vietcong, Communist guerrillas in South Vietnam, as the National Liberation Front (NLF) of Vietnam; President Kennedy sent Vice President Johnson to study the crisis in Vietnam. |

# Kennedy and Vietnam

President Kennedy shared Eisenhower's belief in the domino theory. He, therefore, continued to support the Diem regime. By 1963, the number of United States "advisers" in South Vietnam totaled about 17,000. That year, 489 Americans died in the fighting in Vietnam.

## Debate Over Involvement

American advisers urged Diem to adopt reforms to broaden his support. Diem, however, brutally suppressed all opponents and ruled as a dictator. On November 2, 1963, the South Vietnamese military overthrew Diem, with the knowledge and approval of the United States. Around the same time, the White House announced that it intended to withdraw all United States military personnel from Vietnam by 1965. Kennedy was unable to keep this promise because he was assassinated.

Vietnam, 1968

## Geography in History

Laos shares a long border with North Vietnam. During the Vietnam War, the dense jungle terrain made it difficult for U.S. and South Vietnamese forces to cut off the supply lines that ran between Laos and North Vietnam.

- How might this role as supplier have had an impact on Laos later in the war?

## Key Themes and Concepts

**Presidential Decisions and Actions**
Without a formal declaration of war by Congress, Presidents Eisenhower, Kennedy, and Johnson all sent U.S. military forces to Vietnam.

- What authorized these presidents to take these actions?

## Key Themes and Concepts

**Foreign Policy**
In 1964, Congress passed the Gulf of Tonkin Resolution. The resolution, which empowered the President to "repel an armed attack against the forces of the United States," was used to escalate U.S. bombings in North Vietnam.

- What obstacles did U.S. troops fighting in Vietnam face?

# Johnson and Escalation

Under the Constitution, only Congress can declare war. However, by 1964, three presidents—Eisenhower, Kennedy, and Johnson—had sent United States aid and troops into Vietnam. Each did so by acting as the commander in chief of the nation's military forces.

## The Tonkin Gulf Resolution

On August 4, 1964, President Johnson escalated the war dramatically. He announced on television that American destroyers had been the victim of an unprovoked attack by North Vietnamese gun boats. (It later appeared that the ships might have been protecting South Vietnamese boats headed into North Vietnamese waters.) The next day, Johnson asked Congress for the authority to order air strikes against North Vietnam. With only two dissenting votes, Congress passed the **Gulf of Tonkin Resolution.** The resolution empowered "the President, as commander in chief, to take all necessary measures to repel any armed attack against the forces of the United States and to prevent further aggression." Johnson used the resolution to justify expansion of the war. By April 1965, U.S. planes regularly bombed North Vietnam.

**A Guerrilla War** At first, United States military leaders expected that the nation's superior technology would guarantee victory. However, they soon found themselves bogged down in a guerrilla war fought in the jungles of Southeast Asia. The enemy did not wear uniforms, and no clear battlefront emerged. Thousands of Vietnamese casualties occurred each month as the United States dropped more bombs on Vietnam, an area about twice the size of New York State, than it had used on Nazi Germany during the heaviest months of fighting during World War II.

**Reasons for War** The massive commitment in Vietnam raised questions in the minds of many Americans about why the United States got involved in Vietnam and why it stayed there. The administration argued that the United States was involved in Vietnam to prevent the fall of Vietnam to communism, to stop the rise of aggressor governments, and to protect the nation's position as a superpower and defender of democracy. However, as the war dragged on, many Americans began to question these motives.

## Resistance to the War

By late 1965, an antiwar movement had begun to take shape in the United States.

**Hawks and Doves** In Congress, there were differences of opinion concerning the war. Some stood solidly behind the president and argued in favor of victory at any cost. These members were known as hawks. Those who favored immediate withdrawal and an end to the war were known as doves.

**Student Protests** College campuses became centers of political protest against the war. The University of California, Berkeley campus, became a leader in anti-Vietnam War protests. The name *Berkeley* became synonymous with the activities of the protest movement. Students organized a new form of protest called teach-ins, or meetings in which speakers, usually promoting unconditional American withdrawal from Vietnam, held study sessions and rallies.

The strongest antiwar group in the 1960s was Students for a Democratic Society (SDS), founded in 1960. SDS was antiestablishment, or against big business and government. It led demonstrations, sit-ins, draft-card burnings, and protests against universities with "pro-establishment" regulations. By 1969, the organization had collapsed into a number of splinter groups. However, SDS's legacy of protest against authority remained a strong force into the 1970s.

**Protest Marches** People of all ages joined in protest marches against the war. The first huge march took place in Washington, D.C., in 1965. In 1967, some 300,000 Americans marched in New York City. That same year, another 50,000 tried to shut down the Pentagon.

**Draft Resisters** In 1967, former Olympic boxing light heavy-weight gold medal winner, Muhammad Ali (Cassius Clay) refused to take the oath of induction into the army after being drafted. He was found guilty of draft evasion but remained free on appeal until 1971, when the Supreme Court overturned his case. By 1968, about 10,000 draft resisters, people unwilling to serve in the military after being drafted, had fled the country for Canada. The nation's youth became increasingly divided as some chose to fight for the United States in Vietnam, while others sought deferments to go to college. A large number of minorities, who could not afford the cost of college, responded to the draft and went to Vietnam. The attitude of American youth became increasingly hostile toward the Johnson administration and all war-related issues. In 1968, Lyndon Johnson announced his decision not to run for a second term as president. This was largely due to his low popularity ratings as a result of his Vietnam War policies.

**Preparing for the Exam**

On the examination, you will need to have a thorough understanding of U.S. foreign policy.

List three reasons President Johnson's administration used to justify U.S. involvement in Vietnam.

1.

2.

3.

**Key Themes and Concepts**

**Reform Movements** College campuses became centers of the antiwar movement in the United States. Students organized teach-ins and other protests aimed at getting the Johnson administration to end U.S. involvement in Vietnam. Protest marches featuring people of all ages took place in major cities.

• In what different ways did young people respond to the draft?

# The 1960s—Political and Social Upheaval

Some political analysts who studied the events of 1968 believed the nation had survived one of the biggest tests to its political institutions since the Civil War. The 1960s had been shaped by two movements: the Civil Rights Movement and the antiwar movement. The political turmoil of the decade helped produce great social upheaval, especially among the nation's youth.

## Cultural Changes

Some young people became disillusioned with traditional American values. For the first time in United States history, thousands of Americans flaunted the use of illegal drugs, often popularized in rock music.

Many young Americans referred to themselves as hippies or flower children. They claimed to be searching for a freer, simpler way of life. Communal living attracted thousands of youths who adopted lifestyles foreign to older Americans. Some spoke of a generation gap between youth and people over 30.

The Civil Rights Movement and the Vietnam War also divided Americans. The assassinations of Robert Kennedy and Dr. Martin Luther King, Jr., heightened emotions.

**Reading Strategy**

**Reinforcing Main Ideas**
Identify three events that occurred during 1968 that caused that year to be associated with political and social upheaval.

## Key Events of 1968

| Month | Event |
|---|---|
| January | • North Vietnam launched the Tet (New Year's) offensive, using Soviet-made jets and weapons for the first time. |
| March | • Eugene McCarthy, a peace candidate and leading "dove," won the Democratic presidential primary in New Hampshire.<br>• Robert Kennedy announced his candidacy for the presidency.<br>• President Johnson announced that he would not seek reelection and that he would devote the remainder of his term to trying to end the war. The war had hurt his popularity with voters. |
| April | • American forces in Vietnam reached 549,000; combat deaths climbed to 22,951.<br>• North Vietnam announced its willingness to enter into peace talks.<br>• An assassin claimed the life of Dr. Martin Luther King, Jr. |
| May | • Preliminary peace talks with the North Vietnamese began, but serious negotiations would not take place for several years. |
| June | • An assassin claimed the life of Robert Kennedy shortly after his victory in the California Democratic presidential primary. |
| August | • The Democratic National Convention nominated Hubert Humphrey amid the worst political rioting and demonstrations any convention had ever experienced; Humphrey (Johnson's Vice President) inherited a divided party and sought election in a divided nation.<br>• The Republican National Convention nominated Richard Nixon, whose only serious challenger was Ronald Reagan.<br>• The American Independent party nominated Governor George Wallace of Alabama, showing that a third party could attract white-backlash voters who opposed the Civil Rights Movement. |
| November | • Nixon won the 1968 election with 43.4% of the popular vote; Humphrey claimed 42.7%; Wallace took 13.5%. |

# Nixon and Vietnam

By 1969, President Nixon faced a national crisis. The Vietnam War had turned into the nation's most costly war. American support for the war was at an all-time low.

## Winding Down the War

Nixon did not bring an end to the war right away. In fact, for a time, he widened American military activities, attacking North Vietnamese supply routes out of Laos and Cambodia.

**Vietnamization** Nixon called for Vietnamization of the war, or a takeover of the ground fighting by Vietnamese soldiers. Both Kennedy and Johnson had favored this approach, but neither had been able to make it work. While Nixon promoted Vietnamization, he also bombed neighboring Cambodia, which he claimed served as a base for North Vietnamese guerrillas.

The bombings triggered a large student protest at Kent State University in Ohio. By the time the National Guard broke up the demonstration, four students lay dead and nine others wounded. More and more Americans were questioning the role of the United States in Vietnam, yet President Nixon increased bombing raids on North Vietnam throughout 1970.

**Peace With Honor** Henry Kissinger, Nixon's chief foreign policy adviser, met in Paris with North Vietnamese officials seeking an end to the war. For several years, negotiations remained deadlocked. Finally, on January 15, 1973, Nixon announced that "peace with honor" had been reached and that a cease-fire would soon take effect.

**Key Themes and Concepts**

**Presidential Decisions and Actions**
• What impact did President Nixon's decision to bomb Cambodia have on student protests?

## The War Powers Act

The War Powers Act, passed over President Nixon's veto in 1973, gave Congress more power in dealing with international conflicts.

| | | |
|---|---|---|
| • The President can send troops overseas, but must inform Congress within 48 hours. | • Troops may not stay overseas more than 60 days without the approval of Congress. | • Congress has the power to force the President to bring troops home. |

## The War Powers Act

In November 1973, Congress passed the War Powers Act over Nixon's veto. This law helped reverse the precedent set by the Gulf of Tonkin Resolution, which gave the President sweeping powers in Vietnam. The War Powers Act included the following provisions:

- The President had to notify Congress within 48 hours of sending troops into a foreign country. At that time, the President would have to give Congress a full accounting of the decision.

- The President had to bring the troops home within 60 days unless both houses voted for them to stay.

**Reading Strategy**

**Problem Solving**
• Why do you think Congress passed the War Powers Act over President Nixon's veto?

For the examination, it will be important to understand the significance of historical events, not just the dates of and participants in those events.

• Overall, was the Vietnam War a success or a failure? Why?

• What enduring lessons were learned from the war?

• How has the Vietnam War continued to be remembered in American society?

## Vietnam and Limits on United States Power

When the United States finally withdrew from Vietnam, the North Vietnamese overran South Vietnam. For two years, the United States poured billions of dollars of aid into South Vietnam. However, on April 30, 1975, the government in Saigon collapsed. Bitterness over the war persisted. When the president asked for funds to evacuate the South Vietnamese who had helped the United States, Congress refused. In the end, some 100,000 people fled the country.

The United States had tried for 20 years to guarantee freedom to the people of South Vietnam. However, the United States ultimately could not count its efforts as a success. In the conflict, some 58,000 Americans died, and another 300,000 were wounded. The United States spent over $150 billion on the war effort. Not only did Vietnam fall to communism, but so did its neighbors Cambodia (Kampuchea) and Laos. Throughout the late 1970s and 1980s, the United States sought to understand the Vietnam experience. It was the subject of films, books, and national monuments such as the Vietnam Veterans Memorial in Washington, D.C.

## Conclusions Drawn from U.S. Involvement in Vietnam

The following is a list of conclusions drawn from the Vietnam War era.

• The American political system acted in response to a variety of public pressures.

• Modern war technology was not always powerful enough if an opponent is armed with a determined spirit of nationalism.

• Successful military efforts required a well-prepared and supportive public. (Compare, for example, the differing experiences in Vietnam and World War II.)

• The United States was committed to a foreign policy that supported the global nature of United States involvement in foreign affairs.

• The United States questioned its role as a police officer to the world.

# The Trend Toward Conservatism: 1972–1985

## Section Overview

After the upheaval of the 1960s, Richard Nixon tried to take the nation into a new direction, but the Watergate affair led to his resignation. His successors, Gerald Ford and Jimmy Carter, struggled with lingering economic troubles. In the 1980s, conservatives Ronald Reagan and George Bush came to power. After the cold war ended, the United States struggled to determine its new role in international relations.

## Key Themes and Concepts

As you review this section, take special note of the following key themes and concepts:

**Presidential Decisions and Actions** How did President Nixon shape a new policy toward China and the Soviet Union?

**Economic Systems** How did economic problems of the 1970s present unique challenges to the Nixon, Ford, and Carter administrations?

## Key People

Mao Zedong

Warren Burger

Gerald Ford

Jimmy Carter

Ronald Reagan

Mikhail Gorbachev

## Key Terms

détente

Watergate affair

stagflation

Camp David Accords

supply-side economics

"Star Wars"

Iran-Contra affair

## Key Supreme Court Cases

*Engel* v. *Vitale* (1962) *

*Gideon* v. *Wainwright* (1963) *

*Miranda* v. *Arizona* (1966)

*Tinker* v. *Des Moines Community School District* (1969)

*New York Times* v. *United States* (1971) *

*Roe* v. *Wade* (1973)

*United States* v. *Nixon* (1974)

The
# Big
# Idea

Beginning in the early 1970s, conservatism replaced liberalism in American politics. During this period:

• President Nixon opened diplomatic relations with China and shaped a policy of détente toward the Soviet Union.

• President Ford pardoned President Nixon following his resignation over the Watergate affair.

• President Reagan supported a domestic program of New Federalism during the 1980s that was begun by President Nixon.

* For information on these cases, see the Landmark Supreme Court Cases chart in the Reference Section.

## An Era of Conservatism, 1972–1990

| 1972 Nixon visits China, USSR | 1974 Nixon resigns | 1978 Camp David Accords | 1983 U.S. invades Grenada | 1990 Operation Desert Shield; Germany reunited |

1970 — 1975 — 1980 — 1985 — 1990

| 1973 Watergate investigation begins | 1977 Panama Canal Treaties | 1979 Iran seizes U.S. hostages | 1987 Iran-Contra Hearings begin |

# From Cold War to Détente

Although President Nixon's main foreign policy objective was ending the Vietnam War, he had other foreign policy interests as well.

## Nixon Doctrine

In 1969, Nixon announced what became known as the Nixon Doctrine. This doctrine stated that the United States would no longer provide direct military protection in Asia. Even though the Vietnam War was not yet concluded, the president promised Americans that there would be no more Vietnams for the United States.

## A New Policy Toward China

President Nixon also adopted a new foreign policy toward China. The United States had not had diplomatic relations with the People's Republic since the 1949 Communist revolution.

**Presidential Visit** In 1971, Nixon stunned Americans by announcing that he had accepted an invitation to visit China. On February 21, 1972, Nixon arrived in China. National Security Adviser Henry Kissinger accompanied the president on his peace mission.

**Opening the Door** After more than 20 years of hostility, President Nixon and Chinese leaders Mao Zedong and Premier Zhou Enlai agreed to open the door to normal diplomatic relations. Nixon's visit cleared the way for economic and cultural exchanges. American manufacturers, for example, now had a new market for their products. By following a policy toward China that was separate from the Soviet Union, Nixon underscored the splits that had occurred within communism. This visit ultimately reduced tensions between the United States and China.

## A New Policy Toward the Soviet Union

Nixon balanced his openness with China by looking for ways to ease tensions with the Soviet Union, China's Communist rival.

**Détente** Nixon and Kissinger shaped a policy called détente. The goal of détente was to bring about a warming in the cold war. In contrast to President Truman's policy of containment, President Nixon's policy of détente was designed to prevent open conflict.

During the Nixon administration, the foreign policy of the United States was shaped by *Realpolitik*, a political philosophy favored by Kissinger. The meaning of *Realpolitik* is power politics. Therefore, in its dealings with China and the Soviet Union, the United States made its decisions based on what it needed to maintain its own strength—regardless of world opinion.

## Turning Point

- Why is President Nixon's visit to China considered a turning point in U.S. foreign policy?

## Key Themes and Concepts

**Foreign Policy**
- As secretary of state, Henry Kissinger favored the political philosophy of *Realpolitik*. In your own words, how would you define *Realpolitik*?

President Nixon underscored his willingness to pursue détente by visiting the Soviet Union in May 1972. He was the first president since World War II to make such a journey.

**SALT** While in Moscow, Nixon opened what became known as the Strategic Arms Limitations Talks (SALT). These talks led to a 1972 agreement called the SALT Agreement. The agreement set limits on the number of defensive missile sites and strategic offensive missiles each nation would keep.

### Nixon's Domestic Policies

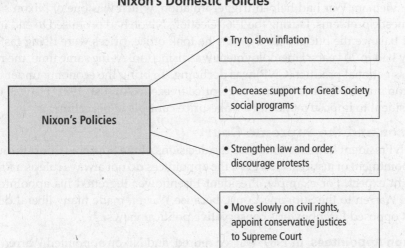

Nixon's Policies

- Try to slow inflation
- Decrease support for Great Society social programs
- Strengthen law and order, discourage protests
- Move slowly on civil rights, appoint conservative justices to Supreme Court

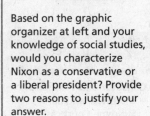

**Analyzing Documents**

Based on the graphic organizer at left and your knowledge of social studies, would you characterize Nixon as a conservative or a liberal president? Provide two reasons to justify your answer.

1.

2.

## Nixon's Domestic Policies

President Nixon was mainly interested in foreign affairs. He knew that he faced a Congress controlled by a Democratic majority. Because of the system of checks and balances, Nixon realized that it would be almost impossible to push Republican policies through Congress. Therefore, he limited his domestic policy goals.

### Nixon's Domestic Initiatives

In 1970, the Occupational Safety and Health Administration (OSHA) was created to ensure safe and healthful working conditions for all working Americans. OSHA assisted states in providing research, information, education, and training in the field of occupational safety and health.

The Environmental Protection Agency (EPA), established in 1970, coordinated federal programs to combat pollution and protect the environment.

The Clean Air Act of 1970 was a major comprehensive federal law addressing topics related to air pollution. It was amended in 1977 to set new goals since many parts of the country did not meet the standards set by the 1970 act. It was amended again in 1990 to address problems such as acid rain, ground level ozone, stratospheric ozone depletion, and air toxins.

On July 12, 1973, President Nixon united several existing federal drug agencies into the Drug Enforcement Administration (DEA), which enforced federal drug laws and conducted investigations of illegal drugs overseas.

In 1974, the Energy Reorganization Act created the Nuclear Regulatory Commission to regulate the nuclear power industry and the Energy Research and Development Administration to manage the nuclear weapon, nuclear reactor, and energy development programs of the federal government. In 1977, under President Carter, the Department of Energy was established. Today, the department ensures energy security and safety.

Preparing for
the Exam

- What did Nixon intend to
  accomplish with his policy
  of New Federalism?

- To what previous
  presidential policy was
  he reacting?

### New Federalism

Like Eisenhower, Nixon wanted to reduce the role of the federal government and turn over more activities to the states. Nixon called this policy the New Federalism. He criticized Johnson's Great Society as too costly and tried to reduce involvement of the federal government in social welfare programs. To achieve this goal, Nixon instituted revenue sharing, a policy in which the federal government gave part of its income to the states to spend on social welfare as they saw fit.

### Curbing Inflation

The Vietnam War had helped trigger inflation, which was one of Nixon's biggest domestic problems. During the 1968 election, Nixon had promised to end inflation and balance the budget. By the time he took office, prices were rising faster than they had in 20 years. Unemployment was rising too. At the same time, the nation's gross national product (GNP) was declining. To bring the economy under control, Nixon implemented a 90-day wage-price freeze in August 1971. He was the first president to impose mandatory wage-price controls in peacetime.

### Nixon and the Supreme Court

Each President hopes to influence the decisions of the Supreme Court through the appointment of justices. However, the appointees do not always rule as a President might expect. For example, President Eisenhower regretted his appointment of Earl Warren to the Supreme Court, because Warren made many liberal decisions that opposed Eisenhower's conservative political views.

Key Themes
and Concepts

Constitutional Principles
- Did these landmark
  Supreme Court cases
  provide more protection
  for individual rights or less
  protection?

- What effects did *Gideon
  v. Wainwright* (1963),
  *Escobedo v. Illinois* (1964),
  *and Miranda v. Arizona*
  (1966) have on people
  who were accused of a
  crime?

**Nixon Appointees** In 1969, Warren retired, and Nixon appointed Warren Burger as chief justice. During his administration, Nixon also had the opportunity to appoint three other justices. Nixon's appointees were all strict constructionists, believing that Congress and the President have only those powers specifically given to them by the Constitution. The "Nixon Court," however, did not overturn many of the liberal rulings of the 1960s, as Nixon had expected.

## Other Domestic Events Under Nixon

Advances in the space program, an increase in the electorate, and additional rights movements occurred in the 1970s.

Key Themes
and Concepts

Science and Technology
- Why was it significant that
  an American was the first
  person to set foot on the
  moon?

### The Space Program

In 1969, American astronaut Neil Armstrong became the first person to walk on the moon. The triumph of seeing Armstrong plant a United States flag on the moon's surface marked a bright spot in an otherwise troubled decade.

### The Twenty-sixth Amendment

In 1971, the Twenty-sixth Amendment to the Constitution was ratified. This amendment extended the vote to people ages 18 and older. By lowering the voting age from 21 to 18, this amendment added almost 12 million new voters to the American electorate. The ratification of this amendment has been seen as a result of the participation of the United States in the Vietnam War, where thousands of Americans between the ages of 18 and 21 died.

Key Themes
and Concepts

Change
- How did passage of the
  Twenty-sixth Amendment
  affect the number of
  voters in the United
  States?

- Would you say that this
  amendment made the
  United States more
  democratic or less
  democratic?

### Women's Rights Movement

In the 1970s, more and more women enrolled in schools of law, medicine, engineering, and business, fields that had been traditionally reserved for men. However, full-time working women in 1971 were paid only 59 percent as much as men. Many of them also did not hold positions equal to their talents. As you read in Section 2, the Equal Rights Amendment failed to win ratification.

## Consumer Rights Movement

A strong consumer rights movement also developed in the early 1970s to address abuses by major American industries. The movement was led by Ralph Nader, a young Washington lawyer who organized a protest in the 1960s against the automotive industry. Nader attracted a number of young volunteers, known as "Nader's Raiders," to his cause. They championed environmental and consumer protection.

# The Watergate Affair

In 1972, the Republicans nominated Nixon for reelection. The Democrats selected George McGovern. President Nixon claimed credit for bringing down inflation and scoring foreign policy triumphs abroad. He swept to victory, carrying the largest popular majority in United States history. Yet less than two years later, Nixon resigned from office.

- **What happened** an illegal break-in to wiretap phones in the Democratic Party headquarters with electronic surveillance equipment
- **Where** Watergate Towers, an apartment complex in Washington, D.C.
- **When** June 17, 1972
- **Who** the Committee to Reelect the President, acting with the knowledge of several high-level Nixon advisers
- **Why** to secure information to undermine the Democratic campaign against Nixon

## The Cover-Up

Police captured the "burglars," who carried evidence linking them to the White House. Nixon did not know about the plan until after it happened. However, he then ordered a cover-up, which was a crime under federal law.

**The Investigation** Reporters from the *Washington Post* probed into the case, now known as the **Watergate affair**, but their reports did not hinder Nixon's reelection. Then in 1973, the Senate set up a committee to look into "illegal, improper, or unethical activities" in the 1972 election. For more than a year, the Senate committee came closer and closer to implicating President Nixon.

**Resignation of Agnew** While the Watergate hearings were under way, the Justice Department charged Vice President Spiro Agnew with income tax evasion. Agnew resigned, and Nixon appointed Gerald R. Ford, the minority leader in the House of Representatives, as Vice President.

**The Tapes** In mid-1973, the Senate committee learned that the White House had kept tape recordings of key conversations between Nixon and his top aides. Nixon refused to turn over the tapes. During the summer, the committee opened the hearings to television. The televised proceedings had the appeal of a soap opera as millions of Americans watched.

**Nixon Resignation** The situation ended when the Supreme Court ordered Nixon to surrender the tapes in its ruling in *United States* v. *Richard Nixon.* Based on evidence in the tapes, the House Judiciary Committee began voting on articles of impeachment against the president. To avoid impeachment, Nixon resigned on August 9, 1974, becoming the first President to do so. On noon of that day, Gerald Ford took the oath of office.

Gerald Ford became the first nonelected president. To fill the office of Vice President, Ford named Nelson Rockefeller, the former governor of New York.

## Key Themes and Concepts

**Reform Movements**
The consumer rights movement of the 1960s, led by Ralph Nader, achieved important reforms, such as improved safety features in U.S.-built automobiles.

- What earlier movement in American history championed the cause of improving products available to the American people?

## Reading Strategy

**Reinforcing Main Ideas**
The Watergate affair was a serious scandal that brought down a president.

- What was the reason behind the Watergate break-in?
- What was Nixon's role?
- How did Nixon's involvement in the Watergate affair lead to his resignation?
- How did the Watergate affair prove that the system of checks and balances works?

From 1974 until 1977, the United States had both a President and Vice President who had not been elected to their offices but had been appointed. Such a situation had not occurred before and has not occurred since.

## Significance of Watergate

Although Nixon was never charged with any specific crimes, President Ford pardoned him. Ford hoped to end what he called "our long national nightmare." Many of Nixon's advisers, however, were found guilty of crimes and sentenced to prison. The incident showed, as Ford put it, that "the Constitution works." The system of checks and balances had stopped Nixon from placing the presidency above the law. However, one impact of the Watergate Scandal was a decline in the public's trust in government.

# The Ford Administration

Many people called Nixon's administration the "Imperial Presidency" because of his disregard of the Constitution. Ford tried to rebuild the image of the President. However, the Watergate affair had disillusioned many Americans.

## Ford's Domestic Policies

From the start, President Ford faced a number of domestic problems.

- *Nixon's Pardon* Many Americans questioned Ford's decision to pardon Nixon when so many of his advisers stood trial and were convicted and jailed.
- *Amnesty Plan* Ford stirred bitter debate when he offered amnesty to thousands of young men who avoided military service in Vietnam by violating draft laws, fleeing the country, or deserting the military.
- *Inflation* In 1973, the Organization of Petroleum Exporting Countries (OPEC) placed an oil embargo on the United States for its support of Israel. The price of oil and gasoline more than doubled, setting off a new round of inflation. Temporary rationing of gasoline and federal incentives to research energy alternatives helped ease shortages. Even so, Americans remained highly dependent on foreign oil. Inflation topped 10 percent, and the nation entered into its worst recession since World War II.

### Turning Point

- Why is the Watergate affair considered a turning point in U.S. history?

### Key Themes and Concepts

**Presidential Decisions and Actions**

Following a Senate investigation into the Watergate affair, President Nixon resigned on August 9, 1974. Vice President Gerald Ford became the first non-elected president in U.S. history. Although President Nixon was never charged with any crime, President Ford issued a pardon to him.

- Why do you think President Ford pardoned President Nixon?

### Analyzing Documents

Based on the chart and your knowledge of social studies, answer the following questions.

- What happened to fuel prices in 1973 and 1974?

- What caused the change in fuel prices in those years?

- How might the change in fuel prices and in all consumer item prices be related?

**Rate of Inflation, 1968–1976**

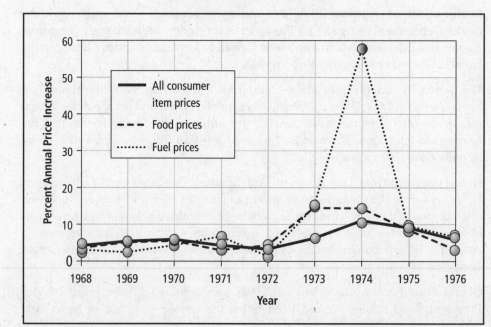

Source: *Statistical Abstract of the United States*

## Ford's Foreign Policies

Henry Kissinger continued working with the Ford administration. Kissinger helped:

- negotiate a cease-fire agreement between Egypt and Israel, thus ending the 1973 Yom Kippur War and OPEC oil embargo.
- continue the policy of détente with the Soviet Union, including the sale of tons of grain to the Soviets and a hookup of Soviet and American space capsules.
- oversee the end of the Vietnam War, including the withdrawal of the last American personnel from Saigon in 1975.

## The Election of 1976

The nation's bicentennial (200th anniversary) in 1976 gave the Ford presidency a boost. However, it was not enough to help Ford completely shake off his negative association with the Nixon years. He lost a close election to the Democratic candidate, James (Jimmy) Earl Carter, former governor of Georgia.

# The Carter Administration

Jimmy Carter won the 1976 election, in part, because of his appeal to the American sense of honesty and integrity. He stated a desire to return to basic American "down home" values. He wanted to prove that an "outsider" could make government more responsive to the people. However, Carter's unfamiliarity with Washington politics proved a disadvantage. First Lady Rosalynn Carter became his most trusted adviser.

## Carter's Domestic Policies

Carter's presidency was made more difficult by changes that had taken place within Congress because of Watergate. Newly elected members tended to question every executive act.

**"Stagflation"** President Carter ran into the same economic woes as Ford—inflation coupled with rising unemployment. The problems were worsened by many welfare programs that increased the cost of government. With the economy apparently stalled in place, economists coined a new term, stagflation, to describe the situation. (The term referred to the stagnation of the economy and simultaneous inflation of prices.)

**Energy Problem** As the world's leading industrial power, the United States was also the world's leading consumer of energy. By the late 1970s, the nation had to import more than 40 percent of its oil. OPEC kept prices high, and American dollars flowed out of the country, worsening the trade deficit—the situation in which a nation buys more foreign goods than it exports abroad. In 1977, President Carter spoke to the American people about the energy crisis. He presented a national energy plan based on ten principles including conservation, environmental protection, and the development of new conventional or alternative sources of energy.

**Corporate Bailouts** Some American corporations were hard hit by stagflation and the decline in purchasing power at home. Foreign imports undersold some American goods, especially automobiles. The Chrysler Corporation and Lockheed Aircraft faced possible bankruptcy. Fearing the effect of massive layoffs on the economy, the federal government authorized huge loans to both corporations to keep them in business.

**Environmental Problems** Acid rain, created by toxic air pollution, continued to threaten forests, lakes, and wildlife in the United States. President Nixon had

### Election of 1976

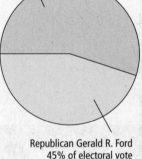

Democrat Jimmy Carter 55% of electoral vote

Republican Gerald R. Ford 45% of electoral vote

## Key Themes and Concepts

**Environment**
In the 1970s, the United States faced a number of environmental problems.

- What steps did Nixon and Carter take to resolve some of these problems?

- Do any of these problems persist today? If so, which ones?

taken steps to end harmful industrial pollution by creating the Environmental Protection Agency. Carter supported environmental programs as well, but inflation and energy shortages prevented him from undertaking ambitious programs to protect the environment. Coal polluted the air, but the nation needed coal to offset oil shortages. The nation needed to clean up the air, but emission devices for cars and factories pushed up prices.

**Nuclear Energy** Carter supported nuclear energy as an alternative to coal and oil. However, in 1979, an accident occurred at the Three Mile Island nuclear plant near Harrisburg, Pennsylvania. Although the problem was brought under control, the incident highlighted the hazards of the nuclear power industry, which by the late 1970s supplied about 4 percent of the nation's energy.

## Carter's Foreign Policy

During his presidency, Carter faced a number of foreign-policy challenges.

**Helsinki Accords** In 1975, the United States and other nations signed the Helsinki Accords, promising to respect basic human rights. Carter believed that the United States should withhold aid from nations that violated human rights.

**Camp David Accords** In 1977, Egyptian President Anwar el-Sadat surprised the world by visiting Israeli Prime Minister Menachem Begin. President Carter seized the opportunity for bringing peace to the Middle East by inviting the two leaders to Camp David, the president's retreat in Maryland. There, Sadat and Begin hammered out the terms for a peace treaty known as the Camp David Accords. The two leaders signed the treaty in 1979. Other Arab nations, however, still refused to recognize Israel.

## Key Themes and Concepts

**Presidential Decisions and Actions**
As you know from your study of United States history, all events are influenced by decisions, actions, and outcomes of earlier times.

- How was Carter's presidency influenced by the shadow of Nixon's presidency?

*President Carter announces the results of the Camp David Accords to a Joint Session of Congress*

**Panama Canal Treaties** In 1977, President Carter signed two treaties promising to turn over control of the Panama Canal to Panama in 1999. The treaties aroused bitter debate, but the Senate narrowly ratified them in 1978.

**Problems With Détente** In June 1979, Carter met with Soviet leader Leonid Brezhnev to negotiate the SALT II Treaty. However, a Soviet invasion of Afghanistan later that year ended détente. Carter cut off grain shipments to the Soviet Union and boycotted the 1980 summer Olympic games held in Moscow. Carter's tough line spurred debate at home.

**Hostage Crisis** The biggest foreign policy crisis for Carter came in Iran. In 1979, a revolution led by Islamic fundamentalists toppled the pro-American shah, Reza Pahlavi. The shah, suffering from terminal cancer, requested treatment in the United States, and Carter agreed. Islamic rebels struck back by seizing the United States embassy in Teheran and holding more than 50 Americans hostage.

### The 1980 Election

During the 1980 presidential campaign, President Carter was haunted by the continuing hostage crisis, persistent energy shortages, and lingering inflation. The conservative Republican candidate, former California governor Ronald Reagan, promised Americans a "new beginning" and a restoration of confidence at home and abroad. Reagan swept to victory, and on the day of his inauguration, Iran released the hostages after more than a year of captivity.

## Reagan and the Challenges of the 1980s

A former actor, Reagan appealed to many Americans with his references to the "good old days" and his patriotic speeches. He used his prepared speeches to promote a conservative approach to government and the economy. He targeted inflation as his top priority and argued that big government was the cause of inflation. "In the present crisis," said Reagan, "government is not the solution to our problem; government is the problem."

### Reagan's First-Term Domestic Policies

During his first term in office, President Reagan supported a domestic program backed by both Eisenhower and Nixon. Like his Republican predecessors, he supported New Federalism, a policy that turned over federal control of some social welfare programs to the states.

**Supply-Side Economics** Reagan called for cuts in taxes on businesses and individuals, especially those with large incomes. The president believed that they would reinvest in more businesses. These businesses would hire more workers and increase the supply of goods and services. Reagan argued that supply-side economics would end inflation without increasing the national debt. His ideas later became known as Reaganomics.

**Balanced Budget** Reagan tried to balance the budget by reducing many social welfare programs. He also made sharp cuts in the Environmental Protection Agency. Despite such efforts, however, the national debt climbed throughout Reagan's presidency.

**"Star Wars"** Reagan felt national security rested on defense and made every effort to fight off cuts in the military budget. He pushed for increased spending on missiles, ships, and bombers. He also asked for funding for the Strategic Defense Initiative (SDI), a massive satellite shield designed to intercept and destroy incoming Soviet missiles. SDI became popularly known as "Star Wars."

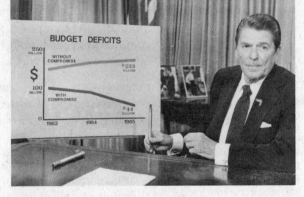

*President Reagan charts budget deficits*

**Farm Aid** In the 1980s, farmers experienced their worst economic problems since the Great Depression. A worldwide recession made it impossible for farmers to sell their surpluses—and to repay their loans. The Reagan administration responded by paying farmers not to plant millions of

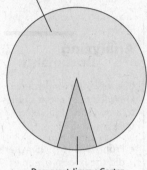

**Election of 1980**

Republican Ronald Reagan
91% of electoral vote

Democrat Jimmy Carter
9% of electoral vote

**Preparing for the Exam**

• What reasons led the American people to elect Ronald Reagan as president in 1980?

acres of land to reduce the supply and raise prices. However, prices did not rise, and the national debt grew.

**Immigration** In an effort to cut down on the number of undocumented workers living in the United States, Congress passed the 1986 Immigration Reform and Control Act, which forbade employers from hiring illegal immigrants. This new legislation did not solve the problem of the thousands of people who enter the United States illegally every year. These immigrants often work in sweatshop type factories, live in substandard housing, and are paid very low wages.

## Analyzing Documents

Use the graph and your knowledge of social studies to answer the following questions.

- From 1982 to 1995, where did the largest group of immigrants to the United States come from?

- How is this different than the origin of most immigrants in the nineteenth century?

### Origin of Immigrants, 1982–1995

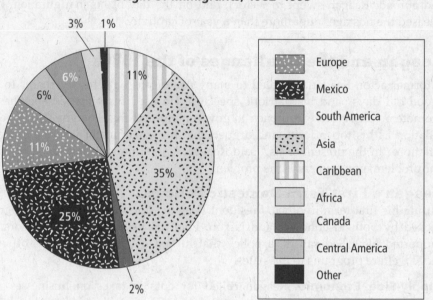

Legend:
- Europe
- Mexico
- South America
- Asia
- Caribbean
- Africa
- Canada
- Central America
- Other

Source: Statistical Abstract of the United States

## Reagan's First-Term Foreign Policy

President Reagan adopted a tough stand toward communism, describing the Soviet Union as an "evil empire."

**Questioning Détente** Reagan's attitude hardened toward communism in December 1981, when the Polish government cracked down on Solidarity, an independent labor party. The president called for economic sanctions to force the communist-backed government to end martial law. A renewal of détente did not take place until Reagan's second term.

**Intervention in Central America** Reagan believed that unstable economic conditions opened the door to communism. He asked for aid to Latin American groups fighting Communist takeovers and approved limited military intervention in some nations.

## Reading Strategy

**Analyzing Cause and Effect**
- What factors contributed to United States military interventions in El Salvador, Nicaragua, and Grenada?

- *El Salvador* Reagan sent arms and military advisers to El Salvador to back anticommunist forces in a civil war. He also pressured the government to hold democratic elections.

- *Nicaragua* In 1979, Marxist guerrillas called the Sandinistas overthrew anticommunist dictator Anastasio Somoza. Because the Sandinistas accepted aid from Cuba and the Soviet Union, Reagan approved aid to the contras, rebels seeking to oust the Sandinistas. Actions by the CIA to help the contras angered Congress, and it cut off aid to the contras in 1987.

- *Grenada* In October 1983, a rebellion in the Caribbean island nation of Grenada raised fears that it might become a Communist base in the Caribbean. To prevent such a possibility, Reagan ordered a surprise United States invasion.

**Turmoil in the Middle East** Religious conflicts in the Middle East increased tensions in an already unstable region. An international peacekeeping force went into Lebanon to try to end bloody fighting between Christians and Muslims. In October 1983, U.S. marines became the target of terrorists when a bomb-laden truck drove into their barracks, killing more than 300 people. In 1984, Reagan admitted the peacekeeping effort had failed and withdrew American troops.

**Terrorism** Global concern was raised by an increase in terrorism, random acts of violence to promote a political cause. In some countries, Islamic fundamentalists engaged in terrorism as part of a jihad, or a struggle to protect the Islamic faith. Charges of terrorism were also leveled against the Soviets in September, 1983, when they shot down a South Korean airliner that strayed into their air space, killing 269 people.

## The Election of 1984
In the presidential election of 1984, Walter Mondale won the Democratic nomination over several contenders including Jesse Jackson, an influential African American minister. Mondale selected Representative Geraldine Ferraro as his running mate. President Reagan campaigned for reelection, with George Bush as his running mate. Reagan won the election and became the first president since Eisenhower to serve two full terms in office.

## Reagan's Second-Term Domestic Policy
Reagan, nicknamed the Great Communicator by some journalists, used his charm and persuasive talents to convince many Americans to support a plan aimed at creating a balanced budget by the early 1990s.

Reagan and his supporters promised to make deep cuts in federal programs. Only a few select programs, such as Social Security and defense, were to be spared. Reagan also called for simplification of tax laws and tax cuts for about 60 percent of Americans. Some people charged that the cuts favored the rich. In fact, by the late 1980s, wealth was more unevenly distributed than at any time since the end of World War II.

**Trade Imbalance** Despite drastic actions by the federal government, the national debt climbed. This was due, in part, to a huge trade imbalance, a situation in which a nation imports more goods than it exports. At the start of Reagan's second term, the trade deficit approached $150 billion.

## Reagan's Second-Term Foreign Policy
President Reagan redirected his foreign policy to meet changes taking place in the Soviet Union. However, an issue that arose out of the United States dealings in the Middle East and Latin America took up much of his attention.

**The Iran-Contra Affair** In 1986, the American public learned that several top presidential aides had sold weapons to Iran in exchange for Iranian help in freeing American hostages held in Lebanon. The money from the sale of arms was then channeled to Nicaragua to support the contras.

Reagan had vowed never to bargain with terrorists or kidnappers. Also, Congress had banned aid to the contras. A congressional committee cleared the president of any wrongdoing in the Iran-Contra affair and concluded that the actions had been illegally undertaken at the direction of Colonel Oliver North and members of the CIA.

### Preparing for the Exam
Terrorism is random acts of violence that promote a political cause. Terrorist acts raised global concern during the 1980s.

- Why do you think terrorists bombed an American marine barracks in Lebanon in 1983?

- What effect did this bombing have on Reagan's policy in Lebanon?

### Election of 1984
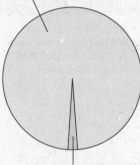

Republican Ronald Reagan 98% of electoral vote

Democrat Walter Mondale 2% of electoral vote

### Key Themes and Concepts

**Presidential Decisions and Actions**
President Reagan supported the policy of New Federalism that had been begun by President Nixon. New Federalism turned over government control of some social programs to the states. As part of New Federalism, Reagan also supported tax cuts for businesses, a balanced federal budget, and increased spending for national defense.

- Why do you think President Reagan supported New Federalism?

## Key Themes and Concepts

**Presidential Decisions and Actions**
Later in 2007, George W. Bush (43) commuted Libby's sentence of 30 months in jail, stating that the sentence was too harsh. Libby avoided any jail time.

In March 2007, Lewis "Scooter" Libby, former Chief of Staff to Vice President Cheney was convicted of lying and obstruction of justice. He was the highest ranking White House official convicted in a government scandal since the Iran-Contra affair during the Reagan administration.

**Renewal of Détente** In 1985, Mikhail Gorbachev became the new charismatic leader of the Soviet Union. Gorbachev criticized Reagan's policy of "Star Wars" and called for a renewal of détente.

Gorbachev helped further relations by announcing his new policies of *glasnost* and *perestroika*. Glasnost called for greater openness, including increased political freedom in the Soviet Union and Eastern Europe. Perestroika allowed a measure of free enterprise to improve economic conditions within the Soviet Union.

**Arms Reductions** In 1987, the United States and Soviet Union reached an agreement to eliminate short-range and medium-range land-based missiles.

### The End of the Cold War

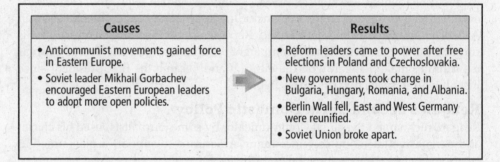

| Causes | Results |
| --- | --- |
| • Anticommunist movements gained force in Eastern Europe.<br>• Soviet leader Mikhail Gorbachev encouraged Eastern European leaders to adopt more open policies. | • Reform leaders came to power after free elections in Poland and Czechoslovakia.<br>• New governments took charge in Bulgaria, Hungary, Romania, and Albania.<br>• Berlin Wall fell, East and West Germany were reunified.<br>• Soviet Union broke apart. |

## Preparing for the Exam

• How did Soviet leader Mikhail Gorbachev work to improve relations with the United States?

**Troubles Elsewhere** Troubles over other foreign policy issues were not so easily resolved. These included the following.

- *Continuing Terrorism* Terrorists continued to claim some American lives. In 1985, for example, Palestinian terrorists killed an American passenger aboard an Italian cruise ship, the *Achille Lauro*. In 1988, a bomb destroyed a Pan Am jet over Scotland.
- *Battling the Drug Trade* First Lady Nancy Reagan launched an antidrug campaign with the slogan, "Just say no!"
- *Ending Apartheid* Many people demanded that Americans divest, or get rid of, investments in South Africa to protest that nation's policy of apartheid, or strict racial segregation and discrimination. In 1986, Congress overrode Reagan's veto and imposed strict economic sanctions against South Africa until it ended apartheid.

## Key Themes and Concepts

**Economic Systems**
• How did Americans protest South Africa's policy of apartheid?

# Approaching and Beginning the 21ˢᵗ Century

## Section Overview

In 1988 George H.W. Bush (41), a conservative Republican from Texas defeated the Democratic candidate, Michael Dukakis for the presidency. After serving one term, President Bush was defeated by Arkansas Governor Bill Clinton. President Clinton served from 1993 until President Bush's son George W. Bush (43) was inaugurated in 2001 after he defeated President Clinton's Vice President Al Gore in the race for the White House.

## Key Themes and Concepts

**Conflict** What domestic and international conflicts caused problems for the United States during this time?

**Culture** How did values of other cultures clash with values of the United States?

**Power** In what ways did the United States government use its power at home and abroad?

## The George H. W. Bush (41) Administration

### Domestic Events

**Economic Troubles** During the election campaign, Bush had promised voters no new taxes. However, as the budget deficit mounted, President Bush was forced to break this promise in 1990. By 1992, an economic recession caused increased layoffs and rising unemployment.

**Savings and Loan Scandal** In 1990, the misuse of funds by savings and loan institutions surfaced. American taxpayers paid hundreds of billions of dollars to bail out the savings and loan industry.

**Supreme Court Appointments** President Bush appointed two new justices to the Supreme Court: David Souter in 1990 and Clarence Thomas in 1991. Thomas was confirmed by the Senate after controversial hearings in which he was charged with sexual harassment by Anita Hill, a former employee.

### Events Abroad

**End of the Cold War** In November 1989, the world watched in amazement as Germans tore down the Berlin Wall—a symbolic reminder of the division between the communist and democratic worlds. Throughout the winter of 1990, Communist governments in Eastern Europe crumbled. In 1990, Gorbachev received the Nobel Peace Prize for relaxing control over former Soviet satellites. In October of that year, East and West Germany were formally reunited. A failed coup by hard-line Communist leaders in 1991 led to the dissolution of the Soviet Union and the 1992 formation of a Commonwealth of Independent States.

**Invasion of Panama** As President, Bush continued Reagan's war on drugs. He ordered United States troops into Panama to capture General Manuel Noriega, the dictator of Panama, and return him to the United States to face drug charges. In 1992, Noriega was sentenced to serve 40 years in federal prison.

## The Big Idea

During the time approaching and beginning the 21ˢᵗ century:

- President George H.W. Bush (41) served during the end of the Cold War.

- President Clinton promoted many ambitious domestic programs during the 1990s.

- President Clinton became the second president to experience an impeachment trial.

- President George W. Bush (43) led the nation in the War on Terrorism following the attacks of September 11, 2001.

- Barack Obama, the first African American president, was inaugurated on January 20, 2009.

**Persian Gulf War** In August 1990, Iraqi leader Saddam Hussein invaded the oil-rich nation of Kuwait. President Bush responded by sending United States troops into Saudi Arabia, with the agreement of Saudi leaders. The United Nations condemned Iraq's actions and approved economic sanctions against Iraq. The UN also authorized a joint military buildup in Saudi Arabia, called Operation Desert Shield.

Operation Desert Shield became **Operation Desert Storm** in January 1991 when the United States with a troop force of over 500,000 (the largest American military commitment since Vietnam) and Allied troops from a number of other nations began a total air assault on Iraq. By the end of February, Bush ordered a cease-fire, and Iraq accepted all UN demands to end the Persian Gulf War. More than 300 Allied lives were lost. The Iraqi death toll was estimated at 100,000.

**Bosnia and the Balkans** The end of the Bush administration was marked by the outbreak of violence in the Balkans. In 1991, Slovenia and Croatia declared their independence from Yugoslavia, and fighting broke out throughout the area. Millions became refugees during the fighting. Bosnian Serbs, led by Slobodan Milosevic, carried out ethnic cleansing, or genocidal warfare, killing thousands of innocent civilians.

## The 1992 Election

In the 1992 presidential election, George Bush ran as the Republican candidate with Dan Quayle as his running mate. The Democrats selected Arkansas governor Bill Clinton as their candidate, with Al Gore as his running mate. Texas billionaire Ross Perot, an independent challenger, also entered the race. Perot ran as a candidate from what he called the Independent Party. In 1996 he ran again as a candidate of the Reform Party. These political parties are known as "Third Parties" because the United States has traditionally had a two party system. The ideas of third party candidates are often incorporated into the platforms of the major parties, although sometimes that doesn't happen until later elections. Third party candidates are often blamed for taking votes from the two major party candidates. This was especially true in the election of 2000. The major issues of the campaign concerned the state of the American economy. In the election, Clinton made Bosnia an issue and promised to take strong action there.

Clinton carried 32 states with a total of 370 electoral votes. Although Perot did not earn any electoral votes, he received over 19 million popular votes. Women, African Americans, and Latino Americans were elected to Congress in record high numbers in 1992.

## The Bill Clinton Administration

### Domestic Issues

**Health-Care Reform** In 1993, President Clinton presented to Congress a health-care reform plan that would ensure health insurance for all Americans. Critics of the plan complained it was too expensive, complex, and would limit choice in health care. In 1994, Congress rejected Clinton's plan. Since the 1990s, the primary issue concerning health care in the United States has been the increasing cost of medical insurance. In the twenty-first century, growing numbers of Americans have been unable to afford health care insurance.

**Social Security** It became clear that the Social Security program, begun during the Great Depression, would run into trouble because of changing demographics. The number of recipients is increasing rapidly due to longer life spans and the

### Election of 1992

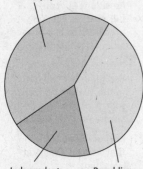

Democrat Bill Clinton 43% of popular vote

Independent Ross Perot 19% of popular vote

Republican George Bush 38% of popular vote

**Preparing for the Exam**

• Was Bill Clinton's victory in the 1992 presidential election decisive? Why or why not?

aging baby boomer generation. Several plans to fund Social Security have been considered, but no plan has been agreed upon.

**Supreme Court Appointees** With his nominations of Ruth Bader Ginsburg and Stephen Breyer, President Clinton became the first Democratic president in 26 years to name a Supreme Court justice.

**The 1994 Congressional Elections** In 1994, Republicans took majority control of Congress for the first time in 40 years.

**The 1996 and 1998 Elections** At the end of 1995, disagreements between Republicans and President Clinton over the budget led to a shutdown of the federal government. During the 1996 presidential campaign, Clinton focused public attention on the Republicans' role in the shutdown. He also adopted several Republican issues by signing welfare reform into law and supporting a balanced budget. Clinton easily won reelection. Republicans maintained their congressional majority after both elections, but Democrats gained five House seats in 1998.

**Scandal and Impeachment** Some of President Clinton's activities were the subject of investigations, including the Whitewater affair, which accused him and his wife Hillary Rodham Clinton of involvement with an illegal real estate scheme in Arkansas. The Clintons were never formally charged.

In 1998, a special prosecutor accused President Clinton of several offenses, including lying under oath about his relationship with a White House intern. On December 19, 1998, the House impeached President Clinton on charges of perjury and obstruction of justice. The Senate acquitted President Clinton two months later. This was similar to President Andrew Johnson's impeachment trial in 1868. Both presidents went through the impeachment process and both won acquittals in the Senate. There was a major difference between the impact of the impeachment on each president. President Andrew Johnson lost power in Washington, whereas President Clinton has remained an extremely popular political figure.

**Economic Prosperity** In the 1990s, the United States enjoyed the longest period of economic growth in its history.

## Foreign Issues

**The Middle East** The Arab-Israeli conflict has long focused attention on the Middle East. Since 1948, Arabs and Israelis have waged four wars. In 1993, the Palestine Liberation Organization and Israel agreed to a measure of Palestinian self-government. However, incidents of violence slowed the peace process. President Clinton continued to try to achieve peace in the Middle East by hosting the Camp David Summit for Israeli and Palestinian leaders. It did not produce lasting peaceful results.

**The Former Yugoslavia** Tensions between ethnic groups in the former Yugoslavia led to war in Bosnia in the early 1990s. The United States helped win

**Key Themes and Concepts**

**Government**
How did the 1994 Congressional elections shift the balance of power in Congress?

**Analyzing Documents**

Examine the cartoon, then answer the questions.

- What does the black spot stand for?

- What is the meaning of the title of the cartoon?

- What is the opinion that this cartoon is trying to convey?

**Key Themes and Concepts**

**Presidential Decisions and Actions**
In the early 1990s, war erupted in the Balkans as the former Yugoslavia fell into a bitter civil war.

- How did President Clinton handle tensions between ethnic groups in the former Yugoslavia in the 1990s?

- What gave President Clinton the authority to take this action?

## Key Themes and Concepts

**Economic Systems**
By the 1990s, the economies of many nations had become more interdependent.

- Name two organizations or agreements designed to improve trade among member nations.

- To which of these does the United States belong?

an agreement between the two sides in 1995. In 1998, violence erupted in Kosovo, where Serbian forces massacred ethnic Albanian civilians. A brief bombing campaign by NATO forced the Serbs to withdraw. Many Serbian leaders then were arrested for war crimes and tried.

**Latin America** In 1994, President Clinton ordered U.S. troops to lead a multinational force in Haiti to restore a legitimate government after years of dictatorships and unrest. During the rest of the decade, millions of dollars in aid was pledged to Haiti by many countries but little has been sent due to the continuing lack of a stable government in that area.

**Global Economy** In 1992, the United States, Canada, and Mexico signed the **North American Free Trade Agreement (NAFTA)** in an effort to break down trade barriers among the three nations. American trade in Europe continued to be strong, despite the formation of the **European Union,** a trade organization designed to break down trade barriers within Europe. The **General Agreement on Trade and Tariffs (GATT)** was formed in 1945 to encourage international trade. In 1995 the World Trade Organization was formed from GATT and included other nations as well.

**Historic Appointment** In late 1996 at the beginning of his second term in office, President Clinton nominated Madeleine K. Albright to be Secretary of State. After being unanimously confirmed by the U.S. Senate, she was sworn in as the 64th Secretary of State in January 1997. Secretary Albright was the first female secretary of state. Since then two women have held that position, Condoleezza Rice in the Bush (43) administration and Hillary Rodham Clinton in the Obama administration.

## The 2000 Election

In the 2000 presidential election, Texas Governor George W. Bush ran as the Republican candidate against the Democrat, Vice President Al Gore. In one of the closest presidential races in history, Florida emerged as the key state because its electoral votes could decide the winner. The Florida vote was so close that a recount of ballots was ordered by law. The election ended when the Supreme Court ruled to discontinue the recounts. Although Gore won the popular vote, Bush won the electoral vote. The election marked the first time the Supreme Court intervened in a presidential election.

The presidential election of 2000 was also the first election since the Hayes/Tilden election of 1876 where the winner of the popular vote—Tilden in 1876 and Gore in 2000—did not win the electoral vote.

This election also popularized the term **Swing State,** which is a term used for a state in which the voters are almost evenly divided between major parties. Candidates and political experts acknowledge that either major party candidate could win the popular vote and therefore that state's electoral votes. Swing states such as Florida, Ohio, and Michigan were also crucial to the elections of 2004 and 2008.

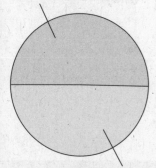

**Election of 2000**

Republican George W. Bush 50.5% of electoral vote

Democrat Al Gore 49.5% of electoral vote

## The George W. Bush (43) Administration

### Domestic Issues

**Taxes and the Economy** President Bush attempted a tax cut and rebates to taxpayers earlier in his administration and in 2008 taxpayers received rebate checks of $300 to $1200. Since 2007, the economy has shown signs of a possible recession, especially in the housing market as thousands of homeowners struggled to meet mortgage payments and others faced bank foreclosures. In 2007, Congress approved an increase in the minimum wage from $5.15 to $5.85 with an increase to $7.25 by 2009. The Federal Reserve Board has lowered its interest rate several times, including a drop of .75 percent, the largest in the history of the Federal Reserve Board. By early spring 2009, the Federal Reserve interest rate was actually at a record breaking 0 percent. All of these actions were an effort to reverse the threat of a recession. By late 2008, the recession was being described as the worst economic downturn since the Great Depression of the 1930s.

**Educational Reform** On January 8, 2002, President Bush signed into law a major educational reform bill called No Child Left Behind. The plan called for increased student and teacher accountability and targeted funds for improving schools. Critics said that it did not accomplish what it needed to do to improve American education.

**Mass Acts of Violence** In 2007, following several years of mass acts of violence in schools and on college campuses, the most deadly shooting rampage in United States history took place, with 33 students, including the killer, dead at Virginia Tech in Blacksburg, Virginia. Later in 2007, a sniper in an Omaha, Nebraska shopping mall killed eight, while in February 2008, another gunman killed five students as well as himself at Northern Illinois University. Each incident of this type of violence renewed the debate among Americans about gun control.

**Immigration Issues** The Bush administration had to deal with several issues relating to immigration, some of which became more serious after the attacks of September 11, 2001. The Real ID Act of 2005 strengthened security requirements at U.S. borders and gave the Director of Homeland Security additional powers. Several proposals were introduced in both houses of Congress to increase border patrols and protection, restrict illegal immigration, and strengthen anti-terrorism laws. There was also extensive discussion over funding bills to construct a wall along the U.S. border between Mexico and the United States. This produced mixed reactions on both sides of the border.

It is estimated that illegal immigrants in the United States today number more than ten million. Immigration was a discussion topic among the 2008 presidential candidates.

**Social Security** In his first term, President Bush wanted to make Social Security reform a primary agenda item. The president's plan to allow younger workers to choose private accounts for a portion of their Social Security contributions drew praise as well as criticism. The president also tried to reform the Medicare program. A major concern with these programs is that the number of Americans eligible for them is growing. There is an increasing senior citizen population due to the aging of the, "baby boom" generation. At the same time there are fewer workers contributing to the system, due to declining American birth rates of the 1970's and 1980's.

**Election 2004** In November 2004, George W. Bush, the Republican incumbent won a close race against challenger, Massachusetts Senator and Vietnam War veteran, John Kerry. The popular vote was Bush, 62,040,606 (51%) to Kerry's 59,028,109 (48%). The state of Ohio ultimately gave the president the needed Electoral votes to win, 286 to 251.

Vice President Dick Cheney continued for a second term. Dr. Condoleezza Rice, former National Security Advisor, became the first African American woman to hold the position of Secretary of State. Within the first few months of being appointed Secretary of State, Rice made trips to Europe, the Middle East, and parts of Asia.

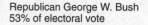

**Election of 2004**

Republican George W. Bush
53% of electoral vote

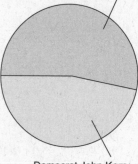

Democrat John Kerry
47% of electoral vote

The Congressional elections of 2006 were a major upset for both President Bush and the majority Republican Party. Democrats took control of both the House of Representatives and the Senate. Nancy Pelosi, a representative from California, was elected by her party to be the first female Speaker of the House of Representatives. This made Speaker Pelosi the highest ranking woman in the history of the United States government. According to the Constitution, the Speaker of the House is second only to the Vice President in succession to the Presidency.

## Foreign Issues

**September 11, 2001 and Resulting Events** President Bush focused largely on foreign policy after the September 11, 2001, attacks on the World Trade Center in New York City and the Pentagon in Washington, D.C. The president called the attacks "acts of war" and committed the country to a campaign against terrorists. American forces attacked military sites and terrorists training camps in Afghanistan. A major goal of this campaign was to aid in the overthrow of the Taliban rule and to find and bring to justice the al-Qaeda leader, Osama bin Laden. Bush urged Americans not to "expect one battle but a lengthy campaign unlike any other we have ever seen."

**The Middle East** Problems between the Israelis and Palestinians continued with repeated incidents of suicide bombers and cross border attacks by both sides. Attempts were made by the United States to develop compromise solutions but episodes of violence delayed peace keeping efforts.

In November 2004, Yasir Arafat, the leader of the Palestine Liberation Organization and recipient of the Nobel Peace Prize, died at 75 after an almost 50-year struggle to gain a permanent homeland for the Palestinian people.

In November 2007, President Bush hosted a Middle East Peace Conference in Annapolis, Maryland, which brought together Israeli Prime Minister Ehud Olmert and Palestinian President Mahmound Abbas, as well as representatives from 49 other countries. The leaders agreed to work on details of a peace treaty. The area continues to be troubled with violence and disagreeing factions.

*The Dome of the Rock, Jerusalem*

**War in Iraq** In late 2002 and early 2003, the Bush administration warned Saddam Hussein to eliminate Iraq's weapons of mass destruction (WMD). Hussein claimed not to have any WMD. The United Nations sent an inspection team, which reported little success finding these weapons. The United States worked to gain United Nations support for an invasion of Iraq. Failing to gain this support, a small number of countries led by the United States and Great Britain attacked Iraq in March 2003. This campaign is known as **Operation Iraqi Freedom.** More than 200,000 American troops were sent to the area. For the first time, the United States military allowed reporters to be "embedded" with the troops. Bush declared an official end to the war on May 1, 2003.

In July 2003, both sons of Saddam Hussein were killed in a shootout with U.S. forces in Mosul, Iraq. Hussein escaped capture until December 2003. An Iraqi Governing Council was established during 2003 with the goal of making Iraq an independent, democratic nation. American casualties continued to rise as the military met resistance. President Bush defended the war on the grounds that a brutal dictator who had terrorist links and was hiding WMD was removed. Given the rising loss of human lives and financial costs to the United States, and the failure to find WMD, critics questioned the Bush administration's activites in Iraq and its long term plan for the country.

During 2004, President Bush and Secretary of Defense Donald Rumsfeld faced serious questions about the treatment of Iraqi prisoners after reports disclosed abuse by American troops. Some soldiers were found guilty and sentenced to prison terms. In January 2005, with American and Coalition Forces' support, the new Iraqi government held its first democratic elections under extremely tight security. Insurgents who opposed the new government and the American presence in Iraq continued violent attacks on both military and civilians in Baghdad and elsewhere. In 2006, President Bush replaced the Secretary of Defense Rumsfeld with Robert Gates, who agreed to continue in that position in President Obama's administration. Early in 2007, the Bush administration was forced to answer questions about the poor treatment of many returning wounded soldiers. At the end of 2007, several Army leaders were dismissed from their jobs as a result of the conditions at Walter Reed Medical Center in Washington.

Although the new Iraqi government made some progress at establishing democracy, the two most powerful Islamic sects, the Shiites and the Sunnis, continued to have difficulties working together. The trial of Saddam Hussein concluded with his being found guilty of multiple murders. He was hanged on December 30, 2006. By 2007, the violent actions of the insurgents moved Iraq into a civil war. Daily violence and loss of life increased as American and coalition troops tried to maintain order. With these events, President Bush's popularity ratings with the American public declined to the lowest levels of his presidency. There was growing antiwar pressure from mainstream Americans as the number of Americans dead and wounded continued to grow. Early in 2007, Great Britain, America's strongest ally in the Iraqi war, began to withdraw its troops from Iraq.

Despite the attempts of Congress to limit the increase of troops in Iraq, President Bush announced a new strategy called a "Surge" in which American troop strength increased to over 160,000. This plan was an effort to control the number of suicide bombers, car bombs, and roadside attacks by Iraqi insurgents that had caused thousands of Iraqi deaths. The Surge did meet with some success, but American war deaths in 2007 increased to their highest level since 2003. The estimates of the cost of the war in Iraq vary widely, but the cost is currently believed to be more than $700 billion.

## Key Themes and Concepts

**Presidential Decisions and Actions**
- How did President Bush's actions during the war in Iraq demonstrate his use of presidential power?

## Turning Point

- Why was the capture, trial, and eventual execution of Saddam Hussein considered a turning point of the war in Iraq?

By the spring of 2010, over 90,000 American troops remained in Iraq with a goal of training Iraqi soldiers to eventually replace the Americans. Over 4,400 American servicemen and women have been killed in Iraq and thousands more have been seriously wounded.

**Preparing for the Exam**

Remember that current topics like Afghanistan and the Taliban, who continue to be a threat to western ideas in that country, are valid topics for both multiple choice and essay questions.

• Why do western nations like the United States continue to oppose the goals of the Taliban?

**Afghanistan** Following the Soviet occupation of Afghanistan from 1979 until the end of the 1980s, millions of Afghans fled their country and Afghan fighters fought a resistance movement to force the Soviets to leave. In the 1990s, a reactionary, extremist Islamic fundamentalist group known as the **Taliban** took over the Afghan government and imposed strict, conservative laws on the population. Women were forced to wear traditional coverings and to remain primarily in their homes. In 2001, NATO forces led by the United States forced the Taliban from power. Many of the surviving Taliban fled across the border into Pakistan where they continued to launch attacks across the border. In 2006, President Bush visited the area under very heavy security to emphasize the desire of the United States to cooperate with that part of Asia. In 2007, Vice President Cheney visited Afghanistan, and suicide bombers attempted to attack the secured compound where the vice president was staying. It is generally believed that Osama bin Laden, the head of the terrorist group al-Qaeda, responsible for the September 11, 2001 attacks, remains at large there or in the rugged mountains of neighboring Pakistan. Bin Laden released his first video in three years in September 2007, declaring that he and al-Qaeda would "continue to escalate the killing and fighting in Iraq." Continued American involvement in Afghanistan is considered crucial to American goals and interests in that part of Asia. Approximately $127 billion has already been spent on the war in Afghanistan. As in the case of the war in Iraq, estimates of total cost vary widely. However, the cost of the war in Afghanistan will likely continue to rise due to a new emphasis by the Obama administration on war efforts there.

**North Korea** In 2007, relations improved between the United States and North Korea. For the first time in five years, U.S. representatives visited North Korea. North Korea agreed to dismantle its nuclear production facilities and to allow international inspectors to visit the country. This was in exchange for a multi-million dollar aid package. The Bush administration also agreed to begin the process of removing North Korea from its list of nations sponsoring terrorism.

**Iran** American foreign policy toward Iran continued to be a difficult problem. Iranian President Mahmoud Ahmadinejad spoke in New York City at Columbia University in September 2007 as well as at the United Nations. The ability of Iran to produce nuclear weapons is of primary concern to the United States. President Bush repeatedly took a hard line position against this possibility.

**Pakistan** During the years after 9/11, Pakistani President Pervez Musharraf generally supported the United States in its efforts in the war on terror. In the fall of 2007, former Pakistani leader Benazir Bhutto returned to Pakistan after eight years of exile. This return was followed by political upheaval and the death of Bhutto at a campaign rally. In 2008 when elections were held, Musharraf's party lost and a new coalition government was formed. It will be crucial to American efforts in this area that favorable diplomatic relations continue with the new government.

**Africa** Early in 2008, President Bush and the First Lady made a visit to several African nations. Throughout the Bush presidency, aid to Africa was a major goal, with funds being directed to the widespread problem of AIDS there. The civil war in Kenya caused thousands of deaths, and the situation of starvation and mass murders in Darfur has drawn world wide attention.

**Cuba** The relationship between the United States and Cuba, the island nation ninety miles from southern Florida, has been troubled since 1959, when Fidel Castro became the Communist leader. On February 19, 2008, Castro announced that he would step down from the Cuban presidency and that he would be succeeded by his brother Raul.

**Kosovo** Since the Clinton administration, the United States has been part of a United Nations peace keeping force in Kosovo, a province of Serbia in the Balkan peninsula. On February 17, 2008, Kosovo declared its independence from Serbia. The following day, the United States, along with several other Western nations, formally recognized the new nation. Russia, in a move suggestive of the Cold War days, sided with Serbia and stated that Kosovo's declaration was a violation of international law.

## The 2008 Election

Early in 2007, several candidates entered the race for the presidency. Some of these candidacies were particularly historic because they represented "firsts" in American history. New York Senator Hillary Clinton was both the first former First Lady and the first female from a major political party (Democratic) to run for President. Illinois Senator Barack Obama, also a Democrat, was the first African American to be considered a serious presidential candidate from a major party.

Please refer to the chart on page 40 of this text that details the steps in becoming a presidential candidate. The state-by-state selection process began on January 3, 2008, with the Iowa caucus, which was followed shortly by the New Hampshire primary. Obama won in Iowa and Clinton won in New Hampshire for the Democrats, setting the stage for weeks of continuing debates and campaign travel for both.

Arizona Senator John McCain, the Republican front runner, took a strong lead over his opponents and several withdrew from the race. In February 2008, Ralph Nader announced that he would run again for president as a third party candidate. In the 2000 election, when Nader ran as a third party candidate, he was blamed for taking votes from the Democratic candidate.

Throughout the spring of 2008, the Democratic frontrunners, Hillary Clinton and Barack Obama, each won primaries. The candidates attracted different groups of voters, and each continued to build large numbers of delegate votes. As the primary season continued, Senator Clinton gradually fell behind both in convention delegates and in campaign money raised. Many sources, ranging from party officials to politicians to the media, urged her to leave the race. Senator Obama stated that Clinton had worked hard and should stay in the race as long as she wanted to do so. Senator Clinton refused to quit, stayed on the primary ballot, and continued to win states until the very last day of the primaries, June 3, 2008. That evening, Obama clinched the Democratic nomination with the required number of delegate votes. Both candidates congratulated each other on their success at bringing so many new voters into the political process. Their candidacies drew thousands of new voters representing several groups, such as younger voters, African Americans, and Hispanics. The increase in eligible Democratic voters concerned the Republican party leadership as they tried to retain control of the White House despite declining popular support for President George W. Bush (43).

The presidential candidates from both parties were not officially chosen until their National Political Conventions. The Democratic Convention was held in Denver, Colorado. At the Democratic Convention, Barack Obama became the Democratic

## Key Themes and Concepts

**Foreign Policy**
- How would the United States and Cuba each benefit from an improved relationship?

## Turning Point

- For what reasons could the election of 2008 be considered a turning point in United States political history?

## Election of 2008

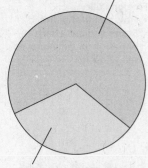

Democrat Barack Obama 68% of electoral vote

Republican John McCain 32% of electoral vote

candidate for president and he selected Senator Joseph Biden of Delaware as his vice presidential running mate. The Republican Convention was held September 1–4, 2008, in Minneapolis, Minnesota. At that time, Senator McCain surprised many people with his choice of Sarah Palin, Governor of Alaska, to be his vice-presidential running mate. While Democratic candidate Biden brought many years of experience in the Senate, including time as Chairman of the Senate Foreign Relations committee, Palin brought executive experience as a state governor to the Republican ticket.

The election results were clear by the evening of Election Day on November 4, 2008. John McCain conceded the election to Barack Obama. The Obama ticket received over 67,000,000 votes to McCain's 58,000,000-plus votes. Ralph Nader took in around 700,000 votes and did not have enough voters to earn one electoral vote. Obama earned 365 electoral votes compared to McCain's 173. The results of the races for the Senate and the House of Representatives also favored the Democrats, and for the first time in a number of years, Democrats controlled both the legislative and executives branches of government.

## The Barack Obama Administration

When President Barack Obama, First Lady Michelle Obama, and their two young daughters moved into the White House following his inauguration on January 20, 2009, they made American history. They were the first African American family to serve in this role. They received encouragement and congratulations from many Americans and many people from foreign nations who looked to the Obama Administration to break with policies of his predecessor, George W. Bush. In the early months of his presidency, President Obama would face a number of serious domestic and foreign issues.

### Domestic Issues

**The Economy** President Obama took office as the United States faced its most serious economic crisis since the Great Depression of the 1930s. The President came into office knowing that an enormous economic stimulus plan would be necessary to solve this crisis. Some major banks had failed and other companies, primarily the massive AIG Insurance company, needed billions of dollars of American taxpayer money, known as "bail out" money to prevent them from collapsing. About $700 billion in what is known as TARP money, or the Troubled Asset Relief Program, was used to help banks that were in danger of failing. The unemployment rate in some parts of the United States was at its highest rate in almost 25 years, between eight and ten percent. Ben Bernanke, the Chairman of the Federal Reserve Board, was called to Capitol Hill several times to explain the policies that the Fed was implementing to remedy the crisis. The President has addressed both Congress and the American public to ask for the support and patience. There has been general support for the President's efforts to keep the three major American automotive companies, General Motors, Ford, and Chrysler, economically afloat. The difference with the money being lent to the auto industry is that it is intended to be paid back to the taxpayers through the government. Other major billion dollar spending plans have received more criticism. A major sticking point with the bailout funds has been the discovery by the White House, Congress, and the public that millions of dollars of taxpayer money went to pay bonuses for executives at failing companies. It is believed that other financial incentives may be required to restore the economic foundations of the United States. Adding to the sense of economic gloom was the revelation of the loss by investors

### Key Themes and Concepts

**Economics**
Adding to the economic crisis of the Obama Administration is the fact that the United States has had a trade deficit for the last two decades. This is a result of the United States importing more than it exports.

of billions of private dollars invested into what was a fraud by a New York City financier, Bernard Madoff. While the troubled economy is the most serious domestic issue facing the him, President Obama has made it clear that he is interested in a number of other issues.

**Health Care** In March 2010 President Obama made history by signing the Health Care Reform Bill. Health care reform had been a major goal of the President and the Democratic Party. They passed the bill with a narrow margin over fierce Republican opposition. The law will be phased in over several years and has provisions to forbid insurance companies to deny health care coverage to applicants, to extend coverage to young adults until they are 26 if living at home and to eventually require all Americans to obtain health care insurance.

*President Barack Obama*

## Other Domestic Issues:

- President Obama visited Washington area schools to stress his interest in educational reform. Millions of dollars of the government stimulus plan is marked for use by the states to improve education.

- Another domestic need that will receive stimulus dollars is the repair of the American infrastructure. High-speed rail lines may be an improvement for New York State, while many states can expect to receive funds to reconstruct crumbling bridges and highways.

- The growing problem of illegal immigration, particularly along the Mexican border, has drawn the president's time and attention.

- One major issue that the Obama administration will face is the Social Security program. The growing number of retiring and aging "baby boomers" has caused concern that funding for Social Security and Medicare, the government medical assistance program, may be inadequate.

## Foreign Issues

President Obama made his first European trip as president in March 2009. One of the major Cabinet appointments that he made early in the formation of his administration was that of his former rival, Hillary Rodham Clinton, to be Secretary of State. This appointment received support in the Senate due to her extensive background and knowledge of foreign affairs. She made official visits to Japan, China, the Middle East, Europe, and Mexico in 2009 and has continued to be a vital part of the Obama administration overseas.

**Wars in Iraq and Afghanistan** President Obama announced plans to "draw down," or to withdraw, troops from Iraq. By August 2010 the U.S. troop strength in Iraq is expected to decrease from 100,000 to 50,000. Simultaneously he said he would increase the number of American troops deployed to Afghanistan by more than 10,000. Although the United States continues to suffer casualties in Iraq, the frequency of those losses has decreased. The crisis in Afghanistan has drawn American attention, as the once-defeated Taliban continued their battle to regain power. There is continuing concern that the Afghan government must be helped in its effort to maintain stability against both the Taliban and terrorist organizations such as al-Qaeda. U.S. troop strength is predicted to increase from 38,000 to 68,000.

**The Middle East** Secretary of State Clinton's trip to the Middle East early in her term indicated that the Obama administration took the issues in the area seriously and desired a peaceful resolution to the problems in the Middle East. Obama and Clinton have both been clear in the American support of Israel against its enemies in the area. By the spring of 2010 tensions grew between Israel and the United States over the expansion of Israeli settlements in border areas.

## Turning Point

In April 2010 President Obama signed a Nuclear Arms Reduction Treaty with Russia. It requires senate approval but if approved, will be the first step in many years taken by nations with nuclear weapons to agree to limit their development.

# Toward a Postindustrial Society: Living in a Global Age

The
**Big
Idea**

Since the end of World War II, the rapid pace of change has turned the world into a "global village." Today:

• technology and growing corporations have helped to increase job growth.

• most people have longer life expectancies, despite diseases such as AIDS.

• population growth and environmental concerns challenge the United States as well as other countries.

## Section Overview

The United States began as a nation of farmers. Today it is one of the leading economic and political powers in the world. Because of the advanced technology of the postindustrial age, the world has become what some call a "global village." Because of increased interdependence, major events in one part of the world have an impact upon the rest of the world.

## Key Themes and Concepts

As you review this section, take special note of the following key themes and concepts:

**Change** What effects do technological change have on American society?

**Places and Regions** How does the United States play a unique role in helping resolve conflicts in other regions of the world?

**Environment** How are concerns about the environment being addressed by activist groups?

**Interdependence** How has the emergence of a global economy strengthened the interdependence of nations?

## Key Terms

| | |
|---|---|
| alternative energy sources | multinational corporations |
| Internet | Earth Day |

## Rapid Pace of Change

Every generation since the Civil War has experienced the effects of the Industrial Revolution. However, the pace of technological change has picked up dramatically since World War II. Today, the United States is moving into a postindustrial age. That is, the American economy no longer rests on the development of new factories and heavy industries, such as the production of steel or coal. Instead, because of technological changes, service-related industries now occupy a larger sector of the economy.

### Technology—What Is It?

Technology is the application of scientific knowledge to commerce and industry. To appreciate the effect of technological change, think of the following situations out of the past.

• George Washington, the nation's first president, never called a member of Congress on the telephone, never rode in a limousine, and never saw his photograph in a newspaper.

• Abraham Lincoln, president during the Civil War, never called generals on the telephone and never listened to battle reports on the radio.

• Franklin Roosevelt, president during World War II, never had a speech transmitted by satellite to Europe and never watched a program on television.

- John F. Kennedy, president in the early 1960s, never wrote a speech on a computer and never ate a snack cooked in a microwave.
- All recent presidents have supported the American space program, but none has yet traveled into space. It is difficult even to imagine the changes that await future presidents.

## The Post-World War II Era

Since the end of World War II, a number of forces have had a great impact upon the economy and upon the lifestyles of Americans.

**Scarce Energy Sources** Scarce oil supplies have led scientists to research **alternative energy sources,** such as solar power and wind power. At the start of the twenty-first century there are already communities in New York State that are utilizing and benefiting from wind power. Other communities in the state as well as nationally are giving serious study to the possibility of developing this natural resource. Nuclear power is being used in some parts of the world. However, the hazards associated with nuclear energy, such as the storage of nuclear waste, have created controversy. The accident at a nuclear power plant at Chernobyl, Ukraine, in 1986 has increased debate even more.

**Use of New Materials** Inventions, such as synthetic plastic, since World War II have replaced wood and steel in many jobs. In some cases, these new materials are lighter and more durable than traditional materials.

**Computer Usage** The prevalent use of computers in American homes and businesses since the 1980s has revolutionized record keeping and the storage of information. Advocates of computers praise their ability to process and store large volumes of information. Critics charge that computers have increased the chances for the invasion of privacy as people access private records without permission, particularly as **Internet** use becomes increasingly widespread. The introduction of automation and computers is considered a cause of job losses in manufacturing industries.

**Security Concerns** The global increase in acts of terrorism, especially the attacks on the Pentagon and the World Trade towers, made some Americans fear that they were not safe. In response, the government took a number of measures. Airport security was tightened, as was security at bridges, tunnels, nuclear power plants, courthouses, and other vulnerable places. The Patriot Act of 2001 gave sweeping new powers to government agencies. To coordinate federal government efforts, the **Homeland Security Act** created a new Cabinet-level department, **Homeland Security.** Its job was to coordinate the efforts of more than 40 federal agencies fighting terror. These agencies include the CIA, FBI, and the National Guard.

In 2002, President Bush and Congress created the independent, bipartisan National Commission on Terrorist Attacks on the United States. After extensive hearings by the Commission, a detailed report was released in the summer of 2004. One of its major recommendations was to unify the United States Intelligence community under the leadership of a new National Intelligence Director. President Bush named John Negroponte, U.S. Ambassador to Iraq, to this position in February 2005. The Commission made a number of other recommendations to improve the security of the United States.

**Growth of Multinational Corporations** Since the 1800s, the organization of American businesses has changed from single ownership and partnerships to corporations. In the post-World War II period, many corporations have become multinational corporations, or businesses with bases of operation in many nations.

**Key Themes and Concepts**

**Change**
The United States faced a rapid pace of change during the Industrial Revolution, but that pace increased dramatically after World War II.

- How did the American economy change after World War II?

**Key Themes and Concepts**

**Science and Technology**
Bill Gates, as founder of Microsoft, became one of the world's richest individuals. Huge fortunes have been made and lost in the computer industry in the last fifteen years. Bill and his wife Melinda administer the charitable Gates Foundation that has given millions of dollars in aid for education and medical research, among other causes.

**Change**
Changes in technology frequently have an impact on the availability of certain jobs. For example, early telephones did not have a dial or push buttons to make a phone call. Instead, a caller placed a call through an operator, who made the phone connections at a switchboard. Once technology improved and direct dialing became available, the need for operators decreased.

• In the 1990s and early 2000s, what impact did technological improvements have on agricultural job opportunities?

How have Americans' lifestyles been influenced by each of the following since the end of World War II?

• average family size

• longer life spans

• expansion of public education

**Analyzing Documents**

Use the chart at right to answer the following questions.

• Between 1994 and 2050, which group of Americans is expected to grow most rapidly?

• Which group of Americans is expected to be a smaller proportion of the U.S. population?

• Which group is expected to remain the same proportion of the overall population?

In the United States during the twentieth century and since the beginning of the twenty-first century, federal prosecutions of corporations such as Standard Oil, AT&T, and Microsoft were based on alleged violations of antitrust laws. There has also been reduced competition in the airline industry, which has ultimately hurt the consumer.

**Job Opportunities** The greatest increases in jobs in the early 2000s promise to be in the service fields. The largest declines will occur in agricultural employment. Technological advances have made it possible for fewer farmers to produce more food, which will continue to reduce the need for agricultural labor.

**New Lifestyles and Longer Life Spans** American attitudes toward family size and divorce have changed since the 1950s. Average family size has declined. After years of expansion, many school districts throughout the nation, including New York's, experienced declining school enrollments in the 1980s. Divorce rates first rose and then remained constant. This created the largest number of single-parent households in the nation's history. At the same time, health-care improvements resulting from new technologies, such as laser surgery and organ transplants, have increased average life spans. This has increased the number of older Americans, who in recent years have organized to protect their rights and improve their lives. Social scientists use the term "the graying of America" to describe the aging of the nation's population.

**Expansion of Public Education** Access to free public education has helped many Americans improve their standard of living. As individuals complete higher levels of education, they have the chance to secure better-paying jobs and more desirable housing. Thus, education helps further social mobility.

**Increasingly Diverse Population** If current trends continue, it is projected that the population of the United States will grow increasingly diverse over the next half century. More of the newest immigrants to the United States come from Asian and Latin American countries, compared with earlier waves of immigration that came from Europe.

**The Changing Ethnic Composition of the United States**

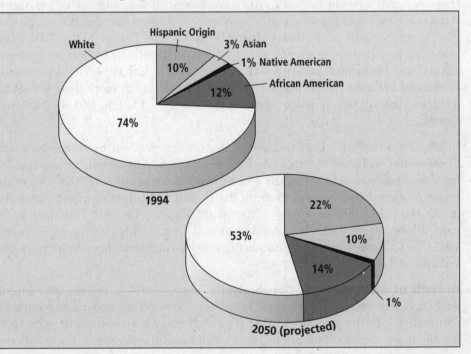

Source: *Statistical Abstract of the United States*

**Dealing With the AIDS Crisis** Since the 1980s, medical researchers have gathered more information about preventing AIDS, or Acquired Immune Deficiency Syndrome. Even so, AIDS has spread through some sectors of the American population at an alarming rate. Without a known cure, scientists and public health officials have tried to increase public awareness and prevention of the disease. Many critics have condemned the federal government for not acting faster to find a cure for AIDS.

**Helping the Homeless** Not everyone enjoyed the prosperity of the post-World War II years. President Johnson's Great Society programs in the 1960s tried to reduce poverty in the United States. However, cuts in social programs during the 1980s caused a significant rise in the number of Americans living below the poverty line. Local communities and private charitable organizations tried to provide relief, but the issue of homelessness has remained a troubling issue.

**Gun Control** The issue of gun control became hotly debated in the late 1990s. Urban violence, as well as a number of highly publicized school shootings, caused millions of Americans to reconsider attitudes toward and the availability of guns in this nation. In May 2000, thousands of American mothers marched in the Million Mom March in Washington, D.C., to focus attention on the need to curb gun violence.

The National Rifle Association continues to be one of the strongest lobbying groups and remains committed to the rights of gun owners. This topic will continue to be a controversial one for years to come. Random gun violence in workplaces, shopping malls, universities, and even health care facilities continues to be a serious problem.

**Right to Life Issues** The United States continues to be a very divided society on the topics of abortion and the right to life/the right to die. In March 2005, President Bush and Congress took unprecedented actions by involving themselves in the case of Terri Schiavo. Schiavo was a terminally ill Florida woman whose right to die had been debated in the Florida courts for many years. Ultimately the decisions of the Florida courts were upheld. This allowed her husband to authorize the removal of a feeding tube which led to her death after a fourteen-year period in which she had been medically determined to be in a persistent vegetative state.

# The United States and Contemporary World Problems

### International Terrorism
Although the attack on New York and Washington, D.C., on September 11, 2001, was aimed at one nation, it mobilized government leaders all over the world. The attacks showed how terrorism has expanded its global reach and has affected the security and stability of all nations.

As the war in Iraq fueled anti-Western attitudes in 2004, terrorists caused almost 200 deaths in a railroad bombing in Spain. Other areas of the world heightened their efforts at limiting the ability of terrorist groups to share information, money, weapons, and personnel.

### Population Growth
Although most developed nations have experienced a decline in their birthrates, the developing nations have an overpopulation problem. Millions of people suffer from malnutrition, living only a marginal existence. Foreign aid from the United States has become of vital economic importance in combating world hunger.

**Preparing for the Exam**

Every ten years since 1790, the United States has conducted a census to count all citizens. In 2010 over 134 million forms have been sent at the cost of over $14,000,000.

• Given the topics on this page and elsewhere in this Unit, what kinds of decisions might the government make based on the statistics it learns from the census?

Interdependence
The concept of a global
community means that
the United States can not
isolate itself from problems
in other countries.
Population growth in
developing nations and
environmental concerns in
nations with essential
ecosystems are two issues
that affect the entire world.

• Why should the
destruction of tropical
rain forests be a concern
to people in other nations,
including the United
States?

Reading
Strategy

Organizing Information
List three ways that environmental activists have raised
public awareness about
environmental issues.

1.

2.

3.

# Environmental Concerns

Because of increased interdependence, an environmental problem in one nation frequently raises global concerns. One example is the destruction of the Brazilian tropical rain forests.

**Environmental Activists** A number of groups have organized to reduce and clean up pollution on the land, in the water, and in the air. Other activist groups work to save endangered species of animals.

Recycling efforts have been organized to reuse paper, glass, plastic, and aluminum. Community organizers have opposed plans to convert vacant lands into dumpsites. Communities have studied the effects of industrial pollution on the groundwater that people drink. In response to public pressure, the federal government has enacted laws requiring automobile manufacturers to put antipollution devices on their cars. Since the first **Earth Day** celebration in 1970, the American people, along with the rest of the world, have begun to realize their obligation to protect the environment for future generations. In 2007, former Vice President Al Gore won a Nobel Peace Prize for his efforts to increase public understanding of issues related to global warming. This followed his widely viewed documentary film, "An Inconvenient Truth," which was about the topic. The phrase "going green" has come to mean the conscious efforts of Americans to conserve energy in all aspects of daily life. Presidents Clinton, Bush (43), and Obama have all directed efforts within the White House itself to increase energy efficiency. Efforts that extend from the First Family to all American families include activities such as recycling, installation of energy efficient light bulbs, the use of solar power where possible, appropriate conservation of heating and cooling sources, and other individual initiatives.

**Natural Disasters** In December 2004, a tsunami, or a giant destructive wave, caused more than 200,000 deaths and left as many as 5,000,000 homeless in parts of Southeast Asia, the Indian subcontinent and East Africa. It was the worst natural disaster in modern history, and the international community joined together in a massive outpouring of financial aid. President Bush committed the United States to $350 million in aid and millions more were donated by Americans directly to private relief agencies. The president also requested his father, former President George H.W. Bush, and former President Bill Clinton to work together to draw attention to the extent of disaster damage in the stricken areas. The two former presidents visited the area and solicited private funds to help in the immediate and long-term needs of the people of the area.

In 2005, unsettled weather patterns continued, and one of the worst hurricane seasons in United States history occurred. In August 2005, Hurricane Katrina caused major flooding in New Orleans, Louisiana, and along the Gulf Coast states of Mississippi and Alabama. About 2,000 people died, thousands of homes were destroyed, and thousands of people were evacuated. Millions of dollars in property damage occurred throughout the area. Businesses, schools, hospitals, hotels, and stores were forced to close, many indefinitely. Media coverage of the hurricane exposed the depth of misery in the area, especially the poverty of large numbers of African Americans. The Bush administration had to defend the slow and inadequate response of the Federal government led by FEMA, the Federal Emergency Management Agency. Shortly after Hurricane Katrina, Hurricane Rita inflicted more damage on the already devasted area and Hurricane Wilma caused major damage in Florida. In November 2007, Congress passed the $23 billion Water Resource Bill, with $3.5 billion specifically earmarked for areas destroyed by Hurricane Katrina. This bill was the first bill passed by Congress after a veto by President Bush (43). In 2007, other natural disasters included tornadoes, snow and ice storms, and high winds that caused over 100 deaths. Wildfires were so extensive in California that at one point over one half million residents were evacuated.

*Flooded neighborhoods in the aftermath of Hurricane Katrina*

In February 2010 Haiti and Chile both experienced major earthquakes. The United States offered aid in both cases. It was especially involved with the disaster in Haiti where there was estimated to be 220,000 deaths and over 1.2 million displaced persons. Haiti has a much lower standard of living and very poor infrastructure as compared to Chile and the damages were felt more severely.

# Questions for Regents Practice

## Multiple Choice

*Directions:* Review the Test-Taking Strategies section of this book. Then answer the following questions, drawn from actual Regents examinations. For each statement or question, choose the *number* of the word or expression that, of those given, best completes the statement or answers the question.

1 The quotations below are from two United States Supreme Court decisions.

I. "Separation of the races does not place a badge of inferiority upon one group over another, thus it is not a violation of the 14th amendment." (1896)

II. "To separate [children in grade school and high school] from others of similar age and qualifications solely because of their race generates a feeling of inferiority as to their status . . . that may affect their hearts and minds in a way unlikely ever to be undone." (1954)

The difference in opinion between these two rulings best shows

(1) a change in judicial philosophy and public attitudes

(2) the persistent efforts of the major political parties to increase equal opportunity

(3) a recognition that democracy depends on economic equality for all citizens

(4) the refusal of the Supreme Court to deal with controversial issues

2 The successful launching of *Sputnik* by the Soviet Union in 1957 signaled the beginning of

(1) American fears that the Soviets had achieved technological superiority

(2) the Cold War with the United States

(3) Soviet aggression in Afghanistan and China

(4) disarmament discussions between the superpowers

3 Which development contributed most to the expansion of suburbs since the 1950s?

(1) construction of interstate highways

(2) invention of the computer

(3) completion of transcontinental railroads

(4) development of jet aircraft

4 When President Dwight D. Eisenhower sent federal troops to Little Rock, Arkansas, during the 1957 school integration crisis, he was exercising his constitutional power as

(1) chief legislator

(2) commander in chief

(3) chief diplomat

(4) head of state

5 Which is a valid conclusion based on United States involvement in the Korean War?

(1) The policy of containment was applied in Asia as well as in Europe.

(2) United Nations economic sanctions are more effective than military action.

(3) The American people will support United States participation in any war, whether declared or undeclared.

(4) United States cooperation with a wartime ally ends when the war ends.

**6** What was the significance of the use of federal marshals to protect African American students in Little Rock, Arkansas, in 1957?

(1) It was the first time martial law had been declared in the United States.

(2) It led to federal takeover of many southern public schools.

(3) It strengthened control of education by state governments.

(4) It showed that the federal government would enforce court decisions on integration.

**7** "We conclude that in the field of public education the doctrine of 'separate but equal' has no place. Separate educational facilities are inherently unequal."

This quotation expresses the Supreme Court decision in the case of

(1) *Plessy* v. *Ferguson*

(2) *Engel* v. *Vitale*

(3) *Tinker* v. *Des Moines Independent Community School District*

(4) *Brown* v. *Board of Education of Topeka, Kansas*

**8** The Supreme Court under Chief Justice Earl Warren had a major impact on the United States in that this Court

(1) became involved in foreign affairs by reviewing the constitutionality of treaties

(2) weakened the judiciary by refusing to deal with controversial issues

(3) supported the idea that states could nullify acts of Congress

(4) followed a policy of judicial activism, leading to broad changes in American society

**9** Segregation in public schools was declared unconstitutional because it violated the

(1) reserved powers provision

(2) due process of law provision

(3) principle of equal protection under the law

(4) principle of a clear and present danger

**10** One similarity between the laws being challenged in the United States Supreme Court cases of *Plessy v. Ferguson* (1896) and *Korematsu v. United States* (1944) is that

(1) specific groups of people were being targeted based on race or ethnicity

(2) state laws were declared unconstitutional

(3) immigrants were relocated to prison camps

(4) federal laws segregating public transportation were upheld

**11** Which list of wars that involved the United States is in the correct chronological order?

(1) Vietnam War → War on Terrorism → Korean War → World War II

(2) Korean War → World War II → Vietnam War → War on Terrorism

(3) World War II → Vietnam War → War on Terrorism → Korean War

(4) World War II → Korean War → Vietnam War → War on Terrorism

**12** The women's movement was strengthened in the 1960s chiefly because

(1) women became increasingly dissatisfied with their status and their roles in society

(2) women were angered by the failure of the voters to elect them to Congress

(3) job discrimination against women and minorities was eliminated

(4) the radical liberation movements of the 1950s had failed

13 "And so my fellow Americans—ask not what your country can do for you—ask what you can do for your country."

When President John F. Kennedy made this statement, he was encouraging the American people to develop

(1) a personal commitment to work for national ideals

(2) an awareness of environmental hazards

(3) a concern for national defense

(4) an appreciation for the contributions of immigrants to American society

14 Which statement about the Cuban missile crisis (1962) is most accurate?

(1) The crisis showed that the United States and the Soviet Union could agree on total disarmament.

(2) The crisis brought the two major world powers very close to war.

(3) The United States wanted to establish missile sites in Cuban territory.

(4) The Communist government in Cuba was overthrown.

15 President Lyndon B. Johnson's Great Society was an effort to solve the problem of

(1) poverty

(2) drug trafficking

(3) overpopulation

(4) illegal immigration

16 One similarity between the actions of Presidents Franklin D. Roosevelt and Lyndon B. Johnson is that both

(1) led the United States to victory in war

(2) expanded the role of government in citizens' lives

(3) vetoed legislation on the issue of rights for minorities

(4) achieved a balanced federal budget during their terms in office

17 "Four Students Killed at Kent State University"

"Gulf of Tonkin Resolution Passed"

"Radical Protesters Disrupt Democratic Convention in Chicago"

These headlines relate to which event in United States history?

(1) Civil War

(2) World War II

(3) Vietnam War

(4) Persian Gulf War

18 During the Vietnam War, serious questions were raised in the United States concerning the

(1) authority of the Supreme Court in regard to national security

(2) extent of the President's powers as commander in chief

(3) loyalty of United States military leaders

(4) role of the North Atlantic Treaty Organization (NATO) in international peacekeeping

19 A major long-term effect of the Vietnam War has been

(1) an end to Communist governments in Asia

(2) a change in United States foreign policy from containment to imperialism

(3) a reluctance to commit United States troops for extended military action abroad

(4) a continued boycott of trade with Asia

20 The outcome of the Watergate scandal reinforced the principle that

(1) national security takes precedence over freedom of the press

(2) the power of executive privilege is greater than the rule of law

(3) the law applies equally to all citizens, including government officials

(4) impeached government officials are immune from criminal prosecution

21 The Camp David accords promoted by President Jimmy Carter were significant because they represented

(1) the first peace agreement between Israel and an Arab nation

(2) the establishment of a worldwide human rights policy

(3) a lasting arms-reduction treaty

(4) the end of the Vietnam War

22 The "trickle down" economic theory of President Herbert Hoover and the "supply side" economic policies under President Ronald Reagan were based on the idea that

(1) balanced budgets are essential to economic success

(2) the federal government needs to assume more responsibility for solving economic problems

(3) economic growth depends on making increased amounts of capital available to businesses

(4) economic stability is the responsibility of federal monetary agencies

23 The North American Free Trade Agreement (NAFTA) between the United States, Mexico, and Canada is meant to

(1) increase commerce and eliminate tariffs

(2) encourage lower labor costs

(3) raise environmental standards

(4) allow citizens to move freely from one nation to another

24 **"Clinton Offers Economic Aid to Russia"**

**"U.S. Sends Peacekeeping Troops to Bosnia"**

**"U.S. Airlifts Food and Medicine to Somalia"**

These headlines illustrate that United States foreign policy during the 1990s stressed

(1) containment

(2) collective security

(3) global involvement

(4) neutrality

25 How does the present-day United States economy differ from the nation's economy in 1900?

(1) Immigrants are no longer a source of labor.

(2) Today's government plays a less active role in the economy.

(3) The United States is less dependent on oil imports.

(4) The growth of service industries is greater today.

# Thematic Essay Question

*Directions:*  Write a well-organized essay that includes an introduction, several paragraphs addressing the task below, and a conclusion.

**Theme:**   **Technological Change**

> Many aspects of United States society have been greatly affected by technological changes.

**Task:**

> Identify *three* aspects of United States society that have been affected by technological change since the beginning of the twentieth century, and for *each*
>
> - Explain how that aspect was affected by a specific technological change
> - Discuss the extent to which the impact of the change was positive or negative

You may use any example from your study of the United States in the twentieth century. Some suggestions you might wish to consider include: environment, politics, agriculture, urbanization, individual rights, or cultural pluralism.

**You are *not* limited to these suggestions.**

**Guidelines:**

**In your essay, be sure to**
- Develop all aspects of the task
- Support the theme with relevant facts, examples, and details
- Use a logical and clear plan of organization, including an introduction and a conclusion that are beyond a simple restatement of the theme

**In developing your answer, be sure to keep these general definitions in mind:**

    (a)  <u>explain</u> **means "to make plain or clear; render understandable or intelligible"**

    (b)  <u>discuss</u> **means "to make observations about something using facts, reasoning, and argument; to present in some detail"**

# Document-Based Question

In developing your answers, be sure to keep this general definition in mind:

>   discuss means "to make observations about something using facts, reasoning, and argument; to present in some detail"

This question is based on the accompanying documents. The question is designed to test your ability to work with historical documents. Some of these documents have been edited for the purposes of this question. As you analyze the documents, take into account the source of each document and any point of view that may be presented in the document.

Historical Context:

>   The Preamble to the United States Constitution reads: "We the people of the United States, in order to form a more perfect union, establish justice, insure domestic tranquility, provide for the common defense, promote the general welfare, and secure the blessings of liberty to ourselves and our posterity, do ordain and establish this Constitution for the United States.

Task:   Using the information from the documents and your knowledge of United States history and government, answer the questions that follow each document in Part A. Your answers to the questions will help you write the Part B essay, in which you will be asked to

>   • Discuss whether the American government, since 1950, has achieved the goals for our nation established in the Preamble to the United States Constitution.

# Document-Based Question

Part A: Short Answer

## Document #1

### Selected Events in African American Civil Rights History (1950s–1960s)

| | |
|---|---|
| **1954** Supreme Court rules in *Brown* v. *Board of Education of Topeka, Kansas* | **1960** Sit-ins by African Americans begin at "whites only" lunch counters |
| **1964** Riots by African Americans occur over discrimination in housing, education, and employment | **1965** President Lyndon B. Johnson signs the Voting Rights Act of 1965 |

| 1950 | 1952 | 1954 | 1956 | 1958 | 1960 | 1962 | 1964 | 1966 | 1968 |
|---|---|---|---|---|---|---|---|---|---|

**1955–56** The actions of Rosa Parks inspire the Montgomery, Alabama bus boycott, resulting in a Supreme Court ruling

**1963** Dr. Martin Luther King Jr. delivers his "I have a dream" speech

**1968** Dr. Martin Luther King Jr. is assassinated

1. What do the events in the time line suggest about the process of achieving "the blessings of liberty" for African Americans during the 1950s and 1960s?

_____

_____

_____

_____

## Document #2

> "One thing became clear: that in the black movement I had been fighting for someone else's oppression, and now there was a way that I could fight for my own freedom, and I was going to be much stronger than I ever was."
>
> —**Cathy Cade, women's rights activist**

2. What experience motivated Cathy Cade to work for the delivery of the "blessings of liberty" to women?

_____

_____

_____

_____

### Document #3

### Selected Great Society Legislation, 1964–1966

| Legislation | Purpose |
|---|---|
| Economic Opportunity Act, 1964 | Created to combat causes of poverty, such as illiteracy and unemployment |
| Volunteers in Service to America (VISTA), 1964 | Sent volunteers to help people in poor communities and set up community action programs to give the poor a voice in defining local housing, health, and education policies |
| Medicare, 1965 | Provided hospital and low-cost medical insurance for most Americans aged 65 and older |
| Medicaid, 1965 | Provided low-cost health insurance for low-income Americans of any age who could not afford private health insurance |
| Elementary and Secondary Education Act of 1965 | Provided education aid to states based on the number of children from low-income households |
| Department of Housing and Urban Development (HUD), 1965 | Established to oversee the nation's housing needs and to develop and rehabilitate urban communities. HUD also provided money for rent subsidies and low-income housing. |
| Water Quality Act, 1965 Clean Water Restoration Act, 1965 | Established water and air quality standards and provided funding for environmental research |
| National Traffic and Motor Vehicle Safety Act, 1966 | Established safety standards for all vehicles to protect consumers. |

3. How did Lyndon Johnson's Great Society "promote the general welfare"?

_____

_____

_____

_____

# Document-Based Question

Document #4

4. What opinion does this cartoon express about how the American government should "provide for the common defense"?

_____

_____

_____

_____

## Document #5

> *"Nixon acts as if the kids had it coming. But shooting into a crowd of students, that is violence. They say it could happen again if the [National] Guard is threatened. They consider stones threat enough to kill children. I think the violence comes from the government."*
>
> **—Mother of Jeffrey Glenn Miller,
> a student killed at Kent State University, quoted in *Life* magazine, May 15, 1970**

5. What opinion did this speaker have about the actions of the National Guard at Kent State University?

_____

_____

_____

_____

6. Who did this speaker blame for the events at Kent State?

_____

_____

_____

_____

## Document #6

> *"He told me they didn't fire those shots to scare the students off. He told me they fired those shots because they knew the students were coming after them, coming for their guns. People are calling my husband a murderer; my husband is not a murderer. He was afraid."*
>
> **—Wife of a member of the National Guard, quoted in *Newsweek* magazine, May 18, 1970**

7. What opinion did this speaker have about the actions of the National Guard at Kent State University?

_____

_____

_____

# Document-Based Question

## Part B

### Essay

*Directions:* Write a well-organized essay that includes an introduction, several paragraphs, and a conclusion. Use evidence from *at least four* of the documents in your essay. Support your response with relevant facts, examples, and details. Include additional outside information.

**Historical Context:**

The Preamble to the United States Constitution reads: "We the people of the United States, in order to form a more perfect union, establish justice, insure domestic tranquility, provide for the common defense, promote the general welfare, and secure the blessings of liberty to ourselves and our posterity, do ordain and establish this Constitution for the United States."

**Task:** Using the information from the documents and your knowledge of United States history and government, write an essay in which you

> • Discuss whether the American government, since 1950, has achieved the goals established for our nation in the Preamble to the United States Constitution

**Guidelines:**

**In your essay, be sure to**
- Develop all aspects of the task
- Incorporate information from *at least four* of the documents
- Incorporate relevant outside information
- Support the theme with relevant facts, examples, and details
- Use a logical and clear plan of organization, including an introduction and a conclusion that are beyond a restatement of the theme

# Presidents of the United States

| | |
|---|---|
| **George Washington**<br>**(1732–1799)**<br><br>*Years in office: 1789–1797*<br>*Federalist*<br>*Vice President: John Adams* | • Commanded the Continental army during the American Revolution<br>• President of the Constitutional Convention<br>• Set precedents that were followed by other presidents, such as forming a cabinet<br>• Strengthened new government through support of Hamilton's financial policies and use of force against the Whiskey Rebellion<br>• Kept peace through Proclamation of Neutrality and Jay Treaty<br>• Set basis of U.S. foreign policy in his Farewell Address |
| **John Adams**<br>**(1735–1826)**<br><br>*Years in office: 1797–1801*<br>*Federalist*<br>*Vice President: Thomas Jefferson* | • American Revolution leader who protested Stamp Act<br>• Helped draft Declaration of Independence<br>• President during times of war in Europe<br>• Alien and Sedition Acts contributed to his unpopularity and the fall of his party |
| **Thomas Jefferson**<br>**(1743–1826)**<br><br>*Years in office: 1801–1809*<br>*Democratic-Republican*<br>*Vice President: Aaron Burr,*<br>*George Clinton* | • Major author of the Declaration of Independence<br>• Opposed Federalists<br>• Favored limited, decentralized government<br>• Opposed Hamilton's financial plan and Alien and Sedition Acts<br>• Negotiated the Louisiana Purchase from France, which doubled the size of the nation |
| **James Madison**<br>**(1751–1836)**<br><br>*Years in office: 1809–1817*<br>*Democratic-Republican*<br>*Vice President: George Clinton,*<br>*Elbridge Gerry* | • Called the "Father of the Constitution"<br>• One author of the Virginia Plan; his journals provide a record of events at the Constitutional Convention<br>• Wrote 29 of *The Federalist Papers*<br>• Proposed the Bill of Rights to Congress<br>• Gained popularity after the War of 1812 |
| **James Monroe**<br>**(1758–1831)**<br><br>*Years in office: 1817–1825*<br>*Democratic-Republican*<br>*Vice President: Daniel Tompkins* | • Established U.S. foreign policy in the Western Hemisphere with the Monroe Doctrine<br>• Settled boundaries with Canada (1818)<br>• Acquired Florida (1819)<br>• President during this "Era of Good Feelings"<br>• Supported and signed Missouri Compromise (1820) |
| **John Quincy Adams**<br>**(1767–1848)**<br><br>*Years in office: 1825–1829*<br>*Democratic-Republican*<br>*Vice President: John Calhoun* | • Became president after election was decided in the House of Representatives<br>• Secretary of State under James Monroe<br>• After leaving office as president, served in House of Representatives; only president to do so |

| | |
|---|---|
| **Andrew Jackson**<br>**(1767–1845)**<br><br>*Years in office: 1829–1837*<br>*Democrat*<br>*Vice President: John Calhoun,*<br>*Martin Van Buren* | • Hero of Battle of New Orleans (War of 1812)<br>• Opposed Calhoun and nullification of 1828 tariff<br>• Vetoed rechartering of Second National Bank<br>• Supported Native American removal policy<br>• Associated with Jacksonian Democracy—the start of mass politics and nominating conventions<br>• Used "spoils system" to give jobs to supporters |
| **Martin Van Buren**<br>**(1782–1862)**<br><br>*Years in office: 1837–1841*<br>*Democrat*<br>*Vice President: Richard Johnson* | • First New Yorker to become president<br>• Served as vice president to Jackson<br>• Opposed Texas annexation because slavery issue divided his party<br>• Presidency weakened by economic crisis of the Panic of 1837<br>• Had major role in creating the Democratic Party from the Democratic-Republicans and the nation's second party system—the Democrats versus the Whigs |
| **William Henry Harrison**<br>**(1774–1841)**<br><br>*Years in office: 1841*<br>*Whig*<br>*Vice President: John Tyler* | • While governor of Indiana Territory, led military actions against Native Americans in the Battle of Tippecanoe (1811)<br>• Elected as first Whig candidate on the slogan "Tippecanoe and Tyler Too"<br>• First president to die in office; served only one month |
| **John Tyler**<br>**(1790–1862)**<br><br>*Years in office: 1841–1845*<br>*Whig*<br>*Vice President: none* | • First vice president to come into presidency on death of president, called "His Accidency"<br>• Texas annexed by congressional vote largely because of his influence<br>• His pro South and pro states rights positions resulted in his expulsion from the Whig Party by its pro nationalism leaders |
| **James K. Polk**<br>**(1795–1849)**<br><br>*Years in office: 1845–1849*<br>*Democrat*<br>*Vice President: George Dallas* | • Foreign policy aimed at fulfilling goal of Manifest Destiny<br>• With slogan "54' 40 or fight!" campaigned for all of Oregon country, settled for Oregon Treaty (1846) with Great Britain, dividing region at $49^{th}$ parallel<br>• Supported Tyler's annexation of Texas and favored acquisition of California<br>• Led nation in Mexican War, 1846–1848<br>• The Treaty of Guadalupe Hidalgo gave the United States the Mexican Cession, which included California |
| **Zachary Taylor**<br>**(1784–1850)**<br><br>*Years in office: 1849–1850*<br>*Whig*<br>*Vice President: Millard Fillmore* | • West Point graduate and military hero of Mexican War, known as "Old Rough and Ready"<br>• A Virginian, a slave owner, and a nationalist—he opposed secession<br>• Died in office after 16 months as president |
| **Millard Fillmore**<br>**(1800–1874)**<br><br>*Years in office: 1850–1853*<br>*Whig*<br>*Vice President: none* | • New Yorker by birth, became president on death of Taylor<br>• Negotiated passage of the Compromise of 1850<br>• Supported enforcement of the Fugitive Slave Law and opposed secessionists angering both Northerners and Southerners<br>• Failure of Compromise of 1850 marked end for Whig Party<br>• In 1856, lost as presidential candidate of the Know-Nothing Party |
| **Franklin Pierce**<br>**(1804–1869)**<br><br>*Years in office: 1853–1857*<br>*Democrat*<br>*Vice President: William King* | • New Englander who supported Kansas-Nebraska Act<br>• Gadsden Purchase ratified during his presidency<br>• Trade treaty with Japan became effective during his administration, due to the efforts of Commodore Matthew Perry |

| | |
|---|---|
| **James Buchanan**<br>**(1791–1868)**<br><br>*Years in office: 1857–1861*<br>*Democrat*<br>*Vice President: John Breckinridge* | • In office when *Dred Scott* v. *Sanford* decision was issued and John Brown's raid at Harper's Ferry occurred<br>• Took no action in response to the secession of South Carolina and six other states, claiming he lacked the power to act |
| **Abraham Lincoln**<br>**(1809–1865)**<br><br>*Years in office: 1861–1865*<br>*Republican*<br>*Vice President: Hannibal Hamlin,*<br>*Andrew Johnson* | • Became nationally known as result of Lincoln-Douglas debates in 1858<br>• First Republican to be elected president<br>• Used war powers of the presidency during Civil War to achieve his goal of preserving the nation<br>• Issued Emancipation Proclamation; gave Gettsyburg Address<br>• Assassinated before he could act on his plans for reconstruction |
| **Andrew Johnson**<br>**(1808–1875)**<br><br>*Years in office: 1865–1869*<br>*Democrat*<br>*Vice President: none* | • Impeached by House after bitter disagreements with Congress over Reconstruction; acquitted by a single vote in Senate<br>• Thirteenth and Fourteenth Amendments ratified during his presidency |
| **Ulysses S. Grant**<br>**(1822–1885)**<br><br>*Years in office: 1869–1877*<br>*Republican*<br>*Vice President: Schuyler Colfax,*<br>*Henry Wilson* | • Civil War military leader who served as General-in-Chief of the Union army<br>• Transcontinental railroad completed and Fifteenth Amendment ratified during his presidency<br>• Crédit Mobilier and the Whiskey Ring scandals marred his presidency |
| **Rutherford B. Hayes**<br>**(1822–1893)**<br><br>*Years in office: 1877–1881*<br>*Republican*<br>*Vice President: William Wheeler* | • Election decided through compromise, preventing a constitutional crisis after a dispute over electoral votes<br>• Federal troops removed from the South, marking the end of Reconstruction |
| **James A. Garfield**<br>**(1831–1881)**<br><br>*Years in office: 1881*<br>*Republican*<br>*Vice President: Chester A. Arthur* | • Assassinated after four months in office |
| **Chester A. Arthur**<br>**(1830–1886)**<br><br>*Years in office: 1881–1885*<br>*Republican*<br>*Vice President: none* | • Vetoed Chinese Exclusion Act (1882) but signed another act reducing the Chinese immigration ban to ten years<br>• Supported Pendleton Act (1883) that enacted civil service reform<br>• Worked to reform American restrictive tariffs |
| **Grover Cleveland**<br>**(1837–1908)**<br><br>*Years in office: 1885–1889;*<br>*1893–1897*<br>*Democrat*<br>*Vice President: Thomas*<br>*Hendricks, Adlai Stevenson* | • Expanded the civil service<br>• Only president to serve two nonconsecutive terms<br>• Served as governor of New York<br>• In second term confronted major depression that began with Panic of 1893<br>• An anti-imperialist, he opposed annexation of Hawaii<br>• In 1894, sent federal troops to end Pullman Strike |

| | |
|---|---|
| **Benjamin Harrison** (1833–1901)<br><br>*Years in office: 1889–1893*<br>*Republican*<br>*Vice President: Levi Morton* | • Elected president with most electoral but not popular votes<br>• Supported Sherman Antitrust Act<br>• Encouraged conservation of forest reserves<br>• Favored U.S. expansion in the Pacific Ocean and building of a canal in Central America<br>• Expanded U.S. Navy |
| **William McKinley** (1843–1901)<br><br>*Years in office: 1897–1901*<br>*Republican*<br>*Vice President: Garret Hobart,*<br>*Theodore Roosevelt* | • President during a period of expansionism marked by Spanish-American War<br>• A high tariff and the Gold Standard Act passed during his administration<br>• Annexed Hawaii<br>• Open Door Policy issued by his secretary of state<br>• Assassinated in 1901 |
| **Theodore Roosevelt** (1858–1919)<br><br>*Years in office: 1901–1909*<br>*Republican*<br>*Vice President: Charles Fairbanks* | • Progressive governor of New York (1899–1900)<br>• Presidential programs called the Square Deal<br>• Known as a trustbuster, conservationist, reformer, and nationalist<br>• Used the power of presidency to regulate economic affairs of the nation and to expand its role in Asia and the Caribbean<br>• Issued the Roosevelt Corollary to the Monroe Doctrine |
| **William Howard Taft** (1857–1903)<br><br>*Years in office: 1909–1913*<br>*Republican*<br>*Vice President: James Sherman* | • Policy of "dollar diplomacy" gave diplomatic and military support to U.S. business investments in Latin America<br>• Continued Progressive Era policies of business regulation, but his conservative tariff and conservation policies split the party |
| **Woodrow Wilson** (1856–1924)<br><br>*Years in office: 1913–1921*<br>*Democrat*<br>*Vice President: Thomas Marshall* | • Progressive Era president whose program was known as New Freedom<br>• Reform regulation included Clayton Antitrust Act, Federal Reserve System, Federal Trade Commission Act, and Underwood Tariff Act (which lowered rates)<br>• Led the nation during World War I<br>• Supported the Treaty of Versailles and League of Nations, which the Senate failed to approve |
| **Warren G. Harding** (1865–1923)<br><br>*Years in office: 1921–1923*<br>*Republican*<br>*Vice President: Calvin Coolidge* | • Led nation into "Roaring Twenties" on a call for "normalcy"<br>• Administration known for corruption and scandals, including the Teapot Dome Scandal<br>• Opened Washington Conference on Naval Disarmament in 1921, although he opposed internationalism |
| **Calvin Coolidge** (1872–1933)<br><br>*Years in office: 1923–1929*<br>*Republican*<br>*Vice President: Charles Dawes* | • Presidency marked by conservative, laissez-faire attitudes toward business<br>• Presided over "Coolidge prosperity"<br>• Kellogg-Briand Pact signed during his administration<br>• Immigration Act (1924), setting national quotas, passed during his presidency |
| **Herbert Hoover** (1874–1964)<br><br>*Years in office: 1929–1933*<br>*Republican*<br>*Vice President: Charles Curtis* | • Used government resources against the Great Depression without success<br>• Supported loans through Reconstruction Finance Corporation<br>• Opposed direct relief<br>• Used federal troops against the World War I veterans' "Bonus Army" |

| | |
|---|---|
| **Franklin D. Roosevelt**<br>**(1882–1945)**<br><br>*Years in office: 1933–1945*<br>*Democrat*<br>*Vice President: John Garner,*<br>*Henry Wallace, Harry S. Truman* | • New Deal policies and leadership in World War II increased the power of the federal government<br>• Tried to expand number of Supreme Court justices when the Court opposed New Deal programs<br>• Pushed for social welfare legislation, such as the Social Security Act<br>• New Deal programs criticized as both inadequate and too extreme<br>• Urged cooperation in Western Hemisphere under the Good Neighbor Policy<br>• Supported Japanese American internment during World War II<br>• Only president to serve more than two terms |
| **Harry S. Truman**<br>**(1884–1972)**<br><br>*Years in office: 1945–1953*<br>*Democrat*<br>*Vice President: Alben Barkley* | • Made decision to drop two atomic bombs on Japan in 1945 to end World War II<br>• Began the policy of containment of communism with the Truman Doctrine<br>• Supported economic recovery in Europe through the Marshall Plan<br>• Continued the New Deal philosophy with his Fair Deal<br>• Entered the Korean War during his presidency |
| **Dwight D. Eisenhower**<br>**(1890–1969)**<br><br>*Years in office: 1953–1961*<br>*Republican*<br>*Vice President: Richard M. Nixon* | • Commander of Allied forces in Europe during World War II<br>• Issued Eisenhower Doctrine<br>• Approved Saint Lawrence Seaway and 1956 Federal Highway Act<br>• Sent troops to Little Rock, Arkansas, to support school desegregation<br>• In office when Alaska and Hawaii became 49th and 50th states |
| **John F. Kennedy**<br>**(1917–1963)**<br><br>*Years in office: 1961–1963*<br>*Democrat*<br>*Vice President: Lyndon B. Johnson* | • Promoted the New Frontier program (which centered on containment), the Peace Corps, and the Alliance for Progress<br>• Successfully resolved the Cuban missile crisis<br>• Assassinated in 1963 |
| **Lyndon B. Johnson**<br>**(1908–1973)**<br><br>*Years in office: 1963–1969*<br>*Democrat*<br>*Vice President: Hubert Humphrey* | • Promoted antipoverty programs and civil rights through his Great Society program<br>• Used the Gulf of Tonkin Resolution to expand the Vietnam War<br>• Division over his war policy led to his decision not to seek reelection<br>• President during a period of active civil rights movements for African Americans and women |
| **Richard M. Nixon**<br>**(1913–1994)**<br><br>*Years in office: 1969–1974*<br>*Republican*<br>*Vice President: Spiro Agnew,*<br>*Gerald R. Ford* | • Pursued a "Vietnamization" policy and increased bombing followed by a 1973 cease-fire in Vietnam<br>• Relaxed relations with USSR and the People's Republic of China<br>• Resigned as president because of Watergate affair |
| **Gerald R. Ford**<br>**(1913–2006)**<br><br>*Years in office: 1974–1977*<br>*Republican*<br>*Vice President: Nelson Rockefeller* | • Only president not to be elected by the American public; appointed as vice president under Nixon and succeeded to the presidency after Nixon's resignation<br>• Pardoned Nixon, for which he was both criticized and praised<br>• Worked to restore faith in government after Watergate crisis |

| | |
|---|---|
| **Jimmy Carter** (1924–   )<br><br>*Years in office: 1977–1981*<br>*Democrat*<br>*Vice President: Walter Mondale* | • Domestic problems included inflation and oil shortages<br>• Supported international human rights and Panama Canal treaties<br>• Opposed the Soviet invasion of Afghanistan<br>• Greatest success was the Camp David Accords, which led to peace between Egypt and Israel |
| **Ronald Reagan** (1911–2004)<br><br>*Years in office: 1981–1989*<br>*Republican*<br>*Vice President:*<br>*George H.W. Bush* | • Took a conservative viewpoint on social issues, such as abortion and prayer in school<br>• Based his supply-side economic policy (or "Reaganomics") on the belief that government works against individual initiative<br>• Presidency marked by trade and federal budget deficits<br>• Arms control agreements signed with the USSR in 1985, 1986, and 1987<br>• Foreign policy aimed at keeping communism out of Latin America<br>• Popularity damaged and foreign policy weakened by Iran-Contra scandal |
| **George H.W. Bush** (1924–   )<br><br>*Years in office: 1989–1993*<br>*Republican*<br>*Vice President:*<br>*J. Danforth Quayle* | • Inherited budget deficit, savings and loan scandal, and legacy of Iran-Contra Affair from the Reagan administration<br>• In office when Cold War ended, and communist governments in Eastern Europe and Soviet Union fell<br>• Led the United States in the Persian Gulf War against Iraq |
| **William (Bill) Clinton** (1946–   )<br><br>*Years in office: 1993–2001*<br>*Democrat*<br>*Vice President: Albert Gore, Jr.* | • Domestic policies centered on health care and social security reform, as well as economic issues, such as reduction of the national deficit<br>• Secured approval of NAFTA (North American Free Trade Agreement)<br>• Backed NATO intervention against Serbia to stop "ethnic cleansing"<br>• Impeached by the House of Representatives in 1998 on charges of perjury and obstruction of justice, but acquitted by the Senate |
| **George W. Bush** (1946–   )<br><br>*Years in office: 2001–2009*<br>*Republican*<br>*Vice President:*<br>*Richard (Dick) B. Cheney* | • Took office after a close election in which a dispute over ballot recounts in Florida was decided by the Supreme Court in *Bush* v. *Gore* (2000)<br>• Conservative domestic agenda included tax cuts, No Child Left Behind, creation of Department of Homeland Security, and attempts to privatize social security<br>• After attacks of September 11, 2001, declared war on international terrorism and ordered U.S. forces into Afghanistan to defeat Taliban and al Qaeda extremists<br>• Led the United States into a war against Iraq<br>• Left office with historically low approval ratings, nation in major recession, and controversy that included Iraq War, treatment of prisoners, conduct of Justice Department, and balancing of liberty versus security in a democracy |
| **Barack H. Obama** (1961–     )<br><br>*Years in office: 2009–*<br>*Democrat*<br>*Vice President:*<br>*Joseph (Joe) R. Biden, Jr.* | • First African American to be elected president<br>• Took office facing a major economic crisis that included high unemployment, collapsing housing market, falling stock market, rising health care costs, and banks and auto companies facing insolvency<br>• Began draw down of U.S. troops in Iraq while increasing troop levels in Afghanistan<br>• Appointed first Hispanic, Justice Sonia Sotomayor, to U.S. Supreme Court<br>• Major legislation passed included Patient Protection and Affordable Health Care Act and American Recovery and Reinvestment Act |

# Landmark Supreme Court Cases

Every Supreme Court case deals with important **constitutional principles.**
Some cases have had such an enduring impact on United States history
and government that they require greater examination. The lasting
significance and central constitutional principles of 32 landmark
Supreme Court cases are outlined briefly in this section. For more
information about the meaning of the constitutional principles, review
Unit 2, Section 1, Part 4.

| Year | Name of Case | Constitutional Principle | Why Decision is Important |
|------|--------------|--------------------------|---------------------------|
| 1803 | *Marbury* v. *Madison* | • Separation of Powers: Checks and Balances<br>• The Judiciary | • Established the Supreme Court's right of *judicial review*—the right to determine the constitutionality of laws<br>• Strengthened the judiciary in relation to other branches of government |
| 1819 | *McCulloch* v. *Maryland* | • Federalism: Federal Supremacy<br>• National Power: *Necessary and Proper Clause*<br>• the Judiciary | • Said no state could tax a federally chartered bank because *the power to tax involves the power to destroy*<br>• Ruling established the principle of national supremacy—that the Constitution and federal laws overrule state laws when the two conflict<br>• Expanded national power by supporting use of *necessary and proper* clause to carry out constitutional powers |
| 1824 | *Gibbons* v. *Ogden* | • Federalism: Federal Supremacy<br>• Property Rights/ Economic Policy: Interstate Commerce<br>• the Judiciary | • States may regulate only what is solely intrastate commerce (within a state)<br>• Congress has power to regulate interstate commerce, including commerce that involved intrastate-interstate activity<br>• Ruling established the basis of congressional regulation of interstate commerce |
| 1832 | *Worchester* v. *Georgia* | • Federalism<br>• National Power<br>• Separation of Powers<br>• Equality<br>• Rights of Ethnic/ Racial Groups | • The Constitution gives the federal, not state governments, exclusive jurisdiction over Native American nations<br>• Treaties between the United States government and Native American nations are the *Supreme Law of the Land*<br>• Therefore, Georgia laws taking jurisdiction of Cherokee people and land were void<br>• President Andrew Jackson defied the ruling and the national policy of Indian Removal followed |

| Year | Name of Case | Constitutional Principle | Why Decision is Important |
|------|--------------|--------------------------|---------------------------|
| 1857 | *Dred Scott* v. *Sanford* | • the Judiciary<br>• Equality<br>• Civil Liberties<br>• Rights of Ethnic/ Racial Groups | • Ruled that African Americans were not citizens (overturned by 14<sup>th</sup> Amendment)<br>• Declared that enslaved people were property of owners<br>• As property, protected by 5<sup>th</sup> amendment, enslaved people could be taken anywhere; therefore, Missouri Compromise was unconstitutional |
| 1883 | *Civil Rights Cases* | • Equality<br>• National Power: Congress<br>• Rights of Ethnic/ Racial Groups: 13<sup>th</sup> and 14<sup>th</sup> Amendments | • Declared 1875 Civil Rights Act unconstitutional<br>• 14<sup>th</sup> Amendment prohibited states from discrimination, not individual actions in the private sector such as in theaters, hotels, and restaurants<br>• Private discrimination was not a violation of the 13<sup>th</sup> Amendment, prohibition against slavery and *involuntary servitude* |
| 1886 | *Wabash, St. Louis & Pacific RR* v. *Illinois* | • Property Rights/ Economic Policy: Interstate Commerce<br>• National Power<br>• Federalism | • Invalidated state law setting railroad rates on the part of an interstate trip within state borders<br>• By declaring it a federal power to regulate rates and by limiting state regulations, Court strengthened Constitution's interstate commerce clause<br>• Ruling paved way for creation in 1887 of Interstate Commerce Commission |
| 1895 | *United States* v. *E.C. Knight Co.* | • National Power: Anti-Trust<br>• the Judiciary<br>• Federalism<br>• Property Rights/ Economic Policy: Interstate Commerce | • While federal government did have the right to regulate some parts of economy, states, under the 10<sup>th</sup> Amendment, could regulate intrastate economic activities such as manufacturing<br>• Refineries were *manufacturing operations*, not commerce; therefore, the Sherman Anti-Trust Act could not be applied to American Sugar Refining Co. although company controlled 90% of sugar processing in the nation |
| 1895 | *In Re Debs* | • National Power: Commerce Clause<br>• Property Rights/ Economic Policy: Commerce Clause and Labor | • Ruled that federal government under commerce clause of Constitution had right to halt 1894 Pullman strike<br>• Said strike hurt *general welfare* of nation by disrupting commerce and mail delivery |

| Year | Name of Case | Constitutional Principle | Why Decision is Important |
|------|--------------|--------------------------|----------------------------|
| 1896 | *Plessy* v. *Ferguson* | • Equality<br>• Rights of Ethnic/Racial Groups 14th Amendment Equal Protection Clause<br>• the Judiciary | • Upheld Louisiana law providing for *equal but separate accommodations for white and colored races*<br>• Said law did not conflict with 13th or 14th Amendments, nor with commerce clause<br>• 14th Amendment was not intended to enforce what Court called *social equality*<br>• Provided legal justification for *separate but equal* segregation policy until overturned in 1954 by *Brown* v. *Board of Education* |
| 1904 | *Northern Securities Co.* v. *United States* | • National Power: Anti-Trust, Commerce Clause<br>• Property Rights/Economic Policy | • Federal suit (part of T. Roosevelt's trust-busting) using Sherman Antitrust Act<br>• Court ruled that the Northern Securities Company was formed only to eliminate competition and ordered it to be dissolved<br>• Congress under commerce clause had authority to regulate any *conspiracy* to eliminate competition |
| 1905 | *Lochner* v. *New York* | • Property Rights/Economic Policy: Contracts<br>• Civil Liberties: 14th Amendment | • Ruled that a New York law limiting bakers to 10-hour days and 60-hour weeks in order to protect public health was unconstitutional because it violated the *right and liberty of an individual to contract*<br>• New York law went beyond *legitimate* police powers of a state |
| 1908 | *Muller* v. *Oregon* | • Civil Liberties: 14th Amendment<br>• Federalism: 10th v. 14th Amendments<br>• Equality<br>• Rights of Women | • Upheld an Oregon law that limited women to a 10-hour work day in laundries or factories in order to protect women's health<br>• Cited the physical differences between men and women when ruling that the need to protect women's health outweighed the liberty to make a contract that was upheld in *Lochner* v. *New York* |
| 1919 | *Schenck* v. *United States* | • Civil Liberties: Limited in Wartime<br>• the Judiciary | • Established limits on free speech; right is not absolute but dependent on circumstances, i.e. person is not protected if falsely shouts fire in a crowded theatre<br>• In this case, Court saw defendants' actions as a *clear and present danger* to security of the nation in wartime |

| Year | Name of Case | Constitutional Principle | Why Decision is Important |
|---|---|---|---|
| 1935 | *Schechter Poultry Corporation* v. *United States* | • Separation of Powers<br>• Property Rights/ Economic Policy: Commerce Clause | • Placed limits on the ability of Congress to delegate legislative powers to president<br>• By narrowly defining interstate commerce also restricted congressional powers to regulate commerce<br>• Declared the New Deal's National Industrial Act unconstitutional |
| 1944 | *Korematsu* v. *United States* | • Civil Liberties: Equal Protection<br>• Presidential Power in Wartime<br>• Rights of Ethnic/ Racial Groups | • Upheld the power of the president in wartime to limit a group's civil liberties<br>• Ruled that forcible relocation of Japanese Americans to Wartime Relocation Agency Camps during World War II was legal |
| 1954 | *Brown* v. *Board of Education* | • Equality: Equal Protection<br>• Federalism<br>• Rights of Ethnic/ Racial Groups | • In this school segregation case, Court overturned *Plessy* v. *Ferguson separate but equal* doctrine<br>• Ruled that *separate educational facilities are inherently* (inseparably) *unequal* and violate the 14th Amendment's *equal protection* clause |
| 1957 | *Watkins* v. *United States* | • Criminal Procedures: Due Process<br>• National Power: Congressional Investigations<br>• Civil Liberties | • Congressional investigations must spell out their legislative purpose and jurisdiction<br>• The Bill of Rights is applicable to congressional investigations<br>• Watkins was within his rights to refuse to testify to matters beyond scope of House Committee on Un-American Activities |
| 1961 | *Mapp* v. *Ohio* | • Criminal Procedures: 4th Amendment<br>• Civil Liberties: 14th Amendment | • Ruled that 4th and 14th Amendments protected citizen from illegal searches<br>• Applied *exclusionary rule* to state courts, i.e. evidence obtained unconstitutionally—in this case without a search warrant—could not be used in federal or state courts |
| 1962 | *Baker* v. *Carr* | • Avenues of Representation: Voting Rights; Equal Protection<br>• Federalism | • Court has jurisdiction over apportionment of seats in state legislatures<br>• Overrepresentation of rural voters and under representation of urban voters was a violation of 14th Amendment's *equal protection* clause<br>• Ruling led to other court cases that established *one person-one vote* concept |

| Year | Name of Case | Constitutional Principle | Why Decision is Important |
|---|---|---|---|
| 1962 | *Engel* v. *Vitale* | • Civil Liberties: Establishment Clause, 1st and 14th Amendments | • Reciting of an official prayer in the schools violated the 1st Amendment's *establishment of religion* clause, which was applied to the states by the 14th Amendment<br>• Although students were not required to say the non-denominational prayer, its recitation in class put them under pressure |
| 1963 | *Gideon* v. *Wainwright* | • Civil Liberties<br>• Criminal Procedures: 6th and 14th Amendments | • Ruled unanimously that the 6th Amendment right to an attorney, which was applied to the states by the 14th Amendment, required that a state provide lawyers for poor people accused of felony crimes, not just capital crimes |
| 1964 | *Heart of Atlanta Motel* v. *United States* | • National Power: Commerce Clause<br>• Civil Liberties: Equal Protection Clause | • Upheld constitutionality of 1964 Civil Rights Act's use of Congressional interstate commerce powers to prohibit discrimination in private facilities whose operations affect interstate commerce |
| 1966 | *Miranda* v. *Arizona* | • Criminal Procedures: Due Process, Self-Incrimination<br>• Civil Liberties: Equal Protection | • Established the requirement prior to questioning to inform those accused of crimes that they have the right to remain silent, the right to a lawyer, and that what they say can be used against them in court<br>• Evidence obtained without this warning may not be used in court under the *exclusionary rule* |
| 1969 | *Tinker* v. *Des Moines Independent Community School District* | • Civil Liberties: 1st Amendment, Student Rights/ Safe School Environment | • While recognizing the authority of schools *to prescribe and control conduct in the schools*, the court ruled that *neither students or teachers shed their constitutional rights to freedom of speech or expression at the schoolhouse gate*<br>• Symbolic, silent expression of opinion in absence of any disorder (wearing of black armbands to protest Vietnam War) is protected under the 1st Amendment |
| 1971 | *New York Times Co.* v. *United States* | • Civil Liberties: Freedom of the Press<br>• National Power | • Court narrowly upheld 1st Amendment right to Freedom of the Press<br>• Ruled that government had not met the *heavy burden of prior restraint* i.e. not made a strong enough case to stop publication of *The Pentagon Papers* on the grounds that national security would be hurt |

| Year | Name of Case | Constitutional Principle | Why Decision is Important |
|------|--------------|--------------------------|---------------------------|
| 1973 | *Roe* v. *Wade* | • Civil Liberties: Right to Privacy<br>• Rights of Women | • Declared state laws making abortions illegal to be unconstitutional while stating certain limits and conditions<br>• Basis of decision was right to privacy, citing primarily the *due process* clause of 14th Amendment |
| 1974 | *United States* v. *Nixon* | • Separation of Powers: Due Process, Executive Power | • By 8-0 vote, Court ruled that Nixon had to turn over the Watergate Tapes to the Special Prosecutor.<br>• No president was above the law; *executive privilege* (confidentiality) was not absolute<br>• Separation of powers does not protect a president from judicial review of *executive privilege*, nor from the needs of the judicial process |
| 1985 | *New Jersey* v. *T.L.O.* | • Civil Liberties: 4th Amendment, Student Rights/ Safe School Environment | • Affirmed that 4th Amendment prohibition on *unreasonable searches and seizures* applied to school officials<br>• But, necessity of maintaining discipline allowed for searches when there are *reasonable grounds* that the law or school rules have been broken compared to police requirement of *probable cause* |
| 1990 | *Cruzan* v. *Director Missouri Department of Health* | • Civil Liberties: Due Process | • Ruled that under *due process* clause, a competent person has the right to refuse life-sustaining treatment<br>• Evidence of the wishes of an incompetent person must be *clear and convincing*; evidence not presented in this case<br>• Cruzan's parents then gathered what Missouri Court agreed was *clear and convincing* evidence and the life support system was removed |
| 1992 | *Planned Parenthood of Southeastern Pennsylvania et al.* v. *Casey* | • Civil Liberties<br>• Rights of Women | • Upheld *Roe* v. *Wade* decision<br>• Determined that Pennsylvania law with provisions such as 24 hour waiting period and parental consent to a minor's abortion did not create *undue burden or substantial obstacles* to abortion<br>• Struck down requirement of husband notification |
| 1995 | *Vernonia School District* v. *Acton* | • Civil Liberties: 4th Amendment, Student Rights/ Safe School Environment | • Ruled that a school's practice of testing athletes randomly for drug use did not violate their rights under 4th and 14th Amendments<br>• Cited schools need to maintain student safety and fulfill its educational mission |

# Important People in United States History and Government

The following list highlights the key people other than presidents who are included in the New York State Core Curriculum for United States History and Government and therefore may be tested on the Regents Examinations. They represent the pluralism that is America.

| | |
|---|---|
| **Ansel Adams** | • Photographer whose natural landscapes of the West are also a statement about the importance of the preservation of the wilderness |
| **Samuel Adams** | • American Revolutionary War leader who helped to organize the Sons of Liberty and the Massachusetts Committee of Correspondence<br>• Signer of the Declaration of Independence |
| **Jane Addams** | • Progressive Era reformer in the social settlement house movement<br>• Founder of Hull House, a Chicago settlement house<br>• Cofounder of Women's International League for Peace and Freedom<br>• Corecipient of the Nobel Peace Prize (1931)<br>• Involved in organizing of the NAACP |
| **Madeleine K. Albright** | • Sworn in as the 64th and first female Secretary of State in January 1997, at the start of President Clinton's second term in office<br>• Previously served as U.S. ambassador to the United Nations |
| **Susan B. Anthony** | • Women's rights leader from 1851 until her death in 1906<br>• Most active for women's suffrage, but also worked for women's property rights and rights of married women |
| **Yasir Arafat** | • Palestinian leader involved in efforts to negotiate peace in the Middle East during President Clinton's administration<br>• Led Palestinians during a number of violent clashes with Israel |
| **Osama bin Laden** | • Leader of the al-Qaeda terrorist network; directed the September 11, 2001, attacks against the World Trade Center and the Pentagon |
| **John Brown** | • Extreme abolitionist who believed in use of violence to promote his cause<br>• His antislavery group killed proslavery settlers at the Pottawatomie Creek Massacre; his raid of Harper's Ferry resulted in his trial and execution<br>• Immortalized by Ralph Waldo Emerson in *John Brown's Body* |
| **William Jennings Bryan** | • Unsuccessful Democratic presidential candidate in 1896 and 1900<br>• Populist who supported farmers and free silver<br>• Orator, religious fundamentalist (Scopes Trial), and anti-imperialist |

| | |
|---|---|
| **John C. Calhoun** | • Outspoken southern leader and advocate of states' rights<br>• Favored nullification and the extension of slavery into the territories<br>• Vice president under Presidents John Quincy Adams and Andrew Jackson; resigned over nullification issue<br>• Secretary of state under President Tyler; successfully pressed for Texas annexation; opposed Mexican War and California statehood |
| **Andrew Carnegie** | • Industrialist and philanthropist who built Carnegie Steel Company<br>• In an article, *The Gospel of Wealth* (1889) he defended Social Darwinism, but also stated that the rich had a duty to help the poor, and improve society in areas they deemed important |
| **Rachel Carson** | • Writer, scientist, and environmentalist whose book, *Silent Spring* (1962), identified the hazards of agricultural pesticides<br>• Inspired the environmental movement and legislation |
| **Fidel Castro** | • Won Cuban revolution against dictator Batista; headed Cuba 1959–2008; limited civil liberties, and nationalized industries<br>• Allied with Soviet Union in 1962 Cuban Missile Crisis<br>• U.S. trade embargo against Cuba under Castro in place since 1962 |
| **Willa Cather** | • Pulitzer Prize winning writer about the struggle of the pioneers settling the frontier<br>• Best known for *My Antonia* (1918) and *Death Comes to the Archbishop* (1927) |
| **Cesar Chavez** | • Latino leader of California farm workers from 1962 until his death in 1993<br>• Organized the United Farm Workers (UFW) to help migrant farm workers gain better pay and working conditions |
| **Winston Churchill** | • Prime minister of Great Britain during World War II |
| **Hillary Rodham Clinton** | • In 2000, became the first First Lady elected to U.S. Senate and first woman elected to statewide office from New York; reelected in 2006<br>• In 2008, ran unsuccessfully for Democratic Party presidential nomination<br>• In 2009, became 67th Secretary of State |
| **Father Charles Coughlin** | • Roman Catholic priest who attacked President Franklin D. Roosevelt and his New Deal programs<br>• Lost popularity because of his pro-fascist, anti-Semitic views |
| **Eugene V. Debs** | • Union organizer and Socialist presidential candidate in every election from the 1890s until World War I |
| **Dorothea Dix** | • Nineteenth-century reformer who revolutionized mental health reform |
| **Stephen Douglas** | • Illinois Senator whose Kansas-Nebraska Act included his idea of popular sovereignty, which increased sectional tensions<br>• Lincoln-Douglas debates (1858) made Lincoln nationally known<br>• Candidate of northern faction of Democratic party in 1860 election |
| **Frederick Douglass** | • Former slave, abolitionist, and lecturer; active in Underground Railroad<br>• Supported Women's Suffrage, attended Seneca Falls Convention |

| | |
|---|---|
| **W.E.B. Du Bois** | • African American civil rights leader, historian, writer, and sociologist<br>• Cofounder of Niagara Movement and of NAACP<br>• Influenced Harlem Renaissance by publishing African Americans in *The Crisis*<br>• Opposed Marcus Garvey's "back to Africa" movement and disagreed with Booker T. Washington by pressing for civil and political, not just economic, equality for African Americans |
| **John Foster Dulles** | • Secretary of state under President Dwight Eisenhower<br>• Made famous the concept of brinkmanship, a foreign policy that brought the United States just to the brink of war |
| **Edward K. "Duke" Ellington** | • Songwriter, band leader, jazz composer, pianist, and a leading figure of the Harlem Renaissance<br>• Famous songs include "Take the A Train" and "Mood Indigo" |
| **Medgar Evers** | • African American activist and NAACP field secretary<br>• Murdered in Mississippi in 1963 by a sniper outside his house |
| **F. Scott Fitzgerald** | • Novelist whose works reflect climate of the "roaring twenties"<br>• Novels include *The Great Gatsby* and *Tender Is the Night* |
| **Henry Ford** | • Industrialist who headed Ford Motor Company<br>• His innovative production methods reduced the cost of producing cars, making it possible for the average person to own an automobile |
| **Benjamin Franklin** | • Philadelphia statesman, diplomat, scientist, and writer in revolutionary period<br>• Drafted the 1754 Albany Plan of Union<br>• Member of Second Continental Congress; served on committee to write the Declaration of Independence, which he signed<br>• Helped persuade France to sign the 1778 Treaty of Alliance against England and helped negotiate the Treaty of Paris of 1783, ending American Revolution; delegate to Constitutional Convention |
| **Betty Friedan** | • Women's rights activist whose book, *The Feminine Mystique* (1963), encouraged women to find their own identity outside marriage<br>• Helped found National Organization for Women (1966) and National Women's Political Caucus (1971) |
| **William Lloyd Garrison** | • Abolitionist editor of newspaper called *The Liberator*, published 1831–1865 demanding immediate end to slavery |
| **Marcus Garvey** | • African American nationalist leader who advocated pride and self-help as a means of empowerment<br>• Founder of the Universal Negro Improvement Association, a nationalist and separatist group that wanted a separate black economy and urged African Americans to emigrate to Africa<br>• Ideas influenced the 1960s Black Power movement |

| | |
|---|---|
| **Bill Gates** | • In 1975 co-founded Microsoft with vision of "a computer on every desk and in every home;" believed "personal computers would change the world"<br>• Philanthropist committed to improving education and public health |
| **Samuel Gompers** | • Organizer and president of American Federation of Labor, a craft union for skilled workers; stressed issues such as wages and hours |
| **Albert A. Gore, Jr.** | • Vice President of the United States (1993–2001); won popular vote but lost electoral vote in 2000 election that went to Supreme Court in *Bush* v. *Gore.*<br>• In 2007 shared the Nobel Peace Prize with the U.N. Intergovernmental Panel on Climate Change, and won an Academy Award for film, *An Inconvenient Truth*, on global warming. |
| **Alexander Hamilton** | • New York delegate at Constitutional Convention who worked for a strong central government<br>• Wrote 51 of *The Federalist Papers* supporting ratifying the Constitution<br>• First secretary of the treasury; promoted U.S. economic development |
| **William Randolph Hearst** | • Newspaper publisher whose yellow journalism style helped create public pressure for the Spanish-American War |
| **Ernest Hemingway** | • Novelist whose writings expressed conflict and concern created by changing American values; 1954 Nobel Prize for Literature winner |
| **Patrick Henry** | • Leader in the American Revolution in Virginia<br>• Member of Continental Congress; supporter of independence<br>• Led movement for addition of the Bill of Rights to the Constitution |
| **Langston Hughes** | • Poet, playwright, and novelist who wrote about the African American experience, especially that of the poor and working class<br>• A leading figure of the Harlem Renaissance |
| **Saddam Hussein** | • Long-time Iraqi dictator who invaded Kuwait causing Persian Gulf war<br>• Removed from power in 2003 during Iraq War and hanged in 2006 |
| **Chiang Kai-shek** | • Leader of the Chinese Nationalists in civil war; when defeated by Mao Zedong in 1949 left China and established a government in Taiwan |
| **Robert Kennedy** | • Attorney general (1961–1963); assassinated in June 1968 |
| **Martin Luther King, Jr.** | • Civil rights leader who advocated civil disobedience and nonviolent demonstrations to achieve change<br>• Founded Southern Christian Leadership Conference, led Montgomery, Alabama bus boycott, and Selma to Mongomery voting rights march<br>• Gave "I Have a Dream" speech; won Nobel Peace Prize<br>• Assassinated in 1968 |

| | |
|---|---|
| **Henry Kissinger** | • Secretary of state under Presidents Nixon and Ford<br>• Deeply involved in foreign policy in Vietnam, China, the Soviet Union, and the Middle East |
| **Robert La Follette** | • Governor of Wisconsin whose program, the "Wisconsin Idea," became the model for progressive reform<br>• Served as United States senator and Progressive leader<br>• Ran for President as the Progressive Party candidate in 1924 |
| **John L. Lewis** | • President of United Mine Workers of America from 1920–1960; led UMWA in 1925 Anthracite Coal Strike<br>• A founder of the Congress of Industrial Organizations (CIO), he worked to organize workers by industry leading to a split in the 1930s between American Federation of Labor and the CIO |
| **Meriwether Lewis and William Clark** | • Explorers who led the 1804–1806 expedition to survey lands included in the Louisiana Purchase; documented the land, plants, animals, and other natural resources from Missouri to Oregon |
| **Sinclair Lewis** | • Novelist whose work *Main Street* attacked middle class values<br>• First American to win Nobel Prize for Literature (1930) |
| **John Locke** | • British Enlightenment writer whose ideas influenced the Declaration of Independence, state constitutions, and the United States Constitution<br>• Believed that people are born free with certain natural rights, including the rights to life, liberty, and property, and must consent to be governed |
| **Henry Cabot Lodge** | • Massachusetts Republican senator whose support of American imperialism and of a powerful navy strongly influenced Theodore Roosevelt<br>• Led successful fight against ratification of the Treaty of Versailles and entry of the United States into the League of Nations<br>• Served as a U.S. representative to Washington Conference |
| **Huey Long** | • Populist governor of Louisiana and U.S. senator<br>• Proposed that income and inheritance taxes on the wealthy be used to give each American a $2,500 income, a car, and a college education<br>• Planned to challenge FDR for president, but was assassinated in 1935 |
| **Douglas MacArthur** | • Led U.S. troops in the Pacific in World War II<br>• Commander of U.S. occupation forces in Japan after World War II<br>• Relieved of command by Truman after publicly disagreeing with him about the conduct of the Korean War |
| **Malcolm X** | • Leader of the 1960s Black Power movement; assassinated in 1965 |
| **Horace Mann** | • Nineteenth century educator; helped create tax-based, nonsectarian public schools as well as better teacher-training institutions |
| **George C. Marshall** | • Army chief of staff during World War II and secretary of state under President Truman; promoted the Marshall Plan, which assisted the economic recovery of Europe after World War II |

| | |
|---|---|
| **John Marshall** | • Chief Justice of the United States (1801–1835)<br>• Established prestige of the Supreme Court and strengthened power of federal government in cases such as *Marbury* v. *Madison* (1803), *McCulloch* v. *Maryland* (1819), and *Gibbons* v. *Ogden* (1824)<br>• First stated the right of judicial review in *Marbury* v. *Madison* (1803) |
| **Thurgood Marshall** | • African American attorney who argued *Brown* v. *Board of Education* before the Supreme Court in 1954 and was appointed to that Court in 1967—the first African American to serve on the Supreme Court |
| **Cotton Mather** | • New England Puritan associated with the concept of the Puritan work ethic (meaning that hard work is its own reward) and an appreciation of thrift and industry<br>• Supported the Salem witch trials |
| **Joseph R. McCarthy** | • Republican Senator of the late 1940s and early 1950s who led a campaign to root out suspected Communists in American life<br>• The term *McCarthyism* came to be associated with an era of government investigation of the private lives of many in public service and in the entertainment industry |
| **Baron de Montesquieu** | • French Enlightenment philosopher who admired the British system of republican government<br>• Influence is seen in separation of powers and in the checks and balances provisions in the Constitution |
| **John Muir** | • Naturalist, conservationist, and writer; influenced President Theodore Roosevelt to protect more land; founded the Sierra Club |
| **Ralph Nader** | • Consumer rights crusader; wrote *Unsafe at Any Speed* (1965) to expose the lack of safety standards for cars<br>• Third party presidential candidate (1996, 2000, 2004, 2008) |
| **Frank Norris** | • Naturalist writer whose 1901 novel, *The Octopus*, told of the struggle between the railroad and California wheat growers |
| **Robert Oppenheimer** | • Physicist who led the American effort to build the first atomic bomb |
| **Thomas Paine** | • English-born writer and political philosopher whose influential pamphlet *Common Sense* (1776) pressed for independence from Great Britain |
| **Rosa Parks** | • African American civil rights activist whose 1955 refusal to give up her seat to a white person led to the Montgomery, Alabama, bus boycott and helped launch the civil rights movement |
| **Frances Perkins** | • Social reformer and political leader<br>• Named secretary of labor under President Franklin D. Roosevelt in 1933, becoming the first woman to serve in a cabinet position |

| | |
|---|---|
| **H. Ross Perot** | • Third-party candidate and billionaire businessman who challenged George Bush and Bill Clinton for the presidency in 1992 with new ideas about balancing the federal budget and about other economic issues |
| **Matthew Perry** | • Led 1853–1854 naval mission to open Japan to world trade and negotiated U.S. trading rights with Japan (Treaty of Kanagawa) |
| **Gifford Pinchot** | • Conservationist and politician who led the Division of Forestry of the Department of Agriculture under President Theodore Roosevelt<br>• Dismissed by Taft after attacking the Secretary of the Interior for removing from federal protection about a million acres of land |
| **Joseph Pulitzer** | • Publisher of the *New York Journal*, whose "yellow journalism" helped provoke the Spanish-American War |
| **Condoleezza Rice** | • Second Secretary of State under President George W. Bush; first female African American to hold that position |
| **Jacob Riis** | • Journalist, photographer, and social reformer of the Progressive Era<br>• Used writings and photographs to show the need for better housing for the poor, such as in his 1890 book *How the Other Half Lives* |
| **Jackie Robinson** | • Professional baseball player<br>• Became the first African American to play in major league baseball when he joined the Brooklyn Dodgers in 1947 |
| **John D. Rockefeller** | • Industrialist and philanthropist<br>• Founder of the Standard Oil Company |
| **Nelson A. Rockefeller** | • Former governor of New York who was appointed Vice President by President Gerald Ford in 1974<br>• Only nonelected Vice President to serve with a nonelected President |
| **Eleanor Roosevelt** | • Political activist and First Lady<br>• Early and long-time activist for rights for African Americans and women during the New Deal as First Lady and as political activist on her own<br>• Played a key role in creation of United Nations Declaration on Human Rights (1948) and heading the UN Commission on Human Rights (1961)<br>• Chaired the Presidential Commission on the Status of Women during the Kennedy Administration |
| **Julius and Ethel Rosenberg** | • Convicted and executed for treason in 1953 during the era of McCarthyism |
| **Jean-Jacques Rousseau** | • French Enlightenment philosopher<br>• Influenced the Declaration of Independence with his arguments in support of government by the consent of the governed |
| **Sacajawea** | • Native American guide for part of the Lewis and Clark expedition<br>• Honored in 2000 with her image on a dollar coin |

| | |
|---|---|
| **Nicola Sacco and Bartolomeo Vanzetti** | • Italian immigrants and anarchists executed for armed robbery and murder at the height of the antiradical, anti-immigrant feelings of the 1920s<br>• Cleared by the Massachusetts governor in 1977, some 50 years later |
| **Margaret Sanger** | • Pioneering advocate of birth control<br>• Organized first American birth control conference in 1921<br>• Founder of a birth-control lobbying group that became Planned Parenthood in 1942 |
| **Upton Sinclair** | • Muckraking journalist of the Progressive Era<br>• Influenced the passage of the 1906 Meat Inspection Act with his novel *The Jungle*, which deals with the exploitation of the poor and the factory conditions that led to contaminated meat |
| **Adam Smith** | • In *The Wealth of Nations* (1776), this Scottish political economist rejected mercantilism and advocated a free enterprise system, the basis of modern capitalism<br>• Argued for free trade, the division of labor, competition, individual freedom, supply and demand, and *laissez-faire* as necessary for a sound economy |
| **Alfred E. Smith** | • Reform governor of New York and first Catholic to run for President<br>• Lost to Hoover in the 1928 election, largely because voters did not want a Catholic President and because Smith favored repeal of the Eighteenth Amendment<br>• Right-wing conservative Democrat who helped organized American Liberty League (1934) and opposed New Deal |
| **Bessie Smith** | • Harlem Renaissance blues singer known as the "Empress of the Blues"<br>• Recorded with prominent jazz musicians, such as Louis Armstrong and Benny Goodman |
| **Elizabeth Cady Stanton** | • Leading crusader for women's rights; also for abolition and temperance<br>• Began women's rights movement with Seneca Falls Convention in New York in 1848; wrote Declaration of Sentiments (1848)<br>• With Susan B. Anthony, cofounded the National Woman Suffrage Association and coedited *Revolution*, a women's rights journal |
| **Lincoln Steffens** | • Muckraking journalist, editor, and reformer; wrote about corruption in government and business in his 1906 novel, *The Shame of the Cities* |
| **John Steinbeck** | • Author whose novels often deal with problems of the working class during the Great Depression<br>• *The Grapes of Wrath* (Pulitzer Prize, 1939) describes the effect of the drought that created the Dust Bowl on a group of farmers forced to leave Oklahoma and work as migrant laborers in California |
| **Harriet Beecher Stowe** | • Writer whose emotional, controversial, and best-selling novel, *Uncle Tom's Cabin* (1852), focused attention on slavery and contributed to the start of the Civil War |

| | |
|---|---|
| **Ida Tarbell** | • Muckraking journalist whose *History of Standard Oil Company* exposed Rockefeller's unfair and often ruthless business practices |
| **Norman Thomas** | • Political leader, minister, and pacifist who ran six times as Socialist party candidate for President<br>• Supporter of moderate social reforms, strongly anticommunist<br>• Helped organize the American Civil Liberties Union and urged nuclear disarmament |
| **Dr. Francis Townsend** | • Opponent of the New Deal who promoted a financially impossible plan to provide government pensions for the elderly |
| **Mark Twain** | • Author and humorist of the late nineteenth and early twentieth centuries, famous, in part, for his homespun stories about life along the Mississippi River<br>• Mark Twain was the pen name of Samuel L. Clemens |
| **Voltaire** | • French Enlightenment philosopher who praised British institutions and rights and influenced framers of the Constitution<br>• Wrote against religious intolerance and persecution |
| **Earl Warren** | • Chief Justice of the United States (1953–1969)<br>• Landmark cases such as *Brown* v. *Board of Education* (1954) and *Miranda* v. *Arizona* (1966) marked his tenure |
| **Booker T. Washington** | • African American educator, author, and leader<br>• Founded Tuskegee Institute (1881) and wrote *Up from Slavery* (1901)<br>• Urged vocational education and self-improvement rather than confrontation as the way for African Americans to gain racial equality |
| **Ida Wells-Barnett** | • African American journalist, suffragist, and reformer<br>• Launched a national crusade against lynching in the 1890s<br>• Cofounder of the NAACP and of the National Association of Colored Women |
| **Edith Wharton** | • 1920s novelist who expressed concern about old versus new values in books such as *The Age of Innocence* (Pulitzer Prize, 1921) |
| **Mao Zedong** | • Leader of the communist Chinese government from 1949 until 1976<br>• Met with President Nixon on Nixon's historic trip to China in 1972 |
| **John Peter Zenger** | • German immigrant, printer and journalist<br>• Tried for criminal libel for criticizing New York governor in his paper; jury found him not guilty on the grounds that he had printed the truth<br>• His case was an early step in establishing freedom of the press |

# Glossary

## A

**abolitionist:** a person seeking the legal end of slavery

**acquit:** to be found not guilty in a trial

**affirmative action:** steps taken to increase the representation of women and minorities, especially in jobs and higher education

**AFL/CIO:** influential labor union resulting from a merger between the American Federation of Labor and the Congress of Industrial Organizations in 1955

**agrarian protest:** demands by farmers for improvements in areas affecting agriculture, especially in the late 1800s

**Agricultural/Agrarian Revolution:** introduction of new farming methods in the 18th century that improved the quality and quantity of farm products and led to the Industrial Revolution

**alien:** a citizen of a foreign country

**alliance:** a group of nations mutually allied by treaty

**Allies:** the World War I alliance of Great Britain, France, Russia, and later the United States; also the World War II alliance of Great Britain, the United States, the Soviet Union, and other nations

**al-Qaeda:** world terrorist organization responsible for September 11, 2001, attacks on the World Trade Center and the Pentagon; led by Osama bin Laden

**amendment:** a change in or addition to a legal document, motion, bylaw, law, or constitution

**American system:** a plan offered by Henry Clay for internal improvements

**annex:** to attach new territory to an existing area, such as a country

**Antifederalist:** a person opposed to the Constitution during the ratification debate of 1787

**anti-Semitism:** prejudice against Jews

**antitrust:** opposed to practices and agreements that restrict trade, such as monopolies, price-fixing, and trusts

**appeasement:** the policy of giving in to an aggressor's demands in order to keep the peace

**appellate jurisdiction:** the authority of a court to review the decisions of inferior (lower) courts

**Articles of Confederation:** the first American constitution

**assassination:** the murder of a public figure

**assembly line:** a method of production in which automobiles or other items being manufactured move past workers and machines and are assembled piece by piece until completed

**assimilation:** the process of becoming part of another culture

**assumption plan:** part of Hamilton's financial plan; called for the new federal government to take over and pay off American Revolution war debts of Continental Congress and states

**atomic age:** a term used to describe period begun by the explosion of the first atomic bomb in 1945

## B

**baby boom:** the rapid growth in the population of the United States between 1945 and 1964

**balance of power:** distribution of political and economic power that prevents any one nation from becoming too strong

**balance of terror:** a balance of power achieved when opposing sides possess nuclear weapons

**balance of trade:** the difference in value between a nation's imports and its exports

**bank holiday:** 1933 banking act that closed banks to prevent collapse of banking system; sound banks then reopened

**bankruptcy:** a court action to release a person or corporation from unpaid debts

**belligerents:** nations fighting a war, usually after a declaration of war

**bicameral legislature:** a lawmaking body composed of two houses

**big business:** corporations or monopolies seen as having too much control over a society and its economy

**Big Stick diplomacy:** foreign policy of President Theodore Roosevelt threatening intervention in Latin American nations to insure their stability

**bill:** a proposal presented to a legislative body for possible enactment as law

**Bill of Attainder:** an act of a legislature that finds a person guilty without a trial; prohibited by the Constitution

**Bill of Rights:** the first ten amendments to the U.S. Constitution, dealing mostly with civil rights

**bipartisan:** supported by two political parties

**Black Codes:** laws passed, especially by southern states after the Civil War, to control the actions and limit the rights of African Americans

**blacklist:** a list, circulated among employers, of people who will not be hired because of their views, beliefs, or actions

**blitzkrieg:** a sudden invasion or "lightning war," first practiced by Germany in World War II

**blockade:** the shutting off of a port to keep people or supplies from moving in or out

**blue-collar worker:** someone who holds an industrial or factory job

**boycott:** an organized refusal to buy or use a product or service, or to deal with a company or group of companies, as a protest or as a means to force them to take some action

**brinkmanship:** the policy of being willing to go "to the brink" of war to preserve peace

**bureaucracy:** a collective term for all of the workers who run the agencies that do the everyday business of government

## C

**cabinet:** the group of officials who head government departments and advise the President

**capitalism:** the economic system based on private initiative, competition, profit, and the private ownership of the means of producing goods and services

**carpetbagger:** pejorative name for a Northerner who went to the South during Reconstruction

**cash crops:** crops grown for sale rather than for family consumption

**census:** gathering information on the nation's population; required by the U.S. Constitution every ten years to determine number of votes a state has in the House of Representatives and the Electoral College

**checks and balances:** the system set up by the U.S. Constitution in which each branch of the federal government has the power to limit the actions of the other branches

**citizen:** a person who by birth or naturalization owes loyalty to, and receives the protection of, a nation's government

**citizenship:** the duties, rights, and privileges of a citizen

**civil disobedience:** nonviolent protest against unjust laws

**civil liberties:** certain rights guaranteed to all citizens of a nation

**civil rights:** rights guaranteed to citizens by the U.S. Constitution and laws of the nation

**civil service:** government jobs for which appointments and promotions are now based on merit rather than on political patronage

**closed shop:** a workplace in which employees must be labor union members in order to be hired

**coalition:** an alliance of political groups

**Cold War:** the state of tension between the United States and the Soviet Union after World War II

**collective bargaining:** the process by which a union negotiates with management for a contract

**collective security:** a system in which member nations agree to take joint action to meet any threat or breach of international peace

**colonialism:** the practice under which a nation takes control of other lands for its economic, military, or other use

**colony:** a settlement of people in a distant land who are ruled by a government of their native land

**commerce clause:** Article I, Section 8, Clause 3 of the U.S. Constitution, which gives Congress the power to regulate interstate and foreign trade

**committee system:** method under which members of the legislative branch form into smaller groups to facilitate such business as considering proposed legislation and holding investigations

**communism:** the economic system based on the collective ownership of property and the means of production, with all individuals expected to contribute to society according to their abilities and to receive from it according to their needs

**compromise:** the resolution of conflict in which concessions are made by all parties to achieve a common goal

**concentration camp:** a place where political opponents or other "enemies" of a nation are forcibly confined, especially those established by Nazi Germany before and during World War II

**concurrent powers:** powers shared by the national and state governments

**confederation:** an alliance of independent states

**conference committee:** a temporary joint committee of both houses of a legislature, created to reconcile differences between the two houses' version of a bill

**conglomerate:** a corporation that owns many different, unrelated businesses

**Congress:** the legislative, or lawmaking, branch of the United States government, made up of the Senate and the House of Representatives

**consent of the governed:** principle that says people are the source of the powers of government

**conservation:** the careful use or preserving of natural resources

**conspicuous consumption:** public enjoyment of costly possessions done in such a way as to emphasize the fact that one can afford such possessions

**constitution:** body of fundamental law, setting out the basic principles, structures, processes, and functions of a government and placing limits on its actions; the supreme law of the United States

**constitutional:** permissible under the Constitution

**Constitutional Convention:** formal meeting of state delegates in Philadelphia in 1787 at which the Constitution was written

**consumer:** person who spends money on goods and services

**consumer goods:** goods produced for use by individuals as opposed to use by businesses

**consumerism:** the practice of protecting consumers; also theory that increased consumption of goods is economically and personally beneficial.

**consumer protection:** measures to shield buyers of goods and services from unsafe products and unfair or illegal sales practices

**containment:** the U.S. policy after World War II of trying to keep the Soviet Union from expanding its area of influence and dominance

**convict:** to be found guilty in a trial

**corporation:** business owned by many investors that raises money by selling stocks or shares to those investors

**court packing:** Franklin Roosevelt's 1937 plan to add justices to the Supreme Court

**credit:** delayed payment for goods or services

**creditor nation:** a nation that is owed money by other nations

**cultural diversity:** many cultures existing in the same society

**cultural pluralism:** the idea that different cultures can exist side by side in the same society, all contributing to the society without losing their identities

**culture:** the way of life of a given people

**custom:** a habit or practice so established that it strongly influences social behavior

## D

**debtor nation:** a nation that owes money to another nation or nations

**Declaration of Independence:** the 1776 document that stated Great Britain's North American colonies had become free and independent of the parent country

**deficit:** the amount by which money spent is greater than money received

**deficit spending:** government practice of spending more money than it takes in from taxes and other revenues

**delegated powers:** powers given by the Constitution to the national government and denied to state governments

**demagogue:** a person who gains political power by rousing the passions of the people

**demobilization:** the process by which a nation reconverts to peacetime status after a war or the threat of war

**democracy:** system of government in which supreme authority rests with the people, either directly or through elected representatives

**Democratic Party:** one of the modern political parties, descended from Jefferson's Democratic-Republican Party; also one of the oldest continuous political parties in the world

**Democratic-Republican Party:** one of the first political parties in the United States, led by Jefferson and other leaders who were opposed to the Federalists; also known as Jeffersonian Republicans

**demography:** the study of populations through statistics

**depression:** a long and severe decline in economic activity

**détente:** the easing of tension between nations

**dictatorship:** form of government in which the power to govern is held by one person or a small group

**direct democracy:** system of government in which the people participate directly in decision-making through the voting process

**direct election of senators:** system put into practice under the Seventeenth Amendment whereby the voters rather than the state legislatures elect members of the U.S. Senate

**disarmament:** reduction of a nation's armed forces or weapons of war

**discrimination:** policy or attitude that denies rights to people based on race, religion, sex, or other characteristics

**disestablishment:** depriving a state church of official support from the government, or never allowing a state church to be founded

**diversity:** variety

**divestiture:** a refusal to hold stock in companies that have operations in South Africa

**division of powers:** basic principle of federalism; the constitutional provisions by which governmental powers are divided between the national and the state governments

**dollar diplomacy:** President Taft's policy of encouraging United States investment in Latin America

**domestic policy:** everything a nation's government says and does in relation to internal matters

**domino theory:** the idea, prevalent during the Vietnam War, that if one Asian nation became Communist, neighboring nations would as well

**due process of law:** constitutional guarantee that government will not deprive any person of life, liberty, or property by any unfair, arbitrary, or unreasonable action

**E**

**economic:** pertaining to production, distribution, and use of wealth

**economic nationalism:** policies focused on improving the economy of one's own nation

**economic programs:** any policies set forward by a government that relate to the workings of its economy

**elastic clause:** Article I, Section 8, Clause 18 of the Constitution, which is the basis for the implied powers of Congress

**Electoral College:** an assembly elected by the voters that meets every four years to formally elect the President of the United States

**electoral votes:** number of votes each state and the District of Columbia can cast for president, equal to the number of senators plus representatives of each state, with 270 electoral votes needed to be elected president

**electorate:** all the persons entitled to vote in a given election

**emancipation:** the act of setting a person or people free

**Emancipation Proclamation:** the Presidential decree, effective January 1, 1863, that freed enslaved people in Confederate-held territory

**embargo:** government prohibition of trade with another nation or nation; also prohibition of ships leaving home ports. *See Embargo Act of 1807, United States embargo against Cuba*

**empathy:** the process of sharing and understanding the feelings or thoughts of another person

**English Bill of Rights:** the 1689 agreement between Parliament and William and Mary which established that representative government and the rule of law outweighed the power of any monarch

**Enlightenment:** Eighteenth-century movement that emphasized science and reason as key to improving society

**entrepreneur:** a person who organizes, operates, and assumes the risks of a business enterprise

**environment:** natural surroundings and all the things that make them up; also the social, cultural, and physical surroundings that affect behavior in a society

**equal protection under the law:** a clause in the Fourteenth Amendment requiring that states apply due process equally, without preference to an individual or group

**espionage:** spying

**ethnic group:** people of foreign birth or descent living in another country

**European Economic Community:** organization, also known as the Common Market, formed in 1957 to ease trade and travel among member European nations

**European Union:** the economic organization of European nations designed to increase the economic power of Europe in the world economy

**excise tax:** taxes levied on the production, transportation, sale, or consumption of goods or services

**executive branch:** part of a government that carries out its laws

**executive power:** the powers of the head of an executive branch of government to carry out the laws

**executive privilege:** the right claimed by presidents to withhold information from the legislative or judicial branches

**expansionism:** desire to enlarge the territory owned or controlled by one's nation

**expatriate:** a person who gives up her or his homeland to live in another country

**expressed powers:** those delegated powers of the national government that are given to it in so many words by the Constitution

### F

**farm output:** total value of products produced by a nation's farms

**fascism:** political philosophy that calls for glorification of the state, a single party system with a strong ruler, and aggressive nationalism

**federal government:** the central or national government

**federalism:** a system of government in which authority is divided between national and state governments; the belief in or advocacy of such a system

**Federalist:** supporter of the Constitution in the ratification debate of 1787, favored a strong national government

**Federalist Party:** one of the first political parties in the United States, organized by those who favored the ratification of the Constitution

**Federal Reserve System:** the nation's central banking system, established in 1913; a system of 12 regional banks overseen by a central board

**feminist movement:** the struggle of women for equality

**First Amendment:** Bill of Rights' guarantee of freedom of religion, speech, press, assembly, and petition

**fiscal policy:** policies relating to a nation's finances

**flapper:** nickname for a young woman in the 1920s who declared her independence from traditional rules

**foreign policy:** the actions and stands that every nation takes in every aspect of its relationships with other countries; everything a nation's government says and does in world affairs

**Fourteen Points:** President Woodrow Wilson's proposal in 1918 for a postwar European peace

**Fourteenth Amendment:** Constitutional amendment that defines "citizen" to reverse Dred Scott decision; its due process and equal protection clauses are aimed at protecting basic rights

**free enterprise:** an economic system based on private ownership, individual enterprise, and competition

**freedom of speech:** the right of freedom of expression guaranteed to Americans by the First Amendment

**freedom of the seas:** right of merchant ships to travel in international waters during peace or war

**frontier:** the border of a country; as defined by the U.S. Bureau of the Census, the edge of settlement beyond which the land was occupied by two or fewer people per square mile

**frontier thesis:** idea set forth by historian Frederick Jackson Turner that the nation's frontier regions shaped its character and institutions

**Fugitive Slave Law:** part of the Compromise of 1850, the Fugitive Slave Law required all citizens to help catch runaway enslaved people

**fundamentalist:** one who believes that the Bible is the literal word of God

### G

**General Agreement on Tariffs and Trade (GATT):** international agreement on reducing tariffs and expanding world trade (1947)

**genocide:** the systematic destruction of a race of people

**Gentlemen's Agreement:** informal agreement between the United States and Japan in 1907 to limit Japanese immigration to this country

**Gettysburg Address:** famous speech by President Abraham Lincoln on the meaning of the Civil War, given in November 1863 at the dedication of a national cemetery on the site of the Battle of Gettysburg

**ghetto:** area in which many members of some minority group live, to which they are restricted by economic pressure or social discrimination

**Gilded Age:** term used to describe the period from 1865 to 1900

**glasnost:** a period of "openness" in relations between the United States and the Soviet Union that began in the late 1980s

**global interdependence:** the idea that the nations of the world must rely on each other in many different ways, including trade, transportation, and communication

**Glorious Revolution:** the bloodless revolution in 1689 in which the English Parliament overthrew James II and replaced him with William and Mary

**gold standard:** a system in which a nation's currency is based on the value of gold

**Good Neighbor Policy:** Franklin D. Roosevelt's policy toward Latin America intended to strengthen relations with the nations of that region

**government:** the complex of offices, personnel, and processes by which a state is ruled, and by which its public policies are made and enforced

**grandfather clause:** laws passed in some southern states giving the right to vote only to people who had that right on January 1, 1867, and their descendants; intended to keep African Americans from voting

**Grangers, The:** organization of farmers founded for social reasons in 1867, which later campaigned for state regulation of railroads and other reforms

**grass-roots support:** political backing from ordinary citizens, especially from rural areas

**Great Compromise:** the plan for a two-house legislature adopted at the Constitutional Convention in 1787 that settled differences between large and small states over representation in Congress

**Great Depression:** period from 1929 to 1941 of severe worldwide economic downturn

**Great Migration:** migration of English Puritans to the Massachusetts Bay Colony beginning in the 1630s; also refers to the migration of African Americans from the South to the North in the early twentieth century

**Great Society:** the name given to President Johnson's domestic program in the 1960s

**gross national product (GNP):** the total value of all the goods and services produced in a nation in a year

**guerrilla warfare:** fighting by stealth and with small bands, which make surprise raids against stronger forces

**H**

*habeas corpus:* a writ of *habeas corpus* (produce the body) requires a person to be brought before a court to determine whether that person is being lawfully jailed

**Harlem Renaissance:** an African American cultural movement centered in New York City from the 1920s to the mid-1930s; focused on African American identity and pride through literature, art, music, dance, and philosophy

**hemisphere:** half of the Earth's surface

**holding company:** a company that gains control of other companies by buying their stock

**Holocaust:** name given to Nazi Germany's persecution of Jews before and during World War II; in this time, more than six million Jews died

**Homestead Act:** 1862 law that offered 160 acres of western land to settlers

**House of Representatives:** lower house of the U.S. Congress in which states are represented according to the size of their populations

**humanitarian:** one who is concerned with the welfare of all people

**human rights:** basic rights that should belong to all people including freedom of speech, religion, and the press

**I**

**immigration:** the movement of people into another nation in order to make a permanent home there

**immigration laws:** laws controlling the movement of people into a country

**immigration quota:** sets limits on numbers of people and/or their nation of origin to limit immigration from those nations

**impeachment:** the process by which the House of Representatives makes an accusation of wrongdoing against the President or other high federal officials

**imperialism:** policy by which one country takes control of another either directly or through economic or political dominance

**implied powers:** those delegated powers of the national government implied by (inferred from) the expressed powers; those powers "necessary and proper" to carry out the expressed powers

**income tax:** a tax levied on individual and corporate earnings permitted by $16^{th}$ amendment (1913)

**incumbent:** person currently occupying a political office at the time of a new election

**indemnities:** money paid by a losing nation to a winning nation after a war

**indentured servant:** person who worked in the colonies for period of three to seven years in exchange for passage, food, housing, clothing; system resulting from labor shortage in colonies

**independence:** freedom from the control, influence, or support of other people or nations

**Indian Removal Policy:** under President Andrew Jackson, the policy of moving all Native Americans to lands west of the Mississippi River in the 1830s

**individual rights:** basic rights that belong to each person

**industrialization:** change from an agricultural society to one based on machine-made goods

**inflation:** an economic condition in which prices rise substantially over a significant period of time

**injunction:** a court order prohibiting a given action; used frequently against workers in nineteenth-century labor-management disputes

**interchangeable parts:** parts made exactly like each other, making the mass production of products on an assembly line possible

**interdependence:** a condition in which parties are reliant on each other

**internal affairs:** public or business matters within the boundaries of a country

**internal improvements:** roads, bridges, canals, and other similar projects funded by the national government

**internationalism:** the belief, held by some Americans in the 1930s, that the United States should aid the victims of international aggression

**international law:** the norms of behavior generally agreed to and followed by the nations of the world in their dealings with each other

**internment camps:** places of confinement, especially in wartime

**interstate commerce:** trade among the states

**intervention:** interference by one nation in the affairs of another

**intrastate commerce:** trade within the borders of a state

**Iron Curtain:** the line between Soviet-dominated Eastern Europe and the West, so-called because the Soviets and their satellite nations prevented the free passage of people, information, and ideas across their borders

**isolationism:** a policy of avoiding alliances and other types of involvement in the affairs of other nations

**isthmus:** a narrow strip or neck of land running from one larger land area to another

## J

**Japanese-American relocation:** policy under which Americans of Japanese ancestry were confined during World War II

**Jim Crow laws:** laws in the Southern states in the nineteenth and twentieth centuries that forced the segregation of the races

**jingoism:** aggressive nationalism

**joint resolution:** legislative measure which must be passed by both houses and approved by the chief executive to become effective; similar to a bill, with the force of law, and often used for unusual or temporary circumstances

**judicial activism:** broad interpretation of the Constitution leading to court-directed change

**judicial branch:** part of the government that decides if laws are carried out fairly

**judicial restraint:** narrow interpretation of the Constitution

**judicial review:** power of the Supreme Court to determine the constitutionality of acts of the legislative and executive branches of the government

**judiciary:** judicial branch of a government, its system of courts

**jurisdiction:** power of a court to hear (to try and decide) a case

**jury:** a group of people who hear evidence in a legal case and give a decision based on that evidence

**justice:** fairness; trial and judgment according to established process of the law

## K

**Know-Nothing Party:** common name for the American party, a nativist political organization formed in 1849

**Korean War:** conflict over the future of the Korean peninsula, fought between 1950 and 1953 and ending in a stalemate

**Ku Klux Klan:** secret society first formed in the South during Reconstruction to ensure white supremacy over blacks; re-formed in the 1920s to express opposition to Jews, Catholics, Bolsheviks, and others considered "un-American"

## L

**labor union:** workers organized as a group to seek higher wages, improve working conditions, and obtain other benefits

**laissez-faire:** noninterference; has come to mean a policy by which the government minimizes its regulation of industry and the economy

**landslide election:** an election in which a victorious candidate gathers an overwhelming percentage of the total votes cast

**law:** rule recognized by a nation, state, or community as binding on its members

**League of Nations:** association of nations to protect the independence of member nations, proposed by President Wilson in his Fourteen Points and formed after World War I

**legislative branch:** the lawmaking agencies of a government

**legislature:** group of people with the power of making laws for a nation or state

**less developed nations:** nations that have not fully industrialized, usually Third World nations

**lifespan:** the lifetime of an individual

**limited government:** basic principle of the American system of government; belief that government is not all-powerful, and may only do those things the people have given it the power to do

**Lincoln-Douglas debates:** the series of political debates between Stephen Douglas and Abraham Lincoln during the Senate campaign of 1858, which catapulted Lincoln to the national spotlight

**literacy:** the ability to read and write

**literacy test:** test of a potential voter's ability to read and write; once used in several states to prevent African Americans and other minorities from voting; now outlawed

**lobby:** to attempt to influence legislation; also, groups that attempt to do so

**lockout:** during a labor dispute, the closing of a business (by locking the gates) to keep employees from entering

**loose interpretation:** a belief that the provisions of the Constitution, especially those granting power to the government, are to be construed in broad terms

**Louisiana Purchase:** purchase by the United States of the Louisiana Territory from France in 1803

**lynch:** to execute someone illegally, by hanging, burning, or other means

**M**

**majority:** at least one more than half (e.g., over 50 percent of the votes in an election)

**Manhattan Project:** secret American program during World War II to develop an atomic bomb

**Manifest Destiny:** a belief held in the first half of the nineteenth century that the United States had a mission to expand its borders to incorporate all land between the Atlantic and Pacific oceans

**margin:** a small part of the total price of a stock purchase deposited with a broker at the time of purchase with the promise to pay the full sum at a later date

**Marshall Court:** the Supreme Court during the tenure of John Marshall as chief justice, in which key decisions were made that strengthened the federal government's role in the nation's economic business

**mass circulation:** reaching a very large audience

**mass production:** rapid manufacture of large numbers of a product

**Mayflower Compact:** agreement signed by Pilgrims before landing at Plymouth

**McCarthyism:** the use of indiscriminate and unfounded accusations and sensationalist investigative methods to suppress political opponents portrayed as subversive; term taken from the name of Senator Joseph McCarthy, who carried out such practices

**melting pot theory:** the idea that different immigrant groups in the United States will lose their old identities and that a new American identity will emerge from the blending of cultures

**mercantilism:** economic theory that a nation's strength came from building up its gold supplies and expanding its trade

**merger:** a combining of two or more companies into a larger company

**Mexican Cession:** lands turned over to the United States after the Mexican War in what is now the states of California, Nevada, Utah, and parts of Wyoming, Colorado, Arizona, and New Mexico

**Mexican War:** conflict between the United States and Mexico from 1846 to 1848, ending with a victory for the United States

**Middle Passage:** transportation by force to European colonies in Western Hemisphere of Africans to be sold as enslaved people; name refers to second of three part transatlantic trade called Triangular Trade

**migration:** historically, a regular, deliberate movement of a group of people to specific locations

**militarism:** policy of building up strong military forces to prepare for war

**minimum wage:** the lowest wage that can be paid to certain workers as set by national or state law

**minority:** less than half

**minority group:** group within a nation that differs from most of the population in race, religion, national origin, and so on

**minor party:** one of the less widely supported political parties in a governmental system

**missionary:** one who attempts to spread the religious ideas of a faith in a foreign land

**mobilization:** a call-up of military forces, usually in preparation for war

**monarchy:** government headed by a single ruler, usually a king or queen

**monetary policy:** actions and positions taken by a government in regard to its system of money

**monopoly:** dominance in or control of a market for certain goods or services by a single company or combination of companies

**Monroe Doctrine:** policy statement of President James Monroe in 1823 warning nations of western Europe not to interfere with the newly independent nations of Latin America

**moral diplomacy:** a term describing President Woodrow Wilson's approach to foreign policy, which emphasized the use of negotiation and arbitration rather than force to settle international disputes

**Mormons:** members of the Church of Jesus Christ of Latter-day Saints; in the 1840s, thousands moved to Utah seeking freedom from religious persecution

**muckraker:** early twentieth-century American journalist who tried to improve society by exposing political corruption, health hazards, and other social problems

**multilateral action:** joint action taken by three or more nations

**municipal government:** the government of a city, town, or village

## N

**National Association for the Advancement of Colored People (NAACP):** an organization founded in 1909 to fight for the rights of African Americans

**national bank:** bank chartered by the federal government

**national government:** in the United States, the federal government

**nationalism:** pride in or devotion to one's country

**National Organization for Women (NOW):** founded in 1966 to work for equal rights for women

**national self interest:** aim of all foreign policy

**nativism:** a belief in the superiority of the way of life of one's home country; in the United States, this was often associated with a desire to limit immigration

**North Atlantic Treaty Organization (NATO):** an alliance formed for mutual defense in 1949 under the North Atlantic Treaty, and now made up of 15 nations stretching from Canada to Turkey

**naturalization:** the process by which a citizen of one country becomes a citizen of another

**natural rights:** rights that all people are entitled to from birth

**Nazism:** belief in the policies of Adolf Hitler

**necessary and proper clause:** another name for the elastic clause, which is the basis of the implied powers of Congress

**negotiation:** talking over an issue by two or more parties with the aim of reaching a mutually agreeable settlement

**neutrality:** the policy of not taking sides in a dispute or a war

**New Deal:** name given to the programs of President Franklin D. Roosevelt

**New Federalism:** name given to the attempt to lessen the federal government's role in its dealings with states during the presidencies of Nixon and Reagan

**New Freedom:** name given to the programs of President Woodrow Wilson

**New Frontier:** name given to the programs of President John F. Kennedy

**New Nationalism:** plan under which Theodore Roosevelt ran for president in 1912

**nominating convention:** political gathering at which a party names candidates for office

**noninvolvement:** policy of taking no side in international disputes, neutrality

**nonrecognition:** refusal to establish formal diplomatic relations with the new government of a nation

**normalcy:** President Warren G. Harding's term for the return to peace after World War I

**North American Free Trade Agreement (NAFTA):** agreement calling for the removal of trade restrictions between the United States, Canada, and Mexico

**nuclear freeze:** a halt in the manufacture and deployment of nuclear weapons

**nuclear power:** energy produced from a controlled atomic reaction

**nuclear waste:** the byproducts of the production of nuclear power

**nullification:** a state's refusal to recognize a federal law

**Nuremberg Trials:** post-World War II trials in which German government and military figures were tried for crimes committed during the war

### O

**Open Door Policy:** policy toward China set out by Secretary of State John Hay allowing any nation to trade in any other nation's sphere of influence

**original jurisdiction:** the court in which a case is heard firsthand

**overproduction:** a condition that exists when the supply of a product exceeds the demand for that product

### P

**pacifist:** a person who is opposed to war and refuses to fight under any circumstances

**pardon:** a release from the punishment or legal consequences of a crime granted by a President or governor

**parliament:** the legislature of Great Britain

**patent and copyright laws:** laws giving rights to inventions, literary, musical, and artistic works to their creators

**patriotism:** love and support of one's nation

**peaceful coexistence:** phrase describing the aim of U.S.–Soviet relations during a time of improved relations between those nations in the 1950s

**per capita income:** income per person

**perestroika:** the restructuring of the Soviet Union's economy under Mikhail Gorbachev that began a move toward free enterprise

**plantation:** large estate farmed by many workers

**political party:** organized group that seeks to control government through the winning of elections and the holding of public office

**political system:** the way a nation is governed

**poll tax:** a tax that must be paid before one can vote, often used in Southern states to discourage or prevent blacks from voting and now banned in national elections by the Twenty-fourth Amendment

**pool:** method of ending competition used by railroads in the late 1800s in which they divided up business in given areas and fixed prices

**popular sovereignty:** basic principle of the American system of government that the people are the only source of any and all governmental power

**popular vote:** votes cast by the people for the electors representing candidates in presidential elections

**Populist movement:** political movement begun by farmers and members of labor unions in the late 1800s seeking to limit the power of big businesses and grant greater say in the governmental process to individuals

**power:** control, authority, right

**preamble:** an introduction to a speech or piece of writing

**prejudice:** unfavorable opinion about people who are of different religion, race, or nationality

**President:** the chief executive of a modern republic, especially of the United States

**primary:** election held before a general election in which voters choose their party's candidates for office

**Progressive Era:** the period from 1900–1920 that saw the greatest action by Progressive reformers

**Progressive movement:** reform movement that worked to correct abuses in American society

**Prohibition:** the period of 1920–1933 when the making and sale of liquor was illegal in the United States

**propaganda:** spreading of ideas or beliefs that help a particular cause and hurt an opposing cause

**protectionism:** belief in policies that favor the protection of domestically produced goods

**protective tariff:** tax on imports designed to discourage their sale and to favor the development of domestic industry

**protectorate:** a country under the protection and partial control of a stronger country

**public opinion:** those attitudes held by a significant number of persons on matters of government and politics; expressed group attitudes

**purchasing power:** the ability to buy goods and services; the value of what money could buy at one time compared to what the same amount could buy at another time

### R

**racial equality:** a condition in which people are treated in the same manner by law and society regardless of their race

**racism:** belief that one race is superior to another

**Radical Republicans:** group of Republicans in Congress who wanted to protect the rights of people freed from slavery in the South and keep rich Southern planters from regaining political power

**ratification:** formal approval; final consent to the effectiveness of a constitution, constitutional amendment, or treaty

**raw materials:** natural substances before processing that will in some way increase their value or usefulness

**recession:** a decline in economic activity usually shorter and less severe than a depression

**Reconstruction:** the period of 1867–1877 when the federal government or local republican governments ruled the Southern states that had seceded

**recovery:** a restoring to a normal condition; one of the aims of FDR's New Deal

**Red Scare:** term used to describe periods in the 1920s and 1950s when American fear and suspicion of communism was at its height

**reform:** change for the better; one of the goals of FDR's New Deal

**regulatory agencies:** parts of the federal bureaucracy charged with overseeing different aspects of the nation's economy

**religious freedom:** the ability to worship as one chooses, guaranteed in this nation by the First Amendment

**reparations:** payments for losses a nation has suffered during a war

**representation:** condition of being acted and spoken for in government

**representative government:** system of government in which voters elect representatives to make laws for them

**republic:** nation in which voters choose representatives to govern them

**Republican Party:** one of the modern political parties, founded in 1854 in opposition to slavery

**reservation:** limited area set aside for Native Americans by the U.S. government

**reserved powers:** those powers held by the state in the American federal system

**revenue:** income

**robber baron:** terms used to describe large-scale entrepreneurs of the late 1800s

**Roosevelt Corollary:** expansion of the Monroe Doctrine announced by President Theodore Roosevelt in 1904 that claimed the United States had the right to intervene in Latin America to preserve law and order

**rural:** in or of the country

### S

**salad bowl theory:** idea that people of different backgrounds can exist side by side in the United States, maintaining their identities while still contributing to the overall society

**salutary neglect:** manner in which England governed the American colonies in the late 1600s and early 1700s, marked by weak enforcement of laws regulating colonial trade

**scalawag:** white Southerner who supported Radical Republicans during Reconstruction

**scarcity:** too small a supply

**secession:** the act of formally withdrawing from membership in a group or organization; in the United States, the withdrawing of 11 southern states from the Union in 1861

**sectionalism:** strong sense of loyalty to a state or section instead of to the whole country

**sedition:** an attempt to incite a rebellion against a national government

**segregation:** separation of people of different races

**Selective Service:** the military draft name first used during World War I

**self-determination:** right of national groups to their own territories and their own forms of government

**Senate:** upper house of the U.S. Congress in which each state has two members

**separate but equal:** principle upheld in *Plessy* v. *Ferguson* (1896) in which the Supreme Court ruled that segregation of public facilities was legal

**separation of church and state:** principle set out in the First Amendment that the government shall take no actions to establish or interfere with the practice of religion

**separation of powers:** the principle that gives the powers of making, enforcing, and interpreting laws to separate legislative, executive, and judicial branches of government

**settlement house:** a private center providing social services for the poor in a needy neighborhood

**sharecropper:** farmer who works land owned by another and gives the landowner part of the harvest

**sitdown strike:** work stoppage in which employees refuse to leave the workplace and occupy it in an attempt to force their employer to come to terms

**slavery:** condition in which one person is the property of another; banned in this country by the Thirteenth Amendment

**social contract theory:** the idea that people agreed to give up some rights and powers to a government that would provide for their safety and well-being

**Social Darwinism:** the belief that the evolutionary idea of "survival of the fittest" applied to societies and businesses

**socialism:** economic and political system based on the public ownership of the means by which goods and services are produced, distributed, and exchanged

**social reform:** efforts to better conditions within a society

**social security:** programs of the federal government to provide economic assistance to the disabled, unemployed, poor, and aged

**social welfare:** programs to promote public well-being

**sovereignty:** absolute power of a state within its own territory

**soviet:** elected assembly in the Soviet Union; (Cap.) pertaining to the Soviet Union

**speculator:** person who invests in a risky business venture in hopes of making a large profit

**spoils system:** system or practice of giving appointed offices as rewards from the successful party in an election; name for the patronage system under President Andrew Jackson

**Square Deal:** name given to programs of President Theodore Roosevelt

**stagflation:** an economic condition characterized by both inflation and recession

**states rights:** idea that individual states had the right to limit the power of the federal government

**stereotype:** a fixed, oversimplified idea about a person or group

**stock market:** place where shares in corporations are traded

**strict interpretation:** a literal reading of the Constitution holding that the federal government has only those powers explicitly delegated to it in the Constitution

**suburbs:** smaller towns surrounding large cities

**suffragists:** people who campaigned for women's right to vote

**summit meetings:** conferences of the heads of two or more nations

**supply-side economics:** the theory that the government can best stimulate the economy by cutting taxes and encouraging investment in business

**supremacy clause:** Article VI, Section 2 of the Constitution, which makes that document and federal laws and treaties the "supreme law of the land"

**Supreme Court:** the highest federal court and the final interpreter of the Constitution

**surplus goods:** extra goods

**swing state:** in a presidential election year, a state that is not clearly for either a Democratic or Republican candidate; the popular vote of the state that determines the electoral vote may be a major factor in the outcome of an election

**T**

**Taliban:** a reactionary, extremist Islamic group that imposed strict conservative laws when it controlled the Afghan government in the 1990s and remains an opponent to westernization

**tariff:** tax placed on goods brought into a country

**technology:** practical application of knowledge

**temperance movement:** campaign against the sale or drinking of alcohol

**tenant farming:** system of farming in which a farmer rents land to farm from a landowner

**territorial integrity:** condition in which a nation's borders are guaranteed against disturbance by other nations

**territory:** a political division of the United States before it becomes a state; a large area of land

**terrorism:** the use of violence, intimidation, and coercion to achieve an end, to gain publicity for a cause, or to disrupt the normal functioning of society

**Tet Offensive:** 1968 attack by Viet Cong and North Vietnamese forces throughout South Vietnam; a turning point in the Vietnam War

**third party:** a political party formed in addition to the Democratic and Republican Parties, which usually promote a limited platform; historically, the two major parties have adopted some aspects of third parties' platforms

**Third World:** during the Cold War, nations in the modern world that professed not to be allied with the Soviet Union and its allies or the United States and its allies, especially the developing nations of Asia, Africa, and Latin America

**three branches of government:** the division of the powers of government into legislative, executive, and judicial functions

**three-fifths compromise:** compromise reached at the Constitutional Convention of 1787 whereby three-fifths of a state's population of enslaved people would be counted for both representation and taxation

**totalitarian:** form of government in which the power to rule embraces all matters of human concern

**tradition:** the handing down of beliefs, customs, and practices from generation to generation

**Trail of Tears:** the forced movement of the Cherokee in 1838–1839 to land west of the Mississippi River

**transcontinental railroad:** railway extending from coast to coast; completed in 1869

**treaty:** a formal agreement concluded between two or more countries

**Treaty of Versailles:** treaty marking the end of World War I that the U.S. Senate refused to ratify

**triangular trade:** trans-Atlantic trade among three regions; in particular in the seventeenth, eighteenth, and early nineteenth centuries with cash crops from colonies, manufactured goods from Europe, and enslaved people from West Africa

**Triple Alliance:** name of the alliance of Germany, Austria-Hungary, and Italy before World War I

**Triple Entente:** name of the alliance of Great Britain, France, and Russia before World War I

**trust:** group of corporations run by a single board of directors

**trustbuster:** person who wanted to break up some or all trusts

**two-party system:** political system in which the candidates of only two major parties have a reasonable chance of winning elections

## U

**unconstitutional:** not permitted by the constitution of a nation

**unilateral action:** an action taken by one nation only

**unitary government:** form of government in which all of the powers are held in a single agency

**universal suffrage:** the right to vote is extended to all adults

**unwritten constitution:** a combination of executive and legislative actions and interpretations and judicial decisions, especially judicial review, as well as customs and traditions such as development of political parties

**urban:** in or of the city

**urbanization:** process by which more of a nation's population becomes concentrated in its cities

## V

**venture capital:** money invested in a new corporation or other business enterprise

**veto:** chief executive's power to reject a bill passed by a legislature

**Vietnam War:** nation's longest war; fought in Southeast Asia from the late 1950s to 1973

**void:** without legal force or effect

## W

**War of 1812:** war between the United States and Great Britain

**War Powers Act:** law passed in 1973 requiring the President to seek congressional approval if troops are sent into action for longer than 60 days

**weapons of mass destruction:** WMD; devices used for large scale and total destruction, i.e. nuclear bombs, nerve gas, chemical warfare

**Whig Party:** one of the first political parties, standing for the limitation of executive power and the defense of liberty; by the 1850s had declined in power

**white-collar worker:** someone holding a job in business or in a profession

**women's rights movement:** the struggle of women for equality

**work ethic:** a belief that hard work is a virtuous end in itself

**World War I:** conflict between Allied Powers and Central Powers from 1914 to 1918

**World War II:** conflict between Allied and Axis nations from 1939 to 1945

## Y

**yellow dog contract:** a contract between an employer and an employee in which the employee agrees not to join a union while employed; this is no longer legal

**yellow journalism:** sensational style of reporting used by some newspapers in the late 1800s

**yellow peril:** derogatory term implying that Asian peoples threatened the ways of life of white Americans

# Index

revolutions. *See specific revolutions*
Rice, Condoleezza, 298–299, A-19
rights. *See also* civil rights movement;
    *specific groups*
        in Bill of Rights, 44
        foundations of American, 20
        natural, 20
        in 1920s, 186–187
        of women, 48, 141–142
right to life issues, 309
Riis, Jacob, 140, A-19
riots, race, 266
rivers. *See specific rivers*
roads and highways, 68, 257
robber barons, 107
Robinson, Jackie, 259, A-19
Rockefeller, John D., 106, A-19
Rockefeller, Nelson A., 287–288, A-19
Rocky Mountain region, 3, 7
*Roe* v. *Wade*, 47, 48, 268, A-12
Rome (ancient), ideas from, 19
Roosevelt, Eleanor, 197–198, 202, 232,
    A-19
Roosevelt, Franklin D., 189, A-5
        court-packing plan of, 204
        elections of, 190, 202
        New Deal and, 196–206
        policies of, 203
        political opposition to, 205–206
        presidential terms of, 52, 220
        quarantine speech of, 219, 220
        World War II and, 222, 224
Roosevelt, Theodore, 136, 144–146, 154,
    A-4
        "big stick" policy of, 158
        as imperialist, 155
        Japan and, 152–153
        Square Deal and, 144–146
Roosevelt Corollary, 152, 157–158, 274
Root-Takahira Agreement (1908), 153
Rosenberg, Julius and Ethel, 239, A-20
Rosenberg case, 232, 239
Rosie the Riveter, 227
Rousseau, Jean-Jacques, 21, A-20
"rule of reason," 146
rural areas
        in Great Depression, 195
        population of, 113
        problems of, 68
Rural Electrification Administration
    (REA, 1935), 199
Russia. *See also* Soviet Union
        Japan and, 152
        Kosovo and, 303
Russian Revolution, 162, 165, 187
Russo-Japanese War, 152
Rust Belt, 257–258

## S

Sacajawea, A-20
Sacco, Nicola, 179, 187, A-20
el-Sadat, Anwar, 290
Saddam Hussein, 296, 301, A-17
Saint Augustine, Florida, 15
*St. Louis* (ship), 226
St. Regis Indian Reservation, 271
"Salary Grab," 98
SALT. *See* Strategic Arms Limitations Talks
    (SALT)
SALT II Treaty, 290
salutary neglect, 23
Samoa, 152–153, 155
Sandinistas, 292
San Francisco, segregation of Asians in,
    152–153
Sanger, Margaret, 142, A-20
sanitation, 68
Santa Fe Trail, 76
Saratoga, Battle of, 25, 26
Saudi Arabia, 296
savings and loan scandal, 295
scalawags, 98
scandals
        under Grant, 98
        under Harding, 180
*Schechter Poultry Corporation* v. *United
    States*, 47, 50, 204, A-10
*Schenck* v. *United States*, 47, 164, A-9
Schiavo, Terri, 309
schools
        desegregation of, 46, 101, 259–260
        for hearing impaired, 271
        reform of, 74, 299
science. *See* industry; technology
Scopes Trial, 179, 188
SDS. *See* Students for a Democratic
    Society (SDS)
seas, freedoms of, 56
SEATO. *See* Southeast Asia Treaty
    Organization (SEATO)
secession, crisis over, 79
Second Amendment, 44
Second Bank of the United States, 67,
    72–73, 147
Second Continental Congress, 25, 26
Second Great Awakening, 74
Second New Deal, 203
Second Seminole War, 74
Second World War. *See* World War II
Secretariat (UN), 232
secret ballot, 72, 143
sectionalism, 65–66, 72–73
security, 301. *See also* national security
Security Council (UN), 232
Sedition Act
        of 1798, 52
        of 1918, 164

segregation, 264–265
        of African Americans, 27, 69, 101
        in armed forces, 179
        of Asians, 152–153
Selective Service Act (1917), 162
self-determination, 165
self-government, 21, 22
Selma March, 260
Seminole Indians, 74
Senate (U.S.), 36, 51
        constitutional powers of, 36–37
        direct election of, 144
Seneca Falls Convention, 75, 141, 267
separate but equal facilities, 101, 142
separation of powers, 22, 33, 49, 54, 204
September 11, 2001, terrorist attacks,
    300
Serbia, 298, 303
servants
        indentured, 15
        in South, 17
Servicemen's Readjustment Act.
    *See* GI Bill of Rights
settlement house movement, 113, 140
settlement(s)
        by ethnic group, 16
        by immigrants, 115–116
        Jamestown as, 13
        Saint Augustine as, 15
Seventeenth Amendment, 45, 144, 148
Seventh Amendment, 44
Seven Years' War, 23
sexism, 268
sexual harassment, 295
sharecroppers, 104
Shays' Rebellion, 28
Sheppard-Towner Act (1921), 186
Sherman Antitrust Act (1890), 108,
    145–146, 148
ships and shipping, in World War I, 161
Sinclair, Upton, 137, 140, A-20
Sioux wars, 118
sit down strike, 201
sit-ins, 264
Sitting Bull (Sioux), 118
Sixteenth Amendment, 45, 144, 147–148
Sixth Amendment, 44
skilled workers, 201
slaves and slavery, 17–19. *See also*
    enslaved
        American Revolution and, 27
        antislavery movement and, 75
        Declaration of Independence and, 26
        Emancipation Proclamation and, 82
        Indians as, 17
        in new states, 28
        North-South conflict over, 77–80
        plantation life and, 71
        resistance and, 19, 71

# Acknowledgments

## Staff Credits:

The people who make up the *United States History and Government Brief Review* team—representing design, editorial, marketing, and production services—are listed below. Bold type denotes the core team members.

**Jane Breen,** Laura Chadwick, **Jennifer McQueeney Creane,** Kerry Dunn, **Thomas Ferreira,** Rebecca Hall, **Linda D. Johnson,** Candi McDowell, Julie Orr, Rachel Youdelman

## Additional Credits:

The Quarasan Group, Inc.: Chicago, IL

Lapiz Digital Services: Chennai, India
Lapiz, Inc.: Boston, MA

## Document-Based Essay Question Writers

Fran Legum and Jane Librett
Department of Instructional Programs and Alternative Schools
Nassau BOCES

Note: Every effort has been made to locate the copyright owner of materials reprinted in this book. Omissions brought to our attention will be corrected in subsequent printings.

## Text and Image Credits:

All uncredited photos copyright © 2011 Pearson Education. Grateful acknowledgment is made to the following for copyrighted material:

**Cover** Stephen Coburn/Shutterstock **Page xii** Adapted from J.S. Pugh, Puck, September 5, 1900; **xxxvi** Copyright Elliott Erwitt/Magnum Photos; **11** *Signing of the Constitution* (1940), Howard Chandler Christy. Oil on canvas, 20' × 30'. House wing of U.S. Capitol, east stairway. Photograph courtesy of Architect of the Capitol; **14** Steve Kelley/Creators News Service; **23** *Join or Die* (May 9, 1754), Benjamin Franklin. Woodcut, published in *Pennsylvania Gazette*/Library of Congress Prints and Photographs Division [LC-USZC4-5315]; **83** *King Andrew the First* (1833), Anonymous. Lithograph on wove paper, 31.7 × 21.4 cm./ Library of Congress Prints and Photographs Division [LC-DIG-ppmsca-15771]; **95** *The Homestead Riot* (1892), W.P. Snyder. Wood engraving, illustration in *Harper's Weekly*, v. 36, no. 1856 (July 16, 1892)/Library of Congress Prints and Photographs Division [LC-USZ62-126046]; **101** *Booker T. Washington Portrait* (ca. 1903), Cheynes Studio, Hampton VA. Photographic print/Library of Congress Prints and Photographs Division [LC-USZ62-49568]; **101** *W.E.B. Du Bois Portrait* (1918), Cornelius M. Battey. Photographic print/Library of Congress Prints and Photographs Division [LC-USZ62-16767]; **106** *John Pierpont Morgan Portrait* (ca. 1902). Photographic print/Library of Congress Prints and Photographs Division [LC-USZ62-94188]; **110** *Great Railway Strikes–The First Meat Train Leaving the Chicago Stockyards Under Escort of United States Cavalry, July 10, 1894,* G.A. Coffin and G.W. Peters. Photomechanical print. Illustration in *Harper's Weekly*, July 28, 1894/Library of Congress Prints and Photographs Division [LC-USZ62-96508]; **112** Frances Benjamin Johnston (1899). Cyanotype/Library of Congress Prints and Photographs Division [LC-USZ62-68344]; **118** *Sitting Bull Portrait* (1885), D.F. Barry. Photographic print/Library of Congress Prints and Photographs Division [LC-USZ62-111147]; **119 L** *William McKinley Portrait*/Library of Congress Prints and Photographs Division; **119 R** *William Jennings Bryan Portrait*/Library of Congress Prints and Photographs Division; **128** Library of Congress, Prints & Photographs Division [LC-USZ62-133890]; **135** *Suffrage Parade, New York, May 6, 1912*/American Press Association (APA)/Library of Congress Prints and Photographs Division [LC-USZC4-5585]; **145** *The Bosses of the Senate* (Illustration in *Puck*, Jan. 23, 1889), lithograph by J. Ottmann after drawing by J. Keppler/Library of Congress Prints and Photographs Division [LC-USZC4-494]; **158** *World's Constable* (cartoon in Judge, Jan. 7, 1905), Louis Dalrymple. Granger Collection, New York; **161** Corbis/Bettmann; **164** Library of Congress, Prints & Photographs Division, WWI Posters, LC-USZC4-8028]; **166** Stock Montage, Inc.; **177** *Workman on the Framework of the Empire State Building* (ca. 1941), Lewis Wickes Hine/Works Progress Administration (WPA)/National Archives and Records Administration (NARA) [NWDNS-69-RH-4K-1]; **181** Library of Congress Prints and Photographs Division [LC-USZ62-110629]; **184** Library of Congress Prints and Photographs Division [LC-D420-2702]; **186** Illustration by John Held, Jr./Time & Life Pictures; **188** Library of Congress Prints and Photographs Division [LC-USZC4-4656]; **195** U.S. Information Agency (1931)/National Archives and Records Administration (NARA) [NWDNS-306-NT-165319c]; **197** *This is One Rabbit that Never Failed Me* cartoon (1938), Clifford Kennedy Berryman; **197** *FDR Plays with Children* cartoon (1938), Clifford Kennedy Berryman/Library of Congress Prints and Photographs Division [LC-USZ62-17300]; **198** National Archives and Records Administration (NARA); **205** FDR cartoon (1937), Clifford Kennedy Berryman/Library of Congress Prints and Photographs Division [LC-USZ62-10046]; **215** Courtesy of Franklin D. Roosevelt Library; **217** J. Howard Miller/Produced by Westinghouse for the War Production Coordinating Committee/NARA Still Picture Branch [NWDNS-179-WP-1563]; **227** Library of Congress Prints and Photographs Division [LC-USW33-028626-C]; **229** *High-School Recess Period, Manzanar Relocation Center, California* (1943), Ansel Adams/Library of Congress, Prints & Photographs Division [LC-DIG-ppprs-00338]; **233** Daniel R. Fitzpatrick/The Granger Collection, New York; **237** Photo Courtesy of U.S. Army; **247** *Trouble with Some of the Pieces* (cartoon in *Punch*, Feb. 7, 1945), Ernest Howard Shepard/Art Archive; **251** Warren K. Leffler/Library of Congress Prints and Photographs Division [LC-DIG-ppmsca-03130]; **269** Dana Fradon (1972)/The New Yorker Magazine/Cartoon Bank **290** Warren K. Leffler (1978)/Library of Congress Prints and Photographs Division [LC-DIG-ppmsca-09791]; **291** Courtesy of the Ronald Reagan Presidential Foundation and Library; **297** Steve Sack/Star Tribune; **300** Dejan Gileski/ Shutterstock; **305** Pete Souza; **311** Petty Officer 2nd Class Kyle Niemi, U.S. Coast Guard/U. S. Army; **320** A 1962 Herblock Cartoon, copyright by The Herb Block Foundation.

**Regents Exams: January 2010 3** Blum et. al. The National Experience: A History of the United States, fifth edition. © 1981 Harcourt Brace Jovanovich; **5** A 1937 Herblock Cartoon, copyright by The Herb Block Foundation; **6** Copyright by Bill Mauldin (1975). Courtesy of Bill Mauldin Estate LLC; **8** Courtesy Joe Heller; **9** Jost, K. (2003, January 10). Stimulating the economy. *CQ Researcher, 13*, 1–24. Federal Deficits and Surpluses graph. Copyright © 2003 CQ Press, a division of SAGE Publications, Inc.; **12** Adapted from Compass Productions; **15** Adapted from USDA and the Kerr Center for Sustainable Agriculture; **16** Adapted from www.geo.msu. edu; **August 2009 5** Gene Elderman, Washington Post, January 7, 1937; **7** Copyright by Bill Mauldin (1973). Courtesy of Bill Mauldin Estate LLC; **9** Clark, C. S. (1997, February 28). Feminism's future. *CQ Researcher, 7*, 169–192. US Women Making Progress graph. Copyright © 1997 CQ Press, a division of SAGE Publications, Inc.; **16** From KENNEDY. The American Spirit, 12E. © 2010 Wadsworth, a part of Cengage Learning, Inc. Reproduced by permission. www.cengage.com/permissions; **21** Clifford Berryman, Washington Star, January 5, 1934. **June 2009 5** Fred O. Seibel/Richmond Times-Dispatch; **6** Theodor Geisel; **7** Rand McNally; **8** A 1975 Herblock Cartoon, copyright by The Herb Block Foundation; **9** Courtesy of The Population Reference Bureau; **10** Courtesy The New York Times; **13** Courtesy of the US Census Bureau; **13** Courtesy of the US Immigration and Naturalization Service; **14** Courtesy of Gary Fields; **14** From A NEW HISTORY OF THE UNITED STATES by Irving Bartlett, copyright 1975 by Holt, Rinehart and Winston, Inc. and reprinted by permission of Houghton Mifflin Harcourt Publishing Company; **18** Courtesy of Library of Congress; **20** Courtesy of Library of Congress; **21** Clifford Kennedy Berryman/ The Washington Post. **January 2009 2** Pearson; **4** Illustration from DISCOVERING AMERICAN HISTORY, VOL. 1, Copyright 1967 by Allen Kownslar and Donald B. Frizzle and published by Holt Rinehart and Winston and reprinted by permission of Houghton Mifflin Harcourt Publishing Company; **6** Courtesy of the US Department of Commerce; **8** Courtesy of the US Census Bureau; **9** Tom Toles/ United Press Syndicate; **10** Courtesy of the National Archives; **14** Courtesy of Library of Congress; **17** The New York Times "Prayer in Public School? It's Nothing New for Many" from *The New York Times, November 22, 1994*. All rights reserved. Used by permission and protected by the Copyright Laws of the United States. The printing, copying, redistribution, or retransmission of the Material without express written permission is prohibited; **18** The Associated Press "Ten Commandments, Other Issues Generating Debate in KY" from The Associated Press, April 13, 2006. Copyright © 2009 The Associated Press. All rights reserved. Used with permission of The Associated Press; **20** Charles Brooks/ Birmingham News. **August 2008 2** Mountain High Maps, courtesy Digital Wisdom; **6** G. R. Spencer/ Reprinted with permission from the Omaha World-Herald; **6** Next Decade Entertainment "Brother Can You Spare a Dime?" by E.Y. "Yip" Harburg and Jap Gorney. Published by Glocca Morra Music (ASCAP) and Gorney Music (ASCAP). Administered by Next Decade Entertainment, Inc. All right reserved. Used by permission; **7** Courtesy of the National Park Service; **8** Dana Summers/ The Orlando Sentinel; **9 L** Etta Hulme/ United Media; **9 R** Courtesy of the US Census Bureau; **13** From KENNEDY. The American Spirit, 12E. © 2010 Wadsworth, a part of Cengage Learning, Inc. Reproduced by permission. www.cengage.com/permissions; **17** Pearson; **21** The New York Times "California Lawmakers Vote to Lower Auto Emissions" from *The New York Times, July 2, 2002* and "Reagan Signs Law Linking Federal Aid to Drinking Age" from *The New York Times, July 18, 1984*. All rights reserved. Used by permission and protected by the Copyright Laws of the United States. The printing, copying, redistribution, or retransmission of the Material without express written permission is prohibited. **June 2008 3** Rex Babin; **4** From American Foreign Policy. Volume 2 Revised, 3E. 1991 Wadsworth, a part of Cengage Learning, Inc. Reproduced by permission.; **6** Random House "Mother to Son" from *The Collected Poems of Langston Hughes* by Langston Hughes, edited by Arnold Rampersad with David Roessel, Associate Editor, copyright © 1994 by the Estate of Langston Hughes. Used by permission of Alfred A. Knopf, a division of Random House, Inc.; **6** Esquire Magazine; **8 L** A 1974 Herblock Cartoon, copyright by The Herb Block Foundation; **8 R** USA Today; **9** Courtesy of the US Census Bureau; **10** Courtesy Rethinking Schools; **19 L** Will Counts Collection at Indiana University Archives; **19 R** Bettmann/ Corbis; **21** Will Counts Collection at Indiana University Archives.

This section contains the Regents Examination in United States History and Government that was given in New York State in January 2010.

Circle your answers to Part I on this exam and write your answers to the thematic essay and document-based essay questions on separate sheets of paper. Be sure to refer to the test-taking strategies in the front of this book as you prepare to answer the test questions.

## Part I

### Answer all questions in this part.

*Directions* (1–50): For each statement or question, write on the separate answer sheet the *number* of the word or expression that, of those given, best completes the statement or answers the question.

1 In which area did good harbors, abundant forests, rocky soil, and a short growing season most influence the colonial economy?

(1) Southern colonies
(2) Middle Atlantic region
(3) Northwest Territory
(4) New England colonies

2 The Mayflower Compact and the Virginia House of Burgesses are most closely associated with

(1) abuses by absolute monarchs
(2) establishment of religious toleration
(3) steps toward colonial self-government
(4) adoption of universal suffrage

3 The authors of the Declaration of Independence used the phrase "Life, Liberty and the pursuit of Happiness" to identify

(1) natural rights        (3) States rights
(2) legal rights          (4) economic rights

4 In order to win ratification of the United States Constitution, supporters agreed to

(1) add a bill of rights
(2) admit new states to the Union
(3) establish an electoral college
(4) give the Senate the power to ratify treaties

5 Which action did Alexander Hamilton support during the 1790s?

(1) restrictions on trade with England
(2) distribution of free land
(3) creation of the national bank
(4) elimination of the whiskey tax

6 Which power did the United States Supreme Court gain through the Court's decision in *Marbury* v. *Madison*?

(1) judicial review
(2) hearing appeals from lower federal courts
(3) deciding cases involving two or more states
(4) judicial independence through lifetime appointments

7 One way in which the Kentucky and Virginia Resolutions (1798) and the South Carolina Ordinance of Nullification (1832) are similar is that each

(1) claimed that individual states have the right to interpret federal laws
(2) formed part of the unwritten constitution
(3) supported the federal government's power to declare war
(4) provided a way for new states to enter the Union

8 During the early 1800s, which factor contributed the most to the start of the Industrial Revolution in the United States?

(1) a restriction on European immigration
(2) the end of the slave labor system
(3) an abundance of natural resources
(4) the availability of electricity

9 A primary goal of the Monroe Doctrine (1823) was to

(1) prevent European intervention in Latin America
(2) create an opportunity for the annexation of Canada
(3) protect the site of a canal across Central America
(4) help European nations establish new Western Hemisphere colonies

10 What was an immediate effect of the completion of the Erie Canal in 1825?

(1) Prices increased for food products along the Atlantic Coast.
(2) Farmers could more easily ship grain to eastern markets.
(3) A territorial conflict began with Canada over the Great Lakes.
(4) Railroads were forced to reduce their shipping rates.

Base your answer to question 11 on the map below and on your knowledge of social studies.

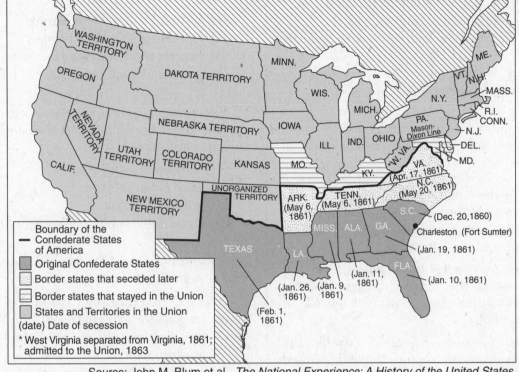

Source: John M. Blum et al., *The National Experience: A History of the United States,*
Harcourt Brace Jovanovich, 1981 (adapted)

11 What is the most accurate title for this map?

(1) Closing the Frontier  (3) A Nation Divided

(2) Results of Reconstruction  (4) Compromise of 1850

12 The Supreme Court ruling in *Dred Scott* v. *Sanford* (1857) helped to increase sectional conflict because the decision

(1) denied Congress the power to regulate slavery in the territories

(2) allowed for the importation of enslaved persons for ten years

(3) prohibited slavery in lands west of the Mississippi River

(4) gave full citizenship to all enslaved persons

13 In 1862, the Homestead Act and the Pacific Railway Act were passed primarily to

(1) achieve Northern victory in the Civil War

(2) develop the Midwest and western parts of the country

(3) improve the lives of freed slaves

(4) expand overseas markets to Asia and Europe

14 Following the Civil War, fewer immigrants settled in the South because

(1) most of the new arrivals chose to settle on the Great Plains

(2) freedmen had been given most of the available farmland in the South

(3) jobs were more plentiful for immigrants on the West Coast

(4) more factories that employed unskilled laborers were located in the North

15 The most direct effect of poll taxes and literacy tests on African Americans was to

(1) prevent them from voting

(2) limit their access to public facilities

(3) block their educational opportunities

(4) deny them economic advancements

16 During the late 1800s, what was a major effect of industrialization on workers in the United States?

(1) Membership in labor unions declined.
(2) Workers migrated to rural regions.
(3) Most factory jobs became service industry jobs.
(4) Skilled craftsmen were replaced by semiskilled machine operators.

Base your answers to questions 17 and 18 on the speakers' statements below and on your knowledge of social studies.

*Speaker A:* Feeding and clothing the poor is a mistake. Just as nature weeds out unfit members, a capitalist society should be allowed to do the same.

*Speaker B:* To provide for the common good and protect the people, the government should pass laws to prevent the sale of alcohol.

*Speaker C:* To promote economic growth, the government should expand United States markets overseas.

*Speaker D:* Since transportation is a public necessity, the government should own and operate the railroads in the public interest.

17 Which speaker would most likely support the theory of Social Darwinism?

(1) A              (3) C
(2) B              (4) D

18 Which third party held beliefs most similar to those expressed by *Speaker D*?

(1) Know-Nothing      (3) Populist
(2) Greenback         (4) Bull Moose

19 During the late 1800s, presidents and governors most often used military force during labor-management conflicts as a way to

(1) support industrialists and end strikes
(2) make employers sign collective bargaining agreements
(3) protect workers from the private armies of employers
(4) replace striking factory workers with soldiers

20 Between 1880 and 1920, the majority of the "new" immigrants to the United States came from

(1) northern and western Europe
(2) southern and eastern Europe
(3) Canada and Latin America
(4) China and Southeast Asia

21 Which factor is most closely associated with the decision of the United States to declare war on Spain in 1898?

(1) isolationist policy
(2) labor union pressure
(3) yellow journalism
(4) unrestricted submarine warfare

22 A major purpose of President Woodrow Wilson's Fourteen Points (1918) was to

(1) ask Congress to enter World War I
(2) set goals for achieving peace after World War I
(3) provide an aid program for rebuilding war-torn nations
(4) retaliate for the sinking of the *Lusitania*

23 The "clear and present danger" doctrine established in *Schenck* v. *United States* (1919) concerned the issue of

(1) freedom of speech
(2) the right to bear arms
(3) the right to an attorney
(4) separation of church and state

24 Why did many United States farmers fail to benefit from the economic prosperity of the 1920s?

(1) No technological advances were made in agriculture.
(2) Levels of farm production declined.
(3) Farm exports were heavily taxed.
(4) Agricultural goods were overproduced.

25 The Scopes trial of the 1920s dealt with a conflict between

(1) communism and capitalism
(2) Protestants and Catholics
(3) science and religion
(4) labor and management

26 Which economic factor contributed most directly to the start of the Great Depression?

(1) low worker productivity
(2) high income taxes
(3) decreasing tariff rates
(4) buying stocks on margin

Base your answer to question 27 on the cartoon below and on your knowledge of social studies.

**"O, death! O, change! O, time!"**

Source: Herblock, *NEA Service*, 1937 (adapted)

27 Which constitutional principle is illustrated in this cartoon?

(1) federalism      (3) States rights
(2) checks and balances      (4) executive privilege

28 What was a guiding principle of the New Deal economic policies?

(1) Pro-business tax breaks would solve the problems associated with urban poverty.
(2) Antitrust legislation would destroy the free market economy of the United States.
(3) Rugged individualism must be allowed to solve social inequality.
(4) Government must assume more responsibility for helping the poor.

29 The Neutrality Acts of 1935 and 1937 were intended to

(1) enforce the policies of the League of Nations
(2) stimulate economic growth in the United States
(3) avoid the policies that drew the nation into World War I
(4) support the use of peacekeeping troops in Europe

30 What was a primary goal of Franklin D. Roosevelt, Winston Churchill, and Joseph Stalin when they met at the Yalta Conference in 1945?

(1) setting up postwar aid for Great Britain
(2) sharing the development of atomic weapons
(3) protecting the colonial empires of the warring nations
(4) settling major wartime issues of the Allied powers

31 What effect did the end of World War II have on American women who worked in defense industries during the war?

(1) They were invited to join labor unions.
(2) Their jobs were taken by returning servicemen.
(3) Their wages were increased to match those of male workers.
(4) Their contributions were rewarded by the government.

32 The war crimes trials in Nuremberg and Tokyo following World War II established the concept that

(1) nations could be made to pay for wartime damages
(2) pardons should be granted to all accused war criminals
(3) those convicted should be given shorter sentences than ordinary criminals
(4) individuals could be held accountable for their actions in a war

33 In the 1960s, which issue was the focus of the Supreme Court decisions in *Mapp* v. *Ohio*, *Gideon* v. *Wainwright*, and *Miranda* v. *Arizona*?

(1) freedom of the press
(2) racial segregation
(3) rights of the accused
(4) interstate commerce

Base your answers to questions 34 and 35 on the passage below and on your knowledge of social studies.

"This Government, as promised, has maintained the closest surveillance of the Soviet Military buildup on the island of Cuba. Within the past week, unmistakable evidence has established the fact that a series of offensive missile sites is now in preparation on that imprisoned island. The purpose of these bases can be none other than to provide a nuclear strike capability against the Western Hemisphere. . . ."

— President John F. Kennedy, October 22, 1962

34 Which action did President Kennedy take following this statement?

(1) urging Allied forces to remove Soviet weapons from Cuba
(2) ordering a naval quarantine of Cuba
(3) breaking off diplomatic relations with the Soviet Union
(4) asking the United Nations to stop grain shipments to the Soviet Union

35 The crisis described in this passage was resolved when

(1) Cuba became a capitalist nation
(2) the United States seized control of Cuba
(3) Soviet Premier Nikita Khruschev met with President Kennedy
(4) the Soviet Union withdrew its missiles from Cuba

36 President Richard Nixon's foreign policy of détente was an attempt to

(1) resolve Middle East conflicts
(2) improve relations with the Soviet Union
(3) defend United States interests in Latin America
(4) increase the power of the United Nations Security Council

37 Which action did President Gerald Ford take in an attempt to end the national controversy over the Watergate affair?

(1) pardoning Richard Nixon
(2) declaring a war on poverty
(3) declining to run for reelection
(4) asking Congress to impeach Richard Nixon

Base your answer to question 38 on the cartoon below and on your knowledge of social studies.

"WELL, GIRLS, AT LEAST THE ONLY WAY WE CAN GO IS UP."

Source: Bill Mauldin, *Chicago Sun-Times*, 1975

38 In the 1970s, many women's rights advocates reacted to the situation shown in the cartoon by

(1) rejecting the provisions of Title IX
(2) opposing affirmative action programs
(3) demanding the right to vote in all elections
(4) supporting the Equal Rights Amendment to the Constitution

39 President Jimmy Carter's decision to pardon Vietnam War draft evaders who had fled to Canada is an example of the president's role as

(1) chief diplomat          (3) chief executive
(2) head of party           (4) world leader

40 The United States Congress can check the executive branch of government by

(1) appointing ambassadors
(2) overriding vetoes
(3) nominating judges
(4) declaring laws unconstitutional

Base your answer to question 41 on the chart below and on your knowledge of social studies.

**Number of Americans Age 85 and Older**

| Year | (in millions) |
|------|------|
| 1900 | 0.1 |
| 1950 | 0.6 |
| 1960 | 0.9 |
| 2000 | 4.2 |
| 2010* | 6.1 |
| 2020* | 7.3 |

*Projected

Source: Federal Interagency Forum on Aging-Related Statistics

41 Which statement is most clearly supported by the information in the chart?

(1) Elderly men outnumber elderly women.
(2) In 1960, more than 10 percent of Americans were age 85 or older.
(3) The number of Americans living past the age of 85 is increasing.
(4) In 1900, only 1 million Americans were age 85.

42 What is one reason for the increases in worldwide oil prices since the 1970s?

(1) construction of the Trans-Alaska oil pipeline
(2) political unrest in the Middle East
(3) promotion of conservation efforts by United States oil companies
(4) doubling of tariffs on oil imports by the United States government

43 The United States has had a trade deficit over the past two decades because the nation

(1) imposed protective tariffs on imports
(2) placed high taxes on exports
(3) refused to enter international free trade agreements
(4) imported more goods than it exported

Base your answer to question 44 on the graphic organizer below and on your knowledge of social studies.

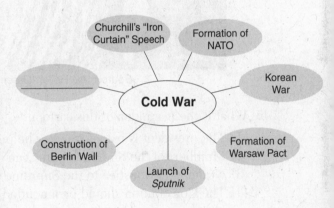

44 Which event best completes this graphic organizer?

(1) Vietnam War          (3) Persian Gulf War
(2) Holocaust            (4) D-Day invasion

Base your answer to question 45 on the cartoon below and on your knowledge of social studies.

SUPREME COURT NOMINEE

Source: Joe Heller, *Green Bay Press-Gazette*, July 20, 2005 (adapted)

45 What is the main idea of this cartoon?

(1) The president is responsible for helping hurricane victims.

(2) Members of the Supreme Court can often ignore political issues.

(3) Nominating a justice to the Supreme Court often creates controversy.

(4) The Constitution should be amended so that Supreme Court Justices are elected.

46 Radical Republicans' passage of the Civil War amendments, President Theodore Roosevelt's Square Deal, and President Lyndon Johnson's Great Society programs were all attempts to

(1) promote the theory of laissez-faire

(2) improve society through government action

(3) reduce the economic role of government

(4) increase the influence of large corporations

47 One way in which the Pearl Harbor attack of December 7, 1941, and the attacks of September 11, 2001, are similar is that both led to

(1) increasing isolation

(2) the creation of a military draft

(3) the impeachment of the president

(4) major changes in United States foreign policy

Base your answer to question 48 on the graph below and on your knowledge of social studies.

**Federal Budget Deficits and Surpluses**
**(1990–2002)**

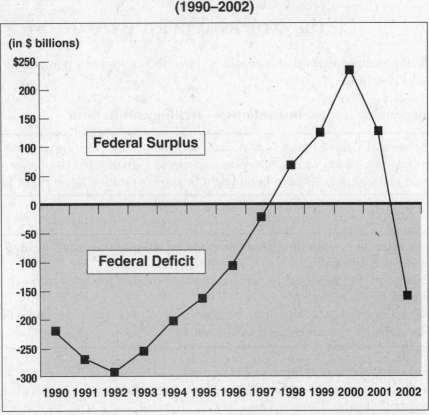

Source: *CQ Researcher,* 2003 (adapted)

48 Which statement about the federal budget is most clearly supported by the information in the graph?

(1) The budget was balanced throughout most of the 1990s.
(2) The budget surplus began declining in 1998.
(3) The budget deficit became smaller between 1992 and 1997.
(4) The budget deficit remained unchanged between 1992 and 2000.

49 The passage of the Alien and Sedition Acts in 1798, the McCarthy hearings in the 1950s, and the passage of the USA Patriot Act in 2001 created controversy because they

(1) required large sums of money to enforce
(2) raised questions about the protection of civil liberties
(3) created alliances with foreign governments
(4) limited the power of the executive branch

50 The policy of Dollar Diplomacy, the Good Neighbor policy, and the Alliance for Progress were designed to

(1) increase United States influence in Latin America
(2) open trade with Southeast Asia
(3) maintain peace with European nations
(4) provide foreign aid to African nations

**Answers to the essay questions are to be written in the separate essay booklet.**

**Part II**

**THEMATIC ESSAY QUESTION**

*Directions:* Write a well-organized essay that includes an introduction, several paragraphs addressing the task below, and a conclusion.

**Theme: Individuals, Groups, Institutions — Writing and Reform**

> Throughout United States history, individuals have used writing as a way to focus attention on issues facing the American people. To resolve the issues raised in these writings, actions have been taken by the government, groups, or individuals.

**Task:**

> Select *two* pieces of writing that have focused attention on issues facing American society and for *each*
> * Describe the historical circumstances surrounding the issue addressed by the author
> * Discuss an action taken by the government *or* a group *or* an individual in response to the issue raised by the author

You may use any piece of writing from your study of United States history that focuses attention on an issue facing American society. Some suggestions you might wish to consider include *Common Sense* by Thomas Paine (1776), *Uncle Tom's Cabin* by Harriet Beecher Stowe (1852), *How the Other Half Lives* by Jacob Riis (1890), *The Jungle* by Upton Sinclair (1906), "I, Too, Sing America" by Langston Hughes (1925), *The Other America* by Michael Harrington (1962), *Silent Spring* by Rachel Carson (1962), *The Feminine Mystique* by Betty Friedan (1963), and "Letter from Birmingham Jail" by Dr. Martin Luther King Jr. (1963).

**You are *not* limited to these suggestions.**

**Guidelines:**

**In your essay, be sure to**
* Develop all aspects of the task
* Support the theme with relevant facts, examples, and details
* Use a logical and clear plan of organization, including an introduction and a conclusion that are beyond a restatement of the theme

**In developing your answer, be sure to keep these general definitions in mind:**

(a) <u>describe</u> means "to illustrate something in words or tell about it"

(b) <u>discuss</u> means "to make observations about something using facts, reasoning, and argument; to present in some detail"

NAME _____  SCHOOL _____

In developing your answers to Part III, be sure to keep this general definition in mind:

<u>discuss</u> means "to make observations about something using facts, reasoning, and argument; to present in some detail"

## Part III

## DOCUMENT-BASED QUESTION

This question is based on the accompanying documents. The question is designed to test your ability to work with historical documents. Some of the documents have been edited for the purposes of the question. As you analyze the documents, take into account the source of each document and any point of view that may be presented in the document.

**Historical Context:**

From colonial times to the present, water has played an important role in the history of the nation. Water resources such as rivers, lakes, oceans, canals, natural harbors, and abundant ground water have influenced the political and economic development of the United States in a number of ways. These ways included exploration and settlement, expansion westward and into the Pacific, agricultural and industrial development, migration patterns, and environmental concerns.

**Task:** Using information from the documents and your knowledge of United States history, answer the questions that follow each document in Part A. Your answers to the questions will help you write the Part B essay, in which you will be asked to

> • Discuss the influence of water on the development of the United States

# Part A
## Short-Answer Questions

*Directions:* Analyze the documents and answer the short-answer questions that follow each document in the space provided.

**Document 1a**

> . . . Nearness to the ocean and to navigable streams as well as local factors of site governed the location of the nucleuses [settlements] at and about which the initial footholds on the Atlantic seaboard were made. How well these elements were recognized by the colonizing agencies early determined success or failure. The James, Potomac, Delaware, Hudson, and Connecticut Rivers became the principal lines of penetration. In most of the English colonies settlers crossed the Fall Line shortly before 1700, set up forts and trading posts along this break in navigation, and entered both the Piedmont in the southern and middle colonies and the hill lands of New England and New York. Always the rivers were the spearheads of penetration. Traders and explorers crossed the mountain barriers to the west and learned of the headwaters of the Ohio; the Dutch and later the English followed the Hudson to and above Albany; the New Englanders advanced rapidly into the Connecticut Valley. Boston, New York, Philadelphia, and smaller settlements approaching urban size became centers of growth and commerce. By 1700 the total population in Colonial America was about 275,000. . . .

Source: Herman R. Friis, "A Series of Population Maps of the Colonies and the United States, 1625–1790," *Geographical Review*, July 1940 (adapted)

**Document 1b**

### The Lewis and Clark Expedition, 1803–1806

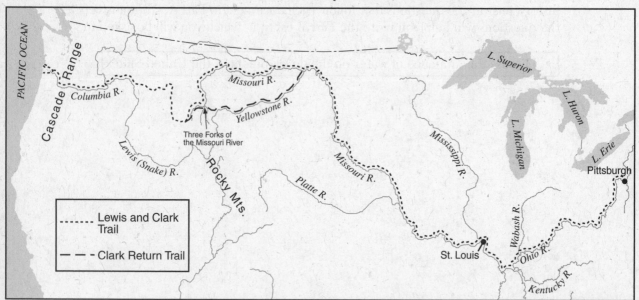

Source: Stephen E. Ambrose, *Undaunted Courage*, Simon and Schuster, 1996 (adapted)

1 Based on these documents, what is **one** way rivers influenced the settlement and exploration of the United States? [1]

_____

_____

Score ☐

## Document 2

According to historian Norman Graebner, expansionists in the 1840s increasingly viewed Oregon and California as "two halves of a single ambition" to stretch the nation's boundary to the Pacific Coast.

... With the Oregon treaty of 1846 the United States had reached the Pacific. Its frontage along the sea from 42° to Fuca Strait and Puget Sound fulfilled half the expansionist dream. On those shores the onward progress of the American pioneer would stop, but commercial expansionists looked beyond to the impetus [momentum] that the possession of Oregon would give to American trade in the Pacific. "Commercially," predicted Benton [United States Senator Thomas Hart Benton from Missouri], "the advantages of Oregon will be great—far greater than any equal portion of the Atlantic States." This Missourian believed that Oriental [Asian] markets and export items would better complement the mercantile [trade] requirements of the United States than would those of Europe. . . .

Source: Norman Graebner, *Empire on the Pacific: A Study in American Continental Expansion*, Ronald Press Co., 1955 (adapted)

2 According to Norman Graebner, what was **one** major reason for the expansion of the United States to the Pacific Coast in the 1840s?  [1]

_____

_____

Score ☐

## Document 3

. . . Mahan was not in the vanguard [forefront] of those imperialists in 1898 who, like Roosevelt, Lodge, Senator Albert J. Beveridge, of Indiana, and others, saw in a victorious war with Spain for Cuba Libre [independence] an opportunity also to annex the distant Philippines. Mahan had seen since 1896 both the need and the opportunity for American commercial expansion in the Pacific and into the markets of China. But there is no persuasive evidence that he linked the annexation of the entire Philippine archipelago with that particular goal. The acquisition of naval coaling stations at Manila, in Guam, and at the mouth of the Yangtze he deemed entirely adequate to sustain future American commercial ambitions in China.

To be sure, he had long advocated the annexation of Hawaii, his arguments invariably [always] centering on defense of the Pacific coast, control of Oriental immigration, and the strategic implications of Japanese expansion into the Central Pacific. He had again demanded Hawaiian annexation as recently as February 1898 when Senator James H. Kyle, of South Dakota, asked him for a statement on the strategic virtues and values of the islands. He cheered in July 1898 when the United States, almost as a national-defense reflex, blinked twice, gulped, and finally swallowed whole the Hawaiian group. As he wrote in mid-August, "In the opinion of the Board, possession of these islands, which happily we now own, is militarily essential, both to our transit to Asia, and to the defense of our Pacific coast." . . .

Source: Robert Seager II, *Alfred Thayer Mahan: The Man and His Letters,*
Naval Institute Press, 1977

3 According to the author, what was *one* reason Alfred Thayer Mahan thought control of Pacific islands was important to the development of the United States? [1]

_____

_____

Score ☐

## Document 4a

. . . The Ogallala Aquifer* (also known as the High Plains Aquifer) is now [in 2000] facing declining water levels and deteriorating water quality. More than 90% of the water pumped from the Ogallala irrigates at least one fifth of all U.S. cropland. This water accounts for 30% of all groundwater used for irrigation in America. Crops that benefit from the aquifer are cotton, corn, alfalfa, soybeans, and wheat. These crops provide the Midwest cattle operations with enormous amounts of feed and account for 40% of the feedlot beef output here in the U.S. Since the advancement of agricultural irrigation in the earlier part of the 20th century, the Ogallala has made it possible so that states such as Nebraska and Kansas can produce large quantities of grain required to feed livestock. . . .

Without irrigation, the High Plains region would have remained a hostile and unproductive frontier environment. Even today dry-land farming remains high-risk farming about which the producers in the region have doubts. But while the Dust Bowl label is appropriate, the High Plains has become one of the most productive farming regions of the world. However, now as groundwater levels decline, workable alternatives for sustainable development have to be further explored. . . .

*An aquifer is an underground source of natural clean water. In the 1930s, farmers lacked the technology to reach the Ogallala Aquifer.

Source: Guru and Horne, *The Ogallala Aquifer,* The Kerr Center for Sustainable Agriculture, 2000 (adapted)

## Document 4b

### Dust Bowl and Ogallala Aquifer

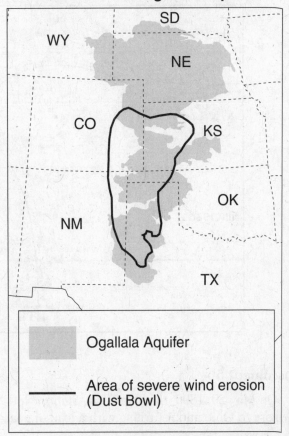

Source: http://www.wadsworth.com and The Kerr Center for Sustainable Agriculture (adapted)

4a Based on these documents, what is *one* reason the Ogallala Aquifer is important to United States farm production in the High Plains region? [1]

_____

_____

Score ☐

b Based on document 4b, how did the lack of water influence parts of the Great Plains in the 1930s? [1]

_____

_____

Score ☐

**Document 5a**

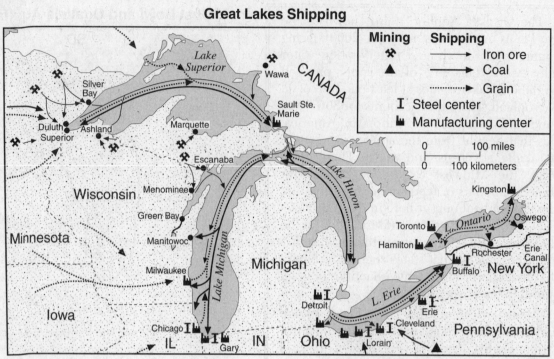

**Great Lakes Shipping**

Source: http://www.geo.msu.edu (adapted)

**Document 5b**

On May 29, 1890, the ship *W. R. Stafford* left Marquette, Michigan, on a routine voyage, carrying a load of iron ore to Ohio and returning with a load of coal.

> . . . Thousands of times that year, hundreds of ships plying [sailing] the Great Lakes between the rich ore fields along the southern and western shores of Lake Superior and the industrial centers in Ohio and Michigan repeated her [the *W. R. Stafford*] schedule. The abundance and quality of the ore these ships transported helped fuel unprecedented industrial growth in the United States in the last decades of the 19th century. Great Lakes transportation played a critical role in that growth. Without this link, it is doubtful the growth of American industry could have occurred as rapidly as it did. . . .

Source: http://www.geo.msu.edu/geogmich/iron_ore__taconite.html

5 Based on these documents, what is **one** way the Great Lakes affected industrialization in the United States? [1]

_____

_____

Score [ ]

## Document 6

This excerpt describes an impact of the Mississippi River flood of 1927.

. . . By early 1928 the exodus of blacks [African Americans] from Washington County [Mississippi], and likely the rest of the Delta, did reach 50 percent. Ever since the end of Reconstruction, blacks had been migrating north and west, out of the South. But it had been only a slow drain, with the South losing about 200,000 blacks between 1900 and 1910. During World War I "the Great Migration" began; the South lost 522,000 blacks between 1910 and 1920, mostly between 1916 and 1919. Now from the floodplain of the Mississippi River, from Arkansas, from Louisiana, from Mississippi, blacks were heading north in even larger numbers. In the 1920s, 872,000 more blacks left the South than returned to it. (In the 1930s the exodus fell off sharply; the number of blacks leaving Arkansas, Louisiana, and Mississippi fell by nearly two-thirds, back to the levels of the early 1900s.)

The favorite destination for Delta blacks was Chicago. They brought the blues to that city, and there the black population exploded, from 44,103 in 1910 to 109,458 in 1920—and 233,903 in 1930. Certainly not all of this exodus came from the floodplain of the Mississippi River. And even within that alluvial empire, the great flood of 1927 was hardly the only reason for blacks to abandon their homes. But for tens of thousands of blacks in the Delta of the Mississippi River, the flood was the final reason. . . .

Source: John M. Barry, *Rising Tide: The Great Mississippi Flood of 1927 and How It Changed America,*
Simon & Schuster, 1997

6 According to this document, what impact did the Mississippi River flood of 1927 have on many African Americans? [1]

_____

_____

Score

**Document 7**

. . . If you begin at the Pacific rim and move inland, you will find large cities, many towns, and prosperous-looking farms until you cross the Sierra Nevada and the Cascades, which block the seasonal weather fronts moving in from the Pacific and wring out their moisture in snows and drenching rains. On the east side of the Sierra-Cascade crest, moisture drops immediately—from as much as 150 inches of precipitation on the western slope to as little as four inches on the eastern—and it doesn't increase much, except at higher elevations, until you have crossed the hundredth meridian, which bisects the Dakotas and Nebraska and Kansas down to Abilene, Texas, and divides the country into its two most significant halves—the one receiving at least twenty inches of precipitation a year, the other generally receiving less. Any place with less than twenty inches of rainfall is hostile terrain to a farmer depending solely on the sky, and a place that receives seven inches or less—as Phoenix, El Paso, and Reno do—is arguably no place to inhabit at all. Everything depends on the manipulation of water—on capturing it behind dams, storing it, and rerouting it in concrete rivers [aqueducts] over distances of hundreds of miles. Were it not for a century and a half of messianic effort [an aggressive crusade] toward that end, the West as we know it would not exist. . . .

Source: Marc Reisner, *Cadillac Desert: The American West and Its Disappearing Water,*
Penguin Books, 1993

7 According to this document, what impact has water had on settlement in the western part of the United States? [1]

_____

_____

Score ☐

**Document 8**

Permission to use this third-party content has not been granted to Pearson. View content at nysedregents.org.

8 Based on this chart, state *two* environmental problems that led to the Clean Water Act. [2]

(1) _____

_____  Score [ ]

(2) _____

_____  Score [ ]

**Document 9**

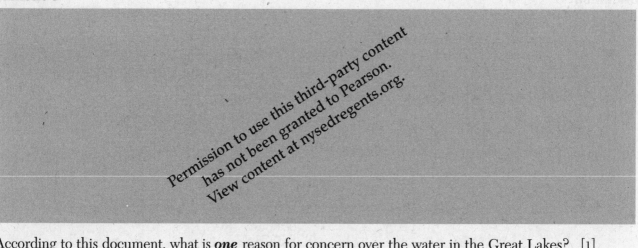

9 According to this document, what is **one** reason for concern over the water in the Great Lakes? [1]

_____

_____

Score ☐

# Part B
## Essay

*Directions:* Write a well-organized essay that includes an introduction, several paragraphs, and a conclusion. Use evidence from *at least **five*** documents in the body of the essay. Support your response with relevant facts, examples, and details. Include additional outside information.

### Historical Context:

From colonial times to the present, water has played an important role in the history of the nation. Water resources such as rivers, lakes, oceans, canals, natural harbors, and abundant ground water have influenced the political and economic development of the United States in a number of ways. These ways included exploration and settlement, expansion westward and into the Pacific, agricultural and industrial development, migration patterns, and environmental concerns.

**Task:** Using information from the documents and your knowledge of United States history, write an essay in which you

> • Discuss the influence of water on the development of the United States

### Guidelines:

**In your essay, be sure to**
- Develop all aspects of the task
- Incorporate information from *at least **five*** documents
- Incorporate relevant outside information
- Support the theme with relevant facts, examples, and details
- Use a logical and clear plan of organization, including an introduction and conclusion that are beyond a restatement of the theme

This section contains the Regents Examination in United States History and Government that was given in New York State in August 2009.

Circle your answers to Part I on this exam and write your answers to the thematic essay and document-based essay questions on separate sheets of paper. Be sure to refer to the test-taking strategies in the front of this book as you prepare to answer the test questions.

# Part I

### Answer all questions in this part.

*Directions* (1–50): For each statement or question, write on the separate answer sheet the *number* of the word or expression that, of those given, best completes the statement or answers the question.

1 Farmers in the Ohio River valley gained the greatest economic benefit when the United States acquired the

(1) Oregon Territory
(2) Gadsden Purchase
(3) Louisiana Territory
(4) Mexican Cession

2 The Mayflower Compact, New England town meetings, and the Virginia House of Burgesses are examples of

(1) early colonial efforts in self-government
(2) colonial protests against British taxation
(3) governments imposed by Parliament
(4) attempts to limit democracy

3 The main purpose for writing the Declaration of Independence was to

(1) declare war on Great Britain
(2) force France to support the Revolutionary War
(3) convince Great Britain to abolish slavery
(4) state the colonists' reasons for separating from Great Britain

4 At the Constitutional Convention of 1787, which problem was solved by the Great Compromise?

(1) developing the method of electing a president
(2) designating control of interstate commerce
(3) outlining the structure of the federal court system
(4) establishing the formula for representation in Congress

5 In the United States Constitution, the power to impeach a federal government official is given to the

(1) House of Representatives
(2) president
(3) state legislatures
(4) Supreme Court

6 A constitutional power specifically delegated to the federal government is the power to

(1) regulate marriage and divorce
(2) establish education standards
(3) declare war
(4) issue driver's licenses

7 To win a presidential election, a candidate must win a

(1) two-thirds vote of the state legislatures
(2) two-thirds vote in Congress
(3) majority of the popular vote
(4) majority of the electoral college vote

8 One goal of Alexander Hamilton's financial plan was the establishment of a

(1) stock exchange
(2) national sales tax
(3) federal income tax
(4) national bank

9 What was one outcome of the Supreme Court decision in *Marbury* v. *Madison* (1803)?

(1) State governments could now determine the constitutionality of federal laws.
(2) The principle of judicial review was established.
(3) Congress expanded its delegated powers.
(4) A method to approve treaties was developed.

10 The Louisiana Purchase initially presented a dilemma for President Thomas Jefferson because he believed it would

(1) lead to war with Great Britain
(2) bankrupt the new nation
(3) force Native American Indians off their lands
(4) violate his strict constructionist view of the Constitution

11 Which statement about the Missouri Compromise (1820) is most accurate?

(1) Slavery was banned west of the Mississippi River.

(2) Unorganized territories would be governed by the United States and Great Britain.

(3) The balance between free and slave states was maintained.

(4) The 36°30' line formed a new boundary between the United States and Canada.

12 Which 19th-century event supported the movement for women's rights?

(1) Seneca Falls Convention

(2) *Dred Scott* decision

(3) formation of the Republican Party

(4) Lincoln-Douglas debates

Base your answer to question 13 on the poster below and on your knowledge of social studies.

# 100 DOLLARS REWARD!

Ranaway from the subscriber on the 27th of July, my Black Woman, named **EMILY,** Seventeen years of age, well grown, black color, has a whining voice. She took with her one dark calico and one blue and white dress, a red corded gingham bonnet; a white striped shawl and slippers. I will pay the above reward if taken near the Ohio river on the Kentucky side, or THREE HUNDRED DOLLARS, if taken in the State of Ohio, and delivered to me near Lewisburg, Mason County, Ky.
**THO'S H. WILLIAMS.**
August 4, 1853.

Source: Ohio Historical Center Archives (adapted)

13 Prior to the Civil War, abolitionists reacted to the situation described in the poster by

(1) supporting the Underground Railroad

(2) opposing the Emancipation Proclamation

(3) banning freed slaves from Northern states

(4) proposing a stricter fugitive slave law

14 Literacy tests and poll taxes were often used to

(1) enforce constitutional amendments added after the Civil War

(2) limit voter participation by African Americans

(3) promote equal educational opportunities for minority persons

(4) provide job training for freedmen

Base your answers to questions 15 and 16 on the song below and on your knowledge of social studies.

We mean to make things over,
we are tired of toil for naught,
With but bare enough to live upon,
and never an hour for thought;
We want to feel the sunshine,
and we want to smell the flowers,
We are sure that God has will'd it,
and we mean to have eight hours.
We're summoning our forces
from the shipyard, shop and mill,

Chorus.
Eight hours for work, eight hours for rest,
eight hours for what we will!
Eight hours for work, eight hours for rest,
eight hours for what we will!
— I.G. Blanchard, "Eight Hours," 1878

15 During the late 1800s, the ideas expressed in these lyrics were the goals of

(1) organizers of labor unions

(2) sharecroppers following the Civil War

(3) Grangers demanding railroad regulation

(4) owners of big businesses

16 In the 1890s, which political party incorporated the chief concern expressed in this song into its platform?

(1) Know-Nothing      (3) Whig

(2) Populist      (4) Bull Moose

17 Society advances when its fittest members are allowed to assert themselves with the least hindrance.

The idea expressed in this statement is most consistent with the

(1) principles of Social Darwinism
(2) concept of assimilation
(3) goals of the Progressive movement
(4) melting pot theory of American culture

18 During the late 1800s, many North American Indian tribes were sent to reservations that were located

(1) along the major rivers and lakes of the Midwest
(2) near large cities in the Northwest
(3) in sparsely populated regions of the West
(4) east of the Mississippi River

19 The closing of the frontier and the growth of industry in the late 1800s are two factors often associated with the

(1) reduction of exports to Asian nations
(2) restoration of a plantation economy in the South
(3) formation of alliances with other nations
(4) rise of United States imperialism

20 Yellow journalists created support for the Spanish-American War by writing articles about the

(1) political popularity of William Jennings Bryan
(2) efforts of the United States to control Mexico
(3) destruction of United States sugar plantations by Hawaiians
(4) sinking of the United States battleship *Maine* in Havana Harbor

21 Muckrakers Ida Tarbell and Upton Sinclair influenced the federal government to

(1) grant citizenship to people who had entered the country illegally
(2) pass legislation to correct harmful business practices
(3) force individual states to regulate monopolies
(4) end racial discrimination in the workplace

Base your answers to questions 22 and 23 on the speakers' statements below and on your knowledge of social studies.

*Speaker A:* Nature should be left as it is found. All unsettled land should be off limits to future settlement or development.

*Speaker B:* Natural resources should be controlled by big business to ensure the economic strength of the United States. Our abundance of land gives us a great advantage for competing in world markets.

*Speaker C:* The natural resources of the United States should be used wisely. We must conserve them for future generations while also using them to serve the people of today.

*Speaker D:* No man or institution owns the land. It is to be shared by everyone and everything in the best interest of all who depend upon its offerings.

22 Which speaker best expresses the environmental views of President Theodore Roosevelt?

(1) A          (3) C
(2) B          (4) D

23 The statement of *Speaker D* is most like views expressed by

(1) Native American Indians
(2) western farmers
(3) railroad companies
(4) European immigrants

24 Many United States senators refused to support membership in the League of Nations because they believed that it would

(1) endanger United States economic growth
(2) force the United States to give up its colonies
(3) grant the president the power to annex new territory
(4) involve the United States in future foreign conflicts

25 Immigration laws passed during the 1920s changed United States policy by

(1) establishing immigration quotas

(2) allowing only skilled workers into the country

(3) favoring immigration from Asia

(4) encouraging an increase in immigration to the United States

26 Henry Ford's use of the assembly line in the production of automobiles led directly to

(1) a decrease in the number of automobiles available

(2) a decrease in the cost of automobiles

(3) an increase in the unemployment rate

(4) an increase in the time needed to produce a single automobile

27 The convictions of Sacco and Vanzetti in the 1920s most closely reflected the

(1) increase in nativist attitudes

(2) federal government's war on crime

(3) corruption of political machines

(4) rise in labor unrest

28 What was one cause of the stock market crash of 1929 and the Great Depression that followed?

(1) Costs associated with World War I had bankrupted the economy.

(2) Speculators had purchased shares of stock on margin with borrowed funds.

(3) Federal tax cuts had caused high inflation.

(4) Low farm production had weakened banks.

29 During the Great Depression, one way New Deal programs tried to stimulate economic recovery was by

(1) raising tariff rates

(2) increasing interest rates

(3) creating public works jobs

(4) lowering the minimum wage

Base your answer to question 30 on the cartoon below and on your knowledge of social studies.

**Let's Harmonize!**

Source: Gene Elderman, *Washington Post*, January 7, 1937 (adapted)

30 The cartoonist is commenting on President Franklin D. Roosevelt's efforts to

(1) win congressional approval for his Supreme Court nominees

(2) gain Supreme Court support for his legislative program

(3) set up a retirement plan for Supreme Court Justices

(4) keep members of Congress off the Supreme Court

31 Which geographic area is most closely associated with the Dust Bowl of the 1930s?

(1) Great Lakes basin

(2) Mississippi River valley

(3) Appalachian Mountains

(4) Great Plains

32 Which series of events leading to World War II is in the correct chronological order?

(1) Neutrality Acts → Japanese attack on Pearl Harbor → Lend-Lease Act → United States declaration of war on Japan

(2) Lend-Lease Act → Neutrality Acts → United States declaration of war on Japan → Japanese attack on Pearl Harbor

(3) United States declaration of war on Japan → Japanese attack on Pearl Harbor → Lend-Lease Act → Neutrality Acts

(4) Neutrality Acts → Lend-Lease Act → Japanese attack on Pearl Harbor → United States declaration of war on Japan

33 Which change in American society occurred during World War II?

(1) African Americans were granted equality in the armed forces.

(2) Women were allowed to enter combat units for the first time.

(3) Congress enacted the first military draft.

(4) Women replaced men in essential wartime industries.

34 Which action was taken by the United States government to help Europe's economic recovery after World War II?

(1) forming the Alliance for Progress

(2) sending troops to Turkey

(3) creating the Marshall Plan

(4) joining the North Atlantic Treaty Organization

35 Issuing the Truman Doctrine, defending South Korea, and sending military advisors to Vietnam were actions taken by the United States to

(1) encourage membership in the United Nations

(2) promote American business in Asia

(3) limit the spread of communism

(4) gain additional overseas colonies

36 The president acted as commander in chief in response to which event of the civil rights movement?

(1) refusal of the governor of Arkansas to obey a federal court order to integrate public schools in Little Rock

(2) desegregation of the city bus system in Montgomery, Alabama

(3) arrest of Martin Luther King Jr. during protests in Birmingham, Alabama

(4) assassination of Medgar Evers in Mississippi

37 Lunch counter sit-ins and the actions of freedom riders are examples of

(1) steps taken in support of the Americans with Disabilities Act

(2) programs dealing with affirmative action

(3) violent acts by the Black Panthers

(4) nonviolent attempts to oppose segregation

38 One way in which President John F. Kennedy's Peace Corps and President Lyndon Johnson's Volunteers in Service to America (VISTA) are similar is that both programs attempted to

(1) increase domestic security

(2) support United States troops fighting overseas

(3) improve the quality of people's lives

(4) provide aid to immigrants coming to the United States

39 The Supreme Court cases of *Gideon* v. *Wainwright* (1963) and *Miranda* v. *Arizona* (1966) dealt with the constitutional principle of

(1) freedom of religion

(2) freedom from unreasonable search

(3) separation of powers

(4) rights of the accused

Base your answers to questions 40 and 41 on the cartoon below and on your knowledge of social studies.

**The Odd Couple**

Source: Bill Mauldin, *Chicago Sun-Times*, 1973 (adapted)

40 The cartoonist is commenting on which Cold War foreign policy?

(1) détente      (3) the domino theory

(2) brinkmanship      (4) collective security

41 Which United States foreign policy decision most clearly reflects the relationship shown in the cartoon?

(1) issuance of the Eisenhower Doctrine

(2) quarantine of Cuba

(3) support of Israel in the Six Day War

(4) negotiation of the Strategic Arms Limitation Treaty (SALT)

42 President Ronald Reagan's supply-side economic policy was successful in

(1) increasing government spending on social programs

(2) lowering tax rates on personal and business income

(3) reducing defense spending

(4) enforcing stricter environmental regulations

43 The rapid westward migration caused by the discovery of gold in California led directly to

(1) the start of the Civil War

(2) the adoption of the Compromise of 1850

(3) increased trade through the Panama Canal

(4) control of the United States Senate by the slave states

Base your answer to question 44 on the statement below and on your knowledge of social studies.

. . . With a profound sense of the solemn and even tragical character of the step I am taking and of the grave responsibilities which it involves, but in unhesitating obedience to what I deem my constitutional duty, I advise that the Congress declare the recent course of the Imperial German Government to be in fact nothing less than war against the government and people of the United States; that it formally accept the status of belligerent which has thus been thrust upon it, and that it take immediate steps not only to put the country in a more thorough state of defense but also to exert all its power and employ all its resources to bring the Government of the German Empire to terms and end the war. . . .

44 Which presidential action is the focus of this statement?

(1) William McKinley's request for war in 1898

(2) Theodore Roosevelt's support for the Panamanian revolt in 1903

(3) William Howard Taft's decision to send troops to Latin America in 1912

(4) Woodrow Wilson's response to unrestricted submarine warfare in 1917

Base your answers to questions 45 and 46 on the table below and on your knowledge of social studies.

**Congressional Bills Vetoed: 1961 to 1993**

| Period | President | Total vetoes | Regular vetoes | Pocket vetoes | Vetoes upheld | Bills passed over veto |
|---|---|---|---|---|---|---|
| 1961–63 | John F. Kennedy | 21 | 12 | 9 | 21 | 0 |
| 1963–69 | Lyndon Johnson | 30 | 16 | 14 | 30 | 0 |
| 1969–74 | Richard Nixon | 43 | 26 | 17 | 36 | 7 |
| 1974–77 | Gerald Ford | 66 | 48 | 18 | 54 | 12 |
| 1977–81 | Jimmy Carter | 31 | 13 | 18 | 29 | 2 |
| 1981–89 | Ronald Reagan | 78 | 39 | 39 | 69 | 9 |
| 1989–93 | George H. W. Bush | 44 | 29 | 15 | 43 | 1 |

Source: U.S. Senate

45 Which statement is accurate about congressional bills vetoed between 1961 and 1993?

(1) Congress was usually able to override a presidential veto.
(2) Pocket vetoes were used more often than regular vetoes.
(3) The majority of presidential vetoes were upheld.
(4) The use of the veto increased steadily between 1961 and 1993.

46 The data in the table illustrate the operation of

(1) executive privilege
(2) checks and balances
(3) congressional immunity
(4) federal supremacy

47 The Pacific [Transcontinental] Railway Act (1862) and the Interstate Highway Act (1956) are both examples of

(1) federally supported internal improvement projects linking the nation
(2) regional construction projects coordinated by southern and western states
(3) military projects required to meet the needs of the defense industry
(4) transportation legislation designed to encourage foreign trade

48 Mark Twain, Langston Hughes, and John Steinbeck made their most important contributions to the United States in the field of

(1) music          (3) literature
(2) politics       (4) business

49 One way in which the New Deal, the Fair Deal, and the Great Society are similar is that these programs

(1) promoted the idea of "rugged individualism"
(2) increased government commitment to the well-being of the people
(3) reduced the amount of money spent on domestic programs
(4) encouraged the states to take a more active role in national defense

Base your answer to question 50 on the graphs below and on your knowledge of social studies.

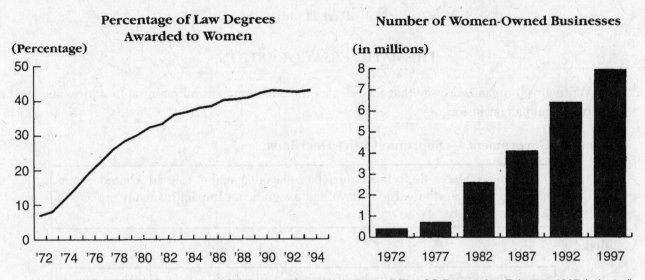

Source: "Feminism's Future," *The CQ Researcher,* February 1997 (adapted)

50 Data from the graphs most clearly support the conclusion that by the mid-1990s, American women as a group

(1) surpassed men in the number of businesses owned and law degrees received
(2) had given up marriage in favor of careers outside the home
(3) had gained more opportunities in professional areas
(4) earned more than men in the legal profession

**Answers to the essay questions are to be written in the separate essay booklet.**

**Part II**

**THEMATIC ESSAY QUESTION**

*Directions:* Write a well-organized essay that includes an introduction, several paragraphs addressing the task below, and a conclusion.

**Theme: Government — Supreme Court Decisions**

> The United States Supreme Court has played a major role in United States history. The Court's decisions have had a significant impact on many aspects of American society.

**Task:**

> Select *two* Supreme Court cases that have had an impact on American society and for *each*
> - Describe the historical circumstances surrounding the case
> - Explain the Supreme Court's decision in the case
> - Discuss an impact this decision has had on American society

You may use any appropriate Supreme Court case from your study of United States history. Some suggestions you might wish to consider include *Worcester* v. *Georgia* (1832), *Dred Scott* v. *Sanford* (1857), *Northern Securities Co.* v. *United States* (1904), *Korematsu* v. *United States* (1944), *Brown* v. *Board of Education of Topeka* (1954), *Heart of Atlanta Motel* v. *United States* (1964), *Miranda* v. *Arizona* (1966), *Roe* v. *Wade* (1973), and *United States* v. *Nixon* (1974).

**You are *not* limited to these suggestions.**

**Guidelines:**

**In your essay, be sure to**
- Develop all aspects of the task
- Support the theme with relevant facts, examples, and details
- Use a logical and clear plan of organization, including an introduction and a conclusion that are beyond a restatement of the theme

**In developing your answer to Part II, be sure to keep these general definitions in mind:**

(a) **describe** means "to illustrate something in words or tell about it"

(b) **explain** means "to make plain or understandable; to give reasons for or causes of; to show the logical development or relationships of"

(c) **discuss** means "to make observations about something using facts, reasoning, and argument; to present in some detail"

NAME _____ SCHOOL _____

In developing your answers to Part III, be sure to keep these general definitions in mind:

    (a) <u>describe</u> means "to illustrate something in words or tell about it"

    (b) <u>explain</u> means "to make plain or understandable; to give reasons for or causes of; to show the logical development or relationships of"

    (c) <u>discuss</u> means "to make observations about something using facts, reasoning, and argument; to present in some detail"

### Part III

### DOCUMENT-BASED QUESTION

This question is based on the accompanying documents. The question is designed to test your ability to work with historical documents. Some of the documents have been edited for the purposes of the question. As you analyze the documents, take into account the source of each document and any point of view that may be presented in the document.

**Historical Context:**

> Historians who have evaluated presidential leadership have generally agreed that **George Washington, Abraham Lincoln,** and **Franklin D. Roosevelt** were great presidents because each successfully addressed a critical challenge faced by the nation during his administration.

**Task:** Using information from the documents and your knowledge of United States history, answer the questions that follow each document in Part A. Your answers to the questions will help you write the Part B essay, in which you will be asked to

> Select *two* presidents mentioned in the historical context and for *each*
> - Describe a challenge that faced the nation during his administration
> - Explain an action taken by the president to address this challenge
> - Discuss the impact of this action on the United States

This page left blank intentionally.

GO ON TO THE NEXT PAGE ⇨

# Part A
# Short-Answer Questions

*Directions:* Analyze the documents and answer the short-answer questions that follow each document in the space provided.

## Document 1

At daybreak on July 16, 1794, about fifty men armed with rifles and clubs marched to the house of John Neville, regional supervisor for collection of the federal excise tax in western Pennsylvania. They demanded that Neville resign his position and turn over to them all records associated with collection of the tax on domestically distilled spirits. He refused. Shots were fired. In the ensuing battle five of the attackers fell wounded. One of them later died. Neville and his slaves, who together had defended the premises from secure positions inside the house, suffered no casualties. The mob dispersed. . . .

The Whiskey Rebellion, as it is traditionally known and studied, had begun. Before it was over, some 7000 western Pennsylvanians advanced against the town of Pittsburgh, threatened its residents, feigned [pretended] an attack on Fort Pitt and the federal arsenal there, banished seven members of the community, and destroyed the property of several others. Violence spread to western Maryland, where a Hagerstown crowd joined in, raised liberty poles, and began a march on the arsenal at Frederick. At about the same time, sympathetic "friends of liberty" arose in Carlisle, Pennsylvania, and back-country regions of Virginia and Kentucky. Reports reached the federal government in Philadelphia that the western country was ablaze and that rebels were negotiating with representatives of Great Britain and Spain, two of the nation's most formidable European competitors, for aid in a frontier-wide separatist movement. In response, President Washington nationalized 12,950 militiamen from New Jersey, Pennsylvania, Maryland, and Virginia—an army approximating in size the Continental force that followed him during the Revolution—and personally led the "Watermelon Army"* west to shatter the insurgency [rebellion]. . . .

Source: Thomas P. Slaughter, *The Whiskey Rebellion: Frontier Epilogue to the American Revolution*, Oxford University Press, 1986

*Watermelon Army was a nickname by whiskey tax rebels mocking the physical fitness and fighting skills of federal troops, particularly those from New Jersey.

1 According to Thomas P. Slaughter, what was *one* problem that resulted from the collection of the federal excise tax in western Pennsylvania? [1]

_____

_____

Score [ ]

**Document 2**

To Major-General Lee

Sir:—I have it in special instruction from the President [George Washington] of the United States, now at this place, to convey to you the following instructions for the general direction of your conduct in the command of the militia army, with which you are charged.

The objects [reasons] for which the militia have been called forth are:

1st. To suppress the combinations [groups] which exist in some of the western counties in Pennsylvania, in opposition to the laws laying duties upon spirits distilled within the United States, and upon stills.

2nd. To cause the laws to be executed.

These objects are to be effected in two ways:

1. By military force.

2. By judiciary process and other civil proceedings.

The objects of the military force are twofold:

1. To overcome any armed opposition which may exist.

2. To countenance [approve] and support the civil officers in the means of executing the laws....
Your obedient servant,
Alexander Hamilton

Source: Alexander Hamilton to Major-General Henry Lee, October 20, 1794,
Henry Cabot Lodge, ed., *The Works of Alexander Hamilton*, Volume VI,
G.P. Putnam's Sons (adapted)

2a According to Alexander Hamilton, what action is President George Washington ordering in response to the Whiskey Rebellion?  [1]

_____

_____

Score ☐

b According to Alexander Hamilton, what is **one** reason President Washington gave this order?  [1]

_____

_____

Score ☐

## Document 3

> . . . The [whiskey] rebellion has long been interpreted as a milestone in the creation of federal authority, and in most respects that is its chief significance. Certainly to the Federalists, who had long been striving for a strong national government, it was a major test: the new government successfully crushed organized and violent resistance to the laws. As Hamilton put it, the rebellion "will do us a great deal of good and add to the solidity [stability] of every thing in this country.". . .

Source: Richard H. Kohn, "The Washington Administration's Decision to Crush the Whiskey Rebellion," *The Journal of American History*, December 1972

3 According to Richard H. Kohn, what was the significance of the Whiskey Rebellion? [1]

_____

_____

Score

Document 4

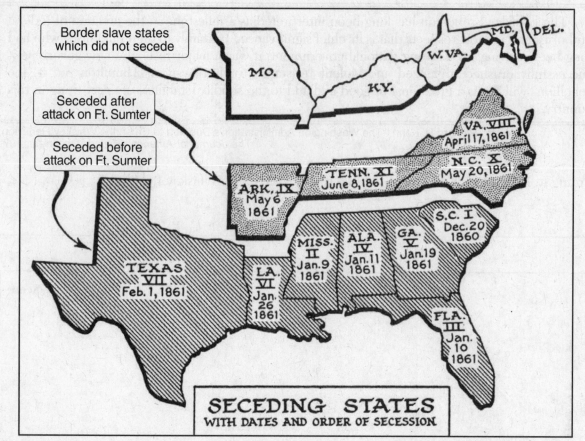

Source: Kennedy and Bailey, eds., *The American Spirit, Volume I: To 1877,* Houghton Mifflin, 2002 (adapted)

4 Based on the information on this map, state **one** problem the United States faced under President Abraham Lincoln. [1]

_____

_____

Score ☐

**Document 5**

> April 15, 1861
>
> By the President of the United States
>
> A Proclamation.
>
> Whereas, the laws of the United States have been for some time past, and now are opposed, and the execution thereof obstructed [interfered with], in the States of South Carolina, Georgia, Alabama, Florida, Mississippi, Louisiana and Texas, by combinations too powerful to be suppressed by the ordinary course of judicial proceedings, or by the powers vested in the Marshals by law,
>
> Now therefore, I, Abraham Lincoln, President of the United States, in virtue of the power in me vested by the Constitution, and the laws, have thought fit to call forth, and hereby do call forth, the militia of the several States of the Union, to the aggregate [total] number of seventy-five thousand [75,000], in order to suppress said combinations, and to cause the laws to be duly executed. The details, for this object, will be immediately communicated to the State authorities through the War Department. . . .
>
> ABRAHAM LINCOLN
>
> By the President
> WILLIAM H. SEWARD, Secretary of State.

Source: Roy P. Basler, ed., *The Collected Works of Abraham Lincoln*, Volume IV, Rutgers University Press (adapted)

5 According to this proclamation, what is **one** action President Abraham Lincoln took to enforce the laws of the United States?  [1]

_____

_____

Score ☐

**Document 6**

... The greatest names in American history are Washington and Lincoln. One is forever associated with the independence of the States and formation of the Federal Union; the other with universal freedom and the preservation of that Union. Washington enforced the Declaration of Independence as against England; Lincoln proclaimed its fulfillment not only to a downtrodden race in America, but to all people for all time, who may seek the protection of our flag. These illustrious men achieved grander results for mankind within a single century— from 1775 to 1865—than any other men ever accomplished in all the years since first the flight of time began. Washington engaged in no ordinary revolution. With him it was not who should rule, but what should rule. He drew his sword, not for a change of rulers upon an established throne, but to establish a new government, which should acknowledge no throne but the tribune [authority] of the people. Lincoln accepted war to save the Union, the safeguard of our liberties, and re-established it on "indestructible foundations" as forever "one and indivisible." To quote his own grand words:

"Now we are contending that this Nation under God, shall have a new birth of freedom; and that government of the people, by the people, for the people, shall not perish from the earth.". . .

Source: William McKinley, Speech at the Marquette Club, Chicago, February 12, 1896, Nicolay and Hay, eds., *Complete Works of Abraham Lincoln*

6 According to William McKinley, what is **one** impact of President Abraham Lincoln's actions on the United States? [1]

_____

_____

Score ☐

**Document 7**

### Interview with Aaron Barkham, a coal miner in West Virginia

. . . It got bad in '29. The Crash caught us with one $20 gold piece. All mines shut down—stores, everything. One day they was workin', the next day the mines shut down. Three or four months later, they opened up. Run two, three days a week, mostly one. They didn't have the privilege of calling their souls their own. Most people by that time was in debt so far to the company itself, they couldn't live.

Some of them been in debt from '29 till today [c. 1970], and never got out. Some of them didn't even try. It seem like whenever they went back to work, they owed so much. The company got their foot on 'em even now. . . .

Source: Studs Terkel, *Hard Times: An Oral History of the Great Depression*, Pantheon Books

7 According to this interview with coal miner Aaron Barkham, what was **one** problem faced by mine workers during the Great Depression? [1]

_____

_____

Score ☐

## Document 8a

... In the consistent development of our previous efforts toward the saving and safeguarding of our national life, I have continued to recognize three related steps. The first was relief, because the primary concern of any Government dominated by the humane ideals of democracy is the simple principle that in a land of vast resources no one should be permitted to starve. Relief was and continues to be our first consideration. It calls for large expenditures and will continue in modified form to do so for a long time to come. We may as well recognize that fact. It comes from the paralysis that arose as the after-effect of that unfortunate decade characterized by a mad chase for unearned riches and an unwillingness of leaders in almost every walk of life to look beyond their own schemes and speculations. In our administration of relief we follow two principles: First, that direct giving shall, wherever possible, be supplemented by provision for useful and remunerative [paid] work and, second, that where families in their existing surroundings will in all human probability never find an opportunity for full self-maintenance, happiness and enjoyment, we will try to give them a new chance in new surroundings. ...

Source: Franklin D. Roosevelt, Address of the President, "Review of the Achievements of the Seventy-third Congress," June 28, 1934, FDR Library

8a According to President Franklin D. Roosevelt, what was **one** action needed to safeguard the life of the nation? [1]

_____

_____

Score ☐

**Document 8b**

Source: Clifford Berryman, *Washington Star*, January 5, 1934, Library of Congress

8b According to this document, what was *one* step taken by President Franklin D. Roosevelt to solve the problems of the Great Depression? [1]

_____

_____

Score

## Document 9

> . . . But was the New Deal answer really successful? Did it work? Other scholarly experts almost uniformly praise and admire Roosevelt, but even the most sympathetic among them add a number of reservations. "The New Deal certainly did not get the country out of the Depression," says Columbia's William Leuchtenburg, author of *Franklin D. Roosevelt and the New Deal*. "As late as 1941, there were still 6 million unemployed, and it was really not until the war that the army of the jobless finally disappeared." "Some of the New Deal legislation was very hastily contrived [planned]," says Williams College's James MacGregor Burns, author of a two-volume Roosevelt biography. Duke's James David Barber, author of *The Presidential Character*, notes that Roosevelt "was not too open about his real intentions, particularly in the court-packing episode.". . .
>
> After all the criticisms, though, the bulk of expert opinion agrees that Roosevelt's New Deal changed American life substantially, changed it permanently and changed it for the better. While the major recovery programs like the NRA and AAA have faded into history, many of Roosevelt's reforms—Social Security, stock market regulation, minimum wage, insured bank deposits—are now taken for granted. . . .
>
> But what actually remains today of the original New Deal? Alexander Heard, 64, who is retiring soon as chancellor of Vanderbilt University, remembers working in the CCC as a youth, remembers it as a time when a new President "restored a sense of confidence and morale and hope—hope being the greatest of all." But what remains? "In a sense," says Heard, "what remains of the New Deal is the United States."

Source: Otto Friedrich, "F.D.R.'s Disputed Legacy," *Time*, February 1, 1982 (adapted)

9 According to this document, what were *two* effects of President Franklin D. Roosevelt's New Deal policies on the nation? [2]

(1) _____

_____

Score ☐

(2) _____

_____

Score ☐

# Part B
# Essay

*Directions:* Write a well-organized essay that includes an introduction, several paragraphs, and a conclusion. Use evidence from *at least four* documents in your essay. Support your response with relevant facts, examples, and details. Include additional outside information.

### Historical Context:

Historians who have evaluated presidential leadership have generally agreed that **George Washington, Abraham Lincoln,** and **Franklin D. Roosevelt** were great presidents because each successfully addressed a critical challenge faced by the nation during his administration.

**Task:** Using information from the documents and your knowledge of United States history, write an essay in which you

Select *two* presidents mentioned in the historical context and for *each*

- Describe a challenge that faced the nation during his administration
- Explain an action taken by the president to address this challenge
- Discuss the impact of this action on the United States

### Guidelines:

**In your essay, be sure to**

- Develop all aspects of the task
- Incorporate information from *at least four* documents
- Incorporate relevant outside information
- Support the theme with relevant facts, examples, and details
- Use a logical and clear plan of organization, including an introduction and conclusion that are beyond a restatement of the theme

This section contains the Regents Examination in United States History and Government that was given in New York State in June 2009.

Circle your answers to Part I on this exam and write your answers to the thematic essay and document-based essay questions on separate sheets of paper. Be sure to refer to the test-taking strategies in the front of this book as you prepare to answer the test questions.

# Part I

## Answer all questions in this part.

*Directions* (1–50): For each statement or question, write on the separate answer sheet the *number* of the word or expression that, of those given, best completes the statement or answers the question.

1 Since the late 1700s, the Mississippi River has been a vital waterway because it

(1) divided the northern territories from the southern territories

(2) allowed American farmers direct access to Canadian markets

(3) connected the Great Lakes to the Atlantic Ocean

(4) provided farmers and merchants an outlet to the Gulf of Mexico

2 During the first half of the 1800s, geographic factors influenced the economy of New England by

(1) encouraging the establishment of large plantations

(2) promoting the growth of trade and manufacturing

(3) increasing the region's reliance on slave labor

(4) supporting rice and indigo farming

3 The British benefited from their mercantilist relationship with the American colonies primarily by

(1) supporting the growth of colonial industries

(2) prohibiting colonists from fishing and fur trading

(3) taking large amounts of gold and silver from the southern colonies

(4) buying raw materials from the colonies and selling them finished products

4 The main reason Great Britian established the Proclamation Line of 1763 was to

(1) avoid conflicts between American colonists and Native American Indians

(2) make a profit by selling the land west of the Appalachian Mountains

(3) prevent American industrial development in the Ohio River valley

(4) allow Canada to control the Great Lakes region

5 The Declaration of Independence (1776) has had a major influence on peoples throughout the world because it

(1) guarantees universal suffrage

(2) establishes a basic set of laws for every nation

(3) provides justification for revolting against unjust governments

(4) describes the importance of a strong central government

6 One accomplishment of the national government under the Articles of Confederation was the passage of legislation establishing

(1) a central banking system

(2) a process for admitting new states to the Union

(3) the president's right to put down rebellions

(4) the ability of Congress to tax the states effectively

7 Disagreement at the Constitutional Convention of 1787 over the Virginia and New Jersey plans was resolved by a compromise that

(1) guaranteed continuation of the slave trade for at least twenty more years

(2) limited the power of the federal government to wage war

(3) provided for construction of a new national capital in the south

(4) created a Congress made up of a Senate and a House of Representatives

8 **"Presidential Candidates Skip Campaigning in Low-Population States"**
**"Winner Of Popular Vote Loses Election"**

These headlines refer to controversial issues most directly related to

(1) judicial review

(2) the electoral college

(3) impeachment

(4) checks and balances

9 "The United States shall guarantee to every state in this Union a republican form of government, and shall protect each of them against invasion; and on application of the legislature, or of the executive (when the legislature cannot be convened), against domestic violence."

— United States Constitution, Article IV, Section 4

According to this excerpt, a goal of the framers of the Constitution was to ensure that the United States

(1) remained neutral during domestic conflicts involving the states
(2) supported the right of each state to resist presidential decisions
(3) provided for the common defense of every state
(4) approved a bill of rights to protect citizens from government tyranny

10 A major reason the Antifederalists opposed the ratification of the United States Constitution was because the Constitution

(1) created a national bank
(2) lacked a provision for a federal court system
(3) failed to provide for the direct election of members of the House of Representatives
(4) changed the balance of power between the state and national governments

11 An example of the use of the unwritten constitution is the creation of the

(1) presidential veto
(2) United States Navy
(3) federal postal system
(4) president's cabinet

12 President George Washington pursued a foreign policy of neutrality during his administration primarily because he believed that

(1) the United States needed time to gain economic and military strength
(2) treaties were prohibited by the Constitution
(3) the United States should not expand by force
(4) alliances should be established with both France and England

13 Many of the decisions made by the Supreme Court while John Marshall was Chief Justice led directly to *Federal Government*

(1) a reduction of federal influence in economic affairs
(2) an increase in the power of the federal government over the states
(3) a greater role for Congress in foreign policy
(4) a limitation on slavery in the states

*east to west*
14 Manifest Destiny was used to justify an American desire to

(1) limit the number of immigrants entering the country
(2) control the area located east of the Appalachian Mountains
(3) expand the United States to the Pacific Ocean
(4) warn European countries against colonizing Latin America

15 In the 1850s, the phrase "Bleeding Kansas" was used to describe clashes between *Pop Plus South*

(1) proslavery and antislavery groups
(2) Spanish landowners and new American settlers
(3) Chinese and Irish railroad workers
(4) Native American Indians and white settlers

16 In the 1850s, why did many runaway slaves go to Canada?

(1) They feared being drafted into the Northern army.
(2) The Fugitive Slave Act kept them at risk in the United States.
(3) More factory jobs were available in Canada.
(4) Northern abolitionists refused to help fugitive slaves.

17 The Homestead Act, the mass killing of buffalo, and the completion of the transcontinental railroad are most closely associated with the

(1) rise of organized labor
(2) building of the Erie Canal
(3) northern migration of African Americans
(4) decline of the Plains Indians

18 Many Southern States tried to limit the effects of Radical Reconstruction by

(1) adopting federal laws mandating segregation
(2) enacting Jim Crow laws
(3) abolishing the Southern sharecropping system
(4) securing passage of new amendments to the United States Constitution

19 The mechanization of agriculture in the United States led directly to

(1) an increase in production
(2) less dependence on railroads by farmers
(3) fewer agricultural exports
(4) the decreasing size of the average farm

20 News organizations were engaging in yellow journalism before the Spanish-American War when

(1) publishers tried to prevent the war
(2) articles about Cuba were fair and balanced
(3) editors exaggerated events to build support for war
(4) writers ignored the situation in Cuba

21 The United States issued the Open Door policy (1899–1900) primarily to

(1) bring democratic government to the Chinese people
(2) secure equal trade opportunities in China
(3) force China to change its immigration policies
(4) use China as a stepping stone to trade with Japan

22 Progressive Era authors such as Jacob Riis and Upton Sinclair are best known for

(1) focusing attention on social conditions
(2) fighting for the civil rights of African Americans
(3) promoting the interests of the American farmer
(4) supporting the goal of woman's suffrage

23 Which type of federal tax was authorized by the 16th amendment in 1913?

(1) excise
(2) import
(3) income
(4) estate

24 ". . . There's no chance of progress and reform in an administration in which war plays the principal part. . . ."

— President-elect Woodrow Wilson, 1913

In this statement, President-elect Wilson was expressing the belief that

(1) the United States should enter World War I immediately
(2) reform movements are strengthened by war
(3) the nation will require a change in leadership if it goes to war
(4) the Progressive movement would be best served by continued peace

25 In *Schenck* v. *United States* (1919), the Supreme Court decided that a "clear and present danger" to the country allowed the federal government to

(1) establish a peacetime draft
(2) restrict first amendment rights
(3) suspend habeas corpus
(4) limit minority voting rights

26 One major reason the United States Senate refused to approve the Treaty of Versailles after World War I was that many senators

(1) were concerned about future United States obligations in foreign affairs
(2) rejected United States colonial practices in Asia
(3) wanted immediate repayment of war debts from France
(4) supported increased foreign aid to Germany

27 National Prohibition, as authorized by the 18th amendment, stated that

(1) Americans must be 18 years old to purchase alcoholic beverages

(2) only imported alcoholic beverages would be sold

(3) alcoholic beverages could be sold only in government-run stores

(4) the manufacture and sale of alcoholic beverages was banned

28 During the 1920s, Congress passed a series of immigration laws that were primarily designed to

(1) increase immigration from Asia

(2) expand the workforce for the growing economy

(3) limit immigration from southern and eastern Europe

(4) prohibit immigration from Latin America

29 During the second half of the 1920s, which economic trend was a major cause of the Great Depression?

(1) deficits in the federal budget

(2) reductions in tariff rates

(3) creation of national and state sales taxes

(4) overproduction and underconsumption

30 President Herbert Hoover's response to the Great Depression was often criticized because it

(1) wasted money on new social programs

(2) caused widespread rioting and looting in major cities

(3) raised taxes on businesses and the wealthy

(4) failed to provide direct relief for the neediest persons

31 A major reason for creating the Tennessee Valley Authority (TVA) in 1933 was to

(1) build and manage a turnpike in the valley

(2) provide health care benefits for southerners

(3) encourage African Americans to settle in the valley

(4) improve economic conditions in a poor rural region

Base your answer to question 32 on the cartoon below and on your knowledge of social studies.

**All Set!**

Source: Fred O. Seibel, *Richmond Times-Dispatch,* January 4, 1936 (adapted)

32 Which statement about President Franklin D. Roosevelt's plans for a second term most accurately expresses the main idea of the cartoon?

(1) Congress will give President Roosevelt a free hand to lead the nation.

(2) The American people will trust Congress to control President Roosevelt.

(3) President Roosevelt will seek direction from the people.

(4) The Great Depression will no longer be a serious concern.

Base your answer to question 33 on the quotation below and on your knowledge of social studies.

. . . I also ask this Congress for authority and for funds sufficient to manufacture additional munitions and war supplies of many kinds, to be turned over to those nations which are now in actual war with aggressor nations.

Our most useful and immediate role is to act as an arsenal for them as well as for ourselves. They do not need man power, but they do need billions of dollars worth of the weapons of defense.

The time is near when they will not be able to pay for them all in ready cash. We cannot, and we will not, tell them that they must surrender, merely because of present inability to pay for the weapons which we know they must have. . . .

— President Franklin D. Roosevelt, Annual Message to Congress, January 6, 1941

33 Which program was President Franklin D. Roosevelt proposing in this speech?

(1) Fair Deal
(2) Great Society
(3) Lend-Lease
(4) Cash and Carry

Base your answer to question 34 on the cartoon below and on your knowledge of social studies.

Source: Dr. Seuss, *PM*, April 7, 1942

34 This World War II cartoon was used to encourage Americans to

(1) buy war bonds
(2) conserve natural resources
(3) serve in the armed forces
(4) work in war industries

35 A major purpose of the GI Bill (1944) was to

(1) replace the draft near the end of World War II
(2) prohibit racial discrimination in the armed forces
(3) provide federal funds for veterans to attend college
(4) increase the number of women working in defense industries

36 In the Truman Doctrine, President Harry Truman pledged to

(1) support Greece in its fight against communist aggression
(2) fight hunger in Africa and Asia
(3) strengthen the United States nuclear arsenal
(4) reject a policy of containment

37 Which factor is most closely associated with McCarthyism?

(1) buildup of Soviet missiles in Cuba
(2) fear of communist influence in the United States
(3) rise of the Communist Party in China
(4) creation of the Warsaw Pact by the Soviet Union

Base your answer to question 38 on the map below and on your knowledge of social studies.

## African American Migration, 1940–1970

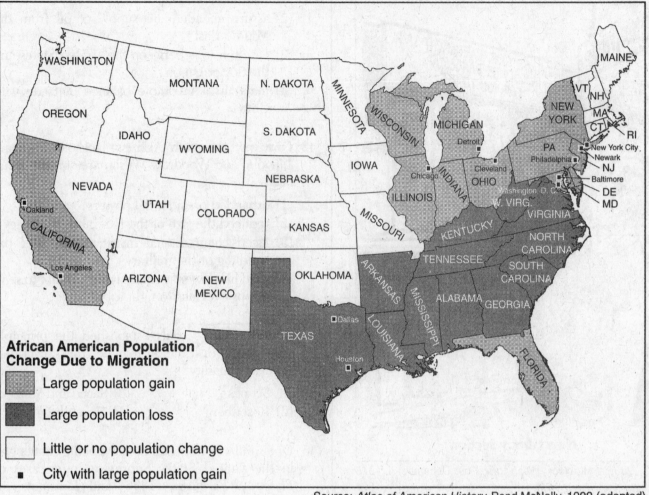

Source: *Atlas of American History,* Rand McNally, 1999 (adapted)

38 The information on the map supports the conclusion that African American migration between 1940 and 1970 was mainly from the

(1) urban areas to rural areas     (3) Mountain states to the West Coast

(2) south to the north     (4) Sun Belt to the Great Plains

---

39 Which development led to the other three?

(1) The United States government increased funding for science and math education.

(2) The Soviet Union launched the *Sputnik* satellite.

(3) A joint Soviet-American space mission was announced.

(4) President John F. Kennedy set the goal of landing a man on the Moon.

40 Which development is most closely associated with the belief in the domino theory?

(1) military involvement in Vietnam

(2) construction of the Berlin Wall

(3) signing of the nuclear test ban treaty

(4) end of the Korean War

Base your answer to question 41 on the cartoon below and on your knowledge of social studies.

**New Library Section**

Source: Herblock, *Washington Post*, December 4, 1975

41 Which statement most accurately describes the main idea of this 1975 cartoon?

(1) The press should not publish materials that damage the reputation of public officials.

(2) The government is improperly hiding information from the public.

(3) Government should restrict the publication of sensitive materials.

(4) Libraries are making too many government reports open to the public.

42 The primary purpose of President Richard Nixon's policy of détente was to

(1) expand United States military involvement in Southeast Asia

(2) assure an adequate supply of oil from the Middle East

(3) ease tensions between the United States and the Soviet Union

(4) maintain a favorable balance of trade with China

43 One way in which Andrew Jackson, Abraham Lincoln, and Woodrow Wilson are similar is that each

(1) expanded presidential powers

(2) reduced the size of the federal bureaucracy

(3) faced congressional investigations over the handling of the military

(4) used his power as commander in chief to send troops overseas to fight a war

44 Which of these trials established the principle that leaders of a nation may be tried for crimes against humanity?

(1) Scopes          (3) Sacco and Vanzetti

(2) Rosenberg       (4) Nuremberg

45 One similarity between the laws being challenged in the United States Supreme Court cases of *Plessy* v. *Ferguson* (1896) and *Korematsu* v. *United States* (1944) is that

(1) specific groups of people were being targeted based on race or ethnicity

(2) state laws were declared unconstitutional

(3) immigrants were relocated to prison camps

(4) federal laws segregating public transportation were upheld

Base your answer to question 46 on the table below and on your knowledge of social studies.

**Projected Change in House Seats in 2010, By State**

| State | House Seats | Projected House Seats | |
|-------|-------------|------------------------|---|
| | 2000 | 2010 | +/− |
| Arizona | 8 | 9 | +1 |
| California | 53 | 54 | +1 |
| Florida | 25 | 27 | +2 |
| Georgia | 13 | 14 | +1 |
| Illinois | 19 | 18 | −1 |
| Massachusetts | 10 | 9 | −1 |
| Missouri | 9 | 8 | −1 |
| Nevada | 3 | 4 | +1 |
| New York | 29 | 27 | −2 |
| Ohio | 18 | 16 | −2 |
| Pennsylvania | 19 | 18 | −1 |
| Texas | 32 | 35 | +3 |

Source: Population Reference Bureau, www.prb.org (adapted)

46 Information from the table supports the conclusion that the

(1) population of the United States is increasing
(2) center of population is moving eastward
(3) distribution of House seats follows shifts in population
(4) number of senators will soon increase

47 **"Eisenhower Sends U.S. Troops to Protect Lebanon"**

**"Kennedy Places Quarantine on Shipment of Soviet Missiles to Cuba"**

**"Johnson Increases U.S. Troop Strength in Vietnam by 125,000"**

Which statement about the Cold War is illustrated by these headlines?

(1) Rivalries between the superpowers often involved conflicts in other nations.
(2) United States military support was most often deployed in Europe.
(3) Communist forces were frequently victorious in Asia.
(4) Summit talks frequently succeeded in limiting international tensions.

48 Which list of wars that involved the United States is in the correct chronological order?

(1) Vietnam War → War on Terrorism → Korean War → World War II
(2) Korean War → World War II → Vietnam War → War on Terrorism
(3) World War II → Vietnam War → War on Terrorism → Korean War
(4) World War II → Korean War → Vietnam War → War on Terrorism

Base your answers to questions 49 and 50 on the graph below and on your knowledge of social studies.

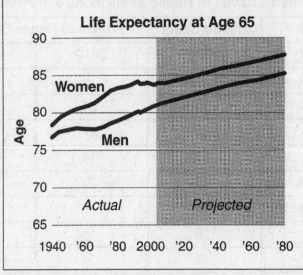

**Life Expectancy at Age 65**

Source: *New York Times,* June 12, 2005 (adapted)

49 Which conclusion about life expectancy at age 65 is most clearly supported by the information in the graph?

(1) Life expectancies for men and women are likely to remain the same.

(2) Life expectancy rates for men show a steady decline since 1980.

(3) By 2040, the life expectancy of men will exceed that of women.

(4) Current life expectancy exceeds age 80 for both men and women.

50 The changes shown between 1940 and 2000 are most likely the result of the

(1) reduction in warfare

(2) improvements in modern medicine

(3) increase in the number of immigrants

(4) decrease in obesity rates

**Answers to the essay questions are to be written in the separate essay booklet.**

## Part II

### THEMATIC ESSAY QUESTION

*Directions:* Write a well-organized essay that includes an introduction, several paragraphs addressing the task below, and a conclusion.

**Theme: Constitutional Principles — Individual Rights**

> Throughout United States history, many different groups have faced discrimination. The federal and state governments have taken actions that have either protected or limited the rights of these groups in American society.

**Task:**

> Select *two* different groups in American society who have faced discrimination and for *each*
> - Describe *one* specific example of discrimination faced by the group
> - Describe *one* action taken by the federal or state governments related to this example of discrimination
> - Discuss how the action taken by the federal or state governments either protected *or* limited the rights of the group

You may use any example from your study of United States history. Some groups you might wish to consider include Native American Indians, African Americans, Asian Americans, Hispanic Americans, women, the elderly, and the disabled.

### You are *not* limited to these suggestions.

**Guidelines:**

**In your essay, be sure to**
- Develop all aspects of the task
- Support the theme with relevant facts, examples, and details
- Use a logical and clear plan of organization, including an introduction and a conclusion that are beyond a restatement of the theme

**In developing your answer to Part II, be sure to keep these general definitions in mind:**

(a) <u>describe</u> means "to illustrate something in words or tell about it"

(b) <u>discuss</u> means "to make observations about something using facts, reasoning, and argument; to present in some detail"

NAME _____ SCHOOL _____

In developing your answers to Part III, be sure to keep this general definition in mind:

> <u>discuss</u> means "to make observations about something using facts, reasoning, and argument; to present in some detail"

## Part III

## DOCUMENT-BASED QUESTION

This question is based on the accompanying documents. The question is designed to test your ability to work with historical documents. Some of the documents have been edited for the purposes of the question. As you analyze the documents, take into account the source of each document and any point of view that may be presented in the document.

### Historical Context:

Between the Civil War and the end of World War I, industrialization played an ever-increasing role in the economic, social, and political development of the United States.

**Task:** Using information from the documents and your knowledge of United States history, answer the questions that follow each document in Part A. Your answers to the questions will help you write the Part B essay, in which you will be asked to

> - Discuss the economic, social, **and/or** political effects of industrialization on the United States between the Civil War (1861–1865) and the end of World War I (1918)

# Part A
# Short-Answer Questions

*Directions:* Analyze the documents and answer the short-answer questions that follow each document in the space provided.

## Document 1a

### Selected Statistics Related to Industrialization

|  | Value of Manufactured Products | Employed in Manufacturing | |
|---|---|---|---|
|  |  | Number of Males | Number of Females |
| 1860 | $1.9 billion | 1.03 million | 270,357 |
| 1870 | $4.2 billion | 1.61 million | 323,506 |
| 1880 | $5.3 billion | 2.01 million | 529,983 |
| 1890 | $9.3 billion | 2.86 million | 503,089 |
| 1900 | $12.9 billion | 4.08 million | 1.03 million |
| 1910 | $20.8 billion | 8.84 million | 1.82 million |

Source: Inter-University Consortium for Political and Social Research, Ann Arbor, MI, and U.S. Census Bureau

## Document 1b

### United States Immigration 1861–1910

| Decade | Total |
|---|---|
| 1861–1870 | 2,314,824 |
| 1871–1880 | 2,812,191 |
| 1881–1890 | 5,246,613 |
| 1891–1900 | 3,687,564* |
| 1901–1910 | 8,795,386 |

*Decline in numbers of immigrants due in part to the Depression of 1893.

Source: U.S. Immigration and Naturalization Service, *Statistical Yearbook of the Immigration and Naturalization Service, 1998,* U.S. Government Printing Office

1 Based on these charts, state *two* trends related to industrialization between 1861 and 1910. [2]

(1) _Poplatio of males and femeley increasing Emoped in manufacturing_
_The value of manfactered is also increasing_

Score ▢

(2) _The value of man Doc(1b) Popleation immigrants from_
_2 million to 8 million_

Score ▢

## Document 2a

### Urbanization, Railroad Mileage, and Industrialization of the United States, 1860–1900

|  | 1860 | 1870 | 1880 | 1890 | 1900 |
|---|---|---|---|---|---|
| Urban Population (millions) | 6.2 | 9.9 | 14.1 | 22.1 | 30.2 |
| % Urban Population | 20% | 25% | 28% | 35% | 40% |
| Number of Cities with Population of 10,000+ | 93 | 168 | 223 | 363 | 440 |
| Railroad Mileage (thousands) | 30.6 | 52.9 | 93.3 | 166.7 | 206.6 |
| Meat Packing Output ($ millions) | not available | 62.1 | 303.6 | 564.7 | 790.3 |

Source: Gary Fields, "Communications, Innovations, and Networks: The National Beef Network of G. F. Swift" (adapted)

## Document 2b

### Union Membership, 1870–1920

| Year | Number of workers, age 10 and over (excluding agricultural workers) | Average annual union membership | Union membership as a percentage of the total number of workers outside agriculture |
|---|---|---|---|
| 1870 | 6,075,000 | 300,000* | 4.9% |
| 1880 | 8,807,000 | 200,000* | 2.3% |
| 1890 | 13,380,000 | 372,000* | 2.7% |
| 1900 | 18,161,000 | 868,000 | 4.8% |
| 1910 | 25,779,000 | 2,140,000 | 8.3% |
| 1920 | 30,985,000 | 5,048,000 | 16.3% |

* Figures for 1870, 1880, and 1890 are estimates.

Source: Irving Bartlett et al., *A New History of the United States*, Holt, Rinehart and Winston,1975 (adapted)

2 Based on these charts, state *two* effects of industrialization on the United States after the Civil War. [2]

(1) 2a) During 1860-1900 the urban population as increase from 6.2 millions to 30.2

Score ☐

(2) union membership (2b) outsid agriculture from 4.9 to 18.3

Score ☐

## Document 3

The resolutions below were proposed at the Populist [People's] Party National Convention.

> 4. *Resolved*, That we condemn the fallacy [myth] of protecting American labor under the present system, which opens our ports to the pauper [poor] and criminal classes of the world, and crowds out our wage-earners; and we denounce the present ineffective laws against contract labor [day laborers], and demand the further restriction of undesirable emigration.
>
> 5. *Resolved*, That we cordially sympathize with the efforts of organized workingmen to shorten the hours of labor, and demand a rigid enforcement of the existing eight-hour law on Government work, and ask that a penalty clause be added to the said law.
>
> 9. *Resolved*, That we oppose any subsidy or national aid to any private corporation for any purpose.

Source: People's Party National Platform, July 4, 1892

3 Based on this document, identify **one** reform proposed at the Populist Party Convention related to industrialization. [1]

demand the further restriction of undesirable emigratio

unions of workers for shorter working hours

Score ☐

## Document 4

The excerpts below are from an Illinois state law passed in 1893.

---

### FACTORIES AND WORKSHOPS.
— —
### INSPECTION

§ 1. Manufacture of certain articles of clothing prohibited in apartments, tenement houses and living rooms, except by families living therein. Every such work shop shall be kept clean, free from vermin [rodents], infectious or contagious matter and to that end shall be subject to inspection as provided in this act. Such work shops shall be reported to the board of health.

§ 2. If upon inspection such work shops shall be found unhealthy or infectious such orders shall be given and action taken as the public health shall require.

§ 4. Children under 14 years of age prohibited from being employed in any manufacturing establishment, factory or work shop in the state. Register of children under 16 years shall be kept. The employment of children between ages of 14 and 16 years prohibited unless an affidavit [legal document] by the parent or guardian shall first be filed in which shall be stated the age date and place of birth. Certificates of physical health may be demanded by the inspectors.

§ 5. No female shall be employed in any factory or workshop more than eight hours in any one day or forty-eight hours in any one week.

---

Source: "Factories and Workshops," *Laws of the State of Illinois, Passed by the Thirty-Eighth General Assembly,* 1893

4 Based on these excerpts, identify *two* ways this 1893 Illinois state law addressed problems caused by industrialization. [2]

(1) To protect children

Score ☐

(2) Female cant work more 8 houry

Score ☐

## Document 5

Hamlin Garland visited Homestead, Pennsylvania, and the Carnegie steel mills to write this article for *McClure's Magazine*.

> . . .The streets of the town were horrible; the buildings were poor; the sidewalks were sunken, swaying, and full of holes, and the crossings were sharp-edged stones set like rocks in a river bed. Everywhere the yellow mud of the street lay kneaded into a sticky mass, through which groups of pale, lean men slouched in faded garments, grimy with the soot and grease of the mills.
>
> The town was as squalid [dirty] and unlovely as could well be imagined, and the people were mainly of the discouraged and sullen type to be found everywhere where labor passes into the brutalizing stage of severity. It had the disorganized and incoherent effect of a town which has feeble public spirit. Big industries at differing eras have produced squads [groups] of squalid tenement-houses far from the central portion of the town, each plant bringing its gangs of foreign laborers in raw masses to camp down like an army around its shops.
>
> Such towns are sown thickly over the hill-lands of Pennsylvania, but this was my first descent into one of them. They are American only in the sense in which they represent the American idea of business. . . .

Source: Hamlin Garland, "Homestead and Its Perilous Trades–Impressions of a Visit,"
*McClure's Magazine*, June 1894

5 Based on Hamlin Garland's observations, what is **one** impact of industrialization on Homestead, Pennsylvania? [1]

Poor People

Score ☐

**This page left blank intentionally.**

GO ON TO THE NEXT PAGE ⟹

[18]

## Document 6a

Clara Lemlich, a labor union leader, sparked the 1909 walkout of shirtwaist [blouse] makers with her call for a strike.

> First let me tell you something about the way we work and what we are paid. There are two kinds of work—regular, that is salary work, and piecework. The regular work pays about $6 a week and the girls have to be at their machines at 7 o'clock in the morning and they stay at them until 8 o'clock at night, with just one-half hour for lunch in that time.
>
> The shops. Well, there is just one row of machines that the daylight ever gets to—that is the front row, nearest the window. The girls at all the other rows of machines back in the shops have to work by gaslight, by day as well as by night. Oh, yes, the shops keep the work going at night, too. . . .

Source: Clara Lemlich, "Life in the Shop," *New York Evening Journal,* November 28, 1909

## Document 6b

Source: *Bain News Service*, New York, February 1910,
Library of Congress

6 Based on these documents, state *two* ways industrialization affected workers. [2]

(1) _women work for lon ways_

Score [ ]

(2) _woren work for long hours_

Score [ ]

**Document 7a**

### THE TRUST GIANT'S POINT OF VIEW,
"What a Funny Little Government"

Source: Horace Taylor, *The Verdict*, January 22, 1900 (adapted)

7a What is the cartoonist's point of view concerning the relationship between government and industrialists such as John D. Rockefeller? [1]

_industrialist more powerful then the government_

Score ▢

**Document 7b**

Source: Clifford K. Berryman, *Washington Evening Star*, October 11, 1907
(adapted)

7b According to the cartoonist, what was President Theodore Roosevelt's policy toward trusts? [1]

Government should have more control

Score ☐

## Document 8

Although they sometimes used controversial methods to accumulate wealth, many industrialists, such as Andrew Carnegie, John D. Rockefeller, and J. P. Morgan, also gave away millions of dollars. This excerpt describes some of the charitable work of Andrew Carnegie.

> . . . But despite his wealth-getting, his wage-cutting, and his responsibility for a bloody labor dispute at his Homestead plant in 1892, Carnegie had not forgotten his heritage of concern for social justice. In his 1889 article "Wealth," he gloried in the cheap steel his leadership had given the American consumer but also proclaimed the moral duty of all possessors of great wealth to plow back their money into philanthropy [charity] with the same judgment, zeal, and leadership they had devoted to getting rich. And he lived up to that precept [principle], paying for thousands of library buildings, setting up trusts and foundations, endowing universities, building Carnegie Hall in New York and the Peace Palace at The Hague, and much more. He once wrote that the man who dies rich dies disgraced. He had some sins to answer for, and it took him a while, but in 1919 at eighty-three Andrew Carnegie died in a state of grace by his own agnostic [non-religious] definition. . . .

Source: Foner and Garraty, eds., "Andrew Carnegie," *The Reader's Companion to American History,*
Houghton Mifflin, 1991

8 According to this document, how did Andrew Carnegie show his concern for social justice? [1]

_____

_____

Score ☐

**Document 9**

... The significance of the American entry into the conflict [World War I] was not at all a military one, at least for twelve to fifteen months after April 1917, since its army was even less prepared for modern campaigning than any of the European forces had been in 1914. But its productive strength, boosted by the billions of dollars of Allied war orders, was unequaled. Its total industrial potential and its share of world manufacturing output was two and a half times that of Germany's now overstrained economy. It could launch merchant ships in their hundreds, a vital requirement in a year when the U-boats were sinking over 500,000 tons a month of British and Allied vessels. It could build destroyers in the astonishing time of three months. It produced half of the world's food exports, which could now be sent to France and Italy as well as to its traditional British market.

In terms of economic power, therefore, the entry of the United States into the war quite transformed the balances, and more than compensated for the collapse of Russia at this same time. . . . the productive resources now arranged against the Central Powers were enormous. . . .

Source: Paul Kennedy, *The Rise and Fall of the Great Powers*, Random House, 1987

9 According to Paul Kennedy, what was *one* effect of United States industrialization on World War I? [1]

_____

_____

Score ☐

# Part B
# Essay

*Directions:* Write a well-organized essay that includes an introduction, several paragraphs, and a conclusion. Use evidence from *at least five* documents in your essay. Support your response with relevant facts, examples, and details. Include additional outside information.

### Historical Context:

Between the Civil War and the end of World War I, industrialization played an ever-increasing role in the economic, social, and political development of the United States.

**Task:** Using information from the documents and your knowledge of United States history, write an essay in which you

> • Discuss the economic, social, ***and/or*** political effects of industrialization on the United States between the Civil War (1861–1865) and the end of World War I (1918)

### Guidelines:

**In your essay, be sure to**
- Develop all aspects of the task
- Incorporate information from *at least five* documents
- Incorporate relevant outside information
- Support the theme with relevant facts, examples, and details
- Use a logical and clear plan of organization, including an introduction and conclusion that are beyond a restatement of the theme

This section contains the Regents Examination in United States History and Government that was given in New York State in January 2009.

Circle your answers to Part I on this exam and write your answers to the thematic essay and document-based essay questions on separate sheets of paper. Be sure to refer to the test-taking strategies in the front of this book as you prepare to answer the test questions.

# Part I

## Answer all questions in this part.

*Directions* (1–50): For each statement or question, write on the separate answer sheet the *number* of the word or expression that, of those given, best completes the statement or answers the question.

Base your answers to questions 1 and 2 on the map below and on your knowledge of social studies.

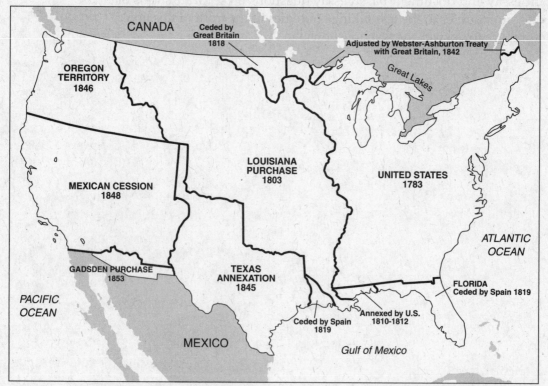

CANADA

Ceded by
Great Britain
1818

Adjusted by Webster-Ashburton Treaty
with Great Britain, 1842

OREGON
TERRITORY
1846

Great Lakes

MEXICAN CESSION
1848

LOUISIANA
PURCHASE
1803

UNITED STATES
1783

ATLANTIC
OCEAN

GADSDEN PURCHASE
1853

TEXAS
ANNEXATION
1845

FLORIDA
Ceded by Spain 1819

PACIFIC
OCEAN

Ceded by Spain
1819

Annexed by U.S.
1810-1812

MEXICO

Gulf of Mexico

Source: Robert A. Divine et al., *America: Past and Present,* Scott, Foresman (adapted)

1  What would be the best title for this map?

(1) British North America Before 1850
(2) United States Territorial Expansion
(3) Colonial North America
(4) Wartime Land Acquisitions

2  The Louisiana Purchase was important to the United States because it

(1) expanded the nation's boundary to the Pacific Ocean
(2) removed the Spanish from North America
(3) closed the western territories to slavery
(4) secured control of the Mississippi River

3 Which geographic feature served as the western boundary for British colonial settlements prior to the Revolutionary War?

(1) Rocky Mountains
(2) Missouri River
(3) Appalachian Mountains
(4) Great Plains

4 "...That to secure these rights, governments are instituted among men, deriving their just powers from the consent of the governed, ..."
— Declaration of Independence

Which provision of the original United States Constitution was most influenced by this ideal?

(1) enabling the president to select a cabinet
(2) providing for direct election of the House of Representatives
(3) allowing the Senate to try articles of impeachment
(4) authorizing the Supreme Court to rule on disputes between states

5 Delegates at the Constitutional Convention of 1787 agreed to the Three-fifths Compromise to solve a dispute directly related to

(1) the power of the presidency
(2) representation in Congress
(3) a decision by the Supreme Court
(4) the addition of a bill of rights

6 Which feature of the United States Constitution traditionally gives the states authority over public education?

(1) reserved powers        (3) fifth amendment
(2) preamble               (4) supremacy clause

7 "**President Wilson Represents the United States at Versailles**"

"**President Reagan Meets with Soviet President Gorbachev**"

"**President Carter Negotiates Camp David Accords**"

Each headline illustrates a time when the president of the United States acted as

(1) chief diplomat
(2) chief legislator
(3) commander in chief
(4) head of a political party

8 Which individual's action was directly protected by the first amendment?

(1) Alexander Graham Bell's invention of the telephone in 1876
(2) Theodore Roosevelt's command of the Rough Riders in 1898
(3) President Franklin D. Roosevelt's election to a third term in 1940
(4) Dr. Martin Luther King Jr.'s leading a march on Washington, D.C., in 1963

Base your answer to question 9 on the quotation below and on your knowledge of social studies.

... The nation deserves and I will select a Supreme Court justice that Americans can be proud of. The nation also deserves a dignified process of confirmation in the United States Senate, characterized by fair treatment, a fair hearing and a fair vote. I will choose a nominee in a timely manner so that the hearing and the vote can be completed before the new Supreme Court term begins. ...
— President George W. Bush, 2005

9 Which constitutional principle is suggested by this quotation?

(1) federalism            (3) States rights
(2) checks and balances   (4) due process

10 In his Farewell Address, President George Washington warned against establishing alliances with European countries because he was concerned primarily about

(1) restrictions on trade with Latin America
(2) French colonization of the Caribbean
(3) United States involvement in foreign wars
(4) protection of the western frontier

11 The Monroe Doctrine (1823) was issued primarily because President James Monroe

(1) wanted to warn European powers against intervention in Latin America
(2) opposed the revolutions taking place in South America
(3) needed to establish a foothold in Panama for a future canal
(4) believed the United States should pursue overseas colonies

Base your answer to question 12 on the map below and on your knowledge of social studies.

**Railroads in 1840 and 1860**

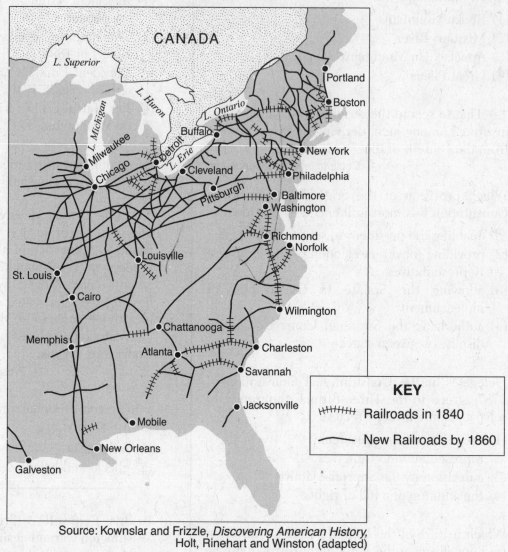

Source: Kownslar and Frizzle, *Discovering American History,*
Holt, Rinehart and Winston (adapted)

12 Based on the map, which statement is a valid conclusion?

(1) Port cities were not connected to railroads.

(2) Railroads were more expensive to build than canals.

(3) Most canals were abandoned before the Civil War.

(●) Railroads were expanding more quickly in the North than in the South.

---

13 President Andrew Jackson's policy toward Native American Indians was created to

(1) encourage Native American Indians to become part of mainstream American society

(●) force Native American Indians to move west of the Mississippi River

(3) improve educational opportunities for Native American Indians

(4) grant citizenship to Native American Indians

14 The publication of *Uncle Tom's Cabin*, written by Harriet Beecher Stowe, contributed to the start of the Civil War by

(1) exposing the dangers of cotton manufacturing

(2) intensifying Northern dislike of slavery

(3) pressuring the president to support emancipation

(●) convincing Congress to ban the importation of slaves

15 Following Reconstruction, the passage of Jim Crow laws in the South limited the effectiveness of

(1) the 14th and 15th amendments
(2) the Freedmen's Bureau
(3) Black Codes
(4) tenant farming and sharecropping

16 During the late 1800s, many United States farmers believed their economic problems would be solved if the federal government would

(1) raise interest rates
(2) outlaw strikes by labor unions
(3) put more money into circulation
(4) regulate the amount of grain that was produced

17 In the late 19th century, critics of big business claimed that monopolies most harmed the economy by

(1) limiting competition
(2) decreasing the urban growth rate
(3) preventing technological innovation
(4) failing to keep pace with European industries

18 In the late 19th century, the ideas of Social Darwinism were used primarily to

(1) encourage the passage of compulsory education laws
(2) explain the differences in income between the rich and the poor
(3) urge Congress to end immigration
(4) support the growth of new political parties

19 The principal reason Congress raised tariff rates in the late 1800s and early 1900s was to

(1) increase personal income taxes
(2) lower prices for American consumers
(3) guarantee high wages to American workers
(4) protect United States businesses from foreign competition

20 Reformers of the early 20th century frequently attacked political machines because the politicians in these organizations often

(1) denied voting rights to the poor
(2) accepted bribes in return for favors
(3) wasted money on military spending
(4) discriminated against migrant workers

Base your answer to question 21 on the song lyrics below and on your knowledge of social studies

## The Uprising of the Twenty Thousands (Dedicated to the Waistmakers [shirt makers] of 1909)

In the black of the winter of nineteen nine,
When we froze and bled on the picket line,
We showed the world that women could fight
And we rose and won with women's might.

Chorus:
Hail the waistmakers of nineteen nine,
Making their stand on the picket line,
Breaking the power of those who reign,
Pointing the way, smashing the chain.

And we gave new courage to the men
Who carried on in nineteen ten
And shoulder to shoulder we'll win through,
Led by the I.L.G.W.U.

— *Let's Sing!*, Educational Department, Internationa
Ladies' Garment Workers' Union, New York City

21 Which type of labor-related action is bes described in this song?

(1) a strike          (3) a boycott
(2) an open shop      (4) an injunction

22 A major purpose of the Progressive movemen (1900–1917) was to

(1) stimulate the economy
(2) support government control of factor production
(3) encourage immigration from southern an eastern Europe
(4) correct the economic and social abuses industrial society

23 Today, the Federal Reserve System attempts t stabilize the economy of the United States by

(1) requiring federal budgets be prepared an presented to Congress
(2) levying and collecting income taxes
(3) regulating interest rates and the mone supply
(4) backing all currency with silver and gold

Base your answer to question 24 on the graph below and on your knowledge of social studies.

**Manufacture of Passenger Cars, 1910–1929**

Source: *Historical Statistics of the United States, Colonial Times to 1970, Part 2*, U. S. Department of Commerce (adapted)

24 The overall trend shown on the graph was primarily the result of

(1) a decline in the economy
(2) the increased use of the assembly line
(3) a shift of the population from urban areas to farms
(4) an increase in the price of automobiles

---

25 What was a major reason the United States entered World War I (1917)?

(1) The Japanese had occupied Manchuria.
(2) Foreign troops had landed on American soil.
(3) The Austro-Hungarian Empire had invaded Belgium.
(4) Germany had resumed unrestricted submarine warfare.

26 What was one effect of the Bolshevik Revolution (October 1917) on the United States?

(1) Nativism increased, leading to the Red Scare.
(2) Federal courts banned anti-immigrant groups.
(3) The Allied powers needed fewer United States troops.
(4) Immigration laws were changed to allow refugees from Russia.

27 What was the effect of the "clear and present danger" ruling established in *Schenck* v. *United States* (1919)?

(1) placing limits on constitutional freedoms
(2) decreasing the president's powers during wartime
(3) limiting the hours women could work in industry
(4) upholding the right of states to regulate child labor

28 The Harlem Renaissance promoted African American culture by

(1) increasing factory employment opportunities for minorities
(2) encouraging immigration from Africa
(3) focusing attention on artistic contributions
(4) bringing an end to legalized racial segregation

29 During the 1920s, the United States changed its immigration policy by passing new laws that

(1) provided incentives to attract more immigrants to factory jobs

(2) encouraged Chinese immigrants to enter the country

(3) allowed unrestricted immigration of war refugees from Vietnam

(4) established quotas that reduced the number of immigrants from certain countries

30 President Franklin D. Roosevelt believed that declaring a bank holiday and creating the Federal Deposit Insurance Corporation (FDIC) would help the nation's banking system by

(1) restoring public confidence in the banks

(2) reducing government regulation of banks

(3) restricting foreign investments

(4) granting tax relief to individuals

31 The Social Security Act (1935) is considered an important program because it

(1) brought about a quick end to the Great Depression

(2) provided employment for those in need of a job

(3) established a progressive income tax

(4) extended support to elderly citizens

32 The policy of Cash and Carry, the Destroyers for Naval Bases Deal, and the Lend-Lease Act were all designed to

(1) contribute to the success of the Axis powers

(2) relieve unemployment caused by the Great Depression

(3) guarantee a third term to President Franklin D. Roosevelt

(4) aid the Allies without involving the United States in war

33 Rationing was used in the United States during World War II as a way to

(1) ensure adequate supplies of scarce natural resources

(2) increase the number of imports

(3) raise production of consumer goods

(4) provide markets for American-made products

34 The post–World War II trials held by the Allied powers in Nuremberg, Germany, and in Japan set an international precedent by

(1) placing blame only on civilian leaders

(2) forcing nations to pay for war damages

(3) returning conquered territories to their peoples

(4) holding individuals accountable for their war crimes

35 The development of the Marshall Plan and the formation of the North Atlantic Treaty Organization (NATO) were part of President Harry Truman's effort to

(1) end the Korean War

(2) limit the spread of communism

(3) provide aid to Asian nations

(4) promote an isolationist foreign policy

36 **"Jackie Robinson Breaks Color Barrier in Major League Baseball"**

**"President Truman Issues Executive Order Desegregating Armed Forces"**

**"NAACP Challenges School Segregation"**

These headlines are most closely associated with

(1) a decline in African American participation in political activities

(2) the beginning of the modern civil rights movement

(3) Southern resistance to the Civil Rights Act of 1964

(4) the effects of affirmative action programs

37 "No person in the United States shall, on the basis of sex, be excluded from participation in, be denied the benefits of, or be subjected to discrimination under any education program or activity receiving Federal financial assistance, . . ."
— Title IX, 1972

The passage of this law affected women across the nation by

(1) granting them the right to own property

(2) guaranteeing them the same wages as male workers

(3) increasing their opportunities to participate in school sports

(4) allowing them the right to seek elective offices

Base your answers to questions 38 and 39 on the graph below and on your knowledge of social studies.

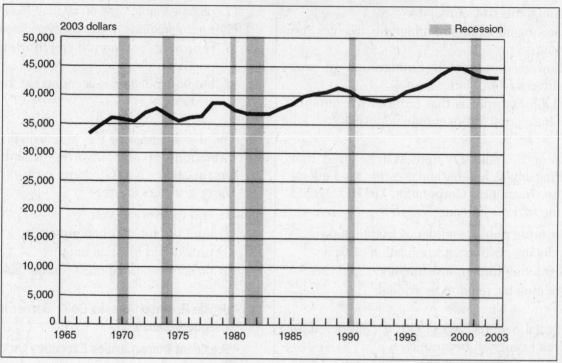

**Real Median Household Income: 1967 to 2003**

Source: U. S. Census Bureau, *Current Population Survey, 1968 to 2004,*
*Annual Social and Economic Supplements* (adapted)

38 Based on the graph, which statement about median household income between 1967 and 2003 is most accurate?

(1) It doubled.

(2) It decreased by about $5,000.

(3) It increased by about $10,000.

(4) It increased by about $50,000.

39 Based on the graph, which development occurred during the year before each recession?

(1) Median household income decreased.

(2) Full employment was achieved.

(3) Median household income stayed the same.

(4) The United States population decreased.

---

40 The passage of the War Powers Act of 1973 was intended to affect the balance of power between the president and Congress by

(1) allowing troops to be sent overseas without the president's consent

(2) requiring the president to remove all United States troops from Southeast Asia

(3) permitting the president to enter treaties without Senate approval

(4) placing limitations on the president's ability to keep troops in hostile situations

41 Which event led to the investigations that resulted in the resignation of President Richard Nixon?

(1) a decision to escalate the war in Vietnam

(2) a presidential decision to freeze wages and prices

(3) a break-in at the headquarters of the Democratic National Committee

(4) an oil embargo by the Organization of Petroleum Exporting Countries (OPEC)

Base your answer to question 42 on the conversation below and on your knowledge of social studies.

*The President:*

Helmut! I am sitting in a meeting with members of our Congress and am calling at the end of this historic day to wish you well.

*Chancellor Kohl:*

Things are going very, very well. I am in Berlin. There were one million people here last night at the very spot where the Wall used to stand—and where President Reagan called on Mr. Gorbachev to open this gate. Words can't describe the feeling. The weather is very nice and warm, fortunately. There were large crowds of young people. Eighty percent were under thirty. It was fantastic. . . .

Source: Telephone conversation between Chancellor Helmut Kohl of Germany and President George H. W. Bush, October 3, 1990

42 This conversation is referring to the

(1) start of the Berlin airlift
(2) expansion of the North Atlantic Treaty Organization (NATO)
(3) end of the Cold War and reunification of Germany
(4) signing of the Nuclear Test Ban Treaty and creation of the Hot Line

43 Which heading best completes the partial outline below?

> I._____
>   A. Desire for new markets
>   B. Creation of a modern navy
>   C. Belief in Anglo-Saxon superiority

(1) Consequences of World War I
(2) Results of the Gentlemen's Agreement
(3) Events Leading to Neutrality
(4) Factors Supporting United States Imperialism

Base your answers to questions 44 and 45 on the cartoon below and on your knowledge of social studies.

Source: Tom Toles, *The Washington Post*, June 26, 2005 (adapted)

44 What is the main idea of this cartoon?

(1) Burning flags is another cause of global warming.
(2) Washington politicians are focusing on the wrong issues.
(3) Respect for the American flag around the world is declining.
(4) Automobiles are mainly responsible for global warming.

45 Based on this cartoon, which action by the federal government would the cartoonist most likely support?

(1) restricting first amendment rights
(2) promoting industrial growth
(3) enforcing environmental regulations
(4) encouraging globalization

Base your answer to question 46 on the chart below and on your knowledge of social studies.

| Political Party | Presidential Nominee | Electoral College Vote | Electoral College Vote Percent | Popular Vote Number | Popular Vote Percent |
|---|---|---|---|---|---|
| Republican | George W. Bush | 271 | 50.4 | 50,456,062 | 47.9 |
| Democratic | Albert Gore, Jr. | 266 | 49.4 | 50,996,582 | 48.4 |
| Green | Ralph Nader | 0 | 0.0 | 2,858,843 | 2.7 |

Source: National Archives and Records Administration, 2000 Presidential Election (adapted)

46 Which generalization about United States presidential elections is most clearly supported by the data in this chart?

(1) A candidate can win the election without a majority of the popular vote.
(2) Third-party candidates have no effect on presidential elections.
(3) Electoral college votes determine the will of the majority of voters.
(4) Voter participation in national elections is declining.

47 The Department of Homeland Security was created as a direct response to the

(1) Persian Gulf War (1991)
(2) Oklahoma City bombing (1995)
(3) terrorist attacks on September 11 (2001)
(4) flooding of New Orleans (2005)

48 • Establishment of the Peace Corps
• Bay of Pigs invasion
• Cuban missile crisis

These events occurred during the presidency of

(1) John F. Kennedy
(2) Lyndon B. Johnson
(3) Richard Nixon
(4) Jimmy Carter

49 The Anthracite Coal Strike (1902), the Wagner Act (1935), and the founding of the United Farm Workers (1962) were important steps in

(1) limiting the growth of labor unions
(2) creating greater equality for women
(3) ending discrimination directed at African Americans in the South
(4) promoting fair labor practices and collective bargaining for workers

50 Which book describes how the Dust Bowl of the 1930s affected farmers of the Great Plains?

(1) *How the Other Half Lives*
(2) *The Jungle*
(3) *The Grapes of Wrath*
(4) *Silent Spring*

**Answers to the essay questions are to be written in the separate essay booklet.**

## Part II

### THEMATIC ESSAY QUESTION

*Directions:* Write a well-organized essay that includes an introduction, several paragraphs addressing the task below, and a conclusion.

### Theme: Movements of People—Migration

> The movement of people *into* and *within* the United States has had a significant impact on the nation. These movements have been both voluntary and involuntary.

**Task:**

> Select *two* periods of migration that had an impact on the United States and for *each*
> - Describe the historical circumstances that led to the migration
> - Discuss the impact of the migration on the United States

You may use any period of migration from your study of United States history. Some suggestions you might wish to consider include colonial settlement (1600s–1700s), westward expansion (1800s), rural to urban migration (1870s–1920s), European immigration (1880–1910), the Dust Bowl (1930s), suburbanization (1950s–1960s), and illegal immigration (1990 to the present).

### You are *not* limited to these suggestions.

**Guidelines:**

**In your essay, be sure to**
- Develop all aspects of the task
- Support the theme with relevant facts, examples, and details
- Use a logical and clear plan of organization, including an introduction and a conclusion that are beyond a restatement of the theme

**In developing your answer to Part II, be sure to keep these general definitions in mind:**

(a) <u>describe</u> means "to illustrate something in words or tell about it"

(b) <u>discuss</u> means "to make observations about something using facts, reasoning, and argument; to present in some detail"

NAME _____    SCHOOL _____

In developing your answers to Part III, be sure to keep this general definition in mind:

> discuss means "to make observations about something using facts, reasoning, and argument; to present in some detail"

## Part III

## DOCUMENT-BASED QUESTION

This question is based on the accompanying documents. The question is designed to test your ability to work with historical documents. Some of the documents have been edited for the purposes of the question. As you analyze the documents, take into account the source of each document and any point of view that may be presented in the document.

**Historical Context:**

> Between 1953 and 1969, the Chief Justice of the United States Supreme Court was Earl Warren. Supreme Court decisions made during the "Warren Court" era led to significant changes in various aspects of life in the United States. Several important court cases affected equal protection under the law, separation of church and state, and the rights of individuals accused of crimes.

**Task:** Using information from the documents and your knowledge of United States history, answer the questions that follow each document in Part A. Your answers to the questions will help you write the Part B essay, in which you will be asked to

> • Discuss how decisions of the Warren Court affected American society

# Part A
# Short-Answer Questions

## Document 1a

> . . . The Warren Court (1953–1969) revolutionized constitutional law and American society. First, the unanimous and watershed [critical] school desegregation ruling, *Brown v. Board of Education*, in 1954 at the end of Warren's first year on the bench. Then, in 1962 *Baker v. Carr* announced the "reapportionment revolution" guaranteeing equal voting rights [to individual voters no matter where they lived]. And throughout the 1960s, the Court handed down a series of rulings on criminal procedure that extended the rights of the accused and sought to ensure equal access to justice for the poor. *Mapp v. Ohio* (1961), extending the exclusionary rule to the states, and *Miranda v. Arizona* (1966), sharply limiting police interrogations of criminal suspects, continue to symbolize the Warren Court's revolution in criminal justice. . . .

Source: David M. O'Brien, "The Supreme Court: From Warren to Burger to Rehnquist," *PS*, Winter 1987

1*a* According to David M. O'Brien, what is **one** effect of the Warren Court on American society?   [1]

_____

_____

Score

## Document 1b

> . . .The Warren Court's revolution in public law promoted acrimony [hostility] and bitterness precisely because it empowered those who had previously not had the opportunity to exercise power. Whether we approve of their behavior or not, there is little doubt that these new groups added dramatically and often disturbingly to the contours of American society. Much of what the Warren Court did was to release dissident minorities from long-standing legal and social strictures [limits]. Critics complained that the Court was the root of the problem; it was fostering subversive [disobedient] action by civil rights advocates, Communist agitators, criminals, smut peddlers, and racketeers who hid behind the Fifth Amendment when called to account. . . .

Source: Kermit Hall, "The Warren Court in Historical Perspective," Bernard Schwartz, ed., *The Warren Court: A Retrospective,* Oxford University Press, 1996

1*b* According to Kermit Hall, what is **one** criticism leveled against the decisions of the Warren Court?   [1]

_____

_____

Score

## Document 2

HIGH COURT BANS
SEGREGATION IN
PUBLIC SCHOOLS

Mrs. Nettie Hunt, sitting on the steps of
the U. S. Supreme Court Building in
Washington, explains the significance of
the Court's May 17, 1954 desegregation
ruling to her daughter, Nikie $3\frac{1}{2}$, in this
November 19, 1954 photo.

Source: "With an Even Hand," Brown v. Board of Education exhibition,
*Library of Congress* (adapted)

2 Based on this photograph and caption, what is the significance of the *Brown* v. *Board of Education*
decision? [1]

_____

_____

Score [ ]

## Document 3a

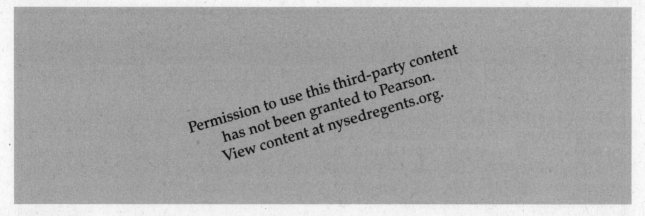

Permission to use this third-party content has not been granted to Pearson. View content at nysedregents.org.

## Document 3b

> . . . Even though the effects of *Brown* were slow in coming—real desegregation only occurred with the 1964 Civil Rights Act and aggressive enforcement by the Department of Justice, which denied federal funds to any segregated school—they were revolutionary. Greenberg [Jack Greenberg, a member of the *Brown* legal team] cites encouraging evidence today as the half-full approach: there are black Cabinet members in Democrat and Republican administrations; blacks hold top management positions in major corporations like Citibank, Xerox, Time Warner, and Merrill Lynch. When Greenberg started practicing law in 1949 there were only two black U.S. Congressmen. Today [2004] there are 39.
>
> *Brown* "broke up the frozen political system in the country at the time," Greenberg notes. Southern congressmen made it a priority to keep African-Americans from obtaining power, but *Brown* allowed for change. Judge Carter [Robert Carter, a member of the *Brown* legal team] believes that the greatest accomplishment of the ruling was to create a black middle class: "The court said everyone was equal, so now you had it by right.". . .

Source: Kristina Dell, "What 'Brown' Means Today," *Time*, May 17, 2004

3 Based on these documents, state **two** effects of the *Brown* v. *Board of Education* Supreme Court decision on American society.   [2]

(1) _____

_____

Score ☐

(2) _____

_____

Score ☐

## Document 4

> **. . . QUESTION**: Mr. President, in the furor [uproar] over the Supreme Court's decision [in *Engel* v. *Vitale*] on prayer in the schools, some members of Congress have been introducing legislation for Constitutional amendments specifically to sanction [permit] prayer or religious exercise in the schools. Can you give us your opinion of the decision itself, and of these moves of the Congress to circumvent [get around] it?
>
> **THE PRESIDENT**: I haven't seen the measures in the Congress and you would have to make a determination of what the language was, and what effect it would have on the First Amendment. The Supreme Court has made its judgment, and a good many people obviously will disagree with it. Others will agree with it. But I think that it is important for us if we are going to maintain our Constitutional principle that we support the Supreme Court decisions even when we may not agree with them.
>
> In addition, we have in this case a very easy remedy, and that is to pray ourselves and I would think that it would be a welcome reminder to every American family that we can pray a good deal more at home, we can attend our churches with a good deal more fidelity, and we can make the true meaning of prayer much more important in the lives of all of our children. That power is very much open to us. . . .

Source: President John F. Kennedy, News Conference, June 27, 1962

4a What was **one** effect of the *Engel* v. *Vitale* decision on public schools in the United States? [1]

_____

_____

Score ☐

b What does President John F. Kennedy suggest as a "remedy" to those who disagree with the Supreme Court's decision in *Engel* v. *Vitale*? [1]

_____

_____

Score ☐

## Document 5

ATLANTA, Nov. 21 — As President Clinton and the new Republican leadership in Congress consider measures that would return organized prayer to public schools, it is worth remembering one thing.

Prayer is already there.

Despite a Supreme Court ruling [*Engel* v. *Vitale*] 32 years ago that classroom prayer and Scripture reading are unconstitutional even if they are voluntary, prayer is increasingly a part of school activities from early-morning moments of silence to lunchtime prayer sessions to pre-football-game prayers for both players and fans.

The most common forms are state-mandated moments of silence at the beginning of the day, which are permissible to the extent they are not meant to be a forum for organized prayer. But, particularly in the South, religious clubs, prayer groups and pro-prayer students and community groups are making religion and prayer part of the school day. . . .

Source: Peter Applebome, "Prayer in Public Schools? It's Nothing New for Many,"
*New York Times*, November 22, 1994

5 According to Peter Applebome, what are *two* ways in which prayer in public schools continued despite the Supreme Court ruling in *Engel* v. *Vitale*? [2]

(1) _____

_____

Score ▢

(2) _____

_____

Score ▢

## Document 6

In the decades following the *Engel* decision, federal courts have continued to hear cases and make rulings on issues involving separation of church and state.

FRANKFORT, Ky. — A civic group will send a Ten Commandments monument back to Frankfort only if political leaders give assurances that it will be displayed publicly, as a new law allows. . . .

The Ten Commandments monument was part of an ever-growing list of religious issues that [Governor Ernie] Fletcher and other political leaders have dealt with this year. . . .

The Eagles [a fraternal organization] donated the Ten Commandments monument to the state in 1971. It was removed from the Capitol grounds and placed in storage in the mid-1980s during a construction project. When political leaders tried to display it again in 2000, the American Civil Liberties Union went to court, claiming the monument was an unconstitutional endorsement of religion. The ACLU won the case. . . .

Lawmakers passed a bill calling for the return of the monument. The same bill granted permission to local governments to post displays of the commandments in courthouses and other public buildings.

Kentucky has been at the center of legal fights in recent years on the posting of the commandments. In one case, *McCreary County v. ACLU* [2005], the U.S. Supreme Court ruled displays inside courthouses in McCreary and Pulaski counties were unconstitutional. In another [lower court case], *Mercer County v. ACLU*, the 6th U.S. Circuit Court of Appeals said a similar display in the Mercer County Courthouse is constitutional because it included other historic documents. . . .

Source: "Ten Commandments, other issues generating debate in Ky.," *Associated Press*, April 13, 2006

6 Based on this article, what is **one** issue in the continuing debate on separation of church and state?  [1]

_____

_____

Score ☐

## Document 7

... along with other Warren Court decisions, *Miranda* has increased public awareness of constitutional rights. The *Miranda* warnings may be the most famous words ever written by the United States Supreme Court. With the widespread dissemination [distribution] of *Miranda* warnings in innumerable [numerous] television shows as well as in the movies and contemporary fiction, the reading of the *Miranda* rights has become a familiar sight and sound to most Americans; *Miranda* has become a household word. As Samuel Walker writes, "[e]very junior high school student knows that suspects are entitled to their '*Miranda* rights.' They often have the details wrong, but the principle that there are limits on police officer behavior, and penalties for breaking those rules, is firmly established." As we have seen, a national poll in 1984 revealed that 93% of those surveyed knew that they had a right to an attorney if arrested, and a national poll in 1991 found that 80% of those surveyed knew that they had a right to remain silent if arrested. Perhaps it should not be surprising that, as many of my research subjects told me, some suspects assert their rights prior to the *Miranda* admonition [warning] or in situations where police warnings are not legally required. Indeed, in the last thirty years, the *Miranda* rights have been so entrenched [well-established] in American popular folklore as to become an indelible part of our collective heritage and consciousness. . . .

Source: Richard A. Leo, "The Impact of 'Miranda' Revisited,"
*The Journal of Criminal Law and Criminology,* Spring 1996 (adapted)

7 According to Richard A. Leo, what is **one** effect of the *Miranda* decision on American society? [1]

_____

_____

Score ☐

## Document 8a

Source: Charles Brooks, *Birmingham News* (adapted)

## Document 8b

> . . . The familiar fact is that the vastly troubled criminal-justice system often exacts no price at all for crime. An adult burglar has only one chance in 412 of going to jail for any single job, according to Gregory Krohm of the Virginia Polytechnic Institute's Center for the Study of Public Choice. For juveniles under 17, the figure is one in 659 burglaries, with a likelihood of only a nine-month term if the 659-to-1 shot comes in. Many critics are convinced that such odds were created in large part by those constitutional-law rulings of the Warren Court that expanded the rights of criminal defendants. Mapp, Escobedo, Miranda and Wade* are still names that enrage law-and-order advocates. But despite all the years of talk and four Nixon appointments, the court has so far been willing only to trim some of the rules, not reverse them. The new rulings obviously add to the work of the courts, and some experts believe that they have hampered the criminal-justice system's capacity to convict guilty offenders, though as yet there have been no studies demonstrating any such significant damage. . . .

Source: "The Crime Wave," *Time*, June 30, 1975

*In *United States* v. *Wade* (1967), the Court ruled that defendants have a right to counsel during police lineups. This does **not** refer to *Roe* v. *Wade*.

8 Based on the cartoon and the *Time* article, what is **one** impact of the rulings of the Warren Court on crime? [1]

_____

_____

Score ▢

## Document 9

WASHINGTON — Refusing to overturn more than three decades of established law enforcement practice, the Supreme Court yesterday strongly reaffirmed its landmark Miranda [*Miranda* v. *Arizona*] decision, which requires police to inform criminal suspects of their rights to remain silent and to be represented by an attorney during interrogation.

In a 7-2 opinion written by Chief Justice William H. Rehnquist, the high court ruled that the requirement that criminal suspects be read their "Miranda rights" is rooted in the Constitution and cannot be overturned by an act of Congress. Federal lawmakers passed legislation seeking to undo the Miranda decision in 1968, two years after the ruling.

The seven justices in the majority left open the question of whether they would have reached the same conclusion as the original five-justice Miranda majority about the constitutional rights of criminal suspects. But citing the court's long tradition of respect for precedent, the justices said there were compelling reasons not to overrule it now.

"Miranda has become embedded in routine police practice to the point where the warnings have become part of our national culture," wrote Rehnquist, a frequent and vocal critic of the Miranda decision during his earlier years on the bench. . . .

Source: "Miranda warnings upheld, Supreme Court says right now deeply rooted,"
*Florida Times Union*, June 27, 2000

9 Based on this article, why did the Supreme Court decide not to overturn the decision in *Miranda* v. *Arizona*? [1]

_____

_____

Score ☐

# Part B
# Essay

*Directions:* Write a well-organized essay that includes an introduction, several paragraphs, and a conclusion. Use evidence from *at least **five*** documents in your essay. Support your response with relevant facts, examples, and details. Include additional outside information.

## Historical Context:

Between 1953 and 1969, the Chief Justice of the United States Supreme Court was Earl Warren. Supreme Court decisions made during the "Warren Court" era led to significant changes in various aspects of life in the United States. Several important court cases affected equal protection under the law, separation of church and state, and the rights of individuals accused of crimes.

**Task:** Using information from the documents and your knowledge of United States history, write an essay in which you

> • Discuss how decisions of the Warren Court affected American society

## Guidelines:

### In your essay, be sure to
- Develop all aspects of the task
- Incorporate information from *at least **five*** documents
- Incorporate relevant outside information
- Support the theme with relevant facts, examples, and details
- Use a logical and clear plan of organization, including an introduction and a conclusion that are beyond a restatement of the theme

This section contains the Regents Examination in United States History and Government that was given in New York State in August 2008.

Circle your answers to Part I on this exam and write your answers to the thematic essay and document-based essay questions on separate sheets of paper. Be sure to refer to the test-taking strategies in the front of this book as you prepare to answer the test questions.

# Part I

## Answer all questions in this part.

*Directions* (1–50): For each statement or question, write on the separate answer sheet the *number* of the word or expression that, of those given, best completes the statement or answers the question.

Base your answers to questions 1 and 2 on the map below and on your knowledge of social studies. Each letter on the map represents a specific geographic feature.

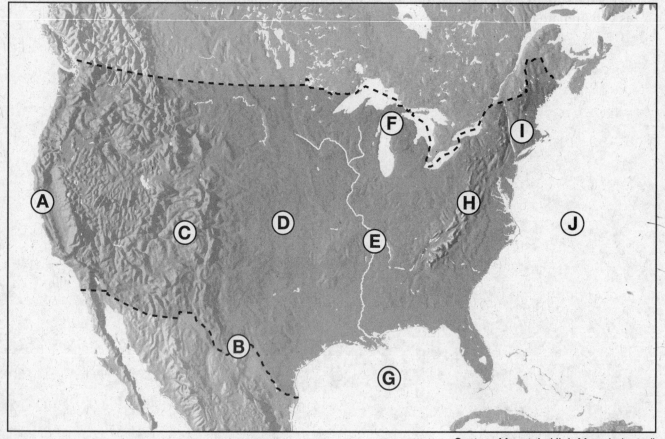

Source: *Mountain High Maps* (adapted)

1 Which geographic feature most limited the westward movement of American colonists before 1750?

    H               (3) C

(2) I                (4) F

2 At the end of the Revolutionary War, which geographic feature became the western boundary of the United States?

(1) A               E

(2) B              (4) G

Base your answer to question 3 on the time line below and on your knowledge of social studies.

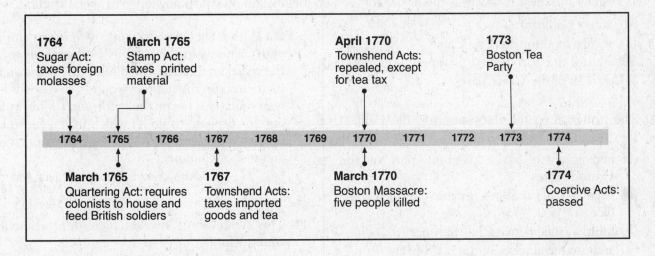

3 Which title is most accurate for this time line?

  (1) Forms of Colonial Protest

  (2) Effects of British Navigation Laws

  (3) Causes of the American Revolution

  (4) Abuse of Power by Colonial Legislatures

---

4 The Land Ordinance of 1785 and the Northwest Ordinance of 1787 are considered achievements under the Articles of Confederation because they

  (1) established processes for settling and governing the western territories

  (2) settled boundary disputes with Great Britain and Spain

  (3) provided the basic methods of collecting taxes and coining money

  (4) created a system of state and federal courts

5 "The powers not delegated to the United States by the Constitution, nor prohibited by it to the States, are reserved to the States respectively, or to the people."

          — United States Constitution, 10th amendment

This part of the Bill of Rights was intended to

  (1) give the people the right to vote on important issues

  (2) reduce the rights of citizens

  (3) limit the powers of the federal government

  (4) assure federal control over the states

6 The creation of the presidential cabinet and political parties are examples of

  (1) the unwritten constitution

  (2) separation of powers

  (3) the elastic clause

  (4) judicial review

7 The term *supreme law of the land* refers to which document?

  (1) Fundamental Orders of Connecticut

  (2) Constitution of the United States

  (3) Articles of Confederation

  (4) Declaration of Independence

8 Which principle of the United States Constitution is intended to ensure that no one branch of government has more power than another branch?

  (1) checks and balances

  (2) federalism

  (3) limited government

  (4) rule of law

9 A geographic and economic motivation for the Louisiana Purchase (1803) was the desire to

(1) annex California
(2) secure land for the Erie Canal
(3) control the port of New Orleans
(4) own all of the Great Lakes

10 The principal goal of the supporters of Manifest Destiny in the 1840s was to

(1) convince Canada to become part of the United States
(2) expand United States territory to the Pacific Ocean
(3) build a canal across Central America
(4) acquire naval bases in the Caribbean

11 The climate and topography of the southeastern United States had a major impact on the history of the United States before 1860 because the region

(1) became the center of commerce and manufacturing
(2) developed as the largest domestic source of steel production
(3) was the area in which most immigrants chose to settle
(4) provided agricultural products that were processed in the North and in Europe

against slavery

12 Abolitionists in the pre–Civil War period were most likely to support the

(1) removal of the Cherokee Indians from Georgia
(2) passage of the Fugitive Slave Act
(3) activities of the Underground Railroad
(4) use of popular sovereignty in the territories

13 Which Supreme Court decision created the need for a constitutional amendment that would grant citizenship to formerly enslaved persons?

(1) *Marbury* v. *Madison*
(2) *McCulloch* v. *Maryland*
(3) *Worcester* v. *Georgia*
(4) *Dred Scott* v. *Sanford*

Base your answer to question 14 on the quotation below and on your knowledge of social studies.

. . . With malice toward none, with charity for all, with firmness in the right as God gives us to see the right, let us strive on to finish the work we are in, to bind up the nation's wounds, to care for him who shall have borne the battle and for his widow and his orphan, to do all which may achieve and cherish a just and lasting peace among ourselves and with all nations.

— Abraham Lincoln, Second Inaugural Address, March 4, 1865

1860-1864

14 This statement reveals President Lincoln's support for

(1) a new peace treaty with Great Britain
(2) universal male suffrage
(3) a fair and generous peace
(4) harsh punishment for Confederate leaders

15 The passage of Jim Crow laws in the South after Reconstruction was aided in part by

(1) a narrow interpretation of the 14th amendment by the United States Supreme Court
(2) a change in the southern economy from agricultural to industrial
(3) the growth of Republican-dominated governments in the South
(4) the rise in European immigration to the South

16 During the late 1800s, pools and trusts were used by big business in an effort to

(1) increase imports
(2) limit competition
(3) improve working conditions
(4) reduce corporate income taxes

17 In the late 1800s, which group most often supported the views of the Populist Party?

(1) factory owners          (3) farmers
(2) nativists               (4) labor unions

18 . . ."You are our employers, but you are not our masters. Under the system of government we have in the United States we are your equals, and we contribute as much, if not more, to the success of industry than do the employers." . . .

— testimony, United States Congress, April 29, 1911

The point of view expressed in the quotation was most likely that of a

(1) recent immigrant responding to discrimination
(2) government official campaigning for re-election
(3) woman demanding the right of suffrage
(4) labor leader speaking about the rights of workers

19 In the late 1800s and early 1900s, many members of Congress supported legislation requiring literacy tests for immigrants in an attempt to

(1) stop illegal immigration from Latin America
(2) provide highly skilled workers for industry
(3) limit the power of urban political machines
(4) restrict immigration from southern and eastern Europe

20 "Hawaiian Planters Urge American Annexation"
"U.S. and Germany Negotiate for Control of the Samoan Islands"
"U.S. Gains Control of Wake Island and Guam"

Which conclusion can best be drawn from these headlines?

(1) The Anti-Imperialist League strongly influenced Congress.
(2) Respect for native cultures motivated United States foreign policy.
(3) United States territorial expansion increased in the Pacific Ocean.
(4) Construction of a railroad to Alaska was a major policy goal.

21 The Federal Reserve System was created in 1913 to

(1) protect endangered species
(2) reduce tariff rates
(3) collect income taxes
(4) regulate the nation's money supply

22 The initiative and referendum are considered democratic reforms because they

(1) permit citizens to have a more direct role in lawmaking
(2) let all registered voters select their state's presidential electors
(3) extend the right to vote to 18-year-old citizens
(4) allow residents of one state to bring lawsuits against residents of another state

23 During the early 1900s, the term *muckrakers* was used to describe

(1) pacifists who demonstrated against war
(2) writers who exposed the evils in American society
(3) newspaper columnists who reported on celebrities
(4) politicians who criticized Progressive Era presidents

24 President Woodrow Wilson's policy of strict neutrality during the early years of World War I was challenged by

(1) German violations of freedom of the seas
(2) British disrespect for the Roosevelt corollary
(3) attacks by Mexicans on United States border towns
(4) the refusal of the League of Nations to supply peacekeepers

25 What was a main result of national Prohibition during the 1920s?

(1) Respect for the law decreased.
(2) Woman's suffrage was restricted.
(3) Racial prejudice increased.
(4) Religious tolerance grew.

26 Which foreign policy did Warren G. Harding support when he used the phrase "return to normalcy" during his presidential campaign of 1920?

(1) appeasement          (3) containment
(2) internationalism     (4) isolationism

27 Which event led to the start of the Great Depression?

(1) Red Scare (1919–1920)

(2) election of President Herbert Hoover (1928)

(3) stock market crash (1929)

(4) passage of the Emergency Banking Act (1933)

Base your answer to question 28 on the cartoon below and on your knowledge of social studies.

### Until He Gets the Key the Door Cannot Be Opened

**"The people in this country whose incomes are less than two thousand dollars a year buy more than two-thirds of the goods sold."**
**— President Roosevelt**

Source: G. R. Spencer, *Omaha World-Herald*, 1934 (adapted)

28 Based on this cartoon, economic recovery would require

(1) fewer regulations by the federal government

(2) increased taxes on the working class

(3) more money in the hands of lower-income families

(4) protective tariffs on foreign goods

Base your answers to questions 29 and 30 on the song below and on your knowledge of social studies.

### Brother, Can You Spare a Dime?

They used to tell me I was building a dream
And so I followed the mob.
When there was earth to plow or guns to bear,
I was always there, right on the job.
They used to tell me I was building a dream
With peace and glory ahead —
Why should I be standing in line, just waiting for bread?

Once I built a railroad, I made it run,
Made it race against time.
Once I built a railroad, now it's done —
Brother, can you spare a dime? . . .

Once in khaki suits, gee, we looked swell
Full of that Yankee Doodle-de-dum.
Half a million boots went slogging through hell,
And I was the kid with the drum. . . .

— E. Y. Harburg and J. Gorney, 1932

29 Which statement most accurately expresses the main idea of this song?

(1) Railroad workers were often overpaid.

(2) The average wage in 1930 was 10 cents an hour.

(3) Soldiers never have difficulty finding jobs when they return from war.

(4) Hard times threaten economic opportunity.

30 Which program was created to deal with the problem identified in this song?

(1) Interstate Commerce Commission (ICC)

(2) Works Progress Administration (WPA)

(3) Federal Trade Commission (FTC)

(4) Federal Deposit Insurance Corporation (FDIC)

31 President Franklin D. Roosevelt's reelection in 1940 created a controversy that eventually led to

(1) the Supreme Court declaring the election unconstitutional

(2) the establishment of presidential term limits

(3) an effort to increase voter participation

(4) an attempt to increase the number of Justices on the Supreme Court

Base your answers to questions 32 and 33 on the map below and on your knowledge of social studies.

### Relocation Centers for Japanese Americans from the West Coast, 1942–1945

Source: National Park Service,
U.S. Department of the Interior (adapted)

32 Which statement is best supported by the information on the map?

(1) Government officials used abandoned mining towns to house Japanese Americans.

(2) Western states did not support the decision to create the relocation centers.

(3) Relocation centers had to be placed near rivers.

(4) The government considered Japanese Americans a threat to national security.

33 The relocation camps shown on the map were mainly a reaction to the

(1) Japanese military attack on Pearl Harbor

(2) capture of Japanese war prisoners

(3) need to train Japanese Americans for military service

(4) attacks by Japanese Americans on United States military bases

34 The D-Day invasion in June 1944 was important to the outcome of World War II because it

(1) opened a new Allied front in Europe

(2) avoided use of the atomic bomb against civilian targets

(3) forced Italy to surrender

(4) stopped Soviet advances in eastern Europe

35 The Marshall Plan (1948–1952) was a United States effort to assist the nations of Europe by

(1) forming a strong military alliance

(2) providing economic aid

(3) sending United States troops to trouble spots

(4) continuing Lend-Lease aid to the Soviet Union

Base your answers to questions 36 and 37 on the statement below and on your knowledge of social studies.

… But this secret, swift, and extraordinary buildup of Communist missiles—in an area well known to have a special and historical relationship to the United States and the nations of the Western Hemisphere, in violation of Soviet assurances, and in defiance of American and hemispheric policy— this sudden, clandestine [secret] decision to station strategic weapons for the first time outside of Soviet soil—is a deliberately provocative and unjustified change in the status quo which cannot be accepted by this country, if our courage and our commitments are ever to be trusted again by either friend or foe. . . .

— President John F. Kennedy, October 22, 1962

36 This statement is most closely associated with the

(1) Bay of Pigs invasion

(2) Cuban missile crisis

(3) United States-Soviet space race

(4) nuclear test ban controversy

37 What is a valid conclusion based on this statement?

(1) Strategic weapons of the United States should be stationed on foreign soil.

(2) An isolationist foreign policy is the most effective way to preserve peace.

(3) Presidential attempts were made to end military alliances.

(4) Geographic location plays an important role in determining foreign policy.

38 **"Martin Luther King Jr. Delivers 'I Have a Dream' Speech to Civil Rights Demonstrators in D.C."**

**"Rachel Carson Awakens Conservationists with Her Book, *Silent Spring*"**

**"Cesar Chavez Organizes Migrant Farm Workers"**

A valid conclusion based on these headlines is that

(1) individuals have a great impact on movements for change

(2) social reforms progress faster with support from big business

(3) the press discouraged efforts at reform in the 1960s

(4) mass movements often continue without strong leaders

Base your answers to questions 39 and 40 on the statement below and on your knowledge of social studies.

. . . In 1961, James Farmer orchestrated and led the famous Freedom Rides through the South, which are renowned for forcing Americans to confront segregation in bus terminals and on interstate buses. In the spring of that year, James Farmer trained a small group of freedom riders, teaching them to deal with the hostility they were likely to encounter using nonviolent resistance. This training would serve them well. . . .

— Senator Charles Robb, "A Tribute to an American Freedom Fighter," U.S. Senate

39 The principal goal of the activity described in this statement was to

(1) achieve racial integration of public facilities

(2) encourage change through violent means

(3) expand voting rights for African Americans

(4) force the president to send military troops into the South

40 The activities described in this statement helped lead to

(1) President Harry Truman's order to desegregate the military

(2) passage of the Civil Rights Act of 1964

(3) ratification of the Equal Rights Amendment

(4) a decision by the Supreme Court to integrate public schools

41 Which term is most commonly used to describe President Richard Nixon's foreign policy toward the Soviet Union?

(1) collective security    (3) détente

(2) brinkmanship    (4) neutrality

42 Since the 1970s, many people have moved from the Midwest and Northeast to the South, Southwest, and West Coast. This migration has resulted in

(1) support for increasing the membership of Congress

(2) a decrease in immigration from Asia and Latin America

(3) increased pressure to eliminate the electoral college

(4) some states gaining and others losing seats in the House of Representatives

Base your answer to question 43 on the cartoon below and on your knowledge of social studies.

Source: Dana Summers, *The Orlando Sentinel*, 1999

43 Which issue in the United States is the focus of this cartoon?

(1) poor diets of many older Americans

(2) high cost of many medicines

(3) increased competition among drug manufacturers

(4) government-controlled prices of prescription drugs

Base your answer to question 44 on the cartoon below and on your knowledge of social studies.

Source: Etta Hulme, *The Fort Worth Star-Telegram*, 2004

44 The graduating student pictured in this cartoon is confronted by a problem caused in part by

(1) cheaper foreign labor
(2) increasing tariff rates
(3) high-cost imports
(4) lack of education

45 **"Gasoline Prices Soar in 2008"**

**"U.S. Oil Consumption and Imports Continue to Rise"**

**"OPEC Votes to Reduce Oil Production"**

Which conclusion is most clearly supported by these headlines?

(1) The United States exports more oil than it imports.
(2) Energy policies are not affected by domestic events.
(3) The demand for alternative energy sources is declining.
(4) United States dependence on foreign oil is a major problem.

Base your answer to question 46 on the graph below and on your knowledge of social studies.

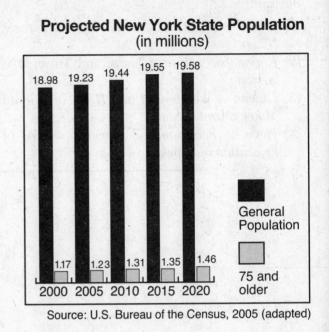

Source: U.S. Bureau of the Census, 2005 (adapted)

46 Which generalization about the projected population in New York State is most clearly supported by the information on the graph?

(1) The death rate will slowly increase by 2020.
(2) The number of citizens 75 and older will double by 2020.
(3) The number of citizens 75 and older will steadily decline by 2020.
(4) The population of both groups shown on the graph will increase by 2020.

47 The decision in *Gibbons* v. *Ogden* (1824) and the decision in *Wabash, St. Louis & Pacific Railroad* v. *Illinois* (1886) addressed the issue of

(1) congressional privileges
(2) regulation of interstate commerce
(3) state taxation of federal property
(4) contract rights

48 Which economic policy argues that government should limit, as much as possible, any interference in the economy?

(1) socialism          (3) mercantilism
(2) laissez-faire      (4) protectionism

49 Which pair of Supreme Court cases demonstrates that the Supreme Court can change an earlier decision?

(1) *Schenck* v. *United States* and *United States* v. *Nixon*

(2) *Korematsu* v. *United States* and *Miranda* v. *Arizona*

(3) *Gideon* v. *Wainwright* and *Heart of Atlanta Motel* v. *United States*

(4) *Plessy* v. *Ferguson* and *Brown* v. *Board of Education of Topeka*

50 The disputed elections of 1876 and 2000 were similar because in both contests the

(1) winner was chosen by a special electoral commission

(2) states were required to hold a second election

(3) winner of the popular vote did not become president

(4) election had to be decided in the House of Representatives

**Answers to the essay questions are to be written in the separate essay booklet.**

## Part II

## THEMATIC ESSAY QUESTION

*Directions:* Write a well-organized essay that includes an introduction, several paragraphs addressing the task below, and a conclusion.

### Theme: Government Role in the Economy

> Throughout history, the United States government has taken various actions to address problems with the nation's economy.

**Task:**

> Choose *two* actions that addressed a problem with the nation's economy and for *each*
> - Discuss the historical circumstance that led to the action
> - Discuss the impact of this action on the economy of the United States

You may use any example from your study of United States history. Some suggestions you might wish to consider include assumption of Revolutionary War debts, building the transcontinental railroad, passage of tariff laws, passage of the Interstate Commerce Act, creation of the Federal Deposit Insurance Corporation, adoption of the Social Security system, passage of federal minimum wage laws, Reagan Era tax cuts, and ratification of the North American Free Trade Agreement (NAFTA).

**You are *not* limited to these suggestions.**

**Guidelines:**

**In your essay, be sure to:**
- Develop all aspects of the task
- Support the theme with relevant facts, examples, and details
- Use a logical and clear plan of organization, including an introduction and a conclusion that are beyond a simple restatement of the theme

**In developing your answer to Part II, be sure to keep this general definition in mind:**

> <u>discuss</u> means "to make observations about something using facts, reasoning, and argument; to present in some detail"

**NAME** _____ **SCHOOL** _____

In developing your answers to Part III, be sure to keep this general definition in mind:

**discuss** means "to make observations about something using facts, reasoning, and argument; to present in some detail"

## Part III

## DOCUMENT-BASED QUESTION

This question is based on the accompanying documents. The question is designed to test your ability to work with historical documents. Some of the documents have been edited for the purposes of the question. As you analyze the documents, take into account the source of each document and any point of view that may be presented in the document.

**Historical Context:**

The automobile has had an important influence on the United States since the early 20th century. Perhaps no other invention has had such a significant impact on production methods, the American landscape, the environment, and American values.

**Task:** Using information from the documents and your knowledge of United States history, answer the questions that follow each document in Part A. Your answers to the questions will help you write the Part B essay, in which you will be asked to

---

- Discuss the political, economic, **and/or** social impacts of the automobile on the United States

---

# Part A
# Short-Answer Questions

## Document 1

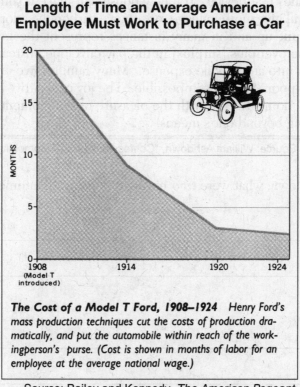

**Length of Time an Average American Employee Must Work to Purchase a Car**

MONTHS

20

15

10

5

0
1908 (Model T introduced)    1914    1920    1924

**The Cost of a Model T Ford, 1908–1924**   Henry Ford's mass production techniques cut the costs of production dramatically, and put the automobile within reach of the workingperson's purse. (Cost is shown in months of labor for an employee at the average national wage.)

Source: Bailey and Kennedy, *The American Pageant*, D.C. Heath and Company, 1987

1 According to Bailey and Kennedy, how did Henry Ford's mass production techniques influence the cost of the automobile?   [1]

_____

_____

Score ☐

## Document 2

> . . . The result [of buying a car] upon the individual is to break down his sense of values. Whether he will or no, he must spend money at every turn. Having succumbed [given in] to the lure of the car, he is quite helpless thereafter. If a new device will make his automobile run smoother or look better, he attaches that device. If a new polish will make it shine brighter, he buys that polish. If a new idea will give more mileage, or remove carbon, he adopts that new idea. These little costs quickly mount up and in many instances represent the margin of safety between income and outgo. The over-plus [surplus] in the pay envelope, instead of going into the bank as a reserve-fund, goes into automobile expense. Many families live on the brink of danger all the time. They are car-poor. Saving is impossible. The joy of security in the future is sacrificed for the pleasure of the moment. And with the pleasure of the moment is mingled the constant anxiety entailed by living beyond one's means. . . .

Source: William Ashdown, "Confessions of an Automobilist," *Atlantic Monthly,* June 1925

2 According to William Ashdown, what were *two* negative impacts of automobile ownership in 1925? [2]

(1) _____

_____

Score ☐

(2) _____

_____

Score ☐

**Document 3**

... Massive and internationally competitive, the automobile industry is the largest single manufacturing enterprise in the United States in terms of total value of products and number of employees. One out of every six U.S. businesses depends on the manufacture, distribution, servicing, or use of motor vehicles. The industry is primarily responsible for the growth of steel and rubber production, and is the largest user of machine tools. Specialized manufacturing requirements have driven advances in petroleum refining, paint and plate-glass manufacturing, and other industrial processes. Gasoline, once a waste product to be burned off, is now one of the most valuable commodities in the world. ...

Source: National Academy of Engineering, 2000

3 Based on this article, state *two* ways the automobile industry has had an impact on the American economy. [2]

(1) _____

_____

Score ☐

(2) _____

_____

Score ☐

## Document 4a

> . . . The automobile allowed a completely different pattern. Today there is often a semi-void of residential population at the heart of a large city, surrounded by rings of less and less densely settled suburbs. These suburbs, primarily dependent on the automobile to function, are where the majority of the country's population lives, a fact that has transformed our politics. Every city that had a major-league baseball team in 1950, with the exception only of New York—ever the exception— has had a drastic loss in population within its city limits over the last four and a half decades, sometimes by as much as 50 percent as people have moved outward, thanks to the automobile.
>
> In more recent years the automobile has had a similar effect on the retail commercial sectors of smaller cities and towns, as shopping malls and superstores such as the Home Depot and Wal-Mart have sucked commerce off Main Street and into the surrounding countryside. . . .

Source: John Steele Gordon, "Engine of Liberation," *American Heritage,* November 1996

4a According to John Steele Gordon, what has been *one* impact of the automobile on cities?  [1]

_____

_____

Score ☐

## Document 4b

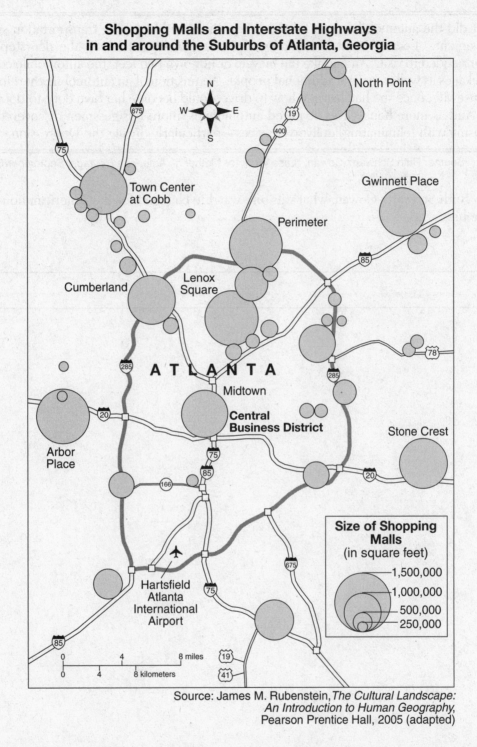

### Shopping Malls and Interstate Highways in and around the Suburbs of Atlanta, Georgia

Source: James M. Rubenstein, *The Cultural Landscape: An Introduction to Human Geography,* Pearson Prentice Hall, 2005 (adapted)

4b Based on the information on this map, what is *one* impact of the automobile on suburbs? [1]

_____

_____

Score

## Document 5

. . . What did the automobile mean for the housewife? Unlike public transportation systems, it was convenient. Located right at her doorstep, it could deposit her at the doorstep that she wanted or needed to visit. And unlike the bicycle or her own two feet, the automobile could carry bulky packages as well as several additional people. Acquisition of an automobile therefore meant that a housewife, once she had learned how to drive, could become her own door-to-door delivery service. And as more housewives acquired automobiles, more businessmen discovered the joys of dispensing with [eliminating] delivery services—particularly during the Depression. . . .

Source: Ruth Schwartz Cowan, "Less Work for Mother?," *American Heritage*, September/October 1987

5 According to Ruth Schwartz Cowan, what was *one* way life changed for the American housewife as a result of the automobile? [1]

_____

_____

Score ☐

## Document 6

| The Influence of the Automobile, 1923–1960 (Selected Years) |
|---|

**1923** Country Club Plaza, the first shopping center, opens in Kansas City.

**1924** In November, 16,833 cars cross the St. John's River into Florida, the beginning of winter motor pilgrimages to Florida.

**1930** Census data suggest that southern cities are becoming more racially segregated as car-owning whites move to suburbs that have no public transportation.

King Kullen, first supermarket, Queens, New York City. Supermarkets are an outgrowth of the auto age, because pedestrians cannot carry large amounts of groceries home.

**1932** One-room rural schools decline because school districts operate 63,000 school buses in the United States.

**1956** Car pools enable Montgomery, Alabama, blacks [African Americans] to boycott successfully the local bus company, beginning the modern civil rights movement.

National Defense and Interstate Highway Act passed. President Eisenhower argues: "In case of atomic attack on our cities, the road net [network] must allow quick evacuation of target areas."

**1957** Sixty-six-year-old gas station operator Harlan Sanders, facing bankruptcy because the interstate has bypassed him, decides to franchise his Kentucky Fried Chicken restaurant.

**1960** Organization of Petroleum Exporting Countries (OPEC) formed.

Source: Clay McShane, *The Automobile: A Chronology of Its Antecedents, Development, and Impact,* Greenwood Press, 1997 (adapted)

6a According to Clay McShane, what were ***two*** economic impacts of the automobile on the United States?  [2]

(1) _____

_____

Score ☐

(2) _____

_____

Score ☐

b According to Clay McShane, what was ***one*** impact of the automobile on race relations in the United States?  [1]

_____

_____

Score ☐

## Document 7

Minor disruptions have begun to appear in the world oil trade in the wake of the renewal of hostilities between the Arabs and the Israelis, and industry executives and Government officials in many countries are waiting to see whether the Arab states will make a serious attempt to use oil as a weapon in the conflict or any political confrontation that follows. The Egyptians are reported to have attacked Israeli-held oil fields in the occupied Sinai, and if true it would be the most ominous event so far in the oil situation. It would be the first direct attack by either side on oil production facilities in any of the conflicts thus far. If the Israelis retaliate it could mean major disruptions of supplies. . . .

Source: William D. Smith, "Conflict Brings Minor Disruptions in Oil Industry: Arab States' Moves Studied for Clues to Intentions," *New York Times,* October 9, 1973

7 According to William D. Smith, what could be *one* impact of the conflicts in the Middle East on the United States? [1]

_____

_____

Score [ ]

## Document 8

WASHINGTON, July 17—President Reagan, appealing for cooperation in ending the "crazy quilt of different states' drinking laws," today signed legislation that would deny some Federal highway funds to states that keep their drinking age under 21.

At a ceremony in the White House Rose Garden, Mr. Reagan praised as "a great national movement" the efforts to raise the drinking age that began years ago among students and parents.

"We know that drinking, plus driving, spell death and disaster," Mr. Reagan told visitors on a sweltering afternoon. "We know that people in the 18–to–20 age group are more likely to be in alcohol-related accidents than those in any other age group."

Mr. Reagan indirectly acknowledged that he once had reservations about a measure that, in effect, seeks to force states to change their policies. In the past, Mr. Reagan has taken the view that certain matters of concern to the states should not be subject to the dictates of the Federal Government.

But in the case of drunken driving, Mr. Reagan said, "The problem is bigger than the individual states.". . .

Source: Steven R. Weisman, "Reagan Signs Law Linking Federal Aid to Drinking Age," *New York Times,* July 18, 1984

8 According to Steven R. Weisman, what was *one* reason President Reagan signed the law linking federal highway funds to the drinking age? [1]

_____

_____

Score [ ]

**Document 9**

... After a long and bitter debate, lawmakers in California today [July 2, 2002] passed the nation's strongest legislation to regulate emissions of the main pollutant that can cause warming of the planet's climate, a step that would require automakers to sell cars that give off the least possible amount of heat-trapping gases. ...

California is the largest market for automobiles in the United States, as well as the state with more serious air pollution problems than any other. Under federal clean air legislation, the state's air quality regulators are allowed to set standards for automobile pollution that are stricter than those imposed by federal law. In the past, many other states have followed California's lead in setting pollution rules on vehicles, and ultimately American automakers have been forced to build cars that meet California's standards and to sell them nationwide. ...

Source: John H. Cushman Jr., "California Lawmakers Vote to Lower Auto Emissions," *New York Times,* July 2, 2002

9 According to John H. Cushman Jr., what is *one* impact of the automobile on the United States? [1]

_____

_____

Score ☐

# Part B
## Essay

*Directions:* Write a well-organized essay that includes an introduction, several paragraphs, and a conclusion. Use evidence from *at least **five*** documents in the body of the essay. Support your response with relevant facts, examples, and details. Include additional outside information.

### Historical Context:

The automobile has had an important influence on the United States since the early 20th century. Perhaps no other invention has had such a significant impact on production methods, the American landscape, the environment, and American values.

**Task:** Using information from the documents and your knowledge of United States history, write an essay in which you

- Discuss the political, economic, ***and/or*** social impacts of the automobile on the United States

### Guidelines:

**In your essay, be sure to**
- Develop all aspects of the task
- Incorporate information from *at least **five*** documents
- Incorporate relevant outside information
- Support the theme with relevant facts, examples, and details
- Use a logical and clear plan of organization, including an introduction and a conclusion that are beyond a restatement of the theme

# Regents Examination – June 2008

This section contains the Regents Examination in United States History and Government that was given in New York State in June 2008.

Circle your answers to Part I on this exam and write your answers to the thematic essay and document-based essay questions on separate sheets of paper. Be sure to refer to the test-taking strategies in the front of this book as you prepare to answer the test questions.

# Part I

## Answer all questions in this part.

*Directions* (1–50): For each statement or question, write on the separate answer sheet the *number* of the word or expression that, of those given, best completes the statement or answers the question.

1 Which geographic factor most helped the United States maintain its foreign policy of neutrality during much of the 1800s?

(1) climate of the Great Plains
(2) oceans on its east and west coasts
(3) large network of navigable rivers
(4) mountain ranges near the Atlantic and Pacific coasts

2 Before 1763, the British policy of salutary neglect toward its American colonies was based on the desire of Great Britain to

(1) treat all English people, including colonists, on an equal basis
(2) benefit from the economic prosperity of the American colonies
(3) encourage manufacturing in the American colonies
(4) ensure that all mercantile regulations were strictly followed

3 A major criticism of the Articles of Confederation was that too much power had been given to the

(1) British monarchy
(2) House of Burgesses
(3) state governments
(4) national government

4 What was the primary reason that slavery became more widespread in the South than in the North?

(1) The abolitionist movement was based in the North.
(2) The textile industry was controlled by southern merchants.
(3) Opposition to slavery by the Anglican Church was stronger in the North.
(4) Geographic factors contributed to the growth of the southern plantation system.

5 Which action can be taken by the United States Supreme Court to illustrate the concept that the Constitution is "the supreme law of the land"?

(1) hiring new federal judges
(2) voting articles of impeachment
(3) declaring a state law unconstitutional
(4) rejecting a presidential nomination to the cabinet

6 Passing marriage and divorce laws, creating vehicle and traffic regulations, and setting high school graduation requirements are examples of powers traditionally

(1) exercised solely by local governments
(2) reserved to the state governments
(3) delegated entirely to the federal government
(4) shared by the national and local governments

7 In the early 1800s, the Mississippi River was important to the United States because it

(1) served as a major highway for trade
(2) led to wars between Great Britain and Spain
(3) divided the Indian territories from the United States
(4) served as a border between the United States and Mexico

8 An example of a primary source of information about the War of 1812 would be a

(1) battle plan for the attack on Fort McHenry
(2) historical novel on the Battle of New Orleans
(3) movie on the life of President James Madison
(4) textbook passage on the naval engagements of the war

9 In the 1840s, the term *Manifest Destiny* was used by many Americans to justify

(1) the extension of slavery into the territories
(2) war with Russia over the Oregon territory
(3) the acquisition of colonies in Latin America
(4) westward expansion into lands claimed by other nations

Base your answer to question 10 on the cartoon below and on your knowledge of social studies.

Source: Rex Babin, *The Sacramento Bee,* June 29, 2004

10 Which constitutional principle is the focus of this cartoon?

(1) individual liberties          (3) freedom of speech
(2) separation of powers          (4) federalism

---

11 Which term refers to the idea that settlers had the right to decide whether slavery would be legal in their territory?

(1) nullification
(2) sectionalism
(3) popular sovereignty
(4) southern secession

12 The Supreme Court decision in *Dred Scott* v. *Sanford* (1857) was significant because it

(1) allowed slavery in California
(2) outlawed slavery in the Southern States
(3) upheld the actions of the Underground Railroad
(4) ruled that Congress could not ban slavery in the territories

13 What was a common purpose of the thr amendments added to the United Stat Constitution between 1865 and 1870?

(1) extending suffrage to Southern women
(2) reforming the sharecropping system
(3) granting rights to African Americans
(4) protecting rights of Southerners accused treason

14 The Radical Republicans in Congress oppos President Abraham Lincoln's plan for Reco struction because Lincoln

(1) called for the imprisonment of m Confederate leaders
(2) rejected the idea of harsh punishments the South
(3) planned to keep Northern troops in the Sou after the war
(4) demanded immediate civil and political rig for formerly enslaved persons

Base your answers to questions 15 and 16 on the map below and on your knowledge of social studies.

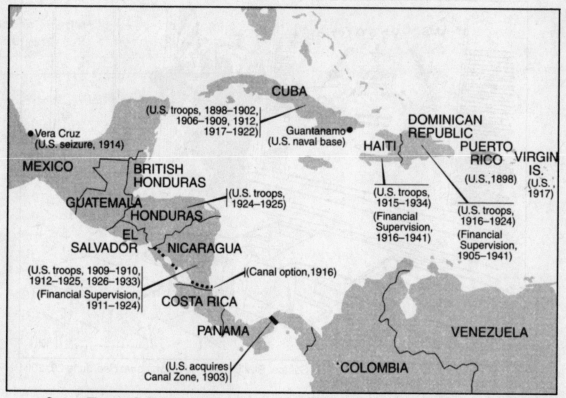

Source: Thomas G. Paterson et al., *American Foreign Policy: A History 1900 to Present*, D. C. Heath, 1991 (adapted)

15 Which title would be the most accurate for this map?

(1) Ending Colonization in Latin America
(2) Promoting Trade with Latin America
(3) Humanitarian Aid in the Western Hemisphere
(4) United States Intervention in the Caribbean Area

16 The United States government justified most of the actions shown on the map by citing the

(1) terms of the Roosevelt corollary to the Monroe Doctrine
(2) threats from Germany after World War I
(3) desire to stop illegal immigration from Latin America
(4) need to protect Latin America from the threat of communism

17 Which statement about the development of the Great Plains in the late 1800s is most accurate?

(1) Great profits could be earned in the steel industry.
(2) Railroads decreased in importance throughout the region.
(3) Immigrants could no longer afford to become farmers.
(4) Mechanized farming became dominant in the region.

18 The Interstate Commerce Act (1887) and the Sherman Antitrust Act (1890) were efforts by the federal government to

(1) regulate some aspects of business
(2) expand the positive features of the trusts
(3) favor big business over small companies
(4) move toward government ownership of key industries

19 In the late 1800s, the Homestead steel strike and the Pullman railcar strike were unsuccessful because

(1) the government supported business owners
(2) most workers refused to take part in the strike
(3) the Supreme Court ruled both strikes were illegal
(4) factory owners hired children to replace the strikers

20 The Supreme Court decision in *Plessy* v. *Ferguson* (1896) upheld a state law that had

(1) banned the hiring of Chinese workers
(2) established racial segregation practices
(3) outlawed the use of prison inmate labor
(4) forced Native American Indians to relocate to reservations

21 The United States promoted its economic interest in China by

(1) intervening in the Sino-Japanese War
(2) passing the Chinese Exclusion Act
(3) encouraging the Boxer Rebellion
(4) adopting the Open Door policy

22 Until the early 20th century, few restrictions on immigration to the United States existed primarily because

(1) industry needed an increasing supply of labor
(2) immigration totals had always been relatively low
(3) labor unions had always favored unrestricted immigration
(4) the Supreme Court had ruled that Congress could not restrict immigration

23 In the early 1900s, the muckrakers provided a service to the American public by

(1) calling for a strong military buildup
(2) lobbying for less government regulation of business
(3) exposing abuses in government and industry
(4) encouraging states to resist federal government authority

Base your answer to question 24 on the cha below and on your knowledge of social studies.

**States and Territories Fully Enfranchising Women Prior to the 19th Amendment**

| State | Date Begun |
| --- | --- |
| Territory of Wyoming | 1869 |
| Wyoming | 1890 |
| Colorado | 1893 |
| Utah | 1896 |
| Idaho | 1896 |
| Arizona | 1912 |
| Washington | 1910 |
| California | 1911 |
| Kansas | 1912 |
| Oregon | 1912 |
| Territory of Alaska | 1913 |
| Montana | 1914 |
| Nevada | 1914 |
| New York | 1917 |
| Michigan | 1918 |
| Oklahoma | 1918 |
| South Dakota | 1918 |

Source: Alexander Keyssar, *The Right to Vote*, Basic Books, 2000 (adapted)

24 Which conclusion about woman's suffrage is be supported by the information in the chart?

(1) Congress did not allow women to vote in th territories.
(2) Before 1917, many of the western states ha granted women the right to vote.
(3) The United States Supreme Court had approve a woman's right to vote in each stat
(4) Women were permitted to vote only in sta elections.

25 After World War I, the United States Sena refused to approve the Treaty of Versailles. Th action reflected the Senate's intention to

(1) provide support for the League of Nations
(2) punish the nations that began the war
(3) return to a policy of isolationism
(4) maintain United States leadership in wor affairs

Base your answer to question 26 on the poem below and on your knowledge of social studies.

**Mother to Son**

Well, son, I'll tell you:
Life for me ain't been no crystal stair.
It's had tacks in it,
And splinters,
And boards torn up,
And places with no carpet on the floor—
Bare.
But all the time
I'se been a-climbin' on,
And reachin' landin's,
And turnin' corners,
And sometimes goin' in the dark
Where there ain't been no light.
So boy, don't you turn back.
Don't you set down on the steps
'Cause you finds it kinder hard.
Don't you fall now—
For I'se still goin', honey,
I'se still climbin',
And life for me ain't been no crystal stair.

—Langston Hughes, 1922

26 One purpose of this poem, written during the Harlem Renaissance, was to

(1) explain the advantages of inner-city life
(2) discuss ideas in the language used by immigrant Americans
(3) ask African Americans to accept things as they are
(4) encourage African Americans to continue their struggle for equality

27 The Scopes trial of 1925 illustrated the

(1) desire for new voting rights laws
(2) need for better private schools
(3) conflict between Protestant fundamentalism and science
(4) effects of the Red Scare on the legal system

28 What was a major cause of the Great Depression?

(1) decrease in the production of goods during most of the 1920s
(2) unequal distribution of wealth in the United States
(3) overregulation of the banking industry
(4) low tariffs on foreign goods

29 The National Labor Relations Act of 1935 (Wagner Act) affected workers by

(1) protecting their right to form unions and bargain collectively
(2) preventing public employee unions from going on strike
(3) providing federal pensions for retired workers
(4) forbidding racial discrimination in employment

Base your answer to question 30 on the cartoon below and on your knowledge of social studies.

**"We saved thirteen points sending Junior to bed without his supper."**

Source: *Esquire Magazine*, 1944 (adapted)

30 Which feature of life on the home front during World War II is most clearly illustrated by this 1944 cartoon?

(1) food rationing
(2) housing shortages
(3) juvenile delinquency
(4) conserving natural resources

31 Prior to the start of World War II, Great Britain and France followed a policy of appeasement when they

(1) rejected an alliance with the Soviet Union
(2) allowed Germany to expand its territory
(3) signed the agreements at the Yalta Conference
(4) opposed United States efforts to rearm

32 The war crimes trials that followed World War II were historically significant because for the first time

(1) nations were asked to pay for war damages
(2) individuals were given immunity from prosecution
(3) nations on both sides were found guilty of causing the war
(4) individuals were held accountable for their actions during wartime

Base your answer to question 33 on the quotation below and on your knowledge of social studies.

. . . I believe that it must be the policy of the United States to support free peoples who are resisting attempted subjugation [control] by armed minorities or by outside pressures.

I believe that we must assist free peoples to work out their own destinies in their own way.

I believe that our help should be primarily through economic and financial aid which is essential to economic stability and orderly political processes. . . .

—President Harry Truman, speech to Congress (Truman Doctrine), March 12, 1947

33 The program described in this quotation was part of the foreign policy of

(1) détente          (3) neutrality
(2) containment       (4) colonialism

34 In both *Schenck* v. *United States* (1919) an *Korematsu* v. *United States* (1944), the Suprem Court ruled that during wartime

(1) civil liberties may be limited
(2) women can fight in combat
(3) drafting of noncitizens is permitted
(4) sale of alcohol is illegal

35 After the end of World War II, many workir women left their factory jobs because they were

(1) fired from their jobs due to poor performanc
(2) unprepared for peacetime employment
(3) forced to give up their jobs to returning wa veterans
(4) dissatisfied with their low wages

36 The Eisenhower Doctrine (1957) was an effort the United States to

(1) gain control of the Suez Canal
(2) take possession of Middle East oil wells
(3) find a homeland for Palestinian refugees
(4) counter the influence of the Soviet Union the Middle East

37 During the 1950s and 1960s, which civil righ leader advocated black separatism?

(1) Medgar Evers       (3) Rosa Parks
(2) James Meredith     (4) Malcolm X

38 The term *Great Society* was used by Preside Lyndon B. Johnson to describe his efforts to

(1) lower taxes for all Americans
(2) win the race for outer space
(3) end poverty and discrimination in the Unit States
(4) improve the nation's armed forces

39 The Berkeley demonstrations, riots at the 19 Democratic National Convention, and the Ke State protest all reflect student disapproval of

(1) the Vietnam War
(2) increases in college tuition
(3) the unequal status of American women
(4) racial segregation

40 Which situation in the 1970s caused the United States to reconsider its dependence on foreign energy resources?

(1) war in Afghanistan
(2) oil embargo by the Organization of Petroleum Exporting Countries (OPEC)
(3) meetings with the Soviet Union to limit nuclear weapons
(4) free-trade agreements with Canada and Mexico

Base your answer to question 41 on the cartoon below and on your knowledge of social studies.

Source: Herblock, "I am Not a Crook,"
*The Washington Post,* May 24, 1974

41 The cartoon is most closely associated with the controversy over the

(1) Watergate affair
(2) war on drugs
(3) Arab-Israeli conflict
(4) Iran hostage crisis

42 One similarity between President Jimmy Carter and President Bill Clinton is that both leaders

(1) attempted to bring peace to the Middle East
(2) supported the federal takeover of public education
(3) testified under oath at United States Senate hearings
(4) proposed treaties to limit trade with Latin America

Base your answer to question 43 on the graph below and on your knowledge of social studies.

### More people getting food stamps

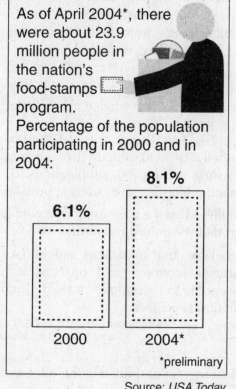

As of April 2004*, there were about 23.9 million people in the nation's food-stamps program.
Percentage of the population participating in 2000 and in 2004:

6.1% — 2000
8.1% — 2004*

*preliminary

Source: *USA Today,*
July 28, 2004 (adapted)

43 Which statement is best supported by the information in this graph?

(1) The surplus of food was greater in 2000 than in 2004.
(2) More money was being spent by consumers at the grocery store in 2000.
(3) The government was helping fewer people in 2004 than in 2000.
(4) More people needed financial assistance to feed their families in 2004.

Base your answer to question 44 on the graph below and on your knowledge of social studies.

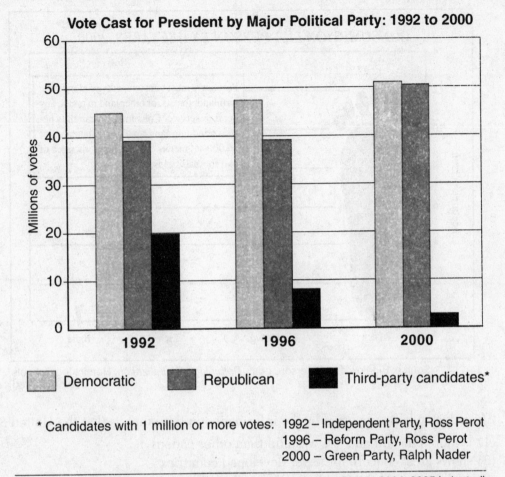

**Vote Cast for President by Major Political Party: 1992 to 2000**

* Candidates with 1 million or more votes:  1992 – Independent Party, Ross Perot
1996 – Reform Party, Ross Perot
2000 – Green Party, Ralph Nader

Source: U. S. Census Bureau, *Statistical Abstract of the United States: 2004–2005* (adapted)

44 Data from this graph support the conclusion that between 1992 and 2000

(1) the Democrats lost more votes to third-party candidates than the Republicans did
(2) third-party candidates received less support in each succeeding presidential election
(3) less than 50 percent of eligible voters participated in elections
(4) the Republicans received more than 40 million votes in each election

45 In 1990, approximately 12 percent of the United States population was over 65. It is estimated that in 2030 that number will climb to nearly 20 percent.

Source: U.S. Census Bureau

The most likely result of this trend will be an increase in the number of

(1) immigrants from Asia
(2) students attending colleges
(3) people receiving Social Security
(4) members of the House of Representatives

46 An initial response of the United States to terrorist attacks of September 11, 2001, was to

(1) aid in the overthrow of Taliban rule Afghanistan
(2) reduce support for Israel
(3) end trade with all Middle Eastern nations
(4) demand an end to communist rule in Iraq

Base your answer to question 47 on the graph below and on your knowledge of social studies.

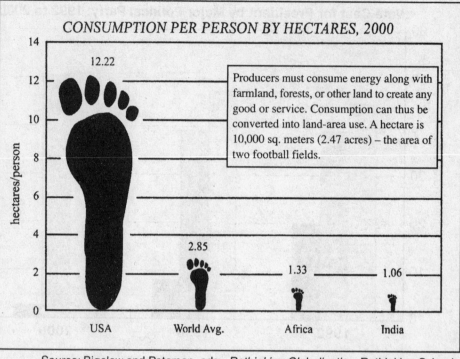

CONSUMPTION PER PERSON BY HECTARES, 2000

Producers must consume energy along with farmland, forests, or other land to create any good or service. Consumption can thus be converted into land-area use. A hectare is 10,000 sq. meters (2.47 acres) – the area of two football fields.

Source: Bigelow and Peterson, eds., *Rethinking Globalization,* Rethinking Schools, 2002 (adapted)

47 A conclusion best supported by the information in this graph is that the United States

(1) is more efficient and less wasteful than other nations
(2) shows great concern for lesser-developed countries
(3) consumes several times the world average of many resources
(4) spends more than other nations on environmental protection

48 One way in which the Gold Rush in 1849 and the Dust Bowl of the 1930s are similar is that both resulted in

(1) a war with other countries
(2) the sale of cheap federal land
(3) an increase in westward migration
(4) the removal of Native American Indians to reservations

49 Samuel Gompers, Eugene V. Debs, and John L. Lewis all influenced the American economy by

(1) supporting free trade between nations
(2) encouraging the use of monopolies
(3) advocating laissez-faire capitalism
(4) working to build unions and improve pay

50 Which category most accurately completes the heading for the partial outline below?

I. Supreme Court Cases that Deal With

   A. *Engel* v. *Vitale* (1962)
   B. *Tinker* v. *Des Moines School District* (1969)
   C. *New Jersey* v. *T.L.O.* (1985)
   D. *Vernonia School District* v. *Acton* (1995)

(1) Right to Counsel
(2) Student Rights
(3) School Integration
(4) Federal Funding of Education

**Answers to the essay questions are to be written in the separate essay booklet.**

**In developing your answer to Part II, be sure to keep this general definition in mind:**

**<u>discuss</u> means "to make observations about something using facts, reasoning, and argument; to present in some detail"**

## Part II

## THEMATIC ESSAY QUESTION

*Directions:* Write a well-organized essay that includes an introduction, several paragraphs addressing the task below, and a conclusion.

**Theme: Change**

> Throughout United States history, individuals other than presidents have played significant roles that led to changes in the nation's economy, government, or society.

**Task:**

> Select *two* important individuals, other than presidents, and the area in which they tried to bring about change, and for *each*
> - Discuss *one* action taken by the individual that led to changes in the nation's economy, government, or society
> - Discuss changes that came about as a result of the individual's action

You may use any important person from your study of United States history (other than a president). Some suggestions you might wish to consider include Frederick Douglass and slavery, Andrew Carnegie and industrialization, Jacob Riis and urban life, Upton Sinclair and consumer protection, Henry Ford and the automobile industry, Margaret Sanger and reproductive rights, Martin Luther King Jr. and civil rights, Cesar Chavez and migrant farmworkers, and Bill Gates and the software industry.

**You are *not* limited to these suggestions. However, you may *not* select a president of the United States.**

**Guidelines:**

**In your essay, be sure to:**
- Develop all aspects of the task
- Support the theme with relevant facts, examples, and details
- Use a logical and clear plan of organization, including an introduction and a conclusion that are beyond a restatement of the theme

NAME _____ SCHOOL _____

In developing your answers to Part III, be sure to keep these general definitions in mind:

   (a) <u>describe</u> means "to illustrate something in words or tell about it"

   (b) <u>explain</u> means "to make plain or understandable; to give reasons for or causes of; to show the logical development or relationships of"

   (c) <u>discuss</u> means "to make observations about something using facts, reasoning, and argument; to present in some detail"

## Part III

### DOCUMENT-BASED QUESTION

This question is based on the accompanying documents. The question is designed to test your ability to work with historical documents. Some of the documents have been edited for the purposes of the question. As you analyze the documents, take into account the source of each document and any point of view that may be presented in the document.

**Historical Context:**

> The president of the United States has been granted power as the commander in chief by the Constitution. While the president has used his military powers to commit troops overseas, he has also used this power to respond to domestic crises. Three such domestic crises were the *Civil War (1861–1865)* during the presidency of Abraham Lincoln, the *Bonus March (1932)* during the presidency of Herbert Hoover, and *Little Rock, Arkansas (1957)* during the presidency of Dwight D. Eisenhower.

**Task:** Using information from the documents and your knowledge of United States history, answer the questions that follow each document in Part A. Your answers to the questions will help you write the Part B essay, in which you will be asked to

---

Choose *two* domestic crises mentioned in the historical context that led presidents to use their military power as commander in chief and for *each*

- Describe the historical circumstances that led to the crisis
- Explain an action taken by the president to resolve the crisis
- Discuss the extent to which the president's action resolved the crisis *or* had an impact on American society

---

## Part A
## Short-Answer Questions

*Directions:* Analyze the documents and answer the short-answer questions that follow each document in th
space provided.

### Document 1

> . . . I [President Abraham Lincoln] would save the Union. I would save it the shortest way under the Constitution. The sooner the national authority can be restored the nearer the Union will be "the Union as it was." If there be those who would not save the Union unless they could at the same time *save* slavery, I do not agree with them. If there be those who would not save the Union unless they could at the same time *destroy* slavery, I do not agree with them. My paramount [most important] object in this struggle [the Civil War] *is* to save the Union, and is *not* either to save or to destroy slavery. If I could save the Union without freeing *any* slave I would do it, and if I could save it by freeing *all* the slaves I would do it; and if I could save it by freeing some and leaving others alone, I would also do that. What I do about slavery and the colored [African American] race, I do because I believe it helps to save the Union; and what I forbear [refrain from doing], I forbear because I do *not* believe it would help save the Union. I shall do *less* whenever I shall believe what I am doing hurts the cause, and I shall do *more* whenever I shall believe doing more will help the cause. I shall try to correct errors when shown to be errors; and I shall adopt new views so fast as they shall appear to be true views. . . .

Source: Abraham Lincoln to Horace Greeley, *New York Tribune*, August 25, 1862

1 According to this document, what is President Abraham Lincoln's main objective in fighting th Civil War? [1]

_____

_____

Score

**Document 2**

> . . . Now, therefore I, Abraham Lincoln, President of the United States, by virtue of the power in me vested as Commander-in-Chief, of the Army and Navy of the United States in time of actual armed rebellion [Civil War] against the authority and government of the United States, and as a fit and necessary war measure for suppressing [stopping] said rebellion, do, on this first day of January, in the year of our Lord one thousand eight hundred and sixty-three, and in accordance with my purpose so to do publicly proclaimed for the full period of one hundred days, from the day first above mentioned, order and designate as the States and parts of States wherein the people thereof respectively, are this day in rebellion against the United States, the following, to wit: . . .
>
> And by virtue of the power, and for the purpose aforesaid, I do order and declare that all persons held as slaves within said designated States [those states in rebellion], and parts of States, are, and henceforward shall be free; and that the Executive government of the United States, including the military and naval authorities thereof, will recognize and maintain the freedom of said persons. . . .

Source: Abraham Lincoln, Emancipation Proclamation, January 1, 1863

2 According to this document, what was President Abraham Lincoln hoping to achieve by issuing the Emancipation Proclamation? [1]

_____

_____

Score ☐

**Document 3a**

> Washington, March 26, 1863
> Hon. Andrew Johnson
> My dear Sir:
>
> I am told you have at least <u>thought</u> of raising a negro [African American] military force. In my opinion the country now needs no specific thing so much as some man of your ability, and position, to go to this work. When I speak of your position, I mean that of an eminent [respected] citizen of a slave-state, and himself a slave-holder. The colored population is the great <u>available</u>, and yet <u>unavailed</u> of, force, for restoring the Union. The bare sight of fifty thousand armed and drilled black soldiers upon the banks of the Mississippi, would end the rebellion at once. And who doubts that we can present that sight if we but take hold in earnest? If you <u>have</u> been thinking of it please do not dismiss the thought.
>
> Yours very truly
> A. Lincoln

Source: Abraham Lincoln to Andrew Johnson, March 26, 1863, Abraham Lincoln Papers, Library of Congress

3a According to this document, what role did Abraham Lincoln think African Americans could play in restorir the Union? [1]

_____

_____

Score

**Document 3b**

> . . . By the end of the Civil War, roughly 179,000 black men (10% of the Union Army) served as soldiers in the U.S. Army and another 19,000 served in the Navy. Nearly 40,000 black soldiers died over the course of the war—30,000 of infection or disease. Black soldiers served in artillery and infantry and performed all noncombat support functions that sustain an army, as well. Black carpenters, chaplains, cooks, guards, laborers, nurses, scouts, spies, steamboat pilots, surgeons, and teamsters also contributed to the war cause. There were nearly 80 black commissioned officers. Black women, who could not formally join the Army, nonetheless served as nurses, spies, and scouts, the most famous being Harriet Tubman, who scouted for the 2nd South Carolina Volunteers. . . .

Source: "The Fight for Equal Rights: Black Soldiers in the Civil War," National Archives & Records Administration

3b Based on this document, state *one* contribution made by African Americans to the war effort. [1]

_____

_____

Score

## Document 4

By June 1932, a large group of World War I veterans had gathered in Washington, D.C., to demand the bonus they had been promised for serving their country. These veterans were known as the Bonus Expeditionary Force (B. E. F.) or Bonus Army. The B. E. F. wanted the bonus early as a form of Depression relief.

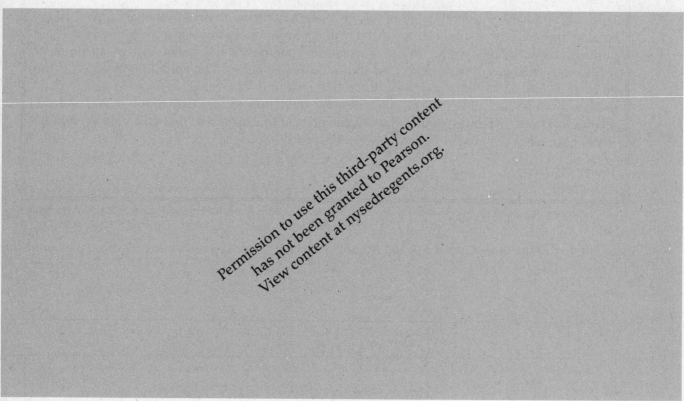

Permission to use this third-party content has not been granted to Pearson. View content at nysedregents.org.

4*a* According to *Time Magazine*, what was likely to happen to the Patman bill when it passed the House of Representatives and was sent to the Senate? [1]

_____

_____

Score ☐

*b* Based on this *Time Magazine* article, identify **one** part of the economy that had already benefited from government spending. [1]

_____

_____

Score ☐

**Document 5**

To: General Douglas MacArthur, Chief of Staff, U.S. Army.

The President has just informed me that the civil government of the District of Columbia has reported to him that it is unable to maintain law and order in the District.

You will have United States troops proceed immediately to the scene of disorder. Cooperate fully with the District of Columbia police force which is now in charge. Surround the affected area and clear it without delay.

Turn over all prisoners to the civil authorities.

In your orders insist that any women and children who may be in the affected area be accorded every consideration and kindness. Use all humanity consistent with the due execution of this order.

> PATRICK J. HURLEY
> Secretary of War.

Source: Patrick J. Hurley, President Hoover's Secretary of War, Washington, D.C., July 28, 1932, Herbert Hoover Presidential Library

5 According to this document, what was General MacArthur ordered to do by President Herbert Hoover Secretary of War in response to the march of the Bonus Army? [1]

_____

_____

Score

## Document 6

... Clark Booth, of the Veterans of Foreign Wars, declared that he had been a Republican all his life up to four days ago and was vice chairman of the Hoover campaign committee in 1928 for the Mobile district, but that Hoover's action in calling out the troops against the Washington veterans "made me a Democrat and I will take the stump against Herbert Hoover."

William Taylor, a veteran of the World War [I] who is also a member of the Alabama Legislature, delivered the chief attack against President Hoover in offering a resolution which was passed unanimously. He declared that "if Hoover had called out troops to keep lobbyists of Wall Street from the White House there would be no depression," adding that the veterans who had gathered in Washington were there only to "attempt to get that to which they are entitled."

"The Democrats will make Hoover pay on March 4 [Inauguration Day] with the aid of the veterans," Mr. Taylor declared, "the President can go back to his home, or return to England where he belongs.". . .

Source: "Assail Hoover in Mobile, Veterans Score Ousting of Bonus Army and 'Republican Prosperity.',"
*New York Times*, August 4, 1932

6 According to this *New York Times* article, what was **one** political impact of President Herbert Hoover's actions against the Bonus Army? [1]

_____

_____

Score [ ]

**Document 7a**

Source: Photograph by Will Counts for *Arkansas Democrat*

**A white student passes through an Arkansas National Guard line as Elizabeth Eckford is turned away on September 4, 1957.**

Source: Clayborne Carson, ed., *Civil Rights Chronicle*, Legacy Publishing

**A mob surrounds Elizabeth Eckford outside Central High School in Little Rock, Arkansas.**

7a Based on these photographs, what happened to Elizabeth Eckford as she tried to attend Central High School on September 4, 1957? [1]

_____

_____

Score

**Document 7b**

> . . . On September 4, after walking a virtual gauntlet of hysterical whites to reach the front door of Central High, the Little Rock Nine were turned back by Arkansas National Guardsmen. The white crowd hooted and cheered, shouted, stomped, and whistled. The segregationist whites of Little Rock did not see the vulnerability or the bravery of the students. Instead, they saw symbols of the South's defeat in the War Between the States, its perceived degradation during the Reconstruction that followed, and the threats to the southern way of life they had been taught to believe was sacrosanct [sacred]. . . .

Source: Clayborne Carson, ed., *Civil Rights Chronicle,* Legacy Publishing

7b According to this document, what was *one* reason some white citizens of Little Rock, Arkansas, did not want the Little Rock Nine to attend Central High School? [1]

_____

_____

Score

## Document 8a

> . . . This morning the mob again gathered in front of the Central High School of Little Rock, obviously for the purpose of again preventing the carrying out of the Court's order relating to the admission of Negro [African American] children to the school.
>
> Whenever normal agencies prove inadequate to the task and it becomes necessary for the Executive Branch of the Federal Government to use its powers and authority to uphold Federal Courts, the President's responsibility is inescapable.
>
> In accordance with that responsibility, I have today issued an Executive Order directing the use of troops under Federal authority to aid in the execution of Federal law at Little Rock, Arkansas. This became necessary when my Proclamation of yesterday was not observed, and the obstruction of justice still continues.
>
> It is important that the reasons for my action be understood by all citizens.
>
> As you know, the Supreme Court of the United States has decided that separate public educational facilities for the races are inherently [by nature] unequal and therefore compulsory school segregation laws are unconstitutional. . . .

Source: Address by President Dwight D. Eisenhower, September 24, 1957

8a (1) Based on this document, what was **one** action taken by President Dwight D. Eisenhower in response to the crisis in Little Rock? [1]

_____

_____

Score [ ]

(2) Based on this document, what was **one** reason President Dwight D. Eisenhower took action in the crisis in Little Rock? [1]

_____

_____

Score [ ]

**Document 8b**

Source: Clayborne Carson, ed., *Civil Rights Chronicle,* Legacy Publishing (adapted)

**On September 25, 1957 federal troops escort the Little Rock Nine
to their classes at Central High School.**

8*b* Based on this photograph, what was the job of the United States Army troops in Little Rock, Arkansas? [

_____

Score

## Document 9

President Dwight D. Eisenhower's actions in Little Rock were an important step in enforcing the Supreme Court's 1954 decision regarding school segregation. However, state and local resistance to school integration continued.

> . . . Little Rock and the developments following in its wake marked the turning of the tide. In September, 1957, desegregation was stalemated. Little Rock broke the stalemate. Virginia early felt the impact of the Little Rock developments. By the end of 1958, the "Old Dominion" state had entrenched itself behind some thirty-four new segregation bulwarks [barriers] — the whole gamut of evasive devices that had spread across the South to prevent desegregation. It was a self-styled program of "massive resistance," a program which other states admittedly sought to duplicate. But as the Bristol (Va.) *Herald-Courier* observed in late 1958, when the showdown came, "'Massive resistance' met every test but one. It could not keep the schools open and segregated.". . .

Source: James W. Vander Zanden, "The Impact of Little Rock," *Journal of Educational Sociology*, April 1962

9 According to James W. Vander Zanden, what are *two* impacts of President Dwight D. Eisenhower's decision to enforce desegregation? [2]

(1) _____

_____

Score [ ]

(2) _____

_____

Score [ ]

# Part B
## Essay

*Directions:* Write a well-organized essay that includes an introduction, several paragraphs, and a conclusion
Use evidence from *at least **four*** documents in the body of the essay. Support your response with
relevant facts, examples, and details. Include additional outside information.

**Historical Context:**

The president of the United States has been granted power as the commander in
chief by the Constitution. While the president has used his military powers to
commit troops overseas, he has also used this power to respond to domestic crises.
Three such domestic crises were the ***Civil War (1861–1865)*** during the
presidency of Abraham Lincoln, the ***Bonus March (1932)*** during the presidency
of Herbert Hoover, and ***Little Rock, Arkansas (1957)*** during the presidency of
Dwight D. Eisenhower.

**Task:** Using information from the documents and your knowledge of United States
history, write an essay in which you

> Choose ***two*** domestic crises mentioned in the historical context that led
> presidents to use their military power as commander in chief and for ***each***
> * Describe the historical circumstances that led to the crisis
> * Explain an action taken by the president to resolve the crisis
> * Discuss the extent to which the president's action resolved the crisis ***or*** had an
>   impact on American society

**Guidelines:**

**In your essay, be sure to**
* Develop all aspects of the task
* Incorporate information from *at least **four*** documents
* Incorporate relevant outside information
* Support the theme with relevant facts, examples, and details
* Use a logical and clear plan of organization, including an introduction and conclusion that
  are beyond a restatement of the theme